BARRON'S
FOREIGN LANGUAGE GUIDES

501
JAPANESE
VERBS

THIRD EDITION

Fully described in all inflections, moods, aspects, and formality levels
in a new easy-to-learn format, alphabetically arranged

by

Roland A. Lange, Ph.D.

Formerly Associate Professor of Japanese
Language and Linguistics
Columbia University, New York

and

Nobuo Akiyama

Professorial Lecturer, Japanese Language
The Paul H. Nitze School of Advanced International Studies
The Johns Hopkins University

All inquiries should be addressed to:
Barron's Educational Series, Inc.
250 Wireless Boulevard
Hauppauge, New York 11788
www.barronseduc.com

Library of Congress Control No. 2006043085

ISBN-13: 978-0-7641-3749-5
ISBN-10: 0-7641-3749-2

Library of Congress Cataloging-in-Publication Data
Lange, Roland A.
   501 Japanese verbs : fully described in all inflections, moods, aspects,
and formality levels in a new easy-to-learn format, alphabetically arranged /
by Roland A. Lange. — 3rd ed.
     p.   cm.
   English and romanized Japanese.
   ISBN-13: 978-0-7641-3749-5
   ISBN-10: 0-7641-3749-2
   1. Japanese language—Verb. I. Title. II. Title: Five hundred one
Japanese verbs.

   PL585.L3 2007
   495.6'5—dc22   2006043085

PRINTED IN THE UNITED STATES OF AMERICA
9 8 7 6 5

Contents

Introduction

This handbook of Japanese verbs is a reference which gives a concise, easy-to-understand description of Japanese verbal inflection and derivation, together with tables showing all the necessary forms of 501 important and widely used Japanese verbs.

Both beginning and advanced students should find *501 Japanese Verbs* helpful. For beginners, it is a valuable aid in learning basic verbal inflection. Most textbooks provide students with just a few examples to illustrate the principles of inflection. This means that students may have no way to check a given form of an unfamiliar verb. With *501 Japanese Verbs* students will be able to quickly verify the form in which they are interested. By presenting the full array of verbal inflection and derivation in tables, this book also enables beginning students to see the language as a system, rather than as a haphazard collection of stems and endings.

More advanced students can also use this presentation of the language to help them organize the many verb forms they have learned into a systematic body of data.

Pronunciation

Japanese isn't difficult to pronounce if you follow a few simple guidelines.

VOWELS

If you have studied Spanish, it may help you to know that Japanese vowels are more like those of Spanish than English. The following vowels are short and pure, with no glide—that is, they are not diphthongs.

Japanese Vowel	English Equivalent	Example
a	as in f**a**ther	*akai (ah-kah-ee) red*
e	as in m**e**n	*ebi (eh-bee) shrimp*
i	as in s**ee**	*imi (ee-mee) meaning*
o	as in b**oa**t	*otoko (oh-toh-koh) male*
u	as in f**oo**d	*uma (oo-mah) horse*

The following vowels are like the ones above, but lengthened.

Japanese Vowel	English Equivalent	Example
ā	as in father, but lengthened	batā (*bah-tāh*) butter
ei	as in men, but lengthened	eigo (*ēh-goh*) English
ii	as in see, but lengthened	iiharu (*ēē-hah-roo*) insist
ō	as in boat, but lengthened	ōsama (*ōh-sah-mah*) king
ū	as in food, but lengthened	yūbin (*yōō-been*) mail

MACRONS
A macron, or bar, above a vowel means it should be lengthened.

Example:

butter   batā   *bah-tāh*

In the above word, the macron above the second vowel means you should hold the sound twice as long as you normally would.

And keep in mind these points:
• Long vowels are important. Pronouncing a long vowel incorrectly can result in a different word or even an unintelligible one.

Example:

obasan (*oh-bah-sahn*) means **aunt**
obāsan (*oh-bāh-sahn*) means **grandmother**

ojisan (*oh-jee-sahn*) means **uncle**
ojiisan (*oh-jēē-sahn*) means **grandfather**

seki (*seh-kee*) means **seat**
seiki (*sēh-kee*) means **century**

• Sometimes the **i** and the **u** aren't pronounced. This usually occurs between voiceless consonants (**p, t, k, ch, f, h, s, sh**), or at the end of a word following a voiceless consonant.

Example:

sukiyaki (*skee-yah-kee*)

This word for a popular Japanese dish begins with **skee**, not **soo**. The **u** is not pronounced.

tabemashita (*tah-beh-mahsh-tah*) **I ate**.
The **i** is not pronounced.

CONSONANTS

With a few exceptions, Japanese consonants are similar to those of English. Note those that are different:

f To make the Japanese **f**, blow air lightly between the lips as if you were just beginning a whistle. (The English **f** is pronounced with a passage of air between the upper teeth and the lower lip.)

g Always pronounce this as in **go**, never as in **age**. You may also hear it pronounced as the **ng** sound in **ring**, but not at the beginning of a word.

r To make the Japanese **r**, lightly touch the tip of your tongue to the bony ridge behind the upper teeth, almost in the English **d** position. This is different from the English **r**. It's more like the Spanish **r**, but it's not trilled.

s Always hiss this as in **so**; never voice it as in **his** or **pleasure**.

And note the following points as well:
- If you have trouble making a consonant the Japanese way, your English pronunciation will be intelligible.

- Some Japanese consonants are doubled. In English, this is just a feature of spelling and often doesn't affect pronunciation. In Japanese, the doubling is important and may change the meaning of a word.

   Example:

   kite kudasai (*kee-teh koo-dah-sah-ee*) means
   Please put it (clothing) on.

   Kitte kudasai (*keet-teh koo-dah-sah-ee*) means
   Please cut it.

In a word with a doubled consonant, don't say the consonant twice—simply hold the sound longer.

LOAN WORDS

If you know English, you may already know more Japanese than you think. There are thousands of English loan words in everyday use in Japan. Most of these common words have been borrowed with no change in meaning. But there is a change in pronunciation. This can be tricky: On the one hand you're secure with the familiar words; on the other, if you pronounce them as you're used to doing, you won't be understood and you won't understand the words when Japanese use them. For example, baseball won't work; **bēsubōru** (beh-soo-boh-roo) will! If you order a beer, you might not get one; say **bīru** (bee-roo) and you will. (Note the long vowel: **biru** with a short vowel means "building.")

Here are a few more examples of familiar words with somewhat different pronunciations in Japanese:

gasoline	ガソリン	*gasorin*
pocket	ポケット	*poketto*
pink	ピンク	*pinku*
ballpoint pen	ボールペン	*bōru pen*
supermarket	スーパー	*sūpā*
yacht	ヨット	*yotto*
handkerchief	ハンカチ	*hankachi*

Speech Levels

When native speakers of English try to learn the Japanese verb system, instead of the familiar distinctions involving number and person, they find distinctions between levels of formality and deference which serve to indicate the speaker's relationship to the person spoken to or about.

Proper use of these grammatical categories requires keen judgment as to the relative social status of speaker and listener, the complexities of overlapping in-group and out-group status, and whether an occasion or relationship is formal or informal. These judgments must be in line with Japanese social views, so students' success will depend upon their knowledge of Japanese social customs and attitudes.

FORMALITY

The two sentences *Ocha o nonda.* and *Ocha o nomimashita.* both mean "I (you, he, she, it, we, they) drank tea," but the second is more formal and polite than the first. The formal sentence with *nomimashita* could be used under any circumstance without giving offense. An adult Japanese would use the sentence with *nonda* only on informal occasions when speaking to persons of lower social status or to persons of the same status with whom he or she was on close terms, such as members of one's immediate family or close friends at school or at work. While formal and informal sentences are used by both men and women, in general, women's speech tends to be more formal and polite than that of men. (Women also tend to make greater use of the honorific and humble deference levels which are discussed below.)

The style of speech is usually kept uniform throughout a conversation, and is determined by the form of the final verb, adjective, or copula in a sentence. It is this which expresses the general tone of the occasion and of the relationship between the speaker and the person spoken to. Since it is the final verb (adjective or copula) which sets the style, other verbs (adjectives or copula) which may occur earlier in the sentence are usually of the shorter, informal type, even in formal speech. For example, the sentence *Kare ga ocha o nonda kara, watakushi mo nomimashita.* "He drank tea, so I drank tea too." is in the formal style even though it contains the informal *nonda*. Students of Japanese must be familiar with both forms of the verb, but should use only the formal sentence style until they have learned to whom and under what circumstances they may use the informal style without offending the person spoken to.

DEFERENCE

While the formality style expresses the speaker's attitude toward the person he or she is speaking to, the deference level expresses the speaker's attitude toward the person he or she is speaking about. As far as verbs are concerned, the deference level shows the speaker's attitude toward the subject of the verb even though the subject of the verb may not be mentioned explicitly in the sentence. There are three basic levels: honorific, plain or neutral, and humble when the subject is a person, and another "neutral-polite" category when the subject is inanimate. The plain level is the most common, with the honorific and humble levels being used when the speaker wishes to express special deference or respect toward someone. The categories of formality and deference operate independently of each other so that each verb form can be classified according to both systems as in the following table, which shows a partial paradigm of the verb *kak.u* "write."

	INFORMAL	FORMAL
Honorific	okaki ni naru	okaki ni narimasu
Neutral	kaku	kakimasu
Humble	okaki suru	okaki shimasu
	okaki itasu	okaki itashimasu

In addition to indicating respect, the use of the humble or honorific level serves to vaguely identify the subject because one never uses the honorific to refer to oneself, nor the humble to refer to the person one is speaking to.* So while *kakimasu* could mean "I (you, he, she, it, we, they) write," *okaki ni narimasu* could not mean "I (or we) write," nor could *okaki shimasu* mean "You write." In the absence of other context, the honorific level will refer to an action of the listener, and the humble level will refer to an action of the speaker.

As with the category of formality, the best guide to proper use of deference levels is a thorough knowledge of Japanese social custom. Until the student gains this he or she can follow the general principle that honorifics are used most often in reference to actions performed by the listener or members of his or her family, and humble forms are used most often in referring to actions performed by the speaker.

*An exception to this is the humble presumptive in which the person spoken to is sometimes covered in an inclusive "we." For example, *Takushī de mairimashō ka* may mean "Shall we (you and I) go by taxi?"

Japanese has two main classes of verbs: those with stems ending in *i* or *e* and those whose stems end in consonants. We shall call them Class I and II respectively. The following is a list of basic inflectional endings (informal) using *ake.ru* "open" and *kats.u* "win" as examples.

Here the dot shows the division between stem and ending, but it will also be used at times to mark the division between the infinitive of a verb and an infinitive-based ending.

For a few verbs, certain sound changes occur at the end of the stem:

- If a verb ends in *-su*, the stem ends in *sh* before a suffix beginning with *i*, or *s* before other suffixes.
- If a verb ends in *-tsu*, the stem ends in *ch* before a suffix beginning with *i*, or *t* before other suffixes.

	Class I	Class II
Infinitive	ake	kach.i
Indicative	ake.ru	kats.u
Imperative I*	ake.ro	kat.e
Presumptive	ake.yō	kat.ō
Provisional	ake.reba	kat.eba
Gerund	ake.te	kat.te
Past Indicative	ake.ta	kat.ta
Past Presumptive	ake.tarō	kat.tarō
Conditional	ake.tara	kat.tara
Alternative	ake.tari	kat.tari

Comparing the endings for the two verb classes we find that in the last five categories they are the same *(-te, -ta, -tarō, -tara,* and *-tari)* but in the first five categories they differ as follows:

	Class I	Class II
Infinitive	—	-i
Indicative	-ru	-u
Imperative	-ro	-e
Presumptive	-yō	-ō
Provisional	-reba	-eba

Except for the discrepancy between the vowels in the two imperative endings, the differences between the endings can be accounted for by a rule to the effect that the initial vowel of a suffix is lost when the stem ends in a vowel (Class I),

*This form is used only by male speakers when speaking harshly. Otherwise it is replaced by more polite informal imperative expressions. Two common ones which we will label informal imperatives II and III are infinitive + *nasai* (imperative of *nasar.u* "to do") and gerund + *kudasai* (imperative of *kudasar.u* "give to me"). Of these the second is the more polite and is the one preferred for general use in making requests.

and the initial consonant of a suffix is lost when the stem ends in a consonant (Class II). For example, *kach-* + *-i* = *kach.i,* but *ake-* + *-i* = *ake;* while *ake-* + *-ru* = *ake.ru,* but *kats-* + *-ru* = *kats.u.*

Turning now to the verb stems we find that Class I *ake-* remains constant throughout the ten categories. This is typical of Class I verb stems, but not of Class II verb stems. *All Class II verb stems which do not end in -t- undergo a change when attached directly to one of the five suffixes which begin with -t- (-te, -ta, -tarō, -tara, and -tari), or -d- (-de, -da, -darō, -dara, and -dari).*

These changes differ according to the final consonant of the stem, but all Class II stems which end in the same consonant undergo the same change. All of the possible changes are illustrated in the following list of examples. *(-te* is used as an example, but the change would be the same before any of the other four *-t-* endings.)

kas- + -te	becomes kashi.te	(kas.u "lend")
kak- + -te	becomes kai.te	(kak.u "write")
kag- + -te	becomes kai.de	(kag.u "sniff")
yob- + -te	becomes yon.de	(yob.u "call")
yom- + -te	becomes yon.de	(yom.u "read")
shin- + -te	becomes shin.de	(shin.u "die")
kar- + -te	becomes kat.te	(kar.u "cut")
ka(w)- + -te	becomes kat.te	(ka(w).u "buy")*

This concludes our outline of inflection, but Japanese verbs have many more forms which are the result of derivation or the addition of various auxiliary endings. Up until now we have considered only informal affirmative forms. Our next step is to cover the formal affirmative, which in both verb classes is derived by attaching the auxiliary verb *-mas.u* to the infinitive of the original verb. The *-mas.u* occurs only as an ending for other verbs and has no substantive meaning of its own, serving only to raise the level of formality of the verb to which it is attached.

In general *-mas.u* behaves like a Class II verb, but it lacks an infinitive and has dual forms in the provisional.

Indicative	-mas.u
Imperative	-mas.e
Presumptive	-mash.ō
Provisional	-mas.eba / -mas.ureba
Gerund	-mashi.te
Past Indicative	-mashi.ta
Past Presumptive	-mashi.tarō
Conditional	-mashi.tara
Alternative	-mashi.tari

*Since in Japanese *w* only occurs before *a,* Class II verbs whose stems end in this sound do not show it in all forms of the verb, but only when the suffix begins with *a.*

All of these forms except the presumptive and the past and nonpast indicative indicate a higher than normal level of formality or politeness. As a rule the imperative -mas.e is only used with honorific verbs such as nasar.u "to do," and kudasar.u "give to me." In the past presumptive the infinitive + mashi.tarō is usually replaced by a combination of the informal past indicative desh.ō (the formal presumptive form of the copula). A similar construction using desh.ō is also used in the nonpast presumptive category. This differs from the -mash.ō form not in degree of formality, but in the identity of the subject and other modal content. Therefore, the -mash.ō form and the informal indicative + desh.ō form will be labeled Presumptive I and II respectively. The two forms using desh.ō are paralleled by informal ones using dar.ō, the informal presumptive form of the copula.

We are now ready to move to the informal negative category. Here we find that, except for the imperative and presumptive, the "verb" is really an adjective derived by adding the adjectival ending -ana.i "negative" to the stem of the verb. The resulting negative adjective inflects like any other adjective. Our earlier juncture rule works for -ana.i too because the initial vowel -a- is lost when it is joined to a Class I stem ending in a vowel.

		Class I	Class II
Indicative		ake.nai	kat.anai
Imperative	I	ake.ru na	kats.u na
	II	ake.nasaru na	kach.i nasaru na
	III	ake.nai de kudasai	kat.anai de kudasai
Presumptive	*I	ake.mai	kats.umai
	II	ake.nai darō	kat.anai darō
Provisional		ake.nakereba	kat.anakereba
Gerund	I	ake.nai de	kat.anai de
	**II	ake.nakute	kat.anakute
Past Indicative		ake.nakatta	kat.anakatta
Past Presumptive		ake.nakattarō	kat.anakattarō
		ake.nakatta darō	kat.anakatta darō
Conditional		ake.nakattara	kat.anakattara
Alternative		ake.nakattari	kat.anakattari

Here we find three informal imperative constructions corresponding to those mentioned in connection with the informal affirmative imperative. The "na" used to form the negative imperative I is a negative command particle.

*In the Class I presumptive I there is optional variation between ake.mai, in which mai follows the stem directly, and ake.ru.mai in which it follows the affirmative nonpast indicative as it does with Class II verbs. We shall use the shorter form in our tables.
**While gerund I has the same range of uses as the affirmative gerund, the negative gerund II is more limited. It is not used with auxiliary "giving" verbs to form polite request or polite command constructions such as negative imperative III.

In the formal negative category we find the *-mas.u* ending again as well as various compounds using the copula.

		Class I	Class II
Indicative		ake.masen	kachi.masen
Imperative		oake nasaimasu na	okachi nasaimasu na
Presumptive	I	ake.masumai	kachi.masumai
	II	ake.nai deshō	kat.anai deshō
Provisional*		ake-masen nara(ba)	kachi.masen nara(ba)
Gerund		ake.masen de	kachi.masen de
Past Indicative		ake.masen deshita	kachi.masen deshita
Past Presumptive		ake.masen deshitarō	kachi.masen deshitarō
		ake.nakatta deshō	kat.anakatta deshō
Conditional		ake.masen deshitara	kachi.masen deshitara
Alternative		ake.masen deshitari	kachi.masen deshitari

The semantic difference between the presumptive I and II is the same as that between the two forms of the affirmative formal presumptive. The imperative, gerund, and alternative forms given here occur only in conjunction with honorifics or when using a very formal style.

Until now we have dealt with derivational endings such as *-mas.u* and *-ana.i* which have a range of inflection only within a given category such as "formal" or "informal negative." *The remaining derivations are different in that they result in new verbs that can themselves take the entire range of inflectional and derivational endings which we have described up to this point.* (See pages 470 and 548 for examples.)

First we will consider the derivation of the passive, potential, causative, and causative passive forms. Since the inflectional endings for these newly derived verbs will be the same as those we have already given for Class I verbs, we will show only their informal affirmative indicative (citation) form in the tables which follow.

	(Original) Class I	(Original) Class II
Passive	ake.rareru	kat.areru
Potential	ake.rareru	kat.eru
Causative	ake.saseru	kat.aseru
Causative Passive	ake.saserareru	kat.aserareru

*Of the two possible provisional forms of the copula: *nara* and *naraba,* the shorter version is used more often in colloquial conversation and is the one we shall use from now on in our tables.

Since the newly formed verbs belong to Class I, the division between stem and ending of the passive would be *akerare.ru, katare.ru,* and so forth. The chief difference between the derivation in original Class I and Class II verbs is that original Class II verbs end up with a separate form for the passive and potential while original Class I verbs use the same derived form for both of these categories. In addition to the causative passive endings shown above (-*saserareru* and -*aserareru*) there are nonstandard shorter endings -*sasareru* and -*asareru* which have the same meaning. We will not include these in the tables in the main body of the text, but they would be used with any verb which takes the longer forms.

The last two categories are the honorific and humble. Two forms are given for each: the second shows the higher level of deference on the part of the speaker.

		Class I	Class II
Honorific	I	oake ni naru	okachi ni naru
	II	oake nasaru	okachi nasaru
Humble	I	oake suru	okachi suru
	II	oake itasu	okachi itasu

This table shows the typical derivation of honorific and humble forms where the infinitive of the original verb becomes a noun by the addition of the prefix *o-* and the inflectional endings are provided by the verbs *nar.u* ("to become"), *nasar.u, su.ru,* and *itas.u* (all "to do"). Of these, *nar.u* and *itas.u* are Class II verbs, but *su.ru* and *nasar.u* are irregular. The student should consult the appropriate tables in the main body of the text to find out the inflectional forms of these two verbs as well as those of the seven other irregular verbs *ar.u, gozar.u, ik.u, irasshar.u, kudasar.u, ku.ru,* and *osshar.u.*

In the honorific and humble categories, a number of common verbs do not follow the typical pattern, but instead use suppletive forms which are not derived from the original verb. For instance, the verbs *nasar.u* and *itas.u* above are, respectively, honorific and humble equivalents of the verb *su.ru.* Normally in such a case there will be only one form each for the honorific and humble categories.

Next we will present tables for the verbs *ake.ru* and *kats.u* showing all the inflectional and derivational categories which we have discussed. The form of these tables is the same as that in the main body of the text. (There is no standard arrangement or list of categories in use for teaching Japanese. The names for the ten basic inflectional categories are from Bernard Bloch's study on inflection, but the content and arrangement of the tables in this book represent the opinion of the original author, Professor Roland A. Lange, as to the most important forms of the Japanese verb and the most convenient arrangement for their presentation.) To help the student learn the distinctions between these verb forms, the Japanese tables are followed by a chart with English translations of each form of *ake.ru.* But first, three forms of the verb—the infinitive, the informal indicative, and the informal gerund—need some additional comment.

THE INFINITIVE

The infinitive is the form of the verb which is used in making compound words. We have already seen how the addition of the prefix *o-* "deference" changes an infinitive into a noun. There are, in addition, a number of nouns which are added to the end of infinitives to form compound nouns. For instance, *kata* "method" and *te* "hand, doer," when added to the infinitive of *tsuka.u* "to use" result in *tsukaikata* "way of using," and *tsukaite* "one who uses." Indeed, there are many infinitives which function as nouns without the addition of other elements. For example:

Infinitive/Noun	Meaning	Verb	Meaning
kangae	"idea"	kangae.ru	"to think, consider"
warai	"laughter"	wara.u	"to laugh"
yorokobi	"joy"	yorokob.u	"to be happy"
nagusame	"consolation"	nagusame.ru	"to console, comfort"
utagai	"doubt, suspicion"	utaga.u	"to doubt, suspect"

To form an adjective from the infinitive, one simply adds one of a number of adjectival endings. We have already seen this happen when the negative ending *-anai* was added to the infinitive of verbs to form the informal nonpast negative indicative, as in *ake.nai.* Other important endings of this type are *-ta.i* "desiderative (want)," *-yasu.i* "easy," and *-nikui* "difficult." By attaching these endings to *kaki* one gets *kakitai, kakiyasui,* and *kakinikui* which mean respectively "want to write," "easy to write," and "difficult to write."

There are also many verbs which are attached to the infinitives of other verbs to make compound verbs. We have already encountered *-mas.u*, which is by far the most common. Three other important ones are *-tagar.u* "non-first-person desiderative" (which, like *-mas.u,* occurs only as an ending in compound verbs), *-hajimeru* "to begin," and *-naosu* "to repair or fix." If we add these to *kaki* we get three new verbs: *kakitagaru* "to wish to write," *kakihajimeru* "to begin to write," and *kakinaosu* "to rewrite." Verbs indicating direction are very productive in combination with verbs of motion. For example, when the infinitive of the verb *tob.u* "to jump, fly" is attached to *agar.u* "rise," *ori.ru* "to descend," *kos.u* "to cross over," and *mawar.u* "revolve," one gets the new verbs *tobiagar.u* "to jump up," *tobiori.ru* "to jump down," *tobikos.u* "to jump over," and *tobimawar.u* "to jump around."

THE INDICATIVE

It is important to remember that all indicative verb forms can function as complete one-word sentences requiring neither subjects nor objects. Thus, the following are all sentences, regardless of whether they are formal or informal, past or nonpast, affirmative or negative.

Akeru.	or Akemasu.	"(Someone) opens/will open (it)."
Aketa.	or Akemashita.	"(Someone) opened (it)."
Akenai.	or Akemasen.	"(Someone) does not/will not open (it)."
Akenakatta.	or Akemasen deshita.	"(Someone) did not open (it)."

When we add more information, such as subject, object, time, and location, the indicative becomes the last word in a longer sentence as in:

Mado o areku, or Mado o akemasu.	"(Someone) opens/will open the window."
Ano hito ga aketa. or Ano hito ga akemashita.	"That person opened (it)."
Kyō wa akenai. or Kyō wa akemasen.	"(Someone) will not open (it) today."

The informal indicative plays a very important role in Japanese modification because it is the form which is used to modify nouns. In Japanese, the modifier, whether it is a verb, adjective, or noun, always precedes the noun it modifies. Since the indicative is a sentence or ends a sentence, one is, in effect, modifying nouns with sentences. For example, the sentence *Mado o aketa.* "(Someone) opened the window," can be used as a modifier in such phrases as the following:

mado o aketa hito	"the person who opened the window"
mado o aketa toki	"the time when (someone) opened the window"
mado o aketa shōko	"the proof that (someone) opened the window"
mado o aketa riyū	"the reason why (someone) opened the window"
mado o aketa kekka	"the result of (someone) having opened the window"

THE INFORMAL GERUND

When ending a sentence (with or without particles), the informal gerund indicates an informal request:

Chotto matte (yo).	"Wait a minute."
Sō ossharanai de.	"Don't say that."
Hayaku kite (yo).	"Come quickly."

Gerunds have many functions when occurring within a sentence. When a sentence simply lists a number of actions without contrasting them or citing one as the cause of the other, all but the last action are often expressed by gerunds. For example, the two sentences *A san wa jūsu o nomimashita.* "Mr. A drank juice." and *B san wa kōhī o nomimashita.* "Mr. B drank coffee." can be combined in one sentence as *A san wa jūsu o nonde, B san wa kōhī o nomimashita.* "Mr. A drank juice, and Mr. B drank coffee." To give strong contrast to these two actions, one would abandon the gerund in favor of an independent clause ending with the indicative: *A san wa jūsu o nonda ga, B san wa kōhī o nomimashita.* "Mr. A drank juice, but Mr. B drank coffee." Similarly, one would use the indicative to show a cause-and-effect relationship as in *A san ga kōhī o nonda kara, B san mo kōhī o nomimashita.* "Mr. A drank coffee, so Mr. B drank coffee too."

A sentence in which the subject of all actions is the same, and which uses a gerund for all but the last verb in the sentence, indicates that the actions were performed in chronological order. For instance: *Kao o aratte, gohan o tabete, gakkō e ikimashita* means "I (you, he, they, etc.) washed my face, ate, and went to school." But *Kao o aratte, gakkō e itte, gohan o tabemashita* means "I (you, he, they, etc.) washed my face, went to school, and ate."

The gerund has no tense, mode, or aspect of its own, so all such information is expressed by the final verb in the sentence. Therefore, if we change the above sentence to *Kao o aratte, gohan o tabete, gakkō e ikimashō,* the meaning becomes "Let's wash our faces, eat, and go to school."

Gerunds within sentences are also used to express manner as in *Eki made aruite ikimashita.* "I (he, they, etc.) went to the station on foot." and *Nani mo iwanai de dete ikimashita.* "I (he, she, etc.) left without saying anything."

We have already seen that in the informal imperative III the gerund combines with the imperative of *kudasar.u* to make a polite request as in *Akete kudasai.* "Please open it." and *Akenai de kudasai.* "Please don't open it." While the gerund may combine with any other verb if the combination makes sense, certain combinations which occur frequently have taken on special fixed meanings. Perhaps the most important of these is the combination of the informal affirmative gerund plus *i.ru* "to exist." Generally speaking, when the gerund of a transitive verb is used with *i.ru,* the combination shows continuing action as in the English progressive, but when the gerund of an intransitive verb is used, the combination shows the existence of a continuing state. A good example of this contrast is seen in comparing combinations using the gerunds of two verbs which mean "to open." *Ake.ru* is transitive and would be used to convey such information as "I opened the door," while *ak.u* is intransitive and is used to convey such information as "The door opened." The transitive gerund *akete* plus *i.ru* means "I (or someone else) am opening it." On the other hand, *aite iru* from *ak.u* means "It is (in the state of being) open," *NOT* "it is opening."

Other productive gerund-verb combinations are those in which the gerund precedes *shima.u* "to finish," *oku* "to put or place," and the various verbs for giving and receiving. That with *shima.u* means "to do something completely, to finish doing something," or "to end up by doing something." That with *ok.u* means "to do something in advance or with reference to the future," while those with verbs for giving and receiving mean "to perform an action for the benefit of another, to have another perform an action for one's own benefit," or simply "to benefit from the action of another." The informal imperative III, which uses the gerund plus the appropriate form of *kudasar.u* "give to me," falls into this last group. Verbs of giving and receiving are discussed at greater length following the main verb tables.

We should also mention the use of the gerund in combination with the particles *mo* and *wa* to express permission and prohibition. In asking for permission one uses the gerund plus *mo* as in *Mite mo ii desu ka.* "May I look (at it)?" To answer that question in the affirmative one might say *Hai (mite mo) ii desu.* "Yes, you may (look at it)." To refuse permission one might use the gerund plus *wa* as in *Iie (mite wa) ikemasen.* "No, you must not (look at it)."

We are now ready for our sample verb tables and tables of English equivalents.

to open　　TRANSITIVE

			AFFIRMATIVE	**NEGATIVE**
Indicative	**INFORMAL**		akeru	akenai
	FORMAL		akemasu	akemasen
Imperative	**INFORMAL**	I	akero	akeru na
		II	akenasai	akenasaru na
		III	akete kudasai	akenai de kudasai
	FORMAL		oake nasaimase	oake nasaimasu na
Presumptive	**INFORMAL**	I	akeyō	akemai
		II	akeru darō	akenai darō
	FORMAL	I	akemashō	akemasumai
		II	akeru deshō	akenai deshō
Provisional	**INFORMAL**		akereba	akenakereba
	FORMAL		akemaseba	akemasen nara
			akemasureba	
Gerund	**INFORMAL**	I	akete	akenai de
		II		akenakute
	FORMAL		akemashite	akemasen de
Past Ind.	**INFORMAL**		aketa	akenakatta
	FORMAL		akemashita	akemasen deshita
Past Presump.	**INFORMAL**		aketarō	akenakattarō
			aketa darō	akenakatta darō
	FORMAL		akemashitarō	akemasen deshitarō
			aketa deshō	akenakatta deshō
Conditional	**INFORMAL**		aketara	akenakattara
	FORMAL		akemashitara	akemasen deshitara
Alternative	**INFORMAL**		aketari	akenakattari
	FORMAL		akemashitari	akemasen deshitari

			INFORMAL AFFIRMATIVE INDICATIVE
Passive			akerareru
Potential			akerareru
Causative			akesaseru
Causative Pass.			akesaserareru
Honorific		I	oake ni naru
		II	oake nasaru
Humble		I	oake suru
		II	oake itasu

			AFFIRMATIVE	NEGATIVE
Indicative	**INFORMAL**		katsu	katanai
	FORMAL		kachimasu	kachimasen
Imperative	**INFORMAL**	I	kate	katsu na
		II	kachinasai	kachinasaru na
		III	katte kudasai	katanai de kudasai
	FORMAL		okachi nasaimase	okachi nasaimasu na
Presumptive	**INFORMAL**	I	katō	katsumai
		II	katsu darō	katanai darō
	FORMAL	I	kachimashō	kachimasumai
		II	katsu deshō	katanai deshō
Provisional	**INFORMAL**		kateba	katanakereba
	FORMAL		kachimaseba	kachimasen nara
			kachimasureba	
Gerund	**INFORMAL**	I	katte	katanai de
		II		katanakute
	FORMAL		kachimashite	kachimasen de
Past Ind.	**INFORMAL**		katta	katanakatta
	FORMAL		kachimashita	kachimasen deshita
Past Presump.	**INFORMAL**		kattarō	katanakattarō
			katta darō	katanakatta darō
	FORMAL		kachimashitarō	kachimasen deshitarō
			katta deshō	katanakatta deshō
Conditional	**INFORMAL**		kattara	katanakattara
	FORMAL		kachimashitara	kachimasen deshitara
Alternative	**INFORMAL**		kattari	katanakattari
	FORMAL		kachimashitari	kachimasen deshitari

		INFORMAL AFFIRMATIVE INDICATIVE
Passive		katareru
Potential		kateru
Causative		kataseru
Causative Pass.		kataserareru
Honorific	I	okachi ni naru
	II	okachi nasaru
Humble	I	
	II	

SAMPLE TABLE OF ENGLISH EQUIVALENTS

In the following table of English equivalents two conventions have been adopted to avoid undue redundancy.

1. The same English translation is used to represent both the formal and informal verb forms, with the understanding that the formal will be more polite in tone.
2. Only affirmative translations are given because except where noted the student can easily deduce the meaning of the corresponding negative form.

The translations offered here, of course, cannot hope to cover all possible cases because meaning is influenced by context. Nevertheless, they should serve to delineate the main semantic boundaries between the various forms.

Infinitive	opening (This form is non-commital as to level of formality, tense, aspect, affirmative, or negative. It merely serves as a base for many endings, and sometimes to end a phrase.)
*Indicative**	I open (it), you open (it), he (she, it) opens (it), we (you, they) open (it)
	or: I (you, he, she, it, we, you, they) will open (it)
Imperative	open (it)! (The Informal Imperative III and the Formal Imperative are closer to "please open it.")
Presumptive	**I:** I am going to open (it), we are going to open (it) or: Let's open (it) (There is no negative form which corresponds to this second meaning of presumptive I.)
	II: I (you, he, she, it, we, they) probably open (it) or: I am probably going to open (it), you are probably going to open (it), he (she, it) is probably going to open (it), we (you, they) are probably going to open (it)
Provisional	if I (you, she, he, it, we, they) open (it)
Gerund	opening (it) (Non-commital as to tense and aspect which are established by the final verb in a clause or sentence.)
Past Indicative	I (you, he, she, it, we, they) opened (it)
	or: I (you, he, she, it, we, they) have opened (it)
	or: I (you, he, she, it, we, they) had opened (it) *(Indicates completed action.)*

*NOTE: In this book and in Japanese dictionaries the informal affirmative indicative is used as the citation form for verbs. This is usually called the "dictionary form."

Past Presumptive	I (you, he, she, it, we, they) probably opened (it)
or:	I (you, he, she, it, we, they) probably have opened (it)
or:	I (you, he, she, it, we, they) probably had opened (it)
Conditional	if I (you, he, she, it, we, they) should open (it)
or:	if I (you, he, she, it, we, they) were to open (it)
or:	when I (you, he, she, it, we, they) open (it)
or:	when I (you, he, she, it, we, they) opened (it)
Alternative	opening (it) and — (Non-commital as to tense and aspect. It merely indicates that two or more actions were, are, or will be performed alternately.)
Passive	is opened (by someone or something)
or:	will be opened (by someone or something)
or:	is opened (by someone) with bad result (for someone else)
or:	will be opened (by someone) with bad result (for someone else) *(This form is sometimes also used as a sort of honorific to show deference for the person who performs the action.)*
Potential	can be opened
or:	can open (it)
Causative	I make (someone) open (it), you make (someone) open (it), he (she, it) makes (someone) open (it), we (you, they) make (someone) open (it)
or:	I (you, he, she, it, we, they) will make (someone) open (it)
or:	I allow (someone) to open (it), you allow (someone) to open (it), he (she, it) allows (someone) to open (it), we (you, they) allow (someone) to open (it)
or:	I (you, he, she, it, we, they) will allow (someone) to open (it)
Causative Pass.	I am made to open (it), you are made to open (it), he (she, it) is made to open (it), we (you, they) are made to open (it)
or:	I (you, he, she, it, we, they) will be made to open (it)
Honorific	you open (it), he (she) opens (it) they open (it)
or:	you, (he, she, they) will open (it) (all showing deference to the subject of the verb.)

Humble	I (we, or a member of my "in group"), open (it)

> *or:* I (we, or a member of my "in group") will open (it)
> *(The speaker shows deference by lowering his own position.)*

LOANWORD + *SURU* VERBS

All of the verbs with which we have dealt thus far have been composed of native Japanese elements. Japanese also has a vast number of verbs derived from foreign loanwords (often nouns) by the addition of the native Japanese verb *suru* "to do." Thus

	shinpai	"worry"	+ suru is shinpai suru "to worry"
	kekkon	"marriage"	+ suru is kekkon suru "to marry"
and	hakken	"discovery"	+ suru is hakken suru "to discover"

Until the mid-nineteenth century, most of these verbs were derived from vocabulary borrowed from Chinese. But from the Meiji period onward an increasing amount of vocabulary has been borrowed from European languages, and from English, French, and German, in particular. These loanwords are assimilated to Japanese in the same manner as the Chinese borrowings. Therefore, one finds in common use today such "Japanese verbs" as *kopī suru* "to copy," *doraibu suru* "to drive," and *sain suru* "to sign."

To communicate effectively in Japanese, students must keep three points firmly in mind when dealing with Japanese verbs based on borrowings from English.

1. The words must be pronounced as they are by Japanese, not as they are in the original English. Remember, they are Japanese verbs.
2. Their meanings may differ as much from the original English as does their pronunciation.
3. They cannot be coined at random by combining any English word with *suru*. Use ones which you have observed Japanese using, and consult a native speaker if in doubt as to whether a particular combination is in use.

On the following pages are one table for verbs of this type derived from Chinese nouns and one for those derived from English nouns. Note that these verbs lack type I honorific and humble forms, that SOME Chinese-derived verbs are prefixed by *go-* rather than *o-* in the formal imperative and honorific forms, and that English-derived verbs are usually not prefixed by either.

benkyō shi   べんきょうする／勉強する   benkyō su.ru

TRANSITIVE   *to study*

			AFFIRMATIVE	NEGATIVE
Indicative	**INFORMAL**		benkyō suru	benkyō shinai
	FORMAL		benkyō shimasu	benkyō shimasen
Imperative	**INFORMAL**	**I**	benkyō shiro	benkyō suru na
		II	benkyō shinasai	benkyō shinasaru na
		III	benkyō shite kudasai	benkyō shinai de kudasai
	FORMAL		gobenkyō nasaimase	gobenkyō nasaimasu na
Presumptive	**INFORMAL**	**I**	benkyō shiyō	benkyō surumai
		II	benkyō suru darō	benkyō shinai darō
	FORMAL	**I**	benkyō shimashō	benkyō shimasumai
		II	benkyō suru deshō	benkyō shinai deshō
Provisional	**INFORMAL**		benkyō sureba	benkyō shinakereba
	FORMAL		benkyō shimaseba	benkyō shimasen nara
			benkyō shimasureba	
Gerund	**INFORMAL**	**I**	benkyō shite	benkyō shinai de
		II		benkyō shinakute
	FORMAL		benkyō shimashite	benkyō shimasen de
Past Ind.	**INFORMAL**		benkyō shita	benkyō shinakatta
	FORMAL		benkyō shimashita	benkyō shimasen deshita
Past Presump.	**INFORMAL**		benkyō shitarō	benkyō shinakattarō
			benkyō shita darō	benkyō shinakatta darō
	FORMAL		benkyō shimashitarō	benkyō shimasen deshitarō
			benkyō shita deshō	benkyō shinakatta deshō
Conditional	**INFORMAL**		benkyō shitara	benkyō shinakattara
	FORMAL		benkyō shimashitara	benkyō shimasen deshitara
Alternative	**INFORMAL**		benkyō shitari	benkyō shinakattari
	FORMAL		benkyō shimashitari	benkyō shimasen deshitari

			INFORMAL AFFIRMATIVE INDICATIVE
Passive			benkyō sareru
Potential			benkyō dekiru
Causative			benkyō saseru
Causative Pass.			benkyō saserareru
Honorific		**I**	
		II	gobenkyō nasaru
Humble		**I**	
		II	benkyō itasu

Introduction   19

to copy   TRANSITIVE

			AFFIRMATIVE	NEGATIVE
Indicative	**INFORMAL**		kopī suru	kopī shinai
	FORMAL		kopī shimasu	kopī shimasen
Imperative	**INFORMAL**	I	kopī shiro	kopī suru na
		II	kopī shinasai	kopī shinasaru na
		III	kopī shite kudasai	kopī shinai de kudasai
	FORMAL		kopī nasaimase	kopī nasaimasu na
Presumptive	**INFORMAL**	I	kopī shiyō	kopī surumai
		II	kopī suru darō	kopī shinai darō
	FORMAL	I	kopī shimashō	kopī shimasumai
		II	kopī suru deshō	kopī shinai deshō
Provisional	**INFORMAL**		kopī sureba	kopī shinakereba
	FORMAL		kopī shimaseba	kopī shimasen nara
			kopī shimasureba	
Gerund	**INFORMAL**	I	kopī shite	kopī shinai de
		II		kopī shinakute
	FORMAL		kopī shimashite	kopī shimasen de
Past Ind.	**INFORMAL**		kopī shita	kopī shinakatta
	FORMAL		kopī shimashita	kopī shimasen deshita
Past Presump.	**INFORMAL**		kopī shitarō	kopī shinakattarō
			kopī shita darō	kopī shinakatta darō
	FORMAL		kopī shimashitarō	kopī shimasen deshitarō
			kopī shita deshō	kopī shinakatta deshō
Conditional	**INFORMAL**		kopī shitara	kopī shinakattara
	FORMAL		kopī shimashitara	kopī shimasen deshitara
Alternative	**INFORMAL**		kopī shitari	kopī shinakattari
	FORMAL		kopī shimashitari	kopī shimasen deshitari

		INFORMAL AFFIRMATIVE INDICATIVE
Passive		kopī sareru
Potential		kopī dekiru
Causative		kopī saseru
Causative Pass.		kopī saserareru
Honorific	I	
	II	kopī nasaru
Humble	I	
	II	kopī itasu

TABLES OF 501 JAPANESE VERBS

We are now ready to enter the main body of the text, which consists of tables of 501 common Japanese verbs showing all of the forms which were presented in our sample tables. The verbs are intransitive unless designated as transitive.

It is likely that students will approach this book looking for two basic types of information. Some will be seeking the inflection and derivation of a Japanese verb whose citation form they already know, while others will be trying to find a Japanese verb which fits a particular meaning in English. To provide for the first case, our verb tables are arranged alphabetically according to the citation form of the verb. Thus students who want to find out a particular form of the verb *taberu* can find it easily on page 481 between *suwaru* and *tadoru*. For the convenience of students who are seeking a verb with a given meaning in English, an English to Japanese index of all 501 verbs is provided beginning on page 635. Here students can look up "begin" and find listed the intransitive verb *hajimaru* and the transitive verb *hajimeru* on pages 110 and 111 respectively. Thus, within the narrow limits of 501 verbs, this text also serves as a sort of Japanese-English, English-Japanese dictionary.

Essential 55 Verb List

ageru	あげる	to give (to second or third person)
aru	ある	to exist, to be (inanimate), to have
aruku	歩く	to walk
benkyō suru	勉強する	to study
dekakeru	出かける	to go out, to leave home
dekiru	出来る	to be able to, to be possible, to be formed, to be ready
deru	出る	to exit, to go, to leave, to go out, to be served
erabu	選ぶ	to select, to choose
hairu	入る	to come in, to enter, to be in, to join
hajimeru	始める	to begin, to start
hanasu	話す	to talk, to speak, to tell
harau	払う	to pay
hataraku	働く	to work
iku	行く	to go
iru	いる	to exist, to be (animate), to have
iu	言う	to say, to tell, to talk about
kaeru	帰る	to go back, to return (to a place)
kaku	書く	to write
kau	買う	to buy
kiku	聞く	to ask, to listen, to hear
kimeru	決める	to decide, to choose
kiru	着る	to put on, to wear (on the body, as with a coat, suit, or dress)
kotaeru	答える	to answer, to respond
kuraberu	比べる	to compare
kuru	来る	to come, to show up
machigaeru	間違える	to make a mistake, to mistake one thing for another
matsu	待つ	to wait, to wait for, to look forward to

miru	見る	to look at, to see, to read
morau	貰う	to receive, to get
motsu	持つ	to have, to hold, to own
narau	習う	to learn
neru	寝る	to sleep, to recline
nomu	飲む	to drink, to swallow
noru	乗る	to get on, to board, to take a ride, to ride
okiru	起きる	to get up, to wake up, to get out of bed
omou	思う	to think, to feel, to believe, to consider, to expect, to regard
oriru	降りる	to get off, to go down
oshieru	教える	to teach, to instruct, to guide, to inform, to show
owaru	終わる	to end, to be finished, to be over
shiru	知る	to know, to get to know, to learn about, to understand
sumu	住む	to reside, to live
suru	する	to do, to make
taberu	食べる	to eat
tanomu	頼む	to ask a favor, to request, to order
tanoshimu	楽しむ	to enjoy, to have fun, to have a good time
tasukeru	助ける	to help, to assist, to rescue, to save
tatsu	立つ	to stand, to be built
toru	取る	to take, to get, to hold, to pick up, to have
tsukau	使う	to use, to operate, to employ
tsuku	着く	to arrive, to get to, to reach
tsukuru	作る	to make, to cook, to create, to build
tsutomeru	勤める	to work for, to be employed
uru	売る	to sell
wakaru	分かる	to understand, to know
yomu	読む	to read

Alphabetical Listing of
501 Japanese Verbs
Fully Described in
All Inflections, Moods, Aspects,
and Formality Levels

あがる／上がる **agar.u**

to rise, to go up

A

			AFFIRMATIVE	NEGATIVE
Indicative	**INFORMAL**		agaru	agaranai
	FORMAL		agarimasu	agarimasen
Imperative	**INFORMAL**	I	agare	agaru na
		II	agarinasai	agarinasaru na
		III	agatte kudasai	agaranai de kudasai
	FORMAL		oagari nasaimase	oagari nasaimasu na
Presumptive	**INFORMAL**	I	agarō	agarumai
		II	agaru darō	agaranai darō
	FORMAL	I	agarimashō	agarimasumai
		II	agaru deshō	agaranai deshō
Provisional	**INFORMAL**		agareba	agaranakereba
	FORMAL		agarimaseba	agarimasen nara
			agarimasureba	
Gerund	**INFORMAL**	I	agatte	agaranai de
		II		agaranakute
	FORMAL		agarimashite	agarimasen de
Past Ind.	**INFORMAL**		agatta	agaranakatta
	FORMAL		agarimashita	agarimasen deshita
Past Presump.	**INFORMAL**		agattarō	agaranakattarō
			agatta darō	agaranakatta darō
	FORMAL		agarimashitarō	agarimasen deshitarō
			agatta deshō	agaranakatta deshō
Conditional	**INFORMAL**		agattara	agaranakattara
	FORMAL		agarimashitara	agarimasen deshitara
Alternative	**INFORMAL**		agattari	agaranakattari
	FORMAL		agarimashitari	agarimasen deshitari

		INFORMAL AFFIRMATIVE INDICATIVE
Passive		agarareru
Potential		agareru
Causative		agaraseru
Causative Pass.		agaraserareru
Honorific	I	oagari ni naru
	II	oagari nasaru
Humble	I	
	II	

to give (to second or third person)　　　TRANSITIVE

			AFFIRMATIVE	NEGATIVE
Indicative	**INFORMAL**		ageru	agenai
	FORMAL		agemasu	agemasen
Imperative	**INFORMAL**	I	agero	ageru na
		II	agenasai	agenasaru na
		III	agete kudasai	agenai de kudasai
	FORMAL		oage nasaimase	oage nasaimasu na
Presumptive	**INFORMAL**	I	ageyō	agemai
		II	ageru darō	agenai darō
	FORMAL	I	agemashō	agemasumai
		II	ageru deshō	agenai deshō
Provisional	**INFORMAL**		agereba	agenakereba
	FORMAL		agemaseba	agemasen nara
			agemasureba	
Gerund	**INFORMAL**	I	agete	agenai de
		II		agenakute
	FORMAL		agemashite	agemasen de
Past Ind.	**INFORMAL**		ageta	agenakatta
	FORMAL		agemashita	agemasen deshita
Past Presump.	**INFORMAL**		agetarō	agenakattarō
			ageta darō	agenakatta darō
	FORMAL		agemashitarō	agemasen deshitarō
			ageta deshō	agenakatta deshō
Conditional	**INFORMAL**		agetara	agenakattara
	FORMAL		agemashitara	agemasen deshitara
Alternative	**INFORMAL**		agetari	agenakattari
	FORMAL		agemashitari	agemasen deshitari

		INFORMAL AFFIRMATIVE INDICATIVE
Passive		agerareru
Potential		agerareru
Causative		agesaseru
Causative Pass.		agesaserareru
Honorific	I	oage ni naru
	II	oage nasaru
Humble	I	sashiageru
	II	

AN ESSENTIAL
55 VERB

28

Ageru あげる

to give (to second or third person)

Ageru is a convenient verb for frequent use. But use this verb with care. Recipients of a thing or a favor should never be first person, and their status should be equal to or lesser than the giver's.

When this verb is used with the gerund form of another verb, it means the giver is doing a favor for, or acting kindly toward, a recipient whose status is equal to or lesser than the giver's.

Sentences Using *Ageru*

Otōto ni, okozukai o agemashita.
弟にお小遣いをあげました。
I gave my younger brother spending money.

Tomodachi wa maitoshi okusan no tanjōbi ni, purezento o agemasu.
友達は毎年奥さんの誕生日に、
プレゼントをあげます。
Every year, my friend gives a present to his wife on her birthday.

Keikan wa ryokōsha ni eki e no michi o oshiete agemashita.
警官は旅行者に駅への道を教えてあげました。
A police officer showed a tourist the way to the station.

Restoran ni tsurete itte ageyō.
レストランに連れていってあげよう。
I'll take you to a restaurant.

Kono hon o agetemo yomanai deshō.
この本をあげても読まないでしょう。
Even if I gave you this book, you wouldn't read it.

Words and Expressions Related to This Verb

Takujisho wa, gogo 3 ji ni kodomotachi ni miruku o ageru.
託児所は、午後3時に子供にミルクをあげる。
The day-care center gives the children milk at 3 P.M. (**ageru**)

Kodomotachi wa, gogo 3 ji ni inu ni miruku o yaru.
子供たちは、午後3時に犬にミルクをやる。
The children give their dog milk at 3 P.M. (**yaru**)

to reveal, to disclose   TRANSITIVE

			AFFIRMATIVE	NEGATIVE
Indicative	**INFORMAL**		akasu	akasanai
	FORMAL		akashimasu	akashimasen
Imperative	**INFORMAL**	I	akase	akasu na
		II	akashinasai	akashinasaru na
		III	akashite kudasai	akasanai de kudasai
	FORMAL		oakashi nasaimase	oakashi nasaimasu na
Presumptive	**INFORMAL**	I	akasō	akasumai
		II	akasu darō	akasanai darō
	FORMAL	I	akashimashō	akashimasumai
		II	akasu deshō	akasanai deshō
Provisional	**INFORMAL**		akaseba	akasanakereba
	FORMAL		akashimaseba	akashimasen nara
			akashimasureba	
Gerund	**INFORMAL**	I	akashite	akasanaide
		II		akasanakute
	FORMAL		akashimasite	akashimasen de
Past Ind.	**INFORMAL**		akashita	akasanakatta
	FORMAL		akashimashita	akashimasen deshita
Past Presump.	**INFORMAL**		akashitarō	akasanakattarō
			akashita darō	akasanakatta darō
	FORMAL		akashimashitarō	akashimasen deshitarō
			akashita deshō	akasanakatta deshō
Conditional	**INFORMAL**		akashitara	akasanakattara
	FORMAL		akashimashitara	akashimasen deshitara
Alternative	**INFORMAL**		akashitari	akasanakattari
	FORMAL		akashimashitari	akashimasen deshitari

		INFORMAL AFFIRMATIVE INDICATIVE
Passive		akasareru
Potential		akaseru
Causative		akasaseru
Causative Pass.		akasaserareru
Honorific	I	oakashi ni naru
	II	oakashi nasaru
Humble	I	oakashi suru
	II	oakashi itasu

あける／開ける **ake.ru**
TRANSITIVE *to open*

A

			AFFIRMATIVE	**NEGATIVE**
Indicative	**INFORMAL**		akeru	akenai
	FORMAL		akemasu	akemasen
Imperative	**INFORMAL**	I	akero	akeru na
		II	akenasai	akenasaru na
		III	akete kudasai	akenai de kudasai
	FORMAL		oake nasaimase	oake nasaimasu na
Presumptive	**INFORMAL**	I	akeyō	akemai
		II	akeru darō	akenai darō
	FORMAL	I	akemashō	akemasumai
		II	akeru deshō	akenai deshō
Provisional	**INFORMAL**		akereba	akenakereba
	FORMAL		akemaseba	akemasen nara
			akemasureba	
Gerund	**INFORMAL**	I	akete	akenai de
		II		akenakute
	FORMAL		akemashite	akemasen de
Past Ind.	**INFORMAL**		aketa	akenakatta
	FORMAL		akemashita	akemasen deshita
Past Presump.	**INFORMAL**		aketarō	akenakattarō
			aketa darō	akenakatta darō
	FORMAL		akemashitarō	akemasen deshitarō
			aketa deshō	akenakatta deshō
Conditional	**INFORMAL**		aketara	akenakattara
	FORMAL		akemashitara	akemasen deshitara
Alternative	**INFORMAL**		aketari	akenakattari
	FORMAL		akemashitari	akemasen deshitari

			INFORMAL AFFIRMATIVE INDICATIVE
Passive			akerareru
Potential			akerareru
Causative			akesaseru
Causative Pass.			akesaserareru
Honorific		I	oake ni naru
		II	oake nasaru
Humble		I	oake suru
		II	oake itasu

akirame

to abandon (an idea), *to resign oneself* (to)　　TRANSITIVE

			AFFIRMATIVE	NEGATIVE
Indicative	**INFORMAL**		akirameru	akiramenai
	FORMAL		akiramemasu	akiramemasen
Imperative	**INFORMAL**	I	akiramero	akirameru na
		II	akiramenasai	akiramenasaru na
		III	akiramete kudasai	akiramenai de kudasai
	FORMAL		oakirame nasaimase	oakirame nasaimasu na
Presumptive	**INFORMAL**	I	akirameyō	akiramemai
		II	akirameru darō	akiramenai darō
	FORMAL	I	akiramemashō	akiramemasumai
		II	akirameru deshō	akiramenai deshō
Provisional	**INFORMAL**		akiramereba	akiramenakereba
	FORMAL		akiramemaseba	akiramemasen nara
			akiramemasureba	
Gerund	**INFORMAL**	I	akiramete	akiramenai de
		II		akiramenakute
	FORMAL		akiramemashite	akiramemasen de
Past Ind.	**INFORMAL**		akirameta	akiramenakatta
	FORMAL		akiramemashita	akiramemasen deshita
Past Presump.	**INFORMAL**		akirametarō	akiramenakattarō
			akirameta darō	akiramenakatta darō
	FORMAL		akiramemashitarō	akiramemasen deshitarō
			akirameta deshō	akiramenakatta deshō
Conditional	**INFORMAL**		akirametara	akiramenakattara
	FORMAL		akiramemashitara	akiramemasen deshitara
Alternative	**INFORMAL**		akirametari	akiramenakattari
	FORMAL		akiramemashitari	akiramemasen deshitari

		INFORMAL AFFIRMATIVE INDICATIVE
Passive		akiramerareru
Potential		akiramerareru
Causative		akiramesaseru
Causative Pass.		akiramesaserareru
Honorific	I	oakirame ni naru
	II	oakirame nasaru
Humble	I	
	II	

あきる／飽きる **aki.ru**
to grow tired of, lose interest in

A

			AFFIRMATIVE	**NEGATIVE**
Indicative	**INFORMAL**		akiru	akinai
	FORMAL		akimasu	akimasen
Imperative	**INFORMAL**	I	akiro	akiru na
		II	akinasai	akinasaru na
		III	akite kudasai	akinai de kudasai
	FORMAL		oaki nasaimase	oaki nasaimasu na
Presumptive	**INFORMAL**	I	akiyō	akimai
		II	akiru darō	akinai darō
	FORMAL	I	akimashō	akimasumai
		II	akiru deshō	akinai deshō
Provisional	**INFORMAL**		akireba	akinakereba
	FORMAL		akimaseba	akimasen nara
			akimasureba	
Gerund	**INFORMAL**	I	akite	akinai de
		II		akinakute
	FORMAL		akimashite	akimasen de
Past Ind.	**INFORMAL**		akita	akinakatta
	FORMAL		akimashita	akimasen deshita
Past Presump.	**INFORMAL**		akitarō	akinakattarō
			akita darō	akinakatta darō
	FORMAL		akimashitarō	akimasen deshitarō
			akita deshō	akinakatta deshō
Conditional	**INFORMAL**		akitara	akinakattara
	FORMAL		akimashitara	akimasen deshitara
Alternative	**INFORMAL**		akitari	akinakattari
	FORMAL		akimashitari	akimasen deshitari

		INFORMAL AFFIRMATIVE INDICATIVE
Passive		akirareru
Potential		akirareru
Causative		akisaseru
Causative Pass.		akisaserareru
Honorific	I	oaki ni naru
	II	oaki nasaru
Humble	I	
	II	

to open, to become vacant

			AFFIRMATIVE	NEGATIVE
Indicative	**INFORMAL**		aku	akanai
	FORMAL		akimasu	akimasen
Imperative	**INFORMAL**	I	ake	akuna
		II		
		III		
	FORMAL			
Presumptive	**INFORMAL**	I	akō	akumai
		II	aku darō	akanai darō
	FORMAL	I	akimashō	akimasumai
		II	aku deshō	akanai deshō
Provisional	**INFORMAL**		akeba	akanakereba
	FORMAL		akimaseba	akimasen nara
			akimasureba	
Gerund	**INFORMAL**	I	aite	akanai de
		II		akanakute
	FORMAL		akimashite	akimasen de
Past Ind.	**INFORMAL**		aita	akanakatta
	FORMAL		akimashita	akimasen deshita
Past Presump.	**INFORMAL**		aitarō	akanakattarō
			aita darō	akanakatta darō
	FORMAL		akimashitarō	akimasen deshitarō
			aita deshō	akanakatta deshō
Conditional	**INFORMAL**		aitara	akanakattara
	FORMAL		akimashitara	akimasen deshitara
Alternative	**INFORMAL**		aitari	akanakattari
	FORMAL		akimashitari	akimasen deshitari

INFORMAL AFFIRMATIVE INDICATIVE

Passive		
Potential		
Causative		
Causative Pass.		
Honorific	I	
	II	
Humble	I	
	II	

あらそう／争う　**araso.u**

TRANSITIVE　*to dispute*

			AFFIRMATIVE	NEGATIVE
Indicative	**INFORMAL**		arasou	arasowanai
	FORMAL		arasoimasu	arasoimasen
Imperative	**INFORMAL**	I	arasoe	arasou na
		II	arasoinasai	arasoinasaru na
		III	arasotte kudasai	arasowanai de kudasai
	FORMAL		oarasoi nasaimase	oarasoi nasaimasu na
Presumptive	**INFORMAL**	I	arasoō	arasoumai
		II	arasou darō	arasowanai darō
	FORMAL	I	arasoimashō	arasoimasumai
		II	arasou deshō	arasowanai deshō
Provisional	**INFORMAL**		arasoeba	arasowanakereba
	FORMAL		arasoimaseba	arasoimasen nara
			arasoimasureba	
Gerund	**INFORMAL**	I	arasotte	arasowanai de
		II		arasowanakute
	FORMAL		arasoimashite	arasoimasen de
Past Ind.	**INFORMAL**		arasotta	arasowanakatta
	FORMAL		arasoimashita	arasoimasen deshita
Past Presump.	**INFORMAL**		arasottarō	arasowanakattarō
			arasotta darō	arasowanakatta darō
	FORMAL		arasoimashitarō	arasoimasen deshitarō
			arasotta deshō	arasowanakatta deshō
Conditional	**INFORMAL**		arasottara	arasowanakattara
	FORMAL		arasoimashitara	arasoimasen deshitara
Alternative	**INFORMAL**		arasottari	arasowanakattari
	FORMAL		arasoimashitari	arasoimasen deshitari

		INFORMAL AFFIRMATIVE INDICATIVE
Passive		arasowareru
Potential		arasoeru
Causative		arasowaseru
Causative Pass.		arasowaserareru
Honorific	I	oarasoi ni naru
	II	oarasoi nasaru
Humble	I	oarasoi suru
	II	oarasoi itasu

to be renewed, to be changed

			AFFIRMATIVE	NEGATIVE
Indicative	**INFORMAL**		aratamaru	aratamaranai
	FORMAL		aratamarimasu	aratamarimasen
Imperative	**INFORMAL**	I	aratamare	aratamaru na
		II	aratamarinasai	aratamarinasaru na
		III	aratamatte kudasai	aratamaranai de kudasai
	FORMAL		oaratamari nasaimase	oaratamari nasaimasu na
Presumptive	**INFORMAL**	I	aratamarō	aratamarumai
		II	aratamaru darō	aratamaranai darō
	FORMAL	I	aratamarimashō	aratamarimasumai
		II	aratamaru deshō	aratamaranai deshō
Provisional	**INFORMAL**		aratamareba	aratamaranakereba
	FORMAL		aratamarimaseba	aratamarimasen nara
			aratamarimasureba	
Gerund	**INFORMAL**	I	aratamatte	aratamaranai de
		II		aratamaranakute
	FORMAL		aratamarimashite	aratamarimasen de
Past Ind.	**INFORMAL**		aratamatta	aratamaranakatta
	FORMAL		aratamarimashita	aratamarimasen deshita
Past Presump.	**INFORMAL**		aratamattarō	aratamaranakattarō
			aratamatta darō	aratamaranakatta darō
	FORMAL		aratamarimashitarō	aratamarimasen deshitarō
			aratamatta deshō	aratamaranakatta deshō
Conditional	**INFORMAL**		aratamattara	aratamaranakattara
	FORMAL		aratamarimashitara	aratamarimasen deshitara
Alternative	**INFORMAL**		aratamattari	aratamaranakattari
	FORMAL		aratamarimashitari	aratamarimasen deshitari

		INFORMAL AFFIRMATIVE INDICATIVE
Passive		aratamarareru
Potential		aratamareru
Causative		aratamaraseru
Causative Pass.		aratamaraserareru
Honorific	I	oaratamari ni naru
	II	oaratamari nasaru
Humble	I	
	II	

あらためる／改める **aratame.ru**
TRANSITIVE *to change, to revise*

A

			AFFIRMATIVE	NEGATIVE
Indicative	**INFORMAL**		aratameru	aratamenai
	FORMAL		aratamemasu	aratamemasen
Imperative	**INFORMAL**	I	aratamero	aratameru na
		II	aratamenasai	aralamenasaru na
		III	aratamete kudasai	aratamenai de kudasai
	FORMAL		oaratame nasaimase	oaratame nasaimasu na
Presumptive	**INFORMAL**	I	aratarneyō	aratamemai
		II	aratameru darō	aratamenai darō
	FORMAL	I	aratamemashō	aratamemasumai
		II	aratameru deshō	aratamenai deshō
Provisional	**INFORMAL**		aratamereba	aratamenakereba
	FORMAL		aratamemaseba	aratamemasen nara
			aralamemasureba	
Gerund	**INFORMAL**	I	aratamete	aratamenai de
		II		aratamenakute
	FORMAL		aratamemashite	aratamemasen de
Past Ind.	**INFORMAL**		aratameta	aratamenakatta
	FORMAL		aratamemashita	aratamemasen deshita
Past Presump.	**INFORMAL**		aratametarō	aralamenakattarō
			aratameta darō	aretamenakatta darō
	FORMAL		aratamemashitarō	aratamemasen deshitarō
			aratameta deshō	aratamenakatta deshō
Conditional	**INFORMAL**		aratametara	aratamenakattara
	FORMAL		aratamemashitara	aratamemasen deshitara
Alternative	**INFORMAL**		aratametari	aratamenakattari
	FORMAL		aratamemashitari	aratamemasen deshitari

		INFORMAL AFFIRMATIVE INDICATIVE
Passive		aratamerareru
Potential		aratamerareru
Causative		aratamesaseru
Causative Pass.		aratamesaserareru
Honorific	I	oaratame ni naru
	II	oaratame nasaru
Humble	I	oaratame suru
	II	oaratame itasu

ara.u あらう／洗う   arai
to wash   TRANSITIVE

			AFFIRMATIVE	NEGATIVE
Indicative	**INFORMAL**		arau	arawanai
	FORMAL		araimasu	araimasen
Imperative	**INFORMAL**	I	arae	arau na
		II	arainasai	arainasaru na
		III	aratte kudasai	arawanai de kudasai
	FORMAL		oarai nasaimase	oarai nasaimasu na
Presumptive	**INFORMAL**	I	araō	araumai
		II	arau darō	arawanai darō
	FORMAL	I	araimashō	araimasumai
		II	arau deshō	arawanai deshō
Provisional	**INFORMAL**		araeba	arawanakereba
	FORMAL		araimaseba	araimasen nara
			araimasureba	
Gerund	**INFORMAL**	I	aratte	arawanai de
		II		arawanakute
	FORMAL		araimashite	araimasen de
Past Ind.	**INFORMAL**		aratta	arawanakatta
	FORMAL		araimashita	araimasen deshita
Past Presump.	**INFORMAL**		arattarō	arawanakattarō
			aratta darō	arawanakatta darō
	FORMAL		araimashitarō	araimasen deshitarō
			aratta deshō	arawanakatta deshō
Conditional	**INFORMAL**		arattara	arawanakattara
	FORMAL		araimashitara	araimasen deshitara
Alternative	**INFORMAL**		arattari	arawanakattari
	FORMAL		araimashitari	araimasen deshitari

		INFORMAL AFFIRMATIVE INDICATIVE
Passive		arawareru
Potential		araeru
Causative		arawaseru
Causative Pass.		arawaserareru
Honorific	I	oarai ni naru
	II	oarai nasaru
Humble	I	oarai suru
	II	oarai itasu

38

araware あらわれる／現われる／表われる／顕われる araware.ru

to appear

			AFFIRMATIVE	NEGATIVE
Indicative	**INFORMAL**		arawareru	arawarenai
	FORMAL		arawaremasu	arawaremasen
Imperative	**INFORMAL**	I	arawarero	arawareru na
		II	arawarenasai	arawarenasaru na
		III	arawarete kudasai	arawarenai de kudasai
	FORMAL			
Presumptive	**INFORMAL**	I	arawareyō	arawaremai
		II	arawareru darō	arawarenai darō
	FORMAL	I	arawaremashō	arawaremasumai
		II	arawareru deshō	arawarenai deshō
Provisional	**INFORMAL**		arawarereba	arawarenakereba
	FORMAL		arawaremaseba arawaremasureba	arawaremasen nara
Gerund	**INFORMAL**	I	arawarete	arawarenai de
		II		arawarenakute
	FORMAL		arawaremashite	arawaremasen de
Past Ind.	**INFORMAL**		arawareta	arawarenakatta
	FORMAL		arawaremashita	arawaremasen deshita
Past Presump.	**INFORMAL**		arawaretarō arawareta darō	arawarenakattarō arawarenakatta darō
	FORMAL		arawaremashitarō arawareta deshō	arawaremasen deshitarō arawarenakatta deshō
Conditional	**INFORMAL**		arawaretara	arawarenakattara
	FORMAL		arawaremashitara	arawaremasen deshitara
Alternative	**INFORMAL**		arawaretari	arawarenakattari
	FORMAL		arawaremashitari	arawaremasen deshitari

		INFORMAL AFFIRMATIVE INDICATIVE
Passive		
Potential		arawarerareru
Causative		arawaresaseru
Causative Pass.		arawaresaserareru
Honorific	I	oaraware ni naru
	II	oaraware nasaru
Humble	I	
	II	

to express, to show up   TRANSITIVE

			AFFIRMATIVE	**NEGATIVE**
Indicative	**INFORMAL**		arawasu	arawasanai
	FORMAL		arawashimasu	arawashimasen
Imperative	**INFORMAL**	I	arawase	arawasu na
		II	arawashinasai	arawashinasaru na
		III	arawashite kudasai	arawasanai de kudasai
	FORMAL		oarawashi nasaimase	oarawashi nasaimasu na
Presumptive	**INFORMAL**	I	arawasō	arawasumai
		II	arawasu darō	arawasanai darō
	FORMAL	I	arawashimashō	arawashimasumai
		II	arawasu deshō	arawasanai deshō
Provisional	**INFORMAL**		arawaseba	arawasanakereba
	FORMAL		arawashimaseba	arawashimasen nara
			arawashimasureba	
Gerund	**INFORMAL**	I	arawashite	arawasanai de
		II		arawasanakute
	FORMAL		arawashimashite	arawashimasen de
Past Ind.	**INFORMAL**		arawashita	arawasanakatta
	FORMAL		arawashimashita	arawashimasen deshita
Past Presump.	**INFORMAL**		arawashitarō	arawasanakattarō
			arawashita darō	arawasanakatta darō
	FORMAL		arawashimashitarō	arawashimasen deshitarō
			arawashita deshō	arawasanakatta deshō
Conditional	**INFORMAL**		arawashitara	arawasanakattara
	FORMAL		arawashimashitara	arawashimasen deshitara
Alternative	**INFORMAL**		arawashitari	arawasanakattari
	FORMAL		arawashimashitari	arawashimasen deshitari

		INFORMAL AFFIRMATIVE INDICATIVE
Passive		arawasareru
Potential		arawaseru
Causative		arawasaseru
Causative Pass.		arawasaserareru
Honorific	I	oarawashi ni naru
	II	oarawashi nasaru
Humble	I	
	II	

ari   ある／有る／在る   **ar.u**

to exist, to be (inanimate), *to have*

                                                      A

			AFFIRMATIVE	**NEGATIVE**
Indicative	**INFORMAL**		aru	nai
	FORMAL		arimasu	arimasen
Imperative	**INFORMAL**	I	are	aru na
		II		
		III		
	FORMAL			
Presumptive	**INFORMAL**	I	arō	arumai
		II	aru darō	nai darō
	FORMAL	I	arimashō	arimasumai
		II	aru deshō	nai deshō
Provisional	**INFORMAL**		areba	nakereba
	FORMAL		arimaseba	arimasen nara
			arimasureba	
Gerund	**INFORMAL**	I	atte	
		II		nakute
	FORMAL		arimashite	arimasen de
Past Ind.	**INFORMAL**		atta	nakatta
	FORMAL		arimashita	arimasen deshita
Past Presump.	**INFORMAL**		attarō	nakattarō
			atta darō	nakatta darō
	FORMAL		arimashitarō	arimasen deshitarō
			atta deshō	nakatta deshō
Conditional	**INFORMAL**		attara	nakattara
	FORMAL		arimashitara	arimasen deshitara
Alternative	**INFORMAL**		attari	nakattari
	FORMAL		arimashitari	arimasen deshitari

	INFORMAL AFFIRMATIVE INDICATIVE
Passive	
Potential	
Causative	
Causative Pass.	
*Polite**	gozaru

*This is neither honorific nor humble (because the subject is inanimate), but rather neutral polite.

AN ESSENTIAL
55 VERB

                                                      41

Aru ある

to exist, to be (inanimate), to have

Aru is a high frequency verb meaning existence or possession. Be careful with *aru* and a similar verb *iru*. The difference between these two verbs is important. *Aru* is used for inanimate things, and *iru* is used for animate things such as people and animals.

Sentences Using *Aru*

Kyōto ni wa, otera to jinja ga takusan arimasu.
京都には、お寺と神社がたくさんあります。
There are a lot of temples and shrines in Kyoto.

Besuto o tsukushita kara kōkai wa arimasen.
ベストを尽くしたから、後悔はありません。
I did my best, so I don't have any regrets.

Tenki yohō ni yoru to, gogo ni wa raiu ga aru deshō.
天気予報によると、午後には雷雨があるでしょう。
According to the weather forecast, there will be thundershowers in the afternoon.

Yoyaku ga nakatta kara, sono resutoran de wa taberaremasen deshita.
予約が無かったので、そのレストランでは食べられませんでした。
We couldn't eat at that restaurant because we didn't have a reservation.

Kono mise ni wa, yasui mono wa arumai.
この店には、安いものはあるまい。
There won't be anything inexpensive at this store.

Words and Expressions Related to This Verb

Tōkyō ni wa, gaikoku ryōri no resutoran ga musū arimasu.
東京には、外国料理のレストランが無数あります。
There are countless numbers of ethnic restaurants in Tokyo. (**aru**)

Tōkyō ni wa, gaikokujin ga ōzei imasu.
東京には、外国人が大勢います。
There are many foreigners in Tokyo. (**iru**)

Ike niwa, koi ga takusan oyoide imashita.
池には鯉が沢山泳いでいました。
There were many carp swimming in the pond. (**iru**)

あるく／歩く **aruk.u**
to walk

A

			AFFIRMATIVE	NEGATIVE
Indicative	**INFORMAL**		aruku	arukanai
	FORMAL		arukimasu	arukimasen
Imperative	**INFORMAL**	I	aruke	aruku na
		II	arukinasai	arukinasaru na
		III	aruite kudasai	arukanai de kudasai
	FORMAL		oaruki nasaimase	oaruki nasaimasu na
Presumptive	**INFORMAL**	I	arukō	arukumai
		II	aruku darō	arukanai darō
	FORMAL	I	arukimashō	arukimasumai
		II	aruku deshō	arukanai deshō
Provisional	**INFORMAL**		arukeba	arukanakereba
	FORMAL		arukimaseba	arukimasen nara
			arukimasureba	
Gerund	**INFORMAL**	I	aruite	arukanai de
		II		arukanakute
	FORMAL		arukimashite	arukimasen de
Past Ind.	**INFORMAL**		aruita	arukanakatta
	FORMAL		arukimashita	arukimasen deshita
Past Presump.	**INFORMAL**		aruitarō	arukanakattarō
			aruita darō	arukanakatta darō
	FORMAL		arukimashitarō	arukimasen deshitarō
			aruita deshō	arukanakatta deshō
Conditional	**INFORMAL**		aruitara	arukanakattara
	FORMAL		arukimashitara	arukimasen deshitara
Alternative	**INFORMAL**		aruitari	arukanakattari
	FORMAL		arukimashitari	arukimasen deshitari

		INFORMAL AFFIRMATIVE INDICATIVE
Passive		arukareru
Potential		arukeru
Causative		arukaseru
Causative Pass.		arukaserareru
Honorific	I	oaruki ni naru
	II	oaruki nasaru
Humble	I	
	II	

AN ESSENTIAL
55 VERB

Aruku 歩く

to walk

Sentences Using *Aruku*

Arukinagara nondari tabetari suru no wa, ogyōgi ga warui to omowarete imasu.

歩きながら飲んだり食べたりするのは、お行儀が悪いと思われています。

It is considered bad manners to drink or to eat while walking.

Arukeba aruku hodo, kanojo wa motto genki ga detekimashita.

歩けば歩くほど、彼女はもっと元気が出てきました。 *The more she walked, the more energy she gained.*

Kenkō no tame ni, ichinichi ni 30 pun wa arukinasai.

健康の為に一日に３０分は歩きなさい。

For your health, walk at least 30 minutes a day.

Ōyuki no naka demo, inu wa soto ni dete arukitagarimashita.

大雪の中でも、犬は外に出て歩きたがりました。

Even during heavy snow, my dog wanted to go out and walk around.

Aruitemo aruitemo, mokutekichi wa tōku omowaremashita.

歩いても歩いても、目的地は遠く思われました。

No matter how much I walked, my destination still seemed far away.

Aruku is an important verb because many Japanese get around by walking and using public transportation rather than driving a car.

Words and Expressions Related to This Verb

aruki michi　歩き道
walking path

aruki zome　歩き初め
baby's first step, a party for baby's first step

hodō　歩道
sidewalk

hokōsha　歩行者
pedestrian

tabe aruki　食べ歩き
restaurant hopping, a gourmet tour

Proverb

Inu mo arukeba, bō ni ataru.
犬も歩けば棒に当たる。
Anyone can have good luck. (Even a dog can come across a stick.)

あそぶ／遊ぶ **asob.u**

to play

			AFFIRMATIVE	NEGATIVE
Indicative	**INFORMAL**		asobu	asobanai
	FORMAL		asobimasu	asobimasen
Imperative	**INFORMAL**	I	asobe	asobu na
		II	asobinasai	asobinasaru na
		III	asonde kudasai	asobanai de kudasai
	FORMAL		oasobi nasaimase	oasobi nasaimasu na
Presumptive	**INFORMAL**	I	asobō	asobumai
		II	asobu darō	asobanai darō
	FORMAL	I	asobimashō	asobimasumai
		II	asobu deshō	asobanai deshō
Provisional	**INFORMAL**		asobeba	asobanakereba
	FORMAL		asobimaseba	asobimasen nara
			asobimasureba	
Gerund	**INFORMAL**	I	asonde	asobanai de
		II		asobanakute
	FORMAL		asobimashite	asobimasen de
Past Ind.	**INFORMAL**		asonda	asobanakatta
	FORMAL		asobimashita	asobimasen deshita
Past Presump.	**INFORMAL**		asondarō	asobanakattarō
			asonda darō	asobanakatta darō
	FORMAL		asobimashitarō	asobimasen deshitarō
			asonda deshō	asobanakatta deshō
Conditional	**INFORMAL**		asondara	asobanakattara
	FORMAL		asobimashitara	asobimasen deshitara
Alternative	**INFORMAL**		asondari	asobanakattari
	FORMAL		asobimashitari	asobimasen deshitari

		INFORMAL AFFIRMATIVE INDICATIVE
Passive		asobareru
Potential		asoberu
Causative		asobaseru
Causative Pass.		asobaserareru
Honorific	I	oasobi ni naru
	II	oasobi nasaru
Humble	I	oasobi suru
	II	oasobi itasu

atar.u あたる／当たる   atari

to strike (against), *to apply to*

			AFFIRMATIVE	NEGATIVE
Indicative	**INFORMAL**		ataru	ataranai
	FORMAL		atarimasu	atarimasen
Imperative	**INFORMAL**	I	atare	ataru na
		II	atarinasai	atarinasaru na
		III	atatte kudasai	ataranai de kudasai
	FORMAL		oatari nasaimase	oatari nasaimasu na
Presumptive	**INFORMAL**	I	atarō	atarumai
		II	ataru darō	ataranai darō
	FORMAL	I	atarimashō	atarimasumai
		II	ataru deshō	ataranai deshō
Provisional	**INFORMAL**		atareba	ataranakereba
	FORMAL		atarimaseba	atarimasen nara
			atarimasureba	
Gerund	**INFORMAL**	I	atatte	ataranai de
		II		ataranakute
	FORMAL		atarimashite	atarimasen de
Past Ind.	**INFORMAL**		atatta	ataranakatta
	FORMAL		atarimashita	atarimasen deshita
Past Presump.	**INFORMAL**		atattarō	ataranakattarō
			atatta darō	ataranakatta darō
	FORMAL		atarimashitarō	atarimasen deshitarō
			atatta deshō	ataranakatta deshō
Conditional	**INFORMAL**		atattara	ataranakattara
	FORMAL		atarimashitara	atarimasen deshitara
Alternative	**INFORMAL**		atattari	ataranakattari
	FORMAL		atarimashitari	atarimasen deshitari

		INFORMAL AFFIRMATIVE INDICATIVE
Passive		atarareru
Potential		atareru
Causative		ataraseru
Causative Pass.		ataraserareru
Honorific	I	oatari ni naru
	II	oatari nasaru
Humble	I	oatari suru
	II	oatari itasu

46

あたたまる／暖まる／温まる　**atatamar.u**

to warm oneself, to get warm

			AFFIRMATIVE	NEGATIVE
Indicative	**INFORMAL**		atatamaru	atatamaranai
	FORMAL		atatamarimasu	atatamarimasen
Imperative	**INFORMAL**	I	atatamare	atatamaru na
		II	atatamarinasai	atatamarinasaru na
		III	atatamatte kudasai	atatamaranai de kudasai
	FORMAL		oatatamari nasaimase	oatatamari nasaimasu na
Presumptive	**INFORMAL**	I	atatamarō	atatamarumai
		II	atatamaru darō	atatamaranai darō
	FORMAL	I	atatamarimashō	atatamarimasumai
		II	atatamaru deshō	atatamaranai deshō
Provisional	**INFORMAL**		atatamareba	atatamaranakereba
	FORMAL		atatamarimaseba	atatamarimasen nara
			atatamarimasureba	
Gerund	**INFORMAL**	I	atatamatte	atatamaranai de
		II		atatamaranakute
	FORMAL		atatamarimashite	atatamarimasen de
Past Ind.	**INFORMAL**		atatamatta	atatamaranakatta
	FORMAL		atatamarimashita	atatamarimasen deshita
Past Presump.	**INFORMAL**		atatamattarō	atatamaranakattarō
			atatamatta darō	atatamaranakatta darō
	FORMAL		atatamarimashitarō	atatamarimasen deshitarō
			atatamatta deshō	atatamaranakatta deshō
Conditional	**INFORMAL**		atatamattara	atatamaranakattara
	FORMAL		atatamarimashitara	atatamarimasen deshitara
Alternative	**INFORMAL**		atatamattari	atatamaranakattari
	FORMAL		atatamarimashitari	atatamarimasen deshitari

		INFORMAL AFFIRMATIVE INDICATIVE
Passive		atatamarareru
Potential		atatamareru
Causative		atatamaraseru
Causative Pass.		atatamaraserareru
Honorific	I	oatatamari ni naru
	II	oatatamari nasaru
Humble	I	
	II	

A

			AFFIRMATIVE	NEGATIVE
Indicative	**INFORMAL**		atatameru	atatamenai
	FORMAL		atatamemasu	atatamemasen
Imperative	**INFORMAL**	I	atatamero	atatameru na
		II	atatamenasai	atatamenasaru na
		III	atatamete kudasai	atatamenai de kudasai
	FORMAL		oatatame nasaimase	oatatame nasaimasu na
Presumptive	**INFORMAL**	I	atatameyō	atatamemai
		II	atatameru darō	atatamenai darō
	FORMAL	I	atatamemashō	atatamemasumai
		II	atatameru deshō	atatamenai deshō
Provisional	**INFORMAL**		atatamereba	atatamenakereba
	FORMAL		atatamemaseba	atatamemasen nara
			atatamemasureba	
Gerund	**INFORMAL**	I	atatamete	atatamenai de
		II		atatamenakute
	FORMAL		atatamemashite	atatamemasen de
Past Ind.	**INFORMAL**		atatameta	atatamenakatta
	FORMAL		atatamemashita	atatamemasen deshita
Past Presump.	**INFORMAL**		atatametarō	atatamenakattarō
			atatameta darō	atatamenakatta darō
	FORMAL		atatamemashitarō	atatamemasen deshitarō
			atatameta deshō	atatamenakatta deshō
Conditional	**INFORMAL**		atatametara	atatamenakattara
	FORMAL		atatamemashitara	atatamemasen deshitara
Alternative	**INFORMAL**		atatametari	atatamenakattari
	FORMAL		atatamemashitari	atatamemasen deshitari

			INFORMAL AFFIRMATIVE INDICATIVE
Passive			atatamerareru
Potential			atatamerareru
Causative			atatamesaseru
Causative Pass.			atatamesaserareru
Honorific		I	oatatame ni naru
		II	oatatame nasaru
Humble		I	oatatame suru
		II	oatatame itasu

atsumari 　　　　あつまる／あつまる／集まる　**atsumar.u**

to gather, to assemble

			AFFIRMATIVE	NEGATIVE
Indicative	**INFORMAL**		atsumaru	atsumaranai
	FORMAL		atsumarimasu	atsumarimasen
Imperative	**INFORMAL**	I	atsumare	atsumaru na
		II	atsumarinasai	atsumarinasaru na
		III	atsumatte kudasai	atsumaranai de kudasai
	FORMAL		oatsumari nasaimase	oatsumari nasaimasu na
Presumptive	**INFORMAL**	I	atsumarō	atsumarumai
		II	atsumaru darō	atsumaranai darō
	FORMAL	I	atsumarimashō	atsumarimasumai
		II	atsumaru deshō	atsumaranai deshō
Provisional	**INFORMAL**		atsumareba	atsumaranakereba
	FORMAL		atsumarimaseba	atsumarimasen nara
			atsumarimasureba	
Gerund	**INFORMAL**	I	atsumatte	atsumaranai de
		II		atsumaranakute
	FORMAL		atsumarimashite	atsumarimasen de
Past Ind.	**INFORMAL**		atsumatta	atsumaranakatta
	FORMAL		atsumarimashita	atsumarimasen deshita
Past Presump.	**INFORMAL**		atsumattarō	atsumaranakattarō
			atsumatta darō	atsumaranakatta darō
	FORMAL		atsumarimashitarō	atsumarimasen deshitarō
			atsumatta deshō	atsumaranakatta deshō
Conditional	**INFORMAL**		atsumattara	atsumaranakattara
	FORMAL		atsumarimashitara	atsumarimasen deshitara
Alternative	**INFORMAL**		atsumattari	atsumaranakattari
	FORMAL		atsumarimashitari	atsumarimasen deshitari

		INFORMAL AFFIRMATIVE INDICATIVE
Passive		atsumarareru
Potential		atsumareru
Causative		atsumaraseru
Causative Pass.		atsumaraserareru
Honorific	I	oatsumari ni naru
	II	oatsumari nasaru
Humble	I	oatsumari suru
	II	oatsumari itasu

to gather, to collect   TRANSITIVE

			AFFIRMATIVE	**NEGATIVE**
Indicative	**INFORMAL**		atsumeru	atsumenai
	FORMAL		atsumemasu	atsumemasen
Imperative	**INFORMAL**	I	atsumero	atsumeru na
		II	atsumenasai	atsumenasaru na
		III	atsumete kudasai	atsumenai de kudasai
	FORMAL		oatsume nasaimase	oatsume nasaimasu na
Presumptive	**INFORMAL**	I	atsumeyō	atsumemai
		II	atsumeru darō	atsumenai darō
	FORMAL	I	atsumemashō	atsumemasumai
		II	atsumeru deshō	atsumenai deshō
Provisional	**INFORMAL**		atsumereba	atsumenakereba
	FORMAL		atsumemaseba	atsumemasen nara
			atsumemasureba	
Gerund	**INFORMAL**	I	atsumete	atsumenai de
		II		atsumenakute
	FORMAL		atsumemashite	atsumemasen de
Past Ind.	**INFORMAL**		atsumeta	atsumenakatta
	FORMAL		atsumemashita	atsumemasen deshita
Past Presump.	**INFORMAL**		atsumetarō	atsumenakattarō
			atsumeta darō	atsumenakatta darō
	FORMAL		atsumemeshitarō	atsumemasen deshitarō
			atsumeta deshō	atsumenakatta deshō
Conditional	**INFORMAL**		atsumetara	atsumenakattara
	FORMAL		atsumemashitara	atsumemasen deshitara
Alternative	**INFORMAL**		atsumetari	atsumenakattari
	FORMAL		atsumemashitari	atsumemasen deshitari

			INFORMAL AFFIRMATIVE INDICATIVE
Passive			atsumerareru
Potential			atsumerareru
Causative			atsumesaseru
Causative Pass.			atsumesaserareru
Honorific		I	oatsume ni naru
		II	oatsume nasaru
Humble		I	oatsume suru
		II	oatsume itasu

ai あう／会う／逢う／合う **a.u**

to meet, to see, to encounter, to fit

A

			AFFIRMATIVE	NEGATIVE
Indicative	**INFORMAL**		au	awanai
	FORMAL		aimasu	aimasen
Imperative	**INFORMAL**	I	ae	au na
		II	ainasai	ainasaru na
		III	atte kudasai	awanai de kudasai
	FORMAL		oai nasaimase	oai nasaimasu na
Presumptive	**INFORMAL**	I	aō	aumai
		II	au darō	awanai darō
	FORMAL	I	aimashō	aimasumai
		II	au deshō	awanai deshō
Provisional	**INFORMAL**		aeba	awanakereba
	FORMAL		aimaseba	aimasen nara
			aimasureba	
Gerund	**INFORMAL**	I	atte	awanai de
		II		awanakute
	FORMAL		aimashite	aimasen de
Past Ind.	**INFORMAL**		atta	awanakatta
	FORMAL		aimashita	aimasen deshita
Past Presump.	**INFORMAL**		attarō	awanakattarō
			atta darō	awanakatta darō
	FORMAL		aimashitarō	aimasen deshitarō
			atta deshō	awanakatta deshō
Conditional	**INFORMAL**		attara	awanakattara
	FORMAL		aimashitara	aimasen deshitara
Alternative	**INFORMAL**		attari	awanakattari
	FORMAL		aimashitari	aimasen deshitari

		INFORMAL AFFIRMATIVE INDICATIVE
Passive		awareru
Potential		aeru
Causative		awaseru
Causative Pass.		awaserareru
Honorific	I	oai ni naru
	II	oai nasaru
Humble	I	oai suru
	II	oai itasu

51

to panic, to lose one's composure

			AFFIRMATIVE	NEGATIVE
Indicative	**INFORMAL**		awateru	awatenai
	FORMAL		awatemasu	awatemasen
Imperative	**INFORMAL**	I	awatero	awateru na
		II	awatenasai	awatenasaru na
		III	awatete kudasai	awatenai de kudasai
	FORMAL		oawate nasaimase	oawate nasaimasu na
Presumptive	**INFORMAL**	I	awateyō	awatemai
		II	awateru darō	awatenai darō
	FORMAL	I	awatemashō	awatemasumai
		II	awateru deshō	awatenai deshō
Provisional	**INFORMAL**		awatereba	awatenakereba
	FORMAL		awatemaseba	awatemasen nara
			awatemasureba	
Gerund	**INFORMAL**	I	awatete	awatenai de
		II		awatenakute
	FORMAL		awatemashite	awatemasen de
Past Ind.	**INFORMAL**		awateta	awatenakatta
	FORMAL		awatemashita	awatemasen deshita
Past Presump.	**INFORMAL**		awatetarō	awatenakattarō
			awateta darō	awatenakatta darō
	FORMAL		awatemashitarō	awatemasen deshitarō
			awateta deshō	awatenakatta deshō
Conditional	**INFORMAL**		awatetara	awatenakattara
	FORMAL		awatemashitara	awatemasen deshitara
Alternative	**INFORMAL**		awatetari	awatenakattari
	FORMAL		awatemashitari	awatemasen deshitari

		INFORMAL AFFIRMATIVE INDICATIVE
Passive		awaterareru
Potential		awaterareru
Causative		awatesaseru
Causative Pass.		awatesaserareru
Honorific	I	oawate ni naru
	II	oawate nasaru
Humble	I	
	II	

あやまる／謝る **ayamar.u**

TRANSITIVE   *to apologize*

A

			AFFIRMATIVE	NEGATIVE
Indicative	**INFORMAL**		ayamaru	ayamaranai
	FORMAL		ayamarimasu	ayamarimasen
Imperative	**INFORMAL**	I	ayamare	ayamaru na
		II	ayamarinasai	ayamarinasaru na
		III	ayamatte kudasai	ayamaranai de kudasai
	FORMAL		oayamari nasaimase	oayamari nasaimasu na
Presumptive	**INFORMAL**	I	ayamarō	ayamarumai
		II	ayamaru darō	ayamaranai darō
	FORMAL	I	ayamarimashō	ayamarimasumai
		II	ayamaru deshō	ayamaranai deshō
Provisional	**INFORMAL**		ayamareba	ayamaranakereba
	FORMAL		ayamarimaseba	ayamarimasen nara
			ayamarimasureba	
Gerund	**INFORMAL**	I	ayamatte	ayamaranai de
		II		ayamaranakute
	FORMAL		ayamarimashite	ayamarimasen de
Past Ind.	**INFORMAL**		ayamatta	ayamaranakatta
	FORMAL		ayamarimashita	ayamarimasen deshita
Past Presump.	**INFORMAL**		ayamattarō	ayamaranakattarō
			ayamatta darō	ayamaranakatta darō
	FORMAL		ayamarimashitarō	ayamarimasen deshitarō
			ayamatta deshō	ayamaranakatta deshō
Conditional	**INFORMAL**		ayamattara	ayamaranakattara
	FORMAL		ayamarimashitara	ayamarimasen deshitara
Alternative	**INFORMAL**		ayamattari	ayamaranakattari
	FORMAL		ayamarimashitari	ayamarimasen deshitari

		INFORMAL AFFIRMATIVE INDICATIVE
Passive		ayamarareru
Potential		ayamareru
Causative		ayamaraseru
Causative Pass.		ayamaraserareru
Honorific	I	oayamari ni naru
	II	oayamari nasaru
Humble	I	oayamari suru
	II	oayamari itasu

to be suspicious of   TRANSITIVE

			AFFIRMATIVE	NEGATIVE
Indicative	**INFORMAL**		ayashimu	ayashimanai
	FORMAL		ayashimimasu	ayashimimasen
Imperative	**INFORMAL**	I	ayashime	ayashimu na
		II	ayashiminasai	ayashiminasaru na
		III	ayashinde kudasai	ayashimanai de kudasai
	FORMAL		oayashimi nasaimase	oayashimi nasaimasu na
Presumptive	**INFORMAL**	I	ayashimō	ayashimumai
		II	ayashimu darō	ayashimanai darō
	FORMAL	I	ayashimimashō	ayashimimasumai
		II	ayashimu deshō	ayashimanai deshō
Provisional	**INFORMAL**		ayashimeba	ayashimanakereba
	FORMAL		ayashimimaseba	ayashimimasen nara
			ayashimimasureba	
Gerund	**INFORMAL**	I	ayashinde	ayashimanai de
		II		ayashimanakute
	FORMAL		ayashimimashite	ayashimimasen de
Past Ind.	**INFORMAL**		ayashinda	ayashimanakatta
	FORMAL		ayashimimashita	ayashimimasen deshita
Past Presump.	**INFORMAL**		ayashindarō	ayashimanakattarō
			ayashinda darō	ayashimanakatta darō
	FORMAL		ayashimimashitarō	ayashimimasen deshitarō
			ayashinda deshō	ayashimanakatta deshō
Conditional	**INFORMAL**		ayashindara	ayashimanakattara
	FORMAL		ayashimimashitara	ayashimimasen deshitara
Alternative	**INFORMAL**		ayashindari	ayashimanakattari
	FORMAL		ayashimimashitari	ayashimimasen deshitari

			INFORMAL AFFIRMATIVE INDICATIVE
Passive			ayashimareru
Potential			ayashimeru
Causative			ayashimaseru
Causative Pass.			ayashimaserareru
Honorific		I	oayashimi ni naru
		II	oayashimi nasaru
Humble		I	oayashimi suru
		II	oayashimi itasu

TRANSITIVE　*to manipulate*

			AFFIRMATIVE	NEGATIVE
Indicative	**INFORMAL**		ayatsuru	ayatsuranai
	FORMAL		ayatsurimasu	ayatsurimasen
Imperative	**INFORMAL**	I	ayatsure	ayatsuru na
		II	ayatsurinasai	ayatsurinasaru na
		III	ayatsutte kudasai	ayatsuranai de kudasai
	FORMAL		oayatsuri nasaimase	oayatsuri nasaimasu na
Presumptive	**INFORMAL**	I	ayatsurō	ayatsurumai
		II	ayatsuru darō	ayatsuranai darō
	FORMAL	I	ayatsurimashō	ayatsurimasumai
		II	ayatsuru deshō	ayatsuranai deshō
Provisional	**INFORMAL**		ayatsureba	ayatsuranakereba
	FORMAL		ayatsurimaseba	ayatsurimasen nara
			ayatsurimasureba	
Gerund	**INFORMAL**	I	ayatsutte	ayatsuranai de
		II		ayatsuranakute
	FORMAL		ayatsurimashite	ayatsurimasen de
Past Ind.	**INFORMAL**		ayatsutta	ayatsuranakatta
	FORMAL		ayatsurimashita	ayatsurimasen deshita
Past Presump.	**INFORMAL**		ayatsuttarō	ayatsuranakattarō
			ayatsutta darō	ayatsuranakatta darō
	FORMAL		ayatsurimashitarō	ayatsurimasen deshitarō
			ayatsutta deshō	ayatsuranakatta deshō
Conditional	**INFORMAL**		ayatsuttara	ayatsuranakattara
	FORMAL		ayatsurimashitara	ayatsurimasen deshitara
Alternative	**INFORMAL**		ayatsuttari	ayatsuranakattari
	FORMAL		ayatsurimashitari	ayatsurimasen deshitari

		INFORMAL AFFIRMATIVE INDICATIVE
Passive		ayatsurareru
Potential		ayatsureru
Causative		ayatsuraseru
Causative Pass.		ayatsuraserareru
Honorific	I	oayatsuri ni naru
	II	oayatsuri nasaru
Humble	I	
	II	

55

to keep, to hold in trust   TRANSITIVE

			AFFIRMATIVE	**NEGATIVE**
Indicative	**INFORMAL**		azukaru	azukaranai
	FORMAL		azukarimasu	azukarimasen
Imperative	**INFORMAL**	I	azukare	azukaru na
		II	azukarinasai	azukarinasaru na
		III	azukatte kudasai	azukaranai de kudasai
	FORMAL		oazukari nasaimase	oazukari nasaimasu na
Presumptive	**INFORMAL**	I	azukarō	azukarumai
		II	azukaru darō	azukaranai darō
	FORMAL	I	azukarimashō	azukarimasumai
		II	azukaru deshō	azukaranai deshō
Provisional	**INFORMAL**		azukareba	azukaranakereba
	FORMAL		azukarimaseba	azukarimasen nara
			azukarimasureba	
Gerund	**INFORMAL**	I	azukatte	azukaranai de
		II		azukaranakute
	FORMAL		azukarimashite	azukarimasen de
Past Ind.	**INFORMAL**		azukatta	azukaranakatta
	FORMAL		azukarimashita	azukarimasen deshita
Past Presump.	**INFORMAL**		azukattarō	azukaranakattarō
			azukatta darō	azukaranakatta darō
	FORMAL		azukarimashitarō	azukarimasen deshitarō
			azukatta deshō	azukaranakatta deshō
Conditional	**INFORMAL**		azukattara	azukaranakattara
	FORMAL		azukarimashitara	azukarimasen deshitara
Alternative	**INFORMAL**		azukattari	azukaranakattari
	FORMAL		azukarimashitari	azukarimasen deshitari

			INFORMAL AFFIRMATIVE INDICATIVE
Passive			azukarareru
Potential			azukareru
Causative			azukaraseru
Causative Pass.			azukaraserareru
Honorific		I	oazukari ni naru
		II	oazukari nasaru
Humble		I	oazukari suru
		II	oazukari itasu

あずける／預ける　**azuke.ru**

to put in someone's charge, to entrust, to deposit

A

			AFFIRMATIVE	NEGATIVE
Indicative	**INFORMAL**		azukeru	azukenai
	FORMAL		azukemasu	azukemasen
Imperative	**INFORMAL**	I	azukero	azukeru na
		II	azukenasai	azukenasaru na
		III	azukete kudasai	azukenai de kudasai
	FORMAL		oazuke nasaimase	oazuke nasaimasu na
Presumptive	**INFORMAL**	I	azukeyō	azukemai
		II	azukeru darō	azukenai darō
	FORMAL	I	azukemashō	azukemasumai
		II	azukeru deshō	azukenai deshō
Provisional	**INFORMAL**		azukereba	azukenakereba
	FORMAL		azukemaseba	azukemasen nara
			azukemasureba	
Gerund	**INFORMAL**	I	azukete	azukenai de
		II		azukenakute
	FORMAL		azukemashite	azukemasen de
Past Ind.	**INFORMAL**		azuketa	azukenakatta
	FORMAL		azukemashita	azukemasen deshita
Past Presump.	**INFORMAL**		azuketarō	azukenakattarō
			azuketa darō	azukenakatta darō
	FORMAL		azukemashitarō	azukemasen deshitarō
			azuketa deshō	azukenakatta deshō
Conditional	**INFORMAL**		azuketara	azukenakattara
	FORMAL		azukemashitara	azukemasen deshitara
Alternative	**INFORMAL**		azuketari	azukenakattari
	FORMAL		azukemashitari	azukemasen deshitari

			INFORMAL AFFIRMATIVE INDICATIVE
Passive			azukerareru
Potential			azukerareru
Causative			azukesaseru
Causative Pass.			azukesaserareru
Honorific		I	oazuke ni naru
		II	oazuke nasaru
Humble		I	oazuke suru
		II	oazuke itasu

			AFFIRMATIVE	NEGATIVE
Indicative	**INFORMAL**		benkyō suru	benkyō shinai
	FORMAL		benkyō shimasu	benkyō shimasen
Imperative	**INFORMAL**	I	benkyō shiro	benkyō suru na
		II	benkyō shinasai	benkyō shinasaru na
		III	benkyō shite kudasai	benkyō shinai de kudasai
	FORMAL		gobenkyō nasaimase	gobenkyō nasaimasu na
Presumptive	**INFORMAL**	I	benkyō shiyō	benkyō surumai
		II	benkyō suru darō	benkyō shinai darō
	FORMAL	I	benkyō shimashō	benkyō shimasumai
		II	benkyō suru deshō	benkyō shinai deshō
Provisional	**INFORMAL**		benkyō sureba	benkyō shinakereba
	FORMAL		benkyō shimaseba	benkyō shimasen nara
			benkyō shimasureba	
Gerund	**INFORMAL**	I	benkyō shite	benkyō shinai de
		II		benkyō shinakute
	FORMAL		benkyō shimashite	benkyō shimasen de
Past Ind.	**INFORMAL**		benkyō shita	benkyō shinakatta
	FORMAL		benkyō shimashita	benkyō shimasen deshita
Past Presump.	**INFORMAL**		benkyō shitarō	benkyō shinakattarō
			benkyō shita darō	benkyō shinakatta darō
	FORMAL		benkyō shimashitarō	benkyō shimasen deshitarō
			benkyō shita deshō	benkyō shinakatta deshō
Conditional	**INFORMAL**		benkyō shitara	benkyō shinakattara
	FORMAL		benkyō shimashitara	benkyō shimasen deshitara
Alternative	**INFORMAL**		benkyō shitari	benkyō shinakattari
	FORMAL		benkyō shimashitari	benkyō shimasen deshitari

			INFORMAL AFFIRMATIVE INDICATIVE
Passive			benkyō sareru
Potential			benkyō dekiru
Causative			benkyō saseru
Causative Pass.			benkyō saserareru
Honorific		I	
		II	gobenkyō nasaru
Humble		I	
		II	benkyō itasu

AN ESSENTIAL
55 VERB

58

AN ESSENTIAL 55 VERB

Benkyō suru
勉強する

to study

Benkyō suru itself is an important verb to refer to both education and personal growth. Because studying and learning are such integral parts of daily life, there are also many other verbs for this, such as *narau* (習う) and *manabu* (学ぶ). A convenient way to form action verbs is to add *suru* to certain *kanji* noun compounds, just as *benkyō* (study) plus *suru* (to do) becomes "to study."

Sentences Using *Benkyō suru*

Ikura benkyō shitemo, wakarimasen deshita.
いくら勉強しても、分かりませんでした。
No matter how much I studied, I didn't understand it.

Isshōkenmei ni benkyō shita node, shiken ni ukatta.
一生懸命に勉強したので、試験に受かった。
Because I studied hard, I passed the exam.

Motto terebi o mite itakatta no ni, chichi ni benkyō saserareta.
もっとテレビを見ていたかったのに、父に勉強させられた。
Although I wanted to keep watching TV, I was forced to study by my father.

Totemo tsukarete ita no de, yūbe wa benkyō dekimasen deshita.
とても疲れていたので、夕べは勉強出来ませんでした。
I was so tired that I couldn't study last night.

Words and Expressions Related to This Verb

Wakai toki kara gaikokugo o manande okeba yaku ni tachimasu.
若い時から外国語を学んでおけば役に立ちます。
It will help you if you keep studying a foreign language from the time you are young. (*manabu*)

Doko de oshūji o naraeba ii desu ka.
どこでお習字を習えばいいですか。
Where is a good place to learn Japanese calligraphy? (*narau*)

Kare ni wa keizaigaku o gakushū suru nōryoku wa nai.
彼には経済学を学習する能力はない。
He doesn't have the ability to study economics. (*gakushū suru*)

bikkuri su.ru　びっくりする

to be startled, to be surprised　TRANSITIVE

bikkuri shi

			AFFIRMATIVE	NEGATIVE
Indicative	**INFORMAL**		bikkuri suru	bikkuri shinai
	FORMAL		bikkuri shimasu	bikkuri shimasen
Imperative	**INFORMAL**	I	bikkuri shiro	bikkuri suru na
		II	bikkuri shinasai	bikkuri shinasaru na
		III	bikkuri shite kudasai	bikkuri shinai de kudasai
	FORMAL		bikkuri nasaimase	bikkuri nasaimasu na
Presumptive	**INFORMAL**	I	bikkuri shiyō	bikkuri surumai
		II	bikkuri suru darō	bikkuri shinai darō
	FORMAL	I	bikkuri shimashō	bikkuri shimasumai
		II	bikkuri suru deshō	bikkuri shinai deshō
Provisional	**INFORMAL**		bikkuri sureba	bikkuri shinakereba
	FORMAL		bikkuri shimaseba	bikkuri shimasen nara
			bikkuri shimasureba	
Gerund	**INFORMAL**	I	bikkuri shite	bikkuri shinai de
		II		bikkuri shinakute
	FORMAL		bikkuri shimashite	bikkuri shimasen de
Past Ind.	**INFORMAL**		bikkuri shita	bikkuri shinakatta
	FORMAL		bikkuri shimashita	bikkuri shimasen deshita
Past Presump.	**INFORMAL**		bikkuri shitarō	bikkuri shinakattarō
			bikkuri shita darō	bikkuri shinakatta darō
	FORMAL		bikkuri shimashitarō	bikkuri shimasen deshitarō
			bikkuri shita deshō	bikkuri shinakatta deshō
Conditional	**INFORMAL**		bikkuri shitara	bikkuri shinakattara
	FORMAL		bikkuri shimashitara	bikkuri shimasen deshitara
Alternative	**INFORMAL**		bikkuri shitari	bikkuri shinakattari
	FORMAL		bikkuri shimashitari	bikkuri shimasen deshitari

		INFORMAL AFFIRMATIVE INDICATIVE
Passive		bikkuri sareru
Potential		bikkuri dekiru
Causative		bikkuri saseru
Causative Pass.		bikkuri saserareru
Honorific	I	
	II	bikkuri nasaru
Humble	I	
	II	bikkuri itasu

ぶつかる **butsukar.u**

to collide with, to hit, to crash, to clash

			AFFIRMATIVE	NEGATIVE
Indicative	**INFORMAL**		butsukaru	butsukaranai
	FORMAL		butsukarimasu	butsukarimasen
Imperative	**INFORMAL**	I	butsukare	butsukaru na
		II	butsukarinasai	butsukarinasaru na
		III	butsukatte kudasai	butsukaranai de kudasai
	FORMAL		obutsukari nasaimase	obutsukari nasaimasu na
Presumptive	**INFORMAL**	I	butsukarō	butsukarumai
		II	butsukaru darō	butsukaranai darō
	FORMAL	I	butsukarimashō	butsukarimasumai
		II	butsukaru deshō	butsukaranai deshō
Provisional	**INFORMAL**		butsukareba	butsukaranakereba
	FORMAL		butsukarimaseba	butsukarimasen nara
			butsukarimasureba	
Gerund	**INFORMAL**	I	butsukatte	butsukaranai de
		II		butsukaranakute
	FORMAL		butsukarimashite	butsukarimasen de
Past Ind.	**INFORMAL**		butsukatta	butsukaranakatta
	FORMAL		butsukarimashita	butsukarimasen deshita
Past Presump.	**INFORMAL**		butsukattarō	butsukaranakattarō
			butsukatta darō	butsukaranakatta darō
	FORMAL		butsukarimashitarō	butsukarimasen deshitarō
			butsukatta deshō	butsukaranakatta deshō
Conditional	**INFORMAL**		butsukattara	butsukaranakattara
	FORMAL		butsukarimashitara	butsukarimasen deshitara
Alternative	**INFORMAL**		butsukattari	butsukaranakattari
	FORMAL		butsukarimashitari	butsukarimasen deshitari

			INFORMAL AFFIRMATIVE INDICATIVE
Passive			butsukarareru
Potential			butsukareru
Causative			butsukaraseru
Causative Pass.			butsukaraserareru
Honorific		I	obutsukari ni naru
		II	obutsukari nasaru
Humble		I	obutsukari suru
		II	obutsukari itasu

			AFFIRMATIVE	NEGATIVE
Indicative	INFORMAL		butsukeru	butsukenai
	FORMAL		butsukemasu	butsukemasen
Imperative	INFORMAL	I	butsukero	butsukeru na
		II	butsukenasai	butsukenasaru na
		III	butsukete kudasai	butsukenai de kudasai
	FORMAL		obutsuke nasaimase	obutsuke nasaimasu na
Presumptive	INFORMAL	I	butsukeyō	butsukemai
		II	butsukeru darō	butsukenai darō
	FORMAL	I	butsukemashō	butsukemasumai
		II	butsukeru deshō	butsukenai deshō
Provisional	INFORMAL		butsukereba	butsukenakereba
	FORMAL		butsukemaseba	butsukemasen nara
			butsukemasureba	
Gerund	INFORMAL	I	butsukete	butsukenai de
		II		butsukenakute
	FORMAL		butsukemashite	butsukemasen de
Past Ind.	INFORMAL		butsuketa	butsukenakatta
	FORMAL		butsukemashita	butsukemasen deshita
Past Presump.	INFORMAL		butsuketarō	butsukenakattarō
			butsuketa darō	butsukenakatta darō
	FORMAL		butsukemashitarō	butsukemasen deshitarō
			butsuketa deshō	butsukenakatta deshō
Conditional	INFORMAL		butsuketara	butsukenakattara
	FORMAL		butsukemashitara	butsukemasen deshitara
Alternative	INFORMAL		butsuketari	butsukenakattari
	FORMAL		butsukemashitari	butsukemasen deshitari

		INFORMAL AFFIRMATIVE INDICATIVE
Passive		butsukerareru
Potential		butsukerareru
Causative		butsukesaseru
Causative Pass.		butsukesaserareru
Honorific	I	obutsuke ni naru
	II	obutsuke nasaru
Humble	I	
	II	

ちがう／違う　**chiga.u**
to be different, to be wrong

			AFFIRMATIVE	NEGATIVE
Indicative	**INFORMAL**		chigau	chigawanai
	FORMAL		chigaimasu	chigaimasen
Imperative	**INFORMAL**	I		
		II		
		III	chigatte kudasai	chigawanai de kudasai
	FORMAL			
Presumptive	**INFORMAL**	I	chigaō	chigaumai
		II	chigau darō	chigawanai darō
	FORMAL	I	chigaimashō	chigaimasumai
		II	chigau deshō	chigawanai deshō
Provisional	**INFORMAL**		chigaeba	chigawanakereba
	FORMAL		chigaimaseba	chigaimasen nara
			chigaimasureba	
Gerund	**INFORMAL**	I	chigatte	chigawanai de
		II		chigawanakute
	FORMAL		chigaimashite	chigaimasen de
Past Ind.	**INFORMAL**		chigatta	chigawanakatta
	FORMAL		chigaimashita	chigaimasen deshita
Past Presump.	**INFORMAL**		chigattarō	chigawanakattarō
			chigatta darō	chigawanakatta darō
	FORMAL		chigaimashitarō	chigaimasen deshitarō
			chigatta deshō	chigawanakatta deshō
Conditional	**INFORMAL**		chigattara	chigawanakattara
	FORMAL		chigaimashitara	chigaimasen deshitara
Alternative	**INFORMAL**		chigattari	chigawanakattari
	FORMAL		chigaimashitari	chigaimasen deshitari

		INFORMAL AFFIRMATIVE INDICATIVE
Passive		
Potential		chigaeru
Causative		chigawaseru
Causative Pass.		chigawaserareru
Honorific	I	
	II	
Humble	I	
	II	

to shorten, to reduce, to shrink TRANSITIVE

			AFFIRMATIVE	**NEGATIVE**
Indicative	**INFORMAL**		chijimeru	chijimenai
	FORMAL		chijimemasu	chijimemasen
Imperative	**INFORMAL**	I	chijimero	chijimeru na
		II	chijimenasai	chijimenasaru na
		III	chijimete kudasai	chijimenai de kudasai
	FORMAL		ochijime nasaimase	ochijime nasaimasu na
Presumptive	**INFORMAL**	I	chijimeyō	chijimemai
		II	chijimeru darō	chijimenai darō
	FORMAL	I	chijimemashō	chijimemasumai
		II	chijimeru deshō	chijimenai deshō
Provisional	**INFORMAL**		chijimereba	chijimenakereba
	FORMAL		chijimemaseba	chijimemasen nara
			chijimemasureba	
Gerund	**INFORMAL**	I	chijimete	chijimenai de
		II		chijimenakute
	FORMAL		chijimemashite	chijimemasen de
Past Ind.	**INFORMAL**		chijimeta	chijimenakatta
	FORMAL		chijimemashita	chijimemasen deshita
Past Presump.	**INFORMAL**		chijimetarō	chijimenakattarō
			chijimeta darō	chijimenakatta darō
	FORMAL		chijimemashitarō	chijimemasen deshitarō
			chijimeta deshō	chijimenakatta deshō
Conditional	**INFORMAL**		chijimetara	chijimenakattara
	FORMAL		chijimemashitara	chijimemasen deshitara
Alternative	**INFORMAL**		chijimetari	chijimenakattari
	FORMAL		chijimemashitari	chijimemasen deshitari

			INFORMAL AFFIRMATIVE INDICATIVE
Passive			chijimerareru
Potential			chijimerareru
Causative			chijimesaseru
Causative Pass.			chijimesaserareru
Honorific		I	ochijime ni naru
		II	ochijime nasaru
Humble		I	ochijime suru
		II	ochijime itasu

to shrink, to dwindle

			AFFIRMATIVE	NEGATIVE
Indicative	**INFORMAL**		chijimu	chijimanai
	FORMAL		chijimimasu	chijimimasen
Imperative	**INFORMAL**	I	chijime	chijimu na
		II		
		III	chijinde kudasai	chijimanai de kudasai
	FORMAL			
Presumptive	**INFORMAL**	I	chijimō	chijimumai
		II	chijimu darō	chijimanai darō
	FORMAL	I	chijimimashō	chijimimasumai
		II	chijimu deshō	chijimanai deshō
Provisional	**INFORMAL**		chijimeba	chijimanakereba
	FORMAL		chijimimaseba	chijimimasen nara
			chijimimasureba	
Gerund	**INFORMAL**	I	chijinde	chijimanai de
		II		chijimanakute
	FORMAL		chijimimashite	chijimimasen de
Past Ind.	**INFORMAL**		chijinda	chijimanakatta
	FORMAL		chijimimashita	chijimimasen deshita
Past Presump.	**INFORMAL**		chijindarō	chijimanakattarō
			chijinda darō	chijimanakatta darō
	FORMAL		chijimimashitarō	chijimimasen deshitarō
			chijinda deshō	chijimanakatta deshō
Conditional	**INFORMAL**		chijindara	chijimanakattara
	FORMAL		chijimimashitara	chijimimasen deshitara
Alternative	**INFORMAL**		chijindari	chijimanakattari
	FORMAL		chijimimashitari	chijimimasen deshitari

		INFORMAL AFFIRMATIVE INDICATIVE
Passive		chijimareru
Potential		chijimeru
Causative		chijimaseru
Causative Pass.		chijimaserareru
Honorific	I	ochijimi ni naru
	II	ochijimi nasaru
Humble	I	
	II	

chika.u　ちかう／誓う　　　　　　　　　　　　　　chikai

to take an oath, to pledge one's word, to promise, to swear　　　TRANSITIVE

			AFFIRMATIVE	NEGATIVE
Indicative	**INFORMAL**		chikau	chikawanai
	FORMAL		chikaimasu	chikaimasen
Imperative	**INFORMAL**	I	chikae	chikau na
		II	chikainasai	chikainasaru na
		III	chikatte kudasai	chikawanai de kudasai
	FORMAL		ochikai nasaimase	ochikai nasaimasu na
Presumptive	**INFORMAL**	I	chikaō	chikaumai
		II	chikau darō	chikawanai darō
	FORMAL	I	chikaimashō	chikaimasumai
		II	chikau deshō	chikawanai deshō
Provisional	**INFORMAL**		chikaeba	chikawanakereba
	FORMAL		chikaimaseba	chikaimasen nara
			chikaimasureba	
Gerund	**INFORMAL**	I	chikatte	chikawanai de
		II		chikawanakute
	FORMAL		chikaimashite	chikaimasen de
Past Ind.	**INFORMAL**		chikatta	chikawanakatta
	FORMAL		chikaimashita	chikaimasen deshita
Past Presump.	**INFORMAL**		chikattarō	chikawanakattarō
			chikatta darō	chikawanakatta darō
	FORMAL		chikaimashitarō	chikaimasen deshitarō
			chikatta deshō	chikawanakatta deshō
Conditional	**INFORMAL**		chikattara	chikawanakattara
	FORMAL		chikaimashitara	chikaimasen deshitara
Alternative	**INFORMAL**		chikattari	chikawanakattari
	FORMAL		chikaimashitari	chikaimasen deshitari

		INFORMAL AFFIRMATIVE INDICATIVE
Passive		chikawareru
Potential		chikaeru
Causative		chikawaseru
Causative Pass.		chikawaserareru
Honorific	I	ochikai ni naru
	II	ochikai nasaru
Humble	I	ochikai suru
	II	ochikai itasu

ちかづく／近づく　**chikazuk.u**

to approach, to get close

			AFFIRMATIVE	NEGATIVE
Indicative	**INFORMAL**		chikazuku	chikazukanai
	FORMAL		chikazukimasu	chikazukimasen
Imperative	**INFORMAL**	I	chikazuke	chikazuku na
		II	chikazukinasai	chikazukinasaru na
		III	chikazuite kudasai	chikazukanai de kudasai
	FORMAL		ochikazuki nasaimase	ochikazuki nasaimasu na
Presumptive	**INFORMAL**	I	chikazukō	chikazukumai
		II	chikazuku darō	chikazukanai darō
	FORMAL	I	chikazukimashō	chikazukimasumai
		II	chikazuku deshō	chikazukanai deshō
Provisional	**INFORMAL**		chikazukeba	chikazukanakereba
	FORMAL		chikazukimaseba	chikazukimasen nara
			chikazukimasureba	
Gerund	**INFORMAL**	I	chikazuite	chikazukanai de
		II		chikazukanakute
	FORMAL		chikazukimashite	chikazukimasen de
Past Ind.	**INFORMAL**		chikazuita	chikazukanakatta
	FORMAL		chikazukimashita	chikazukimasen deshita
Past Presump.	**INFORMAL**		chikazuitarō	chikazukanakattarō
			chikazuita darō	chikazukanakatta darō
	FORMAL		chikazukimashitarō	chikazukimasen deshitarō
			chikazuita deshō	chikazukanakatta deshō
Conditional	**INFORMAL**		chikazuitara	chikazukanakattara
	FORMAL		chikazukimashitara	chikazukimasen deshitara
Alternative	**INFORMAL**		chikazuitari	chikazukanakattari
	FORMAL		chikazukimashitari	chikazukimasen deshitari

			INFORMAL AFFIRMATIVE INDICATIVE
Passive			chikazukareru
Potential			chikazukeru
Causative			chikazukaseru
Causative Pass.			chikazukaserareru
Honorific		I	ochikazuki ni naru
		II	ochikazuki nasaru
Humble		I	ochikazuki suru
		II	ochikazuki itasu

chirakar.u ちらかる／散らかる   chirakari

to be in disorder, to be scattered about, to be untidy

			AFFIRMATIVE	NEGATIVE
Indicative	**INFORMAL**		chirakaru	chirakaranai
	FORMAL		chirakarimasu	chirakarimasen
Imperative	**INFORMAL**	I	chirakare	chirakaru na
		II		
		III	chirakatte kudasai	chirakaranai de kudasai
	FORMAL		ochirakari nasaimase	ochirakari nasaimasu na
Presumptive	**INFORMAL**	I	chirakarō	chirakarumai
		II	chirakaru darō	chirakaranai darō
	FORMAL	I	chirakarimashō	chirakarimasumai
		II	chirakaru deshō	chirakaranai deshō
Provisional	**INFORMAL**		chirakareba	chirakaranakereba
	FORMAL		chirakarimaseba	chirakarimasen nara
			chirakarimasureba	
Gerund	**INFORMAL**	I	chirakatte	chirakaranai de
		II		chirakaranakute
	FORMAL		chirakarimashite	chirakarimasen de
Past Ind.	**INFORMAL**		chirakatta	chirakaranakatta
	FORMAL		chirakarimashita	chirakarimasen deshita
Past Presump.	**INFORMAL**		chirakattarō	chirakaranakattarō
			chirakatta darō	chirakaranakatta darō
	FORMAL		chirakarimashitarō	chirakarimasen deshitarō
			chirakatta deshō	chirakaranakatta deshō
Conditional	**INFORMAL**		chirakattara	chirakaranakatta
	FORMAL		chirakarimashitara	chirakarimasen deshitara
Alternative	**INFORMAL**		chirakattari	chirakaranakattari
	FORMAL		chirakarimashitari	chirakarimasen deshitari

		INFORMAL AFFIRMATIVE INDICATIVE
Passive		chirakarareru
Potential		chirakareru
Causative		chirakaraseru
Causative Pass.		chirakaraserareru
Honorific	I	ochirakari ni naru
	II	ochirakari nasaru
Humble	I	
	II	

68

chirakashi

ちらかす／散らかす **chirakas.u**

TRANSITIVE *to scatter, to make a mess*

			AFFIRMATIVE	NEGATIVE
Indicative	**INFORMAL**		chirakasu	chirakasanai
	FORMAL		chirakashimasu	chirakashimasen
Imperative	**INFORMAL**	I	chirakase	chirakasu na
		II	chirakashinasai	chirakashinasaru na
		III	chirakashite kudasai	chirakasanai de kudasai
	FORMAL		ochirakashi nasaimase	ochirakashi nasaimasu na
Presumptive	**INFORMAL**	I	chirakasō	chirakasumai
		II	chirakasu darō	chirakasanai darō
	FORMAL	I	chirakashimashō	chirakashimasumai
		II	chirakasu deshō	chirakasanai deshō
Provisional	**INFORMAL**		chirakaseba	chirakasanakereba
	FORMAL		chirakashimaseba	chirakashimasen nara
			chirakashimasureba	
Gerund	**INFORMAL**	I	chirakashite	chirakasanai de
		II		chirakasanakute
	FORMAL		chirakashimashite	chirakashimasen de
Past Ind.	**INFORMAL**		chirakashita	chirakasanakatta
	FORMAL		chirakashimashita	chirakashimasen deshita
Past Presump.	**INFORMAL**		chirakashitarō	chirakasanakattarō
			chirakashita darō	chirakasanakatta darō
	FORMAL		chirakarimashitarō	chirakarimasen deshitarō
			chirakashita deshō	chirakasanakatta deshō
Conditional	**INFORMAL**		chirakashitara	chirakasanakattara
	FORMAL		chirakashimashitara	chirakashimasen deshitara
Alternative	**INFORMAL**		chirakashitari	chirakasanakattari
	FORMAL		chirakashimashitari	chirakashimasen deshitari

INFORMAL AFFIRMATIVE INDICATIVE

Passive		chirakasareru
Potential		chirakaseru
Causative		chirakasaseru
Causative Pass.		chirakasaserareru
Honorific	I	ochirakashi ni naru
	II	ochirakashi nasaru
Humble	I	ochirakashi suru
	II	ochirakashi itasu

to scatter, to disperse

			AFFIRMATIVE	NEGATIVE
Indicative	INFORMAL		chiru	chiranai
	FORMAL		chirimasu	chirimasen
Imperative	INFORMAL	I	chire	chiru na
		II	chirinasai	chirinasaru na
		III	chitte kudasai	chiranai de kudasai
	FORMAL		ochiri nasaimase	ochiri nasaimasu na
Presumptive	INFORMAL	I	chirō	chirumai
		II	chiru darō	chiranai darō
	FORMAL	I	chirimashō	chirimasumai
		II	chiru deshō	chiranai deshō
Provisional	INFORMAL		chireba	chiranakereba
	FORMAL		chirimaseba	chirimasen nara
			chirimasureba	
Gerund	INFORMAL	I	chitte	chiranai de
		II		chiranakute
	FORMAL		chirimashite	chirimasen de
Past Ind.	INFORMAL		chitta	chiranakatta
	FORMAL		chirimashita	chirimasen deshita
Past Presump.	INFORMAL		chittarō	chiranakattarō
			chitta darō	chiranakatta darō
	FORMAL		chirimashitarō	chirimasen deshitarō
			chitta deshō	chiranakatta deshō
Conditional	INFORMAL		chittara	chiranakattara
	FORMAL		chirimashitara	chirimasen deshitara
Alternative	INFORMAL		chittari	chiranakattari
	FORMAL		chirimashitari	chirimasen deshitari

		INFORMAL AFFIRMATIVE INDICATIVE
Passive		chirareru
Potential		chireru
Causative		chiraseru
Causative Pass.		chiraserareru
Honorific	I	ochiri ni naru
	II	ochiri nasaru
Humble	I	
	II	

D

			AFFIRMATIVE	NEGATIVE
Indicative	INFORMAL		daku	dakanai
	FORMAL		dakimasu	dakimasen
Imperative	INFORMAL	I	dake	daku na
		II	dakinasai	dakinasaru na
		III	daite kudasai	dakanai de kudasai
	FORMAL		odaki nasaimase	odaki nasaimasu na
Presumptive	INFORMAL	I	dakō	dakumai
		II	daku darō	dakanai darō
	FORMAL	I	dakimashō	dakimasumai
		II	daku deshō	dakanai deshō
Provisional	INFORMAL		dakeba	dakanakereba
	FORMAL		dakimaseba	dakimasen nara
			dakimasureba	
Gerund	INFORMAL	I	daite	dakanai de
		II		dakanakute
	FORMAL		dakimashite	dakimasen de
Past Ind.	INFORMAL		daita	dakanakatta
	FORMAL		dakimashita	dakimasen deshita
Past Presump.	INFORMAL		daitarō	dakanakattarō
			daita darō	dakanakatta darō
	FORMAL		dakimashitarō	dakimasen deshitarō
			daita deshō	dakanakatta deshō
Conditional	INFORMAL		daitara	dakanakattara
	FORMAL		dakimashitara	dakimasen deshitara
Alternative	INFORMAL		daitari	dakanakattari
	FORMAL		dakimashitari	dakimasen deshitari

			INFORMAL AFFIRMATIVE INDICATIVE
Passive			dakareru
Potential			dakeru
Causative			dakaseru
Causative Pass.			dakaserareru
Honorific		I	odaki ni naru
		II	odaki nasaru
Humble		I	odaki suru
		II	odaki itasu

to not speak, to stop talking

			AFFIRMATIVE	**NEGATIVE**
Indicative	**INFORMAL**		damaru	damaranai
	FORMAL		damarimasu	damarimasen
Imperative	**INFORMAL**	I	damare	damaru na
		II	damarinasai	damarinasaru na
		III	damatte kudasai	damaranai de kudasai
	FORMAL		odamari nasaimase	odamari nasaimasu na
Presumptive	**INFORMAL**	I	damarō	damarumai
		II	damaru darō	damaranai darō
	FORMAL	I	damarimashō	damarimasumai
		II	damaru deshō	damaranai deshō
Provisional	**INFORMAL**		damareba	damaranakereba
	FORMAL		damarimaseba	damarimasen nara
			damarimasureba	
Gerund	**INFORMAL**	I	damatte	damaranai de
		II		damaranakute
	FORMAL		damarimashite	damarimasen de
Past Ind.	**INFORMAL**		damatta	damaranakatta
	FORMAL		damarimashita	damarimasen deshita
Past Presump.	**INFORMAL**		damattarō	damaranakattarō
			damatta darō	damaranakatta darō
	FORMAL		damarimashitarō	damarimasen deshitarō
			damatta deshō	damaranakatta deshō
Conditional	**INFORMAL**		damattara	damaranakattara
	FORMAL		damarimashitara	damarimasen deshitara
Alternative	**INFORMAL**		damattari	damaranakattari
	FORMAL		damarimashitari	damarimasen deshitari

			INFORMAL AFFIRMATIVE INDICATIVE
Passive			damarareru
Potential			damareru
Causative			damaraseru
Causative Pass.			damaraserareru
Honorific		I	odamari ni naru
		II	odamari nasaru
Humble		I	odamari suru
		II	odamari itasu

だます／騙す **damas.u**

TRANSITIVE *to trick, to deceive*

			AFFIRMATIVE	NEGATIVE
Indicative	**INFORMAL**		damasu	damasanai
	FORMAL		damashimasu	damashimasen
Imperative	**INFORMAL**	I	damase	damasu na
		II	damashinasai	damashinasaru na
		III	damashite kudasai	damasanai de kudasai
	FORMAL		odamashi nasaimase	odamashi nasaimasu na
Presumptive	**INFORMAL**	I	damasō	damasumai
		II	damasu darō	damasanai darō
	FORMAL	I	damashimashō	damashimasumai
		II	damasu deshō	damasanai deshō
Provisional	**INFORMAL**		damaseba	damasanakereba
	FORMAL		damashimaseba	damashimasen nara
			damashimasureba	
Gerund	**INFORMAL**	I	damashite	damasanai de
		II		damasanakute
	FORMAL		damashimashite	damashimasen de
Past Ind.	**INFORMAL**		damashita	damasanakatta
	FORMAL		damashimashita	damashimasen deshita
Past Presump.	**INFORMAL**		damashitarō	damasanakattarō
			damashita darō	damasanakatta darō
	FORMAL		damashimashitarō	damashimasen deshitarō
			damashita deshō	damasanakatta deshō
Conditional	**INFORMAL**		damashitara	damasanakattara
	FORMAL		damashimashitara	damashimasen deshitara
Alternative	**INFORMAL**		damashitari	damasanakattari
	FORMAL		damashimashitari	damashimasen deshitari

		INFORMAL AFFIRMATIVE INDICATIVE
Passive		damasareru
Potential		damaseru
Causative		damasaseru
Causative Pass.		damasaserareru
Honorific	I	odamashi ni naru
	II	odamashi nasaru
Humble	I	odamashi suru
	II	odamashi itasu

73

to get out, to put out, to send, to submit　　TRANSITIVE

			AFFIRMATIVE	**NEGATIVE**
Indicative	**INFORMAL**		dasu	dasanai
	FORMAL		dashimasu	dashimasen
Imperative	**INFORMAL**	I	dase	dasu na
		II	dashinasai	dashinasaru na
		III	dashite kudasai	dasanai de kudasai
	FORMAL		odashi nasaimase	odashi nasaimasu na
Presumptive	**INFORMAL**	I	dasō	dasumai
		II	dasu darō	dasanai darō
	FORMAL	I	dashimashō	dashimasumai
		II	dasu deshō	dasanai deshō
Provisional	**INFORMAL**		daseba	dasanakereba
	FORMAL		dashimaseba	dashimasen nara
			dashimasureba	
Gerund	**INFORMAL**	I	dashite	dasanai de
		II		dasanakute
	FORMAL		dashimashite	dashimasen de
Past Ind.	**INFORMAL**		dashita	dasanakatta
	FORMAL		dashimashita	dashimasen deshita
Past Presump.	**INFORMAL**		dashitarō	dasanakattarō
			dashita darō	dasanakatta darō
	FORMAL		dashimashitarō	dashimasen deshitarō
			dashita deshō	dasanakatta deshō
Conditional	**INFORMAL**		dashitara	dasanakattara
	FORMAL		dashimashitara	dashimasen deshitara
Alternative	**INFORMAL**		dashitari	dasanakattari
	FORMAL		dashimashitari	dashimasen deshitari

		INFORMAL AFFIRMATIVE INDICATIVE
Passive		dasareru
Potential		daseru
Causative		dasaseru
Causative Pass.		dasaserareru
Honorific	I	odashi ni naru
	II	odashi nasaru
Humble	I	odashi suru
	II	odashi itasu

to encounter, to meet

			AFFIRMATIVE	NEGATIVE
Indicative	**INFORMAL**		deau	deawanai
	FORMAL		deaimasu	deaimasen
Imperative	**INFORMAL**	I		
		II		
		III		
	FORMAL			
Presumptive	**INFORMAL**	I	deaō	deaumai
		II	deau darō	deawanai darō
	FORMAL	I	deaimashō	deaimasumai
		II	deau deshō	deawanai deshō
Provisional	**INFORMAL**		deaeba	deawanakereba
	FORMAL		deaimaseba	deaimasen nara
			deaimasureba	
Gerund	**INFORMAL**	I	deatte	deawanai de
		II		deawanakute
	FORMAL		deaimashite	deaimasen de
Past Ind.	**INFORMAL**		deatta	deawanakatta
	FORMAL		deaimashita	deaimasen deshita
Past Presump.	**INFORMAL**		deattarō	deawanakattarō
			deatta darō	deawanakatta darō
	FORMAL		deaimashitarō	deaimasen deshitarō
			deatta deshō	deawanakatta deshō
Conditional	**INFORMAL**		deattara	deawanakattara
	FORMAL		deaimashitara	deaimasen deshitara
Alternative	**INFORMAL**		deattari	deawanakattari
	FORMAL		deaimashitari	deaimasen deshitari

		INFORMAL AFFIRMATIVE INDICATIVE
Passive		deawareru
Potential		deaeru
Causative		deawaseru
Causative Pass.		deawaserareru
Honorific	I	odeai ni naru
	II	odeai nasaru
Humble	I	
	II	

to go out, to leave home

			AFFIRMATIVE	NEGATIVE
Indicative	INFORMAL		dekakeru	dekakenai
	FORMAL		dekakemasu	dekakemasen
Imperative	INFORMAL	I	dekakero	dekakeru na
		II	dekakemasai	dekakenasaru na
		III	dekakete kudasai	dekakenai de kudasai
	FORMAL		odekake nasaimase	odekake nasaimasu na
Presumptive	INFORMAL	I	dekakeyō	dekakemai
		II	dekakeru darō	dekakenai darō
	FORMAL	I	dekakemashō	dekakemasumai
		II	dekakeru deshō	dekakenai deshō
Provisional	INFORMAL		dekakereba	dekakenakereba
	FORMAL		dekakemaseba	dekakemasen nara
			dekakemasureba	
Gerund	INFORMAL	I	dekakete	dekakenai de
		II		dekakenakute
	FORMAL		dekakemashite	dekakemasen de
Past Ind.	INFORMAL		dekaketa	dekakenakatta
	FORMAL		dekakemashita	dekakemasen deshita
Past Presump.	INFORMAL		dekaketarō	dekakenakattarō
			dekaketa darō	dekakenakatta darō
	FORMAL		dekakemashitarō	dekakemasen deshitarō
			dekaketa deshō	dekakenakatta deshō
Conditional	INFORMAL		dekaketara	dekakenakattara
	FORMAL		dekakemashitara	dekakemasen deshitara
Alternative	INFORMAL		dekaketari	dekakenakattari
	FORMAL		dekakemashitari	dekakemasen deshitari

		INFORMAL AFFIRMATIVE INDICATIVE
Passive		dekakerareru
Potential		dekakerareru
Causative		dekakesaseru
Causative Pass.		dekakesaserareru
Honorific	I	odekake ni naru
	II	odekake nasaru
Humble	I	odekake suru
	II	odekake itasu

AN ESSENTIAL 55 VERB

Dekakeru 出かける

D

to go out, to leave home

Sentences Using *Dekakeru*

Dekakeru magiwa ni totsuzen okyaku ga kita.
出かける間際に突然お客が来た。
Just as I was leaving home, some guests suddenly arrived.

Ima dekakenai to yakusoku ni ma ni aimasen yo.
今出かけないと、約束に間に合いませんよ。
If you don't leave now, you won't be on time for your appointment.

Sumimasen ga, ima、kanai wa dekakete orimasu.
すみませんが、今、家内は出かけております。
I'm sorry, but my wife is out now.

Ano hi ni dekakenakattara, kōtsū jiko ni awanakatta darō ni.
あの日に出かけなかったら、交通事故にあわなかっただろうに。
If I hadn't left home that day, I wouldn't have been involved in a traffic accident.

Dekaketakutemo okane ga nai.
出かけたくてもお金がない。
I want to go out, but I have no money.

Soto wa hidoi arashi desu. Kyō wa odekake nasaimasu na.
外はひどい嵐です。今日はお出かけなさいますな。
There's a terrible storm out there. You shouldn't go out today.

Dekakeru has cultural significance in Japan. Whenever you leave your house, you announce your departure by saying *"Itte mairimasu!"* (I'm going out!) If you run into neighbors right after that, they may greet you by saying *"Ohayō gozaimasu. Odekake desu ka."* (Good morning. Are you going out?) Strange? Not to the Japanese. They're not being nosy, just friendly. You don't need to say where you are going. The ritual response is *"Hai, chotto soko made."* (Yes, just nearby.)

Words and Expressions Related to This Verb

dekake saki　出かけ先
destination

dekake tsuide ni　出かけついでに
while out

gaishutsu suru　外出する
to go out, to leave home, office, etc.

77

to be able to, to be possible, to be formed, to be ready

			AFFIRMATIVE	**NEGATIVE**
Indicative	**INFORMAL**		dekiru	dekinai
	FORMAL		dekimasu	dekimasen
Imperative	**INFORMAL**	I		
		II		
		III		
	FORMAL			
Presumptive	**INFORMAL**	I	dekiyō	dekimai
		II	dekiru darō	dekinai darō
	FORMAL	I	dekimashō	dekimasumai
		II	dekiru deshō	dekinai deshō
Provisional	**INFORMAL**		dekireba	dekinakereba
	FORMAL		dekimaseba	dekimasen nara
			dekimasureba	
Gerund	**INFORMAL**	I	dekite	dekinai de
		II		dekinakute
	FORMAL		dekimashite	dekimasen de
Past Ind.	**INFORMAL**		dekita	dekinakatta
	FORMAL		dekimashita	dekimasen deshita
Past Presump.	**INFORMAL**		dekitarō	dekinakattarō
			dekita darō	dekinakatta darō
	FORMAL		dekimashitarō	dekimasen deshitarō
			dekita deshō	dekinakatta deshō
Conditional	**INFORMAL**		dekitara	dekinakattara
	FORMAL		dekimashitara	dekimasen deshitara
Alternative	**INFORMAL**		dekitari	dekinakattari
	FORMAL		dekimashitari	dekimasen deshitari

		INFORMAL AFFIRMATIVE INDICATIVE
Passive		
Potential		
Causative		
Causative Pass.		
Honorific	I	odeki ni naru
	II	odeki nasaru
Humble	I	
	II	

AN ESSENTIAL 55 VERB

Dekiru 出来る

D

to be able to, to be possible,
to be formed, to be ready

Sentences Using *Dekiru*

Nihongo ga dekimasu ka.
日本語が出来ますか。
Can you speak Japanese?

Dekireba, ashita no gogo ni ome ni
kakaritai no desu ga.
出来れば、明日の午後にお目にかかり
たいのですが。
*If possible, I'd like to see you
tomorrow afternoon.*

Dekinakattara gomennasai.
出来なかったらごめんなさい。
If I can't do it, I'm sorry.

Dekitemo dekinakutemo, kekka o
shirasete kudasai.
出来ても出来なくても、結果を知らせ
て下さい。
*Whether you could or couldn't do it,
please let me know the result.*

Ano kata wa konpyūta wa
dekimasumai.
あの方はコンピュータは出来ますま
い。
*I guess he isn't able to use a
computer.*

Sono shigoto wa, ashita made ni wa
dekimasen.
その仕事は、明日までには出来ま
せん。
*It's impossible to finish that work
by tomorrow.*

Dekiru (can do) and ***dekinai*** (can't do)
are a pair of verbs you will need to use
often. If you're in Japan, people are
interested in you, and they want to know
what you can do or can't do. Also, you
might want to know what's proper for
you to do or not to do. You might want
to tell them your capabilities and
limitations too.

Words and Expressions
Related to This Verb

kanō　可能
possible

fukanō　不可能
impossible

nōryoku　能力
ability, capability

Kanojo niwa, Supeingo o hon-yaku
suru nōryoku ga arimasu.
彼女には、スペイン語を翻訳する能力
があります。
She is capable of translating Spanish.

to exit, to go, to leave, to go out, to be served

			AFFIRMATIVE	NEGATIVE
Indicative	**INFORMAL**		deru	denai
	FORMAL		demasu	demasen
Imperative	**INFORMAL**	I	dero	deru na
		II	denasai	denasaru na
		III	dete kudasai	denai de kudasai
	FORMAL		ode nasaimase	ode nasaimasu na
Presumptive	**INFORMAL**	I	deyō	demai
		II	deru darō	denai darō
	FORMAL	I	demashō	demasumai
		II	deru deshō	denai deshō
Provisional	**INFORMAL**		dereba	denakereba
	FORMAL		demaseba	demasen nara
			demasureba	
Gerund	**INFORMAL**	I	dete	denai de
		II		denakute
	FORMAL		demashite	demasen de
Past Ind.	**INFORMAL**		deta	denakatta
	FORMAL		demashita	demasen deshita
Past Presump.	**INFORMAL**		detarō	denakattarō
			deta darō	denakatta darō
	FORMAL		demashitarō	demasen deshitarō
			deta deshō	denakatta deshō
Conditional	**INFORMAL**		detara	denakattara
	FORMAL		demashitara	demasen deshitara
Alternative	**INFORMAL**		detari	denakattari
	FORMAL		demashitari	demasen deshitari

			INFORMAL AFFIRMATIVE INDICATIVE
Passive			derareru
Potential			derareru
Causative			desaseru
Causative Pass.			desaserareru
Honorific		I	ode ni naru
		II	ode nasaru
Humble		I	
		II	

**AN ESSENTIAL
55 VERB**

80

AN ESSENTIAL 55 VERB

Deru 出る

D

to exit, to go, to leave,
to go out, to be served

Sentences Using *Deru*

Ie o dete ma mo naku, ame ga
hageshiku futte kimashita.
家を出て間もなく、雨が激しく降って
きました。
*Soon after I left home, it began to
rain heavily.*

Yūbe no pātī niwa, sushi to yakitori
mo demashita.
夕べのパーティーには、鮨と焼き鳥も
出ました。
*At the party last night, sushi and
yakitori were served, among other
things.*

Kotori ga subako kara detari haittari
shite imasu.
小鳥が巣箱から出たり入ったりしてい
ます。
*Little birds are going in and out of
the birdhouse.*

Washinton yuki no ni bin wa, 11 ji 10
pun ni deru.
ワシントン行きの2便は、11時10分
に出る。
*Flight Number Two for Washington,
D.C., will depart at 11:10 A.M.*

Deru and **hairu** (to come in, to enter) are
another pair of useful verbs. **Deru** is
similar to **dekakeru**, but the difference is
that the subject of **dekakeru** is always
animate, while the subject of **deru** can be
animate or inanimate.

Words and Expressions Related to This Verb

shuppatsu suru　出発する
to leave, to depart

shusseki suru　出席する
to attend

deiri　出入り
going in and out, comings and goings

dekasegi　出稼ぎ
*to emigrate, to live and work away
from home*

demakase　出まかせ
nonsense, irresponsible words

deokure　出遅れ
late start

Proverb

Deru kui wa utareru.
出る杭は打たれる。
*Tall trees catch much wind. (An
extruding stake will be pounded
down.)*

81

to select, to choose   TRANSITIVE

			AFFIRMATIVE	NEGATIVE
Indicative	**INFORMAL**		erabu	erabanai
	FORMAL		erabimasu	erabimasen
Imperative	**INFORMAL**	I	erabe	erabu na
		II	erabinasai	erabinasaru na
		III	erande kudasai	erabanai de kudasai
	FORMAL		oerabi nasaimase	oerabi nasaimasu na
Presumptive	**INFORMAL**	I	erabō	erabumai
		II	erabu darō	erabanai darō
	FORMAL	I	erabimashō	erabimasumai
		II	erabu deshō	erabanai deshō
Provisional	**INFORMAL**		erabeba	erabanakereba
	FORMAL		erabimaseba	erabimasen nara
			erabimasureba	
Gerund	**INFORMAL**	I	erande	erabanai de
		II		erabanakute
	FORMAL		erabimashite	erabimasen de
Past Ind.	**INFORMAL**		eranda	erabanakatta
	FORMAL		erabimashita	erabimasen deshita
Past Presump.	**INFORMAL**		erandarō	erabanakattarō
			eranda darō	erabanakatta darō
	FORMAL		erabimashitarō	erabimasen deshitarō
			eranda deshō	erabanakatta deshō
Conditional	**INFORMAL**		erandara	erabanakattara
	FORMAL		erabimashitara	erabimasen deshitara
Alternative	**INFORMAL**		erandari	erabanakattari
	FORMAL		erabimashitari	erabimasen deshitari

		INFORMAL AFFIRMATIVE INDICATIVE
Passive		erabareru
Potential		eraberu
Causative		erabaseru
Causative Pass.		erabaserareru
Honorific	I	oerabi ni naru
	II	oerabi nasaru
Humble	I	oerabi suru
	II	oerabi itasu

AN ESSENTIAL
55 VERB

Erabu 選ぶ

to select, to choose **E**

Sentences Using *Erabu*

Kare wa chīmu no kyaputen ni
erabareta.
彼はチームのキャプテンに選ばれた。
He was chosen captain of the team.

Dore o erandemo onaji desu.
どれを選んでも同じです。
*Whichever you choose, they are all
the same.*

Dare o erandara ii ka, wakaranakatta.
誰を選んだら良いか、分からなかっ
た。
I didn't know whom I should choose.

Shachō ni erabarenakattara kaisha o
yameru.
社長に選ばれなかったら会社を辞め
る。
*If I am not chosen as the company
president, I will quit the company.*

Iinkai no menbā wa zen-in itchi de
kanojo o gichō ni eranda.
委員会のメンバーは全員一致で彼女を
議長に選んだ。
*The members of the committee chose
her as the chairperson unanimously.*

Erabu is a verb you will need often in
Japan. Places to go, things to see, things
to buy, delicious food to eat—you will be
choosing all day long. Choose carefully
and you'll be rewarded!

Words and Expressions Related to This Verb

sentaku suru 選択する
to select, to choose

senbetsu suru 選別する
to sort, to select

senshutsu suru 選出する
to elect

sentakushi 選択肢
choices

senkyo 選挙
election

daitōryō sen 大統領選
presidential election

e.ru える／得る

e

to get   TRANSITIVE

			AFFIRMATIVE	**NEGATIVE**
Indicative	**INFORMAL**		eru	enai
	FORMAL		emasu	emasen
Imperative	**INFORMAL**	I	ero	eru na
		II	enasai	enasaru na
		III	ete kudasai	enai de kudasai
	FORMAL			
Presumptive	**INFORMAL**	I	eyō	emai
		II	eru darō	enai darō
	FORMAL	I	emashō	emasumai
		II	eru deshō	enai deshō
Provisional	**INFORMAL**		ereba	enakereba
	FORMAL		emaseba	emasen nara
			emasureba	
Gerund	**INFORMAL**	I	ete	enai de
		II		enakute
	FORMAL		emashite	emasen de
Past Ind.	**INFORMAL**		eta	enakatta
	FORMAL		emashita	emasen deshita
Past Presump.	**INFORMAL**		etarō	enakattarō
			eta darō	enakatta darō
	FORMAL		emashitarō	emasen deshitarō
			eta deshō	enakatta deshō
Conditional	**INFORMAL**		etara	enakattara
	FORMAL		emashitara	emasen deshitara
Alternative	**INFORMAL**		etari	enakattari
	FORMAL		emashitari	emasen deshitari

		INFORMAL AFFIRMATIVE INDICATIVE
Passive		erareru
Potential		erareru
Causative		esaseru
Causative Pass.		esaserareru
Honorific	I	oe ni naru
	II	oe nasaru
Humble	I	
	II	oe itasu

			AFFIRMATIVE	NEGATIVE
Indicative	**INFORMAL**		fueru	fuenai
	FORMAL		fuemasu	fuemasen
Imperative	**INFORMAL**	I	fuero	fueru na
		II	fuenasai	fuenasaru na
		III	fuete kudasai	fuenai de kudasai
	FORMAL		ofue nasaimase	ofue nasaimasu na
Presumptive	**INFORMAL**	I	fueyō	fuemai
		II	fueru darō	fuenai darō
	FORMAL	I	fuemashō	fuemasumai
		II	fueru deshō	fuenai deshō
Provisional	**INFORMAL**		fuereba	fuenakereba
	FORMAL		fuemaseba	fuemasen nara
			fuemasureba	
Gerund	**INFORMAL**	I	fuete	fuenai de
		II		fuenakute
	FORMAL		fuemashite	fuemasen de
Past Ind.	**INFORMAL**		fueta	fuenakatta
	FORMAL		fuemashita	fuemasen deshita
Past Presump.	**INFORMAL**		fuetarō	fuenakattarō
			fueta darō	fuenakatta darō
	FORMAL		fuemashitarō	fuemasen deshitarō
			fueta deshō	fuenakatta deshō
Conditional	**INFORMAL**		fuetara	fuenakattara
	FORMAL		fuemashitara	fuemasen deshitara
Alternative	**INFORMAL**		fuetari	fuenakattari
	FORMAL		fuemashitari	fuemasen deshitari

		INFORMAL AFFIRMATIVE INDICATIVE
Passive		fuerareru
Potential		fuerareru
Causative		fuesaseru
Causative Pass.		fuesaserareru
Honorific	I	ofue ni naru
	II	ofue nasaru
Humble	I	
	II	

85

to become deep

			AFFIRMATIVE	NEGATIVE
Indicative	**INFORMAL**		fukamaru	fukamaranai
	FORMAL		fukamarimasu	fukamarimasen
Imperative	**INFORMAL**	I	fukamare	fukamaru na
		II	fukamarinasai	fukamarinasaru na
		III	fukamatte kudasai	fukamaranai de kudasai
	FORMAL			
Presumptive	**INFORMAL**	I	fukamarō	fukamarumai
		II	fukamaru darō	fukamaranai darō
	FORMAL	I	fukamarimashō	fukamarimasumai
		II	fukamaru deshō	fukamaranai deshō
Provisional	**INFORMAL**		fukamareba	fukamaranakereba
	FORMAL		fukamarimaseba	fukamarimasen nara
			fukamarimasureba	
Gerund	**INFORMAL**	I	fukamatte	fukamaranai de
		II		fukamaranakute
	FORMAL		fukamarimashite	fukamarimasen de
Past Ind.	**INFORMAL**		fukamatta	fukamaranakatta
	FORMAL		fukamarimashita	fukamarimasen deshita
Past Presump.	**INFORMAL**		fukamattarō	fukamaranakattarō
			fukamatta darō	fukamaranakatta darō
	FORMAL		fukamarimashitarō	fukamarimasen deshitarō
			fukamatta deshō	fukamaranakatta deshō
Conditional	**INFORMAL**		fukamattara	fukamaranakattara
	FORMAL		fukamarimashitara	fukamarimasen deshitara
Alternative	**INFORMAL**		fukamattari	fukamaranakattari
	FORMAL		fukamarimashitari	fukamarimasen deshitari

		INFORMAL AFFIRMATIVE INDICATIVE
Passive		fukamarareru
Potential		fukamareru
Causative		fukamaraseru
Causative Pass.		fukamaraserareru
Honorific	I	ofukamari ni naru
	II	ofukamari nasaru
Humble	I	
	II	

ふかめる／深める　**fukame.ru**

			AFFIRMATIVE	**NEGATIVE**
Indicative	**INFORMAL**		fukameru	fukamenai
	FORMAL		fukamemasu	fukamemasen
Imperative	**INFORMAL**	I	fukamero	fukameru na
		II	fukamenasai	fukamenasaru na
		III	fukamete kudasai	fukamenai de kudasai
	FORMAL		ofukame nasaimase	ofukame nasaimasu na
Presumptive	**INFORMAL**	I	fukameyō	fukamemai
		II	fukameru darō	fukamenai darō
	FORMAL	I	fukamemashō	fukamemasumai
		II	fukameru deshō	fukamenai deshō
Provisional	**INFORMAL**		fukamereba	fukamenakereba
	FORMAL		fukamemaseba	fukamemasen nara
			fukamemasureba	
Gerund	**INFORMAL**	I	fukamete	fukamenai de
		II		fukamenakute
	FORMAL		fukamemashite	fukamemasen de
Past Ind.	**INFORMAL**		fukameta	fukamenakatta
	FORMAL		fukamemashita	fukamemasen deshita
Past Presump.	**INFORMAL**		fukametarō	fukamenakattarō
			fukameta darō	fukamenakatta darō
	FORMAL		fukamemashitarō	fukamemasen deshitarō
			fukameta deshō	fukamenakatta deshō
Conditional	**INFORMAL**		fukametara	fukamenakattara
	FORMAL		fukamemashitara	fukamemasen deshitara
Alternative	**INFORMAL**		fukametari	fukamenakattari
	FORMAL		fukamemashitari	fukamemasen deshitari

			INFORMAL AFFIRMATIVE INDICATIVE
Passive			fukamerareru
Potential			fukamerareru
Causative			fukamesaseru
Causative Pass.			fukamesaserareru
Honorific		I	ofukame ni naru
		II	ofukame nasaru
Humble		I	ofukame suru
		II	ofukame itasu

fuk.u　ふく／吹く　　　　　　　　　　　　　　　　　　　**fuki**

to blow　　TRANSITIVE

			AFFIRMATIVE	**NEGATIVE**
Indicative	**INFORMAL**		fuku	fukanai
	FORMAL		fukimasu	fukimasen
Imperative	**INFORMAL**	I	fuke	fuku na
		II	fukinasai	fukinasaru na
		III	fuite kudasai	fukanai de kudasai
	FORMAL		ofuki nasaimase	ofuki nasaimasu na
Presumptive	**INFORMAL**	I	fukō	fukumai
		II	fuku darō	fukanai darō
	FORMAL	I	fukimashō	fukimasumai
		II	fuku deshō	fukanai deshō
Provisional	**INFORMAL**		fukeba	fukanakereba
	FORMAL		fukimaseba	fukimasen nara
			fukimasureba	
Gerund	**INFORMAL**	I	fuite	fukanai de
		II		fukanakute
	FORMAL		fukimashite	fukimasen de
Past Ind.	**INFORMAL**		fuita	fukanakatta
	FORMAL		fukimashita	fukimasen deshita
Past Presump.	**INFORMAL**		fuitarō	fukanakattarō
			fuita darō	fukanakatta darō
	FORMAL		fukimashitarō	fukimasen deshitarō
			fuita deshō	fukanakatta deshō
Conditional	**INFORMAL**		fuitara	fukanakattara
	FORMAL		fukimashitara	fukimasen deshitara
Alternative	**INFORMAL**		fuitari	fukanakattari
	FORMAL		fukimashitari	fukimasen deshitari

			INFORMAL AFFIRMATIVE INDICATIVE
Passive			fukareru
Potential			fukeru
Causative			fukaseru
Causative Pass.			fukaserareru
Honorific		I	ofuki ni naru
		II	ofuki nasaru
Humble		I	ofuki suru
		II	ofuki itasu

88

ふく／拭く **fuk.u**

TRANSITIVE   *to wipe*

			AFFIRMATIVE	NEGATIVE
Indicative	**INFORMAL**		fuku	fukanai
	FORMAL		fukimasu	fukimasen
Imperative	**INFORMAL**	I	fuke	fuku na
		II	fukinasai	fukinasaru na
		III	fuite kudasai	fukanai de kudasai
	FORMAL		ofuki nasaimase	ofuki nasaimasu na
Presumptive	**INFORMAL**	I	fukō	fukumai
		II	fuku darō	fukanai darō
	FORMAL	I	fukimashō	fukimasumai
		II	fuku deshō	fukanai deshō
Provisional	**INFORMAL**		fukeba	fukanakereba
	FORMAL		fukimaseba	fukimasen nara
			fukimasureba	
Gerund	**INFORMAL**	I	fuite	fukanai de
		II		fukanakute
	FORMAL		fukimashite	fukimasen de
Past Ind.	**INFORMAL**		fuita	fukanakatta
	FORMAL		fukimashita	fukimasen deshita
Past Presump.	**INFORMAL**		fuitarō	fukanakattarō
			fuita darō	fukanakatta darō
	FORMAL		fukimashitarō	fukimasen deshitarō
			fuita deshō	fukanakatta deshō
Conditional	**INFORMAL**		fuitara	fukanakattara
	FORMAL		fukimashitara	fukimasen deshitara
Alternative	**INFORMAL**		fuitari	fukanakattari
	FORMAL		fukimashitari	fukimasen deshitari

			INFORMAL AFFIRMATIVE INDICATIVE
Passive			fukareru
Potential			fukeru
Causative			fukaseru
Causative Pass.			fukaserareru
Honorific		I	ofuki ni naru
		II	ofuki nasaru
Humble		I	ofuki suru
		II	ofuki itasu

F

to include   TRANSITIVE

			AFFIRMATIVE	NEGATIVE
Indicative	**INFORMAL**		fukumeru	fukumenai
	FORMAL		fukumemasu	fukumemasen
Imperative	**INFORMAL**	I	fukumero	fukumeru na
		II	fukumenasai	fukumenasaru na
		III	fukumete kudasai	fukumenai de kudasai
	FORMAL		ofukume nasaimase	ofukume nasaimasu na
Presumptive	**INFORMAL**	I	fukumeyō	fukumemai
		II	fukumeru darō	fukumenai darō
	FORMAL	I	fukumemashō	fukumemasumai
		II	fukumeru deshō	fukumenai deshō
Provisional	**INFORMAL**		fukumereba	fukumenakereba
	FORMAL		fukumemaseba	fukumemasen nara
			fukumemasureba	
Gerund	**INFORMAL**	I	fukumete	fukumenai de
		II		fukumenakute
	FORMAL		fukumemashite	fukumemasen de
Past Ind.	**INFORMAL**		fukumeta	fukumenakatta
	FORMAL		fukumemashita	fukumemasen deshita
Past Presump.	**INFORMAL**		fukumetarō	fukumenakattarō
			fukumeta darō	fukumenakatta darō
	FORMAL		fukumemashitarō	fukumemasen deshitarō
			fukumeta deshō	fukumenakatta deshō
Conditional	**INFORMAL**		fukumetara	fukumenakattara
	FORMAL		fukumemashitara	fukumemasen deshitara
Alternative	**INFORMAL**		fukumetari	fukumenakattari
	FORMAL		fukumemashitari	fukumemasen deshitari

		INFORMAL AFFIRMATIVE INDICATIVE
Passive		fukumerareru
Potential		fukamerareru
Causative		fukamesaseru
Causative Pass.		fukamesaserareru
Honorific	I	ofukume ni naru
	II	ofukume nasaru
Humble	I	ofukume suru
	II	ofukume itasu

ふくむ／含む **fukum.u**

TRANSITIVE *to include, to contain, to imply*

			AFFIRMATIVE	NEGATIVE
Indicative	**INFORMAL**		fukumu	fukumanai
	FORMAL		fukumimasu	fukumimasen
Imperative	**INFORMAL**	I	fukume	fukumu na
		II	fukuminasai	fukuminasaru na
		III	fukunde kudasai	fukumanai de kudasai
	FORMAL		ofukumi nasaimase	ofukumi nasaimasu na
Presumptive	**INFORMAL**	I	fukumō	fukumumai
		II	fukumu darō	fukumanai darō
	FORMAL	I	fukumimashō	fukumimasumai
		II	fukumu deshō	fukumanai deshō
Provisional	**INFORMAL**		fukumeba	fukumanakereba
	FORMAL		fukumimaseba	fukumimasen nara
			fukumimasureba	
Gerund	**INFORMAL**	I	fukunde	fukumanai de
		II		fukumanakute
	FORMAL		fukumimashite	fukumimasen de
Past Ind.	**INFORMAL**		fukunda	fukumanakatta
	FORMAL		fukumimashita	fukumimasen deshita
Past Presump.	**INFORMAL**		fukundarō	fukumanakattarō
			fukunda darō	fukumanakatta darō
	FORMAL		fukumimashitarō	fukumimasen deshitarō
			fukunda deshō	fukukmanakatta deshō
Conditional	**INFORMAL**		fukundara	fukumanakattara
	FORMAL		fukumimashitara	fukumimasen deshitara
Alternative	**INFORMAL**		fukundari	fukumanakattari
	FORMAL		fukumimashitari	fukumimasen deshitari

		INFORMAL AFFIRMATIVE INDICATIVE
Passive		fukumareru
Potential		
Causative		fukumaseru
Causative Pass.		fukumaserareru
Honorific	I	ofukumi ni naru
	II	ofukumi nasaru
Humble	I	ofukumi suru
	II	ofukumi itasu

fum.u　ふむ／踏む　　　　　　　　　　　　　　　　　**fumi**
to step on　　TRANSITIVE

			AFFIRMATIVE	NEGATIVE
Indicative	**INFORMAL**		fumu	fumanai
	FORMAL		fumimasu	fumimasen
Imperative	**INFORMAL**	I	fume	fumu na
		II	fuminasai	fuminasaru nil.
		III	funde kudasai	fumanai de kudasai
	FORMAL		ofumi nasaimase	ofumi nasaimasu na
Presumptive	**INFORMAL**	I	fumō	fumumai
		II	fumu darō	fumanai darō
	FORMAL	I	fumimashō	fumimasumai
		II	fumu deshō	fumanai deshō
Provisional	**INFORMAL**		fumeba	fumanakereba
	FORMAL		fumimaseba	fumimasen nara
			fumimasureba	
Gerund	**INFORMAL**	I	funde	fumanai de
		II		fumanakute
	FORMAL		fumimashite	fumimasen de
Past Ind.	**INFORMAL**		funda	fumanakatta
	FORMAL		fumimashita	fumimasen deshita
Past Presump.	**INFORMAL**		fundarō	fumanakattarō
			funda darō	fumanakatta darō
	FORMAL		fumimashitarō	fumimasen deshitarō
			funda deshō	fumanakatta deshō
Conditional	**INFORMAL**		fundara	fumanakattara
	FORMAL		fumimashitara	fumimasen deshitara
Alternative	**INFORMAL**		fundari	fumanakattari
	FORMAL		fumimashitari	fumimasen deshitari

			INFORMAL AFFIRMATIVE INDICATIVE
Passive			fumareru
Potential			fumeru
Causative			fumaseru
Causative Pass.			fumaserareru
Honorific		I	ofumi ni naru
		II	ofumi nasaru
Humble		I	ofumi suru
		II	ofumi itasu

			AFFIRMATIVE	NEGATIVE
Indicative	**INFORMAL**		fureru	furenai
	FORMAL		furemasu	furemasen
Imperative	**INFORMAL**	I	furero	fureru na
		II	furenasai	furenasaru na
		III	furete kudasai	furenai de kudasai
	FORMAL		ofure nasaimase	ofure nasaimasu na
Presumptive	**INFORMAL**	I	fureyō	furemai
		II	fureru darō	furenai darō
	FORMAL	I	furemashō	furemasumai
		II	fureru deshō	furenai deshō
Provisional	**INFORMAL**		furereba	furenakereba
	FORMAL		furemaseba / furemasureba	furemasen nara
Gerund	**INFORMAL**	I	furete	furenai de
		II		furenakute
	FORMAL		furemashite	furemasen de
Past Ind.	**INFORMAL**		fureta	furenakatta
	FORMAL		furemashita	furemasen deshita
Past Presump.	**INFORMAL**		furetarō / fureta darō	furenakattarō / furenakatta darō
	FORMAL		furemashitarō / fureta deshō	furemasen deshitarō / furenakatta deshō
Conditional	**INFORMAL**		furetara	furenakattara
	FORMAL		furemashitara	furemasen deshitara
Alternative	**INFORMAL**		furetari	furenakattari
	FORMAL		furemashitari	furemasen deshitari

		INFORMAL AFFIRMATIVE INDICATIVE
Passive		furerareru
Potential		furerareru
Causative		furesaseru
Causative Pass.		furesaserareru
Honorific	I	ofure ni naru
	II	ofure nasaru
Humble	I	ofure suru
	II	ofure itasu

furikaer.u ふりかえる／振り返る **furikaeri**

to look back, to think back TRANSITIVE

			AFFIRMATIVE	NEGATIVE
Indicative	**INFORMAL**		furikaeru	furikaeranai
	FORMAL		furikaerimasu	furikaerimasen
Imperative	**INFORMAL**	I	furikaere	furikaeru na
		II	furikaerinasai	furikaerinasaru na
		III	furikaette kudasai	furikaeranai de kudasai
	FORMAL		ofurikaeri nasaimase	ofurikaeri nasaimasu na
Presumptive	**INFORMAL**	I	furikaerō	furikaerumai
		II	furikaeru darō	furikaeranai darō
	FORMAL	I	furikaerimashō	furikaerimasumai
		II	furikaeru deshō	furikaeranai deshō
Provisional	**INFORMAL**		furikaereba	furikaeranakereba
	FORMAL		furikaerimaseba	furikaerimasen nara
			furikaerimasureba	
Gerund	**INFORMAL**	I	furikaette	furikaeranai de
		II		furikaeranakute
	FORMAL		furikaerimashite	furikaerimasen de
Past Ind.	**INFORMAL**		furikaetta	furikaeranakatta
	FORMAL		furikaerimashita	furikaerimasen deshita
Past Presump.	**INFORMAL**		furikaettarō	furikaeranakattarō
			furikaetta darō	furikaeranakatta darō
	FORMAL		furikaerimashitarō	furikaerimasen deshitarō
			furikaetta deshō	furikaeranakatta deshō
Conditional	**INFORMAL**		furikaettara	furikaeranakattara
	FORMAL		furikaerimashitara	furikaerimasen deshitara
Alternative	**INFORMAL**		furikaettari	furikaeranakattari
	FORMAL		furikaerimashitari	furikaerimasen deshitari

		INFORMAL AFFIRMATIVE INDICATIVE
Passive		furikaerareru
Potential		furikaereru
Causative		furikaeraseru
Causative Pass.		furikaeraserareru
Honorific	I	ofurikaeri ni naru
	II	ofurikaeri nasaru
Humble	I	
	II	

94

ふる／降る　fur.u
to fall from the sky

			AFFIRMATIVE	NEGATIVE
Indicative	**INFORMAL**		furu	furanai
	FORMAL		furimasu	furimasen
Imperative	**INFORMAL**	I	fure	furu na
		II	furinasai	furinasaru na
		III	futte kudasai	furanai de kudasai
	FORMAL			
Presumptive	**INFORMAL**	I	furō	furumai
		II	furu darō	furanai darō
	FORMAL	I	furimashō	furimasumai
		II	furu deshō	furanai deshō
Provisional	**INFORMAL**		fureba	furanakereba
	FORMAL		furimaseba	furimasen nara
			furimasureba	
Gerund	**INFORMAL**	I	futte	furanai de
		II		furanakute
	FORMAL		furimashite	furimasen de
Past Ind.	**INFORMAL**		futta	furanakatta
	FORMAL		furimashita	furimasen deshita
Past Presump.	**INFORMAL**		futtarō	furanakattarō
			futta darō	furanakatta darō
	FORMAL		furimashitarō	furimasen deshitarō
			futta deshō	furanakatta deshō
Conditional	**INFORMAL**		futtara	furanakattara
	FORMAL		furimashitara	furimasen deshitara
Alternative	**INFORMAL**		futtari	furanakattari
	FORMAL		furimashitari	furimasen deshitari

		INFORMAL AFFIRMATIVE INDICATIVE
Passive		furareru
Potential		fureru
Causative		furaseru
Causative Pass.		furaserareru
Honorific	I	
	II	
Humble	I	
	II	

F

to tremble

			AFFIRMATIVE	NEGATIVE
Indicative	**INFORMAL**		furueru	furuenai
	FORMAL		furuemasu	furuemasen
Imperative	**INFORMAL**	I	furuero	furueru na
		II	furuenasai	furuenasaru na
		III	furuete kudasai	furuenai de kudasai
	FORMAL		ofurue nasaimase	ofurue nasaimasu na
Presumptive	**INFORMAL**	I	furueyō	furuemai
		II	furueru darō	furuenai darō
	FORMAL	I	furuemashō	furuemasumai
		II	furueru deshō	furuenai deshō
Provisional	**INFORMAL**		furuereba	furuenakereba
	FORMAL		furuemaseba	furuemasen nara
			furuemasureba	
Gerund	**INFORMAL**	I	furuete	furuenai de
		II		furuenakute
	FORMAL		furuemashite	furuemasen de
Past Ind.	**INFORMAL**		furueta	furuenakatta
	FORMAL		furuemashita	furuemasen deshita
Past Presump.	**INFORMAL**		furuetarō	furuenakattarō
			furueta darō	furuenakatta darō
	FORMAL		furuemashitarō	furuemasen deshitarō
			furueta deshō	furuenakatta deshō
Conditional	**INFORMAL**		furuetara	furuenakattara
	FORMAL		furuemashitara	furuemasen deshitara
Alternative	**INFORMAL**		furuetari	furuenakattari
	FORMAL		furuemashitari	furuemasen deshitari

		INFORMAL AFFIRMATIVE INDICATIVE
Passive		furuerareru
Potential		furuerareru
Causative		furuesaseru
Causative Pass.		furuesaserareru
Honorific	I	ofurue ni naru
	II	ofurue nasaru
Humble	I	
	II	

ふさがる／塞がる　**fusagar.u**

to be closed, to be taken, to be blocked off

			AFFIRMATIVE	NEGATIVE
Indicative	**INFORMAL**		fusagaru	fusagaranai
	FORMAL		fusagarimasu	fusagarimasen
Imperative	**INFORMAL**	I	fusagare	fusagaru na
		II	fusagarinasai	fusagarinasaru na
		III		
	FORMAL			
Presumptive	**INFORMAL**	I	fusagarō	fusagarumai
		II	fusagaru darō	fusagaranai darō
	FORMAL	I	fusagarimashō	fusagarimasumai
		II	fusagaru deshō	fusagaranai deshō
Provisional	**INFORMAL**		fusagareba	fusagaranakereba
	FORMAL		fusagarimaseba	fusagarimasen nara
			fusagarimasureba	
Gerund	**INFORMAL**	I	fusagatte	fusagaranai de
		II		fusagaranakute
	FORMAL		fusagarimashite	fusagarimasen de
Past Ind.	**INFORMAL**		fusagatta	fusagaranakatta
	FORMAL		fusagarimashita	fusagarimasen deshita
Past Presump.	**INFORMAL**		fusagattarō	fusagaranakattarō
			fusagatta darō	fusagaranakatta darō
	FORMAL		fusagarimashitarō	fusagarimasen deshitarō
			fusagatta deshō	fusagaranakatta deshō
Conditional	**INFORMAL**		fusagattara	fusagaranakattara
	FORMAL		fusagarimashitara	fusagarimasen deshitara
Alternative	**INFORMAL**		fusagattari	fusagaranakattari
	FORMAL		fusagarimashitari	fusagarimasen deshitari

		INFORMAL AFFIRMATIVE INDICATIVE
Passive		fusagarareru
Potential		fusagareru
Causative		fusagaraseru
Causative Pass.		fusagaraserareru
Honorific	I	ofusagari ni naru
	II	ofusagari nasaru
Humble	I	
	II	

F

fusag.u ふさぐ／塞ぐ   **fusagi**

to close, to cover, to block up   TRANSITIVE

			AFFIRMATIVE	NEGATIVE
Indicative	**INFORMAL**		fusagu	fusaganai
	FORMAL		fusagimasu	fusagimasen
Imperative	**INFORMAL**	I	fusage	fusagu na
		II	fusaginasai	fusaginasaru na
		III	fusaide kudasai	fusaganai de kudasai
	FORMAL		ofusagi nasaimase	ofusagi nasaimasu na
Presumptive	**INFORMAL**	I	fusagō	fusagumai
		II	fusagu darō	fusaganai darō
	FORMAL	I	fusagimashō	fusagimasumai
		II	fusagu deshō	fusaganai deshō
Provisional	**INFORMAL**		fusageba	fusaganakereba
	FORMAL		fusagimaseba	fusagimasen nara
			fusagimasureba	
Gerund	**INFORMAL**	I	fusaide	fusaganai de
		II		fusaganakute
	FORMAL		fusagimashite	fusagimasen de
Past Ind.	**INFORMAL**		fusaida	fusaganakatta
	FORMAL		fusagimashita	fusagimasen deshita
Past Presump.	**INFORMAL**		fusaidarō	fusaganakattarō
			fusaida darō	fusaganakatta darō
	FORMAL		fusagimashitarō	fusagimasen deshitarō
			fusaida deshō	fusaganakatta deshō
Conditional	**INFORMAL**		fusaidara	fusaganakattara
	FORMAL		fusagimashitara	fusagimasen deshitara
Alternative	**INFORMAL**		fusaidari	fusaganakattari
	FORMAL		fusagimashitari	fusagimasen deshitari

			INFORMAL AFFIRMATIVE INDICATIVE
Passive			fusagareru
Potential			fusageru
Causative			fusagaseru
Causative Pass.			fusagaserareru
Honorific		I	ofusagi ni naru
		II	ofusagi nasaru
Humble		I	ofusagi suru
		II	ofusagi itasu

TRANSITIVE   *to prevent, to defend*

			AFFIRMATIVE	NEGATIVE
Indicative	**INFORMAL**		fusegu	fuseganai
	FORMAL		fusegimasu	fusegimasen
Imperative	**INFORMAL**	I	fusege	fusegu na
		II	fuseginasai	fuseginasaru na
		III	fuseide kudasai	fuseganai de kudasai
	FORMAL		ofusegi nasaimase	ofusegi nasaimasu na
Presumptive	**INFORMAL**	I	fusegō	fusegumai
		II	fusegu darō	fuseganai darō
	FORMAL	I	fusegimashō	fusegimasumai
		II	fusegu deshō	fuseganai deshō
Provisional	**INFORMAL**		fusegeba	fuseganakereba
	FORMAL		fusegimaseba	fusegimasen nara
			fusegimasureba	
Gerund	**INFORMAL**	I	fuseide	fuseganai de
		II		fuseganakute
	FORMAL		fusegimashite	fusegimasen de
Past Ind.	**INFORMAL**		fuseida	fuseganakatta
	FORMAL		fusegimashita	fusegimasen deshita
Past Presump.	**INFORMAL**		fuseidarō	fuseganakattarō
			fuseida darō	fuseganakatta darō
	FORMAL		fusegimashitarō	fusegimasen deshitarō
			fuseida deshō	fuseganakatta deshō
Conditional	**INFORMAL**		fuseidara	fuseganakattara
	FORMAL		fusegimashitara	fusegimasen deshitara
Alternative	**INFORMAL**		fuseidari	fuseganakattari
	FORMAL		fusegimashitari	fusegimasen deshitari

			INFORMAL AFFIRMATIVE INDICATIVE
Passive			fusegareru
Potential			fusegeru
Causative			fusegaseru
Causative Pass.			fusegaserareru
Honorific		I	ofusegi ni naru
		II	ofusegi nasaru
Humble		I	ofusegi suru
		II	ofusegi itasu

F

to lay (something) *face down*　　TRANSITIVE

			AFFIRMATIVE	NEGATIVE
Indicative	**INFORMAL**		fuseru	fusenai
	FORMAL		fusemasu	fusemasen
Imperative	**INFORMAL**	I	fusero	fuseru na
		II	fusenasai	fusenasaru na
		III	fusete kudasai	fusenai de kudasai
	FORMAL		ofuse nasaimase	ofuse nasaimasu na
Presumptive	**INFORMAL**	I	fuseyō	fusemai
		II	fuseru darō	fusenai darō
	FORMAL	I	fusemashō	fusemasumai
		II	fuseru deshō	fusenai deshō
Provisional	**INFORMAL**		fusereba	fusenakereba
	FORMAL		fusemaseba	fusemasen nara
			fusemasureba	
Gerund	**INFORMAL**	I	fusete	fusenai de
		II		fusenakute
	FORMAL		fusemashite	fusemasen de
Past Ind.	**INFORMAL**		fuseta	fusenakatta
	FORMAL		fusemashita	fusemasen deshita
Past Presump.	**INFORMAL**		fusetarō	fusenakattaro
			fuseta darō	fusenakatta darō
	FORMAL		fusemashitarō	fusemasen deshitarō
			fuseta deshō	fusenakatta deshō
Conditional	**INFORMAL**		fusetara	fusenakattara
	FORMAL		fusemashitara	fusemasen deshitara
Alternative	**INFORMAL**		fusetari	fusenakattari
	FORMAL		fusemashitari	fusemasen deshitari

		INFORMAL AFFIRMATIVE INDICATIVE
Passive		fuserareru
Potential		fuserareru
Causative		fusesaseru
Causative Pass.		fusesaserareru
Honorific	I	ofuse ni naru
	II	ofuse nasaru
Humble	I	ofuse suru
	II	ofuse itasu

fuseri

ふせる／臥せる **fuser.u**
to lie down

			AFFIRMATIVE	NEGATIVE
Indicative	**INFORMAL**		fuseru	fuseranai
	FORMAL		fuserimasu	fuserimasen
Imperative	**INFORMAL**	I	fusero	fuseru na
		II	fuserinasai	fuserinasaru na
		III	fusette kudasai	fuseranai de kudasai
	FORMAL		ofuseri nasaimase	ofuseri nasaimasu na
Presumptive	**INFORMAL**	I	fuserō	fuserumai
		II	fuseru darō	fuseranai darō
	FORMAL	I	fuserimashō	fuserimasumai
		II	fuseru deshō	fuseranai deshō
Provisional	**INFORMAL**		fusereba	fuseranakereba
	FORMAL		fuserimaseba	fuserimasen nara
			fuserimasureba	
Gerund	**INFORMAL**	I	fusette	fuseranai de
		II		fuseranakute
	FORMAL		fuserimashite	fuserimasen de
Past Ind.	**INFORMAL**		fusetta	fuseranakatta
	FORMAL		fuserimashita	fuserimasen deshita
Past Presump.	**INFORMAL**		fusettarō	fuseranakattarō
			fusetta darō	fuseranakatta darō
	FORMAL		fuserimashitarō	fuserimasen deshitarō
			fusetta deshō	fuseranakatta deshō
Conditional	**INFORMAL**		fusettara	fuseranakattara
	FORMAL		fuserimashitara	fuserimasen deshitara
Alternative	**INFORMAL**		fusettari	fuseranakattari
	FORMAL		fuserimashitari	fuserimasen deshitari

		INFORMAL AFFIRMATIVE INDICATIVE
Passive		fuserareru
Potential		fusereru
Causative		fuseraseru
Causative Pass.		fuseraserareru
Honorific	I	ofuseri ni naru
	II	ofuseri nasaru
Humble	I	
	II	

F

101

futor.u　ふとる／太る／肥る　　　　　　　　　　futori

to gain weight, to become fat

			AFFIRMATIVE	NEGATIVE
Indicative	**INFORMAL**		futoru	futoranai
	FORMAL		futorimasu	futorimasen
Imperative	**INFORMAL**	I	futore	futoru na
		II	futorinasai	futorinasaru na
		III	futotte kudasai	futoranai de kudasai
	FORMAL		ofutori nasaimase	ofutori nasaimasu na
Presumptive	**INFORMAL**	I	futorō	futorumai
		II	futoru darō	futoranai darō
	FORMAL	I	futorimashō	futorimasumai
		II	futoru deshō	futoranai deshō
Provisional	**INFORMAL**		futoreba	futoranakereba
	FORMAL		futorimaseba	futorimasen nara
			futorimasureba	
Gerund	**INFORMAL**	I	futotte	futoranai de
		II		futoranakute
	FORMAL		futorimashite	futorimasen de
Past Ind.	**INFORMAL**		futotta	futoranakatta
	FORMAL		futorimashita	futorimasen deshita
Past Presump.	**INFORMAL**		futottarō	futoranakattarō
			futotta darō	futoranakatta darō
	FORMAL		futorimashitarō	futorimasen deshitarō
			futotta deshō	futoranakatta deshō
Conditional	**INFORMAL**		futottara	futoranakattara
	FORMAL		futorimashitara	futorimasen deshitara
Alternative	**INFORMAL**		futottari	futoranakattari
	FORMAL		futorimashitari	futorimasen deshitari

		INFORMAL AFFIRMATIVE INDICATIVE
Passive		futorareru
Potential		futoreru
Causative		futoraseru
Causative Pass.		futoraserareru
Honorific	I	ofutori ni naru
	II	ofutori nasaru
Humble	I	
	II	

102

ふやす／増やす　**fuyas.u**

TRANSITIVE　　*to increase* (something)

			AFFIRMATIVE	**NEGATIVE**
Indicative	**INFORMAL**		fuyasu	fuyasanai
	FORMAL		fuyashimasu	fuyashimasen
Imperative	**INFORMAL**	I	fuyase	fuyasu na
		II	fuyashinasai	fuyashinasaru na
		III	fuyashite kudasai	fuyasanai de kudasai
	FORMAL		ofuyashi nasaimase	ofuyashi nasaimasu na
Presumptive	**INFORMAL**	I	fuyasō	fuyasumai
		II	fuyasu darō	fuyasanai darō
	FORMAL	I	fuyashimashō	fuyashimasumai
		II	fuyasu deshō	fuyasanai deshō
Provisional	**INFORMAL**		fuyaseba	fuyasanakereba
	FORMAL		fuyashimaseba	fuyashimasen nara
			fuyashimasureba	
Gerund	**INFORMAL**	I	fuyashite	fuyasanai de
		II		fuyasanakute
	FORMAL		fuyashimashite	fuyashimasen de
Past Ind.	**INFORMAL**		fuyashita	fuyasanakatta
	FORMAL		fuyashimashita	fuyashimasen deshita
Past Presump.	**INFORMAL**		fuyashitarō	fuyasanakattarō
			fuyashita darō	fuyasanakatta darō
	FORMAL		fuyashimashitarō	fuyashimasen deshitarō
			fuyashita deshō	fuyasanakatta deshō
Conditional	**INFORMAL**		fuyashitara	fuyasanakattara
	FORMAL		fuyashimashitara	fuyashimasen deshitara
Alternative	**INFORMAL**		fuyashitari	fuyasanakattari
	FORMAL		fuyashimashitari	fuyashimasen deshitari

			INFORMAL AFFIRMATIVE INDICATIVE
Passive			fuyasareru
Potential			fuyaseru
Causative			fuyasaseru
Causative Pass.			fuyasaserareru
Honorific		I	ofuyashi ni naru
		II	ofuyashi nasaru
Humble		I	ofuyashi suru
		II	ofuyashi itasu

ganbar.u がんばる／頑張る　　　　　　　　　　　ganbari

to stand firm, to do one's best

			AFFIRMATIVE	NEGATIVE
Indicative	**INFORMAL**		ganbaru	ganbaranai
	FORMAL		ganbarimasu	ganbarimasen
Imperative	**INFORMAL**	I	ganbare	ganbaru na
		II	ganbarinasai	ganbarinasaru na
		III	ganbatte kudasai	ganbaranai de kudasai
	FORMAL		oganbari nasaimase	oganbari nasaimasu na
Presumptive	**INFORMAL**	I	ganbarō	ganbarumai
		II	ganbaru darō	ganbaranai darō
	FORMAL	I	ganbarimashō	ganbarimasumai
		II	ganbaru deshō	ganbaranai deshō
Provisional	**INFORMAL**		ganbareba	ganbaranakereba
	FORMAL		ganbarimaseba	ganbarimasen nara
			ganbarimasureba	
Gerund	**INFORMAL**	I	ganbatte	ganbaranai de
		II		ganbaranakute
	FORMAL		ganbarimashite	ganbarimasen de
Past Ind.	**INFORMAL**		ganbatta	ganbaranakatta
	FORMAL		ganbarimashita	ganbarimasen deshita
Past Presump.	**INFORMAL**		ganbattarō	ganbaranakattarō
			ganbatta darō	ganbaranakatta darō
	FORMAL		ganbarimashitarō	ganbarimasen deshitarō
			ganbatta deshō	ganbaranakatta deshō
Conditional	**INFORMAL**		ganbattara	ganbaranakattara
	FORMAL		ganbarimashitara	ganbarimasen deshitara
Alternative	**INFORMAL**		ganbattari	ganbaranakattari
	FORMAL		ganbarimashitari	ganbarimasen deshitari

		INFORMAL AFFIRMATIVE INDICATIVE
Passive		ganbarareru
Potential		ganbareru
Causative		ganbaraseru
Causative Pass.		ganbaraserareru
Honorific	I	oganbari ni naru
	II	oganbari nasaru
Humble	I	
	II	

104

ござる／御座る　**gozar.u**

to exist (inanimate neutral polite)*

			AFFIRMATIVE	NEGATIVE
Indicative	**INFORMAL**		gozaru	
	FORMAL		gozaimasu	gozaimasen
Imperative	**INFORMAL**	I		
		II		
		III		
	FORMAL			
Presumptive	**INFORMAL**	I	gozarō	gozarumai
		II		
	FORMAL	I	gozaimashō	gozaimasumai
		II		
Provisional	**INFORMAL**			
	FORMAL		gozaimaseba	gozaimasen nara
			gozaimasureba	
Gerund	**INFORMAL**	I		
		II		
	FORMAL		gozaimashite	gozaimasen de
Past Ind.	**INFORMAL**			
	FORMAL		gozaimashita	gozaimasen deshita
Past Presump.	**INFORMAL**			
	FORMAL		gozaimashitarō	gozaimasen deshitarō
Conditional	**INFORMAL**			
	FORMAL		gozaimashitara	gozaimasen deshitara
Alternative	**INFORMAL**			
	FORMAL		gozaimashitari	gozaimasen deshitari

		INFORMAL AFFIRMATIVE INDICATIVE
Passive		
Potential		
Causative		
Causative Pass.		
Honorific	I	
	II	
Humble	I	
	II	

*The forms *gozaru*, *gozarō*, and *gozarumai* are rarely used in standard conversation,
being replaced by their formal equivalents.

to encourage   TRANSITIVE

			AFFIRMATIVE	**NEGATIVE**
Indicative	**INFORMAL**		hagemasu	hagemasanai
	FORMAL		hagemashimasu	hagemashimasen
Imperative	**INFORMAL**	I	hagemase	hagemasu na
		II	hagemashinasai	hagemashinasaru na
		III	hagemashite kudasai	hagemasanai de kudasai
	FORMAL		ohagemashi nasaimase	ohagemashi nasaimasu na
Presumptive	**INFORMAL**	I	hagemasō	hagemasumai
		II	hagemasu darō	hagemasanai darō
	FORMAL	I	hagemashimashō	hagemashimasumai
		II	hagemasu deshō	hagemasanai deshō
Provisional	**INFORMAL**		hagemaseba	hagemasanakereba
	FORMAL		hagemashimaseha	hagemashimasen nara
			hagemashimasureba	
Gerund	**INFORMAL**	I	hagemashite	hagemasanai de
		II		hagemasanakute
	FORMAL		hagemashimashite	hagemashimasen de
Past Ind.	**INFORMAL**		hagemashita	hagemasanakatta
	FORMAL		hagemashimashita	hagemashimasen deshita
Past Presump.	**INFORMAL**		hagemashitarō	hagemasanakattarō
			hagemashita darō	hagemasanakatta darō
	FORMAL		hagemashimashitarō	hagemashimasen deshitarō
			hagemashita deshō	hagemasanakatta deshō
Conditional	**INFORMAL**		hagemashitara	hagemasanakattara
	FORMAL		hagemashimashitara	hagemashimasen deshitara
Alternative	**INFORMAL**		hagemashitari	hagemasanakattari
	FORMAL		hagemashimashitari	hagemashimasen deshitari

			INFORMAL AFFIRMATIVE INDICATIVE
Passive			hagemasareru
Potential			hagemaseru
Causative			hagemasaseru
Causative Pass.			hagemasaserareru
Honorific		I	ohagemashi ni naru
		II	ohagemashi nasaru
Humble		I	ohagemashi suru
		II	ohagemashi itasu

106

はげむ／励む　**hagem.u**

to strive, to make every effort

			AFFIRMATIVE	NEGATIVE
Indicative	**INFORMAL**		hagemu	hagemanai
	FORMAL		hagemimasu	hagemimasen
Imperative	**INFORMAL**	I	hageme	hagemu na
		II	hageminasai	hageminasaru na
		III	hagende kudasai	hagemanai de kudasai
	FORMAL		ohagemi nasaimase	ohagemi nasaimasu na
Presumptive	**INFORMAL**	I	hagemō	hagemumai
		II	hagemu darō	hagemanai darō
	FORMAL	I	hagemimashō	hagemimasumai
		II	hagemu deshō	hagemanai deshō
Provisional	**INFORMAL**		hagemeba	hagemanakereba
	FORMAL		hagemimaseba	hagemimasen nara
			hagemimasureba	
Gerund	**INFORMAL**	I	hagende	hagemanai de
		II		hagemanakute
	FORMAL		hagemimashite	hagemimasen de
Past Ind.	**INFORMAL**		hagenda	hagemanakatta
	FORMAL		hagemimashita	hagemimasen deshita
Past Presump.	**INFORMAL**		hagendarō	hagemanakattarō
			hagenda darō	hagemanakatta darō
	FORMAL		hagemimashitarō	hagemimasen deshitarō
			hagenda deshō	hagemanakatta deshō
Conditional	**INFORMAL**		hagendara	hagemanakattara
	FORMAL		hagemimashitara	hagemimasen deshitara
Alternative	**INFORMAL**		hagendari	hagemanakattari
	FORMAL		hagemimashitari	hagemimasen deshitari

		INFORMAL AFFIRMATIVE INDICATIVE
Passive		hagemareru
Potential		hagemeru
Causative		hagemaseru
Causative Pass.		hagemaserareru

Honorific	I	ohagemi ni naru
	II	ohagemi nasaru
Humble	I	
	II	

H

			AFFIRMATIVE	**NEGATIVE**
Indicative	**INFORMAL**		hairu	hairanai
	FORMAL		hairimasu	hairimasen
Imperative	**INFORMAL**	I	haire	hairu na
		II	hairinasai	hairinasaru na
		III	haitte kudasai	hairanai de kudasai
	FORMAL		ohairi nasaimase	ohairi nasaimasu na
Presumptive	**INFORMAL**	I	hairō	hairumai
		II	hairu darō	hairanai darō
	FORMAL	I	hairimashō	hairimasumai
		II	hairu deshō	hairanai deshō
Provisional	**INFORMAL**		haireba	hairanakereba
	FORMAL		hairimaseba	hairimasen nara
			hairimasureba	
Gerund	**INFORMAL**	I	haitte	hairanai de
		II		hairanakute
	FORMAL		hairimashite	hairimasen de
Past Ind.	**INFORMAL**		haitta	hairanakatta
	FORMAL		hairimashita	hairimasen deshita
Past Presump.	**INFORMAL**		haittarō	hairanakattarō
			haitta darō	hairanakatta darō
	FORMAL		hairimashitarō	hairimasen deshitarō
			haitta deshō	hairanakatta deshō
Conditional	**INFORMAL**		haittara	hairanakattara
	FORMAL		hairimashitara	hairimasen deshitara
Alternative	**INFORMAL**		haittari	hairanakattari
	FORMAL		hairimashitari	hairimasen deshitari

		INFORMAL AFFIRMATIVE INDICATIVE
Passive		hairareru
Potential		haireru
Causative		hairaseru
Causative Pass.		hairaserareru
Honorific	I	ohairi ni naru
	II	ohairi nasaru
Humble	I	ohairi suru
	II	ohairi itasu

AN ESSENTIAL 55 VERB

AN ESSENTIAL 55 VERB

Hairu 入る

to come in, to enter, to be in, to join

Hairu is used for many actions and situations. You can get a lot of mileage out of this verb. Just imagine what happens when an act of *hairu* takes place, and you can get the meaning of this verb.

Sentences Using *Hairu*

Kare wa daigaku o shotsugyō shite, ginkō ni haitta.
彼は大学を卒業して銀行に入った。
After graduating from a university, he started working for a bank.

Sono resutoran wa daininki nanode, yoyaku nashi niwa hairenai deshō.
そのレストランは大人気なので、予約無しには入れないでしょう。
That restaurant is so popular that you won't be able to eat there without a reservation.

Kono furui manshon no biru nimo, yatto haisupīdo no intānetto ga haitta.
この古いマンションのビルにも、やっとハイスピードのインターネットが入った。
Even at this old apartment building, high-speed Internet became available.

Michi de hirotta saifu niwa, taikin ga haitte ita.
道で拾った財布には大金が入っていた。
There was a large sum of money in the wallet I found in the street.

Nihon niwa ōkii jishin ga ōi kara, jishin hoken ni haitta hō ga ii deshō.
日本には大きい地震が多いから、火災保険に入った方がいいでしょう。
Because there are many big earthquakes in Japan, you'd better buy earthquake insurance.

Words and Expressions Related to This Verb

mimi ni hairu   耳に入る
to hear

me ni hairu   目に入る
to see

atama ni hairu   頭に入る
to remember, to learn, to memorize

nyūyoku   入浴
taking a bath, bathing, a bath

nyūjō   入場
entrance, admission

nyūin   入院
hospitalization

H

109

hajimar.u　はじまる／始まる

to begin

hajimari

			AFFIRMATIVE	NEGATIVE
Indicative	**INFORMAL**		hajimaru	hajimaranai
	FORMAL		hajimarimasu	hajimarimasen
Imperative	**INFORMAL**	I	hajimare	hajimaru na
		II		
		III	hajimatte kudasai	hajimaranai de kudasai
	FORMAL			
Presumptive	**INFORMAL**	I	hajimarō	hajimarumai
		II	hajimaru darō	hajimaranai darō
	FORMAL	I	hajimarimashō	hajimarimasumai
		II	hajimaru deshō	hajimaranai deshō
Provisional	**INFORMAL**		hajimareba	hajimaranakereba
	FORMAL		hajimarimaseba	hajimarimasen nara
			hajimarimasureba	
Gerund	**INFORMAL**	I	hajimatte	hajimaranai de
		II		hajimaranakute
	FORMAL		hajimarimashite	hajimarimasen de
Past Ind.	**INFORMAL**		hajimatta	hajimaranakatta
	FORMAL		hajimarimashita	hajimarimasen deshita
Past Presump.	**INFORMAL**		hajimattarō	hajimaranakattarō
			hajimatta darō	hajimaranakatta darō
	FORMAL		hajimarimashitarō	hajimarimasen deshitarō
			hajimatta deshō	hajimaranakatta deshō
Conditional	**INFORMAL**		hajimattara	hajimaranakattara
	FORMAL		hajimarimashitara	hajimarimasen deshitara
Alternative	**INFORMAL**		hajimattari	hajimaranakattari
	FORMAL		hajimarimashitari	hajimarimasen deshitari

		INFORMAL AFFIRMATIVE INDICATIVE
Passive		
Potential		
Causative		hajimaraseru
Causative Pass.		
Honorific	I	
	II	
Humble	I	
	II	

110

はじめる／始める　**hajime.ru**
TRANSITIVE　　*to begin, to start*

			AFFIRMATIVE	NEGATIVE
Indicative	**INFORMAL**		hajimeru	hajimenai
	FORMAL		hajimemasu	hajimemasen
Imperative	**INFORMAL**	I	hajimero	hajimeru na
		II	hajimenasai	hajimenasaru na
		III	hajimete kudasai	hajimenai de kudasai
	FORMAL		ohajime nasaimase	ohajime nasaimasu na
Presumptive	**INFORMAL**	I	hajimeyō	hajimemai
		II	hajimeru darō	hajimenai darō
	FORMAL	I	hajimemashō	hajimemasumai
		II	hajimeru deshō	hajimenai deshō
Provisional	**INFORMAL**		hajimereba	hajimenakereba
	FORMAL		hajimemaseba	hajimemasen nara
			hajimemasureba	
Gerund	**INFORMAL**	I	hajimete	hajimenai de
		II		hajimenakute
	FORMAL		hajimemashite	hajimemasen de
Past Ind.	**INFORMAL**		hajimeta	hajimenakatta
	FORMAL		hajimemashita	hajimemasen deshita
Past Presump.	**INFORMAL**		hajimetarō	hajimenakattarō
			hajimeta darō	hajimenakatta darō
	FORMAL		hajimemashitarō	hajimemasen deshitarō
			hajimeta deshō	hajimenakatta deshō
Conditional	**INFORMAL**		hajimetara	hajimenakattara
	FORMAL		hajimemashitara	hajimemasen deshitara
Alternative	**INFORMAL**		hajimetari	hajimenakattari
	FORMAL		hajimemashitari	hajimemasen deshitari

			INFORMAL AFFIRMATIVE INDICATIVE
Passive			hajimerareru
Potential			hajimerareru
Causative			hajimesaseru
Causative Pass.			hajimesaserareru
Honorific		I	ohajime ni naru
		II	ohajime nasaru
Humble		I	ohajime suru
		II	ohajime itasu

AN ESSENTIAL 55 VERB

Hajimeru 始める

to begin, to start

Sentences Using *Hajimeru*

Hajimetara tochū de yametewa
narimasen.
始めたら途中で止めてはなりません。
*Once you start, you can't stop in the
middle.*

Saisho kara keikaku ga shippai suru
koto ga wakatte itara, hajimenakatta
darō.
最初から計画が失敗することが分かっ
ていたら、始めなかっただろう。
*If I had known the plan would fail,
I wouldn't have started.*

Sugu ni hajimenakereba, shimekiri ni
ma ni awanai.
直ぐに始めなければ、締め切りに間に
合わない。
*If I don't begin now, I won't be able
to meet the deadline.*

Kare ga daietto o hajimete kara ichi
nen ni narimasu ga, taijū ga
nakanaka herimasen.
彼がダイエットを始めてから１年に
なりますが、体重がなかなか減りませ
ん。
*It has been a year since he started
dieting, but his weight doesn't come
down easily.*

Yuki ga furi hajimeta node, isoide ie
ni kaerimashita.
雪が降り始めたので、急いで家に帰り
ました。
*When the snow began falling, I
hurried back home.*

Hajimeru is a verb you need because you
have to start somewhere to get anything
done: learning Japanese and the Japanese
verb system, karate, sushi-making, and
much more. You'll enjoy the challenges
as well as the fun.

Words and Expressions Related to This Verb

kaishi suru　開始する
to begin, to start

hajimari　始まり
the beginning, the start

hajime　始め
the beginning, the start

hajime kara owari made
始めから終わりまで
from the beginning to the end

Proverb

Au wa wakare no hajime.
逢うは別れの始め。
*Inevitable parting starts right at the
moment of meeting. (Meeting is the
beginning of parting.)*

hakari

はかる／計る／測る／量る　**hakar.u**

TRANSITIVE　　*to measure*

			AFFIRMATIVE	NEGATIVE
Indicative	**INFORMAL**		hakaru	hakaranai
	FORMAL		hakarimasu	hakarimasen
Imperative	**INFORMAL**	I	hakare	hakaru na
		II	hakarinasai	hakarinasaru na
		III	hakatte kudasai	hakaranai de kudasai
	FORMAL		ohakari nasaimase	ohakari nasaimasu na
Presumptive	**INFORMAL**	I	hakarō	hakarumai
		II	hakaru darō	hakaranai darō
	FORMAL	I	hakarimashō	hakarimasumai
		II	hakaru deshō	hakaranai deshō
Provisional	**INFORMAL**		hakareba	hakaranakereba
	FORMAL		hakarimaseba	hakarimasen nara
			hakarimasureba	
Gerund	**INFORMAL**	I	hakatte	hakaranai de
		II		hakaranakute
	FORMAL		hakarimashite	hakarimasen de
Past Ind.	**INFORMAL**		hakatta	hakaranakatta
	FORMAL		hakarimashita	hakarimasen deshita
Past Presump.	**INFORMAL**		hakattarō	hakaranakattarō
			hakatta darō	hakaranakatta darō
	FORMAL		hakarimashitarō	hakarimasen deshitarō
			hakatta deshō	hakaranakatta deshō
Conditional	**INFORMAL**		hakattara	hakaranakattara
	FORMAL		hakarimashitara	hakarimasen deshitara
Alternative	**INFORMAL**		hakattari	hakaranakattari
	FORMAL		hakarimashitari	hakarimasen deshitari

		INFORMAL AFFIRMATIVE INDICATIVE
Passive		hakarareru
Potential		hakareru
Causative		hakaraseru
Causative Pass.		hakaraserareru
Honorific	I	ohakari ni naru
	II	ohakari nasaru
Humble	I	ohakari suru
	II	ohakari itasu

H

113

to plan, to plot　　TRANSITIVE

			AFFIRMATIVE	NEGATIVE
Indicative	**INFORMAL**		hakaru	hakaranai
	FORMAL		hakarimasu	hakarimasen
Imperative	**INFORMAL**	I	hakare	hakaru na
		II	hakarinasai	hakarinasaru na
		III	hakatte kudasai	hakaranai de kudasai
	FORMAL		ohakari nasaimase	ohakari nasaimasu na
Presumptive	**INFORMAL**	I	hakarō	hakarumai
		II	hakaru darō	hakaranai darō
	FORMAL	I	hakarimashō	hakarimasumai
		II	hakaru deshō	hakaranai deshō
Provisional	**INFORMAL**		hakareba	hakaranakereba
	FORMAL		hakarimaseba	hakarimasen nara
			hakarimasureba	
Gerund	**INFORMAL**	I	hakatte	hakaranai de
		II		hakaranakute
	FORMAL		hakarimashite	hakarimasen de
Past Ind.	**INFORMAL**		hakatta	hakaranakatta
	FORMAL		hakarimashita	hakarimasen deshita
Past Presump.	**INFORMAL**		hakattarō	hakaranakattarō
			hakatta darō	hakaranakatta darō
	FORMAL		hakarimashitarō	hakarimasen deshitarō
			hakatta deshō	hakaranakatta deshō
Conditional	**INFORMAL**		hakattara	hakaranakattara
	FORMAL		hakarimashitara	hakarimasen deshitara
Alternative	**INFORMAL**		hakattari	hakaranakattari
	FORMAL		hakarimashitari	hakarimasen deshitari

		INFORMAL AFFIRMATIVE INDICATIVE
Passive		hakarareru
Potential		hakareru
Causative		hakaraseru
Causative Pass.		hakaraserareru
Honorific	I	ohakari ni naru
	II	ohakari nasaru
Humble	I	ohakari suru
	II	ohakari itasu

はこぶ／運ぶ **hakob.u**

TRANSITIVE   *to carry*

			AFFIRMATIVE	NEGATIVE
Indicative	**INFORMAL**		hakobu	hakobanai
	FORMAL		hakobimasu	hakobimasen
Imperative	**INFORMAL**	I	hakobe	hakobu na
		II	hakobinasai	hakobinasaru na
		III	hakonde kudasai	hakobanai de kudasai
	FORMAL		ohakobi nasaimase	ohakobi nasaimasu na
Presumptive	**INFORMAL**	I	hakobō	hakobumai
		II	hakobu darō	hakobanai darō
	FORMAL	I	hakobimashō	hakobimasumai
		II	hakobu deshō	hakobanai deshō
Provisional	**INFORMAL**		hakobeba	hakobanakereba
	FORMAL		hakobimaseba	hakobimasen nara
			hakobimasureba	
Gerund	**INFORMAL**	I	hakonde	hakobanai de
		II		hakobarakute
	FORMAL		hakobimashite	hakobimasen de
Past Ind.	**INFORMAL**		hakonda	hakobanakatta
	FORMAL		hakobimashita	hakobimasen deshita
Past Presump.	**INFORMAL**		hakondarō	hakobanakattarō
			hakonda darō	hakobanakatta darō
	FORMAL		hakobimashitarō	hakobimasen deshitarō
			hakonda deshō	hakobanakatta deshō
Conditional	**INFORMAL**		hakondara	hakobanakattara
	FORMAL		hakobimashitara	hakobimasen deshitara
Alternative	**INFORMAL**		hakondari	hakobanakattari
	FORMAL		hakobimashitari	hakobimasen deshitari

			INFORMAL AFFIRMATIVE INDICATIVE
Passive			hakobareru
Potential			hakoberu
Causative			hakobaseru
Causative Pass.			hakobaserareru
Honorific		I	ohakobi ni naru
		II	ohakobi nasaru
Humble		I	ohakobi suru
		II	ohakobi itasu

H

to put on or wear on the feet or legs (shoes, socks, skirt, trousers)   TRANSITIVE

			AFFIRMATIVE	**NEGATIVE**
Indicative	**INFORMAL**		haku	hakanai
	FORMAL		hakimasu	hakimasen
Imperative	**INFORMAL**	I	hake	haku na
		II	hakinasai	hakinasaru na
		III	haite kudasai	hakanai de kudasai
	FORMAL		ohaki nasaimase	ohaki nashimasu na
Presumptive	**INFORMAL**	I	hakō	hakumai
		II	haku darō	hakanai darō
	FORMAL	I	hakimashō	hakimasumai
		II	haku deshō	hakanai deshō
Provisional	**INFORMAL**		hakeba	hakanakereba
	FORMAL		hakimaseba	hakimasen nara
			hakimasureba	
Gerund	**INFORMAL**	I	haite	hakanai de
		II		hakanakute
	FORMAL		hakimashite	hakimasen de
Past Ind.	**INFORMAL**		haita	hakanakatta
	FORMAL		hakimashita	hakimasen deshita
Past Presump.	**INFORMAL**		haitarō	hakanakattarō
			haita darō	hakanakatta darō
	FORMAL		hakimashitarō	hakimasen deshitarō
			haita deshō	hakanakatta deshō
Conditional	**INFORMAL**		haitara	hakanakattara
	FORMAL		hakimashitara	hakimasen deshitara
Alternative	**INFORMAL**		haitari	hakanakattari
	FORMAL		hakimashitari	hakimasen deshitari

		INFORMAL AFFIRMATIVE INDICATIVE
Passive		hakareru
Potential		hakeru
Causative		hakaseru
Causative Pass.		hakaserareru
Honorific	I	ohaki ni naru
	II	ohaki nasaru
Humble	I	ohaki suru
	II	ohaki itasu

			AFFIRMATIVE	NEGATIVE
Indicative	**INFORMAL**		hanareru	hanarenai
	FORMAL		hanaremasu	hanaremasen
Imperative	**INFORMAL**	I	hanarero	hanareru na
		II	hanarenasai	hanarenasaru na
		III	hanarete kudasai	hanarenai de kudasai
	FORMAL		ohanare nasaimase	ohanare nasaimasu na
Presumptive	**INFORMAL**	I	hanareyō	hanaremai
		II	hanareru darō	hanarenai darō
	FORMAL	I	hanaremashō	hanaremasumai
		II	hanareru deshō	hanarenai deshō
Provisional	**INFORMAL**		hanarereba	hanarenakereba
	FORMAL		hanaremaseba	hanaremasen nara
			hanaremasureba	
Gerund	**INFORMAL**	I	hanarete	hanarenai de
		II		hanarenakute
	FORMAL		hanaremashite	hanaremasen de
Past Ind.	**INFORMAL**		hanareta	hanarenakatta
	FORMAL		hanaremashita	hanaremasen deshita
Past Presump.	**INFORMAL**		hanaretarō	hanarenakattarō
			hanareta darō	hanarenakatta darō
	FORMAL		hanaremashitarō	hanaremasen deshitarō
			hanareta deshō	hanarenakatta deshō
Conditional	**INFORMAL**		hanaretara	hanarenakattara
	FORMAL		hanaremashitara	hanaremasen deshitara
Alternative	**INFORMAL**		hanaretari	hanarenakattari
	FORMAL		hanaremashitari	hanaremasen deshitari

		INFORMAL AFFIRMATIVE INDICATIVE
Passive		hanarerareru
Potential		hanarerareru
Causative		hanaresaseru
Causative Pass.		hanaresaserareru
Honorific	I	ohanare ni naru
	II	ohanare nasaru
Humble	I	ohanare suru
	II	ohanare itasu

H

117

to release, to set free   TRANSITIVE

			AFFIRMATIVE	**NEGATIVE**
Indicative	**INFORMAL**		hanasu	hanasanai
	FORMAL		hanashimasu	hanashimasen
Imperative	**INFORMAL**	I	hanase	hanasu na
		II	hanashinasai	hanashinasaru na
		III	hanashite kudasai	hanasanai de kudasai
	FORMAL		ohanashi nasaimase	ohanashi nasaimasu na
Presumptive	**INFORMAL**	I	hanasō	hanasumai
		II	hanasu darō	hanasanai darō
	FORMAL	I	hanashimashō	hanashimasumai
		II	hanasu deshō	hanasanai deshō
Provisional	**INFORMAL**		hanaseba	hanasanakereba
	FORMAL		hanashimaseba	hanashimasen nara
			hanashimasureba	
Gerund	**INFORMAL**	I	hanashite	hanasanai de
		II		hanasanakute
	FORMAL		hanashimashite	hanashimasen de
Past Ind.	**INFORMAL**		hanashita	hanasanakatta
	FORMAL		hanashimashita	hanashimasen deshita
Past Presump.	**INFORMAL**		hanashitarō	hanasanakattarō
			hanashita darō	hanasanakatta darō
	FORMAL		hanashimashitarō	hanashimasen deshitarō
			hanashita deshō	hanasanakatta deshō
Conditional	**INFORMAL**		hanashitara	hanasanakattara
	FORMAL		hanashimashitara	hanashimasen deshitara
Alternative	**INFORMAL**		hanashitari	hanasanakattari
	FORMAL		hanashimashitari	hanashimasen deshitari

		INFORMAL AFFIRMATIVE INDICATIVE
Passive		hanasareru
Potential		hanaseru
Causative		hanasaseru
Causative Pass.		hanasaserareru
Honorific	I	ohanashi ni naru
	II	ohanashi nasaru
Humble	I	ohanashi suru
	II	ohanashi itasu

hanasi

はなす／話す **hanas.u**

TRANSITIVE   *to talk, to speak, to tell*

			AFFIRMATIVE	NEGATIVE
Indicative	**INFORMAL**		hanasu	hanasanai
	FORMAL		hanashimasu	hanashimasen
Imperative	**INFORMAL**	I	hanase	hanasu na
		II	hanashinasai	hanashinasaru na
		III	hanashite kudasai	hanasanai de kudasai
	FORMAL		ohanashi nasaimase	ohanashi nasaimasu na
Presumptive	**INFORMAL**	I	hanasō	hanasumai
		II	hanasu darō	hanasanai darō
	FORMAL	I	hanashimashō	hanashimasumai
		II	hanasu deshō	hanasanai deshō
Provisional	**INFORMAL**		hanaseba	hanasanakereba
	FORMAL		hanashimaseba	hanashimasen nara
			hanashimasureba	
Gerund	**INFORMAL**	I	hanashite	hanasanai de
		II		hanasanakute
	FORMAL		hanashimashite	hanashimasen de
Past Ind.	**INFORMAL**		hanashita	hanasanakatta
	FORMAL		hanashimashita	hanashimasen deshita
Past Presump.	**INFORMAL**		hanashitarō	hanasanakattarō
			hanashita darō	hanasanakatta darō
	FORMAL		hanashimashitarō	hanashimasen deshitarō
			hanashita deshō	hanasanakatta deshō
Conditional	**INFORMAL**		hanashitara	hanasanakattara
	FORMAL		hanashimashitara	hanashimasen deshitara
Alternative	**INFORMAL**		hanashitari	hanasanakattari
	FORMAL		hanashimashitari	hanashimasen deshitari

			INFORMAL AFFIRMATIVE INDICATIVE
Passive			hanasareru
Potential			hanaseru
Causative			hanasaseru
Causative Pass.			hanasaserareru
Honorific		I	ohanashi ni naru
		II	ohanashi nasaru
Humble		I	ohanashi suru
		II	ohanashi itasu

AN ESSENTIAL 55 VERB

Hanasu 話す

to talk, to speak, to tell

Sentences Using *Hanasu*

Nihongo ga motto hanasetara
shiawase desu.
日本語がもっと話せたら幸せです。
*I'd be happy if I could speak Japanese
better.*

Kare wa kanojo ni ikura hanashitemo
wakatte moraemasen deshita.
彼は彼女にいくら話しても分かっても
らえませんでした。
*No matter how much he talked with
her, he wasn't able to be understood
by her.*

Ano oisha to hanashitai no desu ga,
shōkai shite moraemasu ka.
あのお医者と話したいのですが、紹介
してもらえますか。
*I'd like to talk to that doctor. Could
you introduce me to him?*

Toshi ue no hito to hanasu toki niwa,
hanashikata ni ki o tsukenasai.
年上の人と話す時には、話し方に気を
つけなさい。
*When you speak to an older person,
watch the way you speak. (Be polite.)*

Hontō no koto o hanashitara,
yurushite moraeru deshō.
本当のことを話したら、許してもらえ
るでしょう。
*If you tell the truth, you'll be
forgiven.*

Hanasu is a verb you will hear and use
often as you strive to speak correct
Japanese. If you want to talk with
the Japanese in their own language,
studying Japanese grammar and verb
conjugations will help you to attain
your goal.

Words and Expressions
Related to This Verb

hanashi aite　話し相手
someone to talk to

hanashi jōzu　話し上手
a good conversationalist

hanashi beta　話し下手
a poor conversationalist

uwasa banashi　うわさ話
gossip

hanashi no koshi o oru
話しの腰を折る
to interrupt a conversation

hanashi ni hana gasaku
話しに花が咲く
*to have a lovely conversation
(Flowers bloom in a conversation.)*

			AFFIRMATIVE	NEGATIVE
Indicative	**INFORMAL**		harau	harawanai
	FORMAL		haraimasu	haraimasen
Imperative	**INFORMAL**	I	harae	harau na
		II	harainasai	harainasaru na
		III	haratte kudasai	harawanai de kudasai
	FORMAL		oharai nasaimase	oharai nasaimasu na
Presumptive	**INFORMAL**	I	haraō	haraumai
		II	harau darō	harawanai darō
	FORMAL	I	haraimashō	haraimasumai
		II	harau deshō	harawanai deshō
Provisional	**INFORMAL**		haraeba	harawanakereba
	FORMAL		haraimaseba	haraimasen nara
			haraimasureba	
Gerund	**INFORMAL**	I	haratte	harawanai de
		II		harawanakute
	FORMAL		haraimashite	haraimasen de
Past Ind.	**INFORMAL**		haratta	harawanakatta
	FORMAL		haraimashita	haraimasen deshita
Past Presump.	**INFORMAL**		harattarō	harawanakattarō
			haratta darō	harawanakatta darō
	FORMAL		haraimashitarō	haraimasen deshitarō
			haratta deshō	harawanakatta deshō
Conditional	**INFORMAL**		harattara	harawanakattara
	FORMAL		haraimashitara	haraimasen deshitara
Alternative	**INFORMAL**		harattari	harawanakattari
	FORMAL		haraimashitari	haraimasen deshitari

			INFORMAL AFFIRMATIVE INDICATIVE
Passive			harawareru
Potential			haraeru
Causative			harawaseru
Causative Pass.			harawaserareru
Honorific		I	oharai ni naru
		II	oharai nasaru
Humble		I	oharai suru
		II	oharai itasu

H

AN ESSENTIAL 55 VERB

Harau 払う

to pay

Sentences Using *Harau*

Kurejitto kādo de haraemasu ka.
クレジットカードで払えますか。
Can I pay with a credit card?

Shachō wa takusan kaimono o
nasaremashita ga, zenbu genkin de
oharai ni nararemashita.
社長はたくさん買い物をなされま
したが、全部現金でお払いになられ
ました。
*The president of my company did a
lot of shopping, and he paid for it all
with cash.*

Kare niwa, tsukizuki ikura harattemo
haraikirenai hodo no shakkin ga aru.
彼には、月々いくら払っても払いきれ
ない程の借金がある。
*He has a debt he can't pay off no
matter how much he pays monthly.*

Kuruma o kattara, haha ga hanbun
haratte kuremashita.
車を買ったら、母が半分払ってくれま
した。
*When I bought a car, my mother paid
half of the price for me.*

Chūsha ihan no chiketto o
harawanakereba narimasen.
駐車違反のチケットを払わなければな
りません。
I have to pay for a parking violation.

Harau is a verb you need for daily life no
matter where you are. In Japan, which
some consider a shopper's paradise,
you'll be buying and paying often.
Although Japan used to be cash-oriented,
now you can usually pay for your
purchases, meals, and hotels with credit
cards. But it's still wise to carry some
cash with you.

Words and Expressions
Related to This Verb

shiharai　支払い
payment

mae barai　前払い
advance payment

miharai　未払い
outstanding payment

chūi o harau　注意を払う
to pay attention

gisei o harau　犠牲を払う
to pay dearly, to pay a heavy price

keii o harau　敬意を払う
to pay one's respects

hare　　　　　　　　　　　　　はれる／晴れる　**hare.ru**

to clear up (sky, suspicion, mood)

			AFFIRMATIVE	NEGATIVE
Indicative	**INFORMAL**		hareru	harenai
	FORMAL		haremasu	haremasen
Imperative	**INFORMAL**	**I**	harero	hareru na
		II		
		III		
	FORMAL			
Presumptive	**INFORMAL**	**I**	hareyō	haremai
		II	hareru darō	harenai darō
	FORMAL	**I**	haremashō	haremasumai
		II	hareru deshō	harenai deshō
Provisional	**INFORMAL**		harereba	harenakereba
	FORMAL		haremaseba	haremasen nara
			haremasureba	
Gerund	**INFORMAL**	**I**	harete	harenai de
		II		harenakute
	FORMAL		haremashite	haremasen de
Past Ind.	**INFORMAL**		hareta	harenakatta
	FORMAL		haremashita	haremasen deshita
Past Presump.	**INFORMAL**		haretarō	harenakattarō
			hareta darō	harenakatta darō
	FORMAL		haremashitarō	haremasen deshitarō
			hareta deshō	harenakatta deshō
Conditional	**INFORMAL**		haretara	harenakattara
	FORMAL		haremashitara	haremasen deshitara
Alternative	**INFORMAL**		haretari	harenakattari
	FORMAL		haremashitari	haremasen deshitari

		INFORMAL AFFIRMATIVE INDICATIVE
Passive		
Potential		
Causative		
Causative Pass.		
Honorific	**I**	
	II	
Humble	**I**	
	II	

H

123

har.u はる／貼る／張る   hari

to stick, to paste, to pitch, to stretch   TRANSITIVE

			AFFIRMATIVE	NEGATIVE
Indicative	**INFORMAL**		haru	haranai
	FORMAL		harimasu	harimasen
Imperative	**INFORMAL**	**I**	hare	haru na
		II	harinasai	harinasaru na
		III	hatte kudasai	haranai de kudasai
	FORMAL		ohari nasaimase	ohari nasaimasu na
Presumptive	**INFORMAL**	**I**	harō	harumai
		II	haru darō	haranai darō
	FORMAL	**I**	harimashō	harimasumai
		II	haru deshō	haranai deshō
Provisional	**INFORMAL**		hareba	haranakereba
	FORMAL		harimaseba	harimasen nara
			harimasureba	
Gerund	**INFORMAL**	**I**	hatte	harani de
		II		haranakute
	FORMAL		harimashite	harimasen de
Past Ind.	**INFORMAL**		hatta	haranakatta
	FORMAL		harimashita	harimasen deshita
Past Presump.	**INFORMAL**		hattarō	haranakattarō
			hatta darō	haranakatta darō
	FORMAL		harimashitarō	harimasen deshitarō
			hatta deshō	haranakatta deshō
Conditional	**INFORMAL**		hattara	haranakattara
	FORMAL		harimashitara	harimasen deshitara
Alternative	**INFORMAL**		hattari	haranakattari
	FORMAL		harimashitari	harimasen deshitari

		INFORMAL AFFIRMATIVE INDICATIVE
Passive		harareru
Potential		hareru
Causative		haraseru
Causative Pass.		haraserareru
Honorific	**I**	ohari ni naru
	II	ohari nasaru
Humble	**I**	ohari suru
	II	ohari itasu

124

はさむ／挟む **hasam.u**

TRANSITIVE · *to catch or hold between two things*

			AFFIRMATIVE	NEGATIVE
Indicative	**INFORMAL**		hasamu	hasamanai
	FORMAL		hasamimasu	hasamimasen
Imperative	**INFORMAL**	I	hasame	hasamu na
		II	hasaminasai	hasaminasaru na
		III	hasande kudasai	hasamanai de kudasai
	FORMAL		ohasami nasaimase	ohasami nasaimasu na
Presumptive	**INFORMAL**	I	hasamō	hasamumai
		II	hasamu darō	hasamanai darō
	FORMAL	I	hasamimashō	hasamimasumai
		II	hasamu deshō	hasamanai deshō
Provisional	**INFORMAL**		hasameba	hasamanakereba
	FORMAL		hasamimaseba	hasamimasen nara
			hasamimasureba	
Gerund	**INFORMAL**	I	hasande	hasamanai de
		II		hasamanakute
	FORMAL		hasamimashite	hasamimasen de
Past Ind.	**INFORMAL**		hasanda	hasamanakatta
	FORMAL		hasamimashita	hasamimasen deshita
Past Presump.	**INFORMAL**		hasandarō	hasamanakattarō
			hasanda darō	hasamanakatta darō
	FORMAL		hasamimashitarō	hasamimasen deshitarō
			hasanda deshō	hasamanakatta deshō
Conditional	**INFORMAL**		hasandara	hasamanakattara
	FORMAL		hasamimashitara	hasamimasen deshitara
Alternative	**INFORMAL**		hasandari	hasamanakattari
	FORMAL		hasamimashitari	hasamimasen deshitari

			INFORMAL AFFIRMATIVE INDICATIVE
Passive			hasamareru
Potential			hasameru
Causative			hasamaseru
Causative Pass.			hasamaserareru
Honorific		I	ohasami ni naru
		II	ohasami nasaru
Humble		I	ohasami suru
		II	ohasami itasu

H

			AFFIRMATIVE	**NEGATIVE**
Indicative	**INFORMAL**		hashiru	hashiranai
	FORMAL		hashirimasu	hashirimasen
Imperative	**INFORMAL**	I	hashire	hashiru na
		II	hashirinasai	hashirinasaru na
		III	hashitte kudasai	hashiranai de kudasai
	FORMAL		ohashiri nasaimase	ohashiri nasaimasu na
Presumptive	**INFORMAL**	I	hashirō	hashirumai
		II	hashiru darō	hashiranai darō
	FORMAL	I	hashirimashō	hashirimasumai
		II	hashiru deshō	hashiranai deshō
Provisional	**INFORMAL**		hashireba	hashiranakereba
	FORMAL		hashirimaseba	hashirimasen nara
			hashirimasureba	
Gerund	**INFORMAL**	I	hashitte	hashiranai de
		II		hashiranakute
	FORMAL		hashirimashite	hashirimasein de
Past Ind.	**INFORMAL**		hashitta	hashiranakatta
	FORMAL		hashirimashita	hashirimasen deshita
Past Presump.	**INFORMAL**		hashittarō	hashiranakattarō
			hashitta darō	hashiranakatta darō
	FORMAL		hashirimashitarō	hashirimasen deshitarō
			hashitta deshō	hashiranakatta deshō
Conditional	**INFORMAL**		hashittara	hashiranakattara
	FORMAL		hashirimashitara	hashirimasen deshitara
Alternative	**INFORMAL**		hashittari	hashiranakattari
	FORMAL		hashirimashitari	hashirimasen deshitari

			INFORMAL AFFIRMATIVE INDICATIVE
Passive			hashirareru
Potential			hashireru
Causative			hashiraseru
Causative Pass.			hashiraserareru
Honorific		I	ohashiri ni naru
		II	ohashiri nasaru
Humble		I	
		II	

			AFFIRMATIVE	NEGATIVE
Indicative	**INFORMAL**		hataraku	hatarakanai
	FORMAL		hatarakimasu	hatarakimasen
Imperative	**INFORMAL**	I	hatarake	hataraku na
		II	hatarakinasai	hatarakinasaru na
		III	hataraite kudasai	hatarakanai de kudasai
	FORMAL		ohataraki nasaimase	ohataraki nasaimasu na
Presumptive	**INFORMAL**	I	hatarakō	hatarakumai
		II	hataraku darō	hatarakanai darō
	FORMAL	I	hatarakimashō	hatarakimasumai
		II	hataraku deshō	hatarakanai deshō
Provisional	**INFORMAL**		hatarakeba	hatarakanakereba
	FORMAL		hatarakimaseba	hatarakimasen nara
			hatarakimasureba	
Gerund	**INFORMAL**	I	hataraite	hatarakanai de
		II		hatarakanakute
	FORMAL		hatarakimashite	hatarakimasen de
Past Ind.	**INFORMAL**		hataraita	hatarakanakatta
	FORMAL		hatarakimashita	hatarakimasen deshita
Past Presump.	**INFORMAL**		hataraitarō	hatarakanakattarō
			hataraita darō	hatarakanakatta darō
	FORMAL		hatarakimashitarō	hatarakimasen deshitarō
			hataraita deshō	hatarakanakatta deshō
Conditional	**INFORMAL**		hataraitara	hatarakanakattara
	FORMAL		hatarakimashitara	hatarakimasen deshitara
Alternative	**INFORMAL**		hataraitari	hatarakanakattari
	FORMAL		hatarakimashitari	hatarakimasen deshitari

		INFORMAL AFFIRMATIVE INDICATIVE
Passive		
Potential		hatarakeru
Causative		hatarakaseru
Causative Pass.		hatarakaserareru
Honorific	I	ohataraki ni naru
	II	ohataraki nasaru
Humble	I	ohataraki suru
	II	ohataraki itasu

AN ESSENTIAL
55 VERB

AN ESSENTIAL 55 VERB

Hataraku 働く

to work

Sentences Using *Hataraku*

Kare wa donna shigoto demo,
hataraku koto o kobamimasen.
彼はどんな仕事でも、働くことを拒み
ません。
*No matter what kind of job it is, he
never refuses to do it.*

Kare wa byōki de ikkagetsu
hatarakenai no ga kutsū deshita.
彼は病気で一ヶ月働けないのが苦痛で
した。
*He felt anguished at not being able to
work for a month because of his
illness.*

Hataraku no ga omoshirokute,
kyūryō o morau no ga warui mitai
desu.
働くのが面白くて、給料をもらうのが
悪いみたいです。
*My work is so enjoyable that I almost
feel guilty receiving a salary.*

Ano kaisha de hataraketara sugoku
shiawase desu.
あの会社で働けたら凄く幸せです。
*If I can work for that company, I'll be
very happy.*

Kanojo wa kono mise de san jū nen
tsuzukete hataraite imasu.
彼女はこの店で３０年続けて働いてい
ます。
*She has been working for this store
continuously for 30 years.*

Hataraku is a verb people often associate
with the Japanese. Things have been
changing, but working hard is still the
norm almost everywhere, in agricultural
and in urban areas alike. In the latter,
long commutes, long hours of work, and
overtime are still common. And after
work, people often go out with
colleagues for a friendly evening of
drinking and eating.

Words and Expressions Related to This Verb

shigoto suru　仕事する
to work

hataraki　働き
work

hataraki mono　働き者
a hard worker, a diligent worker

tada bataraki　ただ働き
unpaid work

Proverb

Hatarakazaru mono, kuu bekarazu.
働かざる者、食うべからず。
*Work hard for a living. (A person
who doesn't work shouldn't eat.)*

128

はやる／流行る　**hayar.u**
to become widespread, to become popular

			AFFIRMATIVE	NEGATIVE
Indicative	**INFORMAL**		hayaru	hayaranai
	FORMAL		hayarimasu	hayarimasen
Imperative	**INFORMAL**	I	hayare	hayaru na
		II		
		III		
	FORMAL			
Presumptive	**INFORMAL**	I	hayarō	hayarumai
		II	hayaru darō	hayaranai darō
	FORMAL	I	hayarimashō	hayarimasumai
		II	hayaru deshō	hayaranai deshō
Provisional	**INFORMAL**		hayareba	hayaranakereba
	FORMAL		hayarimaseba	hayarimasen nara
			hayarimasureba	
Gerund	**INFORMAL**	I	hayatte	hayaranai de
		II		hayaranakute
	FORMAL		hayarimashite	hayarimasen de
Past Ind.	**INFORMAL**		hayatta	hayaranakatta
	FORMAL		hayarimashita	hayarimasen deshita
Past Presump.	**INFORMAL**		hayattarō	hayaranakattarō
			hayatta darō	hayaranakatta darō
	FORMAL		hayarimashitarō	hayarimasen deshitarō
			hayatta deshō	hayaranakatta deshō
Conditional	**INFORMAL**		hayattara	hayaranakattara
	FORMAL		hayarimashitara	hayarimasen deshitara
Alternative	**INFORMAL**		hayattari	hayaranakattari
	FORMAL		hayarimashitari	hayarimasen deshitari

			INFORMAL AFFIRMATIVE INDICATIVE
Passive			
Potential			
Causative			hayaraseru
Causative Pass.			hayaraserareru
Honorific		I	ohayari ni naru
		II	
Humble		I	
		II	

H

to come off, to go wide of the mark

			AFFIRMATIVE	NEGATIVE
Indicative	INFORMAL		hazureru	hazurenai
	FORMAL		hazuremasu	hazuremasen
Imperative	INFORMAL	I	hazurero	hazureru na
		II	hazurenasai	hazurenasaru na
		III	hazurete kudasai	hazurenai de kudasai
	FORMAL			
Presumptive	INFORMAL	I	hazureyō	hazuremai
		II	hazureru darō	hazurenai darō
	FORMAL	I	hazuremashō	hazuremasumai
		II	hazureru deshō	hazurenai deshō
Provisional	INFORMAL		hazurereba	hazurenakereba
	FORMAL		hazuremaseba	hazuremasen nara
			hazuremasureba	
Gerund	INFORMAL	I	hazurete	hazurenai de
		II		hazurenakute
	FORMAL		hazuremashite	hazuremasen de
Past Ind.	INFORMAL		hazureta	hazurenakatta
	FORMAL		hazuremashita	hazuremasen deshita
Past Presump.	INFORMAL		hazuretarō	hazurenakattarō
			hazureta darō	hazurenakatta darō
	FORMAL		hazuremashitarō	hazuremasen deshitarō
			hazureta deshō	hazurenakatta deshō
Conditional	INFORMAL		hazuretara	hazurenakattara
	FORMAL		hazuremashitara	hazuremasen deshitara
Alternative	INFORMAL		hazuretari	hazurenakattari
	FORMAL		hazuremashitari	hazuremasen deshitari

		INFORMAL AFFIRMATIVE INDICATIVE
Passive		
Potential		
Causative		hazuresaseru
Causative Pass.		hazuresaserareru
Honorific	I	ohazure ni naru
	II	ohazure nasaru
Humble	I	
	II	

TRANSITIVE　　*to remove, to unfasten*

			AFFIRMATIVE	NEGATIVE
Indicative	**INFORMAL**		hazusu	hazusanai
	FORMAL		hazushimasu	hazushimasen
Imperative	**INFORMAL**	**I**	hazuse	hazusu na
		II	hazushinasai	hazushinasaru na
		III	hazushite kudasai	hazusanai de kudasai
	FORMAL		ohazushi nasaimase	ohazushi nasaimasu na
Presumptive	**INFORMAL**	**I**	hazusō	hazusumai
		II	hazusu darō	hazusanai darō
	FORMAL	**I**	hazushimashō	hazushimasumai
		II	hazusu deshō	hazusanai deshō
Provisional	**INFORMAL**		hazuseba	hazusanakereba
	FORMAL		hazushimaseba	hazushimasen nara
			hazushimasureba	
Gerund	**INFORMAL**	**I**	hazushite	hazusanai de
		II		hazusanakute
	FORMAL		hazushimashite	hazushimasen de
Past Ind.	**INFORMAL**		hazushita	hazusanakatta
	FORMAL		hazushimashita	hazushimasen deshita
Past Presump.	**INFORMAL**		hazushitarō	hazusanakattarō
			hazushita darō	hazusanakatta darō
	FORMAL		hazushimashitarō	hazushimasen deshitarō
			hazushita deshō	hazusanakatta deshō
Conditional	**INFORMAL**		hazushitara	hazusanakattara
	FORMAL		hazushimashitara	hazushimasen deshitara
Alternative	**INFORMAL**		hazushitari	hazusanakattari
	FORMAL		hazushimashitari	hazushimasen deshitari

			INFORMAL AFFIRMATIVE INDICATIVE
Passive			hazusareru
Potential			hazuseru
Causative			hazusaseru
Causative Pass.			hazusaserareru
Honorific		**I**	ohazushi ni naru
		II	ohazushi nasaru
Humble		**I**	ohazushi suru
		II	ohazushi itasu

H

131

heras.u へらす／減らす   **herashi**

to reduce, to cut down, to decrease   TRANSITIVE

			AFFIRMATIVE	NEGATIVE
Indicative	**INFORMAL**		herasu	herasanai
	FORMAL		herashimasu	herashimasen
Imperative	**INFORMAL**	I	herase	herasu na
		II	herashinasai	herashinasaru na
		III	herashite kudasai	herasanai de kudasai
	FORMAL		oherashi nasaimase	oherashi nasaimasu na
Presumptive	**INFORMAL**	I	herasō	herasumai
		II	herasu darō	herasanai darō
	FORMAL	I	herashimashō	herashimasumai
		II	herasu deshō	herasanai deshō
Provisional	**INFORMAL**		heraseba	herasanakereba
	FORMAL		herashimaseba	herashimasen nara
			herashimasureba	
Gerund	**INFORMAL**	I	herashite	herasanai de
		II		herasanakute
	FORMAL		herashimashite	herashimasen de
Past Ind.	**INFORMAL**		herashita	herasanakatta
	FORMAL		herashimashita	herashimasen deshita
Past Presump.	**INFORMAL**		herashitarō	herasanakattarō
			herashita darō	herasanakatta darō
	FORMAL		herashimashitarō	herashimasen deshitarō
			herashita deshō	herasanakatta deshō
Conditional	**INFORMAL**		herashitara	herasanakattara
	FORMAL		herashimashitara	herashimasen deshistara
Alternative	**INFORMAL**		herashitari	herasanakattari
	FORMAL		herashimashitari	herashimasen deshitari

			INFORMAL AFFIRMATIVE INDICATIVE
Passive			herasareru
Potential			heraseru
Causative			herasaseru
Causative Pass.			herasaserareru
Honorific		I	oherashi ni naru
		II	oherashi nasaru
Humble		I	oherashi suru
		II	oherashi itasu

へる／経る **he.ru**

TRANSITIVE *to pass through, to go by*

			AFFIRMATIVE	NEGATIVE
Indicative	INFORMAL		heru	henai
	FORMAL		hemasu	hemasen
Imperative	INFORMAL	I	hero	heru na
		II	henasai	henasaru na
		III	hete kudasai	henai de kudasai
	FORMAL		ohe nasaimase	ohe nasaimasu na
Presumptive	INFORMAL	I	heyō	hemai
		II	heru darō	henai darō
	FORMAL	I	hemashō	hemasumai
		II	heru deshō	henai deshō
Provisional	INFORMAL		hereba	henakereba
	FORMAL		hemaseba	hemasen nara
			hemasureba	
Gerund	INFORMAL	I	hete	henai de
		II		henakute
	FORMAL		hemashite	hemasen de
Past Ind.	INFORMAL		heta	henakatta
	FORMAL		hemashita	hemasen deshita
Past Presump.	INFORMAL		hetarō	henakattarō
			heta darō	henakatta darō
	FORMAL		hemashitarō	hemasen deshitarō
			heta deshō	henakatta deshō
Conditional	INFORMAL		hetara	henakattara
	FORMAL		hemashitara	hemasen deshitara
Alternative	INFORMAL		hetari	henakattari
	FORMAL		hemashitari	hemasen deshitari

		INFORMAL AFFIRMATIVE INDICATIVE
Passive		
Potential		herareru
Causative		hesaseru
Causative Pass.		hesaserareru
Honorific	I	ohe ni naru
	II	ohe nasaru
Humble	I	
	II	

133

			AFFIRMATIVE	NEGATIVE
Indicative	**INFORMAL**		heru	heranai
	FORMAL		herimasu	herimasen
Imperative	**INFORMAL**	I		
		II		
		III		
	FORMAL			
Presumptive	**INFORMAL**	I	herō	herumai
		II	heru darō	heranai darō
	FORMAL	I	herimashō	herimasumai
		II	heru deshō	heranai deshō
Provisional	**INFORMAL**		hereba	heranakereba
	FORMAL		herimaseba	herimasen nara
			herimasureba	
Gerund	**INFORMAL**	I	hette	heranai de
		II		heranakute
	FORMAL		herimashite	herimasen de
Past Ind.	**INFORMAL**		hetta	heranakatta
	FORMAL		herimashita	herimasen deshita
Past Presump.	**INFORMAL**		hettarō	heranakattarō
			hetta darō	heranakatta darō
	FORMAL		herimashitarō	herimasen deshitarō
			hetta deshō	heranakatta deshō
Conditional	**INFORMAL**		hettara	heranakattara
	FORMAL		herimashitara	herimasen deshitara
Alternative	**INFORMAL**		hettari	heranakattari
	FORMAL		herimashitari	herimasen deshitari

			INFORMAL AFFIRMATIVE INDICATIVE
Passive			herareru
Potential			hereru
Causative			heraseru
Causative Pass.			heraserareru
Honorific		I	oheri ni naru
		II	oheri nasaru
Humble		I	
		II	

hikae

ひかえる／控える **hikae.ru**

to refrain from, to face, to write down

			AFFIRMATIVE	NEGATIVE
Indicative	**INFORMAL**		hikaeru	hikaenai
	FORMAL		hikaemasu	hikaemasen
Imperative	**INFORMAL**	I	hikaero	hikaeru na
		II	hikaenasai	hikaenasaru na
		III	hikaete kudasai	hikaenai de kudasai
	FORMAL		ohikae nasaimase	ohikae nasaimasu na
Presumptive	**INFORMAL**	I	hikeyō	hikaemai
		II	hikaeru darō	hikaenai darō
	FORMAL	I	hikaemashō	hikaemasumai
		II	hikaeru deshō	hikaerai deshō
Provisional	**INFORMAL**		hikaereba	hikaenakereba
	FORMAL		hikaemaseba	hikaemasen nara
			hikaemasureba	
Gerund	**INFORMAL**	I	hikaete	hikaenai de
		II		hikaenakute
	FORMAL		hikaemashite	hikaemasen de
Past Ind.	**INFORMAL**		hikaeta	hikaenakatta
	FORMAL		hikaemashita	hikaemasen deshita
Past Presump.	**INFORMAL**		hikaetarō	hikaenakattarō
			hikaeta darō	hikaenakatta darō
	FORMAL		hikaemashitarō	hikaemasen deshitarō
			hikaeta deshō	hikaenakatta deshō
Conditional	**INFORMAL**		hikaetara	hikaenakattara
	FORMAL		hikaemashitara	hikaemasen deshitara
Alternative	**INFORMAL**		hikaetari	hikaenakattari
	FORMAL		hikaemashitari	hikaemasen deshitari

		INFORMAL AFFIRMATIVE INDICATIVE
Passive		hikaerareru
Potential		hikaerareru
Causative		hikaesaseru
Causative Pass.		hikaesaserareru
Honorific	I	ohikae ni naru
	II	ohikae nasaru
Humble	I	ohikae suru
	II	ohikae itasu

135

hikar.u ひかる／光る   hikari

to shine, to glitter

			AFFIRMATIVE	NEGATIVE
Indicative	**INFORMAL**		hikaru	hikaranai
	FORMAL		hikarimasu	hikarimasen
Imperative	**INFORMAL**	I	hikare	hikaru na
		II	hikarinasai	hikarinasaru na
		III	hikatte kudasai	hikaranai de kudasai
	FORMAL		ohikari nasaimase	ohikari nasaimasu na
Presumptive	**INFORMAL**	I	hikarō	hikarumai
		II	hikaru darō	hikaranai darō
	FORMAL	I	hikarimashō	hikarimasumai
		II	hikaru deshō	hikaranai deshō
Provisional	**INFORMAL**		hikareba	hikaranakereba
	FORMAL		hikarimaseba	hikarimasen nara
			hikarimasureba	
Gerund	**INFORMAL**	I	hikatte	hikaranai de
		II		hikaranakute
	FORMAL		hikarimashite	hikarimasen de
Past Ind.	**INFORMAL**		hikatta	hikaranakatta
	FORMAL		hikarimashita	hikarimasen deshita
Past Presump.	**INFORMAL**		hikattarō	hikaranakattarō
			hikatta darō	hikaranakatta darō
	FORMAL		hikarimashitarō	hikarimasen deshitarō
			hikatta deshō	hikaranakatta deshō
Conditional	**INFORMAL**		hikattara	hikaranakattara
	FORMAL		hikarimashitara	hikarimasen deshitara
Alternative	**INFORMAL**		hikattari	hikaranakattari
	FORMAL		hikarimashitari	hikarimasen deshitari

			INFORMAL AFFIRMATIVE INDICATIVE
Passive			hikarareru
Potential			hikareru
Causative			hikaraseru
Causative Pass.			hikaraserareru
Honorific		I	ohikari ni naru
		II	ohikari nasaru
Humble		I	
		II	

136

ひきうける／引き受ける　hikiuke.ru

TRANSITIVE　　*to undertake, to take charge of*

			AFFIRMATIVE	NEGATIVE
Indicative	**INFORMAL**		hikiukeru	hikiukenai
	FORMAL		hikiukemasu	hikiukemasen
Imperative	**INFORMAL**	I	hikiukero	hikiukeru na
		II	hikiukenasai	hikiukenasaru na
		III	hikiukete kudasai	hikiukenai de kudasai
	FORMAL		ohikiuke nasaimase	ohikiuke nasaimasu na
Presumptive	**INFORMAL**	I	hikiukeyō	hikiukemai
		II	hikiukeru darō	hikiukenai darō
	FORMAL	I	hikiukemashō	hikiukemasumai
		II	hikiukeru deshō	hikiukenai deshō
Provisional	**INFORMAL**		hikiukereba	hikiukenakereba
	FORMAL		hikiukemaseba	hikiukemasen nara
			hikiukemasureba	
Gerund	**INFORMAL**	I	hikiukete	hikiukenai de
		II		hikiukenakute
	FORMAL		hikiukemashite	hikiukemasen de
Past Ind.	**INFORMAL**		hikiuketa	hikiukenakatta
	FORMAL		hikiukemashita	hikiukemasen deshita
Past Presump.	**INFORMAL**		hikiuketarō	hikiukenakattarō
			hikiuketa darō	hikiukenakatta darō
	FORMAL		hikiukemashitarō	hikiukemasen deshitarō
			hikiuketa deshō	hikiukenakatta deshō
Conditional	**INFORMAL**		hikiuketara	hikiukenakattara
	FORMAL		hikiukemashitara	hikiukemasen deshitara
Alternative	**INFORMAL**		hikiuketari	hikiukenakattari
	FORMAL		hikiukemashitari	hikiukemasen deshitari

H

			INFORMAL AFFIRMATIVE INDICATIVE
Passive			hikiukerareru
Potential			hikiukerareru
Causative			hikiukesaseru
Causative Pass.			hikiukesaserareru
Honorific		I	ohikiuke ni naru
		II	ohikiuke nasaru
Humble		I	ohikiuke suru
		II	ohikiuke itasu

137

to pull   TRANSITIVE

			AFFIRMATIVE	NEGATIVE
Indicative	**INFORMAL**		hiku	hikanai
	FORMAL		hikimasu	hikimasen
Imperative	**INFORMAL**	I	hike	hiku na
		II	hikinasai	hikinasaru na
		III	hiite kudasai	hikanai de kudasai
	FORMAL		ohiki nasaimase	ohiki nasaimasu na
Presumptive	**INFORMAL**	I	hikō	hikumai
		II	hiku darō	hikanai darō
	FORMAL	I	hikimashō	hikimasumai
		II	hiku deshō	hikanai deshō
Provisional	**INFORMAL**		hikeba	hikanakereba
	FORMAL		hikimaseba	hikimasen nara
			hikimasureba	
Gerund	**INFORMAL**	I	hiite	hikanai de
		II		hikanakute
	FORMAL		hikimashite	hikimasen de
Past Ind.	**INFORMAL**		hiita	hikanakatta
	FORMAL		hikimashita	hikimasen deshita
Past Presump.	**INFORMAL**		hiitarō	hikanakattarō
			hiita darō	hikanakatta darō
	FORMAL		hikimashitarō	hikimasen deshitarō
			hiita deshō	hikanakatta deshō
Conditional	**INFORMAL**		hittara	hikanakattara
	FORMAL		hikimashitara	hikimasen deshitara
Alternative	**INFORMAL**		hiitari	hikanakattari
	FORMAL		hikimashitari	hikimasen deshitari

		INFORMAL AFFIRMATIVE INDICATIVE
Passive		hikareru
Potential		hikeru
Causative		hikaseru
Causative Pass.		hikaserareru
Honorific	I	ohiki ni naru
	II	ohiki nasaru
Humble	I	ohiki suru
	II	ohiki itasu

TRANSITIVE　　*to bend , to twist*

			AFFIRMATIVE	NEGATIVE
Indicative	**INFORMAL**		hineru	hineranai
	FORMAL		hinerimasu	hinerimasen
Imperative	**INFORMAL**	I	hinere	hineru na
		II	hinerinasai	hinerinasaru na
		III	hinette kudasai	hineranai de kudasai
	FORMAL		ohineri nasaimase	ohineri nasaimasu na
Presumptive	**INFORMAL**	I	hinerō	hinerumai
		II	hineru darō	hineranai darō
	FORMAL	I	hinerimashō	hinerimasumai
		II	hineru deshō	hineranai deshō
Provisional	**INFORMAL**		hinereba	hineranakereba
	FORMAL		hinerimaseba	hinerimasen nara
			hinerimasureba	
Gerund	**INFORMAL**	I	hinette	hineranai de
		II		hineranakute
	FORMAL		hinerimashite	hinerimasen de
Past Ind.	**INFORMAL**		hinetta	hineranakatta
	FORMAL		hinerimashita	hinerimasen deshita
Past Presump.	**INFORMAL**		hinettarō	hineranakattarō
			hinetta darō	hineranakatta darō
	FORMAL		hinerimashitarō	hinerimasen deshitarō
			hinetta deshō	hineranakatta deshō
Conditional	**INFORMAL**		hinettara	hineranakattara
	FORMAL		hinerimashitara	hinerimasen deshitara
Alternative	**INFORMAL**		hinettari	hineranakattari
	FORMAL		hinerimashitari	hinerimasen deshitari

			INFORMAL AFFIRMATIVE INDICATIVE
Passive			hinerareru
Potential			hinereru
Causative			hineraseru
Causative Pass.			hineraserareru
Honorific		I	ohineri ni naru
		II	ohineri nasaru
Humble		I	ohineri suru
		II	ohineri itasu

hirak.u ひらく／開く   hiraki

to open, to hold (a party, etc.)   TRANSITIVE

			AFFIRMATIVE	NEGATIVE
Indicative	**INFORMAL**		hiraku	hirakanai
	FORMAL		hirakimasu	hirakimasen
Imperative	**INFORMAL**	I	hirake	hiraku na
		II	hirakinasai	hirakinasaru na
		III	hiraite kudasai	hirakanai de kudasai
	FORMAL		ohiraki nasaimase	ohiraki nasaimasu na
Presumptive	**INFORMAL**	I	hirakō	hirakumai
		II	hiraku darō	hirakanai darō
	FORMAL	I	hirakimashō	hirakimasumai
		II	hiraku deshō	hirakanai deshō
Provisional	**INFORMAL**		hirakeba	hirakanakereba
	FORMAL		hirakimaseba	hirakimasen nara
			hirakimasureba	
Gerund	**INFORMAL**	I	hiraite	hirakanai de
		II		hirakanakute
	FORMAL		hirakimashite	hirakimasen de
Past Ind.	**INFORMAL**		hiraita	hirakanakatta
	FORMAL		hirakimashita	hirakimasen deshita
Past Presump.	**INFORMAL**		hiraitarō	hirakanakattarō
			hiraita darō	hirakanakatta darō
	FORMAL		hirakimashitarō	hirakimasen deshitarō
			hiraita deshō	hirakanakatta deshō
Conditional	**INFORMAL**		hiraitara	hirakanakattara
	FORMAL		hirakimashitara	hirakimasen deshitara
Alternative	**INFORMAL**		hiraitari	hirakanakattari
	FORMAL		hirakimashitari	hirakimasen deshitari

		INFORMAL AFFIRMATIVE INDICATIVE
Passive		hirakareru
Potential		hirakeru
Causative		hirakaseru
Causative Pass.		hirakaserareru
Honorific	I	ohiraki ni naru
	II	ohiraki nasaru
Humble	I	ohiraki suru
	II	ohiraki itasu

140

ひろまる／広まる　**hiromar.u**

to spread, to become popular

			AFFIRMATIVE	NEGATIVE
Indicative	**INFORMAL**		hiromaru	hiromaranai
	FORMAL		hiromarimasu	hiromarimasen
Imperative	**INFORMAL**	I	hiromare	hiromaru na
		II	hiromarinasai	hiromarinasaru na
		III	hiromatte kudasai	hiromaranai de kudasai
	FORMAL		ohiromari nasaimase	ohiromari nasaimasu na
Presumptive	**INFORMAL**	I	hiromarō	hiromarumai
		II	hiromaru darō	hiromaranai darō
	FORMAL	I	hiromarimashō	hiromarimasumai
		II	hiromaru deshō	hiromaranai deshō
Provisional	**INFORMAL**		hiromareba	hiromaranakereba
	FORMAL		hiromarimaseba	hiromarimasen nara
			hiromarimasureba	
Gerund	**INFORMAL**	I	hiromatte	hiromaranai de
		II		hiromaranakute
	FORMAL		hiromarimashite	hiromarimasen de
Past Ind.	**INFORMAL**		hiromatta	hiromaranakatta
	FORMAL		hiromarimashita	hiromarimasen desha
Past Presump.	**INFORMAL**		hiromattarō	hiromaranakattarō
			hiromatta darō	hiromaranakatta darō
	FORMAL		hiromarimashitarō	hiromarimasen deshitarō
			hiromatta deshō	hiromaranakatta deshō
Conditional	**INFORMAL**		hiromattara	hiromaranakattara
	FORMAL		hiromarimashitara	hiromarimasen deshitara
Alternative	**INFORMAL**		hiromattari	hiromaranakattari
	FORMAL		hiromarimashitari	hiromarimasen deshitari

		INFORMAL AFFIRMATIVE INDICATIVE
Passive		hiromarareru
Potential		hiromareru
Causative		hiromaraseru
Causative Pass.		hiromaraserareru
Honorific	I	
	II	
Humble	I	
	II	

H

141

hirome.ru ひろめる／広める   hirome

to spread, to make popular   TRANSITIVE

			AFFIRMATIVE	NEGATIVE
Indicative	**INFORMAL**		hiromeru	hiromenai
	FORMAL		hiromemasu	hiromemasen
Imperative	**INFORMAL**	I	hiromero	hiromeru na
		II	hiromenasai	hiromenasaru na
		III	hiromete kudasai	hiromenai de kudasai
	FORMAL		ohirome nasaimase	ohirome nasaimasu na
Presumptive	**INFORMAL**	I	hiromeyō	hiromemai
		II	hiromeru darō	hiromenai darō
	FORMAL	I	hiromemashō	hiromemasumai
		II	hiromeru deshō	hiromenai deshō
Provisional	**INFORMAL**		hiromereba	hiromenakereba
	FORMAL		hiromemaseba	hiromemasen nara
			hiromemasureba	
Gerund	**INFORMAL**	I	hiromete	hiromenai de
		II		hiromenakute
	FORMAL		hiromemashite	hiromemasen de
Past Ind.	**INFORMAL**		hirometa	hiromenakatta
	FORMAL		hiromemashita	hiromemasen deshita
Past Presump.	**INFORMAL**		hirometarō	hiromenakattarō
			hirometa darō	hiromenakatta darō
	FORMAL		hiromemashitarō	hiromemasen deshitarō
			hirometa deshō	hiromenakatta deshō
Conditional	**INFORMAL**		hirometara	hiromenakattara
	FORMAL		hiromemashitara	hiromemasen deshitara
Alternative	**INFORMAL**		hirometari	hiromenakattari
	FORMAL		hiromemashitari	hiromemasen deshitari

		INFORMAL AFFIRMATIVE INDICATIVE
Passive		hiromerareru
Potential		hiromerareru
Causative		hiromesaseru
Causative Pass.		hiromesaserareru
Honorific	I	ohirome ni naru
	II	ohirome nasaru
Humble	I	ohirome suru
	II	ohirome itasu

hiroi

TRANSITIVE　*to pick up* (from ground, etc.), *to find* (by accident)

			AFFIRMATIVE	NEGATIVE
Indicative	**INFORMAL**		hirou	hirowanai
	FORMAL		hiroimasu	hiroimasen
Imperative	**INFORMAL**	I	hiroe	hirou na
		II	hiroinasai	hiroinasaru na
		III	hirotte kudasai	hirowanai de kudasai
	FORMAL		ohiroi nasaimase	ohiroi nasaimasu na
Presumptive	**INFORMAL**	I	hiroō	hiroumai
		II	hirou darō	hirowanai darō
	FORMAL	I	hiroimashō	hiroimasumai
		II	hirou deshō	hirowanai deshō
Provisional	**INFORMAL**		hiroeba	hirowanakereba
	FORMAL		hiroimaseba	hiroimasen nara
			hiroimasureba	
Gerund	**INFORMAL**	I	hirotte	hirowanai de
		II		hirowanakute
	FORMAL		hiroimashite	hiroimasen de
Past Ind.	**INFORMAL**		hirotta	hirowanakatta
	FORMAL		hiroimashita	hiroimasen deshita
Past Presump.	**INFORMAL**		hirottarō	hirowanakattarō
			hirotta darō	hirowanakatta darō
	FORMAL		hiroimashitarō	hiroimasen deshitarō
			hirotta deshō	hirowanakatta deshō
Conditional	**INFORMAL**		hirottara	hirowanakattara
	FORMAL		hiroimashitara	hiroimasen deshitara
Alternative	**INFORMAL**		hirottari	hirowanakattari
	FORMAL		hiroimashitari	hiroimasen deshitari

		INFORMAL AFFIRMATIVE INDICATIVE
Passive		hirowareru
Potential		hiroeru
Causative		hirowaseru
Causative Pass.		hirowaserareru

Honorific	I	ohiroi ni naru
	II	ohiroi nasaru
Humble	I	ohiroi suru
	II	ohiroi itasu

H

143

to make fun of, to tease　　　TRANSITIVE

			AFFIRMATIVE	NEGATIVE
Indicative	**INFORMAL**		hiyakasu	hiyakasanai
	FORMAL		hiyakashimasu	hiyakashimasen
Imperative	**INFORMAL**	I	hiyakase	hiyakasu na
		II	hiyakashinasai	hiyakashinasaru na
		III	hiyakashite kudasai	hiyakasanai de kudasai
	FORMAL		ohiyakashi nasaimase	ohiyakashi nasaimasu na
Presumptive	**INFORMAL**	I	hiyakasō	hiyakasumai
		II	hiyakasu darō	hiyakasanai darō
	FORMAL	I	hiyakashimashō	hiyakashimasumai
		II	hiyakasu deshō	hiyakasanai deshō
Provisional	**INFORMAL**		hiyakaseba	hiyakasanakereba
	FORMAL		hiyakashimaseba	hiyakashimasen nara
			hiyakashimasureba	
Gerund	**INFORMAL**	I	hiyakashite	hiyakasanai de
		II		hiyakasanakute
	FORMAL		hiyakashimashite	hiyakashimasen de
Past Ind.	**INFORMAL**		hiyakashita	hiyakasanakatta
	FORMAL		hiyakashimashita	hiyakashimasen deshita
Past Presump.	**INFORMAL**		hiyakashitarō	hiyakasanakattarō
			hiyakashita darō	hiyakasanakatta darō
	FORMAL		hiyakashimashitarō	hiyakashimasen deshitarō
			hiyakashita deshō	hiyakasanakatta deshō
Conditional	**INFORMAL**		hiyakashitara	hiyakasanakattara
	FORMAL		hiyakashimashitara	hiyakashimasen deshitara
Alternative	**INFORMAL**		hiyakashitari	hiyakasanakattari
	FORMAL		hiyakashimashitari	hiyakashimasen deshitari

			INFORMAL AFFIRMATIVE INDICATIVE
Passive			hiyakasareru
Potential			hiyakaseru
Causative			hiyakasaseru
Causative Pass.			hiyakasaserareru
Honorific		I	ohiyakashi ni naru
		II	ohiyakashi nasaru
Humble		I	ohiyakashi suru
		II	ohiyakashi itasu

			AFFIRMATIVE	NEGATIVE
Indicative	**INFORMAL**		hiyasu	hiyasanai
	FORMAL		hiyashimasu	hiyashimasen
Imperative	**INFORMAL**	I	hiyase	hiyasu na
		II	hiyashinasai	hiyashinasaru na
		III	hiyashite kudasai	hiyasanai de kudasai
	FORMAL		ohiyashi nasaimase	ohiyashi nasaimasu na
Presumptive	**INFORMAL**	I	hiyasō	hiyasumai
		II	hiyasu darō	hiyasanai darō
	FORMAL	I	hiyashimashō	hiyashimasumai
		II	hiyasu deshō	hiyasanai deshō
Provisional	**INFORMAL**		hiyaseba	hiyasanakereba
	FORMAL		hiyashimaseba	hiyashimasen nara
			hiyashimasureba	
Gerund	**INFORMAL**	I	hiyashite	hiyasanai de
		II		hiyasanakute
	FORMAL		hiyashimashite	hiyashimasen de
Past Ind.	**INFORMAL**		hiyashita	hiyasanakatta
	FORMAL		hiyashimashita	hiyashimasen deshita
Past Presump.	**INFORMAL**		hiyashitarō	hiyasanakattarō
			hiyashita darō	hiyasanakatta darō
	FORMAL		hiyashimashitarō	hiyashimasen deshitarō
			hiyashita deshō	hiyasanakatta deshō
Conditional	**INFORMAL**		hiyashitara	hiyasanakattara
	FORMAL		hiyashimashitara	hiyashimasen deshitara
Alternative	**INFORMAL**		hiyashitari	hiyasanakattari
	FORMAL		hiyashimashitari	hiyashimasen deshitari

		INFORMAL AFFIRMATIVE INDICATIVE
Passive		hiyasareru
Potential		hiyaseru
Causative		hiyasaseru
Causative Pass.		hiyasaserareru
Honorific	I	ohiyashi ni naru
	II	ohiyashi nasaru
Humble	I	ohiyashi suru
	II	ohiyashi itasu

H

to come loose, to come untied

			AFFIRMATIVE	NEGATIVE
Indicative	**INFORMAL**		hodokeru	hodokenai
	FORMAL		hodokemasu	hodokemasen
Imperative	**INFORMAL**	I	hodokero	hodokeru na
		II		
		III		
	FORMAL			
Presumptive	**INFORMAL**	I	hodokeyō	hodokemai
		II	hodokeru darō	hodokenai darō
	FORMAL	I	hodokemashō	hodokemasumai
		II	hodokeru deshō	hodokenai deshō
Provisional	**INFORMAL**		hodokereba	hodokenakereba
	FORMAL		hodokemaseba	hodokemasen nara
			hodokemasureba	
Gerund	**INFORMAL**	I	hodokete	hodokenai de
		II		hodokenakute
	FORMAL		hodokemashite	hodokemasen de
Past Ind.	**INFORMAL**		hodoketa	hodokenakatta
	FORMAL		hodokemashita	hodokemasen deshita
Past Presump.	**INFORMAL**		hodoketarō	hodokenattarō
			hodoketa darō	hodokenakatta darō
	FORMAL		hodokemashitarō	hodokemasen deshitarō
			hodoketa deshō	hodokenakatta deshō
Conditional	**INFORMAL**		hodoketara	hodokenakattara
	FORMAL		hodokemashitara	hodokemasen deshitara
Alternative	**INFORMAL**		hodoketari	hodokenakattari
	FORMAL		hodokemashitari	hodokemasen deshitari

		INFORMAL AFFIRMATIVE INDICATIVE
Passive		hodokerareru
Potential		hodokerareru
Causative		hodokesaseru
Causative Pass.		hodokesaserareru
Honorific	I	
	II	
Humble	I	
	II	

ほどく／解く　**hodok.u**

TRANSITIVE　*to untie*

			AFFIRMATIVE	**NEGATIVE**
Indicative	**INFORMAL**		hodoku	hodokanai
	FORMAL		hodokimasu	hodokimasen
Imperative	**INFORMAL**	I	hodoke	hodoku na
		II	hodokinasai	hodokinasaru na
		III	hodoite kudasai	hodokanai de kudasai
	FORMAL		ohodoki nasaimase	ohodoki nasaimasu na
Presumptive	**INFORMAL**	I	hodokō	hodokumai
		II	hodoku darō	hodokanai darō
	FORMAL	I	hodokimashō	hodokimasumai
		II	hodoku deshō	hodokanai deshō
Provisional	**INFORMAL**		hodokeba	hodokanakereba
	FORMAL		hodokimaseba	hodokimasen nara
			hodokimasureba	
Gerund	**INFORMAL**	I	hodoite	hodokanai de
		II		hodokanakute
	FORMAL		hodokimashite	hodokimasen de
Past Ind.	**INFORMAL**		hodoita	hodokanakatta
	FORMAL		hodokimashita	hodokimasen deshita
Past Presump.	**INFORMAL**		hodoitarō	hodokanakattarō
			hodoita darō	hodokanakatta darō
	FORMAL		hodokimashitarō	hodokimasen deshitarō
			hodoita deshō	hodokanakatta deshō
Conditional	**INFORMAL**		hodoitara	hodokanakattara
	FORMAL		hodokimashitara	hodokimasen deshitara
Alternative	**INFORMAL**		hodoitari	hodokanakattari
	FORMAL		hodokimashitari	hodokimasen deshitari

		INFORMAL AFFIRMATIVE INDICATIVE
Passive		hodokareru
Potential		hodokeru
Causative		hodokaseru
Causative Pass.		hodokaserareru
Honorific	I	ohodoki ni naru
	II	ohodoki nasaru
Humble	I	ohodoki suru
	II	ohodoki itasu

H

home.ru ほめる／褒める   **home**

to praise   TRANSITIVE

			AFFIRMATIVE	NEGATIVE
Indicative	**INFORMAL**		homeru	homenai
	FORMAL		homemasu	homemasen
Imperative	**INFORMAL**	I	homero	homeru na
		II	homenasai	homenasaru na
		III	homete kudasai	homenai de kudasai
	FORMAL		ohome nasaimase	ohome nasaimasu na
Presumptive	**INFORMAL**	I	homeyō	homemai
		II	homeru darō	homenai darō
	FORMAL	I	homemashō	homemasumai
		II	homeru deshō	homenai deshō
Provisional	**INFORMAL**		homereba	homenakereba
	FORMAL		homemaseba	homemasen nara
			homemasureba	
Gerund	**INFORMAL**	I	homete	homenai de
		II		homenakute
	FORMAL		homemashite	homemasen de
Past Ind.	**INFORMAL**		hometa	homenakatta
	FORMAL		homemashita	homemasen deshita
Past Presump.	**INFORMAL**		hometarō	homenakattarō
			hometa darō	homenakatta darō
	FORMAL		homemashitarō	homemasen deshitarō
			hometa deshō	homenakatta deshō
Conditional	**INFORMAL**		hometara	homenakattara
	FORMAL		homemashitara	homemasen deshitara
Alternative	**INFORMAL**		hometari	homenakattari
	FORMAL		homemashitari	homemasen deshitari

		INFORMAL AFFIRMATIVE INDICATIVE
Passive		homerareru
Potential		homerareru
Causative		homesaseru
Causative Pass.		homesaserareru
Honorific	I	ohome ni naru
	II	ohome nasaru
Humble	I	ohome suru
	II	ohome itasu

148

honomekashi　　ほのめかす／仄めかす　honomekas.u

TRANSITIVE　　*to hint*

			AFFIRMATIVE	NEGATIVE
Indicative	INFORMAL		honomekasu	honomekasanai
	FORMAL		honomekashimasu	honomekashimasen
Imperative	INFORMAL	I	honomekase	honomekasu na
		II	honomekashinasai	honomekashinasaru na
		III	honomekashite kudasai	honomekasanai de kudasai
	FORMAL		ohonomekashi nasaimase	ohonomekashi nasaimasu na
Presumptive	INFORMAL	I	honomekasō	honomekasumai
		II	honomekasu darō	honomekasanai darō
	FORMAL	I	honomekashimashō	honomekashimasumai
		II	honomekasu deshō	honomekasanai deshō
Provisional	INFORMAL		honomekaseba	honomekasanakereba
	FORMAL		honomekashimaseba	honomekashimasen nara
			honomekashimasureba	
Gerund	INFORMAL	I	honomekashite	honomekasanai de
		II		honomekasanakute
	FORMAL		honomekashimashite	honomekashimasen de
Past Ind.	INFORMAL		honomekashita	honomekasanakatta
	FORMAL		honomekashimashita	honomekashimasen deshita
Past Presump.	INFORMAL		honomekashitarō	honomekasanakattarō
			honomekashita darō	honomekasanakatta darō
	FORMAL		honomekashimashitarō	honomekashimasen deshitarō
			honomekashita deshō	honomekasanakatta deshō
Conditional	INFORMAL		honomekashitara	honomekasanakattara
	FORMAL		honomekashimashitara	honomekashimasen deshitara
Alternative	INFORMAL		honomekashitari	honomekasanakattari
	FORMAL		honomekashimashitari	honomekashimasen deshitari

		INFORMAL AFFIRMATIVE INDICATIVE
Passive		honomekasareru
Potential		honomekaseru
Causative		honomekasaseru
Causative Pass.		honomekasaserareru
Honorific	I	ohonomekashi ni naru
	II	ohonomekashi nasaru
Humble	I	ohonomekashi suru
	II	ohonomekashi itasu

H

149

to fall in love

			AFFIRMATIVE	NEGATIVE
Indicative	**INFORMAL**		horeru	horenai
	FORMAL		horemasu	horemasen
Imperative	**INFORMAL**	I	horero	horeru na
		II	horenasai	horenasaru na
		III	horete kudasai	horenai de kudasai
	FORMAL		ohore nasaimase	ohore nasaimasu na
Presumptive	**INFORMAL**	I	horeyō	horemai
		II	horeru darō	horenai darō
	FORMAL	I	horemashō	horemasumai
		II	horeru deshō	horenai deshō
Provisional	**INFORMAL**		horereba	horenakereba
	FORMAL		horemaseba	horemasen nara
			horemasureba	
Gerund	**INFORMAL**	I	horete	horenai de
		II		horenakute
	FORMAL		horemashite	horemasen de
Past Ind.	**INFORMAL**		horeta	horenakatta
	FORMAL		horemashita	horemasen deshita
Past Presump.	**INFORMAL**		horetarō	horenakattarō
			horeta darō	horenakatta darō
	FORMAL		horemashitarō	horemasen deshitarō
			horeta deshō	horenakatta deshō
Conditional	**INFORMAL**		horetara	horenakattara
	FORMAL		horemashitara	horemasen deshitara
Alternative	**INFORMAL**		horetari	horenakattari
	FORMAL		horemashitari	horemasen deshitari

			INFORMAL AFFIRMATIVE INDICATIVE
Passive			horerareru
Potential			horerareru
Causative			horesaseru
Causative Pass.			horesaserareru
Honorific		I	ohore ni naru
		II	ohore nasaru
Humble		I	ohore suru
		II	ohore itasu

150

ほろびる／滅びる　horobi.ru

to fall into ruin, to perish

			AFFIRMATIVE	NEGATIVE
Indicative	**INFORMAL**		horobiru	horobinai
	FORMAL		horobimasu	horobimasen
Imperative	**INFORMAL**	I	horobiro	horobiru na
		II	horobinasai	horobinasaru na
		III	horobite kudasai	horobinai de kudasai
	FORMAL			ohorobi nasaimasu na
Presumptive	**INFORMAL**	I	horobiyō	horobimai
		II	horobiru darō	horobinai darō
	FORMAL	I	horobimashō	horobimasumai
		II	horobiru deshō	horobinai deshō
Provisional	**INFORMAL**		horobireba	horobinakereba
	FORMAL		horobimaseba	horobimasen nara
			horobimasureba	
Gerund	**INFORMAL**	I	horobite	horobinai de
		II		horobinakute
	FORMAL		horobimashite	horobimasen de
Past Ind.	**INFORMAL**		horobita	horobinakatta
	FORMAL		horobimashita	horobimasen deshita
Past Presump.	**INFORMAL**		horobitarō	horobinakattarō
			horobita darō	horobinakatta darō
	FORMAL		horobimashitarō	horobimasen deshitarō
			horobita deshō	horobinakatta deshō
Conditional	**INFORMAL**		horobitara	horobinakattara
	FORMAL		horobimashitara	horobimasen deshitara
Alternative	**INFORMAL**		horobitari	horobinakattari
	FORMAL		horobimashitari	horobimasen deshitari

		INFORMAL AFFIRMATIVE INDICATIVE
Passive		horobirareru
Potential		horobirareru
Causative		horobisaseru
Causative Pass.		horobisaserareru
Honorific	I	ohorobi ni naru
	II	ohorobi nasaru
Humble	I	
	II	

to ruin, to destroy　　TRANSITIVE

			AFFIRMATIVE	NEGATIVE
Indicative	**INFORMAL**		horobosu	horobosanai
	FORMAL		horoboshimasu	horoboshimasen
Imperative	**INFORMAL**	I	horobose	horobosu na
		II	horoboshinasai	horoboshinasaru na
		III	horoboshite kudasai	horobosanai de kudasai
	FORMAL		ohoroboshi nasaimase	ohoroboshi nasaimasu na
Presumptive	**INFORMAL**	I	horobosō	horobosumai
		II	horobosu darō	horobosanai darō
	FORMAL	I	horoboshimashō	horoboshimasumai
		II	horobosu deshō	horobosanai deshō
Provisional	**INFORMAL**		horoboseba	horobosanakereba
	FORMAL		horoboshimaseba	horoboshimasen nara
			horoboshimasureba	
Gerund	**INFORMAL**	I	horoboshite	horobosanai de
		II		horobosanakute
	FORMAL		horoboshimashite	horoboshimasen de
Past Ind.	**INFORMAL**		horoboshita	horobosanakatta
	FORMAL		horoboshimashita	horoboshimasen deshita
Past Presump.	**INFORMAL**		horoboshitarō	horobosanakattarō
			horoboshita darō	horobosanakatta darō
	FORMAL		horoboshimashitarō	horoboshimasen deshitarō
			horoboshita deshō	horobosanakatta deshō
Conditional	**INFORMAL**		horoboshitara	horobosanakattara
	FORMAL		horoboshimashitara	horoboshimasen deshitara
Alternative	**INFORMAL**		horoboshitari	horobosanakattari
	FORMAL		horoboshimashitari	horoboshimasen deshitari

			INFORMAL AFFIRMATIVE INDICATIVE
Passive			horobosareru
Potential			horoboseru
Causative			horobosaseru
Causative Pass.			horobosaserareru
Honorific		I	ohoroboshi ni naru
		II	ohoroboshi nasaru
Humble		I	ohoroboshi suru
		II	ohoroboshi itasu

ほる／掘る　**hor.u**
TRANSITIVE　*to dig*

			AFFIRMATIVE	NEGATIVE
Indicative	**INFORMAL**		horu	horanai
	FORMAL		horimasu	horimasen
Imperative	**INFORMAL**	I	hore	horu na
		II	horinasai	horinasaru na
		III	hotte kudasai	horanai de kudasai
	FORMAL		ohori nasaimase	ohori nasaimasu na
Presumptive	**INFORMAL**	I	horō	horumai
		II	horu darō	horanai darō
	FORMAL	I	horimashō	horimasumai
		II	horu deshō	horanai deshō
Provisional	**INFORMAL**		horeba	horanakereba
	FORMAL		horimaseba	horimasen nara
			horimasureba	
Gerund	**INFORMAL**	I	hotte	horanai de
		II		horanakute
	FORMAL		horimashite	horimasen de
Past Ind.	**INFORMAL**		hotta	horanakatta
	FORMAL		horimashita	horimasen deshita
Past Presump.	**INFORMAL**		hottarō	horanakattarō
			hotta darō	horanakatta darō
	FORMAL		horimashitarō	horimasen deshitarō
			hotta deshō	horanakatta deshō
Conditional	**INFORMAL**		hottara	horanakattara
	FORMAL		horimashitara	horimasen deshitara
Alternative	**INFORMAL**		hottari	horanakattari
	FORMAL		horimashitari	horimasen deshitari

		INFORMAL AFFIRMATIVE INDICATIVE
Passive		horareru
Potential		horeru
Causative		horaseru
Causative Pass.		horaserareru
Honorific	I	ohori ni naru
	II	ohori nasaru
Humble	I	ohori suru
	II	ohori itasu

H

hoshigar.u　ほしがる／欲しがる　　　　　hoshigari
to want, to desire　　TRANSITIVE

			AFFIRMATIVE	NEGATIVE
Indicative	**INFORMAL**		hoshigaru	hoshigaranai
	FORMAL		hoshigarimasu	hoshigarimasen
Imperative	**INFORMAL**	I	hoshigare	hoshigaru na
		II	hoshigarinasai	hoshigarinasaru na
		III	hoshigatte kudasai	hoshigaranai de kudasai
	FORMAL		ohoshigari nasaimase	ohoshigari nasaimasu na
Presumptive	**INFORMAL**	I	hoshigarō	hoshigarumai
		II	hoshigaru darō	hoshigaranai darō
	FORMAL	I	hoshigarimashō	hoshigarimasumai
		II	hoshigaru deshō	hoshigaranai deshō
Provisional	**INFORMAL**		hoshigareba	hoshigaranakereba
	FORMAL		hoshigarimaseba	hoshigarimasen nara
			hoshigarimasureba	
Gerund	**INFORMAL**	I	hoshigatte	hoshigaranai de
		II		hoshigaranakute
	FORMAL		hoshigarimashite	hoshigarimasen de
Past Ind.	**INFORMAL**		hoshigatta	hoshigaranakatta
	FORMAL		hoshigarimashita	hoshigarimasen deshita
Past Presump.	**INFORMAL**		hoshigattarō	hoshigaranakattarō
			hoshigatta darō	hoshigaranakatta darō
	FORMAL		hoshigarimashitarō	hoshigarimasen deshitarō
			hoshigatta deshō	hoshigaranakatta deshō
Conditional	**INFORMAL**		hoshigattara	hoshigaranakattara
	FORMAL		hoshigarimashitara	hoshigarimasen deshitara
Alternative	**INFORMAL**		hoshigattari	hoshigaranakattari
	FORMAL		hoshigarimashitari	hoshigarimasen deshitari

		INFORMAL AFFIRMATIVE INDICATIVE
Passive		hoshigarareru
Potential		hoshigareru
Causative		hoshigaraseru
Causative Pass.		hoshigaraserareru
Honorific	I	ohoshigari ni naru
	II	ohoshigari nasaru
Humble	I	
	II	

ほす／干す **hos.u**

TRANSITIVE   *to dry, to air*

			AFFIRMATIVE	NEGATIVE
Indicative	**INFORMAL**		hosu	hosanai
	FORMAL		hoshimasu	hoshimasen
Imperative	**INFORMAL**	I	hose	hosu na
		II	hoshinasai	hoshinasaru na
		III	hoshite kudasai	hosanai de kudasai
	FORMAL		ohoshi nasaimase	ohoshi nasaimasu na
Presumptive	**INFORMAL**	I	hosō	hosumai
		II	hosu darō	hosanai darō
	FORMAL	I	hoshimashō	hoshimasumai
		II	hosu deshō	hosanai deshō
Provisional	**INFORMAL**		hoseba	hosanakereba
	FORMAL		hoshimaseba	hoshimasen nara
			hoshimasureba	
Gerund	**INFORMAL**	I	hoshite	hosanai de
		II		hosanakute
	FORMAL		hoshimashite	hoshimasen de
Past Ind.	**INFORMAL**		hoshita	hosanakatta
	FORMAL		hoshimashita	hoshimasen deshita
Past Presump.	**INFORMAL**		hoshitarō	hosanakattarō
			hoshita darō	hosanakatta darō
	FORMAL		hoshimashitarō	hoshimasen deshitarō
			hoshita deshō	hosanakatta deshō
Conditional	**INFORMAL**		hoshitara	hosanakattara
	FORMAL		hoshimashitara	hoshimasen deshitara
Alternative	**INFORMAL**		hoshitari	hosanakattari
	FORMAL		hoshimashitari	hoshimasen deshitari

		INFORMAL AFFIRMATIVE INDICATIVE
Passive		hosareru
Potential		hoseru
Causative		hosaseru
Causative Pass.		hosaserareru
Honorific	I	ohoshi ni naru
	II	ohoshi nasaru
Humble	I	ohoshi suru
	II	ohoshi itasu

H

ibar.u いばる／威張る   ibari

to boast, to put on airs   TRANSITIVE

			AFFIRMATIVE	NEGATIVE
Indicative	**INFORMAL**		ibaru	ibaranai
	FORMAL		ibarimasu	ibarimasen
Imperative	**INFORMAL**	I	ibare	ibaru na
		II	ibarinasai	ibarinasaru na
		III	ibatte kudasai	ibaranai de kudasai
	FORMAL		oibari nasaimase	oibari nasaimasu na
Presumptive	**INFORMAL**	I	ibarō	ibarumai
		II	ibaru darō	ibaranai darō
	FORMAL	I	ibarimashō	ibarimasumai
		II	ibaru deshō	ibaranai deshō
Provisional	**INFORMAL**		ibareba	ibaranakereba
	FORMAL		ibarimaseba	ibarimasen nara
			ibarimasureba	
Gerund	**INFORMAL**	I	ibatte	ibaranai de
		II		ibaranakute
	FORMAL		ibarimashite	ibarimasen de
Past Ind.	**INFORMAL**		ibatta	ibaranakatta
	FORMAL		ibarimashita	ibarimasen deshita
Past Presump.	**INFORMAL**		ibattarō	ibaranakattarō
			ibatta darō	ibaranakatta darō
	FORMAL		ibarimashitarō	ibarimasen deshitarō
			ibatta deshō	ibaranakatta deshō
Conditional	**INFORMAL**		ibattara	ibaranakattara
	FORMAL		ibarimashitara	ibarimasen deshitara
Alternative	**INFORMAL**		ibattari	ibaranakattari
	FORMAL		ibarimashitari	ibarimasen deshitari

		INFORMAL AFFIRMATIVE INDICATIVE
Passive		ibarareru
Potential		ibareru
Causative		ibaraseru
Causative Pass.		ibaraserareru
Honorific	I	oibari ni naru
	II	oibari nasaru
Humble	I	
	II	

いいあらわす／言い表す　**iiarawas.u**

			AFFIRMATIVE	NEGATIVE
Indicative	**INFORMAL**		iiarawasu	iiarawasanai
	FORMAL		iiarawashimasu	iiarawashimasen
Imperative	**INFORMAL**	I	iiarawase	iiarawasu na
		II	iiarawashinasai	iiarawashinasaru na
		III	iiarawashite kudasai	iiarawasanai de kudasai
	FORMAL		oiiarawashi nasaimase	oiiarawashi nasaimasu na
Presumptive	**INFORMAL**	I	iiarawasō	iiarawasumai
		II	iiarawasu darō	iiarawasanai darō
	FORMAL	I	iiarawashimashō	iiarawashimasumai
		II	iiarawasu deshō	iiarawasanai deshō
Provisional	**INFORMAL**		iiarawaseba	iiarawasanakereba
	FORMAL		iiarawashimaseba	iiarawashimasen nara
			iiarawashimasureba	
Gerund	**INFORMAL**	I	iiarawashite	iiarawasanai de
		II		iiarawasanakute
	FORMAL		iiarawashimashite	iiarawashimasen de
Past Ind.	**INFORMAL**		iiarawashita	iiarawasanakatta
	FORMAL		iiarawashimashita	iiarawashimasen deshita
Past Presump.	**INFORMAL**		iiarawashitarō	iiarawasanakattarō
			iiarawashita darō	iiarawasanakatta darō
	FORMAL		iiarawashimashitarō	iiarawashimasen deshitarō
			iiarawashita deshō	iiarawasanakatta deshō
Conditional	**INFORMAL**		iiarawashitara	iiarawasanakattara
	FORMAL		iiarawashimashitara	iiarawashimasen deshitara
Alternative	**INFORMAL**		iiarawashitari	iiarawasanakattari
	FORMAL		iiarawashimashitari	iiarawashimasen deshitari

			INFORMAL AFFIRMATIVE INDICATIVE
Passive			iiarawasareru
Potential			iiarawaseru
Causative			iiarawasaseru
Causative Pass.			iiarawasaserareru
Honorific		I	oiiarawashi ni naru
		II	oiiarawashi nasaru
Humble		I	
		II	

157

iidas.u　いいだす／言い出す　　　　　　　　　　　　iidashi

to start talking, to suggest　　　TRANSITIVE

			AFFIRMATIVE	NEGATIVE
Indicative	INFORMAL		iidasu	iidasanai
	FORMAL		iidashimasu	iidashimasen
Imperative	INFORMAL	I	iidase	iidasu na
		II	iidashinasai	iidashinasaru na
		III	iidashite kudasai	iidasanai de kudasai
	FORMAL		oiidashi nasaimase	oiidashi nasaimasu na
Presumptive	INFORMAL	I	iidasō	iidasumai
		II	iidasu darō	iidasanai darō
	FORMAL	I	iidashimashō	iidashimasumai
		II	iidasu deshō	iidasanai deshō
Provisional	INFORMAL		iidaseba	iidasanakereba
	FORMAL		iidashimaseba	iidashimasen nara
			iidashimasureba	
Gerund	INFORMAL	I	iidashite	iidasanai de
		II		iidasanakute
	FORMAL		iidashimashite	iidashimasen de
Past Ind.	INFORMAL		iidashita	iidasanakatta
	FORMAL		iidashimashita	iidashimasen deshita
Past Presump.	INFORMAL		iidashitarō	iidasanakattarō
			iidashita darō	iidasanakatta darō
	FORMAL		iidashimashitarō	iidashimasen deshitarō
			iidashita deshō	iidasanakatta deshō
Conditional	INFORMAL		iidashitara	iidasanakattara
	FORMAL		iidashimashitara	iidashimasen deshitara
Alternative	INFORMAL		iidashitari	iidasanakattari
	FORMAL		iidashimashitari	iidashimasen deshitari

		INFORMAL AFFIRMATIVE INDICATIVE
Passive		iidasareru
Potential		iidaseru
Causative		iidasaseru
Causative Pass.		iidasaserareru
Honorific	I	oiidashi ni naru
	II	oiidashi nasaru
Humble	I	
	II	

158

いいふらす／言い触らす　**iifuras.u**

TRANSITIVE　*to spread* (a story), *to circulate (a rumor)*

			AFFIRMATIVE	NEGATIVE
Indicative	**INFORMAL**		iifurasu	iifurasanai
	FORMAL		iifurashimasu	iifurashimasen
Imperative	**INFORMAL**	I	iifurase	iifurasu na
		II	iifurashinasai	iifurashinasaru na
		III	iifurashite kudasai	iifurasanai de kudasai
	FORMAL		oiifurashi nasaimase	oiifurashi nasaimasu na
Presumptive	**INFORMAL**	I	iifurasō	iifurasumai
		II	iifurasu darō	iifurasanai darō
	FORMAL	I	iifurashimashō	iifurashimasumai
		II	iifurasu deshō	iifurasanai deshō
Provisional	**INFORMAL**		iifuraseba	iifurasanakereba
	FORMAL		iifurashimaseba	iifurashimasen nara
Gerund			iifurashite	iifurasanai de
	INFORMAL	I		iifurasanakute
		II	iifurashimashite	iifurashimasen de
	FORMAL			
Past Ind.			iifurashita	iifurasanakatta
	INFORMAL		iifurashimashita	iifurashimasen deshita
	FORMAL			
Past Presump.			iifurashitarō	iifurasanakattarō
	INFORMAL		iifurashita darō	iifurasanakatta darō
			iifurashimashitarō	iifurashimasen deshitarō
	FORMAL		iifurashita deshō	iifurasanakatta deshō
Conditional			iifurashitara	iifurasanakattara
	INFORMAL		iifurashimashitara	iifurashimasen deshitara
	FORMAL			
Alternative			iifurashitari	iifurasanakattari
	INFORMAL		iifurashimashitari	iifurashimasen deshitari
	FORMAL			

			INFORMAL AFFIRMATIVE INDICATIVE
Passive			iifurasareru
Potential			iifuraseru
Causative			iifurasaseru
Causative Pass.			iifurasaserareru
Honorific		I	oiifurashi ni naru
		II	oiifurashi nasaru
Humble		I	
		II	

iikaes.u　いいかえす／言い返す　　　　　iikaeshi
to talk back, to retort

			AFFIRMATIVE	NEGATIVE
Indicative	**INFORMAL**		iikaesu	iikaesanai
	FORMAL		iikaeshimasu	iikaeshimasen
Imperative	**INFORMAL**	I	iikaese	iikaesu na
		II	iikaeshinasai	iikaeshinasaru na
		III	iikaeshite kudasai	iikaesanai de kudasai
	FORMAL		oiikaeshi nasaimase	oiikaeshi nasaimasu na
Presumptive	**INFORMAL**	I	iikaesō	iikaesumai
		II	iikaesu darō	iikaesanai darō
	FORMAL	I	iikaeshimashō	iikaeshimasumai
		II	iikaesu deshō	iikaesanai deshō
Provisional	**INFORMAL**		iikaeseba	iikaesanakereba
	FORMAL		iikaeshimaseba	iikaeshimasen nara
			iikaeshimasureba	
Gerund	**INFORMAL**	I	iikaeshite	iikaesanai de
		II		iikaesanakute
	FORMAL		iikaeshimashite	iikaeshimasen de
Past Ind.	**INFORMAL**		iikaeshita	iikaesanakatta
	FORMAL		iikaeshimashita	iikaeshimasen deshita
Past Presump.	**INFORMAL**		iikaeshitarō	iikaesanakattarō
			iikaeshita darō	iikaesakatta darō
	FORMAL		iikaeshimashitarō	iikaeshimasen deshitarō
			iikaeshita deshō	iikaesanakatta deshō
Conditional	**INFORMAL**		iikaeshitara	iikaesanakattara
	FORMAL		iikaeshimashitara	iikaeshimasen deshitara
Alternative	**INFORMAL**		iikaeshitari	iikaesanakattari
	FORMAL		iikaeshimashitari	iikaeshimasen deshitari

			INFORMAL AFFIRMATIVE INDICATIVE
Passive			iikaesareru
Potential			iikaeseru
Causative			iikaesaseru
Causative Pass.			iikaesaserareru
Honorific		I	oiikaeshi ni naru
		II	oiikaeshi nasaru
Humble		I	oiikaeshi suru
		II	oiikaeshi itasu

いいなおす／言い直す iinaos.u

TRANSITIVE   *to rephrase, to correct oneself*

			AFFIRMATIVE	NEGATIVE
Indicative	**INFORMAL**		iinaosu	iinaosanai
	FORMAL		iinaoshimasu	iinaoshimasen
Imperative	**INFORMAL**	I	iinaose	iinaosu na
		II	iinaoshinasai	iinaoshinasaru na
		III	iinaoshite kudasai	iinosanai de kudasai
	FORMAL		oiinaoshi nasaimase	oiinaoshi nasaimasu na
Presumptive	**INFORMAL**	I	iinaosō	iinaosumai
		II	iinaosu darō	iinaosanai darō
	FORMAL	I	iinaoshimashō	iinaoshimasumai
		II	iinaosu deshō	iinaosanai deshō
Provisional	**INFORMAL**		iinaoseba	iinaosanakereba
	FORMAL		iinaoshimaseba	iinaoshimasen nara
			iinaoshimasureba	
Gerund	**INFORMAL**	I	iinaoshite	iinaosanai de
		II		iinaosanakute
	FORMAL		iinaoshimashite	iinaoshimasen de
Past Ind.	**INFORMAL**		iinaoshita	iinaosanakatta
	FORMAL		iinaoshimashita	iinaoshimasen deshita
Past Presump.	**INFORMAL**		iinaoshitarō	iinaosanakattarō
			iinaoshita darō	iinaosanakatta darō
	FORMAL		iinaoshimashitarō	iinaoshimasen deshitarō
			iinaoshita deshō	iinaosanakatta deshō
Conditional	**INFORMAL**		iinaoshitara	iinaosanakattara
	FORMAL		iinaoshimashitara	iinashimasen deshitara
Alternative	**INFORMAL**		iinaoshitari	iinaosanakattari
	FORMAL		iinaoshimashitari	iinaoshimasen deshitari

		INFORMAL AFFIRMATIVE INDICATIVE
Passive		iinaosareru
Potential		iinaoseru
Causative		iinaosaseru
Causative Pass.		iinaosaserareru
Honorific	I	oiinaoshi ni naru
	II	oiinaoshi nasaru
Humble	I	
	II	oiinaoshi itasu

to tell (a person to do something), *to command*   TRANSITIVE

			AFFIRMATIVE	NEGATIVE
Indicative	INFORMAL		iitsukeru	iitsukenai
	FORMAL		iitsukemasu	iitsukemasen
Imperative	INFORMAL	I	iitsukero	iitsukeru na
		II	iitsukenasai	iitsukenasaru na
		III	iitsukete kudasai	iitsukenai de kudasai
	FORMAL		oiitsuke nasaimase	oiitsuke nasaimasu na
Presumptive	INFORMAL	I	iitsukeyō	iitsukemai
		II	iitsukeru darō	iitsukenai darō
	FORMAL	I	iitsukemashō	iitsukemasumai
		II	iitsukeru deshō	iitsukenai deshō
Provisional	INFORMAL		iitsukereba	iitsukenakereba
	FORMAL		iitsukemaseba	iitsukemasen nara
			iitsukemasureba	
Gerund	INFORMAL	I	iitsukete	iitsukenai de
		II		iitsukenakute
	FORMAL		iitsukemashite	iitsukemasen de
Past Ind.	INFORMAL		iitsuketa	iitsukenakatta
	FORMAL		iitsukemashita	iitsukemasen deshita
Past Presump.	INFORMAL		iitsuketarō	iitsukenakattarō
			iitsuketa darō	iitsukenakatta darō
	FORMAL		iitsukemashitarō	iitsukemasen deshitarō
			iitsuketa deshō	iitsukenakatta deshō
Conditional	INFORMAL		iitsuketara	iitsukenakattara
	FORMAL		iitsukemashitara	iitsukemasen deshitara
Alternative	INFORMAL		iitsuketari	iitsukenakattari
	FORMAL		iitsukemashitari	iitsukemasen deshitari

		INFORMAL AFFIRMATIVE INDICATIVE
Passive		iitsukerareru
Potential		iitsukerareru
Causative		iitsukesaseru
Causative Pass.		iitsukesaserareru

Honorific	I	oiitsuke ni naru
	II	oiitsuke nasaru
Humble	I	
	II	

ijime

いじめる／苛める **ijime.ru**

TRANSITIVE   *to bully, to torment*

			AFFIRMATIVE	NEGATIVE
Indicative	**INFORMAL**		ijimeru	ijimenai
	FORMAL		ijimemasu	ijimemasen
Imperative	**INFORMAL**	I	ijimero	ijimeru na
		II	ijimenasai	ijimenasaru na
		III	ijimete kudasai	ijimenai de kudasai
	FORMAL		oijime nasaimase	oijime nasaimasu na
Presumptive	**INFORMAL**	I	ijimeyō	ijimemai
		II	ijimeru darō	ijimenai darō
	FORMAL	I	ijimemashō	ijimemasumai
		II	ijimeru deshō	ijimenai deshō
Provisional	**INFORMAL**		ijimereba	ijimenakereba
	FORMAL		ijimemaseba	ijimemasen nara
			ijimemasureba	
Gerund	**INFORMAL**	I	ijimete	ijimenai de
		II		ijimenakute
	FORMAL		ijimemashite	ijimemasen de
Past Ind.	**INFORMAL**		ijimeta	ijimenakatta
	FORMAL		ijimemashita	ijimemasen deshita
Past Presump.	**INFORMAL**		ijimetarō	ijimenakattarō
			ijimeta darō	ijimenakatta darō
	FORMAL		ijimemashitarō	ijimemasen deshitarō
			ijimeta deshō	ijimenakatta deshō
Conditional	**INFORMAL**		ijimetara	ijimenakattara
	FORMAL		ijimemashitara	ijimemasen deshitara
Alternative	**INFORMAL**		ijimetari	ijimenakattari
	FORMAL		ijimemashitari	ijimemasen deshitari

			INFORMAL AFFIRMATIVE INDICATIVE
Passive			ijimerareru
Potential			ijimerareru
Causative			ijimesaseru
Causative Pass.			ijimesaserareru
Honorific		I	oijime ni naru
		II	oijime nasaru
Humble		I	oijime suru
		II	oijime itasu

163

to touch, to fool with　　TRANSITIVE

			AFFIRMATIVE	NEGATIVE
Indicative	**INFORMAL**		ijiru	ijiranai
	FORMAL		ijirimasu	ijirimasen
Imperative	**INFORMAL**	**I**	ijire	ijiru na
		II	ijirinasai	ijirinasaru na
		III	ijitte kudasai	ijiranai de kudasai
	FORMAL		oijiri nasaimase	oijiri nasaimasu na
Presumptive	**INFORMAL**	**I**	ijirō	ijirumai
		II	ijiru darō	ijiranai darō
	FORMAL	**I**	ijirimashō	ijirimasumai
		II	ijiru deshō	ijiranai deshō
Provisional	**INFORMAL**		ijireba	ijiranakereba
	FORMAL		ijirimaseba	ijirimasen nara
			ijirimasureba	
Gerund	**INFORMAL**	**I**	ijitte	ijiranai de
		II		ijiranakute
	FORMAL		ijirimashite	ijirimasen de
Past Ind.	**INFORMAL**		ijitta	ijiranakatta
	FORMAL		ijirimashita	ijirimasen deshita
Past Presump.	**INFORMAL**		ijittarō	ijiranakattarō
			ijitta darō	ijiranakatta darō
	FORMAL		ijirimashitarō	ijirimasen deshitarō
			ijitta deshō	ijiranakatta deshō
Conditional	**INFORMAL**		ijittara	ijiranakattara
	FORMAL		ijirimashitara	ijirimasen deshitara
Alternative	**INFORMAL**		ijittari	ijiranakattari
	FORMAL		ijirimashitari	ijirimasen deshitari

			INFORMAL AFFIRMATIVE INDICATIVE
Passive			ijirareru
Potential			ijireru
Causative			ijiraseru
Causative Pass.			ijiraserareru
Honorific		**I**	oijiri ni naru
		II	oijiri nasaru
Humble		**I**	oijiri suru
		II	oijiri itasu

いきる／生きる **iki.ru**

to be alive

			AFFIRMATIVE	**NEGATIVE**
Indicative	**INFORMAL**		ikiru	ikinai
	FORMAL		ikimasu	ikimasen
Imperative	**INFORMAL**	I	ikiro	ikiru na
		II	ikinasai	ikinasaru na
		III	ikite kudasai	ikinai de kudasai
	FORMAL		oiki nasaimase	oiki nasaimasu na
Presumptive	**INFORMAL**	I	ikiyō	ikimai
		II	ikiru darō	ikinai darō
	FORMAL	I	ikimashō	ikimasumai
		II	ikiru deshō	ikinai deshō
Provisional	**INFORMAL**		ikireba	ikinakereba
	FORMAL		ikimaseba	ikimasen nara
			ikimasureba	
Gerund	**INFORMAL**	I	ikite	ikinai de
		II		ikinakute
	FORMAL		ikimashite	ikimasen de
Past Ind.	**INFORMAL**		ikita	ikinakatta
	FORMAL		ikimashita	ikimasen deshita
Past Presump.	**INFORMAL**		ikitarō	ikinakattarō
			ikita darō	ikinakatta darō
	FORMAL		ikimashitarō	ikimasen deshitarō
			ikita deshō	ikinakatta deshō
Conditional	**INFORMAL**		ikitara	ikinakattara
	FORMAL		ikimashitara	ikimasen deshitara
Alternative	**INFORMAL**		ikitari	ikinakattari
	FORMAL		ikimashitari	ikimasen deshitari

		INFORMAL AFFIRMATIVE INDICATIVE
Passive		ikirareru
Potential		ikirareru
Causative		ikisaseru
Causative Pass.		ikisaserareru
Honorific	I	oiki ni naru
	II	oiki nasaru
Humble	I	
	II	

165

to go

			AFFIRMATIVE	NEGATIVE
Indicative	**INFORMAL**		iku	ikanai
	FORMAL		ikimasu	ikimasen
Imperative	**INFORMAL**	I	ike	iku na
		II	ikinasai	ikinasaru na
		III	itte kudasai	ikanai de kudasai
	FORMAL		oide nasaimase	oide nasaimasu na
Presumptive	**INFORMAL**	I	ikō	ikumai
		II	iku darō	ikanai darō
	FORMAL	I	ikimashō	ikimasumai
		II	iku deshō	ikanai deshō
Provisional	**INFORMAL**		ikeba	ikanakereba
	FORMAL		ikimaseba	ikimasen nara
			ikimasureba	
Gerund	**INFORMAL**	I	itte	ikanai de
		II		ikanakute
	FORMAL		ikimashite	ikimasen de
Past Ind.	**INFORMAL**		itta	ikanakatta
	FORMAL		ikimashita	ikimasen deshita
Past Presump.	**INFORMAL**		ittarō	ikanakattarō
			itta darō	ikanakatta darō
	FORMAL		ikimashitarō	ikimasen deshitarō
			itta deshō	ikanakatta deshō
Conditional	**INFORMAL**		ittara	ikanakattara
	FORMAL		ikimashitara	ikimasen deshitara
Alternative	**INFORMAL**		ittari	ikanakattari
	FORMAL		ikimashitari	ikimasen deshitari

		INFORMAL AFFIRMATIVE INDICATIVE	
Passive		ikareru	
Potential		ikareru	ikeru
Causative		ikaseru	
Causative Pass.		ikaserareru	
Honorific	I	irassharu	{ oide ni naru (I)
	II		oide nasaru (II)
Humble	I		
	II	mairu	

**AN ESSENTIAL
55 VERB**

Iku　行く

to go

Sentences Using *Iku*

Nihon dewa iku beki tokoro ga
takusan arumasu.
日本では行くべきところがたくさんあ
ります。
I have many places I should go to.

Bijutsukan ni ittara, mō shimatte
imashita.
美術館に行ったら、もう閉まっていま
した。
*When we went to the art museum, it
was already closed.*

Ashita no kaigi niwa, watakushi no
kawari ni itte moraemasu ka.
明日の会議には、私の代わりに行って
もらえますか？
*Would you go to the meeting
tomorrow instead of me?*

Kanojo wa konban no pātī niwa
ikumai.
彼女は今晩のパーティーには行くま
い。
*Probably she won't go to the party
tonight.*

Watakushi ga ikanakereba, mondai
wa kaiketsu shinai.
私が行かなければ、問題は解決しな
い。
*If I don't go, the problems won't be
solved.*

Iku is a verb you'll need when you're
on the go in Japan, seeing and doing and
enjoying wonderful places and things.
No matter how you go, you'll find it
easy to get around. Public transportation
is efficient, and most station names for
train and subway lines are written in
both Japanese and romaji. So you can
read and pronounce them to help you
get to your destination.

I

Words and Expressions Related to This Verb

ikichigau　行き違う
*to just miss each other (paths don't
cross)*

ikisugiru　行き過ぎる
to go past, to go too far

Kyōto yuki　京都行き
for Kyoto

ikisaki　行き先
destination

ikidomari　行き止まり
a dead end

yukusue　行く末
future

to admonish, to caution   TRANSITIVE

			AFFIRMATIVE	**NEGATIVE**
Indicative	**INFORMAL**		imashimeru	imashimenai
	FORMAL		imashimemasu	imashimemasen
Imperative	**INFORMAL**	I	imashimero	imashimeru na
		II	imashimenasai	imashimenasaru na
		III	imashimete kudasai	imashimenai de kudasai
	FORMAL		oimashime nasaimase	oimashime nasaimasu na
Presumptive	**INFORMAL**	I	imashimeyō	imashimenai
		II	imashimeru darō	imashimenai darō
	FORMAL	I	imashimemashō	imashimemasumai
		II	imashimeru deshō	imashimenai deshō
Provisional	**INFORMAL**		imashimereba	imashimenakereba
	FORMAL		imashimemaseba	imashimemasen nara
			imashimemasureba	
Gerund	**INFORMAL**	I	imashimete	imashimenai de
		II		imashimenakute
	FORMAL		imashimemashite	imashimemasen de
Past Ind.	**INFORMAL**		imashimeta	imashimenakatta
	FORMAL		imashimemashita	imashimemasen deshita
Past Presump.	**INFORMAL**		imashimetarō	imashimenakattarō
			imashimeta darō	imashimenakatta darō
	FORMAL		imashimemashitarō	imashimemasen deshitarō
			imashimeta deshō	imashimenakatta deshō
Conditional	**INFORMAL**		imashimetara	imashimenakattara
	FORMAL		imashimemashitara	imashimemasen deshitara
Alternative	**INFORMAL**		imashimetari	imashimenakattari
	FORMAL		imashimemashitari	imashimemasen deshitari

		INFORMAL AFFIRMATIVE INDICATIVE
Passive		imashimerareru
Potential		imashimerareru
Causative		imashimesaseru
Causative Pass.		imashimesaserareru
Honorific	I	oimashime ni naru
	II	oimashime nasaru
Humble	I	oimashime suru
	II	oimashime itasu

inoari

いなおる／居直る **inoar.u**

to assume a threatening attitude

			AFFIRMATIVE	NEGATIVE
Indicative	**INFORMAL**		inaoru	inaoranai
	FORMAL		inaorimasu	inaorimasen
Imperative	**INFORMAL**	I	inaore	inaoru na
		II	inaorinasai	inaorinasaru na
		III	inaotte kudasai	inaoranai de kudasai
	FORMAL		oinaori nasaimase	oinaori nasaimasu na
Presumptive	**INFORMAL**	I	inaorō	inaorumai
		II	inaoru darō	inaoranai darō
	FORMAL	I	inaorimashō	inaorimasumai
		II	inaoru deshō	inaoranai deshō
Provisional	**INFORMAL**		inaoreba	inaoranakereba
	FORMAL		inaorimaseba	inaorimasen nara
			inaorimasureba	
Gerund	**INFORMAL**	I	inaotte	inaoranai de
		II		inaoranakute
	FORMAL		inaorimashite	inaorimasen de
Past Ind.	**INFORMAL**		inaotta	inaoranakatta
	FORMAL		inaorimashita	inaorimasen deshita
Past Presump.	**INFORMAL**		inaottarō	inaoranakattarō
			inaotta darō	inaoranakatta darō
	FORMAL		inaorimashitarō	inaorimasen deshitarō
			inaotta deshō	inaoranakatta deshō
Conditional	**INFORMAL**		inaottara	inaoranakattara
	FORMAL		inaorimashitara	inaorimasen deshitara
Alternative	**INFORMAL**		inaottari	inaoranakattari
	FORMAL		inaorimashitari	inaorimasen deshitari

		INFORMAL AFFIRMATIVE INDICATIVE
Passive		inaorareru
Potential		inaoreru
Causative		inaoraseru
Causative Pass.		inaoraserareru
Honorific	I	oinaori ni naru
	II	oinaori nasaru
Humble	I	
	II	

to pray, to wish for　　TRANSITIVE

			AFFIRMATIVE	NEGATIVE
Indicative	**INFORMAL**		inoru	inoranai
	FORMAL		inorimasu	inorimasen
Imperative	**INFORMAL**	I	inore	inoru na
		II	inorinasai	inorinasaru na
		III	inotte kudasai	inoranai de kudasai
	FORMAL		oinori nasaimase	oinori nasaimasu na
Presumptive	**INFORMAL**	I	inorō	inorumai
		II	inoru darō	inoranai darō
	FORMAL	I	inorimashō	inorimasumai
		II	inoru deshō	inoranai deshō
Provisional	**INFORMAL**		inoreba	inoranakereba
	FORMAL		inorimaseba	inorimasen nara
			inorimasureba	
Gerund	**INFORMAL**	I	inotte	inoranai de
		II		inoranakute
	FORMAL		inorimashite	inorimasen de
Past Ind.	**INFORMAL**		inotta	inoranakatta
	FORMAL		inorimashita	inorimasen deshita
Past Presump.	**INFORMAL**		inottarō	inoranakattarō
			inotta darō	inoranakatta darō
	FORMAL		inorimashitarō	inorimasen deshitarō
			inotta deshō	inoranakatta deshō
Conditional	**INFORMAL**		inottara	inoranakattara
	FORMAL		inorimashitara	inorimasen deshitara
Alternative	**INFORMAL**		inottari	inoranakattari
	FORMAL		inorimashitari	inorimasen deshitari

		INFORMAL AFFIRMATIVE INDICATIVE
Passive		inorareru
Potential		inoreru
Causative		inoraseru
Causative Pass.		inoraserareru
Honorific	I	oinori ni naru
	II	oinori nasaru
Humble	I	oinori suru
	II	oinori itasu

いらっしゃる **irasshar.u**

to come, to go, to exist (animate honorific)

			AFFIRMATIVE	NEGATIVE
Indicative	**INFORMAL**		irassharu	irassharanai
	FORMAL		irasshaimasu	irasshaimasen
Imperative	**INFORMAL**	I	irasshai	irassharu na
		II		
		III	irasshatte kudasai	irassharanai de kudasai
	FORMAL		irasshaimase	irasshaimasu na
Presumptive	**INFORMAL**	I	irassharō	irassharumai
		II	irassharu darō	irassharanai darō
	FORMAL	I	irasshaimashō	irasshaimasumai
		II	irassharu deshō	irassharanai deshō
Provisional	**INFORMAL**		irasshareba	irassharanakereba
	FORMAL		irasshaimaseba	irasshaimasen nara
			irasshaimasureba	
Gerund	**INFORMAL**	I	irasshatte*	irassharanai de
		II		irassharanakute
	FORMAL		irasshaimashite	irasshaimasen de
Past Ind.	**INFORMAL**		irasshatta*	irassharanakatta
	FORMAL		irasshaimashita	irasshaimasen deshita
Past Presump.	**INFORMAL**		irasshattarō*	irassharanakattarō
			irasshatta darō	irassharanakatta darō
	FORMAL		irasshaimashitarō	irasshaimasen deshitarō
			irasshatta deshō	irassharanakatta deshō
Conditional	**INFORMAL**		irasshattara*	irassharanakattara
	FORMAL		irasshaimashitara	irasshaimasen deshitara
Alternative	**INFORMAL**		irasshattari*	irassharanakattari
	FORMAL		irasshaimashitari	irasshaimasen deshitari

		INFORMAL AFFIRMATIVE INDICATIVE
Passive		
Potential		
Causative		
Causative Pass.		
Honorific	I	
	II	
Humble	I	
	II	

*Shorter forms: *irashite, irashita, irashitarō, irashitara,* and *irashitari* also occur in the same environments as the longer forms given above.

to put in, to take in, to let in　　　　TRANSITIVE

			AFFIRMATIVE	NEGATIVE
Indicative	**INFORMAL**		ireru	irenai
	FORMAL		iremasu	iremasen
Imperative	**INFORMAL**	I	irero	ireru na
		II	irenasai	irenasaru na
		III	irete kudasai	irenai de kudasai
	FORMAL		oire nasaimase	oire nasaimasu na
Presumptive	**INFORMAL**	I	ireyō	iremai
		II	ireru darō	irenai darō
	FORMAL	I	iremashō	iremasumai
		II	ireru deshō	irenai deshō
Provisional	**INFORMAL**		irereba	irenakereba
	FORMAL		iremaseba	iremasen nara
			iremasureba	
Gerund	**INFORMAL**	I	irete	irenai de
		II		irenakute
	FORMAL		iremashite	iremasen de
Past Ind.	**INFORMAL**		ireta	irenakatta
	FORMAL		iremashita	iremasen deshita
Past Presump.	**INFORMAL**		iretarō	irenakattarō
			ireta darō	irenakatta darō
	FORMAL		iremashitarō	iremasen deshitarō
			ireta deshō	irenakatta deshō
Conditional	**INFORMAL**		iretara	irenakattara
	FORMAL		iremashitara	iremasen deshitara
Alternative	**INFORMAL**		iretari	irenakattari
	FORMAL		iremashitari	iremasen deshitari

			INFORMAL AFFIRMATIVE INDICATIVE
Passive			irerareru
Potential			irerareru
Causative			iresaseru
Causative Pass.			iresaserareru
Honorific		I	oire ni naru
		II	oire nasaru
Humble		I	oire suru
		II	oire itasu

いる／居る　**i.ru**
to exist, to be (animate), *to have*

			AFFIRMATIVE	**NEGATIVE**
Indicative	**INFORMAL**		iru	inai
	FORMAL		imasu	imasen
Imperative	**INFORMAL**	I	iro	iru na
		II	inasai	inasaru na
		III	ite kudasai	inai de kudasai
	FORMAL		oide nasaimase	oide nasaimasu na
Presumptive	**INFORMAL**	I	iyō	imai
		II	iru darō	inai darō
	FORMAL	I	imashō	imasumai
		II	iru deshō	inai deshō
Provisional	**INFORMAL**		ireba	inakereba
	FORMAL		imaseba	imasen nara
			imasureba	
Gerund	**INFORMAL**	I	ite	inai de
		II		inakute
	FORMAL		imashite	imasen de
Past Ind.	**INFORMAL**		ita	inakatta
	FORMAL		imashita	imasen deshita
Past Presump.	**INFORMAL**		itarō	inakattarō
			ita darō	inakatta darō
	FORMAL		imashitarō	imasen deshitarō
			ita deshō	inakatta deshō
Conditional	**INFORMAL**		itara	inakattara
	FORMAL		imashitara	imasen deshitara
Alternative	**INFORMAL**		itari	inakattari
	FORMAL		imashitari	imasen deshitari

		INFORMAL AFFIRMATIVE INDICATIVE	
Passive		irareru	
Potential		irareru	
Causative		isaseru	
Causative Pass.		isaserareru	
Honorific	I	irassharu	oide ni naru
	II		
Humble	I	oru	
	II		

AN ESSENTIAL
55 VERB

AN ESSENTIAL 55 VERB

Iru いる

to exist, to be (animate), to have

Iru is an essential verb for interpersonal relationships and, of course, for giving and receiving all sorts of information. The possibilities for using this verb are endless.

Sentences Using *Iru*

Yūbe itsumo no sushiya ni ittara, kiniiri no itamae ga byōki de inakatta.
夕べいつもの鮨屋に行ったら、気に入りの板前が病気でいなかった。
I went to my regular sushi shop last night, but my favorite chef wasn't there because he was sick.

Moshimoshi, Suzuki san desu ka. Hanako san wa irasshaimasu ka.
もしもし、鈴木さんですか。花子さんはいらっしゃいますか。
Hello, is this the Suzuki residence? Is Hanako san home? (telephone)

Tomodachi niwa inu ga ni hiki to neko ga go hiki imasu.
友達には犬が二匹と猫が五匹います。
My friend has two dogs and five cats.

Kyō wa ie ni ite benkyō shinasai.
今日は家にいて勉強しなさい。
You should stay home and study today.

Watakushi ga inakutemo, dareka iru hazu desu.
私がいなくても、誰かいるはずです。
Even if I'm not here, someone will be here.

Words and Expressions Related to This Verb

iawaseru　い合わせる
to happen to be (somewhere)

irusu o tsukau　居留守を使う
to pretend not to be (somewhere)

idokoro　居所
one's whereabouts

Proverb

Oni no inu ma ni sentaku.
鬼の居ぬ間に洗濯
When the cat is away, the mice will play. (to do laundry while the demon is away)

いる／要る　**ir.u**

to be necessary, to need

			AFFIRMATIVE	NEGATIVE
Indicative	**INFORMAL**		iru	iranai
	FORMAL		irimasu	irimasen
Imperative	**INFORMAL**	I		
		II		
		III		
	FORMAL			
Presumptive	**INFORMAL**	I	irō	irumai
		II	iru darō	iranai darō
	FORMAL	I	irimashō	irimasumai
		II	iru deshō	iranai deshō
Provisional	**INFORMAL**		ireba	iranakereba
	FORMAL		irimaseba	irimasen nara
			irimasureba	
Gerund	**INFORMAL**	I	itte	iranai de
		II		iranakute
	FORMAL		irimashite	irimasen de
Past Ind.	**INFORMAL**		itta	iranakatta
	FORMAL		irimashita	irimasen deshita
Past Presump.	**INFORMAL**		ittarō	iranakattarō
			itta darō	iranakatta darō
	FORMAL		irimashitarō	irimasen deshitarō
			itta deshō	iranakatta deshō
Conditional	**INFORMAL**		ittara	iranakattara
	FORMAL		irimashitara	irimasen deshitara
Alternative	**INFORMAL**		ittari	iranakattari
	FORMAL		irimashitari	irimasen deshitari

INFORMAL AFFIRMATIVE INDICATIVE

Passive		
Potential		
Causative		
Causative Pass.		
Honorific	I	
	II	
Humble	I	
	II	

isog.u　いそぐ／急ぐ

to hurry　　TRANSITIVE

			AFFIRMATIVE	NEGATIVE
Indicative	**INFORMAL**		isogu	isoganai
	FORMAL		isogimasu	isogimasen
Imperative	**INFORMAL**	I	isoge	isogu na
		II	isoginasai	isoginasaru na
		III	isoide kudasai	isoganai de kudasai
	FORMAL		oisogi nasaimase	oisogi nasaimasu na
Presumptive	**INFORMAL**	I	isogō	isogumai
		II	isogu darō	isoganai darō
	FORMAL	I	isogimashō	isogimasumai
		II	isogu deshō	isoganai deshō
Provisional	**INFORMAL**		isogeba	isoganakereba
	FORMAL		isogimaseba	isogimasen nara
			isogimasureba	
Gerund	**INFORMAL**	I	isoide	isoganai de
		II		isoganakute
	FORMAL		isogimashite	isogimasen de
Past Ind.	**INFORMAL**		isoida	isoganakatta
	FORMAL		isogimashita	isogimasen deshita
Past Presump.	**INFORMAL**		isoidarō	isoganakattarō
			isoida darō	isoganakatta darō
	FORMAL		isogimashitarō	isogimasen deshitarō
			isoida deshō	isoganakatta deshō
Conditional	**INFORMAL**		isoidara	isoganakattara
	FORMAL		isogimashitara	isogimasen deshitara
Alternative	**INFORMAL**		isoidari	isoganakattari
	FORMAL		isogimashitari	isogimasen deshitari

		INFORMAL AFFIRMATIVE INDICATIVE
Passive		isogareru
Potential		isogeru
Causative		isogaseru
Causative Pass.		isogaserareru
Honorific	I	oisogi ni naru
	II	oisogi nasaru
Humble	I	
	II	

いただく／頂く　**itadak.u**

TRANSITIVE　　*to receive, to take food or drink* (humble)

			AFFIRMATIVE	NEGATIVE
Indicative	**INFORMAL**		itadaku	itadakanai
	FORMAL		iladakimasu	itadakimasen
Imperative	**INFORMAL**	I		
		II		
		III		
	FORMAL			
Presumptive	**INFORMAL**	I	itadakō	itadakumai
		II	itadaku darō	itadakanai darō
	FORMAL	I	itadakimashō	itadakimasumai
		II	itadaku deshō	itadakanai deshō
Provisional	**INFORMAL**		itadakeba	itadakanakereba
	FORMAL		itadakimaseba	itadakimasen nara
			itadakimasureba	
Gerund	**INFORMAL**	I	itadaite	itadakanai de
		II		itadakanakute
	FORMAL		itadakimashite	iladakimasen de
Past Ind.	**INFORMAL**		itadaita	itadakanakatta
	FORMAL		itadakimashita	itadakimasen deshita
Past Presump.	**INFORMAL**		itadaitarō	itadakanakattarō
			itadaita darō	itadakanakatta darō
	FORMAL		itadakimashitarō	itadakimasen deshitarō
			itadaita deshō	itadakanakatta deshō
Conditional	**INFORMAL**		itadaitara	itadakanakattara
	FORMAL		itadakimashitara	itadakimasen deshitara
Alternative	**INFORMAL**		itadaitari	itadakanakattari
	FORMAL		itadakimashitari	itadakimasen deshitari

		INFORMAL AFFIRMATIVE INDICATIVE
Passive		
Potential		itadakeru
Causative		itadakaseru
Causative Pass.		itadakaserareru
Honorific	I	
	II	
Humble	I	
	II	

177

to hurt, to become hurt, spoiled, or damaged

			AFFIRMATIVE	NEGATIVE
Indicative	**INFORMAL**		itamu	itamanai
	FORMAL		itamimasu	itamimasen
Imperative	**INFORMAL**	**I**		
		II		
		III		
	FORMAL			
Presumptive	**INFORMAL**	**I**	itamō	itamumai
		II	itamu darō	itamanai darō
	FORMAL	**I**	itamimashō	itamimasumai
		II	itamu deshō	itamanai deshō
Provisional	**INFORMAL**		itameba	itamanakereba
	FORMAL		itamimaseba	itamimasen nara
			itamimasureba	
Gerund	**INFORMAL**	**I**	itande	itamanai de
		II		itamanakute
	FORMAL		itamimashite	itamimasen de
Past Ind.	**INFORMAL**		itanda	itamanakatta
	FORMAL		itamimashita	itamimasen deshita
Past Presump.	**INFORMAL**		itandarō	itamanakattarō
			itanda darō	itamanakatta darō
	FORMAL		itamimashitarō	itamimasen deshitarō
			itanda deshō	itamanakatta deshō
Conditional	**INFORMAL**		itandara	itamanakattara
	FORMAL		itamimashitara	itamimasen deshitara
Alternative	**INFORMAL**		itandari	itamanakattari
	FORMAL		itamimashitari	itamimasen deshitari

		INFORMAL AFFIRMATIVE INDICATIVE
Passive		itamareru
Potential		itameru
Causative		itamaseru
Causative Pass.		itamaserareru
Honorific	**I**	oitami ni naru
	II	oitami nasaru
Humble	**I**	
	II	

いたす／致す **itas.u**

TRANSITIVE　　*to do* (humble)

			AFFIRMATIVE	NEGATIVE
Indicative	**INFORMAL**		itasu	itasanai
	FORMAL		itashimasu	itashimasen
Imperative	**INFORMAL**	I	itase	itasu na
		II		
		III		
	FORMAL			
Presumptive	**INFORMAL**	I	itasō	itasumai
		II	itasu darō	itasanai darō
	FORMAL	I	itashimashō	itashimasumai
		II	itasu deshō	itasanai deshō
Provisional	**INFORMAL**		itaseba	itasanakereba
	FORMAL		itashimaseba	itashimasen nara
			itashimasureba	
Gerund	**INFORMAL**	I	itashite	itasanai de
		II		itasanakute
	FORMAL		itashimashite	itashimasen de
Past Ind.	**INFORMAL**		itashita	itasanakatta
	FORMAL		itashimashita	itashimasen deshita
Past Presump.	**INFORMAL**		itashitarō	itasanakattarō
			itashita darō	itasanakatta darō
	FORMAL		itashimashitarō	itashimasen deshitarō
			itashita deshō	itasanakatta deshō
Conditional	**INFORMAL**		itashitara	itasanakattara
	FORMAL		itashimashitara	itashimasen deshitara
Alternative	**INFORMAL**		itashitari	itasanakattari
	FORMAL		itashimashitari	itashimasen deshitari

		INFORMAL AFFIRMATIVE INDICATIVE
Passive		
Potential		
Causative		
Causative Pass.		
Honorific	I	
	II	
Humble	I	
	II	

179

itsuwar.u　いつわる／偽る

to lie, to deceive　　TRANSITIVE

itsuwari

			AFFIRMATIVE	NEGATIVE
Indicative	**INFORMAL**		itsuwaru	itsuwaranai
	FORMAL		itsuwarimasu	itsuwarimasen
Imperative	**INFORMAL**	I	itsuware	itsuwaru na
		II	itsuwarinasai	itsuwarinasaru na
		III	itsuwatte kudasai	itsuwaranai de kudasai
	FORMAL		oitsuwari nasaimase	oitsuwari nasaimasu na
Presumptive	**INFORMAL**	I	itsuwarō	itsuwarumai
		II	itsuwaru darō	itsuwaranai darō
	FORMAL	I	itsuwarimashō	itsuwarimasumai
		II	itsuwaru deshō	itsuwaranai deshō
Provisional	**INFORMAL**		itsuwareba	itsuwaranakereba
	FORMAL		itsuwarimaseba	itsuwarimasen nara
			itsuwarimasureba	
Gerund	**INFORMAL**	I	itsuwatte	itsuwaranai de
		II		itsuwaranakute
	FORMAL		itsuwarimashite	itsuwarimasen de
Past Ind.	**INFORMAL**		itsuwatta	itsuwaranakatta
	FORMAL		itsuwarimashita	itsuwarimasen deshita
Past Presump.	**INFORMAL**		itsuwattarō	itsuwaranakattarō
			itsuwatta darō	itsuwaranakatta darō
	FORMAL		itsuwarimashitarō	itsuwarimasen deshitarō
			itsuwatta deshō	itsuwaranakatta deshō
Conditional	**INFORMAL**		itsuwattara	itsuwaranakattara
	FORMAL		itsuwarimashitara	itsuwarimasen deshitara
Alternative	**INFORMAL**		itsuwattari	itsuwaranakattari
	FORMAL		itsuwarimashitari	itsuwarimasen deshitari

			INFORMAL AFFIRMATIVE INDICATIVE
Passive			itsuwarareru
Potential			itsuwareru
Causative			itsuwaraseru
Causative Pass.			itsuwaraserareru
Honorific		I	oitsuwari ni naru
		II	oitsuwari nasaru
Humble		I	oitsuwari suru
		II	oitsuwari itasu

180

TRANSITIVE *to say, to talk about, to tell*

			AFFIRMATIVE	NEGATIVE
Indicative	**INFORMAL**		iu	iwanai
	FORMAL		iimasu	iimasen
Imperative	**INFORMAL**	**I**	ie	iu na
		II	iinasai	iinasaru na
		III	itte kudasai	iwanai de kudasai
	FORMAL		osshaimase	osshaimasu na
Presumptive	**INFORMAL**	**I**	iō	iumai
		II	iu darō	iwanai darō
	FORMAL	**I**	iimashō	iimasumai
		II	iu deshō	iwanai deshō
Provisional	**INFORMAL**		ieba	iwanakereba
	FORMAL		iimaseba	iimasen nara
			iimasureba	
Gerund	**INFORMAL**	**I**	itte	iwanai de
		II		iwanakute
	FORMAL		iimashite	iimasen de
Past Ind.	**INFORMAL**		itta	iwanakatta
	FORMAL		iimashita	iimasen deshita
Past Presump.	**INFORMAL**		ittarō	iwanakattamo
			itta darō	iwanakatta darō
	FORMAL		iimashitarō	iimasen deshitarō
			itta deshō	iwanakatta deshō
Conditional	**INFORMAL**		ittara	iwanakattara
	FORMAL		iimashitara	iimasen deshitara
Alternative	**INFORMAL**		ittari	iwanakattari
	FORMAL		iimashitari	iimasen deshitari

INFORMAL AFFIRMATIVE INDICATIVE

Passive		iwareru
Potential		ieru
Causative		iwaseru
Causative Pass.		iwaserareru
Honorific	**I**	ossharu
	II	
Humble	**I**	mōsu
	II	

AN ESSENTIAL 55 VERB

AN ESSENTIAL 55 VERB

Iu 言う

to say, to talk about, to tell

Sentences Using *Iu*

Kanojo wa, itsumo iitai koto ga takusan aru.
彼女は、いつも言いたいことがたくさんある。
She always has plenty of things to say.

Ima sugu ni iwanakereba, tsugi no kikai ga itsu aru ka wakarimasen yo.
今すぐに言わなければ、次ぎの機会がいつあるか分かりませんよ。
If you don't say it immediately, you don't know when the next opportunity will be.

Iwanai de ii koto o itte wa naranai.
言わないで良いことを言ってはならない。
You shouldn't say what you don't need to say.

Shinjitsu o ittara wakatte moraemasu.
真実を言ったら分かってもらえます。
If you tell the truth, you'll be understood.

Kore ijō, iu beki koto wa arimasen.
これ以上、言うべきことはありません。
I have nothing more to say.

Iu is a verb in constant use by everyone. And your efforts to say things in Japanese will be greatly appreciated in Japan even if your Japanese is limited.

Words and Expressions Related to This Verb

noberu　述べる
to state, to express

kataru　語る
to talk, to tell

iinaosu　言い直す
to restate, to correct oneself

iimachigaeru　言い間違える
to misstate

iiwake　言い訳
an excuse

Proverb

Iwanu ga hana.
言わぬが花。
It's better left unsaid.
(Saying nothing is the flower.)

いわう／祝う　**iwa.u**

TRANSITIVE　*to celebrate, to congratulate*

			AFFIRMATIVE	**NEGATIVE**
Indicative	**INFORMAL**		iwau	iwawanai
	FORMAL		iwaimasu	iwaimasen
Imperative	**INFORMAL**	I	iwae	iwau na
		II	iwainasai	iwainasaru na
		III	iwatte kudasai	iwawanai de kudasai
	FORMAL		oiwai nasaimase	oiwai nasaimasu na
Presumptive	**INFORMAL**	I	iwaō	iwaumai
		II	iwau darō	iwawanai darō
	FORMAL	I	iwaimashō	iwaimasumai
		II	iwau deshō	iwawanai deshō
Provisional	**INFORMAL**		iwaeba	iwawanakereba
	FORMAL		iwaimaseba	iwaimasen nara
			iwaimasureba	
Gerund	**INFORMAL**	I	iwatte	iwawanai de
		II		iwawanakute
	FORMAL		iwaimashite	iwaimasen de
Past Ind.	**INFORMAL**		iwatta	iwawanakatta
	FORMAL		iwaimashita	iwaimasen deshita
Past Presump.	**INFORMAL**		iwattarō	iwawanakattarō
			iwatta darō	iwawanakatta darō
	FORMAL		iwaimashitarō	iwaimasen deshitarō
			iwatta deshō	iwawanakatta deshō
Conditional	**INFORMAL**		iwattara	iwawanakattara
	FORMAL		iwaimashitara	iwaimasen deshitara
Alternative	**INFORMAL**		iwattari	iwawanakattari
	FORMAL		iwaimashitari	iwaimasen deshitari

			INFORMAL AFFIRMATIVE INDICATIVE
Passive			iwawareru
Potential			iwaeru
Causative			iwawaseru
Causative Pass.			iwawaserareru
Honorific		I	oiwai ni naru
		II	oiwai nasaru
Humble		I	oiwai suru
		II	oiwai itasu

iyagar.u いやがる／嫌がる   iyagari
to dislike, to hate   TRANSITIVE

			AFFIRMATIVE	NEGATIVE
Indicative	INFORMAL		iyagaru	iyagaranai
	FORMAL		iyagarimasu	iyagarimasen
Imperative	INFORMAL	I	iyagare	iyagaru na
		II	iyagarinasai	iyagarinasaru na
		III	iyagatte kudasai	iyagaranai de kudasai
	FORMAL		oiyagari nasaimase	oiyagari nasaimasu na
Presumptive	INFORMAL	I	iyagarō	iyagarumai
		II	iyagaru darō	iyagaranai darō
	FORMAL	I	iyagarimashō	iyagarimasumai
		II	iyagaru deshō	iyagaranai deshō
Provisional	INFORMAL		iyagareba	iyagaranakereba
	FORMAL		iyagarimaseba	iyagarimasen nara
			iyagarimasureba	
Gerund	INFORMAL	I	iyagatte	iyagaranai de
		II		iyagaranakute
	FORMAL		iyagarimashite	iyagarimasen de
Past Ind.	INFORMAL		iyagatta	iyagaranakatta
	FORMAL		iyagarimashita	iyagarimasen deshita
Past Presump.	INFORMAL		iyagattarō	iyagaranakattarō
			iyagatta darō	iyagaranakatta darō
	FORMAL		iyagarimashitarō	iyagarimasen deshitarō
			iyagatta deshō	iyagaranakatta deshō
Conditional	INFORMAL		iyagattara	iyagaranakattara
	FORMAL		iyagarimashitara	iyagarimasen deshitara
Alternative	INFORMAL		iyagattari	iyagaranakattari
	FORMAL		iyagarimashitari	iyagarimasen deshitari

		INFORMAL AFFIRMATIVE INDICATIVE
Passive		iyagarareru
Potential		
Causative		iyagaraseru
Causative Pass.		iyagaraserareru
Honorific	I	oiyagari ni naru
	II	oiyagari nasaru
Humble	I	
	II	

184

じゅくす／熟す **jukus.u**
to get ripe, to ripen, to mature

			AFFIRMATIVE	**NEGATIVE**
Indicative	**INFORMAL**		jukusu	jukusanai
	FORMAL		jukushimasu	jukushimasen
Imperative	**INFORMAL**	I	jukuse	jukusu na
		II	jukushinasai	jukushinarasaru na
		III	jukushite kudasai	jukusanai de kudasai
	FORMAL			
Presumptive	**INFORMAL**	I	jukusō	jukusumai
		II	jukusu darō	jukusanai darō
	FORMAL	I	jukushimashō	jukushimasumai
		II	jukusu deshō	jukusanai deshō
Provisional	**INFORMAL**		jukuseba	jukusanakereba
	FORMAL		jukushimaseba	jukushimasen nara
			jukushimasureba	
Gerund	**INFORMAL**	I	jukushite	jukusanai de
		II		jukushite
	FORMAL		jukushimashite	jukushimasen de
Past Ind.	**INFORMAL**		jukushita	jukusanakatta
	FORMAL		jukushimashita	jukushimasen deshita
Past Presump.	**INFORMAL**		jukushitarō	jukusanakattarō
			jukushita darō	jukusanakatta darō
	FORMAL		jukushimashitarō	jukushimasen deshitarō
			jukushita deshō	jukusanakatta deshō
Conditional	**INFORMAL**		jukushitara	jukusanakattara
	FORMAL		jukushimashitara	jukushimasen deshitara
Alternative	**INFORMAL**		jukushitari	jukusanakattari
	FORMAL		jukushimashitari	jukushimasen deshitari

J

		INFORMAL AFFIRMATIVE INDICATIVE
Passive		
Potential		jukuseru
Causative		jukusaseru
Causative Pass.		jukusaserareru
Honorific	I	ojukushi ni naru
	II	ojukushi nasaru
Humble	I	
	II	

to protect, to take a person under one's wing   TRANSITIVE

			AFFIRMATIVE	NEGATIVE
Indicative	**INFORMAL**		kabau	kabawanai
	FORMAL		kabaimasu	kabaimasen
Imperative	**INFORMAL**	I	kabae	kabau na
		II	kabainasai	kabainasaru na
		III	kabatte kudasai	kabawanai de kudasai
	FORMAL		okabai nasaimase	okabai nasaimasu na
Presumptive	**INFORMAL**	I	kabaō	kabaumai
		II	kabau darō	kabawanai darō
	FORMAL	I	kabaimashō	kabaimasumai
		II	kabau deshō	kabawanai deshō
Provisional	**INFORMAL**		kabaeba	kabawanakereba
	FORMAL		kabaimaseba	kabaimasen nara
			kabaimasureba	
Gerund	**INFORMAL**	I	kabatte	kabawanai de
		II		kabawanakute
	FORMAL		kabaimashite	kabaimasen de
Past Ind.	**INFORMAL**		kabatta	kabawanakatta
	FORMAL		kabaimashita	kabaimasen deshita
Past Presump.	**INFORMAL**		kabattarō	kabawanakattarō
			kabatta darō	kabawanakatta darō
	FORMAL		kabaimashitarō	kabaimasen deshitarō
			kabatta deshō	kabawanakatta deshō
Conditional	**INFORMAL**		kabattara	kabawanakattara
	FORMAL		kabaimashitara	kabaimasen deshitara
Alternative	**INFORMAL**		kabattari	kabawanakattari
	FORMAL		kabaimashitari	kabaimasen deshitari

			INFORMAL AFFIRMATIVE INDICATIVE
Passive			kabawareru
Potential			kabaeru
Causative			kabawaseru
Causative Pass.			kabawaserareru
Honorific		I	okabai ni naru
		II	okabai nasaru
Humble		I	okabai suru
		II	okabai itasu

kaburi

かぶる／被る　**kabur.u**

TRANSITIVE *to wear on one's head, to put on*

			AFFIRMATIVE	**NEGATIVE**
Indicative	**INFORMAL**		kaburu	kaburanai
	FORMAL		kaburimasu	kaburimasen
Imperative	**INFORMAL**	I	kabure	kaburu na
		II	kaburinasai	kaburinasaru na
		III	kabutte kudasai	kaburanai de kudasai
	FORMAL		okaburi nasaimase	okaburi nasaimasu na
Presumptive	**INFORMAL**	I	kaburō	kaburumai
		II	kaburu darō	kaburanai darō
	FORMAL	I	kaburimashō	kaburimasumai
		II	kaburu deshō	kaburanai deshō
Provisional	**INFORMAL**		kabureba	kaburanakereba
	FORMAL		kaburimaseba	kaburimasen nara
			kaburimasureba	
Gerund	**INFORMAL**	I	kabutte	kaburanai de
		II		kaburanakute
	FORMAL		kaburimashite	kaburimasen de
Past Ind.	**INFORMAL**		kabutta	kaburanakatta
	FORMAL		kaburimashita	kaburimasen deshita
Past Presump.	**INFORMAL**		kabuttarō	kaburanakattarō
			kabutta darō	kaburanakatta darō
	FORMAL		kaburimashitarō	kaburimasen deshitarō
			kabutta deshō	kaburanakatta deshō
Conditional	**INFORMAL**		kabuttara	kaburanakattara
	FORMAL		kaburimashitara	kaburimasen deshitara
Alternative	**INFORMAL**		kabuttari	kaburanakattari
	FORMAL		kaburimashitari	kaburimasen deshitari

		INFORMAL AFFIRMATIVE INDICATIVE
Passive		kaburareru
Potential		kabureru
Causative		kaburaseru
Causative Pass.		kaburaserareru
Honorific	I	okaburi ni naru
	II	okaburi nasaru
Humble	I	okaburi suru
	II	okaburi itasu

K

187

kae.ru　かえる／変える／代える／替える／換える　**kae**

to change　TRANSITIVE

			AFFIRMATIVE	NEGATIVE
Indicative	**INFORMAL**		kaeru	kaenai
	FORMAL		kaemasu	kaemasen
Imperative	**INFORMAL**	I	kaero	kaeru na
		II	kaenasai	kaenasaru na
		III	kaete kudasai	kaenai de kudasai
	FORMAL		okae nasaimase	okae nasaimasu na
Presumptive	**INFORMAL**	I	kaeyō	kaemai
		II	kaeru darō	kaenai darō
	FORMAL	I	kaemashō	kaemasumai
		II	kaeru deshō	kaenai deshō
Provisional	**INFORMAL**		kaereba	kaenakereba
	FORMAL		kaemaseba	kaemasen nara
			kaemasureba	
Gerund	**INFORMAL**	I	kaete	kaenai de
		II		kaenakute
	FORMAL		kaemashite	kaemasen de
Past Ind.	**INFORMAL**		kaeta	kaenakatta
	FORMAL		kaemashita	kaemasen deshita
Past Presump.	**INFORMAL**		kaetarō	kaenakattarō
			kaeta darō	kaenakatta darō
	FORMAL		kaemashitarō	kaemasen deshitarō
			kaeta deshō	kaenakatta deshō
Conditional	**INFORMAL**		kaetara	kaenakattara
	FORMAL		kaemashitara	kaemasen deshitara
Alternative	**INFORMAL**		kaetari	kaenakattari
	FORMAL		kaemashitari	kaemasen deshitari

		INFORMAL AFFIRMATIVE INDICATIVE
Passive		kaerareru
Potential		kaerareru
Causative		kaesaseru
Causative Pass.		kaesaserareru
Honorific	I	okae ni naru
	II	okae nasaru
Humble	I	okae suru
	II	okae itasu

to go back, to return (to a place)

			AFFIRMATIVE	NEGATIVE
Indicative	**INFORMAL**		kaeru	kaeranai
	FORMAL		kaerimasu	kaerimasen
Imperative	**INFORMAL**	I	kaere	kaeru na
		II	kaerinasai	kaerinasaru na
		III	kaette kudasai	kaeranai de kudasai
	FORMAL		okaeri nasaimase	okaeri nasaimasu na
Presumptive	**INFORMAL**	I	kaerō	kaerumai
		II	kaeru darō	kaeranai darō
	FORMAL	I	kaerimashō	kaerimasumai
		II	kaeru deshō	kaeranai deshō
Provisional	**INFORMAL**		kaereba	kaeranakereba
	FORMAL		kaerimaseba	kaerimasen nara
			kaerimasureba	
Gerund	**INFORMAL**	I	kaette	kaeranai de
		II		kaeranakute
	FORMAL		kaerimashite	kaerimasen de
Past Ind.	**INFORMAL**		kaetta	kaeranakatta
	FORMAL		kaerimashita	kaerimasen deshita
Past Presump.	**INFORMAL**		kaettarō	kaeranakattarō
			kaetta darō	kaeranakatta darō
	FORMAL		kaerimashitarō	kaerimasen deshitarō
			kaetta deshō	kaeranakatta deshō
Conditional	**INFORMAL**		kaettara	kaeranakattara
	FORMAL		kaerimashitara	kaerimasen deshitara
Alternative	**INFORMAL**		kaettari	kaeranakattari
	FORMAL		kaerimashitari	kaerimasen deshitari

			INFORMAL AFFIRMATIVE INDICATIVE
Passive			kaerareru
Potential			kaereru
Causative			kaeraseru
Causative Pass.			kaeraserareru
Honorific		I	okaeri ni naru
		II	okaeri nasaru
Humble		I	
		II	

**AN ESSENTIAL
55 VERB**

Kaeru 帰る

to go back, to return (to a place)

Sentences Using *Kaeru*

Shigoto ga isogashikute, ie ni kaeritakutemo kaeremasen.
仕事が忙しくて、家に帰りたくても帰れません。
I want to go back home, but I can't because I'm too busy with work.

Hisashiburi ni kokyō ni kaettara, amari no henka ni odorokimashita.
久しぶりに故郷に帰ったら、余りの変化に驚きました。
When I went back to my hometown after a long time away, I was so surprised at the big changes.

Kanojo wa Amerika no daigaku de benkyō shite iru keredo, sotsugyō shitemo Nihon niwa kaerumai.
彼女はアメリカの大学で勉強しているけれど、卒業しても日本には帰るまい。
She's studying at an American college, but probably she won't go back to Japan after graduation.

Gogo jū ji made ni ie ni kaeranai to, chichi ni shikararemasu.
午後１０時までに家に帰らないと、父に叱られます。
If I don't return home by 10 P.M., I'll be scolded by my father.

Shitenchō wa sengetsu Nihon e okaeri ni narimashita.
支店長は先月日本へお帰りになりました。
The manager of the branch office went back to Japan last month.

Kaeru is a verb you use every day. You go back home after a long day of work or classes, or after a brief trip to the market. You return to your hotel after a day of sightseeing or shopping when you are traveling. And when you return from a trip to Japan, you may want to go back there immediately!

Words and Expressions Related to This Verb

modoru　戻る
to go back, to return

kaeri　帰り
return

kaerimichi　帰り道
on one's way home

kitaku　帰宅
going home

kikoku　帰国
returning to one's own country

kaeshi

かえす／返す **kaes.u**

TRANSITIVE *to return* (something to someone)

			AFFIRMATIVE	NEGATIVE
Indicative	**INFORMAL**		kaesu	kaesanai
	FORMAL		kaeshimasu	kaeshimasen
Imperative	**INFORMAL**	I	kaese	kaesu na
		II	kaeshinasai	kaeshinasaru na
		III	kaeshite kudasai	kaesanai de kudasai
	FORMAL		okaeshi nasaimase	okaeshi nasaimasu na
Presumptive	**INFORMAL**	I	kaesō	kaesumai
		II	kaesu darō	kaesanai darō
	FORMAL	I	kaeshimashō	kaeshimasumai
		II	kaesu deshō	kaesanai deshō
Provisional	**INFORMAL**		kaeseba	kaesanakereba
	FORMAL		kaeshimaseba	kaeshimasen nara
			kaeshimasureba	
Gerund	**INFORMAL**	I	kaeshite	kaesanai de
		II		kaesanakute
	FORMAL		kaeshimashite	kaeshimasen de
Past Ind.	**INFORMAL**		kaeshita	kaesanakatta
	FORMAL		kaeshimashita	kaeshimasen deshita
Past Presump.	**INFORMAL**		kaeshitarō	kaesanakattarō
			kaeshita darō	kaesanakatta darō
	FORMAL		kaeshimashitarō	kaeshimasen deshitarō
			kaeshita deshō	kaesanakatta deshō
Conditional	**INFORMAL**		kaeshitara	kaesanakattara
	FORMAL		kaeshimashitara	kaeshimasen deshitara
Alternative	**INFORMAL**		kaeshitari	kaesanakattari
	FORMAL		kaeshimashitari	kaeshimasen deshitari

K

		INFORMAL AFFIRMATIVE INDICATIVE
Passive		kaesareru
Potential		kaeseru
Causative		kaesaseru
Causative Pass.		kaesaserareru
Honorific	I	okaeshi ni naru
	II	okaeshi nasaru
Humble	I	okaeshi suru
	II	okaeshi itasu

kagayak.u　かがやく／輝く　　　　　　　　　　kagayaki
to shine, to sparkle

			AFFIRMATIVE	NEGATIVE
Indicative	**INFORMAL**		kagayaku	kagayakanai
	FORMAL		kagayakimasu	kagayakimasen
Imperative	**INFORMAL**	I	kagayake	kagayaku na
		II	kagayakinasai	kagayakinasaru na
		III	kagayaite kudasai	kagayakanai de kudasai
	FORMAL		okagayaki nasaimase	okagayaki nasaimasu na
Presumptive	**INFORMAL**	I	kagayakō	kagayakumai
		II	kagayaku darō	kagayakanai darō
	FORMAL	I	kagayakimashō	kagayakimasumai
		II	kagayaku deshō	kagayakanai deshō
Provisional	**INFORMAL**		kagayakeba	kagayakanakereba
	FORMAL		kagayakimaseba	kagayakimasen nara
			kagayakimasureba	
Gerund	**INFORMAL**	I	kagayaite	kagayakanai de
		II		kagayakanakute
	FORMAL		kagayakimashite	kagayakimasen de
Past Ind.	**INFORMAL**		kagayaita	kagayakanakatta
	FORMAL		kagayakimashita	kagayakimasen deshita
Past Presump.	**INFORMAL**		kagayaitarō	kagayakanakattarō
			kagayaita darō	kagayakanakatta darō
	FORMAL		kagayakimashitarō	kagayakimasen deshitarō
			kagayaita deshō	kagayakanakatta deshō
Conditional	**INFORMAL**		kagayaitara	kagayakanakattara
	FORMAL		kagayakimashitara	kagayakimasen deshitara
Alternative	**INFORMAL**		kagayaitari	kagayakanakattari
	FORMAL		kagayakimashitari	kagayakimasen deshitari

		INFORMAL AFFIRMATIVE INDICATIVE
Passive		kagayakareru
Potential		kagayakeru
Causative		kagayakaseru
Causative Pass.		kagayakaserareru
Honorific	I	okagayaki ni naru
	II	okagayaki nasaru
Humble	I	
	II	

かぎる／限る **kagir.u**

TRANSITIVE   *to limit, to restrict*

			AFFIRMATIVE	NEGATIVE
Indicative	**INFORMAL**		kagiru	kagiranai
	FORMAL		kagirimasu	kagirimasen
Imperative	**INFORMAL**	I	kagire	kagiru na
		II	kagirinasai	kagirinasaru na
		III	kagitte kudasai	kagiranai de kudasai
	FORMAL		okagiri nasaimase	okagiri nasaimasu na
Presumptive	**INFORMAL**	I	kagirō	kagirumai
		II	kagiru darō	kagiranai darō
	FORMAL	I	kagirimashō	kagirimasumai
		II	kagiru deshō	kagiranai deshō
Provisional	**INFORMAL**		kagireba	kagiranakereba
	FORMAL		kagirimaseba	kagirimasen nara
			kagirimasureba	
Gerund	**INFORMAL**	I	kagitte	kagiranai de
		II		kagiranakute
	FORMAL		kagirimashite	kagirimasen de
Past Ind.	**INFORMAL**		kagitta	kagiranakatta
	FORMAL		kagirimashita	kagirimasen deshita
Past Presump.	**INFORMAL**		kagittarō	kagiranakattarō
			kagitta darō	kagiranakatta darō
	FORMAL		kagirimashitarō	kagirimasen deshitarō
			kagitta deshō	kagiranakatta deshō
Conditional	**INFORMAL**		kagittara	kagiranakattara
	FORMAL		kagirimashitara	kagirimasen deshitara
Alternative	**INFORMAL**		kagittari	kagiranakattari
	FORMAL		kagirimashitari	kagirimasen deshitari

		INFORMAL AFFIRMATIVE INDICATIVE
Passive		kagirareru
Potential		kagireru
Causative		kagiraseru
Causative Pass.		kagiraserareru
Honorific	I	okagiri ni naru
	II	okagiri nasaru
Humble	I	okagiri suru
	II	okagiri itasu

kajir.u かじる

to gnaw, to nibble TRANSITIVE

kaji

			AFFIRMATIVE	NEGATIVE
Indicative	**INFORMAL**		kajiru	kajiranai
	FORMAL		kajirimasu	kajirimasen
Imperative	**INFORMAL**	I	kajire	kajiru na
		II	kajirinasai	kajirinasaru na
		III	kajitte kudasai	kajiranai de kudasai
	FORMAL		okajiri nasaimase	okajiri nasaimasu na
Presumptive	**INFORMAL**	I	kajirō	kajirumai
		II	kajiru darō	kajiranai darō
	FORMAL	I	kajirimashō	kajirimasumai
		II	kajiru deshō	kajiranai deshō
Provisional	**INFORMAL**		kajireba	kajiranakereba
	FORMAL		kajirimaseba	kajirimasen nara
			kajirimasureba	
Gerund	**INFORMAL**	I	kajitte	kajiranai de
		II		kajiranakute
	FORMAL		kajirimashite	kajirimasen de
Past Ind.	**INFORMAL**		kajitta	kajiranakatta
	FORMAL		kajirimashita	kajirimasen deshita
Past Presump.	**INFORMAL**		kajittarō	kajiranakattarō
			kajitta darō	kajiranakatta darō
	FORMAL		kajirimashitarō	kajirimasen deshitarō
			kajitta deshō	kajiranakatta deshō
Conditional	**INFORMAL**		kajittara	kajiranakattara
	FORMAL		kajirimashitara	kajirimasen deshitara
Alternative	**INFORMAL**		kajittari	kajiranakattari
	FORMAL		kajirimashitari	kajirimasen deshitari

		INFORMAL AFFIRMATIVE INDICATIVE
Passive		kajirareru
Potential		kajireru
Causative		kajiraseru
Causative Pass.		kajiraserareru
Honorific	I	okajiri ni naru
	II	okajiri nasaru
Humble	I	
	II	

kakae

かかえる／抱える **kakae.ru**

TRANSITIVE   *to hold in one's arms, to have*

			AFFIRMATIVE	NEGATIVE
Indicative	**INFORMAL**		kakaeru	kakaenai
	FORMAL		kakaemasu	kakaemasen
Imperative	**INFORMAL**	I	kakaero	kakaeru na
		II	kakaenasai	kakaenasaru na
		III	kakaete kudasai	kakaenai de kudasai
	FORMAL		okakae nasaimase	okakae nasaimasu na
Presumptive	**INFORMAL**	I	kakaeyō	kakaemai
		II	kakaeru darō	kakaenai darō
	FORMAL	I	kakaemashō	kakaemasumai
		II	kakaeru deshō	kakaenai deshō
Provisional	**INFORMAL**		kakaereba	kakaenakereba
	FORMAL		kakaemaseba	kakaemasen nara
			kakaemasureba	
Gerund	**INFORMAL**	I	kakaete	kakaenai de
		II		kakaenakute
	FORMAL		kakaemashite	kakaemasen de
Past Ind.	**INFORMAL**		kakaeta	kakaenakatta
	FORMAL		kakaemashita	kakaemasen deshita
Past Presump.	**INFORMAL**		kakaetarō	kakaenakattarō
			kakaeta darō	kakaenakatta darō
	FORMAL		kakaemashitarō	kakaemasen deshitarō
			kakaeta deshō	kakaenakatta deshō
Conditional	**INFORMAL**		kakaetara	kakaenakattara
	FORMAL		kakaemashitara	kakaemasen deshitara
Alternative	**INFORMAL**		kakaetari	kakaenakattari
	FORMAL		kakaemashitari	kakaemasen deshitari

			INFORMAL AFFIRMATIVE INDICATIVE
Passive			kakaerareru
Potential			kakaerareru
Causative			kakaesaseru
Causative Pass.			kakaesaserareru
Honorific		I	okakae ni naru
		II	okakae nasaru
Humble		I	okakae suru
		II	okakae itasu

to raise (a flag), *to hold up*   TRANSITIVE

			AFFIRMATIVE	**NEGATIVE**
Indicative	**INFORMAL**		kakageru	kakagenai
	FORMAL		kakagemasu	kakagemasen
Imperative	**INFORMAL**	I	kakagero	kakageru na
		II	kakagenasai	kakagenasaru na
		III	kakagete kudasai	kakagenai de kudasai
	FORMAL		okakage nasaimase	okakage nasaimasu na
Presumptive	**INFORMAL**	I	kakageyō	kakagemai
		II	kakageru darō	kakagenai darō
	FORMAL	I	kakagemashō	kakagemasumai
		II	kakageru deshō	kakagenai deshō
Provisional	**INFORMAL**		kakagereba	kakagenakereba
	FORMAL		kakagemaseba	kakagemasen nara
			kakagemasureba	
Gerund	**INFORMAL**	I	kakagete	kakagenai de
		II		kakagenakute
	FORMAL		kakagemashite	kakagemasen de
Past Ind.	**INFORMAL**		kakageta	kakagenakatta
	FORMAL		kakagemashita	kakagemasen deshita
Past Presump.	**INFORMAL**		kakagetarō	kakagenakattarō
			kakageta darō	kakagenakatta darō
	FORMAL		kakagemashitarō	kakagemasen deshitarō
			kakageta deshō	kakagenakatta deshō
Conditional	**INFORMAL**		kakagetara	kakagenakattara
	FORMAL		kakagemashitara	kakagemasen deshitara
Alternative	**INFORMAL**		kakagetari	kakagenakattari
	FORMAL		kakagemashitari	kakagemasen deshitari

		INFORMAL AFFIRMATIVE INDICATIVE
Passive		kakagerareru
Potential		kakagerareru
Causative		kakagesaseru
Causative Pass.		kakagesaserareru
Honorific	I	okakage ni naru
	II	okakage nasaru
Humble	I	okakage suru
	II	okakage itasu

　　　　　　　　　　　かかる／懸かる／掛かる　**kakar.u**

to begin (work), *to be hanging* (from), *to require* (time, money, etc.)

			AFFIRMATIVE	NEGATIVE
Indicative	**INFORMAL**		kakaru	kakaranai
	FORMAL		kakarimasu	kakarimasen
Imperative	**INFORMAL**	I	kakare	kakaru na
		II	kakarinasai	kakarinasaru na
		III	kakatte kudasai	kakaranai de kudasai
	FORMAL		okakari nasaimase	okakari nasaimasu na
Presumptive	**INFORMAL**	I	kakarō	kakarumai
		II	kakaru darō	kakaranai darō
	FORMAL	I	kakarimashō	kakarimasumai
		II	kakaru deshō	kakaranai deshō
Provisional	**INFORMAL**		kakareba	kakaranakereba
	FORMAL		kakarimaseba	kakarimasen nara
			kakarirnasureba	
Gerund	**INFORMAL**	I	kakatte	kakaranai de
		II		kakaranakute
	FORMAL		kakarimashite	kakarimasen de
Past Ind.	**INFORMAL**		kakatta	kakaranakatta
	FORMAL		kakarimashita	kakarimasen deshita
Past Presump.	**INFORMAL**		kakattarō	kakaranakattarō
			kakatta darō	kakaranakatta darō
	FORMAL		kakarimashitarō	kakarimasen deshitarō
			kakatta deshō	kakaranakatta deshō
Conditional	**INFORMAL**		kakattara	kakaranakattara
	FORMAL		kakarimashitara	kakarimasen deshitara
Alternative	**INFORMAL**		kakattari	kakaranakattari
	FORMAL		kakarimashitari	kakarimasen deshitari

		INFORMAL AFFIRMATIVE INDICATIVE
Passive		kakarareru
Potential		kakareru
Causative		kakaraseru
Causative Pass.		kakaraserareru
Honorific	I	okakari ni naru
	II	okakari nasaru
Humble	I	okakari suru
	II	okakari itasu

197

to affect, to get involved in, to take part in

			AFFIRMATIVE	NEGATIVE
Indicative	**INFORMAL**		kakawaru	kakawaranai
	FORMAL		kakawarimasu	kakawarimasen
Imperative	**INFORMAL**	I	kakaware	kakawaru na
		II	kakawarinasai	kakawarinasaru na
		III	kakawatte kudasai	kakawaranai de kudasai
	FORMAL		okakawari nasaimase	okakawari nasaimasu na
Presumptive	**INFORMAL**	I	kakawarō	kakawarumai
		II	kakawaru darō	kakawaranai darō
	FORMAL	I	kakawarimashō	kakawarimasumai
		II	kakawaru deshō	kakawaranai deshō
Provisional	**INFORMAL**		kakawareba	kakawaranakereba
	FORMAL		kakawarimaseba	kakawarimasen nara
			kakawarimasureba	
Gerund	**INFORMAL**	I	kakawatte	kakawaranai de
		II		kakawaranakute
	FORMAL		kakawarimashite	kakawarimasen de
Past Ind.	**INFORMAL**		kakawatta	kakawaranakatta
	FORMAL		kakawarimashita	kakawarimasen deshita
Past Presump.	**INFORMAL**		kakawattarō	kakawaranakattarō
			kakawatta darō	kakawaranakatta darō
	FORMAL		kakawarimashitarō	kakawarimasen deshitarō
			kakawatta deshō	kakawaranakatta deshō
Conditional	**INFORMAL**		kakawattara	kakawaranakattara
	FORMAL		kakawarimashitara	kakawarimasen deshitara
Alternative	**INFORMAL**		kakawattari	kakawaranakattari
	FORMAL		kakawarimashitari	kakawarimasen deshitari

		INFORMAL AFFIRMATIVE INDICATIVE
Passive		kakawarareru
Potential		kakawareru
Causative		kakawaraseru
Causative Pass.		kakawaraserareru
Honorific	I	okakawari ni naru
	II	okakawari nasaru
Humble	I	okakawari suru
	II	okakawari itasu

kake

かける **kake.ru**

TRANSITIVE   *to hang, to sit, to telephone, to lock*

			AFFIRMATIVE	NEGATIVE
Indicative	**INFORMAL**		kakeru	kakenai
	FORMAL		kakemasu	kakemasen
Imperative	**INFORMAL**	I	kakero	kakeru na
		II	kakenasai	kakenasaru na
		III	kakete kudasai	kakenai de kudasai
	FORMAL		okake nasaimase	okake nasaimasu na
Presumptive	**INFORMAL**	I	kakeyō	kakemai
		II	kakeru darō	kakenai darō
	FORMAL	I	kakemashō	kakemasumai
		II	kakeru deshō	kakenai deshō
Provisional	**INFORMAL**		kakereba	kakenakereba
	FORMAL		kakemaseba	kakemasen nara
			kakemasureba	
Gerund	**INFORMAL**	I	kakete	kakenai de
		II		kakenakute
	FORMAL		kakemashite	kakemasen de
Past Ind.	**INFORMAL**		kaketa	kakenakatta
	FORMAL		kakemashita	kakemasen deshita
Past Presump.	**INFORMAL**		kaketarō	kakenakattarō
			kaketa darō	kakenakatta darō
	FORMAL		kakemashitarō	kakemasen deshitarō
			kaketa deshō	kakenakatta deshō
Conditional	**INFORMAL**		kaketara	kakenakattara
	FORMAL		kakemashitara	kakemasen deshitara
Alternative	**INFORMAL**		kaketari	kakenakattari
	FORMAL		kakemashitari	kakemasen deshitari

		INFORMAL AFFIRMATIVE INDICATIVE
Passive		kakerareru
Potential		kakerareru
Causative		kakesaseru
Causative Pass.		kakesaserareru
Honorific	I	okake ni naru
	II	okake nasaru
Humble	I	okake suru
	II	okake itasu

K

199

to wager, to risk　　TRANSITIVE

			AFFIRMATIVE	NEGATIVE
Indicative	**INFORMAL**		kakeru	kakenai
	FORMAL		kakemasu	kakemasen
Imperative	**INFORMAL**	I	kakero	kakeru na
		II	kakenasai	kakenasaru na
		III	kakete kudasai	kakenai de kudasai
	FORMAL		okake nasaimase	okake nasaimasu na
Presumptive	**INFORMAL**	I	kakeyō	kakemai
		II	kakeru darō	kakenai darō
	FORMAL	I	kakemashō	kakemasumai
		II	kakeru deshō	kakenai deshō
Provisional	**INFORMAL**		kakereba	kakenakereba
	FORMAL		kakemaseba	kakemasen nara
			kakemasureba	
Gerund	**INFORMAL**	I	kakete	kakenai de
		II		kakenakute
	FORMAL		kakemashite	kakemasen de
Past Ind.	**INFORMAL**		kaketa	kakenakatta
	FORMAL		kakemashita	kakemasen deshita
Past Presump.	**INFORMAL**		kaketarō	kakenakattarō
			kaketa darō	kakenakatta darō
	FORMAL		kakemashitarō	kakemasen deshitarō
			kaketa deshō	kakenakatta deshō
Conditional	**INFORMAL**		kaketara	kakenakattara
	FORMAL		kakemashitara	kakemasen deshitara
Alternative	**INFORMAL**		kaketari	kakenakattari
	FORMAL		kakemashitari	kakemasen deshitari

		INFORMAL AFFIRMATIVE INDICATIVE
Passive		kakerareru
Potential		kakerareru
Causative		kakesaseru
Causative Pass.		kakesaserareru
Honorific	I	okake ni naru
	II	okake nasaru
Humble	I	okake suru
	II	okake itasu

かこむ／囲む **kakom.u**

TRANSITIVE *to enclose, to surround*

			AFFIRMATIVE	NEGATIVE
Indicative	**INFORMAL**		kakomu	kakomanai
	FORMAL		kakomimasu	kakomimasen
Imperative	**INFORMAL**	I	kakome	kakomu na
		II	kakominasai	kakominasaru na
		III	kakonde kudasai	kakomanai de kudasai
	FORMAL		okakomi nasaimase	okakomi nasaimasu na
Presumptive	**INFORMAL**	I	kakomō	kakomumai
		II	kakomu darō	kakomanai darō
	FORMAL	I	kakomimashō	kakomimasumai
		II	kakomu deshō	kakomanai deshō
Provisional	**INFORMAL**		kakomeba	kakomanakereba
	FORMAL		kakomimaseba	kakomimasen nara
			kakomimasureba	
Gerund	**INFORMAL**	I	kakonde	kakomanai de
		II		kakomanakute
	FORMAL		kakomimashite	kakomimasen de
Past Ind.	**INFORMAL**		kakonda	kakomanakatta
	FORMAL		kakomimashita	kakomimasen deshita
Past Presump.	**INFORMAL**		kakondarō	kakomanakattarō
			kakonda darō	kakomanakatta darō
	FORMAL		kakomimashitarō	kakomimasen deshitarō
			kakonda deshō	kakomanakatta deshō
Conditional	**INFORMAL**		kakondara	kakomanakattara
	FORMAL		kakomimashitara	kakomimasen deshitara
Alternative	**INFORMAL**		kakondari	kakomanakattari
	FORMAL		kakomimashitari	kakomimasen deshitari

K

		INFORMAL AFFIRMATIVE INDICATIVE
Passive		kakomareru
Potential		kakomeru
Causative		kakomaseru
Causative Pass.		kakomaserareru
Honorific	I	okakomi ni naru
	II	okakomi nasaru
Humble	I	okakomi suru
	II	okakomi itasu

			AFFIRMATIVE	NEGATIVE
Indicative	**INFORMAL**		kaku	kakanai
	FORMAL		kakimasu	kakimasen
Imperative	**INFORMAL**	I	kake	kaku na
		II	kakinasai	kakinasaru na
		III	kaite kudasai	kakanai de kudasai
	FORMAL		okaki nasaimase	okaki nasaimasu na
Presumptive	**INFORMAL**	I	kakō	kakumai
		II	kaku darō	kakanai darō
	FORMAL	I	kakimashō	kakimasumai
		II	kaku deshō	kakanai deshō
Provisional	**INFORMAL**		kakeba	kakanakereba
	FORMAL		kakimaseba	kakimasen nara
			kakimasureba	
Gerund	**INFORMAL**	I	kaite	kakanai de
		II		kakanakute
	FORMAL		kakimashite	kakimasen de
Past Ind.	**INFORMAL**		kaita	kakanakatta
	FORMAL		kakimashita	kakimasen deshita
Past Presump.	**INFORMAL**		kaitarō	kakanakattarō
			kaita darō	kakanakatta darō
	FORMAL		kakimashitarō	kakimasen deshitarō
			kaita deshō	kakanakatta deshō
Conditional	**INFORMAL**		kaitara	kakanakattara
	FORMAL		kakimashitara	kakimasen deshitara
Alternative	**INFORMAL**		kaitari	kakanakattari
	FORMAL		kakimashitari	kakimasen deshitari

		INFORMAL AFFIRMATIVE INDICATIVE
Passive		kakareru
Potential		kakeru
Causative		kakaseru
Causative Pass.		kakaserareru
Honorific	I	okaki ni naru
	II	okaki nasaru
Humble	I	okaki suru
	II	okaki itasu

AN ESSENTIAL 55 VERB

202

Kaku 書く

to write

Sentences Using *Kaku*

Kanji, katakana, hiragana ga kakemasu ka.
漢字、カタカナ、ひらがなが書けますか。
Can you write kanji, katakana and hiragana?

Nihongo wa hanasemasu ga, kaitari yondari suru no wa muzukashii desu.
日本語は話せますが、書いたり読んだりするのは難しいです。
I can speak Japanese, but writing and reading are difficult.

Ano sakka wa hon o takusan kaite iru.
あの作家は本を沢山書いている。
That writer has written many books.

Orei jō o wasurezu ni kakinasai.
お礼状を忘れずに書きなさい。
Don't forget to write thank-you letters.

Konpyūta wa benri da keredo, kanji no kakikata o wasurete shimau.
コンピュータは便利だけれど、漢字の書き方を忘れてしまう。
Computers are convenient, but you tend to forget how to write kanji.

Kaku and its meaning are important in most languages. The Japanese especially take writing seriously. They think one's written characters show the writer's character. Writing characters beautifully is a form of art: the characters are praised and the writers are admired.

K

Words and Expressions Related to This Verb

kakitoru　書き取る
to write down, to take notes

kakikomu　書き込む
to write in, to fill in

kakiageru　書き上げる
to finish writing

tegaki　手書き
handwriting

yomikaki　読み書き
reading and writing

kaki jōzu　書き上手
a good writer (handwriting)

to lack, to chip   TRANSITIVE

			AFFIRMATIVE	**NEGATIVE**
Indicative	**INFORMAL**		kaku	kakanai
	FORMAL		kakimasu	kakimasen
Imperative	**INFORMAL**	I	kake	kaku na
		II	kakinasai	kakinasaru na
		III	kaite kudasai	kakanai de kudasai
	FORMAL		okaki nasaimase	okaki nasaimasu na
Presumptive	**INFORMAL**	I	kakō	kakumai
		II	kaku darō	kakanai darō
	FORMAL	I	kakimashō	kakimasumai
		II	kaku deshō	kakanai deshō
Provisional	**INFORMAL**		kakeba	kakanakereba
	FORMAL		kakimaseba	kakimasen nara
			kakimasureba	
Gerund	**INFORMAL**	I	kaite	kakanai de
		II		kakanakute
	FORMAL		kakimashite	kakimasen de
Past Ind.	**INFORMAL**		kaita	kakanakatta
	FORMAL		kakimashita	kakimasen deshita
Past Presump.	**INFORMAL**		kaitarō	kakanakattarō
			kaita darō	kakanakatta darō
	FORMAL		kakimashitarō	kakimasen deshitarō
			kaita deshō	kakanakatta deshō
Conditional	**INFORMAL**		kaitara	kakanakattara
	FORMAL		kakimashitara	kakimasen deshitara
Alternative	**INFORMAL**		kaitari	kakanakattari
	FORMAL		kakimashitari	kakimasen deshitari

			INFORMAL AFFIRMATIVE INDICATIVE
Passive			kakareru
Potential			kakeru
Causative			kakaseru
Causative Pass.			kakaserareru
Honorific		I	okaki ni naru
		II	okaki nasaru
Humble		I	okaki suru
		II	okaki itasu

かくれる／隠れる **kakure.ru**

to hide (oneself)

			AFFIRMATIVE	NEGATIVE
Indicative	**INFORMAL**		kakureru	kakurenai
	FORMAL		kakuremasu	kakuremasen
Imperative	**INFORMAL**	I	kakurero	kakureru na
		II	kakurenasai	kakurenasaru na
		III	kakurete kudasai	kakurenai de kudasai
	FORMAL		okakure nasaimase	okakure nasaimasu na
Presumptive	**INFORMAL**	I	kakureyō	kakuremai
		II	kakureru darō	kakurenai darō
	FORMAL	I	kakuremashō	kakuremasumai
		II	kakureru deshō	kakurenai deshō
Provisional	**INFORMAL**		kakurereba	kakurenakereba
	FORMAL		kakuremaseba	kakuremasen nara
			kakuremasureba	
Gerund	**INFORMAL**	I	kakurete	kakurenai de
		II		kakurenakute
	FORMAL		kakuremashite	kakuremasen de
Past Ind.	**INFORMAL**		kakureta	kakurenakatta
	FORMAL		kakuremashita	kakuremasen deshita
Past Presump.	**INFORMAL**		kakuretarō	kakurenakattarō
			kakureta darō	kakurenakatta darō
	FORMAL		kakuremashitarō	kakuremasen deshitarō
			kakureta deshō	kakurenakatta deshō
Conditional	**INFORMAL**		kakuretara	kakurenakattara
	FORMAL		kakuremashitara	kakuremasen deshitara
Alternative	**INFORMAL**		kakuretari	kakurenakattari
	FORMAL		kakuremashitari	kakuremasen deshitari

			INFORMAL AFFIRMATIVE INDICATIVE
Passive			kakurerareru
Potential			kakurerareru
Causative			kakuresaseru
Causative Pass.			kakuresaserareru
Honorific		I	okakure ni naru
		II	okakure nasaru
Humble		I	
		II	

K

to hide (something)   TRANSITIVE

			AFFIRMATIVE	NEGATIVE
Indicative	**INFORMAL**		kakusu	kakusanai
	FORMAL		kakushimasu	kakushimasen
Imperative	**INFORMAL**	I	kakuse	kakusu na
		II	kakushinasai	kakushinasaru na
		III	kakushite kudasai	kakusanai de kudasai
	FORMAL		okakushi nasaimase	okakushi nasaimasu na
Presumptive	**INFORMAL**	I	kakusō	kakusumai
		II	kakusu darō	kakusanai darō
	FORMAL	I	kakushimashō	kakushimasumai
		II	kakusu deshō	kakusanai deshō
Provisional	**INFORMAL**		kakuseba	kakusanakereba
	FORMAL		kakushimaseba	kakushimasen nara
			kakushimasureba	
Gerund	**INFORMAL**	I	kakushite	kakusanai de
		II		kakusanakute
	FORMAL		kakushimashite	kakushimasen de
Past Ind.	**INFORMAL**		kakushita	kakusanakatta
	FORMAL		kakushimashita	kakushimasen deshita
Past Presump.	**INFORMAL**		kakushitarō	kakusanakattarō
			kakushita darō	kakusanakatta darō
	FORMAL		kakushimashitarō	kakushimasen deshitarō
			kakushita deshō	kakusanakatta deshō
Conditional	**INFORMAL**		kakushitara	kakusanakattara
	FORMAL		kakushimashitara	kakushimasen deshitara
Alternative	**INFORMAL**		kakushitari	kakusanakattari
	FORMAL		kakushimashitari	kakushimasen deshitari

		INFORMAL AFFIRMATIVE INDICATIVE
Passive		kakusareru
Potential		kakuseru
Causative		kakusaseru
Causative Pass.		kakusaserareru
Honorific	I	okakushi ni naru
	II	okakushi nasaru
Humble	I	okakushi suru
	II	okakushi itasu

かまえる／構える   kamae.ru

TRANSITIVE   *to assume a defensive posture, to stand prepared*

			AFFIRMATIVE	NEGATIVE
Indicative	**INFORMAL**		kamaeru	kamaenai
	FORMAL		kamaemasu	kamaemasen
Imperative	**INFORMAL**	I	kamaero	kamaeru na
		II	kamaenasai	kamaenasaru na
		III	kamaete kudasai	kamaenai de kudasai
	FORMAL		okamae nasaimase	okamae nasaimasu na
Presumptive	**INFORMAL**	I	kamaeyō	kamaemai
		II	kamaeru darō	kamaenai darō
	FORMAL	I	kamaemashō	kamaemasumai
		II	kamaeru deshō	kamaenai deshō
Provisional	**INFORMAL**		kamaereba	kamaenakereba
	FORMAL		kamaemaseba	kamaemasen nara
			kamaemasureba	
Gerund	**INFORMAL**	I	kamaete	kamaenai de
		II		kamaenakute
	FORMAL		kamaemashite	kamaemasen de
Past Ind.	**INFORMAL**		kamaeta	kamaenakatta
	FORMAL		kamaemashita	kamaemasen deshita
Past Presump.	**INFORMAL**		kamaetarō	kamaenakattarō
			kamaeta darō	kamaenakatta darō
	FORMAL		kamaemashitarō	kamaemasen deshitarō
			kamaeta deshō	kamaenakatta deshō
Conditional	**INFORMAL**		kamaetara	kamaenakattara
	FORMAL		kamaemashitara	kamaemasen deshitara
Alternative	**INFORMAL**		kamaetari	kamaenakattari
	FORMAL		kamaemashitari	kamaemasen deshitari

		INFORMAL AFFIRMATIVE INDICATIVE
Passive		kamaerareru
Potential		kamaerareru
Causative		kamaesaseru
Causative Pass.		kamaesaserareru
Honorific	I	okamae ni naru
	II	okamae nasaru
Humble	I	
	II	

K

207

kama.u かまう／構う   kamai

to mind, to care about   TRANSITIVE

			AFFIRMATIVE	**NEGATIVE**
Indicative	**INFORMAL**		kamau	kamawanai
	FORMAL		kamaimasu	kamaimasen
Imperative	**INFORMAL**	I	kamae	kamau na
		II	kamainasai	kamainasaru na
		III	kamatte kudasai	kamawanai de kudasai
	FORMAL		okamai nasaimase	okamai nasaimasu na
Presumptive	**INFORMAL**	I	kamaō	kamaumai
		II	kamau darō	kamawanai darō
	FORMAL	I	kamaimashō	kamaimasumai
		II	kamau deshō	kamawanai deshō
Provisional	**INFORMAL**		kamaeba	kamawanakereba
	FORMAL		kamaimaseba	kamaimasen nara
			kamaimasureba	
Gerund	**INFORMAL**	I	kamatte	kamawanai de
		II		kamawanakute
	FORMAL		kamaimashite	kamaimasen de
Past Ind.	**INFORMAL**		kamatta	kamawanakatta
	FORMAL		kamaimashita	kamaimasen deshita
Past Presump.	**INFORMAL**		kamattarō	kamawanakattarō
			kamatta darō	kamawanakatta darō
	FORMAL		kamaimashitarō	kamaimasen deshitarō
			kamatta deshō	kamawanakatta deshō
Conditional	**INFORMAL**		kamattara	kamawanakattara
	FORMAL		kamaimashitara	kamaimasen deshitara
Alternative	**INFORMAL**		kamattari	kamawanakattari
	FORMAL		kamaimashitari	kamaimasen deshitari

			INFORMAL AFFIRMATIVE INDICATIVE
Passive			kamawareru
Potential			kamaeru
Causative			kamawaseru
Causative Pass.			kamawaserareru

Honorific		I	okamai ni naru
		II	okamai nasaru
Humble		I	okamai suru
		II	okamai itasu

TRANSITIVE   *to bite*

			AFFIRMATIVE	**NEGATIVE**
Indicative	**INFORMAL**		kamu	kamanai
	FORMAL		kamimasu	kamimasen
Imperative	**INFORMAL**	I	kame	kamu na
		II	kaminasai	kaminasaru na
		III	kande kudasai	kamanai de kudasai
	FORMAL		okami nasaimase	okami nasaimasu na
Presumptive	**INFORMAL**	I	kamō	kamumai
		II	kamu darō	kamanai darō
	FORMAL	I	kamimashō	kamimasumai
		II	kamu deshō	kamanai deshō
Provisional	**INFORMAL**		kameba	kamanakereba
	FORMAL		kamimaseba	kamimasen nara
			kamimasureba	
Gerund	**INFORMAL**	I	kande	kamanai de
		II		kamanakute
	FORMAL		kamimashite	kamimasen de
Past Ind.	**INFORMAL**		kanda	kamanakatta
	FORMAL		kamimashita	kamimasen deshita
Past Presump.	**INFORMAL**		kandarō	kamanakattarō
			kanda darō	kamanakatta darō
	FORMAL		kamimashitarō	kamimasen deshitarō
			kanda deshō	kamanakatta deshō
Conditional	**INFORMAL**		kandara	kamanakattara
	FORMAL		kamimashitara	kamimasen deshitara
Alternative	**INFORMAL**		kandari	kamanakattari
	FORMAL		kamimashitari	kamimasen deshitari

			INFORMAL AFFIRMATIVE INDICATIVE
Passive			kamareru
Potential			kameru
Causative			kamaseru
Causative Pass.			kamaserareru
Honorific		I	okami ni naru
		II	okami nasaru
Humble		I	okami suru
		II	okami itasu

K

to grant a request, to answer one's prayers   TRANSITIVE

			AFFIRMATIVE	**NEGATIVE**
Indicative	**INFORMAL**		kanaeru	kanaenai
	FORMAL		kanaemasu	kanaemasen
Imperative	**INFORMAL**	I	kanaero	kanaeru na
		II	kanaenasai	kanaenasaru na
		III	kanaete kudasai	kanaenai de kudasai
	FORMAL		okanae nasaimase	okanae nasaimasu na
Presumptive	**INFORMAL**	I	kanaeyō	kanaemai
		II	kanaeru darō	kanaenai darō
	FORMAL	I	kanaemashō	kanaemasumai
		II	kanaeru deshō	kanaenai deshō
Provisional	**INFORMAL**		kanaereba	kanaenakereba
	FORMAL		kanaemaseba	kanaemasen nara
			kanaemasureba	
Gerund	**INFORMAL**	I	kanaete	kanaenai de
		II		kanaenakute
	FORMAL		kanaemashite	kanaemasen de
Past Ind.	**INFORMAL**		kanaeta	kanaenakatta
	FORMAL		kanaemashita	kanaemasen deshita
Past Presump.	**INFORMAL**		kanaetarō	kanaenakattarō
			kanaeta darō	kanaenakatta darō
	FORMAL		kanaemashitarō	kanaemasen deshitarō
			kanaeta deshō	kanaenakatta deshō
Conditional	**INFORMAL**		kanaetara	kanaenakattara
	FORMAL		kanaemashitara	kanaemasen deshitara
Alternative	**INFORMAL**		kanaetari	kanaenakattari
	FORMAL		kanaemashitari	kanaemasen deshitari

		INFORMAL AFFIRMATIVE INDICATIVE
Passive		kanaerareru
Potential		kanaerareru
Causative		kanaesaseru
Causative Pass.		kanaesaserareru
Honorific	I	okanae ni naru
	II	okanae nasaru
Humble	I	okanae suru
	II	okanae itasu

210

かなしむ／悲しむ **kanashim.u**

TRANSITIVE *to be sad, to grieve*

			AFFIRMATIVE	NEGATIVE
Indicative	**INFORMAL**		kanashimu	kanashimanai
	FORMAL		kanashimimasu	kanashimimasen
Imperative	**INFORMAL**	I	kanashime	kanashimu na
		II	kanashiminasai	kanashiminasaru na
		III	kanashinde kudasai	kanashimanai de kudasai
	FORMAL		okanashimi nasaimase	okanashimi nasaimasu na
Presumptive	**INFORMAL**	I	kanashimō	kanashimumai
		II	kanashimu darō	kanashimanai darō
	FORMAL	I	kanashimimashō	kanashimimasumai
		II	kanashimu deshō	kanashimanai deshō
Provisional	**INFORMAL**		kanashimeba	kanashimanakereba
	FORMAL		kanashimimaseba	kanashimimasen nara
			kanashimimasureba	
Gerund	**INFORMAL**	I	kanashinde	kanashimanai de
		II		kanashimanakute
	FORMAL		kanashimimashite	kanashimimasen de
Past Ind.	**INFORMAL**		kanashinda	kanashimanakatta
	FORMAL		kanashimimashita	kanashimimasen deshita
Past Presump.	**INFORMAL**		kanashindarō	kanashimanakattarō
			kanashinda darō	kanashimanakatta darō
	FORMAL		kanashimimashitarō	kanashimimasen deshitarō
			kanashinda deshō	kanashimanakatta deshō
Conditional	**INFORMAL**		kanashindara	kanashimanakattara
	FORMAL		kanashimimashitara	kanashimimasen deshitara
Alternative	**INFORMAL**		kanashindari	kanashimanakattari
	FORMAL		kanashimimashitari	kanashimimasen deshitari

		INFORMAL AFFIRMATIVE INDICATIVE
Passive		kanashimareru
Potential		kanashimeru
Causative		kanashimaseru
Causative Pass.		kanashimaserareru
Honorific	I	okanashimi ni naru
	II	okanashimi nasaru
Humble	I	okanashimi suru
	II	okanashimi itasu

211

to suit, to conform to

			AFFIRMATIVE	**NEGATIVE**
Indicative	**INFORMAL**		kanau	kanawanai
	FORMAL		kanaimasu	kanaimasen
Imperative	**INFORMAL**	I		
		II		
		III		
	FORMAL			
Presumptive	**INFORMAL**	I	kanaō	kanaumai
		II	kanau darō	kanawanai darō
	FORMAL	I	kanaimashō	kanaimasumai
		II	kanau deshō	kanawanai deshō
Provisional	**INFORMAL**		kanaeba	kanawanakereba
	FORMAL		kanaimaseba	kanaimasen nara
			kanaimasureba	
Gerund	**INFORMAL**	I	kanatte	kanawanai de
		II		kanawanakute
	FORMAL		kanaimashite	kanaimasen de
Past Ind.	**INFORMAL**		kanatta	kanawanakatta
	FORMAL		kanaimashita	kanaimasen deshita
Past Presump.	**INFORMAL**		kanattarō	kanawanakattarō
			kanatta darō	kanawanakatta darō
	FORMAL		kanaimashitarō	kanaimasen deshitarō
			kanatta deshō	kanawanakatta deshō
Conditional	**INFORMAL**		kanattara	kanawanakattara
	FORMAL		kanaimashitara	kanaimasen deshitara
Alternative	**INFORMAL**		kanattari	kanawanakattari
	FORMAL		kanaimashitari	kanaimasen deshitari

		INFORMAL AFFIRMATIVE INDICATIVE
Passive		kanawareru
Potential		kanaeru
Causative		kanawaseru
Causative Pass.		kanawaserareru
Honorific	I	
	II	
Humble	I	
	II	

kangae

かんがえる／考える **kangae.ru**

TRANSITIVE *to consider, to think about, to think of*

			AFFIRMATIVE	**NEGATIVE**
Indicative	**INFORMAL**		kangaeru	kangaenai
	FORMAL		kangaemasu	kangaemasen
Imperative	**INFORMAL**	I	kangaero	kangaeru na
		II	kangaenasai	kangaenasaru na
		III	kangaete kudasai	kangaenai de kudasai
	FORMAL		okangae nasaimase	okangae nasaimasu na
Presumptive	**INFORMAL**	I	kangaeyō	kangaemai
		II	kangaeru darō	kangaenai darō
	FORMAL	I	kangaemashō	kangaemasumai
		II	kangaeru deshō	kangaenai deshō
Provisional	**INFORMAL**		kangaereba	kangaenakereba
	FORMAL		kangaemaseba	kangaemasen nara
			kangaemasureba	
Gerund	**INFORMAL**	I	kangaete	kangaenai de
		II		kangaenakute
	FORMAL		kangaemashite	kangaemasen de
Past Ind.	**INFORMAL**		kangaeta	kangaenakatta
	FORMAL		kangaemashita	kangaemasen deshita
Past Presump.	**INFORMAL**		kangaetarō	kangaenakattarō
			kangaeta darō	kangaenakatta darō
	FORMAL		kangaemashitarō	kangaemasen deshitarō
			kangaeta deshō	kangaenakatta deshō
Conditional	**INFORMAL**		kangaetara	kangaenakattara
	FORMAL		kangaemashitara	kangaemasen deshitara
Alternative	**INFORMAL**		kangaetari	kangaenakattari
	FORMAL		kangaemashitari	kangaemasen deshitari

			INFORMAL AFFIRMATIVE INDICATIVE
Passive			kangaerareru
Potential			kangaerareru
Causative			kangaesaseru
Causative Pass.			kangaesaserareru
Honorific		I	okangae ni naru
		II	okangae nasaru
Humble		I	
		II	

K

213

to feel, to sense　　TRANSITIVE

			AFFIRMATIVE	NEGATIVE
Indicative	INFORMAL		kanjiru	kanjinai
	FORMAL		kanjimasu	kanjimasen
Imperative	INFORMAL	I	kanjiro	kanjiru na
		II	kanjinasai	kanjinasaru na
		III	kanjite kudasai	kanjinai de kudasai
	FORMAL		okanji nasaimase	okanji nasaimasu na
Presumptive	INFORMAL	I	kanjiyō	kanjimai
		II	kanjiru darō	kanjinai darō
	FORMAL	I	kanjimashō	kanjimasumai
		II	kanjiru deshō	kanjinai deshō
Provisional	INFORMAL		kanjireba	kanjinakereba
	FORMAL		kanjimaseba	kanjimasen nara
			kanjimasureba	
Gerund	INFORMAL	I	kanjite	kanjinai de
		II		kanjinakute
	FORMAL		kanjimashite	kanjimasen de
Past Ind.	INFORMAL		kanjita	kanjinakatta
	FORMAL		kanjimashita	kanjimasen deshita
Past Presump.	INFORMAL		kanjitarō	kanjinakattarō
			kanjita darō	kanjinakatta darō
	FORMAL		kanjimashitarō	kanjimasen deshitarō
			kanjita deshō	kanjinakatta deshō
Conditional	INFORMAL		kanjitara	kanjinakattara
	FORMAL		kanjimashitara	kanjimasen deshitara
Alternative	INFORMAL		kanjitari	kanjinakattari
	FORMAL		kanjimashitari	kanjimasen deshitari

		INFORMAL AFFIRMATIVE INDICATIVE
Passive		kanjirareru
Potential		kanjirareru
Causative		kanjisaseru
Causative Pass.		kanjisaserareru
Honorific	I	okanji ni naru
	II	okanji nasaru
Humble	I	
	II	

からかう **karaka.u**

TRANSITIVE *to tease, to play jokes on*

			AFFIRMATIVE	NEGATIVE
Indicative	**INFORMAL**		karakau	karakawanai
	FORMAL		karakaimasu	karakaimasen
Imperative	**INFORMAL**	I	karakae	karakau na
		II	karakainasai	karakainasaru na
		III	karakatte kudasai	karakawanai de kudasai
	FORMAL		okarakai nasaimase	okarakai nasaimasu na
Presumptive	**INFORMAL**	I	karakaō	karakaumai
		II	karakau darō	karakawanai darō
	FORMAL	I	karakaimashō	karakaimasumai
		II	karakau deshō	karakawanai deshō
Provisional	**INFORMAL**		karakaeba	karakawanakereba
	FORMAL		karakaimaseba	karakaimasen nara
			karakaimasureba	
Gerund	**INFORMAL**	I	karakatte	karakawanai de
		II		karakawanakute
	FORMAL		karakaimashite	karakaimasen de
Past Ind.	**INFORMAL**		karakatta	karakawanakatta
	FORMAL		karakaimashita	karakaimasen deshita
Past Presump.	**INFORMAL**		karakattarō	karakawanakattarō
			karakatta darō	karakawanakatta darō
	FORMAL		karakaimashitarō	karakaimasen deshitarō
			karakatta deshō	karakawanakatta deshō
Conditional	**INFORMAL**		karakattara	karakawanakattara
	FORMAL		karakaimashitara	karakaimasen deshitara
Alternative	**INFORMAL**		karakattari	karakawanakattari
	FORMAL		karakaimashitari	karakaimasen deshitari

			INFORMAL AFFIRMATIVE INDICATIVE
Passive			karakawareru
Potential			karakaeru
Causative			karakawaseru
Causative Pass.			karakawaserareru
Honorific		I	okarakai ni naru
		II	okarakai nasaru
Humble		I	okarakai suru
		II	okarakai itasu

kare.ru かれる／枯れる

to wither, to die (a plant)

			AFFIRMATIVE	NEGATIVE
Indicative	**INFORMAL**		kareru	karenai
	FORMAL		karemasu	karemasen
Imperative	**INFORMAL**	I	karero	kareru na
		II		
		III		
	FORMAL			
Presumptive	**INFORMAL**	I	kareyō	karemai
		II	kareru darō	karenai darō
	FORMAL	I	karemashō	karemasumai
		II	kareru deshō	karenai deshō
Provisional	**INFORMAL**		karereba	karenakereba
	FORMAL		karemaseba	karemasen nara
			karemasureba	
Gerund	**INFORMAL**	I	karete	karenai de
		II		karenakute
	FORMAL		karemashite	karemasen de
Past Ind.	**INFORMAL**		kareta	karenakatta
	FORMAL		karemashita	karemasen deshita
Past Presump.	**INFORMAL**		karetarō	karenakattarō
			kareta darō	karenakatta darō
	FORMAL		karemashitarō	karemasen deshitarō
			kareta deshō	karenakatta deshō
Conditional	**INFORMAL**		karetara	karenakattara
	FORMAL		karemashitara	karemasen deshitara
Alternative	**INFORMAL**		karetari	karenakattari
	FORMAL		karemashitari	karemasen deshitari

		INFORMAL AFFIRMATIVE INDICATIVE
Passive		karerareru
Potential		karerareru
Causative		karesaseru
Causative Pass.		karesaserareru
Honorific	I	
	II	
Humble	I	
	II	

kari

			AFFIRMATIVE	NEGATIVE
Indicative	**INFORMAL**		kariru	karinai
	FORMAL		karimasu	karimasen
Imperative	**INFORMAL**	I	kariro	kariru na
		II	karinasai	karinasaru na
		III	karite kudasai	karinai de kudasai
	FORMAL		okari nasaimase	okari nasaimasu na
Presumptive	**INFORMAL**	I	kariyō	karimai
		II	kariru darō	karinai darō
	FORMAL	I	karimashō	karimasumai
		II	kariru deshō	karinai deshō
Provisional	**INFORMAL**		karireba	karinakereba
	FORMAL		karimaseba	karimasen nara
			karimasureba	
Gerund	**INFORMAL**	I	karite	karinai de
		II		karinakute
	FORMAL		karimashite	karimasen de
Past Ind.	**INFORMAL**		karita	karinakatta
	FORMAL		karimashita	karimasen deshita
Past Presump.	**INFORMAL**		karitarō	karinakattarō
			karita darō	karinakatta darō
	FORMAL		karimashitarō	karimasen deshitarō
			karita deshō	karinakatta deshō
Conditional	**INFORMAL**		karitara	karinakattara
	FORMAL		karimashitara	karimasen deshitara
Alternative	**INFORMAL**		karitari	karinakattari
	FORMAL		karimashitari	karimasen deshitari

		INFORMAL AFFIRMATIVE INDICATIVE
Passive		karirareru
Potential		karirareru
Causative		karisaseru
Causative Pass.		karisaserareru
Honorific	I	okari ni naru
	II	okari nasaru
Humble	I	okari suru
	II	okari itasu

K

kasanar.u　かさなる／重なる　　　　　　　　　　　　**kasanari**
to be piled up, to overlap

			AFFIRMATIVE	NEGATIVE
Indicative	**INFORMAL**		kasanaru	kasanaranai
	FORMAL		kasanarimasu	kasanarimasen
Imperative	**INFORMAL**	I	kasanare	kasanaru na
		II	kasanarinasai	kasanarinasaru na
		III	kasanatte kudasai	kasanaranai de kudasai
	FORMAL		okasanari nasaimase	okasanari nasaimasu na
Presumptive	**INFORMAL**	I	kasanarō	kasanarumai
		II	kasanaru darō	kasanaranai darō
	FORMAL	I	kasanarimashō	kasanarimasumai
		II	kasanaru deshō	kasanaranai deshō
Provisional	**INFORMAL**		kasanareba	kasanaranakereba
	FORMAL		kasanarimaseba	kasanarimasen nara
			kasanarimasureba	
Gerund	**INFORMAL**	I	kasanatte	kasanaranai de
		II		kasanaranakute
	FORMAL		kasanarimashite	kasanarimasen de
Past Ind.	**INFORMAL**		kasanatta	kasanaranakatta
	FORMAL		kasanarimashita	kasanarimasen deshita
Past Presump.	**INFORMAL**		kasanattarō	kasanaranakattarō
			kasanatta darō	kasanaranakatta darō
	FORMAL		kasanarimashitarō	kasanarimasen deshitarō
			kasanatta deshō	kasanaranakatta deshō
Conditional	**INFORMAL**		kasanattara	kasanaranakattara
	FORMAL		kasanarimashitara	kasanarimasen deshitara
Alternative	**INFORMAL**		kasanattari	kasanaranakattari
	FORMAL		kasanarimashitari	kasanarimasen deshitari

		INFORMAL AFFIRMATIVE INDICATIVE
Passive		kasanarareru
Potential		kasanareru
Causative		kasanaraseru
Causative Pass.		kasanaraserareru
Honorific	I	okasanari ni naru
	II	okasanari nasaru
Humble	I	
	II	

かさねる／重ねる　**kasane.ru**

TRANSITIVE　　*to pile up, to repeat*

			AFFIRMATIVE	NEGATIVE
Indicative	**INFORMAL**		kasaneru	kasanenai
	FORMAL		kasanemasu	kasanemasen
Imperative	**INFORMAL**	I	kasanero	kasaneru na
		II	kasanenasai	kasanenasaru na
		III	kasanete kudasai	kasanenai de kudasai
	FORMAL		okasane nasaimase	okasane nasaimasu na
Presumptive	**INFORMAL**	I	kasaneyō	kasanemai
		II	kasaneru darō	kasanenai darō
	FORMAL	I	kasanemashō	kasanemasumai
		II	kasaneru deshō	kasanenai deshō
Provisional	**INFORMAL**		kasanereba	kasanenakereba
	FORMAL		kasanemaseba	kasanemasen nara
			kasanemasureba	
Gerund	**INFORMAL**	I	kasanete	kasanenai de
		II		kasanenakute
	FORMAL		kasanemashite	kasanemasen de
Past Ind.	**INFORMAL**		kasaneta	kasanenakatta
	FORMAL		kasanemashita	kasanemasen deshita
Past Presump.	**INFORMAL**		kasanetarō	kasanenakattarō
			kasaneta darō	kasanenakatta darō
	FORMAL		kasanemashitarō	kasanemasen deshitarō
			kasaneta deshō	kasanenakatta deshō
Conditional	**INFORMAL**		kasanetara	kasanenakattara
	FORMAL		kasanemashitara	kasanemasen deshitara
Alternative	**INFORMAL**		kasanetari	kasanenakattari
	FORMAL		kasanemashitari	kasanemasen deshitari

K

		INFORMAL AFFIRMATIVE INDICATIVE
Passive		kasanerareru
Potential		kasanerareru
Causative		kasanesaseru
Causative Pass.		kasanesaserareru
Honorific	I	okasane ni naru
	II	okasane nasaru
Humble	I	okasane suru
	II	okasane itasu

kaseg.u　かせぐ／稼ぐ

to earn one's living, to make money　　TRANSITIVE

kasegi

			AFFIRMATIVE	NEGATIVE
Indicative	INFORMAL		kasegu	kaseganai
	FORMAL		kasegimasu	kasegimasen
Imperative	INFORMAL	I	kasege	kasegu na
		II	kaseginasai	kaseginasaru na
		III	kaseide kudasai	kaseganai de kudasai
	FORMAL		okasegi nasaimase	okasegi nasaimasu na
Presumptive	INFORMAL	I	kasegō	kasegumai
		II	kasegu darō	kaseganai darō
	FORMAL	I	kasegimashō	kasegimasumai
		II	kasegu deshō	kaseganai deshō
Provisional	INFORMAL		kasegeba	kaseganakereba
	FORMAL		kasegimaseba	kasegimasen nara
			kasegimasureba	
Gerund	INFORMAL	I	kaseide	kaseganai de
		II		kaseganakute
	FORMAL		kasegimashite	kasegimasen de
Past Ind.	INFORMAL		kaseida	kaseganakatta
	FORMAL		kasegimashita	kasegimasen deshita
Past Presump.	INFORMAL		kaseidarō	kaseganakattarō
			kaseida darō	kaseganakatta darō
	FORMAL		kasegimashitarō	kasegimasen deshitarō
			kaseida deshō	kaseganakatta deshō
Conditional	INFORMAL		kaseidara	kaseganakattara
	FORMAL		kasegimashitara	kasegimasen deshitara
Alternative	INFORMAL		kaseidari	kaseganakattari
	FORMAL		kasegimashitari	kasegimasen deshitari

		INFORMAL AFFIRMATIVE INDICATIVE
Passive		kasegareru
Potential		kasegeru
Causative		kasegaseru
Causative Pass.		kasegaserareru
Honorific	I	okasegi ni naru
	II	okasegi nasaru
Humble	I	okasegi suru
	II	okasegi itasu

220

かす／貸す **kas.u**

TRANSITIVE *to lend, to rent (to)*

			AFFIRMATIVE	NEGATIVE
Indicative	**INFORMAL**		kasu	kasanai
	FORMAL		kashimasu	kashimasen
Imperative	**INFORMAL**	I	kase	kasu na
		II	kashinasai	kashinasaru na
		III	kashite kudasai	kasanai de kudasai
	FORMAL		okashi nasaimase	okashi nasaimasu na
Presumptive	**INFORMAL**	I	kasō	kasumai
		II	kasu darō	kasanai darō
	FORMAL	I	kashimashō	kashimasumai
		II	kasu deshō	kasanai deshō
Provisional	**INFORMAL**		kaseba	kasanakereba
	FORMAL		kashimaseba	kashimasen nara
			kashimasureba	
Gerund	**INFORMAL**	I	kashite	kasanai de
		II		kasanakute
	FORMAL		kashimashite	kashimasen de
Past Ind.	**INFORMAL**		kashita	kasanakatta
	FORMAL		kashimashita	kashimasen deshita
Past Presump.	**INFORMAL**		kashitarō	kasanakattarō
			kashita darō	kasanakatta darō
	FORMAL		kashimashitarō	kashimasen deshitarō
			kashita deshō	kasanakatta deshō
Conditional	**INFORMAL**		kashitara	kasanakattara
	FORMAL		kashimashitara	kashimasen deshitara
Alternative	**INFORMAL**		kashitari	kasanakattari
	FORMAL		kashimashitari	kashimasen deshitari

K

			INFORMAL AFFIRMATIVE INDICATIVE
Passive			kasareru
Potential			kaseru
Causative			kasaseru
Causative Pass.			kasaserareru
Honorific		I	okashi ni naru
		II	okashi nasaru
Humble		I	okashi suru
		II	okashi itasu

to be hazy, to become blurred

			AFFIRMATIVE	NEGATIVE
Indicative	**INFORMAL**		kasumu	kasumanai
	FORMAL		kasumimasu	kasumimasen
Imperative	**INFORMAL**	I	kasume	kasumu na
		II	kasuminasai	kasuminasaru na
		III	kasunde kudasai	kasumanai de kudasai
	FORMAL		okasumi nasaimase	okasumi nasaimasu na
Presumptive	**INFORMAL**	I	kasumō	kasumumai
		II	kasumu darō	kasumanai darō
	FORMAL	I	kasumimashō	kasumimasumai
		II	kasumu deshō	kasumanai deshō
Provisional	**INFORMAL**		kasumeba	kasumanakereba
	FORMAL		kasumimaseba	kasumimasen nara
			kasumimasureba	
Gerund	**INFORMAL**	I	kasunde	kasumanai de
		II		kasumanakute
	FORMAL		kasumimashite	kasumimasen de
Past Ind.	**INFORMAL**		kasunda	kasumanakatta
	FORMAL		kasumimashita	kasumimasen deshita
Past Presump.	**INFORMAL**		kasundarō	kasumanakattarō
			kasunda darō	kasumanakatta darō
	FORMAL		kasumimashitarō	kasumimasen deshitarō
			kasunda deshō	kasumanakatta deshō
Conditional	**INFORMAL**		kasundara	kasumanakattara
	FORMAL		kasumimashitara	kasumimasen deshitara
Alternative	**INFORMAL**		kasundari	kasumanakattari
	FORMAL		kasumimashitari	kasumimasen deshitari

		INFORMAL AFFIRMATIVE INDICATIVE
Passive		kasumareru
Potential		kasumeru
Causative		kasumaseru
Causative Pass.		kasumaserareru
Honorific	I	
	II	
Humble	I	
	II	

katamari

to become hard, to bunch up, to take shape

			AFFIRMATIVE	NEGATIVE
Indicative	INFORMAL		katamaru	katamaranai
	FORMAL		katamarimasu	katamarimasen
Imperative	INFORMAL	I	katamare	katamaru na
		II	katamarinasai	katamarinasaru na
		III	katamatte kudasai	katamaranai de kudasai
	FORMAL		okatamari nasaimase	okatamari nasaimasu na
Presumptive	INFORMAL	I	katamarō	katamarumai
		II	katamaru darō	katamaranai darō
	FORMAL	I	katamarimashō	katamarimasumai
		II	katamaru deshō	katamaranai deshō
Provisional	INFORMAL		katamareba	katamaranakereba
	FORMAL		katamarimaseba	katamarimasen nara
			katamarimasureba	
Gerund	INFORMAL	I	katamatte	katamaranai de
		II		katamaranakute
	FORMAL		katamarimashite	katamarimasen de
Past Ind.	INFORMAL		katamatta	katamaranakatta
	FORMAL		katamarimashita	katamarimasen deshita
Past Presump.	INFORMAL		katamattarō	katamaranakattarō
			katamatta darō	katamaranakatta darō
	FORMAL		katamarimashitarō	katamarimasen deshitarō
			katamatta deshō	katamaranakatta deshō
Conditional	INFORMAL		katamattara	katamaranakattara
	FORMAL		katamarimashitara	katamarimasen deshitara
Alternative	INFORMAL		katamattari	katamaranakattari
	FORMAL		katamarimashitari	katamarimasen deshitari

		INFORMAL AFFIRMATIVE INDICATIVE
Passive		katamarareru
Potential		katamareru
Causative		katamaraseru
Causative Pass.		katamaraserareru
Honorific	I	okatamari ni naru
	II	okatamari nasaru
Humble	I	
	II	

to harden, to strengthen　　　TRANSITIVE

			AFFIRMATIVE	NEGATIVE
Indicative	**INFORMAL**		katameru	katamenai
	FORMAL		katamemasu	katamemasen
Imperative	**INFORMAL**	I	katamero	katameru na
		II	katamenasai	katamenasaru na
		III	katamete kudasai	katamenai de kudasai
	FORMAL		okatame nasaimase	okatame nasaimasu na
Presumptive	**INFORMAL**	I	katameyō	katamemai
		II	katameru darō	katamenai darō
	FORMAL	I	katamemashō	katamemasumai
		II	katameru deshō	katamenai deshō
Provisional	**INFORMAL**		katamereba	katamenakereba
	FORMAL		katamemaseba	katamemasen nara
			katamemasureba	
Gerund	**INFORMAL**	I	katamete	katamenai de
		II		katamenakute
	FORMAL		katamemashite	katamemasen de
Past Ind.	**INFORMAL**		katameta	katamenakatta
	FORMAL		katamemashita	katamemasen deshita
Past Presump.	**INFORMAL**		katametarō	katamenakattarō
			katameta darō	katamenakatta darō
	FORMAL		katamemashitarō	katamemasen deshitarō
			katameta deshō	katamenakatta deshō
Conditional	**INFORMAL**		katametara	katamenakattara
	FORMAL		katamemashitara	katamemasen deshitara
Alternative	**INFORMAL**		katametari	katamenakattari
	FORMAL		katamemashitari	katamemasen deshitari

		INFORMAL AFFIRMATIVE INDICATIVE
Passive		katamerareru
Potential		katamerareru
Causative		katamesaseru
Causative Pass.		katamesaserareru
Honorific	I	okatame ni naru
	II	okatame nasaru
Humble	I	okatame suru
	II	okatame itasu

かたむく／傾く　**katamuk.u**

to lean (toward), *to tilt*

			AFFIRMATIVE	NEGATIVE
Indicative	**INFORMAL**		katamuku	katamukanai
	FORMAL		katamukimasu	katamukimasen
Imperative	**INFORMAL**	I	katamuke	katamuku na
		II	katamukinasai	katamukinasaru na
		III	katamuite kudasai	katamukanai de kudasai
	FORMAL		okatamuki nasaimase	okatamuki nasaimasu na
Presumptive	**INFORMAL**	I	katamukō	katamukumai
		II	katamuku darō	katamukanai darō
	FORMAL	I	katamukimashō	katamukimasumai
		II	katamuku deshō	katamukanai deshō
Provisional	**INFORMAL**		katamukeba	katamukanakereba
	FORMAL		katamukimaseba	katamukimasen nara
			katamukimasureba	
Gerund	**INFORMAL**	I	katamuite	katamukanai de
		II		katamukanakute
	FORMAL		katamukimashite	katamukimasen de
Past Ind.	**INFORMAL**		katamuita	katamukanakatta
	FORMAL		katamukimashita	katamukimasen deshita
Past Presump.	**INFORMAL**		katamuitarō	katamukanakattarō
			katamuita darō	katamukanakatta darō
	FORMAL		katamukimashitarō	katamukimasen deshitarō
			katamuita deshō	katamukanakatta deshō
Conditional	**INFORMAL**		katamuitara	katamukanakattara
	FORMAL		katamukimashitara	katamukimasen deshitara
Alternative	**INFORMAL**		katamuitari	katamukanakattari
	FORMAL		katamukimashitari	katamukimasen deshitari

		INFORMAL AFFIRMATIVE INDICATIVE
Passive		katamukareru
Potential		katamukeru
Causative		katamukaseru
Causative Pass.		katamukaserareru
Honorific	I	okatamuki ni naru
	II	okatamuki nasaru
Humble	I	
	II	

K

to straighten up things, to finish   TRANSITIVE

			AFFIRMATIVE	**NEGATIVE**
Indicative	**INFORMAL**		katazukeru	katazukenai
	FORMAL		katazukemasu	katazukemasen
Imperative	**INFORMAL**	**I**	katazukero	katazukeru na
		II	katazukenasai	katazukenasaru na
		III	katazukete kudasai	katazukenai de kudasai
	FORMAL		okatazuke nasaimase	okatazuke nasaimasu na
Presumptive	**INFORMAL**	**I**	katazukeyō	katazukemai
		II	katazukeru darō	katazukenai darō
	FORMAL	**I**	katazukemashō	katazukemasumai
		II	katazukeru deshō	katazukenai deshō
Provisional	**INFORMAL**		katazukereba	katazukenakereba
	FORMAL		katazukemaseba	katazukemasen nara
			katazukemasureba	
Gerund	**INFORMAL**	**I**	katazukete	katazukenai de
		II		katazukenakute
	FORMAL		katazukemashite	katazukemasen de
Past Ind.	**INFORMAL**		katazuketa	katazukenakatta
	FORMAL		katazukemashita	katazukemasen deshita
Past Presump.	**INFORMAL**		katazuketarō	katazukenakattarō
			katazuketa darō	katazukenakatta darō
	FORMAL		katazukemashitarō	katazukemasen deshitarō
			katazuketa deshō	katazukenakatta deshō
Conditional	**INFORMAL**		katazuketara	katazukenakattara
	FORMAL		katazukemashitara	katazukemasen deshitara
Alternative	**INFORMAL**		katazuketari	katazukenakattari
	FORMAL		katazukemashitari	katazukemasen deshitari

		INFORMAL AFFIRMATIVE INDICATIVE
Passive		katazukerareru
Potential		katazukerareru
Causative		katazukesaseru
Causative Pass.		katazukesaserareru
Honorific	**I**	okatazuke ni naru
	II	okatazuke nasaru
Humble	**I**	okatazuke suru
	II	okatazuke itasu

to win

			AFFIRMATIVE	NEGATIVE
Indicative	**INFORMAL**		katsu	katanai
	FORMAL		kachimasu	kachimasen
Imperative	**INFORMAL**	I	kate	katsu na
		II	kachinasai	kachinasaru na
		III	katte kudasai	katanai de kudasai
	FORMAL		okachi nasaimase	okachi nasaimasu na
Presumptive	**INFORMAL**	I	katō	katsumai
		II	katsu darō	katanai darō
	FORMAL	I	kachimashō	kachimasumai
		II	katsu deshō	katanai deshō
Provisional	**INFORMAL**		kateba	katanakereba
	FORMAL		kachimaseba	kachimasen nara
			kachimasureba	
Gerund	**INFORMAL**	I	katte	katanai de
		II		katanakute
	FORMAL		kachimashite	kachimasen de
Past Ind.	**INFORMAL**		katta	katanakatta
	FORMAL		kachimashita	kachimasen deshita
Past Presump.	**INFORMAL**		kattarō	katanakattarō
			katta darō	katanakatta darō
	FORMAL		kachimashitarō	kachimasen deshitarō
			katta deshō	katanakatta deshō
Conditional	**INFORMAL**		kattara	katanakattara
	FORMAL		kachimashitara	kachimasen deshitara
Alternative	**INFORMAL**		kattari	katanakattari
	FORMAL		kachimashitari	kachimasen deshitari

		INFORMAL AFFIRMATIVE INDICATIVE
Passive		katareru
Potential		kateru
Causative		kataseru
Causative Pass.		kataserareru
Honorific	I	okachi ni naru
	II	okachi nasaru
Humble	I	
	II	

K

227

to carry on one's shoulder(s)   TRANSITIVE

			AFFIRMATIVE	**NEGATIVE**
Indicative	**INFORMAL**		katsugu	katsuganai
	FORMAL		katsugimasu	katsugimasen
Imperative	**INFORMAL**	I	katsuge	katsugu na
		II	katsuginasai	katsuginasaru na
		III	katsuide kudasai	katsuganai de kudasai
	FORMAL		okatsugi nasaimase	okatsugi nasaimasu na
Presumptive	**INFORMAL**	I	katsugō	katsugumai
		II	katsugu darō	katsuganai darō
	FORMAL	I	katsugimashō	katsugimasumai
		II	katsugu deshō	katsuganai deshō
Provisional	**INFORMAL**		katsugeba	katsuganakereba
	FORMAL		katsugimaseba	katsugimasen nara
			katsugimasureba	
Gerund	**INFORMAL**	I	katsuide	katsuganai de
		II		katsuganakute
	FORMAL		katsugimashite	katsugimasen de
Past Ind.	**INFORMAL**		katsuida	katsuganakatta
	FORMAL		katsugimashita	katsugimasen deshita
Past Presump.	**INFORMAL**		katsuidarō	katsuganakattarō
			katsuida darō	katsuganakatta darō
	FORMAL		katsugimashitarō	katsugimasen deshitarō
			katsuida deshō	katsuganakatta deshō
Conditional	**INFORMAL**		katsuidara	katsuganakattara
	FORMAL		katsugimashitara	katsugimasen deshitara
Alternative	**INFORMAL**		katsuidari	katsuganakattari
	FORMAL		katsugimashitari	katsugimasen deshitari

		INFORMAL AFFIRMATIVE INDICATIVE
Passive		katsugareru
Potential		katsugeru
Causative		katsugaseru
Causative Pass.		katsugaserareru
Honorific	I	okatsugi ni naru
	II	okatsugi nasaru
Humble	I	okatsugi suru
	II	okatsugi itasu

かう／買う **ka.u**

TRANSITIVE   *to buy*

			AFFIRMATIVE	**NEGATIVE**
Indicative	**INFORMAL**		kau	kawanai
	FORMAL		kaimasu	kaimasen
Imperative	**INFORMAL**	I	kae	kau na
		II	kainasai	kainasaru na
		III	katte kudasai	kawanai de kudasai
	FORMAL		okai nasaimase	okai nasaimasu na
Presumptive	**INFORMAL**	I	kaō	kaumai
		II	kau darō	kawanai darō
	FORMAL	I	kaimashō	kaimasumai
		II	kau deshō	kawanai deshō
Provisional	**INFORMAL**		kaeba	kawanakereba
	FORMAL		kaimaseba	kaimasen nara
			kaimasureba	
Gerund	**INFORMAL**	I	katte	kawanai de
		II		kawanakute
	FORMAL		kaimashite	kaimasen de
Past Ind.	**INFORMAL**		katta	kawanakatta
	FORMAL		kaimashita	kaimasen deshita
Past Presump.	**INFORMAL**		kattarō	kawanakattarō
			katta darō	kawanakatta darō
	FORMAL		kaimashitarō	kaimasen deshitarō
			katta deshō	kawanakatta deshō
Conditional	**INFORMAL**		kattara	kawanakattara
	FORMAL		kaimashitara	kaimasen deshitara
Alternative	**INFORMAL**		kattari	kawanakattari
	FORMAL		kaimashitari	kaimasen deshitari

		INFORMAL AFFIRMATIVE INDICATIVE
Passive		kawareru
Potential		kaeru
Causative		kawaseru
Causative Pass.		kawaserareru
Honorific	I	okai ni naru
	II	okai nasaru
Humble	I	okai suru
	II	okai itasu

K

AN ESSENTIAL
55 VERB

Kau 買う

to buy

Sentences Using *Kau*

Kattemo Kattemo kaitai mono ga
motto aru.
買っても買っても買いたいものがもっ
とある。
*After buying and buying, there are
still more things I want to buy.*

Subarashii kottō hin no tsubo ga atta
kedo, nedan ga takasugite kaenakatta.
素晴らしい骨董品のつぼがあったけ
ど、値段が高過ぎて買えなかった。
*There was a wonderful antique jar,
but I couldn't buy it because it was
too expensive.*

Nihon dewa, Nihon no dezainā no
irui o kau tsumori desu.
日本では、日本のデザイナーの衣類を
買うつもりです。
*In Japan, I'm planning to buy clothes
by Japanese designers.*

Kesa sūpā de katte kita pan wa,
totemo oishikatta desu.
今朝スーパーで買って来たパンはとて
も美味しかったです。
*The bread I bought at a supermarket
was really delicious.*

Kinjo no kudamonoya de banana to
ringo o kattara, omake shite
kuremashita.
近所の果物屋でバナナとリンゴを買っ
たら、おまけしてくれました。
*They gave me a discount when I
bought bananas and apples at the
fruit shop in the neighborhood.*

Kau is a verb you need for buying
everything from daily necessities,
clothing, and souvenirs to luxury items.
With polite, pleasant service the norm,
buying things is fun in Japan, and
shopping is easy because you don't
haggle over prices.

Words and Expressions Related to This Verb

kōnyū suru　購入する
to buy, to purchase

kaimono suru　買い物する
to shop

kaimono　買い物
shopping

nedan　値段
price

Proverb

Yasumono gai no zeni ushinai.
安物買いの銭失い。
*You waste your money by buying
cheap things.*

かう／飼う **ka.u**

TRANSITIVE   *to keep* (an animal)

			AFFIRMATIVE	NEGATIVE
Indicative	**INFORMAL**		kau	kawanai
	FORMAL		kaimasu	kaimasen
Imperative	**INFORMAL**	I	kae	kau na
		II	kainasai	kainasaru na
		III	katte kudasai	kawanai de kudasai
	FORMAL		okai nasaimase	okai nasaimasu na
Presumptive	**INFORMAL**	I	kaō	kaumai
		II	kau darō	kawanai darō
	FORMAL	I	kaimashō	kaimasumai
		II	kau deshō	kawanai deshō
Provisional	**INFORMAL**		kaeba	kawanakereba
	FORMAL		kaimaseba	kaimasen nara
			kaimasureba	
Gerund	**INFORMAL**	I	katte	kawanai de
		II		kawanakute
	FORMAL		kaimashite	kaimasen de
Past Ind.	**INFORMAL**		katta	kawanakatta
	FORMAL		kaimashita	kaimasen deshita
Past Presump.	**INFORMAL**		kattarō	kawanakattarō
			katta darō	kawanakatta darō
	FORMAL		kaimashitarō	kaimasen deshitarō
			katta deshō	kawanakatta deshō
Conditional	**INFORMAL**		kattara	kawanakattara
	FORMAL		kaimashitara	kaimasen deshitara
Alternative	**INFORMAL**		kattari	kawanakattari
	FORMAL		kaimashitari	kaimasen deshitari

			INFORMAL AFFIRMATIVE INDICATIVE
Passive			kawareru
Potential			kaeru
Causative			kawaseru
Causative Pass.			kawaserareru
Honorific		I	okai ni naru
		II	okai nasaru
Humble		I	okai suru
		II	okai itasu

K

kawaigar.u かわいがる／可愛がる   kawaigari

to love tenderly, to be affectionate   TRANSITIVE

			AFFIRMATIVE	NEGATIVE
Indicative	**INFORMAL**		kawaigaru	kawaigaranai
	FORMAL		kawaigarimasu	kawaigarimasen
Imperative	**INFORMAL**	I	kawaigare	kawaigaru na
		II	kawaigarinasai	kawaigarinasaru na
		III	kawaigatte kudasai	kawaigaranai de kudasai
	FORMAL		okawaigari nasaimase	okawaigari nasaimasu na
Presumptive	**INFORMAL**	I	kawaigarō	kawaigarumai
		II	kawaigaru darō	kawaigaranai darō
	FORMAL	I	kawaigarimashō	kawaigarimasumai
		II	kawaigaru deshō	kawaigaranai deshō
Provisional	**INFORMAL**		kawaigareba	kawaigaranakereba
	FORMAL		kawaigarimaseba	kawaigarimasen nara
			kawaigarimasureba	
Gerund	**INFORMAL**	I	kawaigatte	kawaigaranai de
		II		kawaigaranakute
	FORMAL		kawaigarimashite	kawaigarimasen de
Past Ind.	**INFORMAL**		kawaigatta	kawaigaranakatta
	FORMAL		kawaigarimashita	kawaigarimasen deshita
Past Presump.	**INFORMAL**		kawaigattarō	kawaigaranakattarō
			kawaigatta darō	kawaigaranakatta darō
	FORMAL		kawaigarimashitarō	kawaigarimasen deshitarō
			kawaigatta deshō	kawaigaranakatta deshō
Conditional	**INFORMAL**		kawaigattara	kawaigaranakattara
	FORMAL		kawaigarimashitara	kawaigarimasen deshitara
Alternative	**INFORMAL**		kawaigattari	kawaigaranakattari
	FORMAL		kawaigarimashitari	kawaigarimasen deshitari

		INFORMAL AFFIRMATIVE INDICATIVE
Passive		kawaigarareru
Potential		kawaigareru
Causative		kawaigaraseru
Causative Pass.		kawaigaraserareru
Honorific	I	okawaigari ni naru
	II	okawaigari nasaru
Humble	I	okawaigari suru
	II	okawaigari itasu

232

かわかす／乾かす **kawakas.u**
TRANSITIVE   *to dry*

			AFFIRMATIVE	**NEGATIVE**
Indicative	**INFORMAL**		kawakasu	kawakasanai
	FORMAL		kawakashimasu	kawakashimasen
Imperative	**INFORMAL**	I	kawakase	kawakasu na
		II	kawakashinasai	kawakashinasaru na
		III	kawakashite kudasai	kawakasanai de kudasai
	FORMAL		okawakashi nasaimase	okawakashi nasaimasu na
Presumptive	**INFORMAL**	I	kawakasō	kawakasumai
		II	kawakasu darō	kawakasanai darō
	FORMAL	I	kawakashimashō	kawakashimasumai
		II	kawakasu deshō	kawakasanai deshō
Provisional	**INFORMAL**		kawakaseba	kawakasanakereba
	FORMAL		kawakashimaseba	kawakashimasen nara
			kawakashimasureba	
Gerund	**INFORMAL**	I	kawakashite	kawakasanai de
		II		kawakasanakute
	FORMAL		kawakashimashite	kawakashimasen de
Past Ind.	**INFORMAL**		kawakashita	kawakasanakatta
	FORMAL		kawakashimashita	kawakashimasen deshita
Past Presump.	**INFORMAL**		kawakashitarō	kawakasanakattarō
			kawakashita darō	kawakasanakatta darō
	FORMAL		kawakashimashitarō	kawakashimasen deshitarō
			kawakashita deshō	kawakasanakatta deshō
Conditional	**INFORMAL**		kawakashitara	kawakasanakattara
	FORMAL		kawakashimashitara	kawakashimasen deshitara
Alternative	**INFORMAL**		kawakashitari	kawakasanakattari
	FORMAL		kawakashimashitari	kawakashimasen deshitari

			INFORMAL AFFIRMATIVE INDICATIVE
Passive			kawakasareru
Potential			kawakaseru
Causative			kawakasaseru
Causative Pass.			kawakasaserareru
Honorific		I	okawakashi ni naru
		II	okawakashi nasaru
Humble		I	okawakashi suru
		II	okawakashi itasu

K

233

to become dry

			AFFIRMATIVE	NEGATIVE
Indicative	**INFORMAL**		kawaku	kawakanai
	FORMAL		kawakimasu	kawakimasen
Imperative	**INFORMAL**	I	kawake	kawaku na
		II		
		III		
	FORMAL			
Presumptive	**INFORMAL**	I	kawakō	kawakumai
		II	kawaku darō	kawakanai darō
	FORMAL	I	kawakimashō	kawakimasumai
		II	kawaku deshō	kawakanai deshō
Provisional	**INFORMAL**		kawakeba	kawakanakereba
	FORMAL		kawakimaseba	kawakimasen nara
			kawakimasureba	
Gerund	**INFORMAL**	I	kawaite	kawakanai de
		II		kawakanakute
	FORMAL		kawakimashite	kawakimasen de
Past Ind.	**INFORMAL**		kawaita	kawakanakatta
	FORMAL		kawakimashita	kawakimasen deshita
Past Presump.	**INFORMAL**		kawaitarō	kawakanakattarō
			kawaita darō	kawakanakatta darō
	FORMAL		kawakimashitarō	kawakimasen deshitarō
			kawaita deshō	kawakanakatta deshō
Conditional	**INFORMAL**		kawaitara	kawakanakattara
	FORMAL		kawakimashitara	kawakimasen deshitara
Alternative	**INFORMAL**		kawaitari	kawakanakattari
	FORMAL		kawakimashitari	kawakimasen deshitari

		INFORMAL AFFIRMATIVE INDICATIVE
Passive		
Potential		
Causative		
Causative Pass.		
Honorific	I	
	II	
Humble	I	
	II	

かわる／変わる **kawar.u**
to change

			AFFIRMATIVE	NEGATIVE
Indicative	**INFORMAL**		kawaru	kawaranai
	FORMAL		kawarimasu	kawarimasen
Imperative	**INFORMAL**	I	kaware	kawaru na
		II	kawarinasai	kawarinasaru na
		III	kawatte kudasai	kawaranai de kudasai
	FORMAL		okawari nasaimase	okawari nasaimasu na
Presumptive	**INFORMAL**	I	kawarō	kawarumai
		II	kawaru darō	kawaranai darō
	FORMAL	I	kawarimashō	kawarimasumai
		II	kawaru deshō	kawaranai deshō
Provisional	**INFORMAL**		kawareba	kawaranakereba
	FORMAL		kawarimaseba	kawarimasen nara
			kawarimasureba	
Gerund	**INFORMAL**	I	kawatte	kawaranai de
		II		kawaranakute
	FORMAL		kawarimashite	kawarimasen de
Past Ind.	**INFORMAL**		kawatta	kawaranakatta
	FORMAL		kawarimashita	kawarimasen deshita
Past Presump.	**INFORMAL**		kawattarō	kawaranakattarō
			kawatta darō	kawaranakatta darō
	FORMAL		kawarimashitarō	kawarimasen deshitarō
			kawatta deshō	kawaranakatta deshō
Conditional	**INFORMAL**		kawattara	kawaranakattara
	FORMAL		kawarimashitara	kawarimasen deshitara
Alternative	**INFORMAL**		kawattari	kawaranakattari
	FORMAL		kawarimashitari	kawarimasen deshitari

			INFORMAL AFFIRMATIVE INDICATIVE
Passive			kawarareru
Potential			kawareru
Causative			kawaraseru
Causative Pass.			kawaraserareru
Honorific		I	okawari ni naru
		II	okawari nasaru
Humble		I	
		II	

kayo.u　かよう／通う　　　　　　　　　　　　　　　kayoi
to commute

			AFFIRMATIVE	NEGATIVE
Indicative	**INFORMAL**		kayou	kayowanai
	FORMAL		kayoimasu	kayoimasen
Imperative	**INFORMAL**	I	kayoe	kayou na
		II	kayoinasai	kayoinasaru na
		III	kayotte kudasai	kayowanai de kudasai
	FORMAL		okayoi nasaimase	okayoi nasaimasu na
Presumptive	**INFORMAL**	I	kayoō	kayoumai
		II	kayou darō	kayowanai darō
	FORMAL	I	kayoimashō	kayoimasumai
		II	kayou deshō	kayowanai deshō
Provisional	**INFORMAL**		kayoeba	kayowanakereba
	FORMAL		kayoimaseba	kayoimasen nara
			kayoimasureba	
Gerund	**INFORMAL**	I	kayotte	kayowanai de
		II		kayowanakute
	FORMAL		kayoimashite	kayoimasen de
Past Ind.	**INFORMAL**		kayotta	kayowanakatta
	FORMAL		kayoimashita	kayoimasen deshita
Past Presump.	**INFORMAL**		kayottarō	kayowanakattarō
			kayotta darō	kayowanakatta darō
	FORMAL		kayoimashitarō	kayoimasen deshitarō
			kayotta deshō	kayowanakatta deshō
Conditional	**INFORMAL**		kayottara	kayowanakattara
	FORMAL		kayoimashitara	kayoimasen deshitara
Alternative	**INFORMAL**		kayottari	kayowanakattari
	FORMAL		kayoimashitari	kayoimasen deshitari

		INFORMAL AFFIRMATIVE INDICATIVE
Passive		kayowareru
Potential		kayoeru
Causative		kayowaseru
Causative Pass.		kayowaserareru
Honorific	I	okayoi ni naru
	II	okayoi nasaru
Humble	I	okayoi suru
	II	okayoi itasu

kazari

TRANSITIVE   *to decorate, to display*

			AFFIRMATIVE	NEGATIVE
Indicative	**INFORMAL**		kazaru	kazaranai
	FORMAL		kazarimasu	kazarimasen
Imperative	**INFORMAL**	I	kazare	kazaru na
		II	kazarinasai	kazarinasaru na
		III	kazatte kudasai	kazaranai de kudasai
	FORMAL		okazari nasaimase	okazari nasaimasu na
Presumptive	**INFORMAL**	I	kazarō	kazarumai
		II	kazaru darō	kazaranai darō
	FORMAL	I	kazarimashō	kazarimasumai
		II	kazaru deshō	kazaranai deshō
Provisional	**INFORMAL**		kazareba	kazaranakereba
	FORMAL		kazarimaseba	kazarimasen nara
			kazarimasureba	
Gerund	**INFORMAL**	I	kazatte	kazaranai de
		II		kazaranakute
	FORMAL		kazarimashite	kazarimasen de
Past Ind.	**INFORMAL**		kazatta	kazaranakatta
	FORMAL		kazarimashita	kazarimasen deshita
Past Presump.	**INFORMAL**		kazattarō	kazaranakattarō
			kazatta darō	kazaranakatta darō
	FORMAL		kazarimashitarō	kazarimasen deshitarō
			kazatta deshō	kazaranakatta deshō
Conditional	**INFORMAL**		kazattara	kazaranakattara
	FORMAL		kazarimashitara	kazarimasen deshitara
Alternative	**INFORMAL**		kazattari	kazaranakattari
	FORMAL		kazarimashitari	kazarimasen deshitari

		INFORMAL AFFIRMATIVE INDICATIVE
Passive		kazarareru
Potential		kazareru
Causative		kazaraseru
Causative Pass.		kazaraserareru
Honorific	I	okazari ni naru
	II	okazari nasaru
Humble	I	okazari suru
	II	okazari itasu

237

			AFFIRMATIVE	NEGATIVE
Indicative	**INFORMAL**		kazoeru	kazoenai
	FORMAL		kazoemasu	kazoemasen
Imperative	**INFORMAL**	I	kazoero	kazoeru na
		II	kazoenasai	kazoenasaru na
		III	kazoete kudasai	kazoenai de kudasai
	FORMAL		okazoe nasaimase	okazoe nasaimasu na
Presumptive	**INFORMAL**	I	kazoeyō	kazoemai
		II	kazoeru darō	kazoenai darō
	FORMAL	I	kazoemashō	kazoemasumai
		II	kazoeru deshō	kazoenai deshō
Provisional	**INFORMAL**		kazoereba	kazoenakereba
	FORMAL		kazoemaseba	kazoemasen nara
			kazoemasureba	
Gerund	**INFORMAL**	I	kazoete	kazoenai de
		II		kazoenakute
	FORMAL		kazoemashite	kazoemasen de
Past Ind.	**INFORMAL**		kazoeta	kazoenakatta
	FORMAL		kazoemashita	kazoemasen deshita
Past Presump.	**INFORMAL**		kazoetarō	kazoenakattarō
			kazoeta darō	kazoenakatta darō
	FORMAL		kazoemashitarō	kazoemasen deshitarō
			kazoeta deshō	kazoenakatta deshō
Conditional	**INFORMAL**		kazoetara	kazoenakattara
	FORMAL		kazoemashitara	kazoemasen deshitara
Alternative	**INFORMAL**		kazoetari	kazoenakattari
	FORMAL		kazoemashitari	kazoemasen deshitari

			INFORMAL AFFIRMATIVE INDICATIVE
Passive			kazoerareru
Potential			kazoerareru
Causative			kazoesaseru
Causative Pass.			kazoesaserareru
Honorific		I	okazoe ni naru
		II	okazoe nasaru
Humble		I	okazoe suru
		II	okazoe itasu

TRANSITIVE　　*to erase, to extinguish, to turn off*

			AFFIRMATIVE	NEGATIVE
Indicative	**INFORMAL**		kesu	kesanai
	FORMAL		keshimasu	keshimasen
Imperative	**INFORMAL**	I	kese	kesu na
		II	keshinasai	keshinasaru na
		III	keshite kudasai	kesanai de kudasai
	FORMAL		okeshi nasaimase	okeshi nasaimasu na
Presumptive	**INFORMAL**	I	kesō	kesumai
		II	kesu darō	kesanai darō
	FORMAL	I	keshimashō	keshimasumai
		II	kesu deshō	kesanai deshō
Provisional	**INFORMAL**		keseba	kesanakereba
	FORMAL		keshimaseba	keshimasen nara
			keshimasureba	
Gerund	**INFORMAL**	I	keshite	kesanai de
		II		kesanakute
	FORMAL		keshimashite	keshimasen de
Past Ind.	**INFORMAL**		keshita	kesanakatta
	FORMAL		keshimashita	keshimasen deshita
Past Presump.	**INFORMAL**		keshitarō	kesanakattarō
			keshita darō	kesanakatta darō
	FORMAL		keshimashitarō	keshimasen deshitarō
			keshita deshō	kesanakatta deshō
Conditional	**INFORMAL**		keshitara	kesanakattara
	FORMAL		keshimashitara	keshimasen deshitara
Alternative	**INFORMAL**		keshitari	kesanakattari
	FORMAL		keshimashitari	keshimasen deshitari

		INFORMAL AFFIRMATIVE INDICATIVE
Passive		kesareru
Potential		keseru
Causative		kesaseru
Causative Pass.		kesaserareru
Honorific	I	okeshi ni naru
	II	okeshi nasaru
Humble	I	okeshi suru
	II	okeshi itasu

K

239

to put on airs

			AFFIRMATIVE	**NEGATIVE**
Indicative	**INFORMAL**		kidoru	kidoranai
	FORMAL		kidorimasu	kidorimasen
Imperative	**INFORMAL**	I	kidore	kidoru na
		II	kidorinasai	kidorinasaru na
		III	kidotte kudasai	kidoranai de kudasai
	FORMAL		okidori nasaimase	okidori nasaimasu na
Presumptive	**INFORMAL**	I	kidorō	kidorumai
		II	kidoru darō	kidoranai darō
	FORMAL	I	kidorimashō	kidorimasumai
		II	kidoru deshō	kidoranai deshō
Provisional	**INFORMAL**		kidoreba	kidoranakereba
	FORMAL		kidorimaseba	kidorimasen nara
			kidorimasureba	
Gerund	**INFORMAL**	I	kidotte	kidoranai de
		II		kidoranakute
	FORMAL		kidorimashite	kidorimasen de
Past Ind.	**INFORMAL**		kidotta	kidoranakatta
	FORMAL		kidorimashita	kidorimasen deshita
Past Presump.	**INFORMAL**		kidottarō	kidoranakattarō
			kidotta darō	kidoranakatta darō
	FORMAL		kidorimashitarō	kidorimasen deshitarō
			kidotta deshō	kidoranakatta deshō
Conditional	**INFORMAL**		kidottara	kidoranakattara
	FORMAL		kidorimashitara	kidorimasen deshitara
Alternative	**INFORMAL**		kidottari	kidoranakattari
	FORMAL		kidorimashitari	kidorimasen deshitari

		INFORMAL AFFIRMATIVE INDICATIVE
Passive		kidorareru
Potential		kidoreru
Causative		kidoraseru
Causative Pass.		kidoraserareru
Honorific	I	okidori ni naru
	II	okidori nasaru
Humble	I	
	II	

きえる／消える kie.ru
to vanish, to be extinguished, to go out

			AFFIRMATIVE	NEGATIVE
Indicative	**INFORMAL**		kieru	kienai
	FORMAL		kiemasu	kiemasen
Imperative	**INFORMAL**	I	kiero	kieru na
		II		
		III		
	FORMAL			
Presumptive	**INFORMAL**	I	kieyō	kiemai
		II	kieru darō	kienai darō
	FORMAL	I	kiemashō	kiemasumai
		II	kieru deshō	kienai deshō
Provisional	**INFORMAL**		kiereba	kienakereba
	FORMAL		kiemaseba	kiemasen nara
			kiemasureba	
Gerund	**INFORMAL**	I	kiete	kienai de
		II		kienakute
	FORMAL		kiemashite	kiemasen de
Past Ind.	**INFORMAL**		kieta	kienakatta
	FORMAL		kiemashita	kiemasen deshita
Past Presump.	**INFORMAL**		kietarō	kienakattarō
			kieta darō	kienakatta darō
	FORMAL		kiemashitarō	kiemasen deshitarō
			kieta deshō	kienakatta deshō
Conditional	**INFORMAL**		kietara	kienakattara
	FORMAL		kiemashitara	kiemasen deshitara
Alternative	**INFORMAL**		kietari	kienakattari
	FORMAL		kiemashitari	kiemasen deshitari

		INFORMAL AFFIRMATIVE INDICATIVE
Passive		kierareru
Potential		kierareru
Causative		kiesaseru
Causative Pass.		kiesaserareru
Honorific	I	
	II	
Humble	I	
	II	

to change clothes　　TRANSITIVE

			AFFIRMATIVE	NEGATIVE
Indicative	**INFORMAL**		kikaeru	kikaenai
	FORMAL		kikaemasu	kikaemasen
Imperative	**INFORMAL**	I	kikaero	kikaeru na
		II	kikaenasai	kikaenasaru na
		III	kikaete kudasai	kikaenai de kudasai
	FORMAL		okikae nasaimase	okikae nasaimasu na
Presumptive	**INFORMAL**	I	kikaeyō	kikaemai
		II	kikaeru darō	kikaenai darō
	FORMAL	I	kikaemashō	kikaemasumai
		II	kikaeru deshō	kikaenai deshō
Provisional	**INFORMAL**		kikaereba	kikaenakereba
	FORMAL		kikaemaseba	kikaemasen nara
			kikaemasureba	
Gerund	**INFORMAL**	I	kikaete	kikaenai de
		II		kikaenakute
	FORMAL		kikaemashite	kikaemasen de
Past Ind.	**INFORMAL**		kikaeta	kikaenakatta
	FORMAL		kikaemashita	kikaemasen deshita
Past Presump.	**INFORMAL**		kikaetarō	kikaenakattarō
			kikaeta darō	kikaenakatta darō
	FORMAL		kikaemashitarō	kikaemasen deshitarō
			kikaeta deshō	kikaenakatta deshō
Conditional	**INFORMAL**		kikaetara	kikaenakattara
	FORMAL		kikaemashitara	kikaemasen deshitara
Alternative	**INFORMAL**		kikaetari	kikaenakattari
	FORMAL		kikaemashitari	kikaemasen deshitari

		INFORMAL AFFIRMATIVE INDICATIVE
Passive		kikaerareru
Potential		kikaerareru
Causative		kikaesaseru
Causative Pass.		kikaesaserareru
Honorific	I	okikae ni naru
	II	okikae nasaru
Humble	I	
	II	

kikoe きこえる／聞こえる kikoe.ru
to be audible, to be able to hear

			AFFIRMATIVE	NEGATIVE
Indicative	**INFORMAL**		kikoeru	kikoenai
	FORMAL		kikoemasu	kikoemasen
Imperative	**INFORMAL**	I		
		II		
		III		
	FORMAL			
Presumptive	**INFORMAL**	I	kikoeyō	kikoemai
		II	kikoeru darō	kikoenai darō
	FORMAL	I	kikoemashō	kikoemasumai
		II	kikoeru deshō	kikoenai deshō
Provisional	**INFORMAL**		kikoereba	kikoenakereba
	FORMAL		kikoemaseba	kikoemasen nara
			kikoemasureba	
Gerund	**INFORMAL**	I	kikoete	kikoenai de
		II		kikoenakute
	FORMAL		kikoemashite	kikoemasen de
Past Ind.	**INFORMAL**		kikoeta	kikoenakatta
	FORMAL		kikoemashita	kikoemasen deshita
Past Presump.	**INFORMAL**		kikoetarō	kikoenakattarō
			kikoeta darō	kikoenakatta darō
	FORMAL		kikoemashitarō	kikoemasen deshitarō
			kikoeta deshō	kikoenakatta deshō
Conditional	**INFORMAL**		kikoetara	kikoenakattara
	FORMAL		kikoemashitara	kikoemasen deshitara
Alternative	**INFORMAL**		kikoetari	kikoenakattari
	FORMAL		kikoemashitari	kikoemasen deshitari

		INFORMAL AFFIRMATIVE INDICATIVE
Passive		
Potential		
Causative		
Causative Pass.		
Honorific	I	
	II	
Humble	I	
	II	

K

243

kik.u きく／聞く   kiki

to ask, to listen, to hear   TRANSITIVE

			AFFIRMATIVE	NEGATIVE
Indicative	**INFORMAL**		kiku	kikanai
	FORMAL		kikimasu	kikimasen
Imperative	**INFORMAL**	I	kike	kiku na
		II	kikinasai	kikinasaru na
		III	kiite kudasai	kikanai de kudasai
	FORMAL		okiki nasaimase	okiki nasaimasu na
Presumptive	**INFORMAL**	I	kikō	kikumai
		II	kiku darō	kikanai darō
	FORMAL	I	kikimashō	kikimasumai
		II	kiku deshō	kikanai deshō
Provisional	**INFORMAL**		kikeba	kikanakereba
	FORMAL		kikimaseba	kikimasen nara
			kikimasureba	
Gerund	**INFORMAL**	I	kiite	kikanai de
		II		kikanakute
	FORMAL		kikimashite	kikimasen de
Past Ind.	**INFORMAL**		kiita	kikanakatta
	FORMAL		kikimashita	kikimasen deshita
Past Presump.	**INFORMAL**		kiitarō	kikanakattarō
			kiita darō	kikanakatta darō
	FORMAL		kikimashitarō	kikimasen deshitarō
			kiita deshō	kikanakatta deshō
Conditional	**INFORMAL**		kiitara	kikanakattara
	FORMAL		kikimashitara	kikimasen deshitara
Alternative	**INFORMAL**		kiitari	kikanakattari
	FORMAL		kikimashitari	kikimasen deshitari

		INFORMAL AFFIRMATIVE INDICATIVE	
Passive		kikareru	
Potential		kikeru*	
Causative		kikaseru	
Causative Pass.		kikaserareru	
Honorific	I	okiki ni naru	
	II	okiki nasaru	
*Humble***		ukagau	uketamawaru

*Only in the sense of "can ask or listen"; "to be audible" is a separate verb *kikoeru*.

**Ukagau* means "to ask," while *uketamawaru* means "to hear or listen."

Kiku 聞く、聴く

to ask, to listen, to hear

Sentences Using *Kiku*

Kare wa mainichi rajio de jazu o kikimasu.
彼は毎日ラジオでジャズを聴きます。
He listens to jazz on the radio every day.

Tenki yohō o kiitara, ashita wa yuki ga furu sō da.
天気予報を聞いたら、明日は雪が降るそうだ。
I listened to the weather forecast, and they said it would snow tomorrow.

Doyōbi no yoru, yūmei na kagakusha no kōen o kiki ni iku tsumori desu.
土曜日の夜、有名な科学者の講演を聞きにいく積もりです。
I'm planning to go to listen to the lecture by a famous scientist.

Shiranai koto o kikaretara, shitte iru furi o shinai de shiranai to hakkiri iinasai.
知らないことを聞かれたら、知っているふりをしないで知らないとはっきり言いなさい。
If you're asked something you don't know, you should say you don't know and not pretend to know.

Teinei ni kiitemo, shitsumon ni kotaete moraenakatta.
丁寧に聞いても、質問に答えてもらえなかった。
Although I asked a question politely, I couldn't get an answer.

Kiku is a verb essential for good communication. You listen to people and you listen to music. Listening while totally surrounded by Japanese sounds is an interesting experience for visitors to Japan. And if you need directions, ask a police officer. Each one is like a living map or GPS. Listen and you'll find your destination easily.

K

Words and Expressions Related to This Verb

tazuneru　尋ねる
to ask

shitsumon suru　質問する
to ask a question

Proverb

kiki mimi o tateru
聞き耳を立てる
to be all ears (to let listening ears stand)

Kiku wa ittoki no haji, kikanu wa matsudai no haji.
聞くは一時の恥、聞かぬは末代の恥。
Don't be shy about asking questions. (Asking questions is a one-time shame, not asking questions is generations of shame.)

kik.u　きく／利く／効く　　　　　　　　　　kiki

to be effective, to work

			AFFIRMATIVE	NEGATIVE
Indicative	**INFORMAL**		kiku	kikanai
	FORMAL		kikimasu	kikimasen
Imperative	**INFORMAL**	I	kike	kiku na
		II		
		III		
	FORMAL			
Presumptive	**INFORMAL**	I	kikō	kikumai
		II	kiku darō	kikanai darō
	FORMAL	I	kikimashō	kikimasumai
		II	kiku deshō	kikanai deshō
Provisional	**INFORMAL**		kikeba	kikanakereba
	FORMAL		kikimaseba	kikimasen nara
			kikimasureba	
Gerund	**INFORMAL**	I	kiite	kikanai de
		II		kikanakute
	FORMAL		kikimashite	kikimasen de
Past Ind.	**INFORMAL**		kiita	kikanakatta
	FORMAL		kikimashita	kikimasen deshita
Past Presump.	**INFORMAL**		kiitarō	kikanakattarō
			kiita darō	kikanakatta darō
	FORMAL		kikimashitarō	kikimasen deshitarō
			kiita deshō	kikanakatta deshō
Conditional	**INFORMAL**		kiitara	kikanakattara
	FORMAL		kikimashitara	kikimasen deshitara
Alternative	**INFORMAL**		kiitari	kikanakattari
	FORMAL		kikimashitari	kikimasen deshitari

		INFORMAL AFFIRMATIVE INDICATIVE
Passive		kikareru
Potential		kikeru
Causative		kikaseru
Causative Pass.		kikaserareru
Honorific	I	
	II	
Humble	I	
	II	

kimari　　　　　　　　きまる／決まる　**kimar.u**
to be decided, to be agreed upon

			AFFIRMATIVE	NEGATIVE
Indicative	**INFORMAL**		kimaru	kimaranai
	FORMAL		kimarimasu	kimarimasen
Imperative	**INFORMAL**	I	kimare	kimaru na
		II		
		III		
	FORMAL			
Presumptive	**INFORMAL**	I	kimarō	kimarumai
		II	kimaru darō	kimaranai darō
	FORMAL	I	kimarimashō	kimarimasumai
		II	kimaru deshō	kimaranai deshō
Provisional	**INFORMAL**		kimareba	kimaranakereba
	FORMAL		kimarimaseba	kimarimasen nara
			kimarimasureba	
Gerund	**INFORMAL**	I	kimatte	kimaranai de
		II		kimaranakute
	FORMAL		kimarimashite	kimarimasen de
Past Ind.	**INFORMAL**		kimatta	kimaranakatta
	FORMAL		kimarimashita	kimarimasen deshita
Past Presump.	**INFORMAL**		kimattarō	kimaranakattarō
			kimatta darō	kimaranakatta darō
	FORMAL		kimarimashitarō	kimarimasen deshitarō
			kimatta deshō	kimaranakatta deshō
Conditional	**INFORMAL**		kimattara	kimaranakattara
	FORMAL		kimarimashitara	kimarimasen deshitara
Alternative	**INFORMAL**		kimattari	kimaranakattari
	FORMAL		kimarimashitari	kimarimasen deshitari

		INFORMAL AFFIRMATIVE INDICATIVE
Passive		kimarareru
Potential		kimareru
Causative		kimaraseru
Causative Pass.		kimaraserareru
Honorific	I	okimari ni naru
	II	okimari nasaru
Humble	I	
	II	

			AFFIRMATIVE	**NEGATIVE**
Indicative	**INFORMAL**		kimeru	kimenai
	FORMAL		kimemasu	kimemasen
Imperative	**INFORMAL**	I	kimero	kimeru na
		II	kimenasai	kimenasaru na
		III	kimete kudasai	kimenai de kudasai
	FORMAL		okime nasaimase	okime nasaimasu na
Presumptive	**INFORMAL**	I	kimeyō	kimemai
		II	kimeru darō	kimenai darō
	FORMAL	I	kimemashō	kimemasumai
		II	kimeru deshō	kimenai deshō
Provisional	**INFORMAL**		kimereba	kimenakereba
	FORMAL		kimemaseba	kimemasen nara
			kimemasureba	
Gerund	**INFORMAL**	I	kimete	kimenai de
		II		kimenakute
	FORMAL		kimemashite	kimemasen de
Past Ind.	**INFORMAL**		kimeta	kimenakatta
	FORMAL		kimemashita	kimemasen deshita
Past Presump.	**INFORMAL**		kimetarō	kimenakattarō
			kimeta darō	kimenakatta darō
	FORMAL		kimemashitarō	kimemasen deshitarō
			kimeta deshō	kimenakatta deshō
Conditional	**INFORMAL**		kimetara	kimenakattara
	FORMAL		kimemashitara	kimemasen deshitara
Alternative	**INFORMAL**		kimetari	kimenakattari
	FORMAL		kimemashitari	kimemasen deshitari

			INFORMAL AFFIRMATIVE INDICATIVE
Passive			kimerareru
Potential			kimerareru
Causative			kimesaseru
Causative Pass.			kimesaserareru
Honorific		I	okime ni naru
		II	okime nasaru
Humble		I	okime suru
		II	okime itasu

AN ESSENTIAL 55 VERB

Kimeru 決める

to decide, to choose

Kimeru is an essential verb because decisions large and small are a big part of everyday life. And if you spend much time with the Japanese, you want to be aware of the general Japanese preference for group consensus rather than deciding things on one's own!

K

Sentences Using *Kimeru*

Kare wa ichido kimeta koto wa kanarazu mamoru.
彼は一度決めたことは必ず守る。
Once he decides, he sticks to his decision.

Dore mo kaitakute, kimeru no ga totemo muzukashikatta.
どれも買いたくて、決めるのがとても難しかった。
It was very difficult to decide as I wanted to buy everything.

Saisho ni kisoku o kimete oitara, kaigi wa konran shinakatta deshō.
最初に規則を決めておいたら、会議は混乱しなかったでしょう。
If they had decided on the rules beforehand, the meeting wouldn't have become chaotic.

Kyōju wa rainen intai suru koto o okime nasaimashita.
教授は来年引退することにお決めなさいました。
Our professor has decided to retire next year.

Nihon niwa dono kurai iru ka hayaku kimeyō.
日本にはどのくらいいるか早く決めよう。
Let's decide as soon as possible how long we'll be in Japan.

Words and Expressions Related to This Verb

kesshin suru　決心する
to make up one's mind, to determine

kettei suru　決定する
to decide, to settle

ketsudan suru　決断する
to resolve, to decide

ketsui　決意
determination, resolution

kaiketsu　解決
solution

kasūketsu　多数決
majority rule

to ban, to prohibit　　TRANSITIVE

			AFFIRMATIVE	NEGATIVE
Indicative	**INFORMAL**		kinjiru	kinjinai
	FORMAL		kinjimasu	kinjimasen
Imperative	**INFORMAL**	I	kinjiro	kinjiru na
		II	kinjinasai	kinjinasaru na
		III	kinjite kudasai	kinjinai de kudasai
	FORMAL		okinji nasaimase	okinji nasaimasu na
Presumptive	**INFORMAL**	I	kinjiyō	kinjimai
		II	kinjiru darō	kinjinai darō
	FORMAL	I	kinjimashō	kinjimasumai
		II	kinjiru deshō	kinjinai deshō
Provisional	**INFORMAL**		kinjireba	kinjinakereba
	FORMAL		kinjimaseba	kinjimasen nara
			kinjimasureba	
Gerund	**INFORMAL**	I	kinjite	kinjinai de
		II		kinjinakute
	FORMAL		kinjimashite	kinjimasen de
Past Ind.	**INFORMAL**		kinjita	kinjinakatta
	FORMAL		kinjimashita	kinjimasen deshita
Past Presump.	**INFORMAL**		kinjitarō	kinjinakattarō
			kinjita darō	kinjinakatta darō
	FORMAL		kinjimashitarō	kinjimasen deshitarō
			kinjita deshō	kinjinakatta deshō
Conditional	**INFORMAL**		kinjitara	kinjinakattara
	FORMAL		kinjimashitara	kinjimasen deshitara
Alternative	**INFORMAL**		kinjitari	kinjinakattari
	FORMAL		kinjimashitari	kinjimasen deshitari

		INFORMAL AFFIRMATIVE INDICATIVE
Passive		kinjirareru
Potential		kinjirareru
Causative		kinjisaseru
Causative Pass.		kinjisaserareru
Honorific	I	okinji ni naru
	II	okinji nasaru
Humble	I	okinji suru
	II	okinji itasu

to be cut off, to break, to run out, to expire

			AFFIRMATIVE	NEGATIVE
Indicative	**INFORMAL**		kireru	kirenai
	FORMAL		kiremasu	kiremasen
Imperative	**INFORMAL**	I	kirero	kireru na
		II	kirenasai	kirenasaru na
		III	kirete kudasai	kirenai de kudasai
	FORMAL			
Presumptive	**INFORMAL**	I	kireyō	kirerumai
		II	kireru darō	kirenai darō
	FORMAL	I	kiremashō	kiremasumai
		II	kireru deshō	kirenai deshō
Provisional	**INFORMAL**		kirereba	kirenakereba
	FORMAL		kiremaseba	kiremasen nara
			kiremasureba	
Gerund	**INFORMAL**	I	kirete	kirenai de
		II		kirenakute
	FORMAL		kiremashite	kiremasen de
Past Ind.	**INFORMAL**		kireta	kirenakatta
	FORMAL		kiremashita	kiremasen deshita
Past Presump.	**INFORMAL**		kiretarō	kirenakattarō
			kireta darō	kirenakatta darō
	FORMAL		kiremashitarō	kiremasen deshitarō
			kireta deshō	kirenakatta deshō
Conditional	**INFORMAL**		kiretara	kirenakattara
	FORMAL		kiremashitara	kiremasen deshitara
Alternative	**INFORMAL**		kiretari	kirenakattari
	FORMAL		kiremashitari	kiremasen deshitari

		INFORMAL AFFIRMATIVE INDICATIVE
Passive		
Potential		
Causative		kiresaseru
Causative Pass.		kiresaserareru
Honorific	I	
	II	
Humble	I	
	II	

K

251

			AFFIRMATIVE	NEGATIVE
Indicative	**INFORMAL**		kiru	kiranai
	FORMAL		kirimasu	kirimasen
Imperative	**INFORMAL**	I	kire	kiru na
		II	kirinasai	kirinasaru na
		III	kitte kudasai	kiranai de kudasai
	FORMAL		okiri nasaimase	okiri nasaimasu na
Presumptive	**INFORMAL**	I	kirō	kirumai
		II	kiru darō	kiranai darō
	FORMAL	I	kirimashō	kirimasumai
		II	kiru deshō	kiranai deshō
Provisional	**INFORMAL**		kireba	kiranakereba
	FORMAL		kirimaseba	kirimasen nara
			kirimasureba	
Gerund	**INFORMAL**	I	kitte	kiranai de
		II		kiranakute
	FORMAL		kirimashite	kirimasen de
Past Ind.	**INFORMAL**		kitta	kiranakatta
	FORMAL		kirimashita	kirimasen deshita
Past Presump.	**INFORMAL**		kittarō	kiranakattarō
			kitta darō	kiranakatta darō
	FORMAL		kirimashitarō	kirimasen deshitarō
			kitta deshō	kiranakatta deshō
Conditional	**INFORMAL**		kittara	kiranakattara
	FORMAL		kirimashitara	kirimasen deshitara
Alternative	**INFORMAL**		kittari	kiranakattari
	FORMAL		kirimashitari	kirimasen deshitari

		INFORMAL AFFIRMATIVE INDICATIVE
Passive		kirareru
Potential		kireru
Causative		kiraseru
Causative Pass.		kiraserareru
Honorific	I	okiri ni naru
	II	okiri nasaru
Humble	I	okiri suru
	II	okiri itasu

TRANSITIVE *to put on, to wear* (on the body as with a coat, suit, or dress)

			AFFIRMATIVE	NEGATIVE
Indicative	**INFORMAL**		kiru	kinai
	FORMAL		kimasu	kimasen
Imperative	**INFORMAL**	I	kiro	kiru na
		II	kinasai	kinasaru na
		III	kite kudasai	kinai de kudasai
	FORMAL		omesi nasaimase	omesi nasaimasu na
Presumptive	**INFORMAL**	I	kiyō	kimai
		II	kiru darō	kinai darō
	FORMAL	I	kimashō	kimasumai
		II	kiru deshō	kinai deshō
Provisional	**INFORMAL**		kireba	kinakereba
	FORMAL		kimaseba	kimasen nara
			kimasureba	
Gerund	**INFORMAL**	I	kite	kinai de
		II		kinakute
	FORMAL		kimashite	kimasen de
Past Ind.	**INFORMAL**		kita	kinakatta
	FORMAL		kimashita	kimasen deshita
Past Presump.	**INFORMAL**		kitarō	kinakattarō
			kita darō	kinakatta darō
	FORMAL		kimashitarō	kimasen deshitarō
			kita deshō	kinakatta deshō
Conditional	**INFORMAL**		kitara	kinakattara
	FORMAL		kimashitara	kimasen deshitara
Alternative	**INFORMAL**		kitari	kinakattari
	FORMAL		kimashitari	kimasen deshitari

		INFORMAL AFFIRMATIVE INDICATIVE
Passive		kirareru
Potential		kirareru
Causative		kisaseru
Causative Pass.		kisaserareru
Honorific	I	omeshi ni naru
	II	omeshi nasaru
Humble	I	
	II	

AN ESSENTIAL 55 VERB

253

Kiru 着る

to put on, to wear (on the body,
as with a coat, suit, or dress)

Sentences Using *Kiru*

Tsuma wa konban no pātī ni kimono
o kite ikimasu.
妻は今晩のパーティーに着物を着ていきます。
*My wife is wearing a kimono to the
party tonight.*

Kare wa donna ni ii mono o kitemo,
misuborashiku mieru.
彼はどんなに良いものを着ても、みすぼらしく見える。
*Even if he wears good clothing, he
still looks shabby.*

Kinō wa hidoku mushiatsukatta node,
sūtsu o kinaide shukkin shimashita.
昨日はひどく蒸し暑かったので、スーツを着ないで出勤しました。
*Because it was really hot and humid
yesterday, I didn't wear a suit to
work.*

Soto wa samui kara, sētā o kinasai.
外は寒いからセーターを着なさい。
It's cold outside, so put a sweater on.

Kiru is a verb you need for all the choices
of clothing in daily life: work, leisure,
special occasions, and more. In Japan,
the mix can be dazzling: school uniforms,
business suits, designer outfits, retro and
cutting edge fashion, kimono and yukata,
festival costumes, traditional work
clothes. It's all there to see and enjoy.

Words and Expressions
Related to This Verb

kikaeru　着替える
to change (one's clothes)

shichaku suru　試着する
to try clothes on

shichaku shitsu　試着室
a fitting room

kasanegi　重ね着
putting on layers of clothes

uwagi　上着
a coat, a jacket

shitagi　下着
underwear

きづかう／気遣う **kizuka.u**

TRANSITIVE   *to worry about, to consider*

			AFFIRMATIVE	**NEGATIVE**
Indicative	**INFORMAL**		kizukau	kizukawanai
	FORMAL		kizukaimasu	kizukaimasen
Imperative	**INFORMAL**	**I**	kizukae	kizukau na
		II	kizukainasai	kizukainasaru na
		III	kizukatte kudasai	kizukawanai de kudasai
	FORMAL		okizukai nasaimase	okizukai nasaimasu na
Presumptive	**INFORMAL**	**I**	kizukaō	kizukaumai
		II	kizukau darō	kizukawanai darō
	FORMAL	**I**	kizukaimashō	kizukaimasumai
		II	kizukau deshō	kizukawanai deshō
Provisional	**INFORMAL**		kizukaeba	kizukawanakereba
	FORMAL		kizukaimaseba	kizukaimasen nara
			kizukaimasureba	
Gerund	**INFORMAL**	**I**	kizukatte	kizukawanai de
		II		kizukawanakute
	FORMAL		kizukaimashite	kizukaimasen de
Past Ind.	**INFORMAL**		kizukatta	kizukawanakatta
	FORMAL		kizukaimashita	kizukaimasen deshita
Past Presump.	**INFORMAL**		kizukattarō	kizukawanakattarō
			kizukatta darō	kizukawanakatta darō
	FORMAL		kizukaimashitarō	kizukaimasen deshitarō
			kizukatta deshō	kizukawanakatta deshō
Conditional	**INFORMAL**		kizukattara	kizukawanakattara
	FORMAL		kizukaimashitara	kizukaimasen deshitara
Alternative	**INFORMAL**		kizukattari	kizukawanakattari
	FORMAL		kizukaimashitari	kizukaimasen deshitari

		INFORMAL AFFIRMATIVE INDICATIVE
Passive		kizukawareru
Potential		kizukaeru
Causative		kizukawaseru
Causative Pass.		kizukawaserareru
Honorific	**I**	okizukai ni naru
	II	okizukai nasaru
Humble	**I**	okizukai suru
	II	oldzukai itasu

to notice, to sense, to realize

			AFFIRMATIVE	NEGATIVE
Indicative	**INFORMAL**		kizuku	kizukanai
	FORMAL		kizukimasu	kizukimasen
Imperative	**INFORMAL**	I	kizuke	kizuku na
		II	kizukinasai	kizukinasaru na
		III	kizuite kudasai	kizukanai de kudasai
	FORMAL		okizuki nasaimase	okizuki nasaimasu na
Presumptive	**INFORMAL**	I	kizukō	kizukumai
		II	kizuku darō	kizukanai darō
	FORMAL	I	kizukimashō	kizukimasumai
		II	kizuku deshō	kizukanai deshō
Provisional	**INFORMAL**		kizukeba	kizukanakereba
	FORMAL		kizukimaseba	kizukimasen nara
			kizukimasureba	
Gerund	**INFORMAL**	I	kizuite	kizukanai de
		II		kizukanakute
	FORMAL		kizukimashite	kizukimasen de
Past Ind.	**INFORMAL**		kizuita	kizukanakatta
	FORMAL		kizukimashita	kizukimasen deshita
Past Presump.	**INFORMAL**		kizuitarō	kizukanakattarō
			kizuita darō	kizukanakatta darō
	FORMAL		kizukimashitarō	kizukimasen deshitarō
			kizuita deshō	kizukanakatta deshō
Conditional	**INFORMAL**		kizuitara	kizukanakattara
	FORMAL		kizukimashitara	kizukimasen deshitara
Alternative	**INFORMAL**		kizuitari	kizukanakattari
	FORMAL		kizukimashitari	kizukimasen deshitari

		INFORMAL AFFIRMATIVE INDICATIVE
Passive		kizukareru
Potential		kizukeru
Causative		kizukaseru
Causative Pass.		kizukaserareru
Honorific	I	okizuki ni naru
	II	okizuki nasaru
Humble	I	
	II	

きずつける／傷つける　**kizutsuke.ru**

TRANSITIVE　　*to wound, to damage, to harm*

			AFFIRMATIVE	**NEGATIVE**
Indicative	**INFORMAL**		kizutsukeru	kizutsukenai
	FORMAL		kizutsukemasu	kizutsukemasen
Imperative	**INFORMAL**	I	kizutsukero	kizutsukeru na
		II	kizutsukenasai	kizutsukenasaru na
		III	kizutsukete kudasai	kizutsukenai de kudasai
	FORMAL		okizutsuke nasaimase	okizutsuke nasaimasu na
Presumptive	**INFORMAL**	I	kizutsukeyō	kizutsukemai
		II	kizutsukeru darō	kizutsukenai darō
	FORMAL	I	kizutsukemashō	kizutsukemasumai
		II	kizutsukeru deshō	kizutsukenai deshō
Provisional	**INFORMAL**		kizutsukereba	kizutsukenakereba
	FORMAL		kizutsukemaseba	kizutsukemasen nara
			kizutsukemasureba	
Gerund	**INFORMAL**	I	kizutsukete	kizukenai de
		II		kizutsukenakute
	FORMAL		kizutsukemashite	kizutsukemasen de
Past Ind.	**INFORMAL**		kizutsuketa	kizutsukenakatta
	FORMAL		kizutsukemashita	kizutsukemasen deshita
Past Presump.	**INFORMAL**		kizutsuketarō	kizutsukenakattarō
			kizutsuketa darō	kizutsukenakatta darō
	FORMAL		kizutsukemashitarō	kizutsukemasen deshitarō
			kizutsuketa deshō	kizutsukenakatta deshō
Conditional	**INFORMAL**		kizutsuketara	kizutsukenakattara
	FORMAL		kizutsukemashitara	kizutsukemasen deshitara
Alternative	**INFORMAL**		kizutsuketari	kizutsukenakattari
	FORMAL		kizutsukemashitari	kizutsukemasen deshitari

			INFORMAL AFFIRMATIVE INDICATIVE
Passive			kizutsukerareru
Potential			kizutsukerareru
Causative			kizutsukesaseru
Causative Pass.			kizutsukesaserareru
Honorific		I	okizutsuke ni naru
		II	okizutsuke nasaru
Humble		I	okizutsuke suru
		II	okizutsuke itasu

K

to spill, to drop, to overflow

			AFFIRMATIVE	NEGATIVE
Indicative	**INFORMAL**		koboreru	koborenai
	FORMAL		koboremasu	koboremasen
Imperative	**INFORMAL**	I	koborero	koboreru na
		II		
		III		
	FORMAL			
Presumptive	**INFORMAL**	I	koboreyō	koboremai
		II	koboreru darō	koborenai darō
	FORMAL	I	koboremashō	koboremasumai
		II	koboreru deshō	koborenai deshō
Provisional	**INFORMAL**		koborereba	koborenakereba
	FORMAL		koboremaseba	koboremasen nara
			koboremasureba	
Gerund	**INFORMAL**	I	koborete	koborenai de
		II		koborenakute
	FORMAL		koboremashite	koboremasen de
Past Ind.	**INFORMAL**		koboreta	koborenakatta
	FORMAL		koboremashita	koboremasen deshita
Past Presump.	**INFORMAL**		koboretarō	koborenakattarō
			koboreta darō	koborenakatta darō
	FORMAL		koboremashitarō	koboremasen deshitarō
			koboreta deshō	koborenakatta deshō
Conditional	**INFORMAL**		koboretara	koborenakattara
	FORMAL		koboremashitara	koboremasen deshitara
Alternative	**INFORMAL**		koboretari	koborenakattari
	FORMAL		koboremashitari	koboremasen deshitari

		INFORMAL AFFIRMATIVE INDICATIVE
Passive		koborerareru
Potential		koborerareru
Causative		koboresaseru
Causative Pass.		
Honorific	I	okobore ni naru
	II	okobore nasaru
Humble	I	
	II	

			AFFIRMATIVE	NEGATIVE

TRANSITIVE — *to spill, to drop, to shed*

			AFFIRMATIVE	NEGATIVE
Indicative	**INFORMAL**		kobosu	kobosanai
	FORMAL		koboshimasu	koboshimasen
Imperative	**INFORMAL**	I	kobose	kobosu na
		II	koboshinasai	koboshinasaru na
		III	koboshite kudasai	kobosanai de kudasai
	FORMAL		okoboshi nasaimase	okoboshi nasaimasu na
Presumptive	**INFORMAL**	I	kobosō	kobosumai
		II	kobosu darō	kobosanai darō
	FORMAL	I	koboshimashō	koboshimasumai
		II	kobosu deshō	kobosanai deshō
Provisional	**INFORMAL**		koboseba	kobosanakereba
	FORMAL		koboshimaseba	koboshimasen nara
			koboshimasureba	
Gerund	**INFORMAL**	I	koboshite	kobosanai de
		II		kobosanakute
	FORMAL		koboshimashite	koboshimasen de
Past Ind.	**INFORMAL**		koboshita	kobosanakatta
	FORMAL		koboshimashita	koboshimasen deshita
Past Presump.	**INFORMAL**		koboshitarō	kobosanakattarō
			koboshita darō	kobosanakatta darō
	FORMAL		koboshimashitarō	koboshimasen deshitarō
			koboshita deshō	kobosanakatta deshō
Conditional	**INFORMAL**		koboshitara	kobosanakattara
	FORMAL		koboshimashitara	koboshimasen deshitara
Alternative	**INFORMAL**		koboshitari	kobosanakattari
	FORMAL		koboshimashitari	koboshimasen deshitari

			INFORMAL AFFIRMATIVE INDICATIVE
Passive			kobosareru
Potential			koboseru
Causative			kobosaseru
Causative Pass.			kobosaserareru
Honorific		I	okoboshi ni naru
		II	okoboshi nasaru
Humble		I	okoboshi suru
		II	okoboshi itasu

K

259

			AFFIRMATIVE	NEGATIVE
Indicative	**INFORMAL**		koeru	koenai
	FORMAL		koemasu	koemasen
Imperative	**INFORMAL**	I	koero	koeru na
		II	koenasai	koenasaru na
		III	koete kudasai	koenai de kudasai
	FORMAL		okoe nasaimase	okoe nasaimasu na
Presumptive	**INFORMAL**	I	koeyō	koemai
		II	koeru darō	koenai darō
	FORMAL	I	koemashō	koemasumai
		II	koeru deshō	koenai deshō
Provisional	**INFORMAL**		koereba	koenakereba
	FORMAL		koemaseba	koemasen nara
			koemasureba	
Gerund	**INFORMAL**	I	koete	koenai de
		II		koenakute
	FORMAL		koemashite	koemasen de
Past Ind.	**INFORMAL**		koeta	koenakatta
	FORMAL		koemashita	koemasen deshita
Past Presump.	**INFORMAL**		koetarō	koenakattarō
			koeta darō	koenakatta darō
	FORMAL		koemashitarō	koemasen deshitarō
			koeta deshō	koenakatta deshō
Conditional	**INFORMAL**		koetara	koenakattara
	FORMAL		koemashitara	koemasen deshitara
Alternative	**INFORMAL**		koetari	koenakattari
	FORMAL		koemashitari	koemasen deshitari

			INFORMAL AFFIRMATIVE INDICATIVE
Passive			koerareru
Potential			koerareru
Causative			koesaseru
Causative Pass.			koesaserareru
Honorific		I	okoe ni naru
		II	okoe nasaru
Humble		I	
		II	

こえる／越える／超える koe.ru

TRANSITIVE *to cross over, to exceed, to pass*

			AFFIRMATIVE	NEGATIVE
Indicative	INFORMAL		koeru	koenai
	FORMAL		koemasu	koemasen
Imperative	INFORMAL	I	koero	koeru na
		II	koenasai	koenasaru na
		III	koete kudasai	koenai de kudasai
	FORMAL		okoe nasaimase	okoe nasaimasu na
Presumptive	INFORMAL	I	koeyō	koemai
		II	koeru darō	koenai darō
	FORMAL	I	koemashō	koemasumai
		II	koeru deshō	koenai deshō
Provisional	INFORMAL		koereba	koenakereba
	FORMAL		koemaseba	koemasen nara
			koemasureba	
Gerund	INFORMAL	I	koete	koenai de
		II		koenakute
	FORMAL		koemashite	koemasen de
Past Ind.	INFORMAL		koeta	koenakatta
	FORMAL		koemashita	koemasen deshita
Past Presump.	INFORMAL		koetarō	koenakattarō
			koeta darō	koenakatta darō
	FORMAL		koemashitarō	koemasen deshitarō
			koeta deshō	koenakatta deshō
Conditional	INFORMAL		koetara	koenakattara
	FORMAL		koemashitara	koemasen deshitara
Alternative	INFORMAL		koetari	koenakattari
	FORMAL		koemashitari	koemasen deshitari

		INFORMAL AFFIRMATIVE INDICATIVE
Passive		koerareru
Potential		koerareru
Causative		koesaseru
Causative Pass.		koesaserareru
Honorific	I	okoe ni naru
	II	okoe nasaru
Humble	I	okoe suru
	II	okoe itasu

261

to be charred, to be burned

			AFFIRMATIVE	NEGATIVE
Indicative	**INFORMAL**		kogeru	kogenai
	FORMAL		kogemasu	kogemasen
Imperative	**INFORMAL**	I	kogero	kogeru na
		II		
		III		
	FORMAL			
Presumptive	**INFORMAL**	I	kogeyō	kogemai
		II	kogeru darō	kogenai darō
	FORMAL	I	kogemashō	kogemasumai
		II	kogeru deshō	kogenai deshō
Provisional	**INFORMAL**		kogereba	kogenakereba
	FORMAL		kogemaseba	kogemasen nara
			kogemasureba	
Gerund	**INFORMAL**	I	kogete	kogenai de
		II		kogenakute
	FORMAL		kogemashite	kogemasen de
Past Ind.	**INFORMAL**		kogeta	kogenakatta
	FORMAL		kogemashita	kogemasen deshita
Past Presump.	**INFORMAL**		kogetarō	kogenakattarō
			kogeta darō	kogenakatta darō
	FORMAL		kogemashitarō	kogemasen deshitarō
			kogeta deshō	kogenakatta deshō
Conditional	**INFORMAL**		kogetara	kogenakattara
	FORMAL		kogemashitara	kogemasen deshitara
Alternative	**INFORMAL**		kogetari	kogenakattari
	FORMAL		kogemashitari	kogemasen deshitari

		INFORMAL AFFIRMATIVE INDICATIVE
Passive		kogerareru
Potential		kogerareru
Causative		kogesaseru
Causative Pass.		kogesaserareru
Honorific	I	okoge ni naru
	II	okoge nasaru
Humble	I	
	II	

こころみる／試みる **kokoromi.ru**

TRANSITIVE   *to try, to test*

			AFFIRMATIVE	NEGATIVE
Indicative	**INFORMAL**		kokoromiru	kokorominai
	FORMAL		kokoromimasu	kokoromimasen
Imperative	**INFORMAL**	I	kokoromiro	kokoromiru na
		II	kokorominasai	kokorominasaru na
		III	kokoromite kudasai	kokorominai de kudasai
	FORMAL		okokoromi nasaimase	okokoromi nasaimasu na
Presumptive	**INFORMAL**	I	kokoromiyō	kokoromimai
		II	kokoromiru darō	kokorominai darō
	FORMAL	I	kokoromimashō	kokoromimasumai
		II	kokoromiru deshō	kokorominai deshō
Provisional	**INFORMAL**		kokoromireba	kokorominakereba
	FORMAL		kokoromimaseba	kokoromimasen nara
			kokoromimasureba	
Gerund	**INFORMAL**	I	kokoromite	kokorominai de
		II		kokorominakute
	FORMAL		kokoromimashite	kokoromimasen de
Past Ind.	**INFORMAL**		kokoromita	kokorominakatta
	FORMAL		kokoromimashita	kokoromimasen deshita
Past Presump.	**INFORMAL**		kokoromitarō	kokorominakattarō
			kokoromita darō	kokorominakatta darō
	FORMAL		kokoromimashitarō	kokoromimasen deshitarō
			kokoromita deshō	kokorominakatta deshō
Conditional	**INFORMAL**		kokoromitara	kokorominakattara
	FORMAL		kokoromimashitara	kokoromimasen deshitara
Alternative	**INFORMAL**		kokoromitari	kokorominakattari
	FORMAL		kokoromimashitari	kokoromimasen deshitari

			INFORMAL AFFIRMATIVE INDICATIVE
Passive			kokoromirareru
Potential			kokoromirareru
Causative			kokoromisaseru
Causative Pass.			kokoromisaserareru
Honorific		I	okokoromi ni naru
		II	okokoromi nasaru
Humble		I	okokoromi suru
		II	okokoromi itasu

kokorozas.u　こころざす／志す　　　　　　　　kokorozashi
to intend, to aspire to　　TRANSITIVE

			AFFIRMATIVE	NEGATIVE
Indicative	INFORMAL		kokorozasu	kokorozasanai
	FORMAL		kokorozashimasu	kokorozashimasen
Imperative	INFORMAL	I	kokorozase	kokorozasu na
		II	kokorozashinasai	kokorozashinasaru na
		III	kokorozashite kudasai	kokorozasanai de kudasai
	FORMAL		okokorozashi nasaimase	okokorozashi nasaimasu na
Presumptive	INFORMAL	I	kokorozasō	kokorozasumai
		II	kokorozasu darō	kokorozasanai darō
	FORMAL	I	kokorozashimashō	kokorozashimasumai
		II	kokorozasu deshō	kokorozasanai deshō
Provisional	INFORMAL		kokorozaseba	kokorozasanakereba
	FORMAL		kokorozashimaseba	kokorozashimasen nara
			kokorozashimasureba	
Gerund	INFORMAL	I	kokorozashite	kokorozasanai de
		II		kokorozasanakute
	FORMAL		kokorozashimashite	kokorozashimasen de
Past Ind.	INFORMAL		kokorozashita	kokorozasanakatta
	FORMAL		kokorozashimashita	kokorozashimasen deshita
Past Presump.	INFORMAL		kokorozashitarō	kokorozasanakattarō
			kokorozashita darō	kokorozasanakatta darō
	FORMAL		kokorozashimashitarō	kokorozashimasen deshitarō
			kokorozashita deshō	kokorozasanakatta deshō
Conditional	INFORMAL		kokorozashitara	kokorozasanakattara
	FORMAL		kokorozashimashitara	kokorozashimasen deshitara
Alternative	INFORMAL		kokorozashitari	kokorozasanakattari
	FORMAL		kokorozashimashitari	kokorozashimasen deshitari

		INFORMAL AFFIRMATIVE INDICATIVE
Passive		kokorozasareru
Potential		kokorozaseru
Causative		kokorozasaseru
Causative Pass.		kokorozasaserareru

Honorific	I	okokorozashi ni naru
	II	okokorozashi nasaru
Humble	I	
	II	

264

こまる／困る **koma.ru**

to be in trouble, to be at a loss, to be in a fix

			AFFIRMATIVE	NEGATIVE
Indicative	**INFORMAL**		komaru	komaranai
	FORMAL		komarimasu	komarimasen
Imperative	**INFORMAL**	I	komare	komaru na
		II	komarinasai	komarinasaru na
		III	komatte kudasai	komaranai de kudasai
	FORMAL		okomari nasaimase	okomari nasaimasu na
Presumptive	**INFORMAL**	I	komarō	komarumai
		II	komaru darō	komaranai darō
	FORMAL	I	komarimashō	komarimasumai
		II	komaru deshō	komaranai deshō
Provisional	**INFORMAL**		komareba	komaranakereba
	FORMAL		komarimaseba	komarimasen nara
			komarimasureba	
Gerund	**INFORMAL**	I	komatte	komaranai de
		II		komaranakute
	FORMAL		komarimashite	komarimasen de
Past Ind.	**INFORMAL**		komatta	komaranakatta
	FORMAL		komarimashita	komarimasen deshita
Past Presump.	**INFORMAL**		komattarō	komaranakattarō
			komatta darō	komaranakatta darō
	FORMAL		komarimashitarō	komarimasen deshitarō
			komatta deshō	komaranakatta deshō
Conditional	**INFORMAL**		komattara	komaranakattara
	FORMAL		komarimashitara	komarimasen deshitara
Alternative	**INFORMAL**		komattari	komaranakattari
	FORMAL		komarimashitari	komarimasen deshitari

		INFORMAL AFFIRMATIVE INDICATIVE
Passive		komarareru
Potential		
Causative		komaraseru
Causative Pass.		komaraserareru
Honorific	I	okomari ni naru
	II	okomari nasaru
Humble	I	
	II	

K

kom.u こむ／込む／混む

to become crowded

			AFFIRMATIVE	NEGATIVE
Indicative	**INFORMAL**		komu	komanai
	FORMAL		komimasu	komimasen
Imperative	**INFORMAL**	I	kome	komu na
		II	konde kudasai	komanai de kudasai
		III		
	FORMAL			
Presumptive	**INFORMAL**	I	komō	komumai
		II	komu darō	komanai darō
	FORMAL	I	komimashō	komimasumai
		II	komu deshō	komanai deshō
Provisional	**INFORMAL**		komeba	komanakereba
	FORMAL		komimaseba	komimasen nara
			komimasureba	
Gerund	**INFORMAL**	I	konde	komanai de
		II		komanakute
	FORMAL		komimashite	komimasen de
Past Ind.	**INFORMAL**		konda	komanakatta
	FORMAL		komimashita	komimasen deshita
Past Presump.	**INFORMAL**		kondarō	komanakattarō
			konda darō	komanakatta darō
	FORMAL		komimashitarō	komimasen deshitarō
			konda deshō	komanakatta deshō
Conditional	**INFORMAL**		kondara	komanakattara
	FORMAL		komimashitara	komimasen deshitara
Alternative	**INFORMAL**		kondari	komanakattari
	FORMAL		komimashitari	komimasen deshitari

	INFORMAL AFFIRMATIVE INDICATIVE
Passive	
Potential	
Causative	
Causative Pass.	
Honorific I	
II	
Humble I	
II	

			AFFIRMATIVE	**NEGATIVE**
Indicative	**INFORMAL**		konomu	konomanai
	FORMAL		konomimasu	konomimasen
Imperative	**INFORMAL**	I	konome	konomu na
		II	konominasai	konominasaru na
		III	kononde kudasai	konomanai de kudasai
	FORMAL		okonomi nasaimase	okonomi nasaimasu na
Presumptive	**INFORMAL**	I	konomō	konomumai
		II	konomu darō	konomanai darō
	FORMAL	I	konomimashō	konomimasumai
		II	konomu deshō	konomanai deshō
Provisional	**INFORMAL**		konomeba	konomanakereba
	FORMAL		konomimaseba	konomimasen nara
			konomimasureba	
Gerund	**INFORMAL**	I	kononde	konomanai de
		II		konomanakute
	FORMAL		konomimashite	konomimasen de
Past Ind.	**INFORMAL**		kononda	konomanakatta
	FORMAL		konomimashita	konomimasen deshita
Past Presump.	**INFORMAL**		konondarō	konomanakattarō
			kononda darō	konomanakatta darō
	FORMAL		konomimashitarō	konomimasen deshitarō
			kononda deshō	konomanakatta deshō
Conditional	**INFORMAL**		konondara	konomanakattara
	FORMAL		konomimashitara	konomimasen deshitara
Alternative	**INFORMAL**		konondari	konomanakattari
	FORMAL		konomimashitari	konomimasen deshitari

		INFORMAL AFFIRMATIVE INDICATIVE
Passive		konomareru
Potential		konomeru
Causative		konomaseru
Causative Pass.		konomaserareru
Honorific	I	okonomi ni naru
	II	okonomi nasaru
Humble	I	
	II	

K

kōr.u こおる／凍る

to freeze (solid)

kōri

			AFFIRMATIVE	NEGATIVE
Indicative	**INFORMAL**		kōru	kōranai
	FORMAL		kōrimasu	kōrimasen
Imperative	**INFORMAL**	I	kōre	kōru na
		II		
		III		
	FORMAL			
Presumptive	**INFORMAL**	I	kōrō	kōrumai
		II	kōru darō	kōranai darō
	FORMAL	I	kōrimashō	kōrimasumai
		II	kōru deshō	kōranai deshō
Provisional	**INFORMAL**		kōreba	kōranakereba
	FORMAL		kōrimaseba	kōrimasen nara
			kōrimasureba	
Gerund	**INFORMAL**	I	kōtte	kōranai de
		II		kōranakute
	FORMAL		kōrimashite	kōrimasen de
Past Ind.	**INFORMAL**		kōtta	kōranakatta
	FORMAL		kōrimashita	kōrimasen deshita
Past Presump.	**INFORMAL**		kōttarō	kōranakattarō
			kōtta darō	kōranakatta darō
	FORMAL		kōrimashitarō	kōrimasen deshitarō
			kōtta deshō	kōranakatta deshō
Conditional	**INFORMAL**		kōttara	kōranakattara
	FORMAL		kōrimashitara	kōrimasen deshitara
Alternative	**INFORMAL**		kōttari	kōranakattari
	FORMAL		kōrimashitari	kōrimasen deshitari

		INFORMAL AFFIRMATIVE INDICATIVE
Passive		kōrareru
Potential		kōreru
Causative		kōraseru
Causative Pass.		kōraserareru
Honorific	I	
	II	
Humble	I	
	II	

korae

こらえる／堪える **korae.ru**

TRANSITIVE   *to endure, to persevere*

			AFFIRMATIVE	NEGATIVE
Indicative	**INFORMAL**		koraeru	koraenai
	FORMAL		koraemasu	koraemasen
Imperative	**INFORMAL**	I	koraero	koraeru na
		II	koraenasai	koraenasaru na
		III	koraete kudasai	koraenai de kudasai
	FORMAL		okorae nasaimase	okorae nasaimasu na
Presumptive	**INFORMAL**	I	koraeyō	koraemai
		II	koraeru darō	koraenai darō
	FORMAL	I	koraemashō	koraemasumai
		II	koraeru deshō	koraenai deshō
Provisional	**INFORMAL**		koraereba	koraenakereba
	FORMAL		koraemaseba	koraemasen nara
			koraemasureba	
Gerund	**INFORMAL**	I	koraete	koraenai de
		II		koraenakute
	FORMAL		koraemashite	koraemasen de
Past Ind.	**INFORMAL**		koraeta	koraenakatta
	FORMAL		koraemashita	koraemasen deshita
Past Presump.	**INFORMAL**		koraetarō	koraenakattarō
			koraeta darō	koraenakatta darō
	FORMAL		koraemashitarō	koraemasen deshitarō
			koraeta deshō	koraenakatta deshō
Conditional	**INFORMAL**		koraetara	koraenakattara
	FORMAL		koraemashitara	koraemasen deshitara
Alternative	**INFORMAL**		koraetari	koraenakattari
	FORMAL		koraemashitari	koraemasen deshitari

		INFORMAL AFFIRMATIVE INDICATIVE
Passive		koraerareru
Potential		koraerareru
Causative		koraesaseru
Causative Pass.		koraesaserareru
Honorific	I	okorae ni naru
	II	okorae nasaru
Humble	I	okorae suru
	II	okorae itasu

K

to concentrate (one's attention), *to devote oneself to*　　TRANSITIVE

			AFFIRMATIVE	**NEGATIVE**
Indicative	**INFORMAL**		korasu	korasanai
	FORMAL		korashimasu	korashimasen
Imperative	**INFORMAL**	I	korase	korasu na
		II	korashinasai	korashinasaru na
		III	korashite kudasai	korasanai de kudasai
	FORMAL		okorashi nasaimase	okorashi nasaimasu na
Presumptive	**INFORMAL**	I	korasō	korasumai
		II	korasu darō	korasanai darō
	FORMAL	I	korashimashō	korashimasumai
		II	korasu deshō	korasanai deshō
Provisional	**INFORMAL**		koraseba	korasanakereba
	FORMAL		korashimaseba	korashimasen nara
			korashimasureba	
Gerund	**INFORMAL**	I	korashite	korasanai de
		II		korasanakute
	FORMAL		korashimashite	korashimasen de
Past Ind.	**INFORMAL**		korashita	korasanakatta
	FORMAL		korashimashita	korashimasen deshita
Past Presump.	**INFORMAL**		korashitarō	korasanakattarō
			korashita darō	korasanakatta darō
	FORMAL		korashimashitarō	korashimasen deshitarō
			korashita deshō	korasanakatta deshō
Conditional	**INFORMAL**		korashitara	korasanakattara
	FORMAL		korashimashitara	korashimasen deshitara
Alternative	**INFORMAL**		korashitari	korasanakattari
	FORMAL		korashimashitari	korashimasen deshitari

			INFORMAL AFFIRMATIVE INDICATIVE
Passive			korasareru
Potential			koraseru
Causative			korasaseru
Causative Pass.			korasaserareru
Honorific		I	okorashi ni naru
		II	okorashi nasaru
Humble		I	okorashi suru
		II	okorashi itasu

ころぶ／転ぶ **korob.u**
to take a spill, to fall down

			AFFIRMATIVE	**NEGATIVE**
Indicative	INFORMAL		korobu	korobanai
	FORMAL		korobimasu	korobimasen
Imperative	INFORMAL	I	korobe	korobu na
		II	korobinasai	korobinasaru na
		III	koronde kudasai	korobanai de kudasai
	FORMAL		okorobi nasaimase	okorobi nasaimasu na
Presumptive	INFORMAL	I	korobō	korobumai
		II	korobu darō	korobanai darō
	FORMAL	I	korobimashō	korobimasumai
		II	korobu deshō	korobanai deshō
Provisional	INFORMAL		korobeba	korobanakereba
	FORMAL		korobimaseba	korobimasen nara
			korobimasureba	
Gerund	INFORMAL	I	koronde	korobanai de
		II		korobanakute
	FORMAL		korobimashite	korobimasen de
Past Ind.	INFORMAL		koronda	korobanakatta
	FORMAL		korobimashita	korobimasen deshita
Past Presump.	INFORMAL		korondarō	korobanakattarō
			koronda darō	korobanakatta darō
	FORMAL		korobimashitarō	korobimasen deshitarō
			koronda deshō	korobanakatta deshō
Conditional	INFORMAL		korondara	korobanakattara
	FORMAL		korobimashitara	korobimasen deshitara
Alternative	INFORMAL		korondari	korobaoakattari
	FORMAL		korobimashitari	korobimasen deshitari

K

		INFORMAL AFFIRMATIVE INDICATIVE
Passive		korobareru
Potential		koroberu
Causative		korobaseru
Causative Pass.		korobaserareru
Honorific	I	okorobi ni naru
	II	okorobi nasaru
Humble	I	
	II	

koros.u　ころす／殺す   **koroshi**

to kill   TRANSITIVE

			AFFIRMATIVE	NEGATIVE
Indicative	**INFORMAL**		korosu	korosanai
	FORMAL		koroshimasu	koroshimasen
Imperative	**INFORMAL**	I	korose	korosu na
		II	koroshinasai	koroshinasaru na
		III	koroshite kudasai	korosanai de kudasai
	FORMAL		okoroshi nasaimase	okoroshi nasaimasu na
Presumptive	**INFORMAL**	I	korosō	korosumai
		II	korosu darō	korosanai darō
	FORMAL	I	koroshimashō	koroshimasumai
		II	korosu deshō	korosanai deshō
Provisional	**INFORMAL**		koroseba	korosanakereba
	FORMAL		koroshimaseba	koroshimasen nara
			koroshimasureba	
Gerund	**INFORMAL**	I	koroshite	korosanai de
		II		korosanakute
	FORMAL		koroshimashite	koroshimasen de
Past Ind.	**INFORMAL**		koroshita	korosanakatta
	FORMAL		koroshimashita	koroshimasen deshita
Past Presump.	**INFORMAL**		koroshitarō	korosanakattarō
			koroshita darō	korosanakatta darō
	FORMAL		koroshimashitarō	koroshimasen deshitarō
			koroshita deshō	korosanakatta deshō
Conditional	**INFORMAL**		koroshitara	korosanakattara
	FORMAL		koroshimashitara	koroshimasen deshitara
Alternative	**INFORMAL**		koroshitari	korosanakattari
	FORMAL		koroshimashitari	koroshimasen deshitari

		INFORMAL AFFIRMATIVE INDICATIVE
Passive		korosareru
Potential		koroseru
Causative		korosaseru
Causative Pass.		korosaserareru
Honorific	I	okoroshi ni naru
	II	okoroshi nasaru
Humble	I	okoroshi suru
	II	okoroshi itasu

koshikake

こしかける／腰掛ける **koshikake.ru**
to sit in (Western Style)

			AFFIRMATIVE	NEGATIVE
Indicative	**INFORMAL**		koshikakeru	koshikakenai
	FORMAL		koshikakemasu	koshikakemasen
Imperative	**INFORMAL**	**I**	koshikakero	koshikakeru na
		II	koshikakenasai	koshikakenasaru na
		III	koshikakete kudasai	koshikakenai de kudasai
	FORMAL		okoshikake nasaimase	okoshikake nasaimasu na
Presumptive	**INFORMAL**	**I**	koshikakeyō	koshikakemai
		II	koshikakeru darō	koshikakenai darō
	FORMAL	**I**	koshikakemashō	koshikakemasumai
		II	koshikakeru deshō	koshikakenai deshō
Provisional	**INFORMAL**		koshikakereba	koshikakenakereba
	FORMAL		koshikakemaseba	koshikakemasen nara
			koshikakemasureba	
Gerund	**INFORMAL**	**I**	koshikakete	koshikakenai de
		II		koshikakenakute
	FORMAL		koshikakemashite	koshikakemasen de
Past Ind.	**INFORMAL**		koshikaketa	koshikakenakatta
	FORMAL		koshikakemashita	koshikakemasen deshita
Past Presump.	**INFORMAL**		koshikaketarō	koshikakenakattarō
			koshikaketa darō	koshikakenakatta darō
	FORMAL		koshikakemashitarō	koshikakemasen deshitarō
			koshikaketa deshō	koshikakenakatta deshō
Conditional	**INFORMAL**		koshikaketara	koshikakenakattara
	FORMAL		koshikakemashitara	koshikakemasen deshitara
Alternative	**INFORMAL**		koshikaketari	koshikakenakattari
	FORMAL		koshikakemashitari	koshikakemasen deshitari

		INFORMAL AFFIRMATIVE INDICATIVE
Passive		koshikakerareru
Potential		koshikakerareru
Causative		koshikakesaseru
Causative Pass.		koshikakesaserareru
Honorific	**I**	okoshikake ni naru
	II	okoshikake nasaru
Humble	**I**	
	II	

koshirae.ru こしらえる

to make, to manufacture   TRANSITIVE

koshirae

			AFFIRMATIVE	**NEGATIVE**
Indicative	**INFORMAL**		koshiraeru	koshiraenai
	FORMAL		koshiraemasu	koshiraemasen
Imperative	**INFORMAL**	I	koshiraero	koshiraeru na
		II	koshiraenasai	koshiraenasaru na
		III	koshiraete kudasai	koshiraenai de kudasai
	FORMAL		okoshirae nasaimase	okoshirae nasaimasu na
Presumptive	**INFORMAL**	I	koshiraeyō	koshiraemai
		II	koshiraeru darō	koshiraenai darō
	FORMAL	I	koshiraemashō	koshiraemasumai
		II	koshiraeru deshō	koshiraenai deshō
Provisional	**INFORMAL**		koshiraereba	koshiraenakereba
	FORMAL		koshiraemaseba	koshiraemasen nara
			koshiraemasureba	
Gerund	**INFORMAL**	I	koshiraete	koshiraenai de
		II		koshiraenakute
	FORMAL		koshiraemashite	koshiraemasen de
Past Ind.	**INFORMAL**		koshiraeta	koshiraenakatta
	FORMAL		koshiraemashita	koshiraemasen deshita
Past Presump.	**INFORMAL**		koshiraetarō	koshiraenakattarō
			koshiraeta darō	koshiraenakatta darō
	FORMAL		koshiraemashitarō	koshiraemasen deshitarō
			koshiraeta deshō	koshiraenakatta deshō
Conditional	**INFORMAL**		koshiraetara	koshiraenakattara
	FORMAL		koshiraemashitara	koshiraemasen deshitara
Alternative	**INFORMAL**		koshiraetari	koshiraenakattari
	FORMAL		koshiraemashitari	koshiraemasen deshitari

		INFORMAL AFFIRMATIVE INDICATIVE
Passive		koshiraerareru
Potential		koshiraerareru
Causative		koshiraesaseru
Causative Pass.		koshiraesaserareru
Honorific	I	okoshirae ni naru
	II	okoshirae nasaru
Humble	I	okoshirae suru
	II	okoshirae itasu

TRANSITIVE *to cross, to pass, to surpass, to move ahead*

			AFFIRMATIVE	NEGATIVE
Indicative	**INFORMAL**		kosu	kosanai
	FORMAL		koshimasu	koshimasen
Imperative	**INFORMAL**	I	kose	kosu na
		II	koshinasai	koshinasaru na
		III	koshite kudasai	kosanai de kudasai
	FORMAL		okoshi nasaimase	okoshi nasaimasu na
Presumptive	**INFORMAL**	I	kosō	kosumai
		II	kosu darō	kosanai darō
	FORMAL	I	koshimashō	koshimasumai
		II	kosu deshō	kosanai deshō
Provisional	**INFORMAL**		koseba	kosanakereba
	FORMAL		koshimaseba	koshimasen nara
			koshimasureba	
Gerund	**INFORMAL**	I	koshite	kosanai de
		II		kosanakute
	FORMAL		koshimashite	koshimasen de
Past Ind.	**INFORMAL**		koshita	kosanakatta
	FORMAL		koshimashita	koshimasen deshita
Past Presump.	**INFORMAL**		koshitarō	kosanakattarō
			koshita darō	kosanakatta darō
	FORMAL		koshimashitarō	koshimasen deshitarō
			koshita deshō	kosanakatta deshō
Conditional	**INFORMAL**		koshitara	kosanakattara
	FORMAL		koshimashitara	koshimasen deshitara
Alternative	**INFORMAL**		koshitari	kosanakattari
	FORMAL		koshimashitari	koshimasen deshitari

		INFORMAL AFFIRMATIVE INDICATIVE
Passive		kosareru
Potential		koseru
Causative		kosaseru
Causative Pass.		kosaserareru
Honorific	I	okoshi ni naru
	II	okoshi nasaru
Humble	I	
	II	

K

275

to answer, to respond

			AFFIRMATIVE	NEGATIVE
Indicative	**INFORMAL**		kotaeru	kotaenai
	FORMAL		kotaemasu	kotaemasen
Imperative	**INFORMAL**	I	kotaero	kotaeru na
		II	kotaenasai	kotaenasaru na
		III	kotaete kudasai	kotaenai de kudasai
	FORMAL		okotae nasaimase	okotae nasaimasu na
Presumptive	**INFORMAL**	I	kotaeyō	kotaemai
		II	kotaeru darō	kotaenai darō
	FORMAL	I	kotaemashō	kotaemasumai
		II	kotaeru deshō	kotaenai deshō
Provisional	**INFORMAL**		kotaereba	kotaenakereba
	FORMAL		kotaemaseba	kotaemasen nara
			kotaemasureba	
Gerund	**INFORMAL**	I	kotaete	kotaenai de
		II		kotaenakute
	FORMAL		kotaemashite	kotaemasen de
Past Ind.	**INFORMAL**		kotaeta	kotaenakatta
	FORMAL		kotaemashita	kotaemasen deshita
Past Presump.	**INFORMAL**		kotaetarō	kotaenakattarō
			kotaeta darō	kotaenakatta darō
	FORMAL		kotaemashitarō	kotaemasen deshitarō
			kotaeta deshō	kotaenakatta deshō
Conditional	**INFORMAL**		kotaetara	kotaenakattara
	FORMAL		kotaemashitara	kotaemasen deshitara
Alternative	**INFORMAL**		kotaetari	kotaenakattari
	FORMAL		kotaemashitari	kotaemasen deshitari

		INFORMAL AFFIRMATIVE INDICATIVE
Passive		kotaerareru
Potential		kotaerareru
Causative		kotaesaseru
Causative Pass.		kotaesaserareru
Honorific	I	okotae ni naru
	II	okotae nasaru
Humble	I	okotae suru
	II	okotae itasu

AN ESSENTIAL
55 VERB

Kotaeru 答える

to answer, to respond

Sentences Using *Kotaeru*

Shiken no shitsumon wa dore mo kotaeru no ga muzukashikatta.
試験の質問はどれも答えるのが難しかった。
All the exam questions were hard to answer.

Watakushi no shitsumon ni kotaete kudasai.
私の質問に答えてください。
Please answer my question.

Kantan ni kotaereba sore de ii desu.
簡単に答えれば、それでいいです。
It's fine if you give a brief answer.

Shitsumon wa nandemo kotaemasu.
質問は何でも答えます。
I will answer all the questions.

Kanojo wa kyōju no shitsumon ni kotaeru koto ga dekinakatta.
彼女は教授の質問に答えることができなかった。
She couldn't answer the professor's question.

Kotaeru is a verb you need often in the give and take of daily life. As one asks and answers questions both simple and complex, the responses can help in finding a destination, landing a job, earning good grades, and making new friends.

K

Words and Expressions Related to This Verb

hentō suru   返答する
to answer, to reply

henji suru   返事する
to answer, to reply

kuchigotae suru   口答えする
to talk back, to retort

ukekotae   受け答え
response, reply

tōben   答弁
answer, explanation

to be different (from)

			AFFIRMATIVE	NEGATIVE
Indicative	**INFORMAL**		kotonaru	kotonaranai
	FORMAL		kotonarimasu	kotonarimasen
Imperative	**INFORMAL**	I	kotonare	kotonaru na
		II	kotonarinasai	kotonarinasaru na
		III	kotonatte kudasai	kotonaranai de kudasai
	FORMAL		okotonari nasaimase	okotonari nasaimasu na
Presumptive	**INFORMAL**	I	kotonarō	kotonarumai
		II	kotonaru darō	kotonaranai darō
	FORMAL	I	kotonarimashō	kotonarimasumai
		II	kotonaru deshō	kotonaranai deshō
Provisional	**INFORMAL**		kotonareba	kotonaranakereba
	FORMAL		kotonarimaseba	kotonarimasen nara
			kotonarimasureba	
Gerund	**INFORMAL**	I	kotonatte	kotonaranai de
		II		kotonaranakute
	FORMAL		kotonarimashite	kotonarimasen de
Past Ind.	**INFORMAL**		kotonatta	kotonaranakatta
	FORMAL		kotonarimashita	kotonarimasen deshita
Past Presump.	**INFORMAL**		kotonattarō	kotonaranakattarō
			kotonatta darō	kotonaranakatta darō
	FORMAL		kotonarimashitarō	kotonarimasen deshitarō
			kotonatta deshō	kotonaranakatta deshō
Conditional	**INFORMAL**		kotonattara	kotonaranakattara
	FORMAL		kotonarimashitara	kotonarimasen deshitara
Alternative	**INFORMAL**		kotonattari	kotonaranakattari
	FORMAL		kotonarimashitari	kotonarimasen deshitari

		INFORMAL AFFIRMATIVE INDICATIVE
Passive		
Potential		kotonaeru
Causative		kotonaraseru
Causative Pass.		kotonaraserareru
Honorific	I	
	II	
Humble	I	
	II	

kotowari

ことわる／断わる **kotowar.u**

TRANSITIVE　*to refuse, to decline*

			AFFIRMATIVE	NEGATIVE
Indicative	**INFORMAL**		kotowaru	kotowaranai
	FORMAL		kotowarimasu	kotowarimasen
Imperative	**INFORMAL**	I	kotoware	kotowaru na
		II	kotowarinasai	kotowarinasaru na
		III	kotowatte kudasai	kotowaranai de kudasai
	FORMAL		okotowari nasaimase	okotowari nasaimasu na
Presumptive	**INFORMAL**	I	kotowarō	kotowarumai
		II	kotowaru darō	kotowaranai darō
	FORMAL	I	kotowarimashō	kotowarimasumai
		II	kotowaru deshō	kotowaranai deshō
Provisional	**INFORMAL**		kotowareba	kotowaranakereba
	FORMAL		kotowarimaseba	kotowarimasen nara
			kotowarimasureba	
Gerund	**INFORMAL**	I	kotowatte	kotowaranai de
		II		kotowaranakute
	FORMAL		kotowarimashite	kotowarimasen de
Past Ind.	**INFORMAL**		kotowatta	kotowaranakatta
	FORMAL		kotowarimashita	kotowarimasen deshita
Past Presump.	**INFORMAL**		kotowattarō	kotowaranakattarō
			kotowatta darō	kotowaranakatta darō
	FORMAL		kotowarimashitarō	kotowarimasen deshitarō
			kotowatta deshō	kotowaranakatta deshō
Conditional	**INFORMAL**		kotowattara	kotowaranakattara
	FORMAL		kotowarimashitara	kotowarimasen deshitara
Alternative	**INFORMAL**		kotowattari	kotowaranakattari
	FORMAL		kotowarimashitari	kotowarimasen deshitari

		INFORMAL AFFIRMATIVE INDICATIVE
Passive		kotowarareru
Potential		kotowareru
Causative		kotowaraseru
Causative Pass.		kotowaraserareru
Honorific	I	okotowari ni naru
	II	okotowari nasaru
Humble	I	okotowari suru
	II	okotowari itasu

kowagar.u こわがる／怖がる

to fear　TRANSITIVE

			AFFIRMATIVE	NEGATIVE
Indicative	**INFORMAL**		kowagaru	kowagaranai
	FORMAL		kowagarimasu	kowagarimasen
Imperative	**INFORMAL**	I	kowagare	kowagaru na
		II	kowagarinasai	kowagarinasaru na
		III	kowagatte kudasai	kowagaranai de kudasai
	FORMAL		okowagari nasaimase	okowagari nasaimasu na
Presumptive	**INFORMAL**	I	kowagarō	kowagarumai
		II	kowagaru darō	kowagaranai darō
	FORMAL	I	kowagarimashō	kowagarimasumai
		II	kowagaru deshō	kowagaranai deshō
Provisional	**INFORMAL**		kowagareba	kowagaranakereba
	FORMAL		kowagarimaseba	kowagarimasen nara
			kowagarimasureba	
Gerund	**INFORMAL**	I	kowagatte	kowagaranai de
		II		kowagaranakute
	FORMAL		kowagarimashite	kowagarimasen de
Past Ind.	**INFORMAL**		kowagatta	kowagaranakatta
	FORMAL		kowagarimashita	kowagarimasen deshita
Past Presump.	**INFORMAL**		kowagattarō	kowagaranakattarō
			kowagatta darō	kowagaranakatta darō
	FORMAL		kowagarimashitarō	kowagarimasen deshitarō
			kowagatta deshō	kowagaranakatta deshō
Conditional	**INFORMAL**		kowagattara	kowagaranakattara
	FORMAL		kowagarimashitara	kowagarimasen deshitara
Alternative	**INFORMAL**		kowagattari	kowagaranakattari
	FORMAL		kowagarimashitari	kowagarimasen deshitari

		INFORMAL AFFIRMATIVE INDICATIVE
Passive		kowagarareru
Potential		
Causative		kowagaraseru
Causative Pass.		kowagaraserareru
Honorific	I	okowagari ni naru
	II	okowagari nasaru
Humble	I	
	II	

こわれる／壊れる **koware.ru**

to break

			AFFIRMATIVE	NEGATIVE
Indicative	**INFORMAL**		kowareru	kowarenai
	FORMAL		kowaremasu	kowaremasen
Imperative	**INFORMAL**	I	kowarero	kowareru na
		II		
		III	kowarete kudasai	kowarenai de kudasai
	FORMAL			
Presumptive	**INFORMAL**	I	kowareyō	kowaremai
		II	kowareru darō	kowarenai darō
	FORMAL	I	kowaremashō	kowaremasumai
		II	kowareru deshō	kowarenai deshō
Provisional	**INFORMAL**		kowarereba	kowarenakereba
	FORMAL		kowaremaseba	kowaremasen nara
			kowaremasureba	
Gerund	**INFORMAL**	I	kowarete	kowarenai de
		II		kowarenakute
	FORMAL		kowaremashite	kowaremasen de
Past Ind.	**INFORMAL**		kowareta	kowarenakatta
	FORMAL		kowaremashita	kowaremasen deshita
Past Presump.	**INFORMAL**		kowaretarō	kowarenakattarō
			kowareta darō	kowarenakatta darō
	FORMAL		kowaremashitarō	kowaremasen deshitarō
			kowareta deshō	kowarenakatta deshō
Conditional	**INFORMAL**		kowaretara	kowarenakattara
	FORMAL		kowaremashitara	kowaremasen deshitara
Alternative	**INFORMAL**		kowaretari	kowarenakattari
	FORMAL		kowaremashitari	kowaremasen deshitari

		INFORMAL AFFIRMATIVE INDICATIVE
Passive		
Potential		kowarerareru
Causative		*
Causative Pass.		*
Honorific	I	okoware ni naru
	II	
Humble	I	
	II	

*See *kowas.u*, the transitive verb for "to break"

281

to smash, to break　　TRANSITIVE

			AFFIRMATIVE	NEGATIVE
Indicative	**INFORMAL**		kowasu	kowasanai
	FORMAL		kowashimasu	kowashimasen
Imperative	**INFORMAL**	I	kowase	kowasu na
		II	kowashinasai	kowashinasaru na
		III	kowashite kudasai	kowasanai de kudasai
	FORMAL		okowashi nasaimase	okowashi nasaimasu na
Presumptive	**INFORMAL**	I	kowasō	kowasumai
		II	kowasu darō	kowasanai darō
	FORMAL	I	kowashimashō	kowashimasumai
		II	kowasu deshō	kowasanai deshō
Provisional	**INFORMAL**		kowaseba	kowasanakereba
	FORMAL		kowashimaseba	kowashimasen nara
			kowashimasureba	
Gerund	**INFORMAL**	I	kowashite	kowasanai de
		II		kowasanakute
	FORMAL		kowashimashite	kowashimasen de
Past Ind.	**INFORMAL**		kowashita	kowasanakatta
	FORMAL		kowashimashita	kowashimasen deshita
Past Presump.	**INFORMAL**		kowashitarō	kowasanakattarō
			kowashita darō	kowasanakatta darō
	FORMAL		kowashimashitarō	kowashimasen deshitarō
			kowashita deshō	kowasanakatta deshō
Conditional	**INFORMAL**		kowashitara	kowasanakattara
	FORMAL		kowashimashitara	kowashimasen deshitara
Alternative	**INFORMAL**		kowashitari	kowasanakattari
	FORMAL		kowashimashitari	kowashimasen deshitari

			INFORMAL AFFIRMATIVE INDICATIVE
Passive			kowasareru
Potential			kowaseru
Causative			kowasaseru
Causative Pass.			kowasaserareru
Honorific		I	okowashi ni naru
		II	okowashi nasaru
Humble		I	okowashi suru
		II	okowashi itasu

kudaki

くだく／砕く **kudak.u**

TRANSITIVE   *to smash, to crush*

			AFFIRMATIVE	NEGATIVE
Indicative	**INFORMAL**		kudaku	kudakanai
	FORMAL		kudakimasu	kudakimasen
Imperative	**INFORMAL**	I	kudake	kudaku na
		II	kudakinasai	kudakinasaru na
		III	kudaite kudasai	kudakanai de kudasai
	FORMAL		okudaki nasaimase	okudaki nasaimasu na
Presumptive	**INFORMAL**	I	kudakō	kudakumai
		II	kudaku darō	kudakanai darō
	FORMAL	I	kudakimashō	kudakimasumai
		II	kudaku deshō	kudakanai deshō
Provisional	**INFORMAL**		kudakeba	kudakanakereba
	FORMAL		kudakimaseba	kudakimasen nara
			kudakimasureba	
Gerund	**INFORMAL**	I	kudaite	kudakanai de
		II		kudakanakute
	FORMAL		kudakimashite	kudakimasen de
Past Ind.	**INFORMAL**		kudaita	kudakanakatta
	FORMAL		kudakimashita	kudakimasen deshita
Past Presump.	**INFORMAL**		kudaitarō	kudakanakattarō
			kudaita darō	kudakanakatta darō
	FORMAL		kudakimashitarō	kudakimasen deshitarō
			kudaita deshō	kudakanakatta deshō
Conditional	**INFORMAL**		kudaitara	kudakanakattara
	FORMAL		kudakimashitara	kudakimasen deshitara
Alternative	**INFORMAL**		kudaitari	kudakanakattari
	FORMAL		kudakimashitari	kudakimasen deshitari

		INFORMAL AFFIRMATIVE INDICATIVE
Passive		kudakareru
Potential		kudakeru
Causative		kudakaseru
Causative Pass.		kudakaserareru
Honorific	I	okudaki ni naru
	II	okudaki nasaru
Humble	I	okudaki suru
	II	okudaki itasu

283

kudasar.u くださる／下さる   kudasai

to give (to me)*   TRANSITIVE

			AFFIRMATIVE	NEGATIVE
Indicative	INFORMAL		kudasaru	kudasaranai
	FORMAL		kudasaimasu	kudasaimasen
Imperative	INFORMAL	I	kudasai	kudasaru na
		II		
		III		
	FORMAL		kudasaimase	kudasaimasu na
Presumptive	INFORMAL	I	kudasarō	kudasarumai
		II	kudasaru darō	kudasaranai darō
	FORMAL	I	kudasaimashō	kudasaimasumai
		II	kudasaru deshō	kudasaranai deshō
Provisional	INFORMAL		kudasareba	kudasaranakereba
	FORMAL		kudasaimaseba	kudasaimasen nara
			kudasaimasureba	
Gerund	INFORMAL	I	kudasatte	kudasaranai de
		II		kudasaranakute
	FORMAL		kudasaimashite	kudasaimasen de
Past Ind.	INFORMAL		kudasatta	kudasaranakatta
	FORMAL		kudasaimashita	kudasaimasen deshita
Past Presump.	INFORMAL		kudasattarō	kudasaranakattarō
			kudasatta darō	kudasaranakatta darō
	FORMAL		kudasaimashitarō	kudasaimasen deshitarō
			kudasatta deshō	kudasaranakatta deshō
Conditional	INFORMAL		kudasattara	kudasaranakattara
	FORMAL		kudasaimashitara	kudasaimasen deshitara
Alternative	INFORMAL		kudasattari	kudasaranakattari
	FORMAL		kudasaimashitari	kudasaimasen deshitari

		INFORMAL AFFIRMATIVE INDICATIVE
Passive		
Potential		
Causative		
Causative Pass.		
Honorific	I	
	II	
Humble	I	
	II	

*Or to a member of my "in group."

284

くどく／口説く **kudok.u**

TRANSITIVE   *to urge, to persuade, to make advances to a woman*

			AFFIRMATIVE	**NEGATIVE**
Indicative	**INFORMAL**		kudoku	kudokanai
	FORMAL		kudokimasu	kudokimasen
Imperative	**INFORMAL**	I	kudoke	kudoku na
		II	kudokinasai	kudokinasaru na
		III	kudoite kudasai	kudokanai de kudasai
	FORMAL		okudoki nasaimase	okudoki nasaimasu na
Presumptive	**INFORMAL**	I	kudokō	kudokumai
		II	kudoku darō	kudokanai darō
	FORMAL	I	kudokimashō	kudokimasumai
		II	kudoku deshō	kudokanai deshō
Provisional	**INFORMAL**		kudokeba	kudokanakereba
	FORMAL		kudokimaseba	kudokimasen nara
			kudokimasureba	
Gerund	**INFORMAL**	I	kudoite	kudokanai de
		II		kudokanakute
	FORMAL		kudokimashite	kudokimasen de
Past Ind.	**INFORMAL**		kudoita	kudokanakatta
	FORMAL		kudokimashita	kudokimasen deshita
Past Presump.	**INFORMAL**		kudoitarō	kudokanakattarō
			kudoita darō	kudokanakatta darō
	FORMAL		kudokimashitarō	kudokimasen deshitarō
			kudoita deshō	kudokanakatta deshō
Conditional	**INFORMAL**		kudoitara	kudokanakattara
	FORMAL		kudokimashitara	kudokimasen deshitara
Alternative	**INFORMAL**		kudoitari	kudokanakattari
	FORMAL		kudokimashitari	kudokimasen deshitari

			INFORMAL AFFIRMATIVE INDICATIVE
Passive			kudokareru
Potential			kudokeru
Causative			kudokaseru
Causative Pass.			kudokaserareru
Honorific		I	okudoki ni naru
		II	okudoki nasaru
Humble		I	okudoki suru
		II	okudoki itasu

K

kuichiga.u　くいちがう／食い違う　　　　　　　　　　kuichigai

to be in discord, to clash

			AFFIRMATIVE	NEGATIVE
Indicative	**INFORMAL**		kuichigau	kuichigawanai
	FORMAL		kuichigaimasu	kuichigaimasen
Imperative	**INFORMAL**	I	kuichigae	kuichigau na
		II	kuichigainasai	kuichigainasaru na
		III	kuichigatte kudasai	kuichigawanai de kudasai
	FORMAL		okuichigai nasaimase	okuichigai nasaimasu na
Presumptive	**INFORMAL**	I	kuichigaō	kuichigaumai
		II	kuichigau darō	kuichigawanai darō
	FORMAL	I	kuichigaimashō	kuichigaimasumai
		II	kuichigau deshō	kuichigawanai deshō
Provisional	**INFORMAL**		kuichigaeba	kuichigawanakereba
	FORMAL		kuichigaimaseba	kuichigaimasen nara
			kuichigaimasureba	
Gerund	**INFORMAL**	I	kuichigatte	kuichigawanai de
		II		kuichigawanakute
	FORMAL		kuichigaimashite	kuichigaimasen de
Past Ind.	**INFORMAL**		kuichigatta	kuichigawanakatta
	FORMAL		kuichigaimashita	kuichigaimasen deshita
Past Presump.	**INFORMAL**		kuichigattarō	kuichigawanakattarō
			kuichigatta darō	kuichigawanakatta darō
	FORMAL		kuichigaimashitarō	kuichigaimasen deshitarō
			kuichigatta deshō	kuichigawanakatta deshō
Conditional	**INFORMAL**		kuichigattara	kuichigawanakattara
	FORMAL		kuichigaimashitara	kuichigaimasen deshitara
Alternative	**INFORMAL**		kuichigattari	kuichigawanakattari
	FORMAL		kuichigaimashitari	kuichigaimasen deshitari

		INFORMAL AFFIRMATIVE INDICATIVE
Passive		kuichigawareru
Potential		kuichigaeru
Causative		kuichigawaseru
Causative Pass.		kuichigawaserareru
Honorific	I	
	II	
Humble	I	
	II	

to get cloudy

			AFFIRMATIVE	NEGATIVE
Indicative	**INFORMAL**		kumoru	kumoranai
	FORMAL		kumorimasu	kumorimasen
Imperative	**INFORMAL**	I	kumore	kumoru na
		II		
		III		
	FORMAL			
Presumptive	**INFORMAL**	I	kumorō	kumorumai
		II	kumoru darō	kumoranai darō
	FORMAL	I	kumorimashō	kumorimasumai
		II	kumoru deshō	kumoranai deshō
Provisional	**INFORMAL**		kumoreba	kumoranakereba
	FORMAL		kumorimaseba	kumorimasen nara
			kumorimasureba	
Gerund	**INFORMAL**	I	kumotte	kumoranai de
		II		kumoranakute
	FORMAL		kumorimashite	kumorimasen de
Past Ind.	**INFORMAL**		kumotta	kumoranakatta
	FORMAL		kumorimashita	kumorimasen deshita
Past Presump.	**INFORMAL**		kumottarō	kumoranakattarō
			kumotta darō	kumoranakatta darō
	FORMAL		kumorimashitarō	kumorimasen deshitarō
			kumotta deshō	kumoranakatta deshō
Conditional	**INFORMAL**		kumottara	kumoranakattara
	FORMAL		kumorimashitara	kumorimasen deshitara
Alternative	**INFORMAL**		kumottari	kumoranakattari
	FORMAL		kumorimashitari	kumorimasen deshitari

		INFORMAL AFFIRMATIVE INDICATIVE
Passive		kumorareru
Potential		
Causative		kumoraseru
Causative Pass.		
Honorific	I	
	II	
Humble	I	
	II	

to put together, to unite, to team up　　　TRANSITIVE

			AFFIRMATIVE	**NEGATIVE**
Indicative	**INFORMAL**		kumu	kumanai
	FORMAL		kumimasu	kumimasen
Imperative	**INFORMAL**	I	kume	kumu na
		II	kuminasai	kuminasaru na
		III	kunde kudasai	kumanai de kudasai
	FORMAL		okumi nasaimase	okumi nasaimasu na
Presumptive	**INFORMAL**	I	kumō	kumumai
		II	kumu darō	kumanai darō
	FORMAL	I	kumimashō	kumimasumai
		II	kumu deshō	kumanai deshō
Provisional	**INFORMAL**		kumeba	kumanakereba
	FORMAL		kumimaseba	kumimasen nara
			kumimasureba	
Gerund	**INFORMAL**	I	kunde	kumanai de
		II		kumanakute
	FORMAL		kumimashite	kumimasen de
Past Ind.	**INFORMAL**		kunda	kumanakatta
	FORMAL		kumimashita	kumimasen deshita
Past Presump.	**INFORMAL**		kundarō	kumanakattarō
			kunda darō	kumanakatta darō
	FORMAL		kumimashitarō	kumimasen deshitarō
			kunda deshō	kumanakatta deshō
Conditional	**INFORMAL**		kundara	kumanakattara
	FORMAL		kumimashitara	kumimasen deshitara
Alternative	**INFORMAL**		kundari	kumanakattari
	FORMAL		kumimashitari	kumimasen deshitari

			INFORMAL AFFIRMATIVE INDICATIVE
Passive			kumareru
Potential			kumeru
Causative			kumaseru
Causative Pass.			kumaserareru
Honorific		I	okumi ni naru
		II	okumi nasaru
Humble		I	okumi suru
		II	okumi itasu

くらべる／比べる　**kurabe.ru**

TRANSITIVE　*to compare*

			AFFIRMATIVE	**NEGATIVE**
Indicative	**INFORMAL**		kuraberu	kurabenai
	FORMAL		kurabemasu	kurabemasen
Imperative	**INFORMAL**	I	kurabero	kuraberu na
		II	kurabenasai	kurabenasaru na
		III	kurabete kudasai	kurabenai de kudasai
	FORMAL		okurabe nasaimase	okurabe nasaimasu na
Presumptive	**INFORMAL**	I	kurabeyō	kurabemai
		II	kuraberu darō	kurabenai darō
	FORMAL	I	kurabemashō	kurabemasumai
		II	kuraberu deshō	kurabenai deshō
Provisional	**INFORMAL**		kurabereba	kurabenakereba
	FORMAL		kurabemaseba	kurabemasen nara
			kurabemasureba	
Gerund	**INFORMAL**	I	kurabete	kurabenai de
		II		kurabenakute
	FORMAL		kurabemashite	kurabemasen de
Past Ind.	**INFORMAL**		kurabeta	kurabenakatta
	FORMAL		kurabemashita	kurabemasen deshita
Past Presump.	**INFORMAL**		kurabetarō	kurabenakattarō
			kurabeta darō	kurabenakatta darō
	FORMAL		kurabemashitarō	kurabemasen deshitarō
			kurabeta deshō	kurabenakatta deshō
Conditional	**INFORMAL**		kurabetara	kurabenakattara
	FORMAL		kurabemashitara	kurabemasen deshitara
Alternative	**INFORMAL**		kurabetari	kurabenakattari
	FORMAL		kurabemashitari	kurabemasen deshitari

		INFORMAL AFFIRMATIVE INDICATIVE
Passive		kuraberareru
Potential		kuraberareru
Causative		kurabesaseru
Causative Pass.		kurabesaserareru
Honorific	I	okurabe ni naru
	II	okurabe nasaru
Humble	I	okurabe suru
	II	okurabe itasu

K

AN ESSENTIAL
55 VERB

Kuraberu 比べる

to compare

Sentences Using *Kuraberu*

Dotchi no seihin ga ii ka wa, kurabete mireba sugu ni wakarimasu.
どっちの製品がいいかは、比べてみれば直ぐに分かります。
If you compare the products, you'll immediately see which one is better.

Ano futari wa amarinimo chigaisugite kurabeyō ga nai.
あの二人は余りにも違い過ぎて比べようが無い。
There is no way to compare them because the two are so different.

Atarashii konpyūta ga hoshikatta node, saisho ni intānetto de nedan o kurabete mimashita.
新しいコンピュータが欲しかったので、最初にインターネットで値段を比べてみました。
Since I wanted a new computer, I compared some prices on the Internet.

Ryotei ga futatsu arukara kurabete, dotchika erabimashō.
旅程が二つあるから比べて、どっちか選びましょう。
Let's compare the two itineraries and choose one.

Ano futago no shimai wa, itsumo nandemo kuraberarete iru.
あの双子の姉妹は、いつも何でも比べられている。
Those twin sisters are always being compared in every way.

Kuraberu is an essential verb for everyday speech. You compare people, places, prices, jobs, candidates, political parties—the list is endless. And if you're studying Japanese, comparing English and Japanese verb usage is helpful, too!

Words and Expressions Related to This Verb

hikaku suru　比較する
to compare

hiritsu　比率
ratio, percentage

hiyu　比喩
a figure of speech

Proverb

Donguri no sei kurabe.
ドングリの背比べ。
They're all the same, all ordinary. (Acorns are comparing their height.)

くらむ／眩む **kuram.u**
to get dizzy, to be blinded

			AFFIRMATIVE	NEGATIVE
Indicative	**INFORMAL**		kuramu	kuramanai
	FORMAL		kuramimasu	kuramimasen
Imperative	**INFORMAL**	I	kurame	kuramu na
		II		
		III		
	FORMAL			
Presumptive	**INFORMAL**	I	kuramō	kuramumai
		II	kuramu darō	kuramanai darō
	FORMAL	I	kuramimashō	kuramimasumai
		II	kuramu deshō	kuramanai deshō
Provisional	**INFORMAL**		kurameba	kuramanakereba
	FORMAL		kuramimaseba	kuramimasen nara
			kuramimasureba	
Gerund	**INFORMAL**	I	kurande	kuramanai de
		II		kuramanakute
	FORMAL		kuramimashite	kuramimasen de
Past Ind.	**INFORMAL**		kuranda	kuramanakatta
	FORMAL		kuramimashita	kuramimasen deshita
Past Presump.	**INFORMAL**		kurandarō	kuramanakattarō
			kuranda darō	kuramanakatta darō
	FORMAL		kuramimashitarō	kuramimasen deshitarō
			kuranda deshō	kuramanakatta deshō
Conditional	**INFORMAL**		kurandara	kuramanakattara
	FORMAL		kuramimashitara	kuramimasen deshitara
Alternative	**INFORMAL**		kurandari	kuramanakattari
	FORMAL		kuramimashitari	kuramimasen deshitari

		INFORMAL AFFIRMATIVE INDICATIVE
Passive		kuramareru
Potential		
Causative		kuramaseru
Causative Pass.		kuramaserareru
Honorific	I	okurami ni naru
	II	okurami nasaru
Humble	I	
	II	

kuras.u くらす／暮らす

to live   TRANSITIVE

kurashi

			AFFIRMATIVE	NEGATIVE
Indicative	**INFORMAL**		kurasu	kurasanai
	FORMAL		kurashimasu	kurashimasen
Imperative	**INFORMAL**	I	kurase	kurasu na
		II	kurashinasai	kurashinasaru na
		III	kurashite kudasai	kurasanai de kudasai
	FORMAL		okurashi nasaimase	okurashi nasaimasu na
Presumptive	**INFORMAL**	I	kurasō	kurasumai
		II	kurasu darō	kurasanai darō
	FORMAL	I	kurashimashō	kurashimasumai
		II	kurasu deshō	kurasanai deshō
Provisional	**INFORMAL**		kuraseba	kurasanakereba
	FORMAL		kurashimaseba	kurashimasen nara
			kurashimasureba	
Gerund	**INFORMAL**	I	kurashite	kurasanai de
		II		kurasanakute
	FORMAL		kurashimashite	kurashimasen de
Past Ind.	**INFORMAL**		kurashita	kurasanakatta
	FORMAL		kurashimashita	kurashimasen deshita
Past Presump.	**INFORMAL**		kurashitarō	kurasanakattarō
			kurashita darō	kurasanakatta darō
	FORMAL		kurashimashitarō	kurashimasen deshitarō
			kurashita deshō	kurasanakatta deshō
Conditional	**INFORMAL**		kurashitara	kurasanakattara
	FORMAL		kurashimashitara	kurashimasen deshitara
Alternative	**INFORMAL**		kurashitari	kurasanakattari
	FORMAL		kurashimashitari	kurashimasen deshitari

		INFORMAL AFFIRMATIVE INDICATIVE
Passive		kurasareru
Potential		kuraseru
Causative		kurasaseru
Causative Pass.		kurasaserareru
Honorific	I	okurashi ni naru
	II	okurashi nasaru
Humble	I	
	II	

TRANSITIVE   *to give* (the giver is someone other than the speaker)

			AFFIRMATIVE	NEGATIVE
Indicative	**INFORMAL**		kureru	kurenai
	FORMAL		kuremasu	kuremasen
Imperative	**INFORMAL**	I	kure	kureru na
		II		
		III		
	FORMAL			
Presumptive	**INFORMAL**	I	kureyō	kuremai
		II	kureru darō	kurenai darō
	FORMAL	I	kuremashō	kuremasumai
		II	kureru deshō	kurenai deshō
Provisional	**INFORMAL**		kurereba	kurenakereba
	FORMAL		kuremaseba	kuremasen nara
			kuremasureba	
Gerund	**INFORMAL**	I	kurete	kurenai de
		II		kurenakute
	FORMAL		kuremashite	kuremasen de
Past Ind.	**INFORMAL**		kureta	kurenakatta
	FORMAL		kuremashita	kuremasen deshita
Past Presump.	**INFORMAL**		kuretarō	kurenakattarō
			kureta darō	kurenakatta darō
	FORMAL		kuremashitarō	kuremasen deshitarō
			kureta deshō	kurenakatta deshō
Conditional	**INFORMAL**		kuretara	kurenakattara
	FORMAL		kuremashitara	kuremasen deshitara
Alternative	**INFORMAL**		kuretari	kurenakattari
	FORMAL		kuremashitari	kuremasen deshitari

		INFORMAL AFFIRMATIVE INDICATIVE
Passive		kurerareru
Potential		kurerareru
Causative		kuresaseru
Causative Pass.		kuresaserareru
Honorific	I	
	II	
Humble	I	
	II	

K

293

to grow dark (at end of the day)

			AFFIRMATIVE	NEGATIVE
Indicative	**INFORMAL**		kureru	kurenai
	FORMAL		kuremasu	kuremasen
Imperative	**INFORMAL**	I	kurero	kureru na
		II	kurenasai	kurenasaru na
		III	kurete kudasai	kurenai de kudasai
	FORMAL			
Presumptive	**INFORMAL**	I	kureyō	kuremai
		II	kureru darō	kurenai darō
	FORMAL	I	kuremashō	kuremasumai
		II	kureru deshō	kurenai deshō
Provisional	**INFORMAL**		kurereba	kurenakereba
	FORMAL		kuremaseba	kuremasen nara
			kuremasureba	
Gerund	**INFORMAL**	I	kurete	kurenai de
		II		kurenakute
	FORMAL		kurernashite	kuremasen de
Past Ind.	**INFORMAL**		kureta	kurenakatta
	FORMAL		kuremashita	kuremasen deshita
Past Presump.	**INFORMAL**		kuretarō	kurenakattarō
			kureta darō	kurenakatta darō
	FORMAL		kuremashitarō	kuremasen deshitarō
			kureta deshō	kurenakatta deshō
Conditional	**INFORMAL**		kuretara	kurenakattara
	FORMAL		kuremashitara	kuremasen deshitara
Alternative	**INFORMAL**		kuretari	kurenakattari
	FORMAL		kuremashitari	kuremasen deshitari

		INFORMAL AFFIRMATIVE INDICATIVE
Passive		kurerareru
Potential		kurerareru
Causative		kuresaseru
Causative Pass.		kuresaserareru
Honorific	I	
	II	
Humble	I	
	II	

くりかえす／繰り返す　**kurikaes.u**

TRANSITIVE　　*to repeat*

			AFFIRMATIVE	**NEGATIVE**
Indicative	**INFORMAL**		kurikaesu	kurikaesanai
	FORMAL		kurikaeshimasu	kurikaeshimasen
Imperative	**INFORMAL**	I	kurikaese	kurikaesu na
		II	kurikaeshinasai	kurikaeshinasaru na
		III	kurikaeshite kudasai	kurikaesanai de kudasai
	FORMAL		okurikaeshi nasaimase	okurikaeshi nasaimasu na
Presumptive	**INFORMAL**	I	kurikaesō	kurikaesumai
		II	kurikaesu darō	kurikaesanai darō
	FORMAL	I	kurikaeshimashō	kurikaeshimasumai
		II	kurikaesu deshō	kurikaesanai deshō
Provisional	**INFORMAL**		kurikaeseba	kurikaesanakereba
	FORMAL		kurikaeshimaseba	kurikaeshimasen nara
			kurikaeshimasureba	
Gerund	**INFORMAL**	I	kurikaeshite	kurikaesanai de
		II		kurikaesanakute
	FORMAL		kurikaeshimashite	kurikaeshimasen de
Past Ind.	**INFORMAL**		kurikaeshita	kurikaesanakatta
	FORMAL		kurikaeshimashita	kurikaeshimasen deshita
Past Presump.	**INFORMAL**		kurikaeshitarō	kurikaesanakattarō
			kurikaeshita darō	kurikaesanakatta darō
	FORMAL		kurikaeshimashitarō	kurikaeshimasen deshitarō
			kurikaeshita deshō	kurikaesanakatta deshō
Conditional	**INFORMAL**		kurikaeshitara	kurikaesanakattara
	FORMAL		kurikaeshimashitara	kurikaeshimasen deshitara
Alternative	**INFORMAL**		kurikaeshitari	kurikaesanakattari
	FORMAL		kurikaeshimashitari	kurikaeshimasen deshitari

K

			INFORMAL AFFIRMATIVE INDICATIVE
Passive			kurikaesareru
Potential			kurikaeseru
Causative			kurikaesaseru
Causative Pass.			kurikaesaserareru
Honorific		I	okurikaeshi ni naru
		II	okurikaeshi nasaru
Humble		I	
		II	

ku.ru　くる／来る

to come, to show up　　TRANSITIVE

			AFFIRMATIVE	NEGATIVE
Indicative	**INFORMAL**		kuru	konai
	FORMAL		kimasu	kimasen
Imperative	**INFORMAL**	I	koi	kuru na
		II	kinasai	kinasaru na
		III	kite kudasai	konai de kudasai
	FORMAL		oide nasaimase	oide nasaimasu na
Presumptive	**INFORMAL**	I	koyō	kurumai
		II	kuru darō	konai darō
	FORMAL	I	kimashō	kimasumai
		II	kuru deshō	konai deshō
Provisional	**INFORMAL**		kureba	konakereba
	FORMAL		kimaseba	kimasen nara
			kimasureba	
Gerund	**INFORMAL**	I	kite	konai de
		II		konakute
	FORMAL		kimashite	kimasen de
Past Ind.	**INFORMAL**		kita	konakatta
	FORMAL		kimashita	kimasen deshita
Past Presump.	**INFORMAL**		kitarō	konakattarō
			kita darō	konakatta darō
	FORMAL		kimashitarō	kimasen deshitarō
			kita deshō	konakatta deshō
Conditional	**INFORMAL**		kitara	konakattara
	FORMAL		kimashitara	kimasen deshitara
Alternative	**INFORMAL**		kitari	konakattari
	FORMAL		kimashitari	kimasen deshitari

		INFORMAL AFFIRMATIVE INDICATIVE	
Passive		korareru	
Potential		korareru	
Causative		kosaseru	
Causative Pass.		kosaserareru	
Honorific	I	irassharu	{ oide ni naru (I)
	II		{ oide nasaru (II)
Humble	I	mairu	
	II		

AN ESSENTIAL
55 VERB

Kuru 来る

to come, to show up

Sentences Using *Kuru*

Kotoshi wa tsuyu ga kuru no ga
osoi desu.
今年は梅雨が来るのが遅いです。
*It's late for the rainy season to come
this year.*

Matte ita tegami wa, kekkyoku
kimasen deshita.
待っていた手紙は、結局、来ませんで
した。
*The letter I was waiting for never
came after all.*

Kitakereba kitemo ii desu.
来たければ来てもいいです。
If you want to come here, you can.

Jikan dōri ni konakattara, matte
inai yo.
時間通りに来なかったら、待っていな
いよ。
*If you don't come on time, we won't
wait for you.*

Anata ga korarenai nara, dareka
kawari ni yokoshite kudasai.
貴方が来られないなら、誰か代わりに
よこして下さい。
*If you can't come, please send
somebody in your place.*

Kuru is an essential verb you'll use often
in everyday speech. People come and
go all the time. And in Japan it's more
common for guests or friends to show
up unexpectedly than it is in some
western countries.

K

Words and Expressions Related to This Verb

raihō suru　来訪する
to visit

rainichi suru　来日する
*to come to Japan, to come to visit
Japan*

raiten suru　来店する
to come to a store

raikyaku　来客
a visitor, a guest

raihin　来賓
an honorable guest

Proverb

Kuru mono wa kobamazu.
来るものは拒まず。
*You should welcome anyone coming
to see you. (You shouldn't reject
anyone who comes to you.)*

to torment, to inflict pain　　　TRANSITIVE

			AFFIRMATIVE	NEGATIVE
Indicative	**INFORMAL**		kurushimeru	kurushimenai
	FORMAL		kurushimemasu	kurushimemasen
Imperative	**INFORMAL**	I	kurushimero	kurushimeru na
		II	kurushimenasai	kurushimenasaru na
		III	kurushimete kudasai	kurushimenai de kudasai
	FORMAL		okurushime nasaimase	okurushime nasaimasu na
Presumptive	**INFORMAL**	I	kurushimeyō	kurushimemai
		II	kurushimeru darō	kurushimenai darō
	FORMAL	I	kurushimemashō	kurushimemasumai
		II	kurushimeru deshō	kurushimenai deshō
Provisional	**INFORMAL**		kurushimereba	kurushimenakereba
	FORMAL		kurushimemaseba	kurushimemasen nara
			kurushimemasureba	
Gerund	**INFORMAL**	I	kurushimete	kurushimenai de
		II		kurushimenakute
	FORMAL		kurushimemashite	kurushimemasen de
Past Ind.	**INFORMAL**		kurushimeta	kurushimenakatta
	FORMAL		kurushimemashita	kurushimemasen deshita
Past Presump.	**INFORMAL**		kurushimetarō	kurushimenakattarō
			kurushimeta darō	kurushimenakatta darō
	FORMAL		kurushimemashitarō	kurushimemasen deshitarō
			kurushimeta deshō	kurushimenakatta deshō
Conditional	**INFORMAL**		kurushimetara	kurushimenakattara
	FORMAL		kurushimemashitara	kurushimemasen deshitara
Alternative	**INFORMAL**		kurushimetari	kurushimenakattari
	FORMAL		kurushimemashitari	kurushimemasen deshitari

		INFORMAL AFFIRMATIVE INDICATIVE
Passive		kurushimerareru
Potential		kurushimerareru
Causative		kurushimesaseru
Causative Pass.		kurushimesaserareru
Honorific	I	okurushime ni naru
	II	okurushime nasaru
Humble	I	okurushime suru
	II	okurushime itasu

to suffer

			AFFIRMATIVE	NEGATIVE
Indicative	**INFORMAL**		kurushimu	kurushimanai
	FORMAL		kurushimimasu	kurushimimasen
Imperative	**INFORMAL**	I	kurushime	kurushimu na
		II	kurushiminasai	kurushiminasaru na
		III	kurushinde kudasai	kurushimanai de kudasai
	FORMAL		okurushimi nasaimase	okurushimi nasaimasu na
Presumptive	**INFORMAL**	I	kurushimō	kurushimumai
		II	kurushimu darō	kurushimanai darō
	FORMAL	I	kurushimimashō	kurushimimasumai
		II	kurushimu deshō	kurushimanai deshō
Provisional	**INFORMAL**		kurushimeba	kurushimanakereba
	FORMAL		kurushimimaseba	kurushimimasen nara
			kurushimimasureba	
Gerund	**INFORMAL**	I	kurushinde	kurushimanai de
		II		kurushimanakute
	FORMAL		kurushimimashite	kurushimimasen de
Past Ind.	**INFORMAL**		kurushinda	kurushimanakatta
	FORMAL		kurushimimashita	kurushimimasen deshita
Past Presump.	**INFORMAL**		kurushindarō	kurushimanakattarō
			kurushinda darō	kurushimanakatta darō
	FORMAL		kurushimimashitarō	kurushimimasen deshitarō
			kurushinda deshō	kurushimanakatta deshō
Conditional	**INFORMAL**		kurushindara	kurushimanakattara
	FORMAL		kurushimimashitara	kurushimimasen deshitara
Alternative	**INFORMAL**		kurushindari	kurushimanakattari
	FORMAL		kurushimimashitari	kurushimimasen deshitari

			INFORMAL AFFIRMATIVE INDICATIVE
Passive			kurushimareru
Potential			kurushimeru
Causative			kurushimaseru
Causative Pass.			kurushimaserareru
Honorific		I	okurushimi ni naru
		II	okurushimi nasaru
Humble		I	
		II	

K

299

kuru.u くるう／狂う   kurui
to go mad, to be out of order (a watch)

			AFFIRMATIVE	NEGATIVE
Indicative	**INFORMAL**		kuruu	kuruwanai
	FORMAL		kuruimasu	kuruimasen
Imperative	**INFORMAL**	I	kurue	kuruu na
		II	kuruinasai	kuruinasaru na
		III	kurutte kudasai	kuruwanai de kudasai
	FORMAL		okurui nasaimase	okurui nasaimasu na
Presumptive	**INFORMAL**	I	kuruō	kuruumai
		II	kuruu darō	kuruwanai darō
	FORMAL	I	kuruimashō	kuruimasumai
		II	kuruu deshō	kuruwanai deshō
Provisional	**INFORMAL**		kurueba	kuruwanakereba
	FORMAL		kuruimaseba	kuruimasen nara
			kuruimasureba	
Gerund	**INFORMAL**	I	kurutte	kuruwanai de
		II		kuruwanakute
	FORMAL		kuruimashite	kuruimasen de
Past Ind.	**INFORMAL**		kurutta	kuruwanakatta
	FORMAL		kuruimashita	kuruimasen deshita
Past Presump.	**INFORMAL**		kuruttarō	kuruwanakattarō
			kurutta darō	kuruwanakatta darō
	FORMAL		kuruimashitarō	kuruimasen deshitarō
			kurutta deshō	kuruwanakatta deshō
Conditional	**INFORMAL**		kuruttara	kuruwanakattara
	FORMAL		kuruimashitara	kuruimasen deshitara
Alternative	**INFORMAL**		kuruttari	kuruwanakattari
	FORMAL		kuruimashitari	kuruimasen deshitari

		INFORMAL AFFIRMATIVE INDICATIVE
Passive		kuruwareru
Potential		kurueru
Causative		kuruwaseru
Causative Pass.		kuruwaserareru
Honorific	I	okurui ni naru
	II	okurui nasaru
Humble	I	
	II	

くさる／腐る　**kusar.u**

to go bad, to decay, to feel depressed

			AFFIRMATIVE	NEGATIVE
Indicative	**INFORMAL**		kusaru	kusaranai
	FORMAL		kusarimasu	kusarimasen
Imperative	**INFORMAL**	I	kusare	kusaru na
		II	kusarinasai	kusarinasaru na
		III	kusatte kudasai	kusaranai de kudasai
	FORMAL		okusari nasaimase	okusari nasaimasu na
Presumptive	**INFORMAL**	I	kusarō	kusarumai
		II	kusaru darō	kusaranai darō
	FORMAL	I	kusarimashō	kusarimasumai
		II	kusaru deshō	kusaranai deshō
Provisional	**INFORMAL**		kusareba	kusaranakereba
	FORMAL		kusarimaseba	kusarimasen nara
			kusarimasureba	
Gerund	**INFORMAL**	I	kusatte	kusaranai de
		II		kusaranakute
	FORMAL		kusarimashite	kusarimasen de
Past Ind.	**INFORMAL**		kusatta	kusaranakatta
	FORMAL		kusarimashita	kusarimasen deshita
Past Presump.	**INFORMAL**		kusattarō	kusaranakattarō
			kusatta darō	kusaranakatta darō
	FORMAL		kusarimashitarō	kusarimasen deshitarō
			kusatta deshō	kusaranakatta deshō
Conditional	**INFORMAL**		kusattara	kusaranakattara
	FORMAL		kusarimashitara	kusarimasen deshitara
Alternative	**INFORMAL**		kusattari	kusaranakattari
	FORMAL		kusarimashitari	kusarimasen deshitari

		INFORMAL AFFIRMATIVE INDICATIVE
Passive		kusarareru
Potential		kusareru
Causative		kusaraseru
Causative Pass.		kusaraserareru
Honorific	I	okusari ni naru
	II	okusari nasaru
Humble	I	
	II	

to plan, to attempt, to scheme   TRANSITIVE

			AFFIRMATIVE	**NEGATIVE**
Indicative	**INFORMAL**		kuwadateru	kuwadatenai
	FORMAL		kuwadatemasu	kuwadatemasen
Imperative	**INFORMAL**	I	kuwadatero	kuwadateru na
		II	kuwadatenasai	kuwadatenasaru na
		III	kuwadatete kudasai	kuwadatenai de kudasai
	FORMAL		okuwadate nasaimase	okuwadate nasaimasu na
Presumptive	**INFORMAL**	I	kuwadateyō	kuwadatemai
		II	kuwadateru darō	kuwadatenai darō
	FORMAL	I	kuwadatemashō	kuwadatemasumai
		II	kuwadateru deshō	kuwadatenai deshō
Provisional	**INFORMAL**		kuwadatereba	kuwadatenakereba
	FORMAL		kuwadatemaseba	kuwadatemasen nara
			kuwadatemasureba	
Gerund	**INFORMAL**	I	kuwadatete	kuwadatenai de
		II		kuwadatenakute
	FORMAL		kuwadatemashite	kuwadatemasen de
Past Ind.	**INFORMAL**		kuwadateta	kuwadatenakatta
	FORMAL		kuwadatemashita	kuwadatemasen deshita
Past Presump.	**INFORMAL**		kuwadatetarō	kuwadatenakattarō
			kuwadateta darō	kuwadatenakatta darō
	FORMAL		kuwadatemashitarō	kuwadatemasen deshitarō
			kuwadateta deshō	kuwadatenakatta deshō
Conditional	**INFORMAL**		kuwadatetara	kuwadatenakattara
	FORMAL		kuwadatemashitara	kuwadatemasen deshitara
Alternative	**INFORMAL**		kuwadatetari	kuwadatenakattari
	FORMAL		kuwadatemashitari	kuwadatemasen deshitari

			INFORMAL AFFIRMATIVE INDICATIVE
Passive			kuwadaterareru
Potential			kuwadaterareru
Causative			kuwadatesaseru
Causative Pass.			kuwadatesaserareru
Honorific		I	okuwadate ni naru
		II	okuwadate nasaru
Humble		I	okuwadate suru
		II	okuwadate itasu

kuwae

くわえる／加える kuwae.ru

TRANSITIVE *to add* (to), *to include* (in)

			AFFIRMATIVE	NEGATIVE
Indicative	INFORMAL		kuwaeru	kuwaenai
	FORMAL		kuwaemasu	kuwaemasen
Imperative	INFORMAL	I	kuwaero	kuwaeru na
		II	kuwaenasai	kuwaenasaru na
		III	kuwaete kudasai	kuwaenai de kudasai
	FORMAL		okuwae nasaimase	okuwae nasaimasu na
Presumptive	INFORMAL	I	kuwaeyō	kuwaemai
		II	kuwaeru darō	kuwaenai darō
	FORMAL	I	kuwaemashō	kuwaemasumai
		II	kuwaeru deshō	kuwaenai deshō
Provisional	INFORMAL		kuwaereba	kuwaenakereba
	FORMAL		kuwaemaseba	kuwaemasen nara
			kuwaemasureba	
Gerund	INFORMAL	I	kuwaete	kuwaenai de
		II		kuwaenakute
	FORMAL		kuwaemashite	kuwaemasen de
Past Ind.	INFORMAL		kuwaeta	kuwaenakatta
	FORMAL		kuwaemashita	kuwaemasen deshita
Past Presump.	INFORMAL		kuwaetarō	kuwaenakattarō
			kuwaeta darō	kuwaenakatta darō
	FORMAL		kuwaemashitarō	kuwaemasen deshitarō
			kuwaeta deshō	kuwaenakatta deshō
Conditional	INFORMAL		kuwaetara	kuwaenakattara
	FORMAL		kuwaemashitara	kuwaemasen deshitara
Alternative	INFORMAL		kuwaetari	kuwaenakattari
	FORMAL		kuwaemashitari	kuwaemasen deshitari

K

			INFORMAL AFFIRMATIVE INDICATIVE
Passive			kuwaerareru
Potential			kuwaerareru
Causative			kuwaesaseru
Causative Pass.			kuwaesaserareru
Honorific		I	okuwae ni naru
		II	okuwae nasaru
Humble		I	okuwae suru
		II	okuwae itasu

303

kuzure.ru　くずれる／崩れる　　　　　　　　　kuzure

to collapse, to cave in

			AFFIRMATIVE	NEGATIVE
Indicative	**INFORMAL**		kuzureru	kuzurenai
	FORMAL		kuzuremasu	kuzuremasen
Imperative	**INFORMAL**	I	kuzurero	kuzureru na
		II	kuzurenasai	kuzurenasaru na
		III	kuzurete kudasai	kuzurenai de kudasai
	FORMAL			
Presumptive	**INFORMAL**	I	kuzureyō	kuzuremai
		II	kuzureru darō	kuzurenai darō
	FORMAL	I	kuzuremashō	kuzuremasumai
		II	kuzureru deshō	kuzurenai deshō
Provisional	**INFORMAL**		kuzurereba	kuzurenakereba
	FORMAL		kuzuremaseba	kuzuremasen nara
			kuzuremasureba	
Gerund	**INFORMAL**	I	kuzurete	kuzurenai de
		II		kuzurenakute
	FORMAL		kuzuremashite	kuzuremasen de
Past Ind.	**INFORMAL**		kuzureta	kuzurenakatta
	FORMAL		kuzuremashita	kuzuremasen deshita
Past Presump.	**INFORMAL**		kuzuretarō	kuzurenakattarō
			kuzureta darō	kuzurenakatta darō
	FORMAL		kuzuremashitarō	kuzuremasen deshitarō
			kuzureta deshō	kuzurenakatta deshō
Conditional	**INFORMAL**		kuzuretara	kuzurenakattara
	FORMAL		kuzuremashitara	kuzuremasen deshitara
Alternative	**INFORMAL**		kuzuretari	kuzurenakattari
	FORMAL		kuzuremashitari	kuzuremasen deshitari

		INFORMAL AFFIRMATIVE INDICATIVE
Passive		kuzurerareru
Potential		
Causative		kuzuresaseru
Causative Pass.		kuzuresaserareru
Honorific	I	okuzure ni naru
	II	okuzure nasaru
Humble	I	
	II	

304

くずす／崩す　kuzus.u
TRANSITIVE　*to destroy, to break down*

			AFFIRMATIVE	**NEGATIVE**
Indicative	**INFORMAL**		kuzusu	kuzusanai
	FORMAL		kuzushimasu	kuzushimasen
Imperative	**INFORMAL**	I	kuzuse	kuzusu na
		II	kuzushinasai	kuzushinasaru na
		III	kuzushite kudasai	kuzusanai de kudasai
	FORMAL		okuzushi nasaimase	okuzushi nasaimasu na
Presumptive	**INFORMAL**	I	kuzusō	kuzusumai
		II	kuzusu darō	kuzusanai darō
	FORMAL	I	kuzushimashō	kuzushimasumai
		II	kuzusu deshō	kuzusanai deshō
Provisional	**INFORMAL**		kuzuseba	kuzusanakereba
	FORMAL		kuzushimaseba	kuzushimasen nara
			kuzushimasureba	
Gerund	**INFORMAL**	I	kuzushite	kuzusanai de
		II		kuzusanakute
	FORMAL		kuzushimashite	kuzushimasen de
Past Ind.	**INFORMAL**		kuzushita	kuzusanakatta
	FORMAL		kuzushimashita	kuzushimasen deshita
Past Presump.	**INFORMAL**		kuzushitarō	kuzusanakattarō
			kuzushita darō	kuzusanakatta darō
	FORMAL		kuzushimashitarō	kuzushimasen deshitarō
			kuzushita deshō	kuzusanakatta deshō
Conditional	**INFORMAL**		kuzushitara	kuzusanakattara
	FORMAL		kuzushimashitara	kuzushimasen deshitara
Alternative	**INFORMAL**		kuzushitari	kuzusanakattari
	FORMAL		kuzushimashitari	kuzushimasen deshitari

		INFORMAL AFFIRMATIVE INDICATIVE
Passive		kuzusareru
Potential		kuzuseru
Causative		kuzusaseru
Causative Pass.		kuzusaserareru
Honorific	I	okuzushi ni naru
	II	okuzushi nasaru
Humble	I	okuzushi suru
	II	okuzushi itasu

K

			AFFIRMATIVE	NEGATIVE
Indicative	INFORMAL		machigaeru	machigaenai
	FORMAL		machigaemasu	machigaemasen
Imperative	INFORMAL	I	machigaero	machigaeru na
		II	machigaenasai	machigaenasaru na
		III	machigaete kudasai	machigaenai de kudasai
	FORMAL		omachigae nasaimase	omachigae nasaimasu na
Presumptive	INFORMAL	I	machigaeyō	machigaemai
		II	machigaeru darō	machigaenai darō
	FORMAL	I	machigaemashō	machigaemasumai
		II	machigaeru deshō	machigaenai deshō
Provisional	INFORMAL		machigaereba	machigaenakereba
	FORMAL		machigaemaseba	machigaemasen nara
			machigaemasureba	
Gerund	INFORMAL	I	machigaete	machigaenai de
		II		machigaenakute
	FORMAL		machigaemashite	machigaemasen de
Past Ind.	INFORMAL		machigaeta	machigaenakatta
	FORMAL		machigaemashita	machigaemasen deshita
Past Presump.	INFORMAL		machigaetarō	machigaenakattarō
			machigaeta darō	machigaenakatta darō
	FORMAL		machigaemashitarō	machigaemasen deshitarō
			machigaeta deshō	machigaenakatta deshō
Conditional	INFORMAL		machigaetara	machigaenakattara
	FORMAL		machigaemashitara	machigaemasen deshitara
Alternative	INFORMAL		machigaetari	machigaenakattari
	FORMAL		machigaemashitari	machigaemasen deshitari

		INFORMAL AFFIRMATIVE INDICATIVE
Passive		machigaerareru
Potential		machigaerareru
Causative		machigaesaseru
Causative Pass.		machigaesaserareru
Honorific	I	omachigae ni naru
	II	omachigae nasaru
Humble	I	
	II	

AN ESSENTIAL
55 VERB

AN ESSENTIAL 55 VERB

Machigaeru
間違える

to make a mistake, to mistake
one thing for another

Machigaeru is an essential verb because everybody makes mistakes. How one handles mistakes is another story!

M

Sentences Using *Machigaeru*

Machigaetara iiwake o suru yori,
sunao ni ayamarinasai.
間違えたら言い訳をするより、素直に
謝りなさい。
*If you make a mistake, apologize
honestly rather than making an
excuse.*

Denwa de, tomodachi no imōto san o
tomodachi to machigaete shimatta.
電話で、友達の妹さんを友達と間違え
てしまった。
*On the telephone, I mistook my
friend's sister for my friend.*

Machigaetemo shinpai sezu ni, shite
minasai.
間違えても心配せずに、してみなさ
い。
*Don't worry about making mistakes;
just go ahead and try it.*

Kinō no pātī de tomodachi no
goshujin to machigaerareta.
昨日のパーティーで、友達のご主人と
間違えられた。
*I was mistaken for my friend's
husband at a party yesterday.*

Shiken no shitsumon wa hitotsu mo
machigaenai de kotaeru koto ga
dekimashita.
試験の質問は一つも間違えないで答え
ることが出来ました。
*I was able to answer the exam
questions without making even one
mistake.*

Words and Expressions Related to This Verb

ayamaru　誤る
to make a mistake

michi o machigaeru　道を間違える
to take the wrong way (direction)

machigaete　間違えて
by mistake

machigai denwa　間違い電話
a wrong number (telephone call)

machiga.u　まちがう／間違う

to be mistaken, to make a mistake

machigai

			AFFIRMATIVE	NEGATIVE
Indicative	**INFORMAL**		machigau	machigawanai
	FORMAL		machigaimasu	machigaimasen
Imperative	**INFORMAL**	I		
		II		
		III		
	FORMAL			
Presumptive	**INFORMAL**	I	machigaō	machigaumai
		II	machigau darō	machigawanai darō
	FORMAL	I	machigaimashō	machigaimasumai
		II	machigau deshō	machigawanai deshō
Provisional	**INFORMAL**		machigaeba	machigawanakereba
	FORMAL		machigaimaseba	machigaimasen nara
			machigaimasureba	
Gerund	**INFORMAL**	I	machigatte	machigawanai de
		II		machigawanakute
	FORMAL		machigaimashite	machigaimasen de
Past Ind.	**INFORMAL**		machigatta	machigawanakatta
	FORMAL		machigaimashita	machigaimasen deshita
Past Presump.	**INFORMAL**		machigattarō	machigawanakattarō
			machigatta darō	machigawanakatta darō
	FORMAL		machigaimashitarō	machigaimasen deshitarō
			machigatta deshō	machigawanakatta deshō
Conditional	**INFORMAL**		machigattara	machigawanakattara
	FORMAL		machigaimashitara	machigaimasen deshitara
Alternative	**INFORMAL**		machigattari	machigawanakattari
	FORMAL		machigaimashitari	machigaimasen deshitari

		INFORMAL AFFIRMATIVE INDICATIVE
Passive		machigawareru
Potential		machigaeru
Causative		machigawaseru
Causative Pass.		machigawaserareru
Honorific	I	omachigai ni naru
	II	omachigai nasaru
Humble	I	
	II	

まがる／曲がる **magar.u**

TRANSITIVE *to turn a corner*

			AFFIRMATIVE	NEGATIVE
Indicative	**INFORMAL**		magaru	magaranai
	FORMAL		magarimasu	magarimasen
Imperative	**INFORMAL**	I	magare	magaru na
		II	magarinasai	magarinasaru na
		III	magatte kudasai	magaranai de kudasai
	FORMAL		omagari nasaimase	omagari nasaimasu na
Presumptive	**INFORMAL**	I	magarō	magarumai
		II	magaru darō	magaranai darō
	FORMAL	I	magarimashō	magarimasumai
		II	magaru deshō	magaranai deshō
Provisional	**INFORMAL**		magareba	magaranakereba
	FORMAL		magarimaseba	magarimasen nara
			magarimasureba	
Gerund	**INFORMAL**	I	magatte	magaranai de
		II		magaranakute
	FORMAL		magarimashite	magarimasen de
Past Ind.	**INFORMAL**		magatta	magaranakatta
	FORMAL		magarimashita	magarimasen deshita
Past Presump.	**INFORMAL**		magattarō	magaranakattarō
			magatta darō	magaranakatta darō
	FORMAL		magarimashitarō	magarimasen deshitarō
			magatta deshō	magaranakatta deshō
Conditional	**INFORMAL**		magattara	magaranakattara
	FORMAL		magarimashitara	magarimasen deshitara
Alternative	**INFORMAL**		magattari	magaranakattari
	FORMAL		magarimashitari	magarimasen deshitari

		INFORMAL AFFIRMATIVE INDICATIVE
Passive		magarareru
Potential		magareru
Causative		magaraseru
Causative Pass.		magaraserareru
Honorific	I	omagari ni naru
	II	omagari nasaru
Humble	I	
	II	

to bend, to twist　　TRANSITIVE

			AFFIRMATIVE	NEGATIVE
Indicative	**INFORMAL**		mageru	magenai
	FORMAL		magemasu	magemasen
Imperative	**INFORMAL**	I	magero	mageru na
		II	magenasai	magenasaru na
		III	magete kudasai	magenai de kudasai
	FORMAL		omage nasaimase	omage nasaimasu na
Presumptive	**INFORMAL**	I	mageyō	magemai
		II	mageru darō	magenai darō
	FORMAL	I	magemashō	magemasumai
		II	mageru deshō	magenai deshō
Provisional	**INFORMAL**		magereba	magenakereba
	FORMAL		magemaseba	magemasen nara
			magemasureba	
Gerund	**INFORMAL**	I	magete	magenai de
		II		magenakute
	FORMAL		magemashite	magemasen de
Past Ind.	**INFORMAL**		mageta	magenakatta
	FORMAL		magemashita	magemasen deshita
Past Presump.	**INFORMAL**		magetarō	magenakattarō
			mageta darō	magenakatta darō
	FORMAL		magemashitarō	magemasen deshitarō
			mageta deshō	magenakatta deshō
Conditional	**INFORMAL**		magetara	magenakattara
	FORMAL		magemashitara	magemasen deshitara
Alternative	**INFORMAL**		magetari	magenakattari
	FORMAL		magemashitari	magemasen deshitari

			INFORMAL AFFIRMATIVE INDICATIVE
Passive			magerareru
Potential			magerareru
Causative			magesaseru
Causative Pass.			magesaserareru
Honorific		I	omage ni naru
		II	omage nasaru
Humble		I	omage suru
		II	omage itasu

TRANSITIVE

to divert (one's attention), *to equivocate*

			AFFIRMATIVE	NEGATIVE
Indicative	**INFORMAL**		magirasu	magirasanai
	FORMAL		magirashimasu	magirashimasen
Imperative	**INFORMAL**	I	magirase	magirasu na
		II	magirashinasai	magirashinasaru na
		III	magirashite kudasai	magirasanai de kudasai
	FORMAL		omagirashi nasaimase	omagirashi nasaimasu na
Presumptive	**INFORMAL**	I	magirasō	magirasumai
		II	magirasu darō	magirasanai darō
	FORMAL	I	magirashimashō	magirashimasumai
		II	magirasu deshō	magirasanai deshō
Provisional	**INFORMAL**		magiraseba	magirasanakereba
	FORMAL		magirashimaseba	magirashimasen nara
			magirashimasureba	
Gerund	**INFORMAL**	I	magirashite	magirasanai de
		II		magirasanakute
	FORMAL		magirashimashite	magirashimasen de
Past Ind.	**INFORMAL**		magirashita	magirasanakatta
	FORMAL		magirashimashita	magirashimasen deshita
Past Presump.	**INFORMAL**		magirashitarō	magirasanakattarō
			magirashita darō	magirasanakatta darō
	FORMAL		magirashimashitarō	magirashimasen deshitarō
			magirashita deshō	magirasanakatta deshō
Conditional	**INFORMAL**		magirashitara	magirasanakattara
	FORMAL		magirashimashitara	magirashimasen deshitara
Alternative	**INFORMAL**		magirashitari	magirasanakattari
	FORMAL		magirashimashitari	magirashimasen deshitari

			INFORMAL AFFIRMATIVE INDICATIVE
Passive			magirasareru
Potential			magiraseru
Causative			magirasaseru
Causative Pass.			magirasaserareru
Honorific		I	omagirashi ni naru
		II	omagirashi nasaru
Humble		I	omagirashi suru
		II	omagirashi itasu

M

to come or go (humble)

			AFFIRMATIVE	NEGATIVE
Indicative	**INFORMAL**		mairu	mairanai
	FORMAL		mairimasu	mairimasen
Imperative	**INFORMAL**	I	maire	mairu na
		II		
		III		
	FORMAL		omairi nasaimase	omairi nasaimasu na
Presumptive	**INFORMAL**	I	mairō	mairumai
		II	mairu darō	mairanai darō
	FORMAL	I	mairimashō	mairimasumai
		II	mairu deshō	mairanai deshō
Provisional	**INFORMAL**		maireba	mairanakereba
	FORMAL		mairimaseba	mairimasen nara
			mairimasureba	
Gerund	**INFORMAL**	I	maitte	mairanai de
		II		mairanakute
	FORMAL		mairimashite	mairimasen de
Past Ind.	**INFORMAL**		maitta	mairanakatta
	FORMAL		mairimashita	mairimasen deshita
Past Presump.	**INFORMAL**		maittarō	mairanakattarō
			maitta darō	mairanakatta darō
	FORMAL		mairimashitarō	mairimasen deshitarō
			maitta deshō	mairanakatta deshō
Conditional	**INFORMAL**		maittara	mairanakattara
	FORMAL		mairimashitara	mairimasen deshitara
Alternative	**INFORMAL**		maittari	mairanakattari
	FORMAL		mairimashitari	mairimasen deshitari

		INFORMAL AFFIRMATIVE INDICATIVE
Passive		
Potential		maireru
Causative		mairaseru
Causative Pass.		mairaserareru
Honorific	I	omairi ni naru
	II	omairi nasaru
Humble	I	omairi suru
	II	omairi itasu

まじる／混じる／交じる **majir.u**

to get mingled with, to join, to be mixed

			AFFIRMATIVE	NEGATIVE
Indicative	**INFORMAL**		majiru	majiranai
	FORMAL		majirimasu	majirimasen
Imperative	**INFORMAL**	I	majire	majiru na
		II	majirinasai	majirinasaru na
		III	majitte kudasai	majiranai de kudasai
	FORMAL		omajiri nasaimase	omajiri nasaimasu na
Presumptive	**INFORMAL**	I	majirō	majirumai
		II	majiru darō	majiranai darō
	FORMAL	I	majirimashō	majirimasumai
		II	majiru deshō	majiranai deshō
Provisional	**INFORMAL**		majireba	majiranakereba
	FORMAL		majirimaseba	majirimasen nara
			majirimasureba	
Gerund	**INFORMAL**	I	majitte	majiranai de
		II		majiranakute
	FORMAL		majirimashite	majirimasen de
Past Ind.	**INFORMAL**		majitta	majiranakatta
	FORMAL		majirimashita	majirimasen deshita
Past Presump.	**INFORMAL**		majittarō	majiranakattarō
			majitta darō	majiranakatta darō
	FORMAL		majirimashitarō	majirimasen deshitarō
			majitta deshō	majiranakatta deshō
Conditional	**INFORMAL**		majittara	majiranakattara
	FORMAL		majirimashitara	majirimasen deshitara
Alternative	**INFORMAL**		majittari	majiranakattari
	FORMAL		majirimashitari	majirimasen deshitari

			INFORMAL AFFIRMATIVE INDICATIVE
Passive			majirareru
Potential			majireru
Causative			majiraseru
Causative Pass.			majiraserareru
Honorific		I	omajiri ni naru
		II	omajiri nasaru
Humble		I	
		II	

M

to leave (a matter) *to someone, to leave things to others*   TRANSITIVE

			AFFIRMATIVE	**NEGATIVE**
Indicative	**INFORMAL**		makaseru	makasenai
	FORMAL		makasemasu	makasemasen
Imperative	**INFORMAL**	I	makasero	makaseru na
		II	makasenasai	makasenasaru na
		III	makasete kudasai	makasenai de kudasai
	FORMAL		omakase nasaimase	omakase nasaimasu na
Presumptive	**INFORMAL**	I	makaseyō	makasemai
		II	makaseru darō	makasenai darō
	FORMAL	I	makasemashō	makasemasumai
		II	makaseru deshō	makasenai deshō
Provisional	**INFORMAL**		makasereba	makasenakereba
	FORMAL		makasemaseba	makasemasen nara
			makasemasureba	
Gerund	**INFORMAL**	I	makasete	makasenai de
		II		makasenakute
	FORMAL		makasemashite	makasemasen de
Past Ind.	**INFORMAL**		makaseta	makasenakatta
	FORMAL		makasemashita	makasemasen deshita
Past Presump.	**INFORMAL**		makasetarō	makasenakattarō
			makaseta darō	makasenakatta darō
	FORMAL		makasemashitarō	makasemasen deshitarō
			makaseta deshō	makasenakatta deshō
Conditional	**INFORMAL**		makasetara	makasenakattara
	FORMAL		makasemashitara	makasemasen deshitara
Alternative	**INFORMAL**		makasetari	makasenakattari
	FORMAL		makasemashitari	makasemasen deshitari

		INFORMAL AFFIRMATIVE INDICATIVE
Passive		makaserareru
Potential		makaserareru
Causative		makasesaseru
Causative Pass.		makasesaserareru
Honorific	I	omakase ni naru
	II	omakase nasaru
Humble	I	omakase suru
	II	omakase itasu

まかす／負かす　**makas.u**

TRANSITIVE　　*to defeat*

			AFFIRMATIVE	**NEGATIVE**
Indicative	**INFORMAL**		makasu	makasanai
	FORMAL		makashimasu	makashimasen
Imperative	**INFORMAL**	I	makase	makasu na
		II	makashinasai	makashinasaru na
		III	makashite kudasai	makasanai de kudasai
	FORMAL		omakashi nasaimase	omakashi nasaimasu na
Presumptive	**INFORMAL**	I	makasō	makasumai
		II	makasu darō	makasanai darō
	FORMAL	I	makashimashō	makashimasumai
		II	makasu deshō	makasanai deshō
Provisional	**INFORMAL**		makaseba	makasanakereba
	FORMAL		makashimaseba	makashimasen nara
			makashimasureba	
Gerund	**INFORMAL**	I	makashite	makasanai de
		II		makasanakute
	FORMAL		makashimashite	makashimasen de
Past Ind.	**INFORMAL**		makashita	makasanakatta
	FORMAL		makashimashita	makashimasen deshita
Past Presump.	**INFORMAL**		makashitarō	makasanakattarō
			makashita darō	makasanakatta darō
	FORMAL		makashimashitarō	makashimasen deshitarō
			makashita deshō	makasanakatta deshō
Conditional	**INFORMAL**		makashitara	makasanakattara
	FORMAL		makashimashitara	makashimasen deshitara
Alternative	**INFORMAL**		makashitari	makasanakattari
	FORMAL		makashimashitari	makashimasen deshitari

			INFORMAL AFFIRMATIVE INDICATIVE
Passive			makasareru
Potential			makaseru
Causative			makasaseru
Causative Pass.			makasaserareru
Honorific		I	omakashi ni naru
		II	omakashi nasaru
Humble		I	omakashi suru
		II	omakashi itasu

M

make.ru まける／負ける   **make**
to be defeated, to lose (a game), *to give a discount*

			AFFIRMATIVE	**NEGATIVE**
Indicative	**INFORMAL**		makeru	makenai
	FORMAL		makemasu	makemasen
Imperative	**INFORMAL**	I	makero	makeru na
		II	makenasai	makenasaru na
		III	makete kudasai	makenai de kudasai
	FORMAL		omake nasaimase	omake nasaimasu na
Presumptive	**INFORMAL**	I	makeyō	makemai
		II	makeru darō	makenai darō
	FORMAL	I	makemashō	makemasumai
		II	makeru deshō	makenai deshō
Provisional	**INFORMAL**		makereba	makenakereba
	FORMAL		makemaseba	makemasen nara
			makemasureba	
Gerund	**INFORMAL**	I	makete	makenai de
		II		makenakute
	FORMAL		makemashite	makemasen de
Past Ind.	**INFORMAL**		maketa	makenakatta
	FORMAL		makemashita	makemasen deshita
Past Presump.	**INFORMAL**		maketarō	makenakattarō
			maketa darō	makenakatta darō
	FORMAL		makemashitarō	makemasen deshitarō
			maketa deshō	makenakatta deshō
Conditional	**INFORMAL**		maketara	makenakattara
	FORMAL		makemashitara	makemasen deshitara
Alternative	**INFORMAL**		maketari	makenakattari
	FORMAL		makemashitari	makemasen deshitari

		INFORMAL AFFIRMATIVE INDICATIVE
Passive		makerareru
Potential		makerareru
Causative		makesaseru
Causative Pass.		makesaserareru
Honorific	I	omake ni naru
	II	omake nasaru
Humble	I	omake suru
	II	omake itasu

まもる／守る／護る　**mamor.u**

			AFFIRMATIVE	NEGATIVE
Indicative	**INFORMAL**		mamoru	mamoranai
	FORMAL		mamorimasu	mamorimasen
Imperative	**INFORMAL**	I	mamore	mamoru na
		II	mamorinasai	mamorinasaru na
		III	mamotte kudasai	mamoranai de kudasai
	FORMAL		omamori nasaimase	omamori nasaimasu na
Presumptive	**INFORMAL**	I	mamorō	mamorumai
		II	mamoru darō	mamoranai darō
	FORMAL	I	mamorimashō	mamorimasumai
		II	mamoru deshō	mamoranai deshō
Provisional	**INFORMAL**		mamoreba	mamoranakereba
	FORMAL		mamorimaseba	mamorimasen nara
			mamorimasureba	
Gerund	**INFORMAL**	I	mamotte	mamoranai de
		II		mamoranakute
	FORMAL		mamorimashite	mamorimasen de
Past Ind.	**INFORMAL**		mamotta	mamoranakatta
	FORMAL		mamorimashita	mamorimasen deshita
Past Presump.	**INFORMAL**		mamottarō	mamoranakattarō
			mamotta darō	mamoranakatta darō
	FORMAL		mamorimashitarō	mamorimasen deshitarō
			mamotta deshō	mamoranakatta deshō
Conditional	**INFORMAL**		mamottara	mamoranakattara
	FORMAL		mamorimashitara	mamorimasen deshitara
Alternative	**INFORMAL**		mamottari	mamoranakattari
	FORMAL		mamorimashitari	mamorimasen deshitari

			INFORMAL AFFIRMATIVE INDICATIVE
Passive			mamorareru
Potential			mamoreru
Causative			mamoraseru
Causative Pass.			mamoraserareru
Honorific		I	omamori ni naru
		II	omamori nasaru
Humble		I	omamori suru
		II	omamori itasu

M

manab.u まなぶ／学ぶ

manabi

to learn, to study   TRANSITIVE

			AFFIRMATIVE	**NEGATIVE**
Indicative	**INFORMAL**		manabu	manabanai
	FORMAL		manabimasu	manabimasen
Imperative	**INFORMAL**	I	manabe	manabu na
		II	manabinasai	manabinasaru na
		III	manande kudasai	manabanai de kudasai
	FORMAL		omanabi nasaimase	omanabi nasaimasu na
Presumptive	**INFORMAL**	I	manabō	manabumai
		II	manabu darō	manabanai darō
	FORMAL	I	manabimashō	manabimasumai
		II	manabu deshō	manabanai deshō
Provisional	**INFORMAL**		manabeba	manabanakereba
	FORMAL		manabimaseba	manabimasen nara
			manabimasureba	
Gerund	**INFORMAL**	I	manande	manabanai de
		II		manabanakute
	FORMAL		manabimashite	manabimasen de
Past Ind.	**INFORMAL**		mananda	manabanakatta
	FORMAL		manabimashita	manabimasen deshita
Past Presump.	**INFORMAL**		manandarō	manabanakattarō
			mananda darō	manabanakatta darō
	FORMAL		manabimashitarō	manabimasen deshitarō
			mananda deshō	manabanakatta deshō
Conditional	**INFORMAL**		manandara	manabanakattara
	FORMAL		manabimashitara	manabimasen deshitara
Alternative	**INFORMAL**		manandari	manabanakattari
	FORMAL		manabimashitari	manabimasen deshitari

		INFORMAL AFFIRMATIVE INDICATIVE
Passive		manabareru
Potential		manaberu
Causative		manabaseru
Causative Pass.		manabaserareru
Honorific	I	omanabi ni naru
	II	omanabi nasaru
Humble	I	omanabi suru
	II	omanabi itasu

			AFFIRMATIVE	NEGATIVE
Indicative	**INFORMAL**		maneku	manekanai
	FORMAL		manekimasu	manekimasen
Imperative	**INFORMAL**	I	maneke	maneku na
		II	manekinasai	manekinasaru na
		III	maneite kudasai	manekanai de kudasai
	FORMAL		omaneki nasaimase	omaneki nasaimasu na
Presumptive	**INFORMAL**	I	manekō	manekumai
		II	maneku darō	manekanai darō
	FORMAL	I	manekimashō	manekimasumai
		II	maneku deshō	manekanai deshō
Provisional	**INFORMAL**		manekeba	manekanakereba
	FORMAL		manekimaseba	manekimasen nara
			manekimasureba	
Gerund	**INFORMAL**	I	maneite	manekanai de
		II		manekanakute
	FORMAL		manekimashite	manekimasen de
Past Ind.	**INFORMAL**		maneita	manekanakatta
	FORMAL		manekimashita	manekimasen deshita
Past Presump.	**INFORMAL**		maneitarō	manekanakattarō
			maneita darō	manekanakatta darō
	FORMAL		manekimashitarō	manekimasen deshitarō
			maneita deshō	manekanakatta deshō
Conditional	**INFORMAL**		maneitara	manekanakattara
	FORMAL		manekimashitara	manekimasen deshitara
Alternative	**INFORMAL**		maneitari	manekanakattari
	FORMAL		manekimashitari	manekimasen deshitari

			INFORMAL AFFIRMATIVE INDICATIVE
Passive			manekareru
Potential			manekeru
Causative			manekaseru
Causative Pass.			manekaserareru
Honorific		I	omaneki ni naru
		II	omaneki nasaru
Humble		I	omaneki suru
		II	omaneki itasu

matome.ru　まとめる

to settle (a dispute), *to arrange* (a matter), *to complete*　TRANSITIVE

			AFFIRMATIVE	NEGATIVE
Indicative	INFORMAL		matomeru	matomenai
	FORMAL		matomemasu	matomemasen
Imperative	INFORMAL	I	matomero	matomeru na
		II	matomenasai	matomenasaru na
		III	matomete kudasai	matomenai de kudasai
	FORMAL		omatome nasaimase	omatome nasaimasu na
Presumptive	INFORMAL	I	matomeyō	matomemai
		II	matomeru darō	matomenai darō
	FORMAL	I	matomemashō	matomemasumai
		II	matomeru deshō	matomenai deshō
Provisional	INFORMAL		matomereba	matomenakereba
	FORMAL		matomemaseba	matomemasen nara
			matomemasureba	
Gerund	INFORMAL	I	matomete	matomenai de
		II		matomenakute
	FORMAL		matomemashite	matomemasen de
Past Ind.	INFORMAL		matometa	matomenakatta
	FORMAL		matomemashita	matomemasen deshita
Past Presump.	INFORMAL		matometarō	matomenakattarō
			matometa darō	matomenakatta darō
	FORMAL		matomemashitarō	matomemasen deshitarō
			matometa deshō	matomenakatta deshō
Conditional	INFORMAL		matometara	matomenakattara
	FORMAL		matomemashitara	matomemasen deshitara
Alternative	INFORMAL		matometari	matomenakattari
	FORMAL		matomemashitari	matomemasen deshitari

		INFORMAL AFFIRMATIVE INDICATIVE
Passive		matomerareru
Potential		matomerareru
Causative		matomesaseru
Causative Pass.		matomesaserareru
Honorific	I	omatome ni naru
	II	omatome nasaru
Humble	I	omatome suru
	II	omatome itasu

まつ／待つ **mats.u**

TRANSITIVE　*to wait, to wait for, to look forward to*

			AFFIRMATIVE	**NEGATIVE**
Indicative	**INFORMAL**		matsu	matanai
	FORMAL		machimasu	machimasen
Imperative	**INFORMAL**	I	mate	matsu na
		II	machinasai	machinasaru na
		III	matte kudasai	matanai de kudasai
	FORMAL		omachi nasaimase	omachi nasaimasu na
Presumptive	**INFORMAL**	I	matō	matsumai
		II	matsu darō	matanai darō
	FORMAL	I	machimashō	machimasumai
		II	matsu deshō	matanai deshō
Provisional	**INFORMAL**		mateba	matanakereba
	FORMAL		machimaseba	machimasen nara
			machimasureba	
Gerund	**INFORMAL**	I	matte	matanai de
		II		matanakute
	FORMAL		machimashite	machimasen de
Past Ind.	**INFORMAL**		matta	matanakatta
	FORMAL		machimashita	machimasen deshita
Past Presump.	**INFORMAL**		mattarō	matanakattarō
			matta darō	matanakatta darō
	FORMAL		machimashitarō	machimasen deshitarō
			matta deshō	matanakatta deshō
Conditional	**INFORMAL**		mattara	matanakattara
	FORMAL		machimashitara	machimasen deshitara
Alternative	**INFORMAL**		mattari	matanakattari
	FORMAL		machimashitari	machimasen deshitari

M

		INFORMAL AFFIRMATIVE INDICATIVE
Passive		matareru
Potential		materu
Causative		mataseru
Causative Pass.		mataserareru
Honorific	I	omachi ni naru
	II	omachi nasaru
Humble	I	omachi suru
	II	omachi itasu

AN ESSENTIAL 55 VERB

AN ESSENTIAL 55 VERB

Matsu 待つ

to wait, to wait for, to look forward to

Matsu is a verb you need as you wait for the right time to do something, wait for someone or something, or look forward to an exciting event.

Sentences Using *Matsu*

Kanojo wa mattemo mattemo kimasen deshita.
彼女は待っても待っても来ませんでした。
I waited and waited for her, but she never came.

Mō juppun matte moraemasu ka.
もう十分待ってもらえますか。
Could you wait for me for 10 more minutes?

Kare wa okusan o matanaide dekakete shimatta.
彼は奥さんを待たないで出かけてしまった。
He left home without waiting for his wife.

Matte itara, kanarazu kikai ga yatte kimasu.
待っていたら、必ず機会がやってきます。
If you wait, an opportunity will always come.

Gaikoku ryokō wa rainen made machimashō.
外国旅行は来年まで待ちましょう。
Let's wait until next year to take an overseas trip.

Words and Expressions Related to This Verb

machiawaseru 待ち合わせる
to arrange to meet

machinozomu 待ち望む
to wait eagerly

matta nashi 待った無し
time is up

machiaishitsu 待合室
a waiting room

Proverb

Mateba kairo no hiyori kana.
待てば海路の日和かな。
After a storm, comes the calm. (If you wait, calm weather for sea routes will come.)

matsuri

まつる／祭る **matsur.u**

TRANSITIVE   *to deify, to worship*

			AFFIRMATIVE	NEGATIVE
Indicative	INFORMAL		matsuru	matsuranai
	FORMAL		matsurimasu	matsurimasen
Imperative	INFORMAL	I	matsure	matsuru na
		II	matsurinasai	matsurinasaru na
		III	matsutte kudasai	matsuranai de kudasai
	FORMAL		omatsuri nasaimase	omatsuri nasaimasu na
Presumptive	INFORMAL	I	matsurō	matsurumai
		II	matsuru darō	matsuranai darō
	FORMAL	I	matsurimashō	matsurimasumai
		II	matsuru deshō	matsuranai deshō
Provisional	INFORMAL		matsureba	matsuranakereba
	FORMAL		matsurimaseba	matsurimasen nara
			matsurimasureba	
Gerund	INFORMAL	I	matsutte	matsuranai de
		II		matsuranakute
	FORMAL		matsurimashite	matsurimasen de
Past Ind.	INFORMAL		matsutta	matsuranakatta
	FORMAL		matsurimashita	matsurimasen deshita
Past Presump.	INFORMAL		matsuttarō	matsuranakattarō
			matsutta darō	matsuranakatta darō
	FORMAL		matsurimashitarō	matsurimasen deshitarō
			matsutta deshō	matsuranakatta deshō
Conditional	INFORMAL		matsuttara	matsuranakattara
	FORMAL		matsurimashitara	matsurimasen deshitara
Alternative	INFORMAL		matsuttari	matsuranakattari
	FORMAL		matsurimashitari	matsurimasen deshitari

		INFORMAL AFFIRMATIVE INDICATIVE
Passive		matsurareru
Potential		matsureru
Causative		matsuraseru
Causative Pass.		matsuraserareru
Honorific	I	omatsuri ni naru
	II	omatsuri nasaru
Humble	I	omatsuri suru
	II	omatsuri itasu

M

323

to be puzzled, to be at a loss

			AFFIRMATIVE	**NEGATIVE**
Indicative	**INFORMAL**		mayou	mayowanai
	FORMAL		mayoimasu	mayoimasen
Imperative	**INFORMAL**	I	mayoe	mayou na
		II	mayoinasai	mayoinasaru na
		III	mayotte kudasai	mayowanai de kudasai
	FORMAL		omayoi nasaimase	omayoi nasaimasu na
Presumptive	**INFORMAL**	I	mayoō	mayoumai
		II	mayou darō	mayowanai darō
	FORMAL	I	mayoimashō	mayoimasumai
		II	mayou deshō	mayowanai deshō
Provisional	**INFORMAL**		mayoeba	mayowanakereba
	FORMAL		mayoimaseba	mayoimasen nara
			mayoimasureba	
Gerund	**INFORMAL**	I	mayotte	mayowanai de
		II		mayowanakute
	FORMAL		mayoimashite	mayoimasen de
Past Ind.	**INFORMAL**		mayotta	mayowanakatta
	FORMAL		mayoimashita	mayoimasen deshita
Past Presump.	**INFORMAL**		mayottarō	mayowanakattarō
			mayotta darō	mayowanakatta darō
	FORMAL		mayoimashitarō	mayoimasen deshitarō
			mayotta deshō	mayowanakatta deshō
Conditional	**INFORMAL**		mayottara	mayowanakattara
	FORMAL		mayoimashitara	mayoimasen deshitara
Alternative	**INFORMAL**		mayottari	mayowanakattari
	FORMAL		mayoimashitari	mayoimasen deshitari

		INFORMAL AFFIRMATIVE INDICATIVE
Passive		mayowareru
Potential		mayoeru
Causative		mayowaseru
Causative Pass.		mayowaserareru
Honorific	I	omayoi ni naru
	II	omayoi nasaru
Humble	I	
	II	

まぜる／混ぜる／交ぜる　**maze.ru**

TRANSITIVE　　*to mix, to blend*

			AFFIRMATIVE	**NEGATIVE**
Indicative	**INFORMAL**		mazeru	mazenai
	FORMAL		mazemasu	mazemasen
Imperative	**INFORMAL**	I	mazero	mazeru na
		II	mazenasai	mazenasaru na
		III	mazete kudasai	mazenai de kudasai
	FORMAL		omaze nasaimase	omaze nasaimasu na
Presumptive	**INFORMAL**	I	mazeyō	mazemai
		II	mazeru darō	mazenai darō
	FORMAL	I	mazemashō	mazemasumai
		II	mazeru deshō	mazenai deshō
Provisional	**INFORMAL**		mazereba	mazenakereba
	FORMAL		mazemaseba	mazemasen nara
			mazemasureba	
Gerund	**INFORMAL**	I	mazete	mazenai de
		II		mazenakute
	FORMAL		mazemashite	mazemasen de
Past Ind.	**INFORMAL**		mazeta	mazenakatta
	FORMAL		mazemashita	mazemasen deshita
Past Presump.	**INFORMAL**		mazetarō	mazenakattarō
			mazeta darō	mazenakatta darō
	FORMAL		mazemashitarō	mazemasen deshitarō
			mazeta deshō	mazenakatta deshō
Conditional	**INFORMAL**		mazetara	mazenakattara
	FORMAL		mazemashitara	mazemasen deshitara
Alternative	**INFORMAL**		mazetari	mazenakattari
	FORMAL		mazemashitari	mazemasen deshitari

			INFORMAL AFFIRMATIVE INDICATIVE
Passive			mazerareru
Potential			mazerareru
Causative			mazesaseru
Causative Pass.			mazesaserareru
Honorific		I	omaze ni naru
		II	omaze nasaru
Humble		I	omaze suru
		II	omaze itasu

M

to stand out, to attract attention, to be conspicuous

			AFFIRMATIVE	**NEGATIVE**
Indicative	INFORMAL		medatsu	medatanai
	FORMAL		medachimasu	medachimasen
Imperative	INFORMAL	I	medate	medatsu na
		II	medachinasai	medachinasaru na
		III	medatte kudasai	medatanai de kudasai
	FORMAL		omedachi nasaimase	omedachi nasaimasu na
Presumptive	INFORMAL	I	medatō	medatsumai
		II	medatsu darō	medatanai darō
	FORMAL	I	medachimashō	medachimasumai
		II	medatsu deshō	medatanai deshō
Provisional	INFORMAL		medateba	medatanakereba
	FORMAL		medachimaseba	medachimasen nara
			medachimasureba	
Gerund	INFORMAL	I	medatte	medatanai de
		II		medatanakute
	FORMAL		medachimashite	medachimasen de
Past Ind.	INFORMAL		medatta	medatanakatta
	FORMAL		medachimashita	medachimasen deshita
Past Presump.	INFORMAL		medattarō	medatanakattarō
			medatta darō	medatanakatta darō
	FORMAL		medachimashitarō	medachimasen deshitarō
			medatta deshō	medatanakatta deshō
Conditional	INFORMAL		medattara	medatanakattara
	FORMAL		medachimashitara	medachimasen deshitara
Alternative	INFORMAL		medattari	medatanakattari
	FORMAL		medachimashitari	medachimasen deshitari

		INFORMAL AFFIRMATIVE INDICATIVE
Passive		
Potential		medateru
Causative		medataseru
Causative Pass.		medataserareru
Honorific	I	omedachi ni naru
	II	omedachi nasaru
Humble	I	
	II	

めしあがる／召し上がる　**meshiagar.u**

TRANSITIVE　　*to eat* (honorific), *to drink* (honorific)

			AFFIRMATIVE	NEGATIVE
Indicative	**INFORMAL**		meshiagaru	meshiagaranai
	FORMAL		meshiagarimasu	meshiagarimasen
Imperative	**INFORMAL**	**I**	meshiagare	
		II		meshiagarinasaru na
		III	meshiagatte kudasai	meshiagaranai de kudasai
	FORMAL		omeshiagari nasaimase	omeshiagari nasaimasu na
Presumptive	**INFORMAL**	**I**	meshiagarō	meshiagarumai
		II	meshiagaru darō	meshiagaranai darō
	FORMAL	**I**	meshiagarimashō	meshiagarimasumai
		II	meshiagaru deshō	meshiagaranai deshō
Provisional	**INFORMAL**		meshiagareba	meshiagaranakereba
	FORMAL		meshiagarimaseba	meshiagarimasen nara
			meshiagarimasureba	
Gerund	**INFORMAL**	**I**	meshiagatte	meshiagaranai de
		II		meshiagaranakute
	FORMAL		meshiagarimashite	meshiagarimasen de
Past Ind.	**INFORMAL**		meshiagatta	meshiagaranakatta
	FORMAL		meshiagarimashita	meshiagarimasen deshita
Past Presump.	**INFORMAL**		meshiagattarō	meshiagaranakattarō
			meshiagatta darō	meshiagaranakatta darō
	FORMAL		meshiagarimashitarō	meshiagarimasen deshitarō
			meshiagatta deshō	meshiagaranakatta deshō
Conditional	**INFORMAL**		meshiagattara	meshiagaranakattara
	FORMAL		meshiagarimashitara	meshiagarimasen deshitara
Alternative	**INFORMAL**		meshiagattari	meshiagaranakattari
	FORMAL		meshiagarimashitari	meshiagarimasen deshitari

M

		INFORMAL AFFIRMATIVE INDICATIVE
Passive		meshiagarareru
Potential		meshiagareru
Causative		meshiagaraseru
Causative Pass.		meshiagaraserareru
Honorific	**I**	omeshiagari ni naru
	II	omeshiagari nasaru
Humble	**I**	
	II	

to be visible, to be able to see, honorific for to come

			AFFIRMATIVE	NEGATIVE
Indicative	**INFORMAL**		mieru	mienai
	FORMAL		miemasu	miemasen
Imperative	**INFORMAL**	I		
		II		
		III		
	FORMAL			
Presumptive	**INFORMAL**	I	mieyō	miemai
		II	mieru darō	mienai darō
	FORMAL	I	miemashō	miemasumai
		II	mieru deshō	mienai deshō
Provisional	**INFORMAL**		miereba	mienakereba
	FORMAL		miemaseba	miemasen nara
			miemasureba	
Gerund	**INFORMAL**	I	miete	mienai de
		II		mienakute
	FORMAL		miemashite	miemasen de
Past Ind.	**INFORMAL**		mieta	mienakatta
	FORMAL		miemashita	miemasen deshita
Past Presump.	**INFORMAL**		mietarō	mienakattarō
			mieta darō	mienakatta darō
	FORMAL		miemashitarō	miemasen deshitarō
			mieta deshō	mienakatta deshō
Conditional	**INFORMAL**		mietara	mienakattara
	FORMAL		miemashitara	miemasen deshitara
Alternative	**INFORMAL**		mietari	mienakattari
	FORMAL		miemashitari	miemasen deshitari

		INFORMAL AFFIRMATIVE INDICATIVE
Passive		
Potential		
Causative		
Causative Pass.		
Honorific	I	omie ni naru
	II	irassharu
Humble	I	
	II	

みがく／磨く　**migak.u**

TRANSITIVE　*to polish*

			AFFIRMATIVE	NEGATIVE
Indicative	**INFORMAL**		migaku	migakanai
	FORMAL		migakimasu	migakimasen
Imperative	**INFORMAL**	I	migake	migaku na
		II	migakinasai	migakinasaru na
		III	migaite kudasai	migakanai de kudasai
	FORMAL		omigaki nasaimase	omigaki nasaimasu na
Presumptive	**INFORMAL**	I	migakō	migakumai
		II	migaku darō	migakanai darō
	FORMAL	I	migakimashō	migakimasumai
		II	migaku deshō	migakanai deshō
Provisional	**INFORMAL**		migakeba	migakanakereba
	FORMAL		migakimaseba	migakimasen nara
			migakimasureba	
Gerund	**INFORMAL**	I	migaite	migakanai de
		II		migakanakute
	FORMAL		migakimashite	migakimasen de
Past Ind.	**INFORMAL**		migaita	migakanakatta
	FORMAL		migakimashita	migakimasen deshita
Past Presump.	**INFORMAL**		migaitarō	migakanakattarō
			migaita darō	migakanakatta darō
	FORMAL		migakimashitarō	migakimasen deshitarō
			migaita deshō	migakanakatta deshō
Conditional	**INFORMAL**		migaitara	migakanakattara
	FORMAL		migakimashitara	migakimasen deshitara
Alternative	**INFORMAL**		migaitari	migakanakattari
	FORMAL		migakimashitari	migakimasen deshitari

			INFORMAL AFFIRMATIVE INDICATIVE
Passive			migakareru
Potential			migakeru
Causative			migakaseru
Causative Pass.			migakaserareru
Honorific		I	omigaki ni naru
		II	omigaki nasaru
Humble		I	omigaki suru
		II	omigaki itasu

M

to stand guard, to keep a lookout   TRANSITIVE

			AFFIRMATIVE	NEGATIVE
Indicative	**INFORMAL**		miharu	miharanai
	FORMAL		miharimasu	miharimasen
Imperative	**INFORMAL**	I	mihare	miharu na
		II	miharinasai	miharinasaru na
		III	mihatte kudasai	miharanai de kudasai
	FORMAL		omihari nasaimase	omihari nasaimasu na
Presumptive	**INFORMAL**	I	miharō	miharumai
		II	miharu darō	miharanai darō
	FORMAL	I	miharimashō	miharimasumai
		II	miharu deshō	miharanai deshō
Provisional	**INFORMAL**		mihareba	miharanakereba
	FORMAL		miharimaseba	miharimasen nara
			miharimasureba	
Gerund	**INFORMAL**	I	mihatte	miharanai de
		II		miharanakute
	FORMAL		miharimashite	miharimasen de
Past Ind.	**INFORMAL**		mihatta	miharanakatta
	FORMAL		miharimashita	miharimasen deshita
Past Presump.	**INFORMAL**		mihattarō	miharanakattarō
			mihatta darō	miharanakatta darō
	FORMAL		miharimashitarō	miharimasen deshitarō
			mihatta deshō	miharanakatta deshō
Conditional	**INFORMAL**		mihattara	miharanakattara
	FORMAL		miharimashitara	miharimasen deshitara
Alternative	**INFORMAL**		mihattari	miharanakattari
	FORMAL		miharimashitari	miharimasen deshitari

			INFORMAL AFFIRMATIVE INDICATIVE
Passive			miharareru
Potential			mihareru
Causative			miharaseru
Causative Pass.			miharaserareru
Honorific		I	omihari ni naru
		II	omihari nasaru
Humble		I	omihari suru
		II	omihari itasu

TRANSITIVE　　　*to look at again, to reconsider, to discover new merits*

			AFFIRMATIVE	**NEGATIVE**
Indicative	**INFORMAL**		minaosu	minaosanai
	FORMAL		minaoshimasu	minaoshimasen
Imperative	**INFORMAL**	I	minaose	minaosu na
		II	minaoshinasai	minaoshinasaru na
		III	minaoshite kudasai	minaosanai de kudasai
	FORMAL		ominaoshi nasaimase	ominaoshi nasaimasu na
Presumptive	**INFORMAL**	I	minaosō	minaosumai
		II	minaosu darō	minaosanai darō
	FORMAL	I	minaoshimashō	minaoshimasumai
		II	minaosu deshō	minaosanai deshō
Provisional	**INFORMAL**		minaoseba	minaosanakereba
	FORMAL		minaoshimaseba	minaoshimasen nara
			minaoshimasureba	
Gerund	**INFORMAL**	I	minaoshite	minaosanai de
		II		minaosanakute
	FORMAL		minaoshimashite	minaoshimasen de
Past Ind.	**INFORMAL**		minaoshita	minaosanakatta
	FORMAL		minaoshimashita	minaoshimasen deshita
Past Presump.	**INFORMAL**		minaoshitarō	minaosanakattarō
			minaoshita darō	minaosanakatta darō
	FORMAL		minaoshimashitarō	minaoshimasen deshitarō
			minaoshita deshō	minaosanakatta deshō
Conditional	**INFORMAL**		minaoshitara	minaosanakattara
	FORMAL		minaoshimashitara	minaoshimasen deshitara
Alternative	**INFORMAL**		minaoshitari	minaosanakattari
	FORMAL		minaoshimashitari	minaoshimasen deshitari

			INFORMAL AFFIRMATIVE INDICATIVE
Passive			minaosareru
Potential			minaoseru
Causative			minaosaseru
Causative Pass.			minaosaserareru
Honorific		I	ominaoshi ni naru
		II	ominaoshi nasaru
Humble		I	ominaoshi suru
		II	ominaoshi itasu

to regard as, to look upon as, to consider   TRANSITIVE

			AFFIRMATIVE	**NEGATIVE**
Indicative	**INFORMAL**		minasu	minasanai
	FORMAL		minashimasu	minashimasen
Imperative	**INFORMAL**	I	minase	minasu na
		II	minashinasai	minashinasaru na
		III	minashite kudasai	minasanai de kudasai
	FORMAL		ominashi nasaimase	ominashi nasaimasu na
Presumptive	**INFORMAL**	I	minasō	minasumai
		II	minasu darō	minasanai darō
	FORMAL	I	minashimashō	minashimasumai
		II	minasu deshō	minasanai deshō
Provisional	**INFORMAL**		minaseba	minasanakereba
	FORMAL		minashimaseba	minashimasen nara
			minashimasureba	
Gerund	**INFORMAL**	I	minashite	minasanai de
		II		minasanakute
	FORMAL		minashimashite	minashimasen de
Past Ind.	**INFORMAL**		minashita	minasanakatta
	FORMAL		minashimashita	minashimasen deshita
Past Presump.	**INFORMAL**		minashitarō	minasanakattarō
			minashita darō	minasanakatta darō
	FORMAL		minashimashitarō	minashimasen deshitarō
			minashita deshō	minasanakatta deshō
Conditional	**INFORMAL**		minashitara	minasanakattara
	FORMAL		minashimashitara	minashimasen deshitara
Alternative	**INFORMAL**		minashitari	minasanakattari
	FORMAL		minashimashitari	minashimasen deshitari

		INFORMAL AFFIRMATIVE INDICATIVE
Passive		minasareru
Potential		minaseru
Causative		minasaseru
Causative Pass.		minasaserareru
Honorific	I	ominashi ni naru
	II	ominashi nasaru
Humble	I	ominashi suru
	II	ominashi itasu

みのがす／見逃す **minogas.u**

TRANSITIVE   *to overlook, to let pass*

			AFFIRMATIVE	**NEGATIVE**
Indicative	**INFORMAL**		minogasu	minogasanai
	FORMAL		minogashimasu	minogashimasen
Imperative	**INFORMAL**	I	minogase	minogasu na
		II	minogashinasai	minogashinasaru na
		III	minogashite kudasai	minogasanai de kudasai
	FORMAL		ominogashi nasaimase	ominogashi nasaimasu na
Presumptive	**INFORMAL**	I	minogasō	minogasumai
		II	minogasu darō	minogasanai darō
	FORMAL	I	minogashimashō	minogashimasumai
		II	minogasu deshō	minogasanai deshō
Provisional	**INFORMAL**		minogaseba	minogasanakereba
	FORMAL		minogashimaseba	minogashimasen nara
			minogashimasureba	
Gerund	**INFORMAL**	I	minogashite	minogasanai de
		II		minogasanakute
	FORMAL		minogashimashite	minogashimasen de
Past Ind.	**INFORMAL**		minogashita	minogasanakatta
	FORMAL		minogashimashita	minogashimasen deshita
Past Presump.	**INFORMAL**		minogashitarō	minogasanakattarō
			minogashita darō	minogasanakatta darō
	FORMAL		minogashimashitarō	minogashimasen deshitarō
			minogashita deshō	minogasanakatta deshō
Conditional	**INFORMAL**		minogashitara	minogasanakattara
	FORMAL		minogashimashitara	minogashimasen deshitara
Alternative	**INFORMAL**		minogashitari	minogasanakattari
	FORMAL		minogashimashitari	minogashimasen deshitari

		INFORMAL AFFIRMATIVE INDICATIVE
Passive		minogasareru
Potential		minogaseru
Causative		minogasaseru
Causative Pass.		minogasaserareru
Honorific	I	ominogashi ni naru
	II	ominogashi nasaru
Humble	I	ominogashi suru
	II	ominogashi itasu

M

minor.u　みのる／実る

to ripen, to bear fruit

minori

			AFFIRMATIVE	NEGATIVE
Indicative	INFORMAL		minoru	minoranai
	FORMAL		minorimasu	minorimasen
Imperative	INFORMAL	I	minore	minoru na
		II	minorinasai	minorinasaru na
		III	minotte kudasai	minoranai de kudasai
	FORMAL		ominori nasaimase	ominori nasaimasu na
Presumptive	INFORMAL	I	minorō	minorumai
		II	minoru darō	minoranai darō
	FORMAL	I	minorimashō	minorimasumai
		II	minoru deshō	minoranai deshō
Provisional	INFORMAL		minoreba	minoranakereba
	FORMAL		minorimaseba	minorimasen nara
			minorimasureba	
Gerund	INFORMAL	I	minotte	minoranai de
		II		minoranakute
	FORMAL		minorimashite	minorimasen de
Past Ind.	INFORMAL		minotta	minoranakatta
	FORMAL		minorimashita	minorimasen deshita
Past Presump.	INFORMAL		minottarō	minoranakattarō
			minotta darō	minoranakatta darō
	FORMAL		minorimashitarō	minorimasen deshitarō
			minotta deshō	minoranakatta deshō
Conditional	INFORMAL		minottara	minoranakattara
	FORMAL		minorimashitara	minorimasen deshitara
Alternative	INFORMAL		minottari	minoranakattari
	FORMAL		minorimashitari	minorimasen deshitari

		INFORMAL AFFIRMATIVE INDICATIVE
Passive		minorareru
Potential		minoreru
Causative		minoraseru
Causative Pass.		minoraserareru
Honorific	I	ominori ni naru
	II	ominori nasaru
Humble	I	
	II	

334

みぬく／見抜く　**minuk.u**

TRANSITIVE　　*to see through, to have an insight into*

			AFFIRMATIVE	NEGATIVE
Indicative	**INFORMAL**		minuku	minukanai
	FORMAL		minukimasu	minukimasen
Imperative	**INFORMAL**	I	minuke	minuku na
		II	minukinasai	minukinasaru na
		III	minuite kudasai	minukanai de kudasai
	FORMAL		ominuki nasaimase	ominuki nasaimasu na
Presumptive	**INFORMAL**	I	minukō	minukumai
		II	minuku darō	minukanai darō
	FORMAL	I	minukimashō	minukimasumai
		II	minuku deshō	minukanai deshō
Provisional	**INFORMAL**		minukeba	minukanakereba
	FORMAL		minukimaseba	minukimasen nara
			minukimasureba	
Gerund	**INFORMAL**	I	minuite	minukanai de
		II		minukanakute
	FORMAL		minukimashite	minukimasen de
Past Ind.	**INFORMAL**		minuita	minukanakatta
	FORMAL		minukimashita	minukimasen deshita
Past Presump.	**INFORMAL**		minuitarō	minukanakattarō
			minuita darō	minukanakatta darō
	FORMAL		minukimashitarō	minukimasen deshitarō
			minuita deshō	minukanakatta deshō
Conditional	**INFORMAL**		minuitara	minukanakattara
	FORMAL		minukimashitara	minukimasen deshitara
Alternative	**INFORMAL**		minuitari	minukanakattari
	FORMAL		minukimashitari	minukimasen deshitari

			INFORMAL AFFIRMATIVE INDICATIVE
Passive			minukareru
Potential			minukeru
Causative			minukaseru
Causative Pass.			minukaserareru
Honorific		I	ominuki ni naru
		II	ominuki nasaru
Humble		I	ominuki suru
		II	ominuki itasu

M

to look (at), *to see, to read*   TRANSITIVE

			AFFIRMATIVE	NEGATIVE
Indicative	**INFORMAL**		miru	minai
	FORMAL		mimasu	mimasen
Imperative	**INFORMAL**	I	miro	miru na
		II	minasai	minasaru na
		III	mite kudasai	minai de kudasai
	FORMAL		goran nasaimase	goran nasaimasu na
Presumptive	**INFORMAL**	I	miyō	mimai
		II	miru darō	minai darō
	FORMAL	I	mimashō	mimasumai
		II	miru deshō	minai deshō
Provisional	**INFORMAL**		mireba	minakereba
	FORMAL		mimaseba	mimasen nara
			mimasureba	
Gerund	**INFORMAL**	I	mite	minai de
		II		minakute
	FORMAL		mimashite	mimasen de
Past Ind.	**INFORMAL**		mita	minakatta
	FORMAL		mimashita	mimasen deshita
Past Presump.	**INFORMAL**		mitarō	minakattarō
			mita darō	minakatta darō
	FORMAL		mimashitarō	mimasen deshitarō
			mita deshō	minakatta deshō
Conditional	**INFORMAL**		mitara	minakattara
	FORMAL		mimashitara	mimasen deshitara
Alternative	**INFORMAL**		mitari	minakattari
	FORMAL		mimashitari	mimasen deshitari

		INFORMAL AFFIRMATIVE INDICATIVE
Passive		mirareru
Potential		mirareru*
Causative		misaseru
Causative Pass.		misaserareru
Honorific	I	goran ni naru
	II	goran nasaru
Humble	I	haiken suru
	II	haiken itasu

AN ESSENTIAL 55 VERB

*This form means "can be seen" in the sense that it exists at the time one wants to look at it. "To be visible" is the separate verb *mieru*.

AN ESSENTIAL 55 VERB

Miru 見る

to look (at), to see, to read

Sentences Using *Miru*

Mitai eiga ga arimasu.
見たい映画があります。
There's a movie I want to see.

Chizu o mireba, sore ga doko ni aru
ka sugu wakarimasu.
地図を見れば、それがどこにあるかす
ぐ分かります。
*If you look at a map, you'll know
immediately where it is.*

Sono shinbun o minai no nara
kaeshite kudasai.
その新聞を見ないのなら返して下さ
い。
*If you're not going to read it, please
return the newspaper to me.*

Mitakunai shashin o misaserareta.
見たくない写真を見させられた。
*I was forced to look at some
photographs I didn't want to see.*

Atarashii kōen o mini ikimashita.
新しい公園を見に行きました。
I went to see a new park.

Miru is verb you use often in Japan,
where there's so much to look at and see
everywhere. And reading Japanese can
add a new dimension to the experience.

Words and Expressions Related to This Verb

M

nagameru　眺める
to look at, to watch

miwatasu　見渡す
to look out over, to gaze over

miharashi　見晴らし
a view

mikake　見かけ
appearance, looks

Proverb

Mizaru, kikazaru, iwazaru.
見ざる、聞かざる、言わざる。
*See no evil, hear no evil, speak
no evil.*

to show　　　TRANSITIVE

			AFFIRMATIVE	**NEGATIVE**
Indicative	**INFORMAL**		miseru	misenai
	FORMAL		misemasu	misemasen
Imperative	**INFORMAL**	I	misero	miseru na
		II	misenasai	misenasaru na
		III	misete kudasai	misenai de kudasai
	FORMAL		omise nasaimase	omise nasaimasu na
Presumptive	**INFORMAL**	I	miseyō	misemai
		II	miseru darō	misenai darō
	FORMAL	I	misemashō	misemasumai
		II	miseru deshō	misenai deshō
Provisional	**INFORMAL**		misereba	misenakereba
	FORMAL		misemaseba	misemasen nara
			misemasureba	
Gerund	**INFORMAL**	I	misete	misenai de
		II	misenakute	
	FORMAL		misemashite	misemasen de
Past Ind.	**INFORMAL**		miseta	misenakatta
	FORMAL		misemashita	misemasen deshita
Past Presump.	**INFORMAL**		misetarō	misenakattarō
			miseta darō	misenakatta darō
	FORMAL		misemashitarō	misemasen deshitarō
			miseta deshō	misenakatta deshō
Conditional	**INFORMAL**		misetara	misenakattara
	FORMAL		misemashitara	misemasen deshitara
Alternative	**INFORMAL**		misetari	misenakattari
	FORMAL		misemashitari	misemasen deshitari

		INFORMAL AFFIRMATIVE INDICATIVE	
Passive		miserareru	
Potential		miserareru	
Causative		misesaseru	
Causative Pass.		misesaserareru	
Honorific	I	omise ni naru	
	II	omise nasaru	
Humble	I	omise suru	goran ni ireru
	II	omise itasu	

みとめる／認める   **mitome.ru**

TRANSITIVE   *to admit, to recognize*

			AFFIRMATIVE	**NEGATIVE**
Indicative	**INFORMAL**		mitomeru	mitomenai
	FORMAL		mitomemasu	mitomemasen
Imperative	**INFORMAL**	I	mitomero	mitomeru na
		II	mitomenasai	mitomenasaru na
		III	mitomete kudasai	mitomenai de kudasai
	FORMAL		omitome nasaimase	omitome nasaimasu na
Presumptive	**INFORMAL**	I	mitomeyō	mitomemai
		II	mitomeru darō	mitomenai darō
	FORMAL	I	mitomemashō	mitomemasumai
		II	mitomeru deshō	mitomenai deshō
Provisional	**INFORMAL**		mitomereba	mitomenakereba
	FORMAL		mitomemaseba	mitomemasen nara
			mitomemasureba	
Gerund	**INFORMAL**	I	mitomete	mitomenai de
		II		mitomenakute
	FORMAL		mitomemashite	mitomemasen de
Past Ind.	**INFORMAL**		mitometa	mitomenakatta
	FORMAL		mitomemashita	mitomemasen deshita
Past Presump.	**INFORMAL**		mitometarō	mitomenakattarō
			mitometa darō	mitomenakatta darō
	FORMAL		mitomemashitarō	mitomemasen deshitarō
			mitometa deshō	mitomenakatta deshō
Conditional	**INFORMAL**		mitometara	mitomenakattara
	FORMAL		mitomemashitara	mitomemasen deshitara
Alternative	**INFORMAL**		mitometari	mitomenakattari
	FORMAL		mitomemashitari	mitomemasen deshitari

			INFORMAL AFFIRMATIVE INDICATIVE
Passive			mitomerareru
Potential			mitomerareru
Causative			mitomesaseru
Causative Pass.			mitomesaserareru
Honorific		I	omitome ni naru
		II	omitome nasaru
Humble		I	omitome suru
		II	omitome itasu

M

mitsukar.u みつかる／見付かる
to be found

mitsukari

			AFFIRMATIVE	NEGATIVE
Indicative	**INFORMAL**		mitsukaru	mitsukaranai
	FORMAL		mitsukarimasu	mitsukarimasen
Imperative	**INFORMAL**	I		
		II		
		III		
	FORMAL			
Presumptive	**INFORMAL**	I	mitsukarō	mitsukarumai
		II	mitsukaru darō	mitsukaranai darō
	FORMAL	I	mitsukarimashō	mitsukarimasumai
		II	mitsukaru deshō	mitsukaranai deshō
Provisional	**INFORMAL**		mitsukareba	mitsukaranakereba
	FORMAL		mitsukarimaseba	mitsukarimasen nara
			mitsukarimasureba	
Gerund	**INFORMAL**	I	mitsukatte	mitsukaranai de
		II		mitsukaranakute
	FORMAL		mitsukarimashite	mitsukarimasen de
Past Ind.	**INFORMAL**		mitsukatta	mitsukaranakatta
	FORMAL		mitsukarimashita	mitsukarimasen deshita
Past Presump.	**INFORMAL**		mitsukattarō	mitsukaranakattarō
			mitsukatta darō	mitsukaranakatta darō
	FORMAL		mitsukarimashitarō	mitsukarimasen deshitarō
			mitsukatta deshō	mitsukaranakatta deshō
Conditional	**INFORMAL**		mitsukattara	mitsukaranakattara
	FORMAL		mitsukarimashitara	mitsukarimasen deshitara
Alternative	**INFORMAL**		mitsukattari	mitsukaranakattari
	FORMAL		mitsukarimashitari	mitsukarimasen deshitari

		INFORMAL AFFIRMATIVE INDICATIVE
Passive		
Potential		
Causative		
Causative Pass.		
Honorific	I	
	II	
Humble	I	
	II	

340

mitsuke

みつける／見付ける　**mitsuke.ru**

TRANSITIVE　　*to find*

			AFFIRMATIVE	NEGATIVE
Indicative	**INFORMAL**		mitsukeru	mitsukenai
	FORMAL		mitsukemasu	mitsukemasen
Imperative	**INFORMAL**	I	mitsukero	mitsukeru na
		II	mitsukenasai	mitsukenasaru na
		III	mitsukete kudasai	mitsukenai de kudasai
	FORMAL		omitsuke nasaimase	omitsuke nasaimasu na
Presumptive	**INFORMAL**	I	mitsukeyō	mitsukemai
		II	mitsukeru darō	mitsukenai darō
	FORMAL	I	mitsukemashō	mitsukemasumai
		II	mitsukeru deshō	mitsukenai deshō
Provisional	**INFORMAL**		mitsukereba	mitsukenakereba
	FORMAL		mitsukemaseba	mitsukemasen nara
			mitsukemasureba	
Gerund	**INFORMAL**	I	mitsukete	mitsukenai de
		II		mitsukenakute
	FORMAL		mitsukemashite	mitsukemasen de
Past Ind.	**INFORMAL**		mitsuketa	mitsukenakatta
	FORMAL		mitsukemashita	mitsukemasen deshita
Past Presump.	**INFORMAL**		mitsuketarō	mitsukenakattarō
			mitsuketa darō	mitsukenakatta darō
	FORMAL		mitsukemashitarō	mitsukemasen deshitarō
			mitsuketa deshō	mitsukenakatta deshō
Conditional	**INFORMAL**		mitsuketara	mitsukenakattara
	FORMAL		mitsukemashitara	mitsukemasen deshitara
Alternative	**INFORMAL**		mitsuketari	mitsukenakattari
	FORMAL		mitsukemashitari	mitsukemasen deshitari

			INFORMAL AFFIRMATIVE INDICATIVE
Passive			mitsukerareru
Potential			mitsukerareru
Causative			mitsukesaseru
Causative Pass.			mitsukesaserareru
Honorific		I	omitsuke ni naru
		II	omitsuke nasaru
Humble		I	omitsuke suru
		II	omitsuke itasu

M

modor.u　もどる／戻る　　　　　　　　　　**modori**
to return, to retrace one's steps, to go back

			AFFIRMATIVE	NEGATIVE
Indicative	**INFORMAL**		modoru	modoranai
	FORMAL		modorimasu	modorimasen
Imperative	**INFORMAL**	I	modore	modoru na
		II	modorinasai	modorinasaru na
		III	modotte kudasai	modoranai de kudasai
	FORMAL		omodori nasaimase	omodori nasaimasu na
Presumptive	**INFORMAL**	I	modorō	modorumai
		II	modoru darō	modoranai darō
	FORMAL	I	modorimashō	modorimasumai
		II	modoru deshō	modoranai deshō
Provisional	**INFORMAL**		modoreba	modoranakereba
	FORMAL		modorimaseba	modorimasen nara
			modorimasureba	
Gerund	**INFORMAL**	I	modotte	modoranai de
		II		modoranakute
	FORMAL		modorimashite	modorlmasen de
Past Ind.	**INFORMAL**		modotta	modoranakatta
	FORMAL		modorimashita	modorimasen deshita
Past Presump.	**INFORMAL**		modottarō	modoranakattarō
			modotta darō	modoranakatta darō
	FORMAL		modorimashitarō	modorimasen deshitarō
			modotta deshō	modoranakatta deshō
Conditional	**INFORMAL**		modottara	modoranakattara
	FORMAL		modorimashitara	modorimasen deshitara
Alternative	**INFORMAL**		modottari	modoranakattari
	FORMAL		modorimashitari	modorimasen deshitari

		INFORMAL AFFIRMATIVE INDICATIVE
Passive		modorareru
Potential		modoreru
Causative		modoraseru
Causative Pass.		modoraserareru
Honorific	I	omodori ni naru
	II	omodori nasaru
Humble	I	omodori suru
	II	omodori itasu

342

modoshi

もどす／戻す **modos.u**

TRANSITIVE   *to put back, to return, to vomit*

			AFFIRMATIVE	NEGATIVE
Indicative	INFORMAL		modosu	modosanai
	FORMAL		modoshimasu	modoshimasen
Imperative	INFORMAL	I	modose	modosu na
		II	modoshinasai	modoshinasaru na
		III	modoshite kudasai	modosanai de kudasai
	FORMAL		omodoshi nasaimase	omodoshi nasaimasu na
Presumptive	INFORMAL	I	modosō	modosumai
		II	modosu darō	modosanai darō
	FORMAL	I	modoshimashō	modoshimasumai
		II	modosu deshō	modosanai deshō
Provisional	INFORMAL		modoseba	modosanakereba
	FORMAL		modoshimaseba	modoshimasen nara
			modoshimasureba	
Gerund	INFORMAL	I	modoshite	modosanai de
		II		modosanakute
	FORMAL		modoshimashite	modoshimasen de
Past Ind.	INFORMAL		modoshita	modosanakatta
	FORMAL		modoshimashita	modoshimasen deshita
Past Presump.	INFORMAL		modoshitarō	modosanakattarō
			modoshita darō	modosanakatta darō
	FORMAL		modoshimashitarō	modoshimasen deshitarō
Conditional	INFORMAL		modoshitara	modosanakattara
	FORMAL		modoshimashitara	modoshimasen deshitara
Alternative	INFORMAL		modoshitari	modosanakattari
	FORMAL		modoshimashitari	modoshimasen deshitari

INFORMAL AFFIRMATIVE INDICATIVE

Passive		modosareru
Potential		modoseru
Causative		modosaseru
Causative Pass.		modosaserareru
Honorific	I	omodoshi ni naru
	II	omodoshi narasaru
Humble	I	omodoshi suru
	II	omodoshi itasu

M

mōkar.u　もうかる／儲かる　　　mōkari

to be profitable, to make money

			AFFIRMATIVE	NEGATIVE
Indicative	INFORMAL		mōkaru	mōkaranai
	FORMAL		mōkarimasu	mōkarimasen
Imperative	INFORMAL	I	mōkare	mōkaru na
		II		
		III		
	FORMAL			
Presumptive	INFORMAL	I	mōkarō	mōkarumai
		II	mōkaru darō	mōkaranai darō
	FORMAL	I	mōkarimashō	mōkarimasumai
		II	mōkaru deshō	mōkaranai deshō
Provisional	INFORMAL		mōkareba	mōkaranakereba
	FORMAL		mōkarimaseba	mōkarimasen nara
			mōkarimasureba	
Gerund	INFORMAL	I	mōkatte	mōkaranai de
		II		mōkaranakute
	FORMAL		mōkarimashite	mōkarimasen de
Past Ind.	INFORMAL		mōkatta	mōkaranakatta
	FORMAL		mōkarimashita	mōkarimasen deshita
Past Presump.	INFORMAL		mōkattarō	mōkaranakattarō
			mōkatta darō	mōkaranakatta darō
	FORMAL		mōkarimashitarō	mōkarimasen deshitarō
			mōkatta deshō	mōkaranakatta deshō
Conditional	INFORMAL		mōkattara	mōkaranakattara
	FORMAL		mōkarimashitara	mōkarimasen deshitara
Alternative	INFORMAL		mōkattari	mōkaranakattari
	FORMAL		mōkarimashitari	mōkarimasen deshitari

		INFORMAL AFFIRMATIVE INDICATIVE
Passive		
Potential		
Causative		mōkaraseru
Causative Pass.		mōkaraserareru
Honorific	I	
	II	
Humble	I	
	II	

344

TRANSITIVE   *to profit, to make money*

			AFFIRMATIVE	NEGATIVE
Indicative	**INFORMAL**		mōkeru	mōkenai
	FORMAL		mōkemasu	mōkemasen
Imperative	**INFORMAL**	I	mōkero	mōkeru na
		II	mōkenasai	mōkenasaru na
		III	mōkete kudasai	mōkenai de kudasai
	FORMAL		omōke nasaimase	omōke nasaimasu na
Presumptive	**INFORMAL**	I	mōkeyō	mōkemai
		II	mōkeru darō	mōkenai darō
	FORMAL	I	mōkemashō	mōkemasumai
		II	mōkeru deshō	mōkenai deshō
Provisional	**INFORMAL**		mōkereba	mōkenakereba
	FORMAL		mōkemaseba	mōkemasen nara
			mōkemasureba	
Gerund	**INFORMAL**	I	mōkete	mōkenai de
		II		mōkenakute
	FORMAL		mōkemashite	mōkemasen de
Past Ind.	**INFORMAL**		mōketa	mōkenakatta
	FORMAL		mōkemashita	mōkemasen deshita
Past Presump.	**INFORMAL**		mōketarō	mōkenakattarō
			mōketa darō	mōkenakatta darō
	FORMAL		mōkemashitarō	mōkemasen deshitarō
			mōketa deshō	mōkenakatta deshō
Conditional	**INFORMAL**		mōketara	mōkenakattara
	FORMAL		mōkemashitara	mōkemasen deshitara
Alternative	**INFORMAL**		mōketari	mōkenakattari
	FORMAL		mōkemashitari	mōkemasen deshitari

		INFORMAL AFFIRMATIVE INDICATIVE
Passive		mōkerareru
Potential		mōkerareru
Causative		mōkesaseru
Causative Pass.		mōkesaserareru
Honorific	I	omōke ni naru
	II	omōke nasaru
Humble	I	
	II	

moras.u　もらす／漏らす
to let leak, to disclose　TRANSITIVE

morashi

			AFFIRMATIVE	NEGATIVE
Indicative	INFORMAL		morasu	morasanai
	FORMAL		morashimasu	morashimasen
Imperative	INFORMAL	I	morase	morasu na
		II	morashinasai	morashinasaru na
		III	morashite kudasai	morasanai de kudasai
	FORMAL		omorashi nasaimase	omorashi nasaimasu na
Presumptive	INFORMAL	I	morasō	morasumai
		II	morasu darō	morasanai darō
	FORMAL	I	morashimashō	morashimasumai
		II	morasu deshō	morasanai deshō
Provisional	INFORMAL		moraseba	morasanakereba
	FORMAL		morashimaseba	morashimasen nara
			morashimasureba	
Gerund	INFORMAL	I	morashite	morasanai de
		II		morasanakute
	FORMAL		morashimashite	morashimasen de
Past Ind.	INFORMAL		morashita	morasanakatta
	FORMAL		morashimashita	morashimasen deshita
Past Presump.	INFORMAL		morashitarō	morasanakattarō
			morashita darō	morasanakatta darō
	FORMAL		morashimashitarō	morashimasen deshitarō
			morashita deshō	morasanakatta deshō
Conditional	INFORMAL		morashitara	morasanakattara
	FORMAL		morashimashitara	morashimasen deshitara
Alternative	INFORMAL		morashitari	morasanakattari
	FORMAL		morashimashitari	morashimasen deshitari

		INFORMAL AFFIRMATIVE INDICATIVE
Passive		morasareru
Potential		moraseru
Causative		morasaseru
Causative Pass.		morasaserareru
Honorific	I	omorashi ni naru
	II	omorashi nasaru
Humble	I	omorashi suru
	II	omorashi itasu

もらう／貰う　**mora.u**

TRANSITIVE　　*to receive, to get*

			AFFIRMATIVE	NEGATIVE
Indicative	**INFORMAL**		morau	morawanai
	FORMAL		moraimasu	moraimasen
Imperative	**INFORMAL**	I	morae	morau na
		II	morainasai	morainasaru na
		III	moratte kudasai	morawanai de kudasai
	FORMAL		omorai nasaimase	omorai nasaimasu na
Presumptive	**INFORMAL**	I	moraō	moraumai
		II	morau darō	morawanai darō
	FORMAL	I	moraimashō	moraimasumai
		II	morau deshō	morawanai deshō
Provisional	**INFORMAL**		moraeba	morawanakereba
	FORMAL		moraimaseba	moraimasen nara
			moraimasureba	
Gerund	**INFORMAL**	I	moratte	morawanai de
		II		morawanakute
	FORMAL		moraimashite	moraimasen de
Past Ind.	**INFORMAL**		moratta	morawanakatta
	FORMAL		moraimashita	moraimasen deshita
Past Presump.	**INFORMAL**		morattarō	morawanakattarō
			moratta darō	morawanakatta darō
	FORMAL		moraimashitarō	moraimasen deshitarō
			moratta deshō	morawanakatta deshō
Conditional	**INFORMAL**		morattara	morawanakattara
	FORMAL		moraimashitara	moraimasen deshitara
Alternative	**INFORMAL**		morattari	morawanakattari
	FORMAL		moraimashitari	moraimasen deshitari

M

		INFORMAL AFFIRMATIVE INDICATIVE
Passive		morawareru
Potential		moraeru
Causative		morawaseru
Causative Pass.		morawaserareru

Honorific	I	omorai ni naru
	II	omorai nasaru
Humble	I	itadaku
	II	

AN ESSENTIAL 55 VERB

Morau もらう

to receive, to get

Morau is an essential verb if you plan to spend any time in Japan. The Japanese are well known for their custom of gift giving for all sorts of occasions. So you'll probably get more gifts than you ever expected. For example, if you invite someone to dinner, even at a restaurant, he or she will usually bring a gift. And in Japan the wedding guests receive gifts!

Sentences Using *Morau*

Tanjōbi no purezento niwa, dejitaru kamera o moraitai.
誕生日のプレゼントには、デジタルカメラをもらいたい。
I'd like to get a digital camera for my birthday.

Shutchō ni moratta ryohi wa jūbun dewa nakatta.
出張にもらった旅費は十分ではなかった。
The travel allowance I received was not sufficient.

Kotoshi wa natsu no bōnasu ga moraenakatta.
今年は夏のボーナスがもらえなかった。
We didn't receive a summer bonus this year.

Kudamono ya de, omake ni banana o ippon moraimashita.
果物屋で、おまけにバナナを一本もらいました。
We got a banana thrown in as an extra at the fruit shop.

Tonari no ie ni koneko ga go hiki umareta node ippiki moraimashita.
隣の家に子猫が5匹生まれたので一匹もらいました。
Five kittens were born at the next door neighbor's, and I got one of them.

Words and Expressions Related to This Verb

itadaku　頂く
to receive, to get (polite)

chōdai suru　頂戴する
to receive, to get (polite)

moraite　貰い手
a receiver, a recipient

moraimono　貰い物
a present, a gift

mono morai　物もらい
a beggar

to leak, to escape

			AFFIRMATIVE	NEGATIVE
Indicative	**INFORMAL**		moreru	morenai
	FORMAL		moremasu	moremasen
Imperative	**INFORMAL**	I		
		II		
		III		
	FORMAL			
Presumptive	**INFORMAL**	I	moreyō	morerumai
		II	moreru darō	morenai darō
	FORMAL	I	moremashō	moremasumai
		II	moreru deshō	morenai deshō
Provisional	**INFORMAL**		morereba	morenakereba
	FORMAL		moremaseba	moremasen nara
			moremasureba	
Gerund	**INFORMAL**	I	morete	morenai de
		II		morenakute
	FORMAL		moremashite	moremasen de
Past Ind.	**INFORMAL**		moreta	morenakatta
	FORMAL		moremashita	moremasen deshita
Past Presump.	**INFORMAL**		moretarō	morenakattarō
			moreta darō	morenakatta darō
	FORMAL		moremashitarō	moremasen deshitarō
			moreta deshō	morenakatta deshō
Conditional	**INFORMAL**		moretara	morenakattara
	FORMAL		moremashitara	moremasen deshitara
Alternative	**INFORMAL**		moretari	morenakattari
	FORMAL		moremashitari	moremasen deshitari

INFORMAL AFFIRMATIVE INDICATIVE

Passive	
Potential	
Causative	
Causative Pass.	
Honorific	I
	II
Humble	I
	II

349

to bring about, to cause   TRANSITIVE

			AFFIRMATIVE	**NEGATIVE**
Indicative	**INFORMAL**		motarasu	motarasanai
	FORMAL		motarashimasu	motarashimasen
Imperative	**INFORMAL**	I	motarase	motarasu na
		II	motarashinasai	motarashinasaru na
		III	motarashite kudasai	motarasanai de kudasai
	FORMAL		omotarashi nasaimase	omotarashi nasaimasu na
Presumptive	**INFORMAL**	I	motarasō	motarasumai
		II	motarasu darō	motarasanai darō
	FORMAL	I	motarashimashō	motarashimasumai
		II	motarasu deshō	motarasanai deshō
Provisional	**INFORMAL**		motaraseba	motarasanakereba
	FORMAL		motarashimaseba	motarashimasen nara
			motarashimasureba	
Gerund	**INFORMAL**	I	motarashite	motarasanai de
		II		motarasanakute
	FORMAL		motarashimashite	motarashimasen de
Past Ind.	**INFORMAL**		motarashita	motarasanakatta
	FORMAL		motarashimashita	motarashimasen deshita
Past Presump.	**INFORMAL**		motarashitarō	motarasanakattarō
			motarashita darō	motarasanakatta darō
	FORMAL		motarashimashitarō	motarashimasen deshitarō
			motarashita deshō	motarasanakatta deshō
Conditional	**INFORMAL**		motarashitara	motarasanakattara
	FORMAL		motarashimashitara	motarashimasen deshitara
Alternative	**INFORMAL**		motarashitari	motarasanakattari
	FORMAL		motarashimashitari	motarashimasen deshitari

			INFORMAL AFFIRMATIVE INDICATIVE
Passive			motarasareru
Potential			motaraseru
Causative			motarasaseru
Causative Pass.			motarasaserareru
Honorific		I	omotarashi ni naru
		II	omotarashi nasaru
Humble		I	omotarashi suru
		II	omotarashi itasu

to be popular

			AFFIRMATIVE	NEGATIVE
Indicative	**INFORMAL**		moteru	motenai
	FORMAL		motemasu	motemasen
Imperative	**INFORMAL**	I		
		II		
		III		
	FORMAL			
Presumptive	**INFORMAL**	I	moteyō	motemai
		II	moteru darō	motenai darō
	FORMAL	I	motemashō	motemasumai
		II	moteru deshō	motenai deshō
Provisional	**INFORMAL**		motereba	motenakereba
	FORMAL		motemaseba	motemasen nara
			motemasureba	
Gerund	**INFORMAL**	I	motete	motenai de
		II		motenakute
	FORMAL		motemashite	motemasen de
Past Ind.	**INFORMAL**		moteta	motenakatta
	FORMAL		motemashita	motemasen deshita
Past Presump.	**INFORMAL**		motetarō	motenakattarō
			moteta darō	motenakatta darō
	FORMAL		motemashitarō	motemasen deshitarō
			moteta deshō	motenakatta deshō
Conditional	**INFORMAL**		motetara	motenakattara
	FORMAL		motemashitara	motemasen deshitara
Alternative	**INFORMAL**		motetari	motenakattari
	FORMAL		motemashitari	motemasen deshitari

		INFORMAL AFFIRMATIVE INDICATIVE
Passive		moterareru
Potential		moterareru
Causative		motesaseru
Causative Pass.		motesaserareru
Honorific	I	omote ni naru
	II	omote nasaru
Humble	I	
	II	

to request, to seek, to ask, to buy   TRANSITIVE

			AFFIRMATIVE	NEGATIVE
Indicative	**INFORMAL**		motomeru	motomenai
	FORMAL		motomemasu	motomemasen
Imperative	**INFORMAL**	I	motomero	motomeru na
		II	motomenasai	motomenasaru na
		III	motomete kudasai	motomenai de kudasai
	FORMAL		omotome nasaimase	omotome nasaimasu na
Presumptive	**INFORMAL**	I	motomeyō	motomemai
		II	motomeru darō	motomenai darō
	FORMAL	I	motomemashō	motomemasumai
		II	motomeru deshō	motomenai deshō
Provisional	**INFORMAL**		motomereba	motomenakereba
	FORMAL		motomemaseba	motomemasen nara
			motomemasureba	
Gerund	**INFORMAL**	I	motomete	motomenai de
		II		motomenakute
	FORMAL		motomemashite	motomemasen de
Past Ind.	**INFORMAL**		motometa	motomenakatta
	FORMAL		motomemashita	motomemasen deshita
Past Presump.	**INFORMAL**		motometarō	motomenakattarō
			motometa darō	motomenakatta darō
	FORMAL		motomemashitarō	motomemasen deshitarō
			motometa deshō	motomenakatta deshō
Conditional	**INFORMAL**		motometara	motomenakattara
	FORMAL		motomemashitara	motomemasen deshitara
Alternative	**INFORMAL**		motometari	motomenakattari
	FORMAL		motomemashitari	motomemasen deshitari

		INFORMAL AFFIRMATIVE INDICATIVE
Passive		motomerareru
Potential		motomerareru
Causative		motomesaseru
Causative Pass.		motomesaserareru
Honorific	I	omotome ni naru
	II	omotome nasaru
Humble	I	omotome suru
	II	omotome itasu

もとづく／基づく　**motozuk.u**

to be based on

			AFFIRMATIVE	NEGATIVE
Indicative	**INFORMAL**		motozuku	motozukanai
	FORMAL		motozukimasu	motozukimasen
Imperative	**INFORMAL**	**I**	motozuke	motozuku na
		II	motozukinasai	motozukinasaru na
		III	motozuite kudasai	motozukanai de kudasai
	FORMAL			
			motozukō	motozukumai
Presumptive	**INFORMAL**	**I**	motozuku darō	motozukanai darō
		II	motozukimashō	motozukimasumai
	FORMAL	**I**	motozuku deshō	motozukanai deshō
		II		
			motozukeba	motozukanakereba
Provisional	**INFORMAL**		motozukimaseba	motozukimasen nara
	FORMAL		motozukimasureba	
			motozuite	motozukanai de
Gerund	**INFORMAL**	**I**		motozukanakute
		II	motozukimashite	motozukimasen de
	FORMAL			
			motozuita	motozukanakatta
Past Ind.	**INFORMAL**		motozukimashita	motozukimasen deshita
	FORMAL			
			motozuitarō	motozukanakattarō
Past Presump.	**INFORMAL**		motozuita darō	motozukanakatta darō
			motozukimashitarō	motozukimasen deshitarō
	FORMAL		motozuita deshō	motozukanakatta deshō
			motozuitara	motozukanakattara
Conditional	**INFORMAL**		motozukimashitara	motozukimasen deshitara
	FORMAL			
			motozuitari	motozukanakattari
Alternative	**INFORMAL**		motozukimashitari	motozukimasen deshitari
	FORMAL			

			INFORMAL AFFIRMATIVE INDICATIVE
Passive			motozukareru
Potential			motozukeru
Causative			motozukaseru
Causative Pass.			motozukaserareru
Honorific		**I**	omotozuki ni naru
		II	omotozuki nasaru
Humble		**I**	
		II	

			AFFIRMATIVE	NEGATIVE
Indicative	**INFORMAL**		motsu	motanai
	FORMAL		mochimasu	mochimasen
Imperative	**INFORMAL**	I	mote	motsu na
		II	mochinasai	mochinasaru na
		III	motte kudasai	motanai de kudasai
	FORMAL		omochi nasaimase	omochi nasaimasu na
Presumptive	**INFORMAL**	I	motō	motsumai
		II	motsu darō	motanai darō
	FORMAL	I	mochimashō	mochimasumai
		II	motsu deshō	motanai deshō
Provisional	**INFORMAL**		moteba	motanakereba
	FORMAL		mochimaseba	mochimasen nara
			mochimasureba	
Gerund	**INFORMAL**	I	motte	motanai de
		II		motanakute
	FORMAL		mochimashite	mochimasen de
Past Ind.	**INFORMAL**		motta	motanakatta
	FORMAL		mochimashita	mochimasen deshita
Past Presump.	**INFORMAL**		mottarō	motanakattarō
			motta darō	motanakatta darō
	FORMAL		mochimashitarō	mochimasen deshitarō
			motta deshō	motanakatta deshō
Conditional	**INFORMAL**		mottara	motanakattara
	FORMAL		mochimashitara	mochimasen deshitara
Alternative	**INFORMAL**		mottari	motanakattari
	FORMAL		mochimashitari	mochimasen deshitari

		INFORMAL AFFIRMATIVE INDICATIVE
Passive		motareru
Potential		moteru
Causative		motaseru
Causative Pass.		motaserareru
Honorific	I	omochi ni naru
	II	omochi nasaru
Humble	I	omochi suru
	II	omochi itasu

AN ESSENTIAL
55 VERB

Motsu 持つ

to have, to hold, to own

Motsu is an essential verb because you often need to refer to things you have or own, such as money, possessions, or opinions, or the lack thereof. You'll get a lot of mileage out of this verb!

M

Sentences Using *Motsu*

Kuruma o nan dai motte imasu ka.
車を何台持っていますか。
How many cars do you have?

Jisho o motte iru nara kashite kudasai.
辞書を持っているなら貸してください。
If you have a dictionary, please lend it to me.

Kanojo wa kankyō mondai ni tsuite tsuyoi iken o motte iru.
彼女は環境問題について強い意見を持っている。
She has strong opinions about environmental issues.

Jitensha wa motte imasen.
自転車は持っていません。
I don't have a bicycle.

Konpyūta wa motte itemo, yoku tsukaemasen.
コンピュータは持っていても、よく使えません。
Although I have a computer, I can't use it well.

Words and Expressions Related to This Verb

shoji suru　所持する
to own, to have

shoyū suru　所有する
to own, to possess

shoji hin　所持品
personal effects, one's belongings

mochinushi　持ち主
owner

kane mochi　金持ち
a rich person, a wealthy person

to greet, to welcome, to meet　　　TRANSITIVE

			AFFIRMATIVE	**NEGATIVE**
Indicative	**INFORMAL**		mukaeru	mukaenai
	FORMAL		mukaemasu	mukaemasen
Imperative	**INFORMAL**	**I**	mukaero	mukaeru na
		II	mukaenasai	mukaenasaru na
		III	mukaete kudasai	mukaenai de kudasai
	FORMAL		omukae nasaimase	omukae nasaimasu na
Presumptive	**INFORMAL**	**I**	mukaeyō	mukaemai
		II	mukaeru darō	mukaenai darō
	FORMAL	**I**	mukaemashō	mukaemasumai
		II	mukaeru deshō	mukaenai deshō
Provisional	**INFORMAL**		mukaereba	mukaenakereba
	FORMAL		mukaemaseba	mukaemasen nara
			mukaemasureba	
Gerund	**INFORMAL**	**I**	mukaete	mukaenai de
		II		mukaenakute
	FORMAL		mukaemashite	mukaemasen de
Past Ind.	**INFORMAL**		mukaeta	mukaenakatta
	FORMAL		mukaemashita	mukaemasen deshita
Past Presump.	**INFORMAL**		mukaetarō	mukaenakattarō
			mukaeta darō	mukaenakatta darō
	FORMAL		mukaemashitarō	mukaemasen deshitarō
			mukaeta deshō	mukaenakatta deshō
Conditional	**INFORMAL**		mukaetara	mukaenakattara
	FORMAL		mukaemashitara	mukaemasen deshitara
Alternative	**INFORMAL**		mukaetari	mukaenakattari
	FORMAL		mukaemashitari	mukaemasen deshitari

			INFORMAL AFFIRMATIVE INDICATIVE
Passive			mukaerareru
Potential			mukaerareru
Causative			mukaesaseru
Causative Pass.			mukaesaserareru

Honorific	**I**	omukae ni naru
	II	omukae nasaru
Humble	**I**	omukae suru
	II	omukae itasu

to face, to head toward, to turn toward

			AFFIRMATIVE	NEGATIVE
Indicative	INFORMAL		mukau	mukawanai
	FORMAL		mukaimasu	mukaimasen
Imperative	INFORMAL	I	mukae	mukau na
		II	mukainasai	mukainasaru na
		III	mukatte kudasai	mukawanai de kudasai
	FORMAL		omukai nasaimase	omukai nasaimasu na
Presumptive	INFORMAL	I	mukaō	mukaumai
		II	mukau darō	mukawanai darō
	FORMAL	I	mukaimashō	mukaimasumai
		II	mukau deshō	mukawanai deshō
Provisional	INFORMAL		mukaeba	mukawanakereba
	FORMAL		mukaimaseba	mukaimasen nara
			mukaimasureba	
Gerund	INFORMAL	I	mukatte	mukawanai de
		II		mukawanakute
	FORMAL		mukaimashite	mukaimasen de
Past Ind.	INFORMAL		mukatta	mukawanakatta
	FORMAL		mukaimashita	mukaimasen deshita
Past Presump.	INFORMAL		mukattarō	mukawanakattarō
			mukatta darō	mukawanakatta darō
	FORMAL		mukaimashitarō	mukaimasen deshitarō
			mukatta deshō	mukawanakatta deshō
Conditional	INFORMAL		mukattara	mukawanakattara
	FORMAL		mukaimashitara	mukaimasen deshitara
Alternative	INFORMAL		mukattari	mukawanakattari
	FORMAL		mukaimashitari	mukaimasen deshitari

		INFORMAL AFFIRMATIVE INDICATIVE
Passive		mukawareru
Potential		mukaeru
Causative		mukawaseru
Causative Pass.		mukawaserareru
Honorific	I	omukai ni naru
	II	omukai nasaru
Humble	I	omukai suru
	II	omukai itasu

to tie, to knot, to make (a contract) TRANSITIVE

			AFFIRMATIVE	NEGATIVE
Indicative	**INFORMAL**		musubu	musubanai
	FORMAL		musubimasu	musubimasen
Imperative	**INFORMAL**	I	musube	musubu na
		II	musubinasai	musubinasaru na
		III	musunde kudasai	musubanai de kudasai
	FORMAL		omusubi nasaimase	omusubi nasaimasu na
Presumptive	**INFORMAL**	I	musubō	musubumai
		II	musubu darō	musubanai darō
	FORMAL	I	musubimashō	musubimasumai
		II	musubu deshō	musubanai deshō
Provisional	**INFORMAL**		musubeba	musubanakereba
	FORMAL		musubimaseba	musubimasen nara
			musubimasureba	
Gerund	**INFORMAL**	I	musunde	musubanai de
		II		musubanakute
	FORMAL		musubimashite	musubimasen de
Past Ind.	**INFORMAL**		musunda	musubanakatta
	FORMAL		musubimashita	musubimasen deshita
Past Presump.	**INFORMAL**		musundarō	musubanakattarō
			musunda darō	musubanakatta darō
	FORMAL		musubimashitarō	musubimasen deshitarō
			musunda deshō	musubanakatta deshō
Conditional	**INFORMAL**		musundara	musubanakattara
	FORMAL		musubimashitara	musubimasen deshitara
Alternative	**INFORMAL**		musundari	musubanakattari
	FORMAL		musubimashitari	musubimasen deshitara

			INFORMAL AFFIRMATIVE INDICATIVE
Passive			musubareru
Potential			musuberu
Causative			musubaseru
Causative Pass.			musubaserareru
Honorific		I	omusubi ni naru
		II	omusubi nasaru
Humble		I	omusubi suru
		II	omusubi itasu

ながめる／眺める **nagame.ru**

TRANSITIVE   *to watch, to look at, to view*

			AFFIRMATIVE	NEGATIVE
Indicative	**INFORMAL**		nagameru	nagamenai
	FORMAL		nagamemasu	nagamemasen
Imperative	**INFORMAL**	I	nagamero	nagameru na
		II	nagamenasai	nagamenasaru na
		III	nagamete kudasai	nagamenai de kudasai
	FORMAL		onagame nasaimase	onagame nasaimasu na
Presumptive	**INFORMAL**	I	nagameyō	nagamemai
		II	nagameru darō	nagamenai darō
	FORMAL	I	nagamemashō	nagamemasumai
		II	nagameru deshō	nagamenai deshō
Provisional	**INFORMAL**		nagamereba	nagamenakereba
	FORMAL		nagamemaseba	nagamemasen nara
			nagamemasureba	
Gerund	**INFORMAL**	I	nagamete	nagamenai de
		II		nagamenakute
	FORMAL		nagamemashite	nagamemasen de
Past Ind.	**INFORMAL**		nagameta	nagamenakatta
	FORMAL		nagamemashita	nagamemasen deshita
Past Presump.	**INFORMAL**		nagametarō	nagamenakattarō
			nagameta darō	nagamenakatta darō
	FORMAL		nagamemashitarō	nagamemasen deshitarō
			nagameta deshō	nagamenakatta deshō
Conditional	**INFORMAL**		nagametara	nagamenakattara
	FORMAL		nagamemashitara	nagamemasen deshitara
Alternative	**INFORMAL**		nagametari	nagamenakattari
	FORMAL		nagamemashitari	nagamemasen deshitari

			INFORMAL AFFIRMATIVE INDICATIVE
Passive			nagamerareru
Potential			nagamerareru
Causative			nagamesaseru
Causative Pass.			nagamesaserareru
Honorific		I	onagame ni naru
		II	onagame nasaru
Humble		I	
		II	

to flow, to be called off

			AFFIRMATIVE	**NEGATIVE**
Indicative	**INFORMAL**		nagareru	nagarenai
	FORMAL		nagaremasu	nagaremasen
Imperative	**INFORMAL**	I	nagarero	nagareru na
		II		
		III	nagarete kudasai	nagarenai de kudasai
	FORMAL			
Presumptive	**INFORMAL**	I	nagareyō	nagaremai
		II	nagareru darō	nagarenai darō
	FORMAL	I	nagaremashō	nagaremasumai
		II	nagareru deshō	nagarenai deshō
Provisional	**INFORMAL**		nagarereba	nagarenakereba
	FORMAL		nagaremaseba	nagaremasen nara
			nagaremasureba	
Gerund	**INFORMAL**	I	nagarete	nagarenai de
		II		nagarenakute
	FORMAL		nagaremashite	nagaremasen de
Past Ind.	**INFORMAL**		nagareta	nagarenakatta
	FORMAL		nagaremashita	nagaremasen deshita
Past Presump.	**INFORMAL**		nagaretarō	nagarenakattarō
			nagareta darō	nagarenakatta darō
	FORMAL		nagaremashitarō	nagaremasen deshitarō
			nagareta deshō	nagarenakatta deshō
Conditional	**INFORMAL**		nagaretara	nagarenakattara
	FORMAL		nagaremashitara	nagaremasen deshitara
Alternative	**INFORMAL**		nagaretari	nagarenakattari
	FORMAL		nagaremashitari	nagaremasen deshitari

		INFORMAL AFFIRMATIVE INDICATIVE
Passive		nagarerareru
Potential		nagarerareru
Causative		nagaresaseru
Causative Pass.		nagaresaserareru
Honorific	I	
	II	
Humble	I	
	II	

nagashi

ながす／流す **nagas.u**

TRANSITIVE   *to pour, to let flow*

			AFFIRMATIVE	NEGATIVE
Indicative	INFORMAL		nagasu	nagasanai
	FORMAL		nagashimasu	nagashimasen
Imperative	INFORMAL	I	nagase	nagasu na
		II	nagashinasai	nagashinasaru na
		III	nagashite kudasai	nagasanai de kudasai
	FORMAL		onagashi nasaimase	onagashi nasaimasu na
Presumptive	INFORMAL	I	nagasō	nagasumai
		II	nagasu darō	nagasanai darō
	FORMAL	I	nagashimashō	nagashimasumai
		II	nagasu deshō	nagasanai deshō
Provisional	INFORMAL		nagaseba	nagasanakereba
	FORMAL		nagashimaseba	nagashimasen nara
			nagashimasureba	
Gerund	INFORMAL	I	nagashite	nagasanai de
		II		nagasanakute
	FORMAL		nagashimashite	nagashimasen de
Past Ind.	INFORMAL		nagashita	nagasanakatta
	FORMAL		nagashimashita	nagashimasen deshita
Past Presump.	INFORMAL		nagashitarō	nagasanakattarō
			nagashita darō	nagasanakatta darō
	FORMAL		nagashimashitarō	nagashimasen deshitarō
			nagashita deshō	nagasanakatta deshō
Conditional	INFORMAL		nagashitara	nagasanakattara
	FORMAL		nagashimashitara	nagashimasen deshitara
Alternative	INFORMAL		nagashitari	nagasanakattari
	FORMAL		nagashimashitari	nagashimasen deshitari

		INFORMAL AFFIRMATIVE INDICATIVE
Passive		nagasareru
Potential		nagaseru
Causative		nagasaseru
Causative Pass.		nagasaserareru
Honorific	I	onagashi ni naru
	II	onagashi nasaru
Humble	I	onagashi suru
	II	onagashi itasu

to throw, to pitch   TRANSITIVE

			AFFIRMATIVE	**NEGATIVE**
Indicative	**INFORMAL**		nageru	nagenai
	FORMAL		nagemasu	nagemasen
Imperative	**INFORMAL**	I	nagero	nageru na
		II	nagenasai	nagenasaru na
		III	nagete kudasai	nagenai de kudasai
	FORMAL		onage nasaimase	onage nasaimasu na
Presumptive	**INFORMAL**	I	nageyō	nagemai
		II	nageru darō	nagenai darō
	FORMAL	I	nagemashō	nagemasumai
		II	nageru deshō	nagenai deshō
Provisional	**INFORMAL**		nagereba	nagenakereba
	FORMAL		nagemaseba	nagemasen nara
			nagemasureba	
Gerund	**INFORMAL**	I	nagete	nagenai de
		II		nagenakute
	FORMAL		nagemashite	nagemasen de
Past Ind.	**INFORMAL**		nageta	nagenakatta
	FORMAL		nagemashita	nagemasen deshita
Past Presump.	**INFORMAL**		nagetarō	nagenakattarō
			nageta darō	nagenakatta darō
	FORMAL		nagemashitarō	nagemasen deshitarō
			nageta deshō	nagenakatta deshō
Conditional	**INFORMAL**		nagetara	nagenakattara
	FORMAL		nagemashitara	nagemasen deshitara
Alternative	**INFORMAL**		nagetari	nagenakattari
	FORMAL		nagemashitari	nagemasen deshitari

		INFORMAL AFFIRMATIVE INDICATIVE
Passive		nagerareru
Potential		nagerareru
Causative		nagesaseru
Causative Pass.		nagesaserareru
Honorific	I	onage ni naru
	II	onage nasaro
Humble	I	onage suru
	II	onage itasu

なぐる／殴る **nagur.u**

TRANSITIVE   *to punch, to hit*

			AFFIRMATIVE	NEGATIVE
Indicative	**INFORMAL**		naguru	naguranai
	FORMAL		nagurimasu	nagurimasen
Imperative	**INFORMAL**	I	nagure	naguru na
		II	nagurinasai	nagurinasaru na
		III	nagutte kudasai	naguranai de kudasai
	FORMAL		onaguri nasaimase	onaguri nasaimasu na
Presumptive	**INFORMAL**	I	nagurō	nagurumai
		II	naguru darō	naguranai darō
	FORMAL	I	nagurimashō	nagurimasumai
		II	naguru deshō	naguranai deshō
Provisional	**INFORMAL**		nagureba	naguranakereba
	FORMAL		nagurimaseba	nagurimasen nara
			nagurimasureba	
Gerund	**INFORMAL**	I	nagutte	naguranai de
		II		naguranakute
	FORMAL		nagurimashite	nagurimasen de
Past Ind.	**INFORMAL**		nagutta	naguranakatta
	FORMAL		nagurimashita	nagurimasen deshita
Past Presump.	**INFORMAL**		naguttarō	naguranakattarō
			nagutta darō	naguranakatta darō
	FORMAL		nagurimashitarō	nagurimasen deshitarō
			nagutta deshō	naguranakatta deshō
Conditional	**INFORMAL**		naguttara	naguranakattara
	FORMAL		nagurimashitara	nagurimasen deshitara
Alternative	**INFORMAL**		naguttari	naguranakattari
	FORMAL		nagurimashitari	nagurimasen deshitari

		INFORMAL AFFIRMATIVE INDICATIVE
Passive		nagurareru
Potential		nagureru
Causative		naguraseru
Causative Pass.		naguraserareru
Honorific	I	onaguri ni naru
	II	onaguri nasaru
Humble	I	onaguri suru
	II	onaguri itasu

to comfort, to console   TRANSITIVE

			AFFIRMATIVE	NEGATIVE
Indicative	**INFORMAL**		nagusameru	nagusamenai
	FORMAL		nagusamemasu	nagusamemasen
Imperative	**INFORMAL**	I	nagusamero	nagusameru na
		II	nagusamenasai	nagusamenasaru na
		III	nagusamete kudasai	nagusamenai de kudasai
	FORMAL		onagusame nasaimase	onagusame nasaimasu na
Presumptive	**INFORMAL**	I	nagusameyō	nagusamemai
		II	nagusameru darō	nagusamenai darō
	FORMAL	I	nagusamemashō	nagusamemasumai
		II	nagusameru deshō	nagusamenai deshō
Provisional	**INFORMAL**		nagusamereba	nagusamenakereba
	FORMAL		nagusamemaseba	nagusamemasen nara
			nagusamemasureba	
Gerund	**INFORMAL**	I	nagusamete	nagusamenai de
		II		nagusamenakute
	FORMAL		nagusamemashite	nagusamemasen de
Past Ind.	**INFORMAL**		nagusameta	nagusamenakatta
	FORMAL		nagusamemashita	nagusamemasen deshita
Past Presump.	**INFORMAL**		nagusametarō	nagusamenakattarō
			nagusameta darō	nagusamenakatta darō
	FORMAL		nagusamemashitarō	nagusamemasen deshitarō
			nagusameta deshō	nagusamenakatta deshō
Conditional	**INFORMAL**		nagusametara	nagusamenakattara
	FORMAL		nagusamemashitara	nagusamemasen deshitara
Alternative	**INFORMAL**		nagusametari	nagusamenakattari
	FORMAL		nagusamemashitari	nagusamemasen deshitari

			INFORMAL AFFIRMATIVE INDICATIVE
Passive			nagusamerareru
Potential			nagusamerareru
Causative			nagusamesaseru
Causative Pass.			nagusamesaserareru
Honorific		I	onagusame ni naru
		II	onagusame nasaru
Humble		I	onagusame suru
		II	onagusame itasu

to become acquainted with, to adapt oneself to, to get used to

			AFFIRMATIVE	NEGATIVE
Indicative	**INFORMAL**		najimu	najimanai
	FORMAL		najimimasu	najimimasen
Imperative	**INFORMAL**	I	najime	najimu na
		II	najiminasai	najiminasaru na
		III	najinde kudasai	najimanai de kudasai
	FORMAL		onajimi nasaimase	onajimi nasaimasu na
Presumptive	**INFORMAL**	I	najimō	najimumai
		II	najimu darō	najimanai darō
	FORMAL	I	najimimashō	najimimasumai
		II	najimu deshō	najimanai deshō
Provisional	**INFORMAL**		najimeba	najimanakereba
	FORMAL		najimimaseba	najimimasen nara
			najimimasureba	
Gerund	**INFORMAL**	I	najinde	najimanai de
		II		najimanakute
	FORMAL		najimimashite	najimimasen de
Past Ind.	**INFORMAL**		najinda	najimanakatta
	FORMAL		najimimashita	najimimasen deshita
Past Presump.	**INFORMAL**		najindarō	najimanakattarō
			najinda darō	najimanakatta darō
	FORMAL		najimimashitarō	najimimasen deshitarō
			najinda deshō	najimanakatta deshō
Conditional	**INFORMAL**		najindara	najimanakattara
	FORMAL		najimimashitara	najimimasen deshitara
Alternative	**INFORMAL**		najindari	najimanakattari
	FORMAL		najimimashitari	najimimasen deshitari

			INFORMAL AFFIRMATIVE INDICATIVE
Passive			najimareru
Potential			najimeru
Causative			najimaseru
Causative Pass.			najimaserareru
Honorific		I	onajimi ni naru
		II	onajimi nasaru
Humble		I	
		II	

nak.u　なく／泣く／鳴く　　　　　　　　　　naki
to cry, to bark, mew, caw, chirp, etc.

			AFFIRMATIVE	NEGATIVE
Indicative	INFORMAL		naku	nakanai
	FORMAL		nakimasu	nakimasen
Imperative	INFORMAL	I	nake	naku na
		II	nakinasai	nakinasaru na
		III	naite kudasai	nakanai de kudasai
	FORMAL		onaki nasaimase	onaki nasaimasu na
Presumptive	INFORMAL	I	nakō	nakumai
		II	naku darō	nakanai darō
	FORMAL	I	nakimashō	nakimasumai
		II	naku deshō	nakanai deshō
Provisional	INFORMAL		nakeba	nakanakereba
	FORMAL		nakimaseba	nakimasen nara
			nakimasureba	
Gerund	INFORMAL	I	naite	nakanai de
		II		nakanakute
	FORMAL		nakimashite	nakimasen de
Past Ind.	INFORMAL		naita	nakanakatta
	FORMAL		nakimashita	nakimasen deshita
Past Presump.	INFORMAL		naitarō	nakanakattarō
			naita darō	nakanakatta darō
	FORMAL		nakimashitarō	nakimasen deshitarō
			naita deshō	nakanakatta deshō
Conditional	INFORMAL		naitara	nakanakattara
	FORMAL		nakimashitara	nakimasen deshitara
Alternative	INFORMAL		naitari	nakanakattari
	FORMAL		nakimashitari	nakimasen deshitari

		INFORMAL AFFIRMATIVE INDICATIVE
Passive		nakareru
Potential		nakeru
Causative		nakaseru
Causative Pass.		nakaserareru
Honorific	I	onaki ni naru
	II	onaki nasaru
Humble	I	onaki suru
	II	onaki itasu

なくなる／無くなる／亡くなる **nakunar.u**

to be missing, to die (polite), *to vanish*

			AFFIRMATIVE	NEGATIVE
Indicative	**INFORMAL**		nakunaru	nakunaranai
	FORMAL		nakunarimasu	nakunarimasen
Imperative	**INFORMAL**	I	nakunare	nakunaru na
		II		nakunarinasaru na
		III		nakunaranai de kudasai
	FORMAL			onakunari nasaimasu na
Presumptive	**INFORMAL**	I	nakunarō	nakunarumai
		II	nakunaru darō	nakunaranai darō
	FORMAL	I	nakunarimashō	nakunarimasumai
		II	nakunaru deshō	nakunaranai deshō
Provisional	**INFORMAL**		nakunareba	nakunaranakereba
	FORMAL		nakunarimaseba	nakunarimasen nara
			nakunarimasureba	
Gerund	**INFORMAL**	I	nakunatte	nakunaranai de
		II		nakunaranakute
	FORMAL		nakunarimashite	nakunarimasen de
Past Ind.	**INFORMAL**		nakunatta	nakunaranakatta
	FORMAL		nakunarimashita	nakunarimasen deshita
Past Presump.	**INFORMAL**		nakunattarō	nakunaranakattarō
			nakunatta darō	nakunaranakatta darō
	FORMAL		nakunarimashitarō	nakunarimasen deshitarō
			nakunatta deshō	nakunaranakatta deshō
Conditional	**INFORMAL**		nakunattara	nakunaranakattara
	FORMAL		nakunarimashitara	nakunarimasen deshitara
Alternative	**INFORMAL**		nakunattari	nakunaranakattari
	FORMAL		nakunarimashitari	nakunarimasen deshitari

		INFORMAL AFFIRMATIVE INDICATIVE
Passive		nakunarareru
Potential		nakunareru
Causative		nakunaraseru
Causative Pass.		nakunaraserareru
Honorific	I	onakunari ni naru
	II	onakunari nasaru
Humble	I	
	II	

to lose, to remove, to do away with   TRANSITIVE

			AFFIRMATIVE	NEGATIVE
Indicative	**INFORMAL**		nakusu	nakusanai
	FORMAL		nakushimasu	nakushimasen
Imperative	**INFORMAL**	I	nakuse	nakusu na
		II	nakushinasai	nakushinasaru na
		III	nakushite kudasai	nakusanai de kudasai
	FORMAL		onakushi nasaimase	onakushi nasaimasu na
Presumptive	**INFORMAL**	I	nakusō	nakusumai
		II	nakusu darō	nakusanai darō
	FORMAL	I	nakushimashō	nakushimasumai
		II	nakusu deshō	nakusanai deshō
Provisional	**INFORMAL**		nakuseba	nakusanakereba
	FORMAL		nakushimaseba	nakushimasen nara
			nakushimasureba	
Gerund	**INFORMAL**	I	nakushite	nakusanai de
		II		nakusanakute
	FORMAL		nakushimashite	nakushimasen de
Past Ind.	**INFORMAL**		nakushita	nakusanakatta
	FORMAL		nakushimashita	nakushimasen deshita
Past Presump.	**INFORMAL**		nakushitarō	nakusanakattarō
			nakushita darō	nakusanakatta darō
	FORMAL		nakushimashitarō	nakushimasen deshitarō
			nakushita deshō	nakusanakatta deshō
Conditional	**INFORMAL**		nakushitara	nakusanakattara
	FORMAL		nakushimashitara	nakushimasen deshitara
Alternative	**INFORMAL**		nakushitari	nakusanakattari
	FORMAL		nakushimashitari	nakushimasen deshitari

			INFORMAL AFFIRMATIVE INDICATIVE
Passive			nakusareru
Potential			nakuseru
Causative			nakusaseru
Causative Pass.			nakusaserareru
Honorific		I	onakushi ni naru
		II	onakushi nasaru
Humble		I	
		II	

なまける／怠ける **namake.ru**

TRANSITIVE *to be lazy, to neglect one's work*

			AFFIRMATIVE	**NEGATIVE**
Indicative	**INFORMAL**		namakeru	namakenai
	FORMAL		namakemasu	namakemasen
Imperative	**INFORMAL**	**I**	namakero	namakeru na
		II		namakenasaru na
		III		namakenai de kudasai
	FORMAL			onamake nasaimasu na
Presumptive	**INFORMAL**	**I**	namakeyō	namakemai
		II	namakeru darō	namakenai darō
	FORMAL	**I**	namakemashō	namakemasumai
		II	namakeru deshō	namakenai deshō
Provisional	**INFORMAL**		namakereba	namakenakereba
	FORMAL		namakemaseba	namakemasen nara
			namakemasureba	
Gerund	**INFORMAL**	**I**	namakete	namakenai de
		II		namakenakute
	FORMAL		namakemashite	namakemasen de
Past Ind.	**INFORMAL**		namaketa	namakenakatta
	FORMAL		namakemashita	namakemasen deshita
Past Presump.	**INFORMAL**		namaketarō	namakenakattarō
			namaketa darō	namakenakatta darō
	FORMAL		namakemashitarō	namakemasen deshitarō
			namaketa deshō	namakenakatta deshō
Conditional	**INFORMAL**		namaketara	namakenakattara
	FORMAL		namakemashitara	namakemasen deshitara
Alternative	**INFORMAL**		namaketari	namakenakattari
	FORMAL		namakemashitari	namakemasen deshitari

			INFORMAL AFFIRMATIVE INDICATIVE
Passive			namakerareru
Potential			namakerareru
Causative			namakesaseru
Causative Pass.			namakesaserareru
Honorific		**I**	onamake ni naru
		II	onamake nasaru
Humble		**I**	
		II	

name.ru　なめる

to lick, to belittle　TRANSITIVE

name

			AFFIRMATIVE	NEGATIVE
Indicative	**INFORMAL**		nameru	namenai
	FORMAL		namemasu	namemasen
Imperative	**INFORMAL**	I	namero	nameru na
		II	namenasai	namenasaru na
		III	namete kudasai	namenai de kudasai
	FORMAL		oname nasaimase	oname nasaimasu na
Presumptive	**INFORMAL**	I	nameyō	namemai
		II	nameru darō	namenai darō
	FORMAL	I	namemashō	namemasumai
		II	nameru deshō	namenai deshō
Provisional	**INFORMAL**		namereba	namenakereba
	FORMAL		namemaseba	namemasen nara
			namemasureba	
Gerund	**INFORMAL**	I	namete	namenai de
		II		namenakute
	FORMAL		namemashite	namemasen de
Past Ind.	**INFORMAL**		nameta	namenakatta
	FORMAL		namemashita	namemasen deshita
Past Presump.	**INFORMAL**		nametarō	namenakattarō
			nameta darō	namenakatta darō
	FORMAL		namemashitarō	namemasen deshitarō
			nameta deshō	namenakatta deshō
Conditional	**INFORMAL**		nametara	namenakattara
	FORMAL		namemashitara	namemasen deshitara
Alternative	**INFORMAL**		nametari	namenakattari
	FORMAL		namemashitari	namemasen deshitari

			INFORMAL AFFIRMATIVE INDICATIVE
Passive			namerareru
Potential			namerareru
Causative			namesaseru
Causative Pass.			namesaserareru
Honorific		I	oname ni naru
		II	oname nasaru
Humble		I	oname suru
		II	oname itasu

なおる／治る／直る　**naor.u**

to recover from illness, to be fixed

			AFFIRMATIVE	NEGATIVE
Indicative	**INFORMAL**		naoru	naoranai
	FORMAL		naorimasu	naorimasen
Imperative	**INFORMAL**	I	naore	naoru na
		II	naorinasai	naorinasaru na
		III	naotte kudasai	naoranai de kudasai
	FORMAL		onaori nasaimase	onaori nasaimasu na
Presumptive	**INFORMAL**	I	naorō	naorumai
		II	naoru darō	naoranai darō
	FORMAL	I	naorimashō	naorimasumai
		II	naoru deshō	naoranai deshō
Provisional	**INFORMAL**		naoreba	naoranakereba
	FORMAL		naorimaseba	naorimasen nara
			naorimasureba	
Gerund	**INFORMAL**	I	naotte	naoranai de
		II		naoranakute
	FORMAL		naorimashite	naorimasen de
Past Ind.	**INFORMAL**		naotta	naoranakatta
	FORMAL		naorimashita	naorimasen deshita
Past Presump.	**INFORMAL**		naottarō	naoranakattarō
			naotta darō	naoranakatta darō
	FORMAL		naorimashitarō	naorimasen deshitaro
			naotta deshō	naoranakatta deshō
Conditional	**INFORMAL**		naottara	naoranakattara
	FORMAL		naorimashitara	naorimasen deshitara
Alternative	**INFORMAL**		naottari	naoranakattari
	FORMAL		naorimashitari	naorimasen deshitari

		INFORMAL AFFIRMATIVE INDICATIVE
Passive		naorareru
Potential		naoreru
Causative		naoraseru
Causative Pass.		naoraserareru
Honorific	I	onaori ni naru
	II	onaori nasaru
Humble	I	
	II	

to repair, to cure　　　TRANSITIVE

			AFFIRMATIVE	NEGATIVE
Indicative	**INFORMAL**		naosu	naosanai
	FORMAL		naoshimasu	naoshimasen
Imperative	**INFORMAL**	I	naose	naosu na
		II	naoshinasai	naoshinasaru na
		III	naoshite kudasai	naosanai de kudasai
	FORMAL		onaoshi nasaimase	onaoshi nasaimasu na
Presumptive	**INFORMAL**	I	naosō	naosumai
		II	naosu darō	naosanai darō
	FORMAL	I	naoshimashō	naoshimasumai
		II	naosu deshō	naosanai deshō
Provisional	**INFORMAL**		naoseba	naosanakereba
	FORMAL		naoshimaseba	naoshimasen nara
			naoshimasureba	
Gerund	**INFORMAL**	I	naoshite	naosanai de
		II		naosanakute
	FORMAL		naoshimashite	naoshimasen de
Past Ind.	**INFORMAL**		naoshita	naosanakatta
	FORMAL		naoshimashita	naoshimasen deshita
Past Presump.	**INFORMAL**		naoshitarō	naosanakattarō
			naoshita darō	naosanakatta darō
	FORMAL		naoshimashitarō	naoshimasen deshitarō
			naoshita deshō	naosanakatta deshō
Conditional	**INFORMAL**		naoshitara	naosanakattara
	FORMAL		naoshimashitara	naoshimasen deshitara
Alternative	**INFORMAL**		naoshitari	naosanakattari
	FORMAL		naoshimashitari	naoshimasen deshitari

			INFORMAL AFFIRMATIVE INDICATIVE
Passive			naosareru
Potential			naoseru
Causative			naosaseru
Causative Pass.			naosaserareru
Honorific		I	onaoshi ni naru
		II	onaoshi nasaru
Humble		I	onaoshi suru
		II	onaoshi itasu

ならべる／並べる **narabe.ru**

TRANSITIVE *to arrange in order, to line up, to list*

			AFFIRMATIVE	NEGATIVE
Indicative	**INFORMAL**		naraberu	narabenai
	FORMAL		narabemasu	narabemasen
Imperative	**INFORMAL**	I	narabero	naraberu na
		II	narabenasai	narabenasaru na
		III	narabete kudasai	narabenai de kudasai
	FORMAL		onarabe nasaimase	onarabe nasaimasu na
Presumptive	**INFORMAL**	I	narabeyō	narabemai
		II	naraberu darō	narabenai darō
	FORMAL	I	narabemashō	narabemasumai
		II	naraberu deshō	narabenai deshō
Provisional	**INFORMAL**		narabereba	narabenakereba
	FORMAL		narabemaseba	narabemasen nara
			narabemasureba	
Gerund	**INFORMAL**	I	narabete	narabenai de
		II		narabenakute
	FORMAL		narabemashite	narabemasen de
Past Ind.	**INFORMAL**		narabeta	narabenakatta
	FORMAL		narabemashita	narabemasen deshita
Past Presump.	**INFORMAL**		narabetarō	narabenakattarō
			narabeta darō	narabenakatta darō
	FORMAL		narabemashitarō	narabemasen deshitarō
			narabeta deshō	narabenakatta deshō
Conditional	**INFORMAL**		narabetara	narabenakattara
	FORMAL		narabemashitara	narabemasen deshitara
Alternative	**INFORMAL**		narabetari	narabenakattari
	FORMAL		narabemashitari	narabemasen deshitari

		INFORMAL AFFIRMATIVE INDICATIVE
Passive		naraberareru
Potential		naraberareru
Causative		narabesaseru
Causative Pass.		narabesaserareru
Honorific	I	onarabe ni naru
	II	onarabe nasaru
Humble	I	onarabe suru
	II	onarabe itasu

to form a line, to equal

			AFFIRMATIVE	NEGATIVE
Indicative	**INFORMAL**		narabu	narabanai
	FORMAL		narabimasu	narabimasen
Imperative	**INFORMAL**	I	narabe	narabu na
		II	narabinasai	narabinasaru na
		III	narande kudasai	narabanai de kudasai
	FORMAL		onarabi nasaimase	onarabi nasaimasu na
Presumptive	**INFORMAL**	I	narabō	narabumai
		II	narabu darō	narabanai darō
	FORMAL	I	narabimashō	narabimasumai
		II	narabu deshō	narabanai deshō
Provisional	**INFORMAL**		narabeba	narabanakereba
	FORMAL		narabimaseba	narabimasen nara
			narabimasureba	
Gerund	**INFORMAL**	I	narande	narabanai de
		II		narabanakute
	FORMAL		narabimashite	narabimasen de
Past Ind.	**INFORMAL**		naranda	narabanakatta
	FORMAL		narabimashita	narabimasen deshita
Past Presump.	**INFORMAL**		narandarō	narabanakattarō
			naranda darō	narabanakatta darō
	FORMAL		narabimashitarō	narabimasen deshitarō
			naranda deshō	narabanakatta deshō
Conditional	**INFORMAL**		narandara	narabanakattara
	FORMAL		narabimashitara	narabimasen deshitara
Alternative	**INFORMAL**		narandari	narabanakattari
	FORMAL		narabimashitari	narabimasen deshitari

		INFORMAL AFFIRMATIVE INDICATIVE
Passive		narabareru
Potential		naraberu
Causative		narabaseru
Causative Pass.		narabaserareru
Honorific	I	onarabi ni naru
	II	onarabi nasaru
Humble	I	onarabi suru
	II	onarabi itasu

ならう／習う **nara.u**

TRANSITIVE *to learn*

			AFFIRMATIVE	NEGATIVE
Indicative	INFORMAL		narau	narawanai
	FORMAL		naraimasu	naraimasen
Imperative	INFORMAL	I	narae	narau na
		II	narainasai	narainasaru na
		III	naratte kudasai	narawanai de kudasai
	FORMAL		onarai nasaimase	onarai nasaimasu na
Presumptive	INFORMAL	I	naraō	naraumai
		II	narau darō	narawanai darō
	FORMAL	I	naraimashō	naraimasumai
		II	narau deshō	narawanai deshō
Provisional	INFORMAL		naraeba	narawanakereba
	FORMAL		naraimaseba	naraimasen nara
			naraimasureba	
Gerund	INFORMAL	I	naratte	narawanai de
		II		narawanakute
	FORMAL		naraimashite	naraimasen de
Past Ind.	INFORMAL		naratta	narawanakatta
	FORMAL		naraimashita	naraimasen deshita
Past Presump.	INFORMAL		narattarō	narawanakattarō
			naratta darō	narawanakatta darō
	FORMAL		naraimashitarō	naraimasen deshitarō
			naratta deshō	narawanakatta deshō
Conditional	INFORMAL		narattara	narawanakattara
	FORMAL		naraimashitara	naraimasen deshitara
Alternative	INFORMAL		narattari	narawanakattari
	FORMAL		naraimashitari	naraimasen deshitari

N

			INFORMAL AFFIRMATIVE INDICATIVE
Passive			narawareru
Potential			naraeru
Causative			narawaseru
Causative Pass.			narawaserareru
Honorific		I	onarai ni naru
		II	onarai nasaru
Humble		I	onarai suru
		II	onarai itasu

AN ESSENTIAL
55 VERB

Narau 習つ

to learn

Sentences Using *Narau*

Eigo no tsugi wa supein go ga naraitai.
英語の次ぎはスペイン語が習いたい。
I'd like to learn Spanish after English.

Kare wa, kodomo no toki ni piano o naratte ita.
彼は子供の時にピアノを習っていた。
He was learning piano when he was a child.

Konpyūta o narainasai.
コンピュータを習いなさい。
You should learn how to use a computer.

Jūdō wa, itsu kara narai hajimemashita ka.
柔道はいつから習い始めましたか。
When did you start learning judo?

Nihon dewa, kadō to sadō o narau tsumori desu.
日本では、華道と茶道を習うつもりです。
I'm planning to learn flower arrangement and tea ceremony.

Narau is an essential verb because you never stop learning! And there's so much to learn in Japan: the traditional martial arts, musical instruments, flower arrangement, tea ceremony, brushstroke painting, the subway system. And, of course, speaking and reading Japanese!

Words and Expressions Related to This Verb

manabu　学ぶ
to learn

gakushū suru　学習する
to learn, to study

tenarai　手習い
writing practice

renshū　練習
practice

Proverb

Narau yori narero.
習うより慣れろ。
Practice makes perfect. (Get used to things rather than learning things.)

なれる／慣れる **nare.ru**
to get used to, to become familiar with

			AFFIRMATIVE	NEGATIVE
Indicative	**INFORMAL**		nareru	narenai
	FORMAL		naremasu	naremasen
Imperative	**INFORMAL**	I	narero	nareru na
		II	narenasai	narenasaru na
		III	narete kudasai	narenai de kudasai
	FORMAL		onare nasaimase	onare nasaimasu na
Presumptive	**INFORMAL**	I	nareyō	narerumai
		II	nareru darō	narenai darō
	FORMAL	I	naremashō	naremasumai
		II	nareru deshō	narenai deshō
Provisional	**INFORMAL**		narereba	narenakereba
	FORMAL		naremaseba	naremasen nara
			naremasureba	
Gerund	**INFORMAL**	I	narete	narenai de
		II		narenakute
	FORMAL		naremashite	naremasen de
Past Ind.	**INFORMAL**		nareta	narenakatta
	FORMAL		naremashita	naremasen deshita
Past Presump.	**INFORMAL**		naretarō	narenakattarō
			nareta darō	narenakatta darō
	FORMAL		naremashitarō	naremasen deshitarō
			mareta deshō	narenakatta deshō
Conditional	**INFORMAL**		naretara	narenakattara
	FORMAL		naremashitara	naremasen deshitara
Alternative	**INFORMAL**		naretari	narenakattari
	FORMAL		naremashitari	naremasen deshitari

			INFORMAL AFFIRMATIVE INDICATIVE
Passive			
Potential			
Causative			naresaseru
Causative Pass.			naresaserareru
Honorific		I	onare ni naru
		II	onare nasaru
Humble		I	
		II	

to become

			AFFIRMATIVE	NEGATIVE
Indicative	**INFORMAL**		naru	naranai
	FORMAL		narimasu	narimasen
Imperative	**INFORMAL**	I	nare	naru na
		II	narinasai	narinasaru na
		III	natte kudasai	naranai de kudasai
	FORMAL		onari nasaimase	onari nasaimasu na
Presumptive	**INFORMAL**	I	narō	narumai
		II	naru darō	naranai darō
	FORMAL	I	narimashō	narimasumai
		II	naru deshō	naranai deshō
Provisional	**INFORMAL**		nareba	naranakereba
	FORMAL		narimaseba	narimasen nara
			narimasureba	
Gerund	**INFORMAL**	I	natte	naranai de
		II		naranakute
	FORMAL		narimashite	narimasen de
Past Ind.	**INFORMAL**		natta	naranakatta
	FORMAL		narimashita	narimasen deshita
Past Presump.	**INFORMAL**		nattarō	naranakattarō
			natta darō	naranakatta darō
	FORMAL		narimashitarō	narimasen deshitarō
			natta deshō	naranakatta deshō
Conditional	**INFORMAL**		nattara	naranakattara
	FORMAL		narimashitara	narimasen deshitara
Alternative	**INFORMAL**		nattari	naranakattari
	FORMAL		narimashitari	narimasen deshitari

		INFORMAL AFFIRMATIVE INDICATIVE
Passive		narareru
Potential		nareru
Causative		naraseru
Causative Pass.		naraserareru
Honorific	I	onari ni naru
	II	onari nasaru
Humble	I	
	II	

nasai

なさる **nasar.u**
TRANSITIVE   *to do* (honorific)

			AFFIRMATIVE	NEGATIVE
Indicative	**INFORMAL**		nasaru	nasaranai
	FORMAL		nasaimasu	nasaimasen
Imperative	**INFORMAL**	I	nasare	nasaru na
		II	nasainasai	nasainasaru na
		III	nasatte kudasai	nasaranai de kudasai
	FORMAL		nasaimase	nasaimasu na
Presumptive	**INFORMAL**	I	nasarō	nasarumai
		II	nasaru darō	nasaranai darō
	FORMAL	I	nasaimashō	nasaimasumai
		II	nasaru deshō	nasaranai deshō
Provisional	**INFORMAL**		nasareba	nasaranakereba
	FORMAL		nasaimaseba	nasaimasen nara
			nasaimasureba	
Gerund	**INFORMAL**	I	nasatte	nasaranai de
		II		nasaranakute
	FORMAL		nasaimashite	nasaimasen de
Past Ind.	**INFORMAL**		nasatta	nasaranakatta
	FORMAL		nasaimashita	nasaimasen deshita
Past Presump.	**INFORMAL**		nasattarō	nasaranakattarō
			nasatta darō	nasaranakatta darō
	FORMAL		nasaimashitarō	nasaimasen deshitarō
			nasatta deshō	nasaranakatta deshō
Conditional	**INFORMAL**		nasattara	nasaranakattara
	FORMAL		nasaimashitara	nasaimasen deshitara
Alternative	**INFORMAL**		nasattari	nasaranakattari
	FORMAL		nasaimashitari	nasaimasen deshitari

		INFORMAL AFFIRMATIVE INDICATIVE
Passive		nasarareru
Potential		nasareru
Causative		nasaraseru
Causative Pass.		nasaraserareru
Honorific	I	
	II	
Humble	I	
	II	

N

379

nemur.u ねむる／眠る   nemuri
to sleep, to go to sleep, to fall asleep

			AFFIRMATIVE	NEGATIVE
Indicative	**INFORMAL**		nemuru	nemuranai
	FORMAL		nemurimasu	nemurimasen
Imperative	**INFORMAL**	I	nemure	nemuru na
		II	nemurinasai	nemurinasaru na
		III	nemutte kudasai	nemuranai de kudasai
	FORMAL		onemuri nasaimase	onemuri nasaimasu na
Presumptive	**INFORMAL**	I	nemurō	nemurumai
		II	nemuru darō	nemuranai darō
	FORMAL	I	nemurimashō	nemurimasumai
		II	nemuru deshō	nemuranai deshō
Provisional	**INFORMAL**		nemureba	nemuranakereba
	FORMAL		nemurimaseba	nemurimasen nara
			nemurimasureba	
Gerund	**INFORMAL**	I	nemutte	nemuranai de
		II		nemuranakute
	FORMAL		nemurimashite	nemurimasen de
Past Ind.	**INFORMAL**		nemutta	nemuranakatta
	FORMAL		nemurimashita	nemurimasen deshita
Past Presump.	**INFORMAL**		nemuttarō	nemuranakattarō
			nemutta darō	nemuranakatta darō
	FORMAL		nemurimashitarō	nemurimasen deshitarō
			nemutta deshō	nemuranakatta deshō
Conditional	**INFORMAL**		nemuttara	nemuranakattara
	FORMAL		nemurimashitara	nemurimasen deshitara
Alternative	**INFORMAL**		nemuttari	nemuranakattari
	FORMAL		nemurimashitari	nemurimasen deshitari

		INFORMAL AFFIRMATIVE INDICATIVE
Passive		nemurareru
Potential		nemureru
Causative		nemuraseru
Causative Pass.		nemuraserareru
Honorific	I	onemuri ni naru
	II	onemuri nasaru
Humble	I	
	II	

ねる／寝る **ne.ru**
to sleep, to recline

			AFFIRMATIVE	**NEGATIVE**
Indicative	**INFORMAL**		neru	nenai
	FORMAL		nemasu	nemasen
Imperative	**INFORMAL**	I	nero	neru na
		II	nenasai	nenasaru na
		III	nete kudasai	nenai de kudasai
	FORMAL		oyasumi nasaimase	oyasumi nasaimasu na
Presumptive	**INFORMAL**	I	neyō	nemai
		II	neru darō	nenai darō
	FORMAL	I	nemashō	nemasumai
		II	neru deshō	nenai deshō
Provisional	**INFORMAL**		nereba	nenakereba
	FORMAL		nemaseba	nemasen nara
			nemasureba	
Gerund	**INFORMAL**	I	nete	nenai de
		II		nenakute
	FORMAL		nemashite	nemasen de
Past Ind.	**INFORMAL**		neta	nenakatta
	FORMAL		nemashita	nemasen deshita
Past Presump.	**INFORMAL**		netarō	nenakattarō
			neta darō	nenakatta darō
	FORMAL		nemashitarō	nemasen deshitarō
			neta deshō	nenakatta deshō
Conditional	**INFORMAL**		netara	nenakattara
	FORMAL		nemashitara	nemasen deshitara
Alternative	**INFORMAL**		netari	nenakattari
	FORMAL		nemashitari	nemasen deshitari

		INFORMAL AFFIRMATIVE INDICATIVE
Passive		nerareru
Potential		nerareru
Causative		nesaseru
Causative Pass.		nesaserareru
Honorific*	I	oyasumi ni naru
	II	oyasumi nasaru
Humble	I	
	II	

N

AN ESSENTIAL
55 VERB

*The formal imperative forms and honorific equivalents for *neru*
are the same as those of its synonym *yasumu*.

Neru 寝る

to sleep, to recline

Sentences Using *Neru*

Netai dake nenasai.
寝たいだけ寝なさい。
Sleep as long as you like.

Itsumo nan ji ni nemasu ka.
いつも何時に寝ますか。
What time do you usually go to bed?

Ikura netemo netarinai.
いくら寝ても寝足りない。
No matter how much sleep I get, it's never enough.

Tappuri nereba genki ni narimasu yo.
たっぷり寝れば元気になりますよ。
If you sleep enough, you'll be refreshed.

Konban wa jū ji made ni nenakereba naranai.
今晩は１０時までに寝なければならない。
I have to go to sleep by ten tonight.

Neru is an essential verb for use in daily life everywhere. In Japan it's especially important because of sleeping arrangements that may be quite different from your own back home. If you're used to a bed, sleeping on a futon on the tatami floor is a whole new experience!

Words and Expressions Related to This Verb

neiru　寝入る
to fall asleep

nesugosu　寝過ごす
to oversleep

nekomu　寝込む
to be sick in bed

nebusoku　寝不足
lack of sleep

netakiri　寝たきり
bedridden

Proverb

netemo sametemo　寝ても覚めても
all the time (awake or asleep)

neta ko o okosu　寝た子を起こす
create problems (wake a sleeping baby)

にげる／逃げる　**nige.ru**
to flee, to run away, to escape

			AFFIRMATIVE	NEGATIVE
Indicative	**INFORMAL**		nigeru	nigenai
	FORMAL		nigemasu	nigemasen
Imperative	**INFORMAL**	I	nigero	nigeru na
		II	nigenasai	nigenasaru na
		III	nigete kudasai	nigenai de kudasai
	FORMAL		onige nasaimase	onige nasaimasu na
Presumptive	**INFORMAL**	I	nigeyō	nigemai
		II	nigeru darō	nigenai darō
	FORMAL	I	nigemashō	nigemasumai
		II	nigeru deshō	nigenai deshō
Provisional	**INFORMAL**		nigereba	nigenakereba
	FORMAL		nigemaseba	nigemasen nara
			nigemasureba	
Gerund	**INFORMAL**	I	nigete	nigenai de
		II		nigenakute
	FORMAL		nigemashite	nigemasen de
Past Ind.	**INFORMAL**		nigeta	nigenakatta
	FORMAL		nigemashita	nigemasen deshita
Past Presump.	**INFORMAL**		nigetarō	nigenakattarō
			nigeta darō	nigenakatta darō
	FORMAL		nigemashitarō	nigemasen deshitarō
			nigeta deshō	nigenakatta deshō
Conditional	**INFORMAL**		nigetara	nigenakattara
	FORMAL		nigemashitara	nigemasen deshitara
Alternative	**INFORMAL**		nigetari	nigenakattari
	FORMAL		nigemashitari	nigemasen deshitari

		INFORMAL AFFIRMATIVE INDICATIVE
Passive		nigerareru
Potential		nigerareru
Causative		nigesaseru
Causative Pass.		nigesaserareru
Honorific	I	onige ni naru
	II	onige nasaru
Humble	I	
	II	

nigir.u にぎる／握る

to grasp, to hold, to understand   TRANSITIVE

nigiri

			AFFIRMATIVE	NEGATIVE
Indicative	**INFORMAL**		nigiru	nigiranai
	FORMAL		nigirimasu	nigirimasen
Imperative	**INFORMAL**	I	nigire	nigiru na
		II	nigirinasai	nigirinasaru na
		III	nigitte kudasai	nigiranai de kudasai
	FORMAL		onigiri nasaimase	onigiri nasaimasu na
Presumptive	**INFORMAL**	I	nigirō	nigirumai
		II	nigiru darō	nigiranai darō
	FORMAL	I	nigirimashō	nigirimasumai
		II	nigiru deshō	nigiranai deshō
Provisional	**INFORMAL**		nigireba	nigiranakereba
	FORMAL		nigirimaseba	nigirimasen nara
			nigirimasureba	
Gerund	**INFORMAL**	I	nigitte	nigiranai de
		II		nigiranakute
	FORMAL		nigirimashite	nigirimasen de
Past Ind.	**INFORMAL**		nigitta	nigiranakatta
	FORMAL		nigirimashita	nigirimasen deshita
Past Presump.	**INFORMAL**		nigittarō	nigiranakattarō
			nigitta darō	nigiranakatta darō
	FORMAL		nigirimashitarō	nigirimasen deshitarō
			nigitta deshō	nigiranakatta deshō
Conditional	**INFORMAL**		nigittara	nigiranakattara
	FORMAL		nigirimashitara	nigirimasen deshitara
Alternative	**INFORMAL**		nigittari	nigiranakattari
	FORMAL		nigirimashitari	nigirimasen deshitari

		INFORMAL AFFIRMATIVE INDICATIVE
Passive		nigirareru
Potential		nigireru
Causative		nigiraseru
Causative Pass.		nigiraserareru
Honorific	I	onigiri ni naru
	II	onigiri nasaru
Humble	I	onigiri suru
	II	onigiri itasu

384

にらむ／睨む　**niram.u**

TRANSITIVE　　*to glare at, to keep an eye on*

			AFFIRMATIVE	**NEGATIVE**
Indicative	**INFORMAL**		niramu	niramanai
	FORMAL		niramimasu	niramimasen
Imperative	**INFORMAL**	I	nirame	niramu na
		II	niraminasai	niraminasaru na
		III	nirande kudasai	niramanai de kudasai
	FORMAL		onirami nasaimase	onirami nasaimasu na
Presumptive	**INFORMAL**	I	niramō	niramumai
		II	niramu darō	niramanai darō
	FORMAL	I	niramimashō	niramimasumai
		II	niramu deshō	niramanai deshō
Provisional	**INFORMAL**		nirameba	niramanakereba
	FORMAL		niramimaseba	niramimasen nara
			niramimasureba	
Gerund	**INFORMAL**	I	nirande	niramanai de
		II		niramanakute
	FORMAL		niramimashite	niramimasen de
Past Ind.	**INFORMAL**		niranda	niramanakatta
	FORMAL		niramimashita	niramimasen deshita
Past Presump.	**INFORMAL**		nirandarō	niramanakattarō
			niranda darō	niramanakatta darō
	FORMAL		niramimashitarō	niramimasen deshitarō
			niranda deshō	niramanakatta deshō
Conditional	**INFORMAL**		nirandara	niramanakattara
	FORMAL		niramimashitara	niramimasen deshitara
Alternative	**INFORMAL**		nirandari	niramanakattari
	FORMAL		niramimashitari	niramimasen deshitari

			INFORMAL AFFIRMATIVE INDICATIVE
Passive			niramareru
Potential			nirameru
Causative			niramaseru
Causative Pass.			niramaserareru
Honorific		I	onirami ni naru
		II	onirami nasaru
Humble		I	onirami suru
		II	onirami itasu

N

to resemble, to be similar to, to look like

			AFFIRMATIVE	NEGATIVE
Indicative	**INFORMAL**		niru	ninai
	FORMAL		nimasu	nimasen
Imperative	**INFORMAL**	I	niro	niru na
		II	ninasai	ninasaru na
		III	nite kudasai	ninai de kudasai
	FORMAL		oni nasaimase	oni nasaimasu na
Presumptive	**INFORMAL**	I	niyō	nimai
		II	niru darō	ninai darō
	FORMAL	I	nimashō	nimasumai
		II	niru deshō	ninai deshō
Provisional	**INFORMAL**		nireba	ninakereba
	FORMAL		nimaseba	nimasen nara
			nimasureba	
Gerund	**INFORMAL**	I	nite	ninai de
		II		ninakute
	FORMAL		nimashite	nimasen de
Past Ind.	**INFORMAL**		nita	ninakatta
	FORMAL		nimashita	nimasen deshita
Past Presump.	**INFORMAL**		nitarō	ninakattarō
			nita darō	ninakatta darō
	FORMAL		nimashitarō	nimasen deshitarō
			nita deshō	ninakatta deshō
Conditional	**INFORMAL**		nitara	ninakattara
	FORMAL		nimashitara	nimasen deshitara
Alternative	**INFORMAL**		nitari	ninakattari
	FORMAL		nimashitari	nimasen deshitari

		INFORMAL AFFIRMATIVE INDICATIVE
Passive		nirareru
Potential		nirareru
Causative		niraseru
Causative Pass.		niraserareru
Honorific	I	
	II	
Humble	I	
	II	

nobashi のばす／延ばす／伸ばす nobas.u

TRANSITIVE *to postpone, to extend, to lengthen*

			AFFIRMATIVE	NEGATIVE
Indicative	INFORMAL		nobasu	nobasanai
	FORMAL		nobashimasu	nobashimasen
Imperative	INFORMAL	I	nobase	nobasu na
		II	nobashinasai	nobashinasaru na
		III	nobashite kudasai	nobasanai de kudasai
	FORMAL		onobashi nasaimase	onobashi nasaimasu na
Presumptive	INFORMAL	I	nobasō	nobasumai
		II	nobasu darō	nobasanai darō
	FORMAL	I	nobashimashō	nobashimasumai
		II	nobasu deshō	nobasanai deshō
Provisional	INFORMAL		nobaseba	nobasanakereba
	FORMAL		nobashimaseba	nobashimasen nara
			nobashimasureba	
Gerund	INFORMAL	I	nobashite	nobasanai de
		II		nobasanakute
	FORMAL		nobashimashite	nobashimasen de
Past Ind.	INFORMAL		nobashita	nobasanakatta
	FORMAL		nobashimashita	nobashimasen deshita
Past Presump.	INFORMAL		nobashitarō	nobasanakattarō
			nobashita darō	nobasanakatta darō
	FORMAL		nobashimashitarō	nobashimasen deshitarō
			nobashita deshō	nobasanakatta deshō
Conditional	INFORMAL		nobashitara	nobasanakattara
	FORMAL		nobashimashitara	nobashimasen deshitara
Alternative	INFORMAL		nobashitari	nobasanakattari
	FORMAL		nobashimashitari	nobashimasen deshitari

		INFORMAL AFFIRMATIVE INDICATIVE
Passive		nobasareru
Potential		nobaseru
Causative		nobasaseru
Causative Pass.		nobasaserareru
Honorific	I	onobashi ni naru
	II	onobashi nasaru
Humble	I	onobashi suru
	II	onobashi itasu

to climb, to go up　　　TRANSITIVE

			AFFIRMATIVE	**NEGATIVE**
Indicative	**INFORMAL**		noboru	noboranai
	FORMAL		noborimasu	noborimasen
Imperative	**INFORMAL**	I	nobore	noboru na
		II	noborinasai	noborinasaru na
		III	nobotte kudasai	noboranai de kudasai
	FORMAL		onobori nasaimase	onobori nasaimasu na
Presumptive	**INFORMAL**	I	noborō	noborumai
		II	noboru darō	noboranai darō
	FORMAL	I	noborimashō	noborimasumai
		II	noboru deshō	noboranai deshō
Provisional	**INFORMAL**		noboreba	noboranakereba
	FORMAL		noborimaseba	noborimasen nara
			noborimasureba	
Gerund	**INFORMAL**	I	nobotte	noboranai de
		II		noboranakute
	FORMAL		noborimashite	noborimasen de
Past Ind.	**INFORMAL**		nobotta	noboranakatta
	FORMAL		noborimashita	noborimasen deshita
Past Presump.	**INFORMAL**		nobottarō	noboranakattarō
			nobotta darō	noboranakatta darō
	FORMAL		noborimashitarō	noborimasen deshitarō
			nobotta deshō	noboranakatta deshō
Conditional	**INFORMAL**		nobottara	noboranakattara
	FORMAL		noborimashitara	noborimasen deshitara
Alternative	**INFORMAL**		nobottari	noboranakattari
	FORMAL		noborimashitari	noborimasen deshitari

			INFORMAL AFFIRMATIVE INDICATIVE
Passive			noborareru
Potential			noboreru
Causative			noboraseru
Causative Pass.			noboraserareru
Honorific		I	onobori ni naru
		II	onobori nasaru
Humble		I	onobori suru
		II	onobori itasu

to be left over, to be left behind, to remain

			AFFIRMATIVE	NEGATIVE
Indicative	**INFORMAL**		nokoru	nokoranai
	FORMAL		nokorimasu	nokorimasen
Imperative	**INFORMAL**	I	nokore	nokoru na
		II	nokorinasai	nokorinasaru na
		III	nokotte kudasai	nokoranaide kudasai
	FORMAL		onokori nasaimase	onokori nasaimasu na
Presumptive	**INFORMAL**	I	nokorō	nokorumai
		II	nokoru darō	nokoranai darō
	FORMAL	I	nokorimashō	nokorimasumai
		II	nokoru deshō	nokoranai deshō
Provisional	**INFORMAL**		nokoreba	nokoranakereba
	FORMAL		nokorimaseba	nokorimasen nara
			nokorimasureba	
Gerund	**INFORMAL**	I	nokotte	nokoranai de
		II		nokoranakute
	FORMAL		nokorimashite	nokorimasen de
Past Ind.	**INFORMAL**		nokotta	nokoranakatta
	FORMAL		nokorimashita	nokorimasen deshita
Past Presump.	**INFORMAL**		nokottarō	nokoranakattarō
			nokotta darō	nokoranakatta darō
	FORMAL		nokorimashitarō	nokorimasen deshitarō
			nokotta deshō	nokoranakatta deshō
Conditional	**INFORMAL**		nokottara	nokoranakattara
	FORMAL		nokorimashitara	nokorimasen deshitara
Alternative	**INFORMAL**		nokottari	nokoranakattari
	FORMAL		nokorimashitari	nokorimasen deshitari

			INFORMAL AFFIRMATIVE INDICATIVE
Passive			nokorareru
Potential			nokoreru
Causative			nokoraseru
Causative Pass.			nokoraserareru
Honorific		I	onokori ni naru
		II	onokori nasaru
Humble		I	onokori suru
		II	onokori itasu

nokos.u のこす／残す

nokoshi

to leave behind, to leave unfinished, to save   TRANSITIVE

			AFFIRMATIVE	NEGATIVE
Indicative	**INFORMAL**		nokosu	nokosanai
	FORMAL		nokoshimasu	nokoshimasen
Imperative	**INFORMAL**	I	nokose	nokosu na
		II	nokoshinasai	nokoshinasaru na
		III	nokoshite kudasai	nokosanai de kudasai
	FORMAL		onokoshi nasaimase	onokoshi nasaimasu na
Presumptive	**INFORMAL**	I	nokosō	nokosumai
		II	nokosu darō	nokosanai darō
	FORMAL	I	nokoshimashō	nokoshimasumai
		II	nokosu deshō	nokosanai deshō
Provisional	**INFORMAL**		nokoseba	nokosanakereba
	FORMAL		nokoshimaseba	nokoshimasen nara
			nokoshimasureba	
Gerund	**INFORMAL**	I	nokoshite	nokosanai de
		II		nokosanakute
	FORMAL		nokoshimashite	nokoshimasen de
Past Ind.	**INFORMAL**		nokoshita	nokosanakatta
	FORMAL		nokoshimashita	nokoshimasen deshita
Past Presump.	**INFORMAL**		nokoshitarō	nokosanakattarō
			nokoshita darō	nokosanakatta darō
	FORMAL		nokoshimashitarō	nokoshimasen deshitarō
			nokoshita deshō	nokosanakatta deshō
Conditional	**INFORMAL**		nokoshitara	nokosanakattara
	FORMAL		nokoshimashitara	nokoshimasen deshitara
Alternative	**INFORMAL**		nokoshitari	nokosanakattari
	FORMAL		nokoshimashitari	nokoshimasen deshitari

		INFORMAL AFFIRMATIVE INDICATIVE
Passive		nokosareru
Potential		nokoseru
Causative		nokosaseru
Causative Pass.		nokosaserareru
Honorific	I	onokoshi ni naru
	II	onokoshi nasaru
Humble	I	onokoshi suru
	II	onokoshi itasu

のむ／飲む／呑む **nom.u**

TRANSITIVE   *to drink, to swallow*

			AFFIRMATIVE	NEGATIVE
Indicative	**INFORMAL**		nomu	nomanai
	FORMAL		nomimasu	nomimasen
Imperative	**INFORMAL**	**I**	nome	nomu na
		II	nominasai	nominasaru na
		III	nonde kudasai	nomanai de kudasai
	FORMAL		meshiagarimase	meshiagarimasu na
			onomi nasaimase	onomi nasaimasu na
Presumptive	**INFORMAL**	**I**	nomō	nomumai
		II	nomu darō	nomanai darō
	FORMAL	**I**	nomimashō	nomimasumai
		II	nomu deshō	nomanai deshō
Provisional	**INFORMAL**		nomeba	nomanakereba
	FORMAL		nomimaseba	nomimasen nara
			nomimasureba	
Gerund	**INFORMAL**	**I**	nonde	nomanai de
		II		nomanakute
	FORMAL		nomimashite	nomimasen de
Past Ind.	**INFORMAL**		nonda	nomanakatta
	FORMAL		nomimashita	nomimasen deshita
Past Presump.	**INFORMAL**		nondarō	nomanakattarō
			nonda darō	nomanakatta darō
	FORMAL		nomimashitarō	nomimasen deshitarō
			nonda deshō	nomanakatta deshō
Conditional	**INFORMAL**		nondara	nomanakattara
	FORMAL		nomimashitara	nomimasen deshitara
Alternative	**INFORMAL**		nondari	nomanakattari
	FORMAL		nomimashitari	nomimasen deshitari

		INFORMAL AFFIRMATIVE INDICATIVE	
Passive		nomareru	
Potential		nomeru	
Causative		nomaseru	
Causative Pass.		nomaserareru	
Honorific		meshiagaru	**I** onomi ni naru
			II onomi nasaru
Humble		itadaku	

AN ESSENTIAL
55 VERB

Nomu 飲む

to drink, to swallow

Sentences Using *Nomu*

Chichi wa maiasa kōhī o san bai nomimasu.
父は毎朝コーヒーを三杯飲みます。
My father drinks three cups of coffee every morning.

Kanojo wa arukōru rui wa issai nomimasen.
彼女はアルコール類はいっさい飲みません。
She doesn't drink alcohol at all.

Ocha ga nomitai. お茶が飲みたい。
I want to drink some Japanese tea.

Osake o nonde unten shinai yō ni.
お酒を飲んで運転しないように。
Don't drink and drive.

Bīru o nomimashō ka.
ビールを飲みましょうか。
Shall we drink some beer?

Nomu is an essential verb for everyday conversation. The Japanese take their coffee seriously, both at home and in excellent coffee shops everywhere. The tea is an art form, from the tea ceremony to the ubiquitous multiple cups of green or roasted Japanese tea offered and consumed daily. The beer and sake are legendary. Bottled water from fine local springs is readily available. And the tap water is safe to drink!

Proverb

geiin bashoku 鯨飲馬食
consuming a huge amount of food and drink (drink like a whale, eat like a horse)

Words and Expressions Related to This Verb

nomikomu 飲み込む
to swallow, to understand, to grasp

inshoku 飲食
eat and drink

nomimizu 飲み水
drinking water

nomi hōdai tabe hōdai
飲み放題食べ放題
all you can drink, all you can eat

のる／乗る　**nor.u**

to get on, to board, to take a ride, to ride

			AFFIRMATIVE	**NEGATIVE**
Indicative	**INFORMAL**		noru	noranai
	FORMAL		norimasu	norimasen
Imperative	**INFORMAL**	I	nore	noru na
		II	norinasai	norinasaru na
		III	notte kudasai	noranai de kudasai
	FORMAL		onori nasaimase	onori nasaimasu na
Presumptive	**INFORMAL**	I	norō	norumai
		II	noru darō	noranai darō
	FORMAL	I	norimashō	norimasumai
		II	noru deshō	noranai deshō
Provisional	**INFORMAL**		noreba	noranakereba
	FORMAL		norimaseba	norimasen nara
			norimasureba	
Gerund	**INFORMAL**	I	notte	noranai de
		II		noranakute
	FORMAL		norimashite	norimasen de
Past Ind.	**INFORMAL**		notta	noranakatta
	FORMAL		norimashita	norimasen deshita
Past Presump.	**INFORMAL**		nottarō	noranakattarō
			notta darō	noranakatta darō
	FORMAL		norimashitarō	norimasen deshitarō
			notta deshō	noranakatta deshō
Conditional	**INFORMAL**		nottara	noranakattara
	FORMAL		norimashitara	norimasen deshitara
Alternative	**INFORMAL**		nottari	noranakattari
	FORMAL		norimashitari	norimasen deshitari

			INFORMAL AFFIRMATIVE INDICATIVE
Passive			norareru
Potential			noreru
Causative			noraseru
Causative Pass.			noraserareru
Honorific		I	onori ni naru
		II	onori nasaru
Humble		I	onori suru
		II	onori itasu

AN ESSENTIAL 55 VERB

Noru 乗る

to get on, to board, to take a ride, to ride

Noru is a verb you'll use often, especially with public transportation such an important part of life in Japan. You'll be boarding the crowded commuter trains, the fast bullet trains, the efficient buses— maybe even riding in a taxi with a white-gloved driver.

Sentences Using *Noru*

Shinkansen ni notta koto ga arimasu ka.
新幹線に乗ったことがありますか。
Have you ever taken the Shinkansen?

Tsūkin densha ga sugoku konde ite norenakatta.
通勤電車が凄く混んでいて乗れなかった。
I couldn't get on the commuter train because it was so crowded.

Jitensha ni noremasu ka.
自転車に乗れますか。
Can you ride a bicycle?

Chikatetsu ni notta hō ga takushī yori hayai desu.
地下鉄に乗った方がタクシーより速いです。
Taking the subway is faster than taking a taxi.

Ginza made takushī ni noru to ikura kakarimasu ka.
銀座までタクシーに乗ると、いくらかかりますか。
If I take a taxi to Ginza, how much will it be?

Words and Expressions Related to This Verb

jōsha suru　乗車する
to get on a train, to get in a car

norikaeru　乗り換える
to change (trains or buses), to transfer

jōsha ken　乗車券
a ticket (train, bus)

jōsha chin　乗車賃
a fare

Proverb

norikakatta fune
乗りかかった船
having obligated oneself (a ship one is about to board)

TRANSITIVE   *to put* (on top of), *to put on board*

			AFFIRMATIVE	**NEGATIVE**
Indicative	**INFORMAL**		noseru	nosenai
	FORMAL		nosemasu	nosemasen
Imperative	**INFORMAL**	I	nosero	noseru na
		II	nosenasai	nosenasaru na
		III	nosete kudasai	nosenai de kudasai
	FORMAL		onose nasaimase	onose nasaimasu na
Presumptive	**INFORMAL**	I	noseyō	nosemai
		II	noseru darō	nosenai darō
	FORMAL	I	nosemashō	nosemasumai
		II	noseru deshō	nosenai deshō
Provisional	**INFORMAL**		nosereba	nosenakereba
	FORMAL		nosemaseba	nosemasen nara
			nosemasureba	
Gerund	**INFORMAL**	I	nosete	nosenai de
		II		nosenakute
	FORMAL		nosemashite	nosemasen de
Past Ind.	**INFORMAL**		noseta	nosenakatta
	FORMAL		nosemashita	nosemasen deshita
Past Presump.	**INFORMAL**		nosetarō	nosenakattarō
			noseta darō	nosenakatta darō
	FORMAL		nosemashitarō	nosemasen deshitarō
			noseta deshō	nosenakatta deshō
Conditional	**INFORMAL**		nosetara	nosenakattara
	FORMAL		nosemashitara	nosemasen deshitara
Alternative	**INFORMAL**		nosetari	nosenakattari
	FORMAL		nosemashitari	nosemasen deshitari

			INFORMAL AFFIRMATIVE INDICATIVE
Passive			noserareru
Potential			noserareru
Causative			nosesaseru
Causative Pass.			nosesaserareru
Honorific		I	onose ni naru
		II	onose nasaru
Humble		I	onose suru
		II	onose itasu

N

to remove, to omit, to look in   TRANSITIVE

			AFFIRMATIVE	**NEGATIVE**
Indicative	**INFORMAL**		nozoku	nozokanai
	FORMAL		nozokimasu	nozokimasen
Imperative	**INFORMAL**	I	nozoke	nozoku na
		II	nozokinasai	nozokinasaru na
		III	nozoite kudasai	nozokanai de kudasai
	FORMAL		onozoki nasaimase	onozoki nasaimasu na
Presumptive	**INFORMAL**	I	nozokō	nozokumai
		II	nozoku darō	nozokanai darō
	FORMAL	I	nozokimashō	nozokimasumai
		II	nozoku deshō	nozokanai deshō
Provisional	**INFORMAL**		nozokeba	nozokanakereba
	FORMAL		nozokimaseba	nozokimasen nara
			nozokimasureba	
Gerund	**INFORMAL**	I	nozoite	nozokanai de
		II		nozokanakute
	FORMAL		nozokimashite	nozokimasen de
Past Ind.	**INFORMAL**		nozoita	nozokanakatta
	FORMAL		nozokimashita	nozokimasen deshita
Past Presump.	**INFORMAL**		nozoitarō	nozokanakattarō
			nozoita darō	nozokanakatta darō
	FORMAL		nozokimashitarō	nozokimasen deshitarō
			nozoita deshō	nozokanakatta deshō
Conditional	**INFORMAL**		nozoitara	nozokanakattara
	FORMAL		nozokimashitara	nozokimasen deshitara
Alternative	**INFORMAL**		nozoitari	nozokanakattari
	FORMAL		nozokimashitari	nozokimasen deshitari

		INFORMAL AFFIRMATIVE INDICATIVE
Passive		nozokareru
Potential		nozokeru
Causative		nozokaseru
Causative Pass.		nozokaserareru
Honorific	I	onozoki ni naru
	II	onozoki nasaru
Humble	I	onozoki suru
	II	onozoki itasu

TRANSITIVE   *to take off, to remove* (clothes, shoes, hats, etc.)

			AFFIRMATIVE	NEGATIVE
Indicative	INFORMAL		nugu	nuganai
	FORMAL		nugimasu	nugimasen
Imperative	INFORMAL	I	nuge	nugu na
		II	nuginasai	nuginasaru na
		III	nuide kudasai	nuganai de kudasai
	FORMAL		onugi nasaimase	onugi nasaimasu na
Presumptive	INFORMAL	I	nugō	nugumai
		II	nugu darō	nuganai darō
	FORMAL	I	nugimashō	nugimasumai
		II	nugu deshō	nuganai deshō
Provisional	INFORMAL		nugeba	nuganakereba
	FORMAL		nugimaseba	nugimasen nara
			nugimasureba	
Gerund	INFORMAL	I	nuide	nuganai de
		II		nuganakute
	FORMAL		nugimashite	nugimasen de
Past Ind.	INFORMAL		nuida	nuganakatta
	FORMAL		nugimashita	nugimasen deshita
Past Presump.	INFORMAL		nuidarō	nuganakattarō
			nuida darō	nuganakatta darō
	FORMAL		nugimashitarō	nugimasen deshitarō
			nuida deshō	nuganakatta deshō
Conditional	INFORMAL		nuidara	nuganakattara
	FORMAL		nugimashitara	nugimasen deshitara
Alternative	INFORMAL		nuidari	nuganakattari
	FORMAL		nugimashitari	nugimasen deshitari

		INFORMAL AFFIRMATIVE INDICATIVE
Passive		nugareru
Potential		nugeru
Causative		nugaseru
Causative Pass.		nugasareru
Honorific	I	onugi ni naru
	II	onugi nasaru
Humble	I	onugi suru
	II	onugi itasu

to get wet

			AFFIRMATIVE	NEGATIVE
Indicative	**INFORMAL**		nureru	nurenai
	FORMAL		nuremasu	nuremasen
Imperative	**INFORMAL**	I	nurero	nureru na
		II	nurenasai	nurenasaru na
		III	nurete kudasai	nurenai de kudasai
	FORMAL		onure nasaimase	onure nasaimasu na
Presumptive	**INFORMAL**	I	nureyō	nuremai
		II	nureru darō	nurenai darō
	FORMAL	I	nuremashō	nuremasumai
		II	nureru deshō	nurenai deshō
Provisional	**INFORMAL**		nurereba	nurenakereba
	FORMAL		nuremaseba	nuremasen nara
			nuremasureba	
Gerund	**INFORMAL**	I	nurete	nurenai de
		II		nurenakute
	FORMAL		nuremashite	nuremasen de
Past Ind.	**INFORMAL**		nureta	nurenakatta
	FORMAL		nuremashita	nuremasen deshita
Past Presump.	**INFORMAL**		nuretarō	nurenakattarō
			nureta darō	nurenakatta darō
	FORMAL		nuremashitarō	nuremasen deshitarō
			nureta deshō	nurenakatta deshō
Conditional	**INFORMAL**		nuretara	nurenakattara
	FORMAL		nuremashitara	nuremasen deshitara
Alternative	**INFORMAL**		nuretari	nurenakattari
	FORMAL		nuremashitari	nuremasen deshitari

		INFORMAL AFFIRMATIVE INDICATIVE
Passive		nurerareru
Potential		nurerareru
Causative		nuresaseru
Causative Pass.		nuresaserareru
Honorific	I	onure ni naru
	II	onure nasaru
Humble	I	
	II	

ぬる／塗る　**nur.u**

TRANSITIVE　　*to paint, to put on, to spread*

			AFFIRMATIVE	NEGATIVE
Indicative	**INFORMAL**		nuru	nuranai
	FORMAL		nurimasu	nurimasen
Imperative	**INFORMAL**	I	nure	nuru na
		II	nurinasai	nurinasaru na
		III	nutte kudasai	nuranai de kudasai
	FORMAL		onuri nasaimase	onuri nasaimasu na
Presumptive	**INFORMAL**	I	nurō	nurumai
		II	nuru darō	nuranai darō
	FORMAL	I	nurimashō	nurimasumai
		II	nuru deshō	nuranai deshō
Provisional	**INFORMAL**		nureba	nuranakereba
	FORMAL		nurimaseba	nurimasen nara
			nurimasureba	
Gerund	**INFORMAL**	I	nutte	nuranai de
		II		nuranakute
	FORMAL		nurimashite	nurimasen de
Past Ind.	**INFORMAL**		nutta	nuranakatta
	FORMAL		nurimashita	nurimasen deshita
Past Presump.	**INFORMAL**		nuttarō	nuranakattarō
			nutta darō	nuranakatta darō
	FORMAL		nurimashitarō	nurimasen deshitarō
			nutta deshō	nuranakatta deshō
Conditional	**INFORMAL**		nuttara	nuranakattara
	FORMAL		nurimashitara	nurimasen deshitara
Alternative	**INFORMAL**		nuttari	nuranakattari
	FORMAL		nurimashitari	nurimasen deshitari

			INFORMAL AFFIRMATIVE INDICATIVE
Passive			nurareru
Potential			nureru
Causative			nuraseru
Causative Pass.			nuraserareru
Honorific		I	onuri ni naru
		II	onuri nasaru
Humble		I	onuri suru
		II	onuri itasu

nusum.u ぬすむ／盗む   nusumi

to steal   TRANSITIVE

			AFFIRMATIVE	NEGATIVE
Indicative	**INFORMAL**		nusumu	nusumanai
	FORMAL		nusumimasu	nusumimasen
Imperative	**INFORMAL**	I	nusume	nusumu na
		II	nusuminasai	nusuminasaru na
		III	nusunde kudasai	nusumanai de kudasai
	FORMAL		onusumi nasaimase	onusumi nasaimasu na
Presumptive	**INFORMAL**	I	nusumō	nusumumai
		II	nusumu darō	nusumanai darō
	FORMAL	I	nusumimashō	nusumimasumai
		II	nusumu deshō	nusumanai deshō
Provisional	**INFORMAL**		nusumeba	nusumanakereba
	FORMAL		nusumimaseba	nusumimasen nara
			nusumimasureba	
Gerund	**INFORMAL**	I	nusunde	nusumanai de
		II		nusumanakute
	FORMAL		nusumimashite	nusumimasen de
Past Ind.	**INFORMAL**		nusunda	nusumanakatta
	FORMAL		nusumimashita	nusumimasen deshita
Past Presump.	**INFORMAL**		nusundarō	nusumanakattarō
			nusunda darō	nusumanakatta darō
	FORMAL		nusumimashitarō	nusumimasen deshitarō
			nusunda deshō	nusumanakatta deshō
Conditional	**INFORMAL**		nusundara	nusumanakattara
	FORMAL		nusumimashitara	nusumimasen deshitara
Alternative	**INFORMAL**		nusundari	nusumanakattari
	FORMAL		nusumimashitari	nusumimasen deshitari

		INFORMAL AFFIRMATIVE INDICATIVE
Passive		nusumareru
Potential		nusumeru
Causative		nusumaseru
Causative Pass.		nusumaserareru
Honorific	I	onusumi ni naru
	II	onusumi nasaru
Humble	I	
	II	

400

おぼえる／覚える　oboe.ru

TRANSITIVE　*to learn, to remember, to memorize*

			AFFIRMATIVE	**NEGATIVE**
Indicative	**INFORMAL**		oboeru	oboenai
	FORMAL		oboemasu	oboemasen
Imperative	**INFORMAL**	**I**	oboero	oboeru na
		II	oboenasai	oboenasaru na
		III	oboete kudasai	oboenai de kudasai
	FORMAL		oboe nasaimase	oboe nasaimasu na
Presumptive	**INFORMAL**	**I**	oboeyō	oboemai
		II	oboeru darō	oboenai darō
	FORMAL	**I**	oboemashō	oboemasumai
		II	oboeru deshō	oboenai deshō
Provisional	**INFORMAL**		oboereba	oboenakereba
	FORMAL		oboemaseba	oboemasen nara
			oboemasureba	
Gerund	**INFORMAL**	**I**	oboete	oboenai de
		II		oboenakute
	FORMAL		oboemashite	oboemasen de
Past Ind.	**INFORMAL**		oboeta	oboenakatta
	FORMAL		oboemashita	oboemasen deshita
Past Presump.	**INFORMAL**		oboetarō	oboenakattarō
			oboeta darō	oboenakatta darō
	FORMAL		oboemashitarō	oboemasen deshitarō
			oboeta deshō	oboenakatta deshō
Conditional	**INFORMAL**		oboetara	oboenakattara
	FORMAL		oboemashitara	oboemasen deshitara
Alternative	**INFORMAL**		oboetari	oboenakattari
	FORMAL		oboemashitari	oboemasen deshitari

		INFORMAL AFFIRMATIVE INDICATIVE
Passive		oboerareru
Potential		oboerareru
Causative		oboesaseru
Causative Pass.		oboesaserareru

Honorific	**I**	ooboe ni naru
	II	ooboe nasaru
Humble	**I**	
	II	

O

401

ochi.ru おちる／落ちる   ochi
to fall, to go down, to fail

			AFFIRMATIVE	NEGATIVE
Indicative	INFORMAL		ochiru	ochinai
	FORMAL		ochimasu	ochimasen
Imperative	INFORMAL	I	ochiro	ochiru na
		II	ochinasai	ochinasaru na
		III	ochite kudasai	ochinai de kudasai
	FORMAL		oochi nasaimase	oochi nasaimasu na
Presumptive	INFORMAL	I	ochiyō	ochirumai
		II	ochiru darō	ochinai darō
	FORMAL	I	ochimashō	ochimasumai
		II	ochiru deshō	ochinai deshō
Provisional	INFORMAL		ochireba	ochinakereba
	FORMAL		ochimaseba	ochimasen nara
			ochimasureba	
Gerund	INFORMAL	I	ochite	ochinai de
		II		ochinakute
	FORMAL		ochimashite	ochimasen de
Past Ind.	INFORMAL		ochita	ochinakatta
	FORMAL		ochimashita	ochimasen deshita
Past Presump.	INFORMAL		ochitarō	ochinakattarō
			ochita darō	ochinakatta darō
	FORMAL		ochimashitarō	ochimasen deshitarō
			ochita deshō	ochinakatta deshō
Conditional	INFORMAL		ochitara	ochinakattara
	FORMAL		ochimashitara	ochimasen deshitara
Alternative	INFORMAL		ochitari	ochinakattari
	FORMAL		ochimashitari	ochimasen deshitari

		INFORMAL AFFIRMATIVE INDICATIVE
Passive		
Potential		
Causative		ochisaseru
Causative Pass.		ochisaserareru
Honorific	I	oochi ni naru
	II	oochi nasaru
Humble	I	
	II	

402

おどろく／驚く **odorok.u**

to be surprised, to be amazed

			AFFIRMATIVE	NEGATIVE
Indicative	**INFORMAL**		odoroku	odorokanai
	FORMAL		odorokimasu	odorokimasen
Imperative	**INFORMAL**	I	odoroke	odoroku na
		II	odorokinasai	odorokinasaru na
		III	odoroite kudasai	odorokanai de kudasai
	FORMAL		oodoroki nasaimase	oodoroki nasaimasu na
Presumptive	**INFORMAL**	I	odorokō	odorokumai
		II	odoroku darō	odorokanai darō
	FORMAL	I	odorokimashō	odorokimasumai
		II	odoroku deshō	odorokanai deshō
Provisional	**INFORMAL**		odorokeba	odorokanakereba
	FORMAL		odorokimaseba	odorokimasen nara
			odorokimasureba	
Gerund	**INFORMAL**	I	odoroite	odorokanai de
		II		odorokanakute
	FORMAL		odorokimashite	odorokimasen de
Past Ind.	**INFORMAL**		odoroita	odorokanakatta
	FORMAL		odorokimashita	odoroldmasen deshita
Past Presump.	**INFORMAL**		odoroitarō	odorokanakattarō
			odoroita darō	odorokanakatta darō
	FORMAL		odorokimashitarō	odorokimasen deshitarō
			odoroita deshō	odorokanakatta deshō
Conditional	**INFORMAL**		odoroitara	odorokanakattara
	FORMAL		odorokimashitara	odorokimasen deshitara
Alternative	**INFORMAL**		odoroitari	odorokanakattari
	FORMAL		odorokimashitari	odorokimasen deshitari

		INFORMAL AFFIRMATIVE INDICATIVE
Passive		odorokareru
Potential		odorokeru
Causative		odorokaseru
Causative Pass.		odorokaserareru
Honorific	I	oodoroki ni naru
	II	oodoroki nasaru
Humble	I	
	II	

odor.u おどる／踊る

to dance

odori

			AFFIRMATIVE	NEGATIVE
Indicative	**INFORMAL**		odoru	odoranai
	FORMAL		odorimasu	odorimasen
Imperative	**INFORMAL**	I	odore	odoru na
		II	odorinasai	odorinasaru na
		III	odotte kudasai	odoranai de kudasai
	FORMAL		oodori nasaimase	oodori nasaimasu na
Presumptive	**INFORMAL**	I	odorō	odorumai
		II	odoru darō	odoranai darō
	FORMAL	I	odorimashō	odorimasumai
		II	odoru deshō	odoranai deshō
Provisional	**INFORMAL**		odoreba	odoranakereba
	FORMAL		odorimaseba	odorimasen nara
			odorimasureba	
Gerund	**INFORMAL**	I	odotte	odoranai de
		II		odoranakute
	FORMAL		odorimashite	odorimasen de
Past Ind.	**INFORMAL**		odotta	odoranakatta
	FORMAL		odorimashita	odorimasen deshita
Past Presump.	**INFORMAL**		odottarō	odoranakattarō
			odotta darō	odoranakatta darō
	FORMAL		odorimashitarō	odorimasen deshitarō
			odotta deshō	odoranakatta deshō
Conditional	**INFORMAL**		odottara	odoranakattara
	FORMAL		odorimashitara	odorimasen deshitara
Alternative	**INFORMAL**		odottari	odoranakattari
	FORMAL		odorimashitari	odorimasen deshitari

		INFORMAL AFFIRMATIVE INDICATIVE
Passive		odorareru
Potential		odoreru
Causative		odoraseru
Causative Pass.		odoraserareru

Honorific	I	oodori ni naru
	II	oodori nasaru
Humble	I	oodori suru
	II	oodori itasu

おきる／起きる　oki.ru

to get up, to wake up

			AFFIRMATIVE	NEGATIVE
Indicative	**INFORMAL**		okiru	okinai
	FORMAL		okimasu	okimasen
Imperative	**INFORMAL**	I	okiro	okiru na
		II	okinasai	okinasaru na
		III	okite kudasai	okinai de kudasai
	FORMAL		ooki nasaimase	ooki nasaimasu na
Presumptive	**INFORMAL**	I	okiyō	okimai
		II	okiru darō	okinai darō
	FORMAL	I	okimashō	okimasumai
		II	okiru deshō	okinai deshō
Provisional	**INFORMAL**		okireba	okinakereba
	FORMAL		okimaseba	okimasen nara
			okimasureba	
Gerund	**INFORMAL**	I	okite	okinai de
		II		okinakute
	FORMAL		okimashite	okimasen de
Past Ind.	**INFORMAL**		okita	okinakatta
	FORMAL		okimashita	okimasen deshita
Past Presump.	**INFORMAL**		okitarō	okinakattarō
			okita darō	okinakatta darō
	FORMAL		okimashitarō	okimasen deshitarō
			okita deshō	okinakatta deshō
Conditional	**INFORMAL**		okitara	okinakattara
	FORMAL		okimashitara	okimasen deshitara
Alternative	**INFORMAL**		okitari	okinakattari
	FORMAL		okimashitari	okimasen deshitari

		INFORMAL AFFIRMATIVE INDICATIVE
Passive		okirareru
Potential		okirareru
Causative		okisaseru
Causative Pass.		okisaserareru
Honorific	I	ooki ni naru
	II	ooki nasaru
Humble	I	ooki suru
	II	ooki itasu

O

AN ESSENTIAL 55 VERB

405

Okiru 起きる

to get up, to wake up, to get out of bed

Okiru is a verb used in many everyday situations. If you stay at a ryokan, or Japanese inn, for example, you'll be asked what time you will wake up and want breakfast served. Or this verb might be used when discussing travel plans and an early departure.

Sentences Using *Okiru*

Ashita wa roku ji ni okinasai.
明日は六時に起きなさい。
You should get up at six tomorrow.

Nan ji ni okitemo kamaimasen.
何時に起きても構いません。
Whenever you get up, it's fine.

Ku ji ni okitara, asa gohan wa owatte imashita.
九時に起きたら、朝ご飯は終わっていました。
When I got up at nine, breakfast was over.

Shichi ji ni okireba, ku ji no kisha ni maniaimasu ka.
七時に起きれば、九時の汽車に間に合いますか。
If I get up at seven, can I make a nine o'clock train?

Byōki dakara okite wa dame desu yo.
病気だから起きてはダメですよ。
You're sick, so you shouldn't get up.

Words and Expressions Related to This Verb

okosu　起こす
to wake someone up

kishō suru　起床する
to get out of bed, to get up

kiritsu suru　起立する
to stand up, to rise

Proverb

Hayaoki wa san mon no toku.
早起きは三文の徳。
The early bird catches the worm. (By getting up early, you gain something nice.)

nanakorobi yaoki
七転び八起き
There is always next time. (falling down seven times, getting up the eighth time)

to get angry

			AFFIRMATIVE	NEGATIVE
Indicative	**INFORMAL**		okoru	okoranai
	FORMAL		okorimasu	okorimasen
Imperative	**INFORMAL**	I	okore	okoru na
		II	okorinasai	okorinasaru na
		III	okotte kudasai	okoranai de kudasai
	FORMAL		ookori nasaimase	ookori nasaimasu na
Presumptive	**INFORMAL**	I	okorō	okorumai
		II	okoru darō	okoranai darō
	FORMAL	I	okorimashō	okorimasumai
		II	okoru deshō	okoranai deshō
Provisional	**INFORMAL**		okoreba	okoranakereba
	FORMAL		okorimaseba	okorimasen nara
			okorimasureba	
Gerund	**INFORMAL**	I	okotte	okoranai de
		II		okoranakute
	FORMAL		okorimashite	okorimasen de
Past Ind.	**INFORMAL**		okotta	okoranakatta
	FORMAL		okorimashita	okorimasen deshita
Past Presump.	**INFORMAL**		okottarō	okoranakattarō
			okotta darō	okoranakatta darō
	FORMAL		okorimashitarō	okorimasen deshitarō
			okotta deshō	okoranakatta deshō
Conditional	**INFORMAL**		okottara	okoranakattara
	FORMAL		okorimashitara	okorimasen deshitara
Alternative	**INFORMAL**		okottari	okoranakattari
	FORMAL		okorimashitari	okorimasen deshitari

		INFORMAL AFFIRMATIVE INDICATIVE
Passive		okorareru
Potential		okoreru
Causative		okoraseru
Causative Pass.		okoraserareru
Honorific	I	ookori ni naru
	II	ookori nasaru
Humble	I	
	II	

407

okos.u おこす／起こす   **okoshi**

to raise up, to awake, to cause   TRANSITIVE

			AFFIRMATIVE	**NEGATIVE**
Indicative	**INFORMAL**		okosu	okosanai
	FORMAL		okoshimasu	okoshimasen
Imperative	**INFORMAL**	I	okose	okosu na
		II	okoshinasai	okoshinasaru na
		III	okoshite kudasai	okosanai de kudasai
	FORMAL		ookoshi nasaimase	ookoshi nasaimasu na
Presumptive	**INFORMAL**	I	okosō	okosumai
		II	okosu darō	okosanai darō
	FORMAL	I	okoshimashō	okoshimasumai
		II	okosu darō	okosanai darō
Provisional	**INFORMAL**		okoseba	okosanakereba
	FORMAL		okoshimaseba	okoshimasen nara
			okoshimasureba	
Gerund	**INFORMAL**	I	okoshite	okosanai de
		II		okosanakute
	FORMAL		okoshimashite	okoshimasen de
Past Ind.	**INFORMAL**		okoshita	okosanakatta
	FORMAL		okoshimashita	okoshimasen deshita
Past Presump.	**INFORMAL**		okoshitarō	okosanakattarō
			okoshita darō	okosanakatta darō
	FORMAL		okoshimashitarō	okoshimasen deshitarō
			okoshita deshō	okosanakatta deshō
Conditional	**INFORMAL**		okoshitara	okosanakattara
	FORMAL		okoshimashitara	okoshimasen deshitara
Alternative	**INFORMAL**		okoshitari	okosanakattari
	FORMAL		okoshimashitari	okoshimasen deshitari

		INFORMAL AFFIRMATIVE INDICATIVE
Passive		okosareru
Potential		okoseru
Causative		okosaseru
Causative Pass.		okosaserareru

Honorific	I	ookoshi ni naru
	II	ookoshi nasaru
Humble	I	ookoshi suru
	II	ookoshi itasu

おく／置く ok.u

TRANSITIVE *to put, to place*

			AFFIRMATIVE	NEGATIVE
Indicative	**INFORMAL**		oku	okanai
	FORMAL		okimasu	okimasen
Imperative	**INFORMAL**	I	oke	oku na
		II	okinasai	okinasaru na
		III	oite kudasai	okanai de kudasai
	FORMAL		ooki nasaimase	ooki nasaimasu na
Presumptive	**INFORMAL**	I	okō	okumai
		II	oku darō	okanai darō
	FORMAL	I	okimashō	okimasumai
		II	oku deshō	okanai deshō
Provisional	**INFORMAL**		okeba	okanakereba
	FORMAL		okimaseba	okimasen nara
			okimasureba	
Gerund	**INFORMAL**	I	oite	okanai de
		II		okanakute
	FORMAL		okimashite	okimasen de
Past Ind.	**INFORMAL**		oita	okanakatta
	FORMAL		okimashita	okimasen deshita
Past Presump.	**INFORMAL**		oitarō	okanakattarō
			oita darō	okanakatta darō
	FORMAL		okimashitarō	okimasen deshitarō
			oita deshō	okanakatta deshō
Conditional	**INFORMAL**		oitara	okanakattara
	FORMAL		okimashitara	okimasen deshitara
Alternative	**INFORMAL**		oitari	okanakattari
	FORMAL		okimashitari	okimasen deshitari

			INFORMAL AFFIRMATIVE INDICATIVE
Passive			okareru
Potential			okeru
Causative			okaseru
Causative Pass.			okaserareru
Honorific		I	ooki ni naru
		II	ooki nasaru
Humble		I	ooki suru
		II	ooki itasu

to be late, to lag behind

			AFFIRMATIVE	NEGATIVE
Indicative	**INFORMAL**		okureru	okurenai
	FORMAL		okuremasu	okuremasen
Imperative	**INFORMAL**	I	okurero	okureru na
		II	okurenasai	okurenasaru na
		III	okurete kudasai	okurenai de kudasai
	FORMAL		ookure nasaimase	ookure nasaimasu na
Presumptive	**INFORMAL**	I	okureyō	okuremai
		II	okureru darō	okurenai darō
	FORMAL	I	okuremashō	okuremasumai
		II	okureru deshō	okurenai deshō
Provisional	**INFORMAL**		okurereba	okurenakereba
	FORMAL		okuremaseba	okuremasen nara
			okuremasureba	
Gerund	**INFORMAL**	I	okurete	okurenai de
		II		okurenakute
	FORMAL		okuremashite	okuremasen de
Past Ind.	**INFORMAL**		okureta	okurenakatta
	FORMAL		okuremashita	okuremasen deshita
Past Presump.	**INFORMAL**		okuretarō	okurenakattarō
			okureta darō	okurenakatta darō
	FORMAL		okuremashitarō	okuremasen deshitarō
			okureta deshō	okurenakatta deshō
Conditional	**INFORMAL**		okuretara	okurenakattara
	FORMAL		okuremashitara	okuremasen deshitara
Alternative	**INFORMAL**		okuretari	okurenakattari
	FORMAL		okuremashitari	okuremasen deshitari

			INFORMAL AFFIRMATIVE INDICATIVE
Passive			okurerareru
Potential			okurerareru
Causative			okuresaseru
Causative Pass.			okuresaserareru
Honorific		I	ookure ni naru
		II	ookure nasaru
Humble		I	
		II	

okuri

おくる／送る **okur.u**

TRANSITIVE　　*to send* (a package), *to see off*, *to accompany* (a person)

			AFFIRMATIVE	**NEGATIVE**
Indicative	**INFORMAL**		okuru	okuranai
	FORMAL		okurimasu	okurimasen
Imperative	**INFORMAL**	I	okure	okuru na
		II	okurinasai	okurinasaru na
		III	okutte kudasai	okuranai de kudasai
	FORMAL		ookuri nasaimase	ookuri nasaimasu na
Presumptive	**INFORMAL**	I	okurō	okurumai
		II	okuru darō	okuranai darō
	FORMAL	I	okurimashō	okurimasumai
		II	okuru deshō	okuranai deshō
Provisional	**INFORMAL**		okureba	okuranakereba
	FORMAL		okurimaseba	okurimasen nara
			okurimasureba	
Gerund	**INFORMAL**	I	okutte	okuranai de
		II		okuranakute
	FORMAL		okurimashite	okurimasen de
Past Ind.	**INFORMAL**		okutta	okuranakatta
	FORMAL		okurimashita	okurimasen deshita
Past Presump.	**INFORMAL**		okuttarō	okuranakattarō
			okutta darō	okuranakatta darō
	FORMAL		okurimashitarō	okurimasen deshitarō
			okutta deshō	okuranakatta deshō
Conditional	**INFORMAL**		okuttara	okuranakattara
	FORMAL		okurimashitara	okurimasen deshitara
Alternative	**INFORMAL**		okuttari	okuranakattari
	FORMAL		okurimashitari	okurimasen deshitari

		INFORMAL AFFIRMATIVE INDICATIVE
Passive		okurareru
Potential		okureru
Causative		okuraseru
Causative Pass.		okuraserareru
Honorific	I	ookuri ni naru
	II	ookuri nasaru
Humble	I	ookuri suru
	II	ookuri itasu

O

omo.u おもう／思う

omoi

to think, to feel, to believe, to consider, to expect, to regard   TRANSITIVE

			AFFIRMATIVE	**NEGATIVE**
Indicative	**INFORMAL**		omou	omowanai
	FORMAL		omoimasu	omoimasen
Imperative	**INFORMAL**	I	omoe	omou na
		II	omoinasai	omoinasaru na
		III	omotte kudasai	omowanai de kudasai
	FORMAL		oomoi nasaimase	oomoi nasaimasu na
Presumptive	**INFORMAL**	I	omoō	omoumai
		II	omou darō	omowanai darō
	FORMAL	I	omoimashō	omoimasumai
		II	omou deshō	omowanai deshō
Provisional	**INFORMAL**		omoeba	omowanakereba
	FORMAL		omoimaseba	omoimasen nara
			omoimasureba	
Gerund	**INFORMAL**	I	omotte	omowanai de
		II		omowanakute
	FORMAL		omoimashite	omoimasen de
Past Ind.	**INFORMAL**		omotta	omowanakatta
	FORMAL		omoimashita	omoimasen deshita
Past Presump.	**INFORMAL**		omottarō	omowanakattarō
			omotta darō	omowanakatta darō
	FORMAL		omoimashitarō	omoimasen deshitarō
			omotta deshō	omowanakatta deshō
Conditional	**INFORMAL**		omottara	omowanakattara
	FORMAL		omoimashitara	omoimasen deshitara
Alternative	**INFORMAL**		omottari	omowanakattari
	FORMAL		omoimashitari	omoimasen deshitari

		INFORMAL AFFIRMATIVE INDICATIVE	
Passive		omowareru	
Potential		omoeru	
Causative		omowaseru	
Causative Pass.		omowaserareru	
Honorific	I	oboshimesu	I oomoi ni naru
	II		II oomoi nasaru
Humble	I		I oomoi suru
	II		II oomoi itasu

AN ESSENTIAL 55 VERB

412

Omou
おもう／思う

to think, to feel, to believe,
to consider, to expect, to regard

Omou is a useful verb you need often. If you think about it, you'll see it's used in a great number of everyday situations and expressions.

Sentences Using *Omou*

Rainen, Nihon ni ikō to omoimasu.
来年、日本に行こうと思います。
I think I'll go to Japan next year.

Kanojo no iken ga tadashii to wa omoimasen.
彼女の意見が正しいとは思いません。
I don't think her opinion is correct.

Ikura omottemo omoidasemasen deshita.
いくら思っても思い出せませんでした。
No matter how much I thought, I couldn't remember.

Ano seijika wa tsugi no shushō da to omowarete iru.
あの政治家は次ぎの首相だと思われている。
That politician is expected to be the next prime minister.

Words and Expressions Related to This Verb

omoitatsu　思い立つ
to decide to do

omowazu　思わず
in spite of oneself

omoichigai　思い違い
misunderstanding

omou zonbun　思う存分
as much as one wants

O

Proverb

Omou nenriki, iwa o mo tōsu.
思う念力、岩をも通す。
*Where there's a will, there's a way.
(The power of will penetrates even a rock.)*

Omoitatsu hi ga kichijitsu.
思い立つ日が吉日。
Strike while the iron is hot. (The day you decide to do things is the auspicious day.)

ore.ru おれる／折れる

to be broken, to snap, to give in

			AFFIRMATIVE	NEGATIVE
Indicative	**INFORMAL**		oreru	orenai
	FORMAL		oremasu	oremasen
Imperative	**INFORMAL**	I	orero	oreru na
		II	orenasai	orenasaru na
		III	orete kudasai	orenai de kudasai
	FORMAL		oore nasaimase	oore nasaimasu na
Presumptive	**INFORMAL**	I	oreyō	orerumai
		II	oreru darō	orenai darō
	FORMAL	I	oremashō	oremasumai
		II	oreru deshō	orenai deshō
Provisional	**INFORMAL**		orereba	orenakereba
	FORMAL		oremaseba	oremasen nara
			oremasureba	
Gerund	**INFORMAL**	I	orete	orenai de
		II		orenakute
	FORMAL		oremashite	oremasen de
Past Ind.	**INFORMAL**		oreta	orenakatta
	FORMAL		oremashita	oremasen deshita
Past Presump.	**INFORMAL**		oretarō	orenakattarō
			oreta darō	orenakatta darō
	FORMAL		oremashitarō	oremasen deshitarō
			oreta deshō	orenakatta deshō
Conditional	**INFORMAL**		oretara	orenakattara
	FORMAL		oremashitara	oremasen deshitara
Alternative	**INFORMAL**		oretari	orenakattari
	FORMAL		oremashitari	oremasen deshitari

		INFORMAL AFFIRMATIVE INDICATIVE
Passive		
Potential		
Causative		oresaseru
Causative Pass.		oresaserareru
Honorific	I	oore ni naru
	II	oore nasaru
Humble	I	oore suru
	II	oore itasu

おりる／降りる／下りる　ori.ru
to get off, to go down

			AFFIRMATIVE	NEGATIVE
Indicative	INFORMAL		oriru	orinai
	FORMAL		orimasu	orimasen
Imperative	INFORMAL	I	oriro	oriru na
		II	orinasai	orinasaru na
		III	orite kudasai	orinai de kudasai
	FORMAL		oori nasaimase	oori nasaimasu na
Presumptive	INFORMAL	I	oriyō	orimai
		II	oriru darō	orinai darō
	FORMAL	I	orimashō	orimasumai
		II	oriru deshō	orinai deshō
Provisional	INFORMAL		orireba	orinakereba
	FORMAL		orimaseba	orirnasen nara
			orimasureba	
Gerund	INFORMAL	I	orite	orinai de
		II		orinakute
	FORMAL		orimashite	orimasen de
Past Ind.	INFORMAL		orita	orinakatta
	FORMAL		orimashita	orimasen deshita
Past Presump.	INFORMAL		oritarō	orinakattarō
			orita darō	orinakatta darō
	FORMAL		orimashitarō	orimasen deshitarō
			orita deshō	orinakatta deshō
Conditional	INFORMAL		oritara	orinakattara
	FORMAL		orimashitara	orimasen deshitara
Alternative	INFORMAL		oritari	orinakattari
	FORMAL		orimashitari	orimasen deshitari

			INFORMAL AFFIRMATIVE INDICATIVE
Passive			orirareru
Potential			orirareru
Causative			orisaseru
Causative Pass.			orisaserareru
Honorific	I		oori ni naru
	II		oori nasaru
Humble	I		oori suru
	II		oori itasu

AN ESSENTIAL 55 VERB

Oriru 降りる

to get off, to go down

Oriru is a verb you need as you travel around Japan, getting off and out of trains, planes, and automobiles, and going down staircases, elevators, and escalators!

Sentences Using *Oriru*

Erebētā wa nana kai de orimasu.
エレベーターは七階で降ります。
You should get off the elevator at the seventh floor.

Ginza de orite Hibiya sen ni
norikaeru to benri desu.
銀座で降りて日比谷線に乗り換えると
便利です。
It's convenient if you get off at Ginza and transfer to the Hibiya Line.

Takushī o oritara, ame ga
furihajimeta.
タクシーを降りたら雨が降り始めた。
The rain started falling when I got out of the cab.

Kaidan o oriru to, sugu migi gawa
desu.
階段を下りると、直ぐ右側です。
If you go down the stairs, it's just there on your right.

Ii resutoran ga aru kara tsugi no eki
de oriyō.
いいレストランがあるから次ぎの駅で
降りよう。
Let's get off at the next station because there's a nice restaurant there.

Words and Expressions Related to This Verb

orosu　降ろす
to disembark

kōsha jō　降車場
disembarking zone

kōsha guchi　降車口
the exit

おさえる／抑える／押さえる **osae.ru**

TRANSITIVE *to restrain, to control, to press down*

			AFFIRMATIVE	NEGATIVE
Indicative	**INFORMAL**		osaeru	osaenai
	FORMAL		osaemasu	osaemasen
Imperative	**INFORMAL**	I	osaero	osaeru na
		II	osaenasai	osaenasaru na
		III	osaete kudasai	osaenai de kudasai
	FORMAL		oosae nasaimase	oosae nasaimasu na
Presumptive	**INFORMAL**	I	osaeyō	osaemai
		II	osaeru darō	osaenai darō
	FORMAL	I	osaemashō	osaemasumai
		II	osaeru deshō	osaenai deshō
Provisional	**INFORMAL**		osaereba	osaenakereba
	FORMAL		osaemaseba	osaemasen nara
			osaemasureba	
Gerund	**INFORMAL**	I	osaete	osaenai de
		II		osaenakute
	FORMAL		osaemashite	osaemasen de
Past Ind.	**INFORMAL**		osaeta	osaenakatta
	FORMAL		osaemashita	osaemasen deshita
Past Presump.	**INFORMAL**		osaetarō	osaenakattarō
			osaeta darō	osaenakatta darō
	FORMAL		osaemashitarō	osaemasen deshitarō
			osaeta deshō	osaenakatta deshō
Conditional	**INFORMAL**		osaetara	osaenakattara
	FORMAL		osaemashitara	osaemasen deshitara
Alternative	**INFORMAL**		osaetari	osaenakattari
	FORMAL		osaemashitari	osaemasen deshitari

			INFORMAL AFFIRMATIVE INDICATIVE
Passive			osaerareru
Potential			osaerareru
Causative			osaesaseru
Causative Pass.			osaesaserareru
Honorific		I	oosae ni naru
		II	oosae nasaru
Humble		I	oosae suru
		II	oosae itasu

O

oshie.ru おしえる／教える

oshie

to teach, to instruct, to guide, to inform, to show TRANSITIVE

			AFFIRMATIVE	**NEGATIVE**
Indicative	**INFORMAL**		oshieru	oshienai
	FORMAL		oshiemasu	oshiemasen
Imperative	**INFORMAL**	I	oshiero	oshieru na
		II	oshienasai	oshienasaru na
		III	oshiete kudasai	oshienai de kudasai
	FORMAL		ooshie nasaimase	ooshie nasaimasu na
Presumptive	**INFORMAL**	I	oshieyō	oshiemai
		II	oshieru darō	oshienai darō
	FORMAL	I	oshiemashō	oshiemasumai
		II	oshieru deshō	oshienai deshō
Provisional	**INFORMAL**		oshiereba	oshienakereba
	FORMAL		oshiemaseba	oshiemasen nara
			oshiemasureba	
Gerund	**INFORMAL**	I	oshiete	oshienai de
		II		oshienakute
	FORMAL		oshiemashite	oshiemasen de
Past Ind.	**INFORMAL**		oshieta	oshienakatta
	FORMAL		oshiemashita	oshiemasen deshita
Past Presump.	**INFORMAL**		oshietarō	oshienakattarō
			oshieta darō	oshienakatta darō
	FORMAL		oshiemashitarō	oshiemasen deshitarō
			oshieta deshō	oshienakatta deshō
Conditional	**INFORMAL**		oshietara	oshienakattara
	FORMAL		oshiemashitara	oshiemasen deshitara
Alternative	**INFORMAL**		oshietari	oshienakattari
	FORMAL		oshiemashitari	oshiemasen deshitari

		INFORMAL AFFIRMATIVE INDICATIVE
Passive		oshierareru
Potential		oshierareru
Causative		oshiesaseru
Causative Pass.		oshiesaserareru
Honorific	I	ooshie ni naru
	II	ooshie nasaru
Humble	I	ooshie suru
	II	ooshie itasu

AN ESSENTIAL 55 VERB

AN ESSENTIAL 55 VERB

Oshieru 教える

to teach, to instruct, to guide,
to inform, to show

Oshieru is a verb used in many common everyday situations. You may inform people of things, show someone the way, teach a friend a game, instruct an employee to prepare a report, or guide someone to your favorite restaurant—the possibilities are endless!

Sentences Using *Oshieru*

Musuko ga go sai ni nattara yakyū o oshiemasu.
息子が五歳になったら野球を教えます。
I'll teach my son baseball when he becomes 5 years old.

Kisha no eki e wa dō ikeba ii ka oshiete kudasai.
汽車の駅へはどう行けばいいか教えてください。
Could you show me how to get to the train station?

Kare ni go o oshietara, sugu ni oboemashita.
彼に碁を教えたら直ぐに覚えました。
When I taught him the board game "go," he learned it in no time.

Haha ni ikebana o oshieraremashita.
母に生け花を教えられました。
I was taught ikebana by my mother.

Nihon go ga naraitai nara, oshiete agemasu yo.
日本語が習いたいなら教えてあげますよ。
If you want to learn Japanese, I'll teach you.

O

Words and Expressions Related to This Verb

kyōiku suru 教育する
to educate

osowaru 教わる
to be taught

sekkyō suru 説教する
to preach, to scold

oshie 教え
teachings, a lesson

Proverb

Oshiuru wa manabu no nakaba.
教うるは学ぶの半ば。
Teaching others teaches yourself.
(Teaching is half of learning.)

to regret, to begrudge, to be reluctant   TRANSITIVE

			AFFIRMATIVE	NEGATIVE
Indicative	**INFORMAL**		oshimu	oshimanai
	FORMAL		oshimimasu	oshimimasen
Imperative	**INFORMAL**	I	oshime	oshimu na
		II	oshiminasai	oshiminasaru na
		III	oshinde kudasai	oshimanai de kudasai
	FORMAL		ooshimi nasaimase	ooshimi nasaimasu na
Presumptive	**INFORMAL**	I	oshimō	oshimumai
		II	oshimu darō	oshimanai darō
	FORMAL	I	oshimimashō	oshimimasumai
		II	oshimu deshō	oshimanai deshō
Provisional	**INFORMAL**		oshimeba	oshimanakereba
	FORMAL		oshimimaseba	oshimimasen nara
			oshimimasureba	
Gerund	**INFORMAL**	I	oshinde	oshimanai de
		II		oshimanakute
	FORMAL		oshimimashite	oshimimasen de
Past Ind.	**INFORMAL**		oshinda	oshimanakatta
	FORMAL		oshimimashita	oshimimasen deshita
Past Presump.	**INFORMAL**		oshindarō	oshimanakattarō
			oshinda darō	oshimanakatta darō
	FORMAL		oshimimashitarō	oshimimasen deshitarō
			oshinda deshō	oshimanakatta deshō
Conditional	**INFORMAL**		oshindara	oshimanakattara
	FORMAL		oshimimashitara	oshimimasen deshitara
Alternative	**INFORMAL**		oshindari	oshimanakattari
	FORMAL		oshimimashitari	oshimimasen deshitari

		INFORMAL AFFIRMATIVE INDICATIVE
Passive		oshimareru
Potential		oshimeru
Causative		oshimaseru
Causative Pass.		oshimaserareru
Honorific	I	ooshimi ni naru
	II	ooshimi nasaru
Humble	I	ooshimi suru
	II	ooshimi itasu

			AFFIRMATIVE	**NEGATIVE**
Indicative	**INFORMAL**		osoreru	osorenai
	FORMAL		osoremasu	osoremasen
Imperative	**INFORMAL**	I	osorero	osoreru na
		II	osorenasai	osorenasaru na
		III	osorete kudasai	osorenai de kudasai
	FORMAL		oosore nasaimase	oosore nasaimasu na
Presumptive	**INFORMAL**	I	osoreyō	osoremai
		II	osoreru darō	osorenai darō
	FORMAL	I	osoremashō	osoremasumai
		II	osoreru deshō	osorenai deshō
Provisional	**INFORMAL**		osorereba	osorenakereba
	FORMAL		osoremaseba	osoremasen nara
			osoremasureba	
Gerund	**INFORMAL**	I	osorete	osorenai de
		II		osorenakute
	FORMAL		osoremashite	osoremasen de
Past Ind.	**INFORMAL**		osoreta	osorenakatta
	FORMAL		osoremashita	osoremasen deshita
Past Presump.	**INFORMAL**		osoretarō	osorenakattarō
			osoreta darō	osorenakatta darō
	FORMAL		osoremashitarō	osoremasen deshitarō
			osoreta deshō	osorenakatta deshō
Conditional	**INFORMAL**		osoretara	osorenakattara
	FORMAL		osoremashitara	osoremasen deshitara
Alternative	**INFORMAL**		osoretari	osorenakattari
	FORMAL		osoremashitari	osoremasen deshitari

		INFORMAL AFFIRMATIVE INDICATIVE
Passive		osorerareru
Potential		osorerareru
Causative		osoresaseru
Causative Pass.		osoresaserareru
Honorific	I	oosore ni naru
	II	oosore nasaru
Humble	I	oosore suru
	II	oosore itasu

O

oso.u おそう／襲う   **osoi**

to attack, to raid   TRANSITIVE

			AFFIRMATIVE	NEGATIVE
Indicative	**INFORMAL**		osou	osowanai
	FORMAL		osoimasu	osoimasen
Imperative	**INFORMAL**	I	osoe	osou na
		II	osoinasai	osoinasaru na
		III	osotte kudasai	osowanai de kudasai
	FORMAL		oosoi nasaimase	oosoi nasaimasu na
Presumptive	**INFORMAL**	I	osoō	osoumai
		II	osou darō	osowanai darō
	FORMAL	I	osoimashō	osoimasumai
		II	osou deshō	osowanai deshō
Provisional	**INFORMAL**		osoeba	osowanakereba
	FORMAL		osoimaseba osoimasureba	osoimasen nara
Gerund	**INFORMAL**	I	osotte	osowanai de
		II		osowanakute
	FORMAL		osoimashite	osoimasen de
Past Ind.	**INFORMAL**		osotta	osowanakatta
	FORMAL		osoimashita	osoimasen deshita
Past Presump.	**INFORMAL**		osottarō osotta darō	osowanakattarō osowanakatta darō
	FORMAL		osoimashitarō osotta deshō	osoimasen deshitarō osowanakatta deshō
Conditional	**INFORMAL**		osottara	osowanakattara
	FORMAL		osoimashitara	osoimasen deshitara
Alternative	**INFORMAL**		osottari	osowanakattari
	FORMAL		osoimashitari	osoimasen deshitari

		INFORMAL AFFIRMATIVE INDICATIVE
Passive		osowareru
Potential		osoeru
Causative		osowaseru
Causative Pass.		osowaserareru
Honorific	I	oosoi ni naru
	II	oosoi nasaru
Humble	I	oosoi suru
	II	oosoi itasu

おっしゃる **osshar.u**

TRANSITIVE   *to say* (honorific)

			AFFIRMATIVE	NEGATIVE
Indicative	**INFORMAL**		ossharu	ossharanai
	FORMAL		osshaimasu	osshaimasen
Imperative	**INFORMAL**	I	osshai	ossharu na
		II	osshainasai	osshainasaru na
		III	osshatte kudasai	ossharanai de kudasai
	FORMAL		osshaimase	osshaimasu na
Presumptive	**INFORMAL**	I	ossharō	ossharumai
		II	ossharu darō	ossharanai darō
	FORMAL	I	osshaimashō	osshaimasumai
		II	ossharu deshō	ossharanai deshō
Provisional	**INFORMAL**		osshareba	ossharanakereba
	FORMAL		osshaimaseba	osshaimasen nara
			osshaimasureba	
Gerund	**INFORMAL**	I	osshatte	ossharanai de
		II		ossharanakute
	FORMAL		osshaimashite	osshaimasen de
Past Ind.	**INFORMAL**		osshatta	ossharanakatta
	FORMAL		osshaimashita	osshaimasen deshita
Past Presump.	**INFORMAL**		osshattarō	ossharanakattarō
			osshatta darō	ossharanakatta darō
	FORMAL		osshaimashitarō	osshaimasen deshitarō
			osshatta deshō	ossharanakatta deshō
Conditional	**INFORMAL**		osshattara	ossharanakattara
	FORMAL		osshaimashitara	osshaimasen deshitara
Alternative	**INFORMAL**		osshattari	ossharanakattari
	FORMAL		osshaimashitari	osshaimasen deshitari

			INFORMAL AFFIRMATIVE INDICATIVE
Passive			
Potential			osshareru
Causative			
Causative Pass.			
Honorific		I	osshai ni naru
		II	osshai nasaru
Humble		I	
		II	

O

to push, to press   TRANSITIVE

			AFFIRMATIVE	NEGATIVE
Indicative	**INFORMAL**		osu	osanai
	FORMAL		oshimasu	oshimasen
Imperative	**INFORMAL**	I	ose	osu na
		II	oshinasai	oshinasaru na
		III	oshite kudasai	osanai de kudasai
	FORMAL		ooshi nasaimase	ooshi nasaimasu na
Presumptive	**INFORMAL**	I	osō	osumai
		II	osu darō	osanai darō
	FORMAL	I	oshimashō	oshimasumai
		II	osu deshō	osanai deshō
Provisional	**INFORMAL**		oseba	osanakereba
	FORMAL		oshimaseba	oshimasen nara
			oshimasureba	
Gerund	**INFORMAL**	I	oshite	osanai de
		II		osanakute
	FORMAL		oshimashite	oshimasen de
Past Ind.	**INFORMAL**		oshita	osanakatta
	FORMAL		oshimashita	oshimasen deshita
Past Presump.	**INFORMAL**		oshitarō	osanakattarō
			oshita darō	osanakatta darō
	FORMAL		oshimashitarō	oshimasen deshitarō
			oshita deshō	osanakatta deshō
Conditional	**INFORMAL**		oshitara	osanakattara
	FORMAL		oshimashitara	oshimasen deshitara
Alternative	**INFORMAL**		oshitari	osanakattari
	FORMAL		oshimashitari	oshimasen deshitari

		INFORMAL AFFIRMATIVE INDICATIVE
Passive		osareru
Potential		oseru
Causative		osaseru
Causative Pass.		osaserareru
Honorific	I	ooshi ni naru
	II	ooshi nasaru
Humble	I	ooshi suru
	II	ooshi itasu

おとる／劣る　**otor.u**

to be inferior to, to be worse than

			AFFIRMATIVE	NEGATIVE
Indicative	**INFORMAL**		otoru	otoranai
	FORMAL		otorimasu	otorimasen
Imperative	**INFORMAL**	I	otore	otoru na
		II	otorinasai	otorinasaru na
		III	ototte kudasai	otoranai de kudasai
	FORMAL		ootori nasaimase	ootori nasaimasu na
Presumptive	**INFORMAL**	I	otorō	otorumai
		II	otoru darō	otoranai darō
	FORMAL	I	otorimashō	otorimasumai
		II	otoru deshō	otoranai deshō
Provisional	**INFORMAL**		otoreba	otoranakereba
	FORMAL		otorimaseba	otorimasen nara
			otorimasureba	
Gerund	**INFORMAL**	I	ototte	otoranai de
		II		otoranakute
	FORMAL		otorimashite	otorimasen de
Past Ind.	**INFORMAL**		ototta	otoranakatta
	FORMAL		otorimashita	otorimasen deshita
Past Presump.	**INFORMAL**		otottarō	otoranakattarō
			ototta darō	otoranakatta darō
	FORMAL		otorimashitarō	otorimasen deshitarō
			ototta deshō	otoranakatta deshō
Conditional	**INFORMAL**		otottara	otoranakattara
	FORMAL		otorimashitara	otorimasen deshitara
Alternative	**INFORMAL**		otottari	otoranakattari
	FORMAL		otorimashitari	otorimasen deshitari

		INFORMAL AFFIRMATIVE INDICATIVE
Passive		otorareru
Potential		otoreru
Causative		otoraseru
Causative Pass.		otoraserareru
Honorific	I	ootori ni naru
	II	ootori nasaru
Humble	I	
	II	

O

otos.u おとす／落とす   otoshi

to drop, to lose   TRANSITIVE

			AFFIRMATIVE	NEGATIVE
Indicative	**INFORMAL**		otosu	otosanai
	FORMAL		otoshimasu	otoshimasen
Imperative	**INFORMAL**	I	otose	otosu na
		II	otoshinasai	otoshinasaru na
		III	otoshite kudasai	otosanai de kudasai
	FORMAL		ootoshi nasaimase	ootoshi nasaimasu na
Presumptive	**INFORMAL**	I	otosō	otosumai
		II	otosu darō	otosanai darō
	FORMAL	I	otoshimashō	otoshimasumai
		II	otosu deshō	otosanai deshō
Provisional	**INFORMAL**		otoseba	otosanakereba
	FORMAL		otoshimaseba	otoshimasen nara
			otoshimasureba	
Gerund	**INFORMAL**	I	otoshite	otosanai de
		II		otosanakute
	FORMAL		otoshimashite	otoshimasen de
Past Ind.	**INFORMAL**		otoshita	otosanakatta
	FORMAL		otoshimashita	otoshimasen deshita
Past Presump.	**INFORMAL**		otoshitarō	otosanakattarō
			otoshita darō	otosanakatta darō
	FORMAL		otoshimashitarō	otoshimasen deshitarō
			otoshita deshō	otosanakatta deshō
Conditional	**INFORMAL**		otoshitara	otosanakattara
	FORMAL		otoshimashitara	otoshimasen deshitara
Alternative	**INFORMAL**		otoshitari	otosanakattari
	FORMAL		otoshimashitari	otoshimasen deshitari

			INFORMAL AFFIRMATIVE INDICATIVE
Passive			otosareru
Potential			otoseru
Causative			otosaseru
Causative Pass.			otosaserareru
Honorific		I	ootoshi ni naru
		II	ootoshi nasaru
Humble		I	ootoshi suru
		II	ootoshi itasu

TRANSITIVE　　*to drive away, to chase, to pursue*

			AFFIRMATIVE	NEGATIVE
Indicative	**INFORMAL**		ou	owanai
	FORMAL		oimasu	oimasen
Imperative	**INFORMAL**	I	oe	ou na
		II	oinasai	oinasaru na
		III	otte kudasai	owanai de kudasai
	FORMAL		ooi nasaimase	ooi nasaimasu na
Presumptive	**INFORMAL**	I	oō	oumai
		II	ou darō	owanai darō
	FORMAL	I	oimashō	oimasumai
		II	ou deshō	owanai deshō
Provisional	**INFORMAL**		oeba	owanakereba
	FORMAL		oimaseba	oimasen nara
			oimasureba	
Gerund	**INFORMAL**	I	otte	owanai de
		II		owanakute
	FORMAL		oimashite	oimasen de
Past Ind.	**INFORMAL**		otta	owanakatta
	FORMAL		oimashita	oimasen deshita
Past Presump.	**INFORMAL**		ottarō	owanakattarō
			otta darō	owanakatta darō
	FORMAL		oimashitarō	oimasen deshitarō
			otta deshō	owanakatta deshō
Conditional	**INFORMAL**		ottara	owanakattara
	FORMAL		oimashitara	oimasen deshitara
Alternative	**INFORMAL**		ottari	owanakattari
	FORMAL		oimashitari	oimasen deshitari

			INFORMAL AFFIRMATIVE INDICATIVE
Passive			owareru
Potential			oeru
Causative			owaseru
Causative Pass.			owaserareru
Honorific		I	ooi ni naru
		II	ooi nasaru
Humble		I	ooi suru
		II	ooi itasu

427

to be indebted, to assume responsibility, to bear   TRANSITIVE

			AFFIRMATIVE	NEGATIVE
Indicative	INFORMAL		ou	owanai
	FORMAL		oimasu	oimasen
Imperative	INFORMAL	I	oe	ou na
		II	oinasai	oinasaru na
		III	otte kudasai	owanai de kudasai
	FORMAL		ooi nasaimase	ooi nasaimasu na
Presumptive	INFORMAL	I	oō	oumai
		II	ou darō	owanai darō
	FORMAL	I	oimashō	oimasumai
		II	ou deshō	owanai deshō
Provisional	INFORMAL		oeba	owanakereba
	FORMAL		oimaseba	oimasen nara
			oimasureba	
Gerund	INFORMAL	I	otte	owanai de
		II		owanakute
	FORMAL		oimashite	oimasen de
Past Ind.	INFORMAL		otta	owanakatta
	FORMAL		oimashita	oimasen deshita
Past Presump.	INFORMAL		ottarō	owanakattarō
			otta darō	owanakatta darō
	FORMAL		oimashitarō	oimasen deshitarō
			otta deshō	owanakatta deshō
Conditional	INFORMAL		ottara	owanakattara
	FORMAL		oimashitara	oimasen deshitara
Alternative	INFORMAL		ottari	owanakattari
	FORMAL		oimashitari	oimasen deshitari

		INFORMAL AFFIRMATIVE INDICATIVE
Passive		owareru
Potential		oeru
Causative		owaseru
Causative Pass.		owaserareru
Honorific	I	ooi ni naru
	II	ooi nasaru
Humble	I	ooi suru
	II	ooi itasu

to end, to be finished, to be over

			AFFIRMATIVE	NEGATIVE
Indicative	**INFORMAL**		owaru	owaranai
	FORMAL		owarimasu	owarimasen
Imperative	**INFORMAL**	I	oware	owaru na
		II		
		III	owatte kudasai	owaranai de kudasai
	FORMAL			
Presumptive	**INFORMAL**	I	owarō	owarumai
		II	owaru darō	owaranai darō
	FORMAL	I	owarimashō	owarimasumai
		II	owaru deshō	owaranai deshō
Provisional	**INFORMAL**		owareba	owaranakereba
	FORMAL		owarimaseba	owarimasen nara
			owarimasureba	
Gerund	**INFORMAL**	I	owatte	owaranai de
		II		owaranakute
	FORMAL		owarimashite	owarimasen de
Past Ind.	**INFORMAL**		owatta	owaranakatta
	FORMAL		owarimashita	owarimasen deshita
Past Presump.	**INFORMAL**		owattarō	owaranakattarō
			owatta darō	owaranakatta darō
	FORMAL		owarimashitarō	owarimasen deshitarō
			owatta deshō	owaranakatta deshō
Conditional	**INFORMAL**		owattara	owaranakattara
	FORMAL		owarimashitara	owarimasen deshitara
Alternative	**INFORMAL**		owattari	owaranakattari
	FORMAL		owarimashitari	owarimasen deshitari

		INFORMAL AFFIRMATIVE INDICATIVE
Passive		owareru
Potential		owaraseru
Causative		owaraseru
Causative Pass.		owaraserareru
Honorific	I	oowari ni naru
	II	oowari nasaru
Humble	I	
	II	

AN ESSENTIAL
55 VERB

Owaru 終わる

Sentences Using *Owaru*

Yūbe no yakyū no shiai wa hikiwake ni owarimashita.
夕べの野球の試合は引き分けに終わりました。
The baseball game last night ended in a tie.

Oji wa ban gohan ga owaru to sugu ni nemasu.
叔父は晩ご飯が終わると直ぐに寝ます。
My uncle goes to sleep right after dinner is over.

Sono kōen wa ni jikan de owaru deshō.
その講演は２時間で終わるでしょう。
The lecture will be over in two hours.

Natsu ga owatta hazu nanoni, mada atsui desu.
夏が終わったはずなのに、まだ暑いです。
Although summer is supposed to be over, it's still hot.

Yūshoku ga owattemo, mada onaka ga suite imasu.
夕食が終わっても、まだお腹がすいています。
Although dinner is finished, I'm still hungry.

to end, to be finished, to be over

Owaru is a verb you can't do without as you describe all the situations or events that have a beginning and an end. As we say in English, when it's over, it's over!

Words and Expressions Related to This Verb

shūryō suru　終了する
to end, to be over

shūshi suru　終始する
to remain the same from beginning to end

ichibu shijū　一部始終
all the details

Proverb

Owari yokereba subete yoshi.
終わりよければ総て良し。
All's well that ends well. (If the end is good, everything is good.)

およぶ／及ぶ　oyob.u

to reach, to extend to, to amount to, to refer to

			AFFIRMATIVE	NEGATIVE
Indicative	**INFORMAL**		oyobu	oyobanai
	FORMAL		oyobimasu	oyobimasen
Imperative	**INFORMAL**	I	oyobe	oyobu na
		II		
		III	oyonde kudasai	oyobanai de kudasai
	FORMAL			
Presumptive	**INFORMAL**	I	oyobō	oyobumai
		II	oyobu darō	oyobanai darō
	FORMAL	I	oyobimashō	oyobimasumai
		II	oyobu deshō	oyobanai deshō
Provisional	**INFORMAL**		oyobeba	oyobanakereba
	FORMAL		oyobimaseba	oyobimasen nara
			oyobimasureba	
Gerund	**INFORMAL**	I	oyonde	oyobanai de
		II		oyobanakute
	FORMAL		oyobimashite	oyobimasen de
Past Ind.	**INFORMAL**		oyonda	oyobanakatta
	FORMAL		oyobimashita	oyobimasen deshita
Past Presump.	**INFORMAL**		oyondarō	oyobanakattarō
			oyonda darō	oyobanakatta darō
	FORMAL		oyobimashitarō	oyobimasen deshitarō
			oyonda deshō	oyobanakatta deshō
Conditional	**INFORMAL**		oyondara	oyobanakattara
	FORMAL		oyobimashitara	oyobimasen deshitara
Alternative	**INFORMAL**		oyondari	oyobanakattari
	FORMAL		oyobimashitari	oyobimasen deshitari

		INFORMAL AFFIRMATIVE INDICATIVE
Passive		oyobareru
Potential		oyoberu
Causative		oyobaseru
Causative Pass.		oyobaserareru
Honorific	I	ooyobi ni naru
	II	ooyobi nasaru
Humble	I	
	II	

O

			AFFIRMATIVE	NEGATIVE
Indicative	**INFORMAL**		oyogu	oyoganai
	FORMAL		oyogimasu	oyogimasen
Imperative	**INFORMAL**	I	oyoge	oyogu na
		II	oyoginasai	oyoginasaru na
		III	oyoide kudasai	oyoganai de kudasai
	FORMAL		ooyogi nasaimase	ooyogi nasaimasu na
Presumptive	**INFORMAL**	I	oyogō	oyogumai
		II	oyogu darō	oyoganai darō
	FORMAL	I	oyogimashō	oyogimasumai
		II	oyogu deshō	oyoganai deshō
Provisional	**INFORMAL**		oyogeba	oyoganakereba
	FORMAL		oyogimaseba	oyogimasen nara
			oyogimasureba	
Gerund	**INFORMAL**	I	oyoide	oyoganai de
		II		oyoganakute
	FORMAL		oyogimashite	oyogimasen de
Past Ind.	**INFORMAL**		oyoida	oyoganakatta
	FORMAL		oyogimashita	oyogimasen deshita
Past Presump.	**INFORMAL**		oyoidarō	oyoganakattarō
			oyoida darō	oyoganakatta darō
	FORMAL		oyogimashitarō	oyogimasen deshitarō
			oyoida deshō	oyoganakatta deshō
Conditional	**INFORMAL**		oyoidara	oyoganakattara
	FORMAL		oyogimashitara	oyogimasen deshitara
Alternative	**INFORMAL**		oyoidari	oyoganakattari
	FORMAL		oyogimashitari	oyogimasen deshitari

			INFORMAL AFFIRMATIVE INDICATIVE
Passive			oyogareru
Potential			oyogeru
Causative			oyogaseru
Causative Pass.			oyogaserareru
Honorific		I	ooyogi ni naru
		II	ooyogi nasaru
Humble		I	
		II	

さだめる／定める　**sadame.ru**

TRANSITIVE　　*to decide, to establish*

			AFFIRMATIVE	NEGATIVE
Indicative	**INFORMAL**		sadameru	sadamenai
	FORMAL		sadamemasu	sadamemasen
Imperative	**INFORMAL**	I	sadamero	sadameru na
		II	sadamenasai	sadamenasaru na
		III	sadamete kudasai	sadamenai de kudasai
	FORMAL		osadame nasaimase	osadame nasaimasu na
Presumptive	**INFORMAL**	I	sadameyō	sadamemai
		II	sadameru darō	sadamenai darō
	FORMAL	I	sadamemashō	sadamemasumai
		II	sadameru deshō	sadamenai deshō
Provisional	**INFORMAL**		sadamereba	sadamenakereba
	FORMAL		sadamemaseba	sadamemasen nara
			sadamemasureba	
Gerund	**INFORMAL**	I	sadamete	sadamenai de
		II		sadamenakute
	FORMAL		sadamemashite	sadamemasen de
Past Ind.	**INFORMAL**		sadameta	sadamenakatta
	FORMAL		sadamamashita	sadamemasen deshita
Past Presump.	**INFORMAL**		sadametarō	sadamenakattarō
			sadameta darō	sadamenakatta darō
	FORMAL		sadamemashitarō	sadamemasen deshitarō
			sadameta deshō	sadamenakatta deshō
Conditional	**INFORMAL**		sadametara	sadamenakattara
	FORMAL		sadamemashitara	sadamemasen deshitara
Alternative	**INFORMAL**		sadametari	sadamenakattari
	FORMAL		sadamemashitari	sadamemasen deshitari

		INFORMAL AFFIRMATIVE INDICATIVE
Passive		sadamerareru
Potential		sadamerareru
Causative		sadamesaseru
Causative Pass.		sadamesaserareru
Honorific	I	osadame ni naru
	II	osadame nasaru
Humble	I	osadame suru
	II	osadame itasu

S

sagar.u　さがる／下がる

to fall, to drop, to hang, to leave

sagari

			AFFIRMATIVE	NEGATIVE
Indicative	**INFORMAL**		sagaru	sagaranai
	FORMAL		sagarimasu	sagarimasen
Imperative	**INFORMAL**	I	sagare	sagaru na
		II	sagarinasai	sagarinasaru na
		III	sadatte kudasai	sagaranai de kudasai
	FORMAL		osagari nasaimase	osagari nasaimasu na
Presumptive	**INFORMAL**	I	sagarō	sagarumai
		II	sagaru darō	sagaranai darō
	FORMAL	I	sagarimashō	sagarimasumai
		II	sagaru deshō	sagaranai deshō
Provisional	**INFORMAL**		sagareba	sagaranakereba
	FORMAL		sagarimaseba	sagarimasen nara
			sagarimasureba	
Gerund	**INFORMAL**	I	sagatte	sagaranai de
		II		sagaranakute
	FORMAL		sagarimashite	sagarimasen de
Past Ind.	**INFORMAL**		sagatta	sagaranakatta
	FORMAL		sagarimashita	sagarimasen deshita
Past Presump.	**INFORMAL**		sagattarō	sagaranakattarō
			sagatta darō	sagaranakatta darō
	FORMAL		sagarimashitarō	sagarimasen deshitarō
			sagatta deshō	sagaranakatta deshō
Conditional	**INFORMAL**		sagattara	sagaranakattara
	FORMAL		sagarimashitara	sagarimasen deshitara
Alternative	**INFORMAL**		sagattari	sagaranakattari
	FORMAL		sawagimashitari	sawagimasen deshitari

		INFORMAL AFFIRMATIVE INDICATIVE
Passive		
Potential		sagareru
Causative		sagaraseru
Causative Pass.		sagaraserareru
Honorific	I	osagari ni naru
	II	osagari nasaru
Humble	I	
	II	

さがす／探す　**sagas.u**

TRANSITIVE　　*to search for, to look for*

			AFFIRMATIVE	NEGATIVE
Indicative	**INFORMAL**		sagasu	sagasanai
	FORMAL		sagashimasu	sagashimasen
Imperative	**INFORMAL**	I	sagase	sagasu na
		II	sagashinasai	sagashinasaru na
		III	sagashite kudasai	sagasanai de kudasai
	FORMAL		osagashi nasaimase	osagashi nasaimasu na
Presumptive	**INFORMAL**	I	sagasō	sagasumai
		II	sagasu darō	sagasanai darō
	FORMAL	I	sagashimashō	sagashimasumai
		II	sagasu deshō	sagasanai deshō
Provisional	**INFORMAL**		sagaseba	sagasanakereba
	FORMAL		sagashimaseba	sagashimasen nara
			sagashimasureba	
Gerund	**INFORMAL**	I	sagashite	sagasanai de
		II		sagasanakute
	FORMAL		sagashimashite	sagashimasen de
Past Ind.	**INFORMAL**		sagashita	sagasanakatta
	FORMAL		sagashimashita	sagashimasen deshita
Past Presump.	**INFORMAL**		sagashitarō	sagasanakattarō
			sagashita darō	sagasanakatta darō
	FORMAL		sagashimashitarō	sagashimasen deshitarō
			sagashita deshō	sagasanakatta deshō
Conditional	**INFORMAL**		sagashitara	sagasanakattara
	FORMAL		sagashimashitara	sagashimasen deshitara
Alternative	**INFORMAL**		sagashitari	sagasanakattari
	FORMAL		sagashimashitari	sagashimasen deshitari

			INFORMAL AFFIRMATIVE INDICATIVE
Passive			sagasareru
Potential			sagaseru
Causative			sagasaseru
Causative Pass.			sagasaserareru
Honorific		I	osagashi ni naru
		II	osagashi nasaru
Humble		I	osagashi suru
		II	osagashi itasu

to lower, to hang, to clear   TRANSITIVE

			AFFIRMATIVE	**NEGATIVE**
Indicative	**INFORMAL**		sageru	sagenai
	FORMAL		sagemasu	sagemasen
Imperative	**INFORMAL**	I	sagero	sageru na
		II	sagenasai	sagenasaru na
		III	sagete kudasai	sagenai de kudasai
	FORMAL		osage nasaimase	osage nasaimasu na
Presumptive	**INFORMAL**	I	sageyō	sagerumai
		II	sageru darō	sagenai darō
	FORMAL	I	sagemashō	sagemasumai
		II	sageru deshō	sagenai deshō
Provisional	**INFORMAL**		sagereba	sagenakereba
	FORMAL		sagemaseba	sagemasen nara
			sagemasureba	
Gerund	**INFORMAL**	I	sagete	sagenai de
		II		sagenakute
	FORMAL		sagemashite	sagemasen de
Past Ind.	**INFORMAL**		sageta	sagenakatta
	FORMAL		sagemashita	sagemasen deshita
Past Presump.	**INFORMAL**		sagetarō	sagenakattarō
			sageta darō	sagenakatta darō
	FORMAL		sagemashitarō	sagemasen deshitarō
			sageta deshō	sagenakatta deshō
Conditional	**INFORMAL**		sagetara	sagenakattara
	FORMAL		sagemashitara	sagemasen deshitara
Alternative	**INFORMAL**		sagetari	sagenakattari
	FORMAL		sagemashitari	sagemasen deshitari

		INFORMAL AFFIRMATIVE INDICATIVE
Passive		sagerareru
Potential		sagerareru
Causative		sagesaseru
Causative Pass.		sagesaserareru
Honorific	I	osage ni naru
	II	osage nasaru
Humble	I	osage suru
	II	osage itasu

to shout, to cry out, to advocate

			AFFIRMATIVE	NEGATIVE
Indicative	**INFORMAL**		sakebu	sakebanai
	FORMAL		sakebimasu	sakebimasen
Imperative	**INFORMAL**	I	sakebe	sakebu na
		II	sakebinasai	sakebinasaru na
		III	sakende kudasai	sakebanai de kudasai
	FORMAL		osakebi nasaimase	osakebi nasaimasu na
Presumptive	**INFORMAL**	I	sakebō	sakebumai
		II	sakebu darō	sakebanai darō
	FORMAL	I	sakebimashō	sakebimasumai
		II	sakebu deshō	sakebanai deshō
Provisional	**INFORMAL**		sakebeba	sakebanakereba
	FORMAL		sakebimaseba	sakebimasen nara
			sakebimasureba	
Gerund	**INFORMAL**	I	sakende	sakebanai de
		II		sakebanakute
	FORMAL		sakebimashite	sakebimasen de
Past Ind.	**INFORMAL**		sakenda	sakebanakatta
	FORMAL		sakebimashita	sakebimasen deshita
Past Presump.	**INFORMAL**		sakendarō	sakebanakattarō
			sakenda darō	sakebanakatta darō
	FORMAL		sakebimashitarō	sakebimasen deshitarō
			sakenda deshō	sakebanakatta deshō
Conditional	**INFORMAL**		sakendara	sakebanakattara
	FORMAL		sakebimashitara	sakebimasen deshitara
Alternative	**INFORMAL**		sakendari	sakebanakattari
	FORMAL		sakebimashitari	sakebimasen deshitari

			INFORMAL AFFIRMATIVE INDICATIVE
Passive			sakebareru
Potential			sakeberu
Causative			sakebaseru
Causative Pass.			sakebaserareru
Honorific		I	osakebi ni naru
		II	osakebi nasaru
Humble		I	osakebi suru
		II	osakebi itasu

to avoid, to stay away from, to dodge　　　TRANSITIVE

			AFFIRMATIVE	**NEGATIVE**
Indicative	**INFORMAL**		sakeru	sakenai
	FORMAL		sakemasu	sakemasen
Imperative	**INFORMAL**	I	sakero	sakeru na
		II	sakenasai	sakenasaru na
		III	sakete kudasai	sakenai de kudasai
	FORMAL		osake nasaimase	osake nasaimasu na
Presumptive	**INFORMAL**	I	sakeyō	sakemai
		II	sakeru darō	sakenai darō
	FORMAL	I	sakemashō	sakemasumai
		II	sakeru deshō	sakenai deshō
Provisional	**INFORMAL**		sakereba	sakenakereba
	FORMAL		sakemaseba	sakemasen nara
			sakemasureba	
Gerund	**INFORMAL**	I	sakete	sakenai de
		II		sakenakute
	FORMAL		sakemashite	sakemasen de
Past Ind.	**INFORMAL**		saketa	sakenakatta
	FORMAL		sakemashita	sakemasen deshita
Past Presump.	**INFORMAL**		saketarō	sakenakattarō
			saketa darō	sakenakatta darō
	FORMAL		sakemashitarō	sakemasen deshitarō
			saketa deshō	sakenakatta deshō
Conditional	**INFORMAL**		saketara	sakenakattara
	FORMAL		sakemashitara	sakemasen deshitara
Alternative	**INFORMAL**		saketari	sakenakattari
	FORMAL		sakemashitari	sakemasen deshitari

		INFORMAL AFFIRMATIVE INDICATIVE
Passive		sakerareru
Potential		sakerareru
Causative		sakesaseru
Causative Pass.		sakesaserareru
Honorific	I	osake ni naru
	II	osake nasaru
Humble	I	osake suru
	II	osake itasu

saki   さく／咲く **sak.u**

to bloom

			AFFIRMATIVE	NEGATIVE
Indicative	INFORMAL		saku	sakanai
	FORMAL		sakimasu	sakimasen
Imperative	INFORMAL	I	sake	saku na
		II	sakinasai	sakinasaru na
		III	saite kudasai	sakanai de kudasai
	FORMAL			
Presumptive	INFORMAL	I	sakō	sakumai
		II	saku darō	sakanai darō
	FORMAL	I	sakimashō	sakimasumai
		II	saku deshō	sakanai deshō
Provisional	INFORMAL		sakeba	sakanakereba
	FORMAL		sakimaseba	sakimasen nara
			sakimasureba	
Gerund	INFORMAL	I	saite	sakanai de
		II		sakanakute
	FORMAL		sakimashite	sakimasen de
Past Ind.	INFORMAL		saita	sakanakatta
	FORMAL		sakimashita	sakimasen deshita
Past Presump.	INFORMAL		saitarō	sakanakattarō
			saita darō	sakanakatta darō
	FORMAL		sakimashitarō	sakimasen deshitarō
			saita deshō	sakanakatta deshō
Conditional	INFORMAL		saitara	sakanakattara
	FORMAL		sakimashitara	sakimasen deshitara
Alternative	INFORMAL		saitari	sakanakattari
	FORMAL		sakimashitari	sakimasen deshitari

		INFORMAL AFFIRMATIVE INDICATIVE
Passive		sakareru
Potential		sakeru
Causative		sakaseru
Causative Pass.		sakaserareru
Honorific	I	osaki ni naru
	II	osaki nasaru
Humble	I	
	II	

S

439

to hinder, to obstruct   TRANSITIVE

			AFFIRMATIVE	NEGATIVE
Indicative	**INFORMAL**		samatageru	samatagenai
	FORMAL		samatagemasu	samatagemasen
Imperative	**INFORMAL**	I	samatagero	samatageru na
		II	samatagenasai	samatagenasaru na
		III	samatagete kudasai	samatagenai de kudasai
	FORMAL		osamatage nasaimase	osamatage nasaimasu na
Presumptive	**INFORMAL**	I	samatageyō	samatagemai
		II	samatageru darō	samatagenai darō
	FORMAL	I	samatagemashō	samatagemasumai
		II	samatageru deshō	samatagenai deshō
Provisional	**INFORMAL**		samatagereba	samatagenakereba
	FORMAL		samatagemaseba	samatagemasen nara
			samatagemasureba	
Gerund	**INFORMAL**	I	samatagete	samatagenai de
		II		samatagenakute
	FORMAL		samatagemashite	samatagemasen de
Past Ind.	**INFORMAL**		samatageta	samatagenakatta
	FORMAL		samatagemashita	samatagemasen deshita
Past Presump.	**INFORMAL**		samatagetarō	samatagenakattarō
			samatageta darō	samatagenakatta darō
	FORMAL		samatagemashitarō	samatagemasen deshitarō
			samatageta deshō	samatagenakatta deshō
Conditional	**INFORMAL**		samatagetara	samatagenakattara
	FORMAL		samatagemashitara	samatagemasen deshitara
Alternative	**INFORMAL**		samatagetari	samatagenakattari
	FORMAL		samatagemashitari	samatagemasen deshitari

			INFORMAL AFFIRMATIVE INDICATIVE
Passive			samatagerareru
Potential			samatagerareru
Causative			samatagesaseru
Causative Pass.			samatagesaserareru
Honorific		I	osamatage ni naru
		II	osamatage nasaru
Humble		I	osamatage suru
		II	osamatage itasu

ささえる／支える　**sasae.ru**

TRANSITIVE　*to support*

			AFFIRMATIVE	**NEGATIVE**
Indicative	**INFORMAL**		sasaeru	sasaenai
	FORMAL		sasaemasu	sasaemasen
Imperative	**INFORMAL**	I	sasaero	sasaeru na
		II	sasaenasai	sasaenasaru na
		III	sasaete kudasai	sasaenai de kudasai
	FORMAL		osasae nasaimase	osasae nasaimasu na
Presumptive	**INFORMAL**	I	sasaeyō	sasaemai
		II	sasaeru darō	sasaenai darō
	FORMAL	I	sasaemashō	sasaemasumai
		II	sasaeru deshō	sasaenai deshō
Provisional	**INFORMAL**		sasaereba	sasaenakereba
	FORMAL		sasaemaseba	sasaemasen nara
			sasaemasureba	
Gerund	**INFORMAL**	I	sasaete	sasaenai de
		II		sasaenakute
	FORMAL		sasaemashite	sasaemasen de
Past Ind.	**INFORMAL**		sasaeta	sasaenakatta
	FORMAL		sasaemashita	sasaemasen deshita
Past Presump.	**INFORMAL**		sasaetarō	sasaenakattarō
			sasaeta darō	sasaenakatta darō
	FORMAL		sasaemashitarō	sasaemasen deshitarō
			sasaeta deshō	sasaenakatta deshō
Conditional	**INFORMAL**		sasaetara	sasaenakattara
	FORMAL		sasaemashitara	sasaemasen deshitara
Alternative	**INFORMAL**		sasaetari	sasaenakattari
	FORMAL		sasaemashitari	sasaemasen deshitari

		INFORMAL AFFIRMATIVE INDICATIVE
Passive		sasaerareru
Potential		sasaerareru
Causative		sasaesaseru
Causative Pass.		sasaesaserareru
Honorific	I	osasae ni naru
	II	osasae nasaru
Humble	I	osasae suru
	II	osasae itasu

S

to invite, to ask, to tempt   TRANSITIVE

			AFFIRMATIVE	NEGATIVE
Indicative	**INFORMAL**		sasou	sasowanai
	FORMAL		sasoimasu	sasoimasen
Imperative	**INFORMAL**	**I**	sasoe	sasou na
		II	sasoinasai	sasoinasaru na
		III	sasotte kudasai	sasowanai de kudasai
	FORMAL		osasoi nasaimase	osasoi nasaimasu na
Presumptive	**INFORMAL**	**I**	sasoō	sasoumai
		II	sasou darō	sasowanai darō
	FORMAL	**I**	sasoimashō	sasoimasumai
		II	sasou deshō	sasowanai deshō
Provisional	**INFORMAL**		sasoeba	sasowanakereba
	FORMAL		sasoimaseba	sasoimasen nara
			sasoimasureba	
Gerund	**INFORMAL**	**I**	sasotte	sasowanai de
		II		sasowanakute
	FORMAL		sasoimashite	sasoimasen de
Past Ind.	**INFORMAL**		sasotta	sasowanakatta
	FORMAL		sasoimashita	sasoimasen deshita
Past Presump.	**INFORMAL**		sasottarō	sasowanakattarō
			sasotta darō	sasowanakatta darō
	FORMAL		sasoimashitarō	sasoimasen deshitarō
			sasotta deshō	sasowanakatta deshō
Conditional	**INFORMAL**		sasottara	sasowanakattara
	FORMAL		sasoimashitara	sasoimasen deshitara
Alternative	**INFORMAL**		sasottari	sasowanakattari
	FORMAL		sasoimashitari	sasoimasen deshitari

			INFORMAL AFFIRMATIVE INDICATIVE
Passive			sasowareru
Potential			sasoeru
Causative			sasowaseru
Causative Pass.			sasowaserareru
Honorific		**I**	osasoi ni naru
		II	osasoi nasaru
Humble		**I**	osasoi suru
		II	osasoi itasu

さす／指す／刺す／差す **sas.u**

TRANSITIVE *to point out, to sting, to stab, to put up*

			AFFIRMATIVE	NEGATIVE
Indicative	**INFORMAL**		sasu	sasanai
	FORMAL		sashimasu	sashimasen
Imperative	**INFORMAL**	I	sase	sasu na
		II	sashinasai	sashinasaru na
		III	sashite kudasai	sasanai de kudasai
	FORMAL		osashi nasaimase	osashi nasaimasu na
Presumptive	**INFORMAL**	I	sasō	sasumai
		II	sasu darō	sasanai darō
	FORMAL	I	sashimashō	sashimasumai
		II	sasu deshō	sasanai deshō
Provisional	**INFORMAL**		saseba	sasanakereba
	FORMAL		sashimaseba	sashimasen nara
			sashimasureba	
Gerund	**INFORMAL**	I	sashite	sasanai de
		II		sasanakute
	FORMAL		sashimashite	sashimasen de
Past Ind.	**INFORMAL**		sashita	sasanakatta
	FORMAL		sashimashita	sashimasen deshita
Past Presump.	**INFORMAL**		sashitarō	sasanakattarō
			sashita darō	sasanakatta darō
	FORMAL		sashimashitarō	sashimasen deshitarō
			sashita deshō	sasanakatta deshō
Conditional	**INFORMAL**		sashitara	sasanakattara
	FORMAL		sashimashitara	sashimasen deshitara
Alternative	**INFORMAL**		sashitari	sasanakattari
	FORMAL		sashimashitari	sashimasen deshitari

		INFORMAL AFFIRMATIVE INDICATIVE
Passive		sasareru
Potential		saseru
Causative		sasaseru
Causative Pass.		sasaserareru
Honorific	I	osashi ni naru
	II	osashi nasaru
Humble	I	osashi suru
	II	osashi itasu

S

to make noise, to be rowdy

			AFFIRMATIVE	NEGATIVE
Indicative	INFORMAL		sawagu	sawaganai
	FORMAL		sawagimasu	sawagimasen
Imperative	INFORMAL	I	sawage	sawagu na
		II	sawaginasai	sawaginasaru na
		III	sawaide kudasai	sawaganai de kudasai
	FORMAL		osawagi nasaimase	osawagi nasaimasu na
Presumptive	INFORMAL	I	sawagō	sawagumai
		II	sawagu darō	sawaganai darō
	FORMAL	I	sawagimashō	sawagimasumai
		II	sawagu deshō	sawaganai deshō
Provisional	INFORMAL		sawageba	sawaganakereba
	FORMAL		sawagimaseba	sawagimasen nara
			sawagimasureba	
Gerund	INFORMAL	I	sawaide	sawaganai de
		II		sawaganakute
	FORMAL		sawagimashite	sawagimasen de
Past Ind.	INFORMAL		sawaida	sawaganakatta
	FORMAL		sawagimashita	sawagimasen deshita
Past Presump.	INFORMAL		sawaidarō	sawaganakattarō
			sawaida darō	sawaganakatta darō
	FORMAL		sawagimashitarō	sawagimasen deshitarō
			sawaida deshō	sawaganakatta deshō
Conditional	INFORMAL		sawaidara	sawaganakattara
	FORMAL		sawagimashitara	sawagimasen deshitara
Alternative	INFORMAL		sawaidari	sawaganakattari
	FORMAL		sawagimashitari	sawagimasen deshitari

		INFORMAL AFFIRMATIVE INDICATIVE
Passive		sawagareru
Potential		sawageru
Causative		sawagaseru
Causative Pass.		sawagaserareru
Honorific	I	osawagi ni naru
	II	osawagi nasaru
Humble	I	osawagi suru
	II	osawagi itasu

さわる／触る **sawar.u**
to touch or feel (with the hands)

			AFFIRMATIVE	NEGATIVE
Indicative	**INFORMAL**		sawaru	sawaranai
	FORMAL		sawarimasu	sawarimasen
Imperative	**INFORMAL**	**I**	saware	sawaru na
		II	sawarinasai	sawarinasaru na
		III	sawatte kudasai	sawaranai de kudasai
	FORMAL		osawari nasaimase	osawari nasaimasu na
Presumptive	**INFORMAL**	**I**	sawarō	sawarumai
		II	sawaru darō	sawaranai darō
	FORMAL	**I**	sawarimashō	sawarimasumai
		II	sawaru deshō	sawaranai deshō
Provisional	**INFORMAL**		sawareba	sawaranakereba
	FORMAL		sawarimaseba	sawarimasen nara
			sawarimasureba	
Gerund	**INFORMAL**	**I**	sawatte	sawaranai de
		II		sawaranakute
	FORMAL		sawarimashite	sawarimasen de
Past Ind.	**INFORMAL**		sawatta	sawaranakatta
	FORMAL		sawarimashita	sawarimasen deshita
Past Presump.	**INFORMAL**		sawattarō	sawaranakattarō
			sawatta darō	sawaranakatta darō
	FORMAL		sawarimashitarō	sawarimasen deshitarō
			sawatta deshō	sawaranakatta deshō
Conditional	**INFORMAL**		sawattara	sawaranakattara
	FORMAL		sawarimashitara	sawarimasen deshitara
Alternative	**INFORMAL**		sawattari	sawaranakattari
	FORMAL		sawarimashitari	sawarimasen deshitari

S

			INFORMAL AFFIRMATIVE INDICATIVE
Passive			sawarareru
Potential			sawareru
Causative			sawaraseru
Causative Pass.			sawaraserareru
Honorific		**I**	osawari ni naru
		II	osawari nasaru
Humble		**I**	osawari suru
		II	osawari itasu

to blame, to torment　　TRANSITIVE

			AFFIRMATIVE	NEGATIVE
Indicative	**INFORMAL**		semeru	semenai
	FORMAL		sememasu	sememasen
Imperative	**INFORMAL**	I	semero	semeru na
		II	semenasai	semenasaru na
		III	semete kudasai	semenai de kudasai
	FORMAL		oseme nasaimase	oseme nasaimasu na
Presumptive	**INFORMAL**	I	semeyō	sememai
		II	semeru darō	semenai darō
	FORMAL	I	sememashō	sememasumai
		II	semeru deshō	semenai deshō
Provisional	**INFORMAL**		semereba	semenakereba
	FORMAL		sememaseba	sememasen nara
			sememasureba	
Gerund	**INFORMAL**	I	semete	semenai de
		II		semenakute
	FORMAL		sememashite	sememasen de
Past Ind.	**INFORMAL**		semeta	semenakatta
	FORMAL		sememashita	sememasen deshita
Past Presump.	**INFORMAL**		semetarō	semenakattarō
			semeta darō	semenakatta darō
	FORMAL		sememashitarō	sememasen deshitarō
			semeta deshō	semenakatta deshō
Conditional	**INFORMAL**		semetara	semenakattara
	FORMAL		sememashitara	sememasen deshitara
Alternative	**INFORMAL**		semetari	semenakattari
	FORMAL		sememashitari	sememasen deshitari

		INFORMAL AFFIRMATIVE INDICATIVE
Passive		semerareru
Potential		semerareru
Causative		semesaseru
Causative Pass.		semesaserareru
Honorific	I	oseme ni naru
	II	oseme nasaru
Humble	I	oseme suru
	II	oseme itasu

しばる／縛る　**shibar.u**

TRANSITIVE　　*to tie up, to bind*

			AFFIRMATIVE	NEGATIVE
Indicative	**INFORMAL**		shibaru	shibaranai
	FORMAL		shibarimasu	shibarimasen
Imperative	**INFORMAL**	**I**	shibare	shibaru na
		II	shibarinasai	shibarinasaru na
		III	shibatte kudasai	shibaranai de kudasai
	FORMAL		oshibari nasaimase	oshibari nasaimasu na
Presumptive	**INFORMAL**	**I**	shibarō	shibarumai
		II	shibaru darō	shibaranai darō
	FORMAL	**I**	shibarimashō	shibarimasumai
		II	shibaru deshō	shibaranai deshō
Provisional	**INFORMAL**		shibareba	shibaranakereba
	FORMAL		shibarimaseba	shibarimasen nara
			shibarimasureba	
Gerund	**INFORMAL**	**I**	shibatte	shibaranai de
		II		shibaranakute
	FORMAL		shibarimashite	shibarimasen de
Past Ind.	**INFORMAL**		shibatta	shibaranakatta
	FORMAL		shibarimashita	shibarimasen deshita
Past Presump.	**INFORMAL**		shibattarō	shibaranakattarō
			shibatta darō	shibaranakatta darō
	FORMAL		shibarimashitarō	shibarimasen deshitarō
			shibatta deshō	shibaranakatta deshō
Conditional	**INFORMAL**		shibattara	shibaranakattara
	FORMAL		shibarimashitara	shibarimasen deshitara
Alternative	**INFORMAL**		shibattari	shibaranakattari
	FORMAL		shibarimashitari	shibarimasen deshitari

			INFORMAL AFFIRMATIVE INDICATIVE
Passive			shibarareru
Potential			shibareru
Causative			shibaraseru
Causative Pass.			shibaraserareru
Honorific		**I**	oshibari ni naru
		II	oshibari nasaru
Humble		**I**	oshibari suru
		II	oshibari itasu

S

shikar.u しかる／叱る   shikari

to scold, to chide   TRANSITIVE

			AFFIRMATIVE	NEGATIVE
Indicative	**INFORMAL**		shikaru	shikaranai
	FORMAL		shikarimasu	shikarimasen
Imperative	**INFORMAL**	I	shikare	shikaru na
		II	shikarinasai	shikarinasaru na
		III	shikatte kudasai	shikaranai de kudasai
	FORMAL		oshikari nasaimase	oshikari nasaimasu na
Presumptive	**INFORMAL**	I	shikarō	shikarumai
		II	shikaru darō	shikaranai darō
	FORMAL	I	shikarimashō	shikarimasumai
		II	shikaru deshō	shikaranai deshō
Provisional	**INFORMAL**		shikareba	shikaranakereba
	FORMAL		shikarimaseba	shikarimasen nara
			shikarimasureba	
Gerund	**INFORMAL**	I	shikatte	shikaranai de
		II		shikaranakute
	FORMAL		shikarimashite	shikarimasen de
Past Ind.	**INFORMAL**		shikatta	shikaranakatta
	FORMAL		shikarimashita	shikarimasen deshita
Past Presump.	**INFORMAL**		shikattarō	shikaranakattarō
			shikatta darō	shikaranakatta darō
	FORMAL		shikarimashitarō	shikarimasen deshitarō
			shikatta deshō	shikaranakatta deshō
Conditional	**INFORMAL**		shikattara	shikaranakattara
	FORMAL		shikarimashitara	shikarimasen deshitara
Alternative	**INFORMAL**		shikattari	shikaranakattari
	FORMAL		shikarimashitari	shikarimasen deshitari

			INFORMAL AFFIRMATIVE INDICATIVE
Passive			shikarareru
Potential			shikareru
Causative			shikaraseru
Causative Pass.			shikaraserareru
Honorific		I	oshikari ni naru
		II	oshikari nasaru
Humble		I	oshikari suru
		II	oshikari itasu

しく／敷く　**shik.u**

			AFFIRMATIVE	NEGATIVE
Indicative	**INFORMAL**		shiku	shikanai
	FORMAL		shikimasu	shikimasen
Imperative	**INFORMAL**	I	shike	shiku na
		II	shikinasai	shikinasaru na
		III	shiite kudasai	shikanai de kudasai
	FORMAL		oshiki nasaimase	oshiki nasaimasu na
Presumptive	**INFORMAL**	I	shikō	shikumai
		II	shiku darō	shikanai darō
	FORMAL	I	shikimashō	shikimasumai
		II	shiku deshō	shikanai deshō
Provisional	**INFORMAL**		shikeba	shikanakereba
	FORMAL		shikimaseba	shikimasen nara
			shikimasureba	
Gerund	**INFORMAL**	I	shiite	shikanai de
		II		shikanakute
	FORMAL		shikimashite	shikimasen de
Past Ind.	**INFORMAL**		shiita	shikanakatta
	FORMAL		shikimashita	shikimasen deshita
Past Presump.	**INFORMAL**		shiitarō	shikanakattarō
			shiita darō	shikanakatta darō
	FORMAL		shikimashitarō	shikimasen deshitarō
			shiita deshō	shikanakatta deshō
Conditional	**INFORMAL**		shiitara	shikanakattara
	FORMAL		shikimashitara	shikimasen deshitara
Alternative	**INFORMAL**		shiitari	shikanakattari
	FORMAL		shikimashitari	shikimasen deshitari

			INFORMAL AFFIRMATIVE INDICATIVE
Passive			shikareru
Potential			shikeru
Causative			shikaseru
Causative Pass.			shikaserareru
Honorific		I	oshiki ni naru
		II	oshiki nasaru
Humble		I	oshiki suru
		II	oshiki itasu

shimar.u しまる／閉まる   shimari

to close (by itself), *to be closed, to be shut*

			AFFIRMATIVE	NEGATIVE
Indicative	**INFORMAL**		shimaru	shimaranai
	FORMAL		shimarimasu	shimarimasen
Imperative	**INFORMAL**	I	shimare	shimaru na
		II		
		III	shimatte kudasai	shimaranai de kudasai
	FORMAL			
Presumptive	**INFORMAL**	I	shimarō	shimarumai
		II	shimaru darō	shimaranai darō
	FORMAL	I	shimarimashō	shimarimasumai
		II	shimaru deshō	shimaranai deshō
Provisional	**INFORMAL**		shimareba	shimaranakereba
	FORMAL		shimarimaseba	shimarimasen nara
			shimarimasureba	
Gerund	**INFORMAL**	I	shimatte	shimaranai de
		II		shimaranakute
	FORMAL		shimarimashite	shimarimasen de
Past Ind.	**INFORMAL**		shimatta	shimaranakatta
	FORMAL		shimarimashita	shimarimasen deshita
Past Presump.	**INFORMAL**		shimattarō	shimaranakattarō
			shimatta darō	shimaranakatta darō
	FORMAL		shimarimashitarō	shimarimasen deshitarō
			shimatta deshō	shimaranakatta deshō
Conditional	**INFORMAL**		shimattara	shimaranakattara
	FORMAL		shimarimashitara	shimarimasen deshitara
Alternative	**INFORMAL**		shimattari	shimaranakattari
	FORMAL		shimarimashitari	shimarimasen deshitari

		INFORMAL AFFIRMATIVE INDICATIVE
Passive		
Potential		
Causative		shimaraseru
Causative Pass.		shimaraserareru
Honorific	I	oshimari ni naru
	II	oshimari nasaru
Humble	I	
	II	

TRANSITIVE   *to put away, to pack away*

			AFFIRMATIVE	NEGATIVE
Indicative	**INFORMAL**		shimau	shimawanai
	FORMAL		shimaimasu	shimaimasen
Imperative	**INFORMAL**	I	shimae	shimau na
		II	shimainasai	shimainasaru na
		III	shimatte kudasai	shimawanai de kudasai
	FORMAL		oshimai nasaimase	oshimai nasaimasu na
Presumptive	**INFORMAL**	I	shimaō	shimaumai
		II	shimau darō	shimawanai darō
	FORMAL	I	shimaimashō	shimaimasumai
		II	shimau deshō	shimawanai deshō
Provisional	**INFORMAL**		shimaeba	shimawanakereba
	FORMAL		shimaimaseba	shimaimasen nara
			shimaimasureba	
Gerund	**INFORMAL**	I	shimatte	shimawanai de
		II		shimawanakute
	FORMAL		shimaimashite	shimaimasen de
Past Ind.	**INFORMAL**		shimatta	shimawanakatta
	FORMAL		shimaimashita	shimaimasen deshita
Past Presump.	**INFORMAL**		shimattarō	shimawanakattarō
			shimatta darō	shimawanakatta darō
	FORMAL		shimaimashitarō	shimaimasen deshitarō
			shimatta deshō	shimawanakatta deshō
Conditional	**INFORMAL**		shimattara	shimawanakattara
	FORMAL		shimaimashitara	shimaimasen deshitara
Alternative	**INFORMAL**		shimattari	shimawanakattari
	FORMAL		shimaimashitari	shimaimasen deshitari

			INFORMAL AFFIRMATIVE INDICATIVE
Passive			shimawareru
Potential			shimaeru
Causative			shimawaseru
Causative Pass.			shimawaserareru
Honorific		I	oshimai ni naru
		II	oshimai nasaru
Humble		I	oshimai suru
		II	oshimai itasu

451

shime.ru しめる／閉める   shime

to shut, to close   TRANSITIVE

			AFFIRMATIVE	NEGATIVE
Indicative	**INFORMAL**		shimeru	shimenai
	FORMAL		shimemasu	shimemasen
Imperative	**INFORMAL**	I	shimero	shimeru na
		II	shimenasai	shimenasaru na
		III	shimete kudasai	shimenai de kudasai
	FORMAL		oshime nasaimase	oshime nasaimasu na
Presumptive	**INFORMAL**	I	shimeyō	shimemai
		II	shimeru darō	shimenai darō
	FORMAL	I	shimemashō	shimemasumai
		II	shimeru deshō	shimenai deshō
Provisional	**INFORMAL**		shimereba	shimenakereba
	FORMAL		shimemaseba	shimemasen nara
			shimemasureba	
Gerund	**INFORMAL**	I	shimete	shimenai de
		II		shimenakute
	FORMAL		shimemashite	shimemasen de
Past Ind.	**INFORMAL**		shimeta	shimenakatta
	FORMAL		shimemashita	shimemasen deshita
Past Presump.	**INFORMAL**		shimetarō	shimenakattarō
			shimeta darō	shimenakatta darō
	FORMAL		shimemashitarō	shimemasen deshitarō
			shimeta deshō	shimenakatta deshō
Conditional	**INFORMAL**		shimetara	shimenakattara
	FORMAL		shimemashitara	shimemasen deshitara
Alternative	**INFORMAL**		shimetari	shimenakattari
	FORMAL		shimemashitari	shimemasen deshitari

		INFORMAL AFFIRMATIVE INDICATIVE
Passive		shimerareru
Potential		shimerareru
Causative		shimesaseru
Causative Pass.		shimesaserareru

Honorific	I	oshime ni naru
	II	oshime nasaru
Humble	I	oshime suru
	II	oshime itasu

452

shimeshi

しめす／示す **shimes.u**

TRANSITIVE *to indicate, to point out, to show*

			AFFIRMATIVE	**NEGATIVE**
Indicative	**INFORMAL**		shimesu	shimesanai
	FORMAL		shimeshimasu	shimeshimasen
Imperative	**INFORMAL**	I	shimese	shimesu na
		II	shimeshinasai	shimeshinasaru na
		III	shimeshite kudasai	shimesanai de kudasai
	FORMAL		oshimeshi nasaimase	oshimeshi nasaimasu na
Presumptive	**INFORMAL**	I	shimesō	shimesumai
		II	shimesu darō	shimesanai darō
	FORMAL	I	shimeshimashō	shimeshimasumai
		II	shimesu deshō	shimesanai deshō
Provisional	**INFORMAL**		shimeseba	shimesanakereba
	FORMAL		shimeshimaseba	shimeshimasen nara
			shimeshimasureba	
Gerund	**INFORMAL**	I	shimeshite	shimesanai de
		II		shimesanakute
	FORMAL		shimeshimashite	shimeshimasen de
Past Ind.	**INFORMAL**		shimeshita	shimesanakatta
	FORMAL		shimeshimashita	shimeshimasen deshita
Past Presump.	**INFORMAL**		shimeshitarō	shimesanakattarō
			shimeshita darō	shimesanakatta darō
	FORMAL		shimeshimashitarō	shimeshimasen deshitarō
			shimeshita deshō	shimesanakatta deshō
Conditional	**INFORMAL**		shimeshitara	shimesanakattara
	FORMAL		shimeshimashitara	shimeshimasen deshitara
Alternative	**INFORMAL**		shimeshitari	shimesanakattari
	FORMAL		shimeshimashitari	shimeshimasen deshitari

S

			INFORMAL AFFIRMATIVE INDICATIVE
Passive			shimesareru
Potential			shimeseru
Causative			shimesaseru
Causative Pass.			shimesaserareru
Honorific		I	oshimeshi ni naru
		II	oshimeshi nasaru
Humble		I	oshimeshi suru
		II	oshimeshi itasu

to believe, to trust TRANSITIVE

			AFFIRMATIVE	**NEGATIVE**
Indicative	**INFORMAL**		shinjiru	shinjinai
	FORMAL		shinjimasu	shinjimasen
Imperative	**INFORMAL**	I	shinjiro	shinjiru na
		II	shinjinasai	shinjinasaru na
		III	shinjite kudasai	shinjinai de kudasai
	FORMAL		oshinji nasaimase	oshinji nasaimasu na
Presumptive	**INFORMAL**	I	shinjiyō	shinjimai
		II	shinjiru darō	shinjinai darō
	FORMAL	I	shinjimashō	shinjimasumai
		II	shinjiru deshō	shinjinai deshō
Provisional	**INFORMAL**		shinjireba	shinjinakereba
	FORMAL		shinjimaseba	shinjimasen nara
			shinjimasureba	
Gerund	**INFORMAL**	I	shinjite	shinjinai de
		II		shinjinakute
	FORMAL		shinjimashite	shinjimasen de
Past Ind.	**INFORMAL**		shinjita	shinjinakatta
	FORMAL		shinjimashita	shinjimasen deshita
Past Presump.	**INFORMAL**		shinjitarō	shinjinakattarō
			shinjita darō	shinjinakatta darō
	FORMAL		shinjimashitarō	shinjimasen deshitarō
			shinjita deshō	shinjinakatta deshō
Conditional	**INFORMAL**		shinjitara	shinjinakattara
	FORMAL		shinjimashitara	shinjimasen deshitara
Alternative	**INFORMAL**		shinjitari	shinjinakattari
	FORMAL		shinjimashitari	shinjimasen deshitari

		INFORMAL AFFIRMATIVE INDICATIVE
Passive		shinjirareru
Potential		shinjirareru
Causative		shinjisaseru
Causative Pass.		shinjisaserareru
Honorific	I	oshinji ni naru
	II	oshinji nasaru
Humble	I	oshinji suru
	II	oshinji itasu

			AFFIRMATIVE	**NEGATIVE**
Indicative	**INFORMAL**		shinu	shinanai
	FORMAL		shinimasu	shinimasen
Imperative	**INFORMAL**	I	shine	shinu na
		II	shininasai	shininasaru na
		III	shinde kudasai	shinanai de kudasai
	FORMAL		onakunari nasaimase	onakunari nasaimasu na
Presumptive	**INFORMAL**	I	shinō	shinumai
		II	shinu darō	shinanai darō
	FORMAL	I	shinimashō	shinimasumai
		II	shinu deshō	shinanai deshō
Provisional	**INFORMAL**		shineba	shinanakereba
	FORMAL		shinimaseba	shinimasen nara
			shinimasureba	
Gerund	**INFORMAL**	I	shinde	shinanai de
		II		shinanakute
	FORMAL		shinimashite	shinimasen de
Past Ind.	**INFORMAL**		shinda	shinanakatta
	FORMAL		shinimashita	shinimasen deshita
Past Presump.	**INFORMAL**		sindarō	shinanakattarō
			shinda darō	shinanakatta darō
	FORMAL		shinimashitarō	shinimasen deshitarō
			shinda deshō	shinanakatta deshō
Conditional	**INFORMAL**		shindara	shinanakattara
	FORMAL		shinimashitara	shinimasen deshitara
Alternative	**INFORMAL**		shindari	shinanakattari
	FORMAL		shinimashitari	shinimasen deshitari

		INFORMAL AFFIRMATIVE INDICATIVE
Passive		shinareru
Potential		shineru
Causative		shinaseru
Causative Pass.		shinaserareru
Honorific	I	onakunari ni naru
	II	onakunari nasaru
Humble	I	
	II	

S

to check, to investigate, to search   TRANSITIVE

			AFFIRMATIVE	NEGATIVE
Indicative	**INFORMAL**		shiraberu	shirabenai
	FORMAL		shirabemasu	shirabemasen
Imperative	**INFORMAL**	I	shirabero	shiraberu na
		II	shirabenasai	shirabenasaru na
		III	shirabete kudasai	shirabenai de kudasai
	FORMAL		oshirabe nasaimase	oshirabe nasaimasu na
Presumptive	**INFORMAL**	I	shirabeyō	shirabemai
		II	shiraberu darō	shirabenai darō
	FORMAL	I	shirabemashō	shirabemasumai
		II	shiraberu deshō	shirabenai deshō
Provisional	**INFORMAL**		shirabereba	shirabenakereba
	FORMAL		shirabemaseba	shirabemasen nara
			shirabemasureba	
Gerund	**INFORMAL**	I	shirabete	shirabenai de
		II		shirabenakute
	FORMAL		shirabemashite	shirabemasen de
Past Ind.	**INFORMAL**		shirabeta	shirabenakatta
	FORMAL		shirabemashita	shirabemasen deshita
Past Presump.	**INFORMAL**		shirabetarō	shirabenakattarō
			shirabeta darō	shirabenakatta darō
	FORMAL		shirabemashitarō	shirabemasen deshitarō
			shirabeta deshō	shirabenakatta deshō
Conditional	**INFORMAL**		shirabetara	shirabenakattara
	FORMAL		shirabemashitara	shirabemasen deshitara
Alternative	**INFORMAL**		shirabetari	shirabenakattari
	FORMAL		shirabemashitari	shirabemasen deshitari

			INFORMAL AFFIRMATIVE INDICATIVE
Passive			shiraberareru
Potential			shiraberareru
Causative			shirabesaseru
Causative Pass.			shirabesaserareru
Honorific		I	oshirabe ni naru
		II	oshirabe nasaru
Humble		I	oshirabe suru
		II	oshirabe itasu

shiri

TRANSITIVE   *to know, to get to know, to learn about, to understand*

しる／知る　**shir.u**

			AFFIRMATIVE	NEGATIVE
Indicative	**INFORMAL**		shiru	shiranai
	FORMAL		shirimasu	shirimasen
Imperative	**INFORMAL**	I	shire	shiru na
		II	shirinasai	shirinasaru na
		III	shitte kudasai	shiranai de kudasai
	FORMAL		oshiri nasaimase	oshiri nasaimasu na
Presumptive	**INFORMAL**	I	shirō	shirumai
		II	shiru darō	shiranai darō
	FORMAL	I	shirimashō	shirimasumai
		II	shiru deshō	shiranai deshō
Provisional	**INFORMAL**		shireba	shiranakereba
	FORMAL		shirimaseba	shirimasen nara
			shirimasureba	
Gerund	**INFORMAL**	I	shitte	shiranai de
		II		shiranakute
	FORMAL		shirimashite	shirimasen de
Past Ind.	**INFORMAL**		shitta	shiranakatta
	FORMAL		shirimashita	shirimasen deshita
Past Presump.	**INFORMAL**		shittarō	shiranakattarō
			shitta darō	shiranakatta darō
	FORMAL		shirimashitarō	shirimasen deshitarō
			shitta deshō	shiranakatta deshō
Conditional	**INFORMAL**		shittara	shiranakattara
	FORMAL		shirimashitara	shirimasen deshitara
Alternative	**INFORMAL**		shittari	shiranakattari
	FORMAL		shirimashitari	shirimasen deshitari

		INFORMAL AFFIRMATIVE INDICATIVE	
Passive		shirareru	
Potential		shireru	
Causative		shiraseru	
Causative Pass.		shiraserareru	
Honorific	I	gozonji de irassharu	I oshiri ni naru
	II		II oshiri nasaru
Humble	I	zonjiru	
	II		

AN ESSENTIAL 55 VERB

Shiru 知る

Sentences Using *Shiru*

Kanojo no mēru adoresu ga shiritai.
彼女のメールアドレスが知りたい。
I'd like to know her e-mail address.

Ano hito ga shiritai no desu ga.
あの人が知りたいのですが。
I'd like to get to know him.

Nihon go o shiranakutemo daijōbu
desu ka.
日本語を知らなくても大丈夫ですか。
Is it okay if I don't know Japanese?

Ano kashu wa yoku shirarete imasu.
あの歌手は良く知られています。
That singer is well known.

Tomodachi ga yūmei na sakka no
musuko da towa shiranakatta.
友達が有名な作家の息子だとは知らな
かった。
*I didn't know my friend was a
famous writer's son.*

to know, to get to know,
to learn about, to understand

Shiru is an essential verb for everyday
conversation and all sorts of situations.
You need to know or get to know many
people, places, and things.

Words and Expressions Related to This Verb

shiriau　知り合う
to get acquainted with

shiritsukusu　知り尽くす
to know thoroughly

chijin　知人
an acquaintance

shirazu shirazu　知らず知らず
without knowing, unwittingly

Proverb

Shiranu ga hotoke.
知らぬが仏。
Ignorance is bliss. (No thing is bliss.)

したがう／従う　**shitaga.u**

to obey, to follow, to comply with

			AFFIRMATIVE	NEGATIVE
Indicative	**INFORMAL**		shitagau	shitagawanai
	FORMAL		shitagaimasu	shitagaimasen
Imperative	**INFORMAL**	I	shitagae	shitagau na
		II	shitagainasai	shitagainasaru na
		III	shitagatte kudasai	shitagawanai de kudasai
	FORMAL		oshitagai nasaimase	oshitagai nasaimasu na
Presumptive	**INFORMAL**	I	shitagaō	shitagaumai
		II	shitagau darō	shitagawanai darō
	FORMAL	I	shitagaimashō	shitagaimasumai
		II	shitagau deshō	shitagawanai deshō
Provisional	**INFORMAL**		shitagaeba	shitagawanakereba
	FORMAL		shitagaimaseba	shitagaimasen nara
			shitagaimasureba	
Gerund	**INFORMAL**	I	shitagatte	shitagawanai de
		II		shitagawanakute
	FORMAL		shitagaimashite	shitagaimasen de
Past Ind.	**INFORMAL**		shitagatta	shitagawanakatta
	FORMAL		shitagaimashita	shitagaimasen deshita
Past Presump.	**INFORMAL**		shitagattarō	shitagawanakattarō
			shitagatta darō	shitagawanakatta darō
	FORMAL		shitagaimashitarō	shitagaimasen deshitarō
			shitagatta deshō	shitagawanakatta deshō
Conditional	**INFORMAL**		shitagattara	shitagawanakattara
	FORMAL		shitagaimashitara	shitagaimasen deshitara
Alternative	**INFORMAL**		shitagattari	shitagawanakattari
	FORMAL		shitagaimashitari	shitagaimasen deshitari

			INFORMAL AFFIRMATIVE INDICATIVE
Passive			shitagawareru
Potential			shitagaeru
Causative			shitagawaseru
Causative Pass.			shitagawaserareru
Honorific		I	oshitagai ni naru
		II	oshitagai nasaru
Humble		I	oshitagai suru
		II	oshitagai itasu

S

shitashim.u　したしむ／親しむ

to get to know, to make friends with

			AFFIRMATIVE	NEGATIVE
Indicative	**INFORMAL**		shitashimu	shitashimanai
	FORMAL		shitashimimasu	shitashimimasen
Imperative	**INFORMAL**	I	shitashime	shitashimu na
		II	shitashiminasai	shitashiminasaru na
		III	shitashinde kudasai	shitashimanai de kudasai
	FORMAL		oshitashimi nasaimase	oshitashimi nasaimasu na
Presumptive	**INFORMAL**	I	shitashimō	shitashimumai
		II	shitashimu darō	shitashimanai darō
	FORMAL	I	shitashimimashō	shitashimimasumai
		II	shitashimu deshō	shitashimanai deshō
Provisional	**INFORMAL**		shitashimeba	shitashimanakereba
	FORMAL		shitashimimaseba	shitashimimasen nara
			shitashimimasureba	
Gerund	**INFORMAL**	I	shitashinde	shitashimanai de
		II		shitashimanakute
	FORMAL		shitashimimashite	shitashimimasen de
Past Ind.	**INFORMAL**		shitashinda	shitashimanakatta
	FORMAL		shitashimimashita	shitashimimasen deshita
Past Presump.	**INFORMAL**		shitashindarō	shitashimanakattarō
			shitashinda darō	shitashimanakatta darō
	FORMAL		shitashimimashitarō	shitashimimasen deshitarō
			shitashinda deshō	shitashimanakatta deshō
Conditional	**INFORMAL**		shitashindara	shitashimanakattara
	FORMAL		shitashimimashitara	shitashimimasen deshitara
Alternative	**INFORMAL**		shitashindari	shitashimanakattari
	FORMAL		shitashimimashitari	shitashimimasen deshitari

		INFORMAL AFFIRMATIVE INDICATIVE
Passive		shitashimareru
Potential		shitashimeru
Causative		shitashimaseru
Causative Pass.		shitashimaserareru
Honorific	I	oshitashimi in naru
	II	oshitashimi nasaru
Humble	I	oshitashimi suru
	II	oshitashimi itasu

			AFFIRMATIVE	NEGATIVE
Indicative	INFORMAL		shizumu	shizumanai
	FORMAL		shizumimasu	shizumimasen
Imperative	INFORMAL	I	shizume	shizumu na
		II	shizuminasai	shizuminasaru na
		III	shizunde kudasai	shizumanai de kudasai
	FORMAL		oshizumi nasaimase	oshizumi nasaimasu na
Presumptive	INFORMAL	I	shizumō	shizumumai
		II	shizumu darō	shizumanai darō
	FORMAL	I	shizumimashō	shizumimasumai
		II	shizumu darō	shizumanai darō
Provisional	INFORMAL		shizumeba	shizumanakereba
	FORMAL		shizumimaseba	shizumimasen nara
			shizumimasureba	
Gerund	INFORMAL	I	shizunde	shizumanai de
		II		shizumanakute
	FORMAL		shizumimashite	shizumimasen de
Past Ind.	INFORMAL		shizunda	shizumanakatta
	FORMAL		shizumimashita	shizumimasen deshita
Past Presump.	INFORMAL		shizundarō	shizumanakattarō
			shizunda darō	shizumanakatta darō
	FORMAL		shizumimashitarō	shizumimasen deshitarō
			shizunda deshō	shizumanakatta deshō
Conditional	INFORMAL		shizundara	shizumanakattara
	FORMAL		shizumimashitara	shizumimasen deshitara
Alternative	INFORMAL		shizundari	shizumanakattari
	FORMAL		shizumimashitari	shizumimasen deshitari

			INFORMAL AFFIRMATIVE INDICATIVE
Passive			shizumareru
Potential			shizumeru
Causative			shizumaseru
Causative Pass.			shizumaserareru
Honorific		I	oshizumi ni naru
		II	oshizumi nasaru
Humble		I	
		II	

461

to raise a child, to bring up, to train　　　TRANSITIVE

			AFFIRMATIVE	NEGATIVE
Indicative	INFORMAL		sodateru	sodatenai
	FORMAL		sodatemasu	sodatemasen
Imperative	INFORMAL	I	sodatero	sodateru na
		II	sodatenasai	sodatenasaru na
		III	sodatete kudasai	sodatenai de kudasai
	FORMAL		osodate nasaimase	osodate nasaimasu na
Presumptive	INFORMAL	I	sodateyō	sodatemai
		II	sodateru darō	sodatenai darō
	FORMAL	I	sodatemashō	sodatemasumai
		II	sodateru deshō	sodatenai deshō
Provisional	INFORMAL		sodatereba	sodatenakereba
	FORMAL		sodatemaseba	sodatemasen nara
			sodatemasureba	
Gerund	INFORMAL	I	sodatete	sodatenai de
		II		sodatenakute
	FORMAL		sodatemashite	sodatemasen de
Past Ind.	INFORMAL		sodateta	sodatenakatta
	FORMAL		sodatemashita	sodatemasen deshita
Past Presump.	INFORMAL		sodatetarō	sodatenakattarō
			sodateta darō	sodatenakatta darō
	FORMAL		sodatemashitarō	sodatemasen deshitarō
			sodateta deshō	sodatenakatta deshō
Conditional	INFORMAL		sodatetara	sodatenakattara
	FORMAL		sodatemashitara	sodatemasen deshitara
Alternative	INFORMAL		sodatetari	sodatenakattari
	FORMAL		sodatemashitari	sodatemasen deshitari

			INFORMAL AFFIRMATIVE INDICATIVE
Passive			sodaterareru
Potential			sodaterareru
Causative			sodatesaseru
Causative Pass.			sodatesaserareru
Honorific		I	osodate ni naru
		II	osodate nasaru
Humble		I	osodate suru
		II	osodate itasu

to grow up, to be raised

			AFFIRMATIVE	NEGATIVE
Indicative	**INFORMAL**		sodatsu	sodatanai
	FORMAL		sodachimasu	sodachimasen
Imperative	**INFORMAL**	I	sodate	sodatsu na
		II	sodachinasai	sodachinasaru na
		III	sodatte kudasai	sodatanai de kudasai
	FORMAL		osodachi nasaimase	osodachi nasaimasu na
Presumptive	**INFORMAL**	I	sodatō	sodatsumai
		II	sodatsu darō	sodatanai darō
	FORMAL	I	sodachimashō	sodachimasumai
		II	sodatsu deshō	sodatanai deshō
Provisional	**INFORMAL**		sodateba	sodatanakereba
	FORMAL		sodachimaseba	sodachimasen nara
			sodachimasureba	
Gerund	**INFORMAL**	I	sodatte	sodatanai de
		II		sodatanakute
	FORMAL		sodachimashite	sodachimasen de
Past Ind.	**INFORMAL**		sodatta	sodatanakatta
	FORMAL		sodachimashita	sodachimasen deshita
Past Presump.	**INFORMAL**		sodattarō	sodatanakattarō
			sodatta darō	sodatanakatta darō
	FORMAL		sodachimashitarō	sodachimasen deshitarō
			sodatta deshō	sodatanakatta deshō
Conditional	**INFORMAL**		sodattara	sodatanakattara
	FORMAL		sodachimashitara	sodachimasen deshitara
Alternative	**INFORMAL**		sodattari	sodatanakattari
	FORMAL		sodachimashitari	sodachimasen deshitari

		INFORMAL AFFIRMATIVE INDICATIVE
Passive		
Potential		
Causative		sodataseru
Causative Pass.		sodataserareru
Honorific	I	osodachi ni naru
	II	osodachi nasaru
Humble	I	
	II	

S

463

to slide, to slip

			AFFIRMATIVE	NEGATIVE
Indicative	**INFORMAL**		suberu	suberanai
	FORMAL		suberimasu	suberimasen
Imperative	**INFORMAL**	I	subere	suberu na
		II	suberinasai	suberinasaru na
		III	subette kudasai	suberanai de kudasai
	FORMAL		osuberi nasaimase	osuberi nasaimasu na
Presumptive	**INFORMAL**	I	suberō	suberumai
		II	suberu darō	suberanai darō
	FORMAL	I	suberimashō	suberimasumai
		II	suberu deshō	suberanai deshō
Provisional	**INFORMAL**		subereba	suberanakereba
	FORMAL		suberimaseba	suberimasen nara
			suberimasureba	
Gerund	**INFORMAL**	I	subette	suberanai de
		II		suberanakute
	FORMAL		suberimashite	suberimasen de
Past Ind.	**INFORMAL**		subetta	suberanakatta
	FORMAL		suberimashita	suberimasen deshita
Past Presump.	**INFORMAL**		subettarō	suberanakattarō
			subetta darō	suberanakatta darō
	FORMAL		suberimashitarō	suberimasen deshitarō
			subetta deshō	suberanakatta deshō
Conditional	**INFORMAL**		subettara	suberanakattara
	FORMAL		suberimashitara	suberimasen deshitara
Alternative	**INFORMAL**		subettari	suberanakattari
	FORMAL		suberimashitari	suberimasen deshitari

		INFORMAL AFFIRMATIVE INDICATIVE
Passive		suberareru
Potential		subereru
Causative		suberaseru
Causative Pass.		suberaserareru
Honorific	I	osuberi ni naru
	II	osuberi nasaru
Humble	I	
	II	

to pass, to exceed

			AFFIRMATIVE	NEGATIVE
Indicative	**INFORMAL**		sugiru	suginai
	FORMAL		sugimasu	sugimasen
Imperative	**INFORMAL**	I	sugiro	sugiru na
		II	suginasai	suginasaru na
		III	sugite kudasai	suginai de kudasai
	FORMAL		osugi nasaimase	osugi nasaimasu na
Presumptive	**INFORMAL**	I	sugiyō	sugimai
		II	sugiru darō	suginai darō
	FORMAL	I	sugimashō	sugimasumai
		II	sugiru deshō	suginai deshō
Provisional	**INFORMAL**		sugireba	suginakereba
	FORMAL		sugimaseba	sugimasen nara
			sugimasureba	
Gerund	**INFORMAL**	I	sugite	suginai de
		II		suginakute
	FORMAL		sugimashite	sugimasen de
Past Ind.	**INFORMAL**		sugita	suginakatta
	FORMAL		sugimashita	sugimasen deshita
Past Presump.	**INFORMAL**		sugitarō	suginakattarō
			sugita darō	suginakatta darō
	FORMAL		sugimashitarō	sugimasen deshitarō
			sugita deshō	suginakatta deshō
Conditional	**INFORMAL**		sugitara	suginakattara
	FORMAL		sugimashitara	sugimasen deshitara
Alternative	**INFORMAL**		sugitari	suginakattari
	FORMAL		sugimashitari	sugimasen deshitari

			INFORMAL AFFIRMATIVE INDICATIVE
Passive			
Potential			
Causative			sugisaseru
Causative Pass.			sugisaserareru
Honorific		I	osugi ni naru
		II	osugi nasaru
Humble		I	
		II	

S

to spend time, to pass time, to live   TRANSITIVE

			AFFIRMATIVE	NEGATIVE
Indicative	**INFORMAL**		sugosu	sugosanai
	FORMAL		sugoshimasu	sugoshimasen
Imperative	**INFORMAL**	I	sugose	sugosu na
		II	sugoshinasai	sugoshinasaru na
		III	sugoshite kudasai	sugosanai de kudasai
	FORMAL		osugoshi nasaimase	osugoshi nasaimasu na
Presumptive	**INFORMAL**	I	sugosō	sugosumai
		II	sugosu darō	sugosanai darō
	FORMAL	I	sugoshimashō	sugoshimasumai
		II	sugosu deshō	sugosanai deshō
Provisional	**INFORMAL**		sugoseba	sugosanakereba
	FORMAL		sugoshimaseba	sugoshimasen nara
			sugoshimasureba	
Gerund	**INFORMAL**	I	sugoshite	sugosanai de
		II		sugosanakute
	FORMAL		sugoshimashite	sugoshimasen de
Past Ind.	**INFORMAL**		sugoshita	sugosanakatta
	FORMAL		sugoshimashita	sugoshimasen deshita
Past Presump.	**INFORMAL**		sugoshitarō	sugosanakattarō
			sugoshita darō	sugosanakatta darō
	FORMAL		sugoshimashitarō	sugoshimasen deshitarō
			sugoshita deshō	sugosanakatta deshō
Conditional	**INFORMAL**		sugoshitara	sugosanakattara
	FORMAL		sugoshimashitara	sugoshimasen deshitara
Alternative	**INFORMAL**		sugoshitari	sugosanakattari
	FORMAL		sugoshimashitari	sugoshimasen deshitari

		INFORMAL AFFIRMATIVE INDICATIVE
Passive		sugosareru
Potential		sugoseru
Causative		sugosaseru
Causative Pass.		sugosaserareru
Honorific	I	osugoshi ni naru
	II	osugoshi nasaru
Humble	I	osugoshi suru
	II	osugoshi itasu

すぐれる／優れる **sugure.ru**
to be excellent, to be superior, to surpass, to excel

			AFFIRMATIVE	**NEGATIVE**
Indicative	**INFORMAL**		sugureru	sugurenai
	FORMAL		suguremasu	suguremasen
Imperative	**INFORMAL**	I	sugurero	sugureru na
		II	sugurenasai	sugurenasaru na
		III	sugurete kudasai	sugurenai de kudasai
	FORMAL		osugure nasaimase	osugure nasaimasu na
Presumptive	**INFORMAL**	I	sugureyō	suguremai
		II	sugureru darō	sugurenai darō
	FORMAL	I	suguremashō	suguremasumai
		II	sugureru deshō	sugurenai deshō
Provisional	**INFORMAL**		sugurereba	sugurenakereba
	FORMAL		suguremaseba	suguremasen nara
			suguremasureba	
Gerund	**INFORMAL**	I	sugurete	sugurenai de
		II		sugurenakute
	FORMAL		suguremashite	suguremasen de
Past Ind.	**INFORMAL**		sugureta	sugurenakatta
	FORMAL		suguremashita	suguremasen deshita
Past Presump.	**INFORMAL**		suguretarō	sugurenakattarō
			sugureta darō	sugurenakatta darō
	FORMAL		suguremashitarō	suguremasen deshitarō
			sugureta deshō	sugurenakatta deshō
Conditional	**INFORMAL**		suguretara	sugurenakattara
	FORMAL		suguremashitara	suguremasen deshitara
Alternative	**INFORMAL**		suguretari	sugurenakattari
	FORMAL		suguremashitari	suguremasen deshitari

		INFORMAL AFFIRMATIVE INDICATIVE
Passive		sugurerareru
Potential		sugurerareru
Causative		suguresaseru
Causative Pass.		suguresaserareru

Honorific	I	osugure ni naru
	II	osugure nasaru
Humble	I	
	II	

S

suk.u すく／空く suki

to become empty, to become uncrowded

			AFFIRMATIVE	NEGATIVE
Indicative	INFORMAL		suku	sukanai
	FORMAL		sukimasu	sukimasen
Imperative	INFORMAL	I	suke	suku na
		II		
		III	suite kudasai	sukanai de kudasai
	FORMAL			
Presumptive	INFORMAL	I	sukō	sukumai
		II	suku darō	sukanai darō
	FORMAL	I	sukimashō	sukimasumai
		II	suku deshō	sukanai deshō
Provisional	INFORMAL		sukeba	sukanakereba
	FORMAL		sukimaseba	sukimasen nara
			sukimasureba	
Gerund	INFORMAL	I	suite	sukanai de
		II		sukanakute
	FORMAL		sukimashite	sukimasen de
Past Ind.	INFORMAL		suita	sukanakatta
	FORMAL		sukimashita	sukimasen deshita
Past Presump.	INFORMAL		suitarō	sukanakattarō
			suita darō	sukanakatta darō
	FORMAL		sukimashitarō	sukimasen deshitarō
			suita deshō	sukanakatta deshō
Conditional	INFORMAL		suitara	sukanakattara
	FORMAL		sukimashitara	sukimasen deshitara
Alternative	INFORMAL		suitari	sukanakattari
	FORMAL		sukimashitari	sukimasen deshitari

		INFORMAL AFFIRMATIVE INDICATIVE
Passive		
Potential		
Causative		sukaseru
Causative Pass.		sukaserareru
Honorific	I	
	II	
Humble	I	
	II	

468

すくう／救う　**suku.u**

TRANSITIVE　　*to rescue, to save*

			AFFIRMATIVE	**NEGATIVE**
Indicative	**INFORMAL**		sukuu	sukuwanai
	FORMAL		sukuimasu	sukuimasen
Imperative	**INFORMAL**	I	sukue	sukuu na
		II	sukuinasai	sukuinasaru na
		III	sukutte kudasai	sukuwanai de kudasai
	FORMAL		osukui nasaimase	osukui nasaimasu na
Presumptive	**INFORMAL**	I	sukuō	sukuumai
		II	sukuu darō	sukuwanai darō
	FORMAL	I	sukuimashō	sukuimasumai
		II	sukuu deshō	sukuwanai deshō
Provisional	**INFORMAL**		sukueba	sukuwanakereba
	FORMAL		sukuimaseba	sukuimasen nara
			sukuimasureba	
Gerund	**INFORMAL**	I	sukutte	sukuwanai de
		II		sukuwanakute
	FORMAL		sukuimashite	sukuimasen de
Past Ind.	**INFORMAL**		sukutta	sukuwanakatta
	FORMAL		sukuimashita	sukuimasen deshita
Past Presump.	**INFORMAL**		sukuttarō	sukuwanakattarō
			sukutta darō	sukuwanakatta darō
	FORMAL		sukuimashitarō	sukuimasen deshitarō
			sukutta deshō	sukuwanakatta deshō
Conditional	**INFORMAL**		sukuttara	sukuwanakattara
	FORMAL		sukuimashitara	sukuimasen deshitara
Alternative	**INFORMAL**		sukuttari	sukuwanakattari
	FORMAL		sukuimashitari	sukuimasen deshitari

			INFORMAL AFFIRMATIVE INDICATIVE
Passive			sukuwareru
Potential			sukueru
Causative			sukuwaseru
Causative Pass.			sukuwaserareru
Honorific		I	osukui ni naru
		II	osukui nasaru
Humble		I	osukui suru
		II	osukui itasu

sumase.ru* すませる／済ませる

to finish, to be over, to end   TRANSITIVE

			AFFIRMATIVE	NEGATIVE
Indicative	**INFORMAL**		sumaseru	sumasenai
	FORMAL		sumasemasu	sumasemasen
Imperative	**INFORMAL**	I	sumasero	sumaseru na
		II	sumasenasai	sumasenasaru na
		III	sumasete kudasai	sumasenai de kudasai
	FORMAL		osumase nasaimase	osumase nasaimasu na
Presumptive	**INFORMAL**	I	sumaseyō	sumasemai
		II	sumaseru darō	sumasenai darō
	FORMAL	I	sumasemashō	sumasemasumai
		II	sumaseru deshō	sumasenai deshō
Provisional	**INFORMAL**		sumasereba	sumasenakereba
	FORMAL		sumasemaseba	sumasemasen nara
			sumasemasureba	
Gerund	**INFORMAL**	I	sumasete	sumasenai de
		II		sumasenakute
	FORMAL		sumasemashite	sumasemasen de
Past Ind.	**INFORMAL**		sumaseta	sumasenakatta
	FORMAL		sumasemashita	sumasemasen deshita
Past Presump.	**INFORMAL**		sumasetarō	sumasenakattarō
			sumaseta darō	sumasenakatta darō
	FORMAL		sumasemashitarō	sumasemasen deshitarō
			sumaseta deshō	sumasenakatta deshō
Conditional	**INFORMAL**		sumasetara	sumasenakattara
	FORMAL		sumasemashitara	sumasemasen deshitara
Alternative	**INFORMAL**		sumasetari	sumasenakattari
	FORMAL		sumasemashitari	sumasemasen deshitari

		INFORMAL AFFIRMATIVE INDICATIVE
Passive		sumaserareru
Potential		sumaserareru
Causative		sumasaseru
Causative Pass.		sumasaserareru
Honorific	I	osumase ni naru
	II	osumase nasaru
Humble	I	osumase suru
	II	osumase itasu

*This is the causative form of *sum.u* "to end" and is given to illustrate the full range of inflection found in this type of derived verb.

すむ／住む **sum.u**
to reside, to live (location)

			AFFIRMATIVE	NEGATIVE
Indicative	**INFORMAL**		sumu	sumanai
	FORMAL		sumimasu	sumimasen
Imperative	**INFORMAL**	I	sume	sumu na
		II	suminasai	suminasaru na
		III	sunde kudasai	sumanai de kudasai
	FORMAL		osumi nasaimase	osumi nasaimasu na
Presumptive	**INFORMAL**	I	sumō	sumumai
		II	sumu darō	sumanai darō
	FORMAL	I	sumimashō	sumimasumai
		II	sumu deshō	sumanai deshō
Provisional	**INFORMAL**		sumeba	sumanakereba
	FORMAL		sumimaseba	sumimasen nara
			sumimasureba	
Gerund	**INFORMAL**	I	sunde	sumanai de
		II		sumanakute
	FORMAL		sumimashite	sumimasen de
Past Ind.	**INFORMAL**		sunda	sumanakatta
	FORMAL		sumimashita	sumimasen deshita
Past Presump.	**INFORMAL**		sundarō	sumanakattarō
			sunda darō	sumanakatta darō
	FORMAL		sumimashitarō	sumimasen deshitarō
			sunda deshō	sumanakatta deshō
Conditional	**INFORMAL**		sundara	sumanakattara
	FORMAL		sumimashitara	sumimasen deshitara
Alternative	**INFORMAL**		sundari	sumanakattari
	FORMAL		sumimashitari	sumimasen deshitari

		INFORMAL AFFIRMATIVE INDICATIVE
Passive		sumareru
Potential		sumeru
Causative		sumaseru
Causative Pass.		sumaserareru
Honorific	I	osumi ni naru
	II	osumi nasaru
Humble	I	
	II	

S

AN ESSENTIAL
55 VERB

Sumu 住む

to reside, to live

Sentences Using *Sumu*

Nihon ni sumitai.
日本に住みたい。
I'd like to live in Japan.

Amerika ni sunda koto ga arimasu.
アメリカに住んだことがあります。
I have lived in the United States.

Kōgai niwa sumitaku arimasen.
郊外には住みたくありません。
I don't want to live in the suburbs.

Kare wa dai toshi niwa suminarete imasen.
彼は大都市には住み慣れていません。
He is not used to living in a large city.

Tomodachi wa ōkii ie ni sunde imasu.
友達は大きい家に住んでいます。
My friend lives in a big house.

Sumu is a verb you'll use often as you ask and answer questions and make statements about where you and others live.

Words and Expressions Related to This Verb

ijū suru　移住する
to emigrate, to immigrate

eijū suru　永住する
to reside permanently

sumai　住まい
a house, a home, a residence

jūsho　住所
an address

Proverb

Sumeba miyako.　住めば都。
Home is where you make it. (No matter where you live, it'll become your palace.)

すむ／済む **sum.u**

to end, to be finished, to be over

			AFFIRMATIVE	NEGATIVE
Indicative	**INFORMAL**		sumu	sumanai
	FORMAL		sumimasu	sumimasen
Imperative	**INFORMAL**	I	sume	sumu na
		II		
		III	sunde kudasai	sumanai de kudasai
	FORMAL			
Presumptive	**INFORMAL**	I	sumō	sumumai
		II	sumu darō	sumanai darō
	FORMAL	I	sumimashō	sumimasumai
		II	sumu deshō	sumanai deshō
Provisional	**INFORMAL**		sumeba	sumanakereba
	FORMAL		sumimaseba	sumimasen nara
			sumimasureba	
Gerund	**INFORMAL**	I	sunde	sumanai de
		II		sumanakute
	FORMAL		sumimashite	sumimasen de
Past Ind.	**INFORMAL**		sunda	sumanakatta
	FORMAL		sumimashita	sumimasen deshita
Past Presump.	**INFORMAL**		sundarō	sumanakattarō
			sunda darō	sumanakatta darō
	FORMAL		sumimashitarō	sumimasen deshitarō
			sunda deshō	sumanakatta deshō
Conditional	**INFORMAL**		sundara	sumanakattara
	FORMAL		sumimashitara	sumimasen deshitara
Alternative	**INFORMAL**		sundari	sumanakattari
	FORMAL		sumimashitari	sumimasen deshitari

		INFORMAL AFFIRMATIVE INDICATIVE
Passive		sumareru
Potential		sumeru
Causative		sumaseru
Causative Pass.		sumaserareru
Honorific	I	osumi ni naru
	II	osumi nasaru
Humble	I	
	II	

S

to do, to make   TRANSITIVE

			AFFIRMATIVE	NEGATIVE
Indicative	**INFORMAL**		suru	shinai
	FORMAL		shimasu	shimasen
Imperative	**INFORMAL**	I	shiro	suru na
		II	shinasai	shinasaru na
		III	shite kudasai	shinai de kudasai
	FORMAL		nasaimase	nasaimasu na
Presumptive	**INFORMAL**	I	shiyō	surumai
		II	suru darō	shinai darō
	FORMAL	I	shimashō	shimasumai
		II	suru deshō	shinai deshō
Provisional	**INFORMAL**		sureba	shinakereba
	FORMAL		shimaseba	shimasen nara
			shimasureba	
Gerund	**INFORMAL**	I	shite	shinai de
		II		shinakute
	FORMAL		shimashite	shimasen de
Past Ind.	**INFORMAL**		shita	shinakatta
	FORMAL		shimashita	shimasen deshita
Past Presump.	**INFORMAL**		shitarō	shinakattarō
			shita darō	shinakatta darō
	FORMAL		shimashitarō	shimasen deshitarō
			shita deshō	shinakatta deshō
Conditional	**INFORMAL**		shitara	shinakattara
	FORMAL		shimashitara	shimasen deshitara
Alternative	**INFORMAL**		shitari	shinakattari
	FORMAL		shimashitari	shimasen deshitari

		INFORMAL AFFIRMATIVE INDICATIVE
Passive		sareru
Potential		dekiru
Causative		saseru
Causative Pass.		saserareru
Honorific	I	nasaru
	II	
Humble	I	itasu
	II	

AN ESSENTIAL
55 VERB

*This is used to derive verbs from Sino-Japanese nouns. For example, *kekkon* ("marriage") plus *su.ru* becomes *kekkon-suru* "to get married."

Suru　する

to do, to make

Sentences Using *Suru*

Sore wa, shitaku arimasen.
それは、したくありません。
I wouldn't like to do that.

Ima sugu ni, shite moraemasu ka.
今直ぐに、してもらえますか。
Could you do it now?

Nihon dewa, shitai koto ga takusan arimasu.
日本では、したいことがたくさんあります。
There are many things I want to do in Japan.

Otōto wa shukudai o shinaide nemutte shimatta.
弟は宿題をしないで眠ってしまった。
My younger brother fell asleep without doing his homework.

Shūmatsu niwa, niwa shigoto o shiyō to omotte imasu.
週末には庭仕事をしようと思っています。
I'm planning to do some yardwork during the weekend.

Suru is a verb you can't do without! Just like its English counterpart, it's one of the most common verbs in the Japanese language. And by combining it with certain nouns, you can create a verb form, as in denwa suru, or make a phone call.

S

Words and Expressions Related to This Verb

okonau　行う
to do, to carry out

shisonjiru　し損じる
to make a mistake

shitogeru　し遂げる
to carry through, to achieve

jikkō suru　実行する
to carry out

kekkō suru　決行する
to carry out

to recommend, to advise　　　TRANSITIVE

			AFFIRMATIVE	**NEGATIVE**
Indicative	**INFORMAL**		susumeru	susumenai
	FORMAL		susumemasu	susumemasen
Imperative	**INFORMAL**	I	susumero	susumeru na
		II	susumenasai	susumenasaru na
		III	susumete kudasai	susumenai de kudasai
	FORMAL		osusume nasaimase	osusume nasaimasu na
Presumptive	**INFORMAL**	I	susumeyō	susumemai
		II	susumeru darō	susumenai darō
	FORMAL	I	susumemashō	susumemasumai
		II	susumeru deshō	susumenai deshō
Provisional	**INFORMAL**		susumereba	susumenakereba
	FORMAL		susumemaseba	susumemasen nara
			susumemasureba	
Gerund	**INFORMAL**	I	susumete	susumenai de
		II		susumenakute
	FORMAL		susumemashite	susumemasen de
Past Ind.	**INFORMAL**		susumeta	susumenakatta
	FORMAL		susumemashita	susumemasen deshita
Past Presump.	**INFORMAL**		susumetarō	susumenakattarō
			susumeta darō	susumenakatta darō
	FORMAL		susumemashitarō	susumemasen deshitarō
			susumeta deshō	susumenakatta deshō
Conditional	**INFORMAL**		susumetara	susumenakattara
	FORMAL		susumemashitara	susumemasen deshitara
Alternative	**INFORMAL**		susumetari	susumenakattari
	FORMAL		susumemashitari	susumemasen deshitari

		INFORMAL AFFIRMATIVE INDICATIVE
Passive		susumerareru
Potential		susumerareru
Causative		susumesaseru
Causative Pass.		susumesaserareru
Honorific	I	osusume ni naru
	II	osusume nasaru
Humble	I	osusume suru
	II	osusume itasu

to go forward, to advance, to progress

			AFFIRMATIVE	NEGATIVE
Indicative	**INFORMAL**		susumu	susumanai
	FORMAL		susumimasu	susumimasen
Imperative	**INFORMAL**	I	susume	susumu na
		II	susuminasai	susuminasaru na
		III	susunde kudasai	susumanai de kudasai
	FORMAL		osusumi nasaimase	osusumi nasaimasu na
Presumptive	**INFORMAL**	I	susumō	susumumai
		II	susumu darō	susumanai darō
	FORMAL	I	susumimashō	susumimasumai
		II	susumu deshō	susumanai deshō
Provisional	**INFORMAL**		susumeba	susumanakereba
	FORMAL		susumimaseba	susumimasen nara
			susumimasureba	
Gerund	**INFORMAL**	I	susunde	susumanai de
		II		susumanakute
	FORMAL		susumimashite	susumimasen de
Past Ind.	**INFORMAL**		susunda	susumanakatta
	FORMAL		susumimashita	susumimasen deshita
Past Presump.	**INFORMAL**		susundarō	susumanakattarō
			susunda darō	susumanakatta darō
	FORMAL		susumimashitarō	susumimasen deshitarō
			susunda deshō	susumanakatta deshō
Conditional	**INFORMAL**		susundara	susumanakattara
	FORMAL		susumimashitara	susumimasen deshitara
Alternative	**INFORMAL**		susundari	susumanakattari
	FORMAL		susumimashitari	susumimasen deshitari

			INFORMAL AFFIRMATIVE INDICATIVE
Passive			susumareru
Potential			susumeru
Causative			susumaseru
Causative Pass.			susumaserareru
Honorific		I	osusumi ni naru
		II	osusumi nasaru
Humble		I	osusumi suru
		II	osusumi itasu

S

to throw away, to abandon TRANSITIVE

			AFFIRMATIVE	**NEGATIVE**
Indicative	**INFORMAL**		suteru	sutenai
	FORMAL		sutemasu	sutemasen
Imperative	**INFORMAL**	I	sutero	suteru na
		II	sutenasai	sutenasaru na
		III	sutete kudasai	sutenai de kudasai
	FORMAL		osute nasaimase	osute nasaimasu na
Presumptive	**INFORMAL**	I	suteyō	sutemai
		II	suteru darō	sutenai darō
	FORMAL	I	sutemashō	sutemasumai
		II	suteru deshō	sutenai deshō
Provisional	**INFORMAL**		sutereba	sutenakereba
	FORMAL		sutemaseba	sutemasen nara
			sutemasureba	
Gerund	**INFORMAL**	I	sutete	sutenai de
		II		sutenakute
	FORMAL		sutemashite	sutemasen de
Past Ind.	**INFORMAL**		suteta	sutenakatta
	FORMAL		sutemashita	sutemasen deshita
Past Presump.	**INFORMAL**		sutetarō	sutenakattarō
			suteta darō	sutenakatta darō
	FORMAL		sutemashitarō	sutemasen deshitarō
			suteta deshō	sutenakatta deshō
Conditional	**INFORMAL**		sutetara	sutenakattara
	FORMAL		sutemashitara	sutemasen deshitara
Alternative	**INFORMAL**		sutetari	sutenakattari
	FORMAL		sutemashitari	sutemasen deshitari

			INFORMAL AFFIRMATIVE INDICATIVE
Passive			suterareru
Potential			suterareru
Causative			sutesaseru
Causative Pass.			sutesaserareru
Honorific		I	osute ni naru
		II	osute nasaru
Humble		I	osute suru
		II	osute itasu

すう／吸う **su.u**

TRANSITIVE   *to sip, to breathe in, to smoke* (a cigarette)

			AFFIRMATIVE	**NEGATIVE**
Indicative	**INFORMAL**		suu	suwanai
	FORMAL		suimasu	suimasen
Imperative	**INFORMAL**	I	sue	suuna
		II	suinasai	suinasaru na
		III	sutte kudasai	suwanai de kudasai
	FORMAL		osui nasaimase	osui nasaimasu na
Presumptive	**INFORMAL**	I	suō	suumai
		II	suu darō	suwanai darō
	FORMAL	I	suimashō	suimasumai
		II	suu deshō	suwanai deshō
Provisional	**INFORMAL**		sueba	suwanakereba
	FORMAL		suimaseba	suimasen nara
			suimasureba	
Gerund	**INFORMAL**	I	sutte	suwanai de
		II		suwanakute
	FORMAL		suimashite	suimasen de
Past Ind.	**INFORMAL**		sutta	suwanakatta
	FORMAL		suimashita	suimasen deshita
Past Presump.	**INFORMAL**		suttarō	suwanakattarō
			sutta darō	suwanakatta darō
	FORMAL		suimashitarō	suimasen deshitarō
			sutta deshō	suwanakatta deshō
Conditional	**INFORMAL**		suttara	suwanakattara
	FORMAL		suimashitara	suimasen deshitara
Alternative	**INFORMAL**		suttari	suwanakattari
	FORMAL		suimashitari	suimasen deshitari

		INFORMAL AFFIRMATIVE INDICATIVE
Passive		suwareru
Potential		sueru
Causative		suwaseru
Causative Pass.		suwasaserareru
Honorific	I	osui ni naru
	II	osui nasaru
Humble	I	osui suru
	II	osui itasu

S

suwar.u　すわる／座る

to sit

suwari

			AFFIRMATIVE	NEGATIVE
Indicative	**INFORMAL**		suwaru	suwaranai
	FORMAL		suwarimasu	suwarimasen
Imperative	**INFORMAL**	I	suware	suwaru na
		II	suwarinasai	suwarinasaru na
		III	suwatte kudasai	suwaranai de kudasai
	FORMAL		osuwari nasaimase	osuwari nasaimasu na
Presumptive	**INFORMAL**	I	suwarō	suwarumai
		II	suwaru darō	suwaranai darō
	FORMAL	I	suwarimashō	suwarimasumai
		II	suwaru deshō	suwaranai deshō
Provisional	**INFORMAL**		suwareba	suwaranakereba
	FORMAL		suwarimaseba	suwarimasen nara
			suwarimasureba	
Gerund	**INFORMAL**	I	suwatte	suwaranai de
		II		suwaranakute
	FORMAL		suwarimashite	suwarimasen de
Past Ind.	**INFORMAL**		suwatta	suwaranakatta
	FORMAL		suwarimashita	suwarimasen deshita
Past Presump.	**INFORMAL**		suwattarō	suwaranakattarō
			suwatta darō	suwaranakatta darō
	FORMAL		suwarimashitarō	suwarimasen deshitarō
			suwatta deshō	suwaranakatta deshō
Conditional	**INFORMAL**		suwattara	suwaranakattara
	FORMAL		suwarimashitara	suwarimasen deshitara
Alternative	**INFORMAL**		suwattari	suwaranakattari
	FORMAL		suwarimashitari	suwarimasen deshitari

		INFORMAL AFFIRMATIVE INDICATIVE
Passive		suwarareru
Potential		suwareru
Causative		suwaraseru
Causative Pass.		suwaraserareru
Honorific	I	osuwari ni naru
	II	osuwari nasaru
Humble	I	
	II	

480

tabe たべる／食べる tabe.ru

TRANSITIVE *to eat*

			AFFIRMATIVE	NEGATIVE
Indicative	**INFORMAL**		taberu	tabenai
	FORMAL		tabemasu	tabemasen
Imperative	**INFORMAL**	I	tabero	taberu na
		II	tabenasai	tabenasaru na
		III	tabete kudasai	tabenai de kudasai
	FORMAL		meshiagarimase	meshiagarimasu na
Presumptive	**INFORMAL**	I	tabeyō	tabemai
		II	taberu darō	tabenai darō
	FORMAL	I	tabemashō	tabemasumai
		II	taberu deshō	tabenai deshō
Provisional	**INFORMAL**		tabereba	tabenakereba
	FORMAL		tabemaseba	tabemasen nara
			tabemasureba	
Gerund	**INFORMAL**	I	tabete	tabenai de
		II		tabenakute
	FORMAL		tabemashite	tabemasen de
Past Ind.	**INFORMAL**		tabeta	tabenakatta
	FORMAL		tabemashita	tabemasen deshita
Past Presump.	**INFORMAL**		tabetarō	tabenakattarō
			tabeta darō	tabenakatta darō
	FORMAL		tabemashitarō	tabemasen deshitarō
			tabeta deshō	tabenakatta deshō
Conditional	**INFORMAL**		tabetara	tabenakattara
	FORMAL		tabemashitara	tabemasen deshitara
Alternative	**INFORMAL**		tabetari	tabenakattari
	FORMAL		tabemashitari	tabemasen deshitari

	INFORMAL AFFIRMATIVE INDICATIVE
Passive	taberareru
Potential	taberareru
Causative	tabesaseru
Causative Pass.	tabesaserareru
Honorific	meshiagaru
Humble	itadaku

AN ESSENTIAL
55 VERB

AN ESSENTIAL
55 VERB

Taberu 食べる

to eat

Sentences Using *Taberu*

Konban wa sukiyaki o tabete, ashita wa sushi o tabemasu.
今晩はすき焼きを食べて、明日は鮨を食べます。
We'll eat sukiyaki tonight and sushi tomorrow.

Taberarenai mono ga arimasu ka.
食べられないものがありますか。
Is there anything you can't eat?

Kanojo wa ikura tabetemo futoranai.
彼女はいくら食べても太らない。
No matter how much she eats, she doesn't get fat.

Kare wa kudamono o tabemasen.
彼は果物を食べません。
He doesn't eat fruit.

Yūbe ōkii bifuteki o tabemashita.
夕べ、大きいビフテキを食べました。
Last night we ate a huge steak.

Proverb

Tade kuu mushi mo sukizuki.
蓼食う虫も好き好き。
Each man to his taste. (Some insects like to eat the fiery hot water pepper plant and others don't.)

Taberu is an essential verb because whether you eat to live or live to eat, you have to do it! The delicious food is one of the great pleasures of being in Japan. Although Japanese cuisine is now enjoyed worldwide, eating sushi in Japan is still a special experience.

Words and Expressions Related to This Verb

shokuji suru　食事する
to have a meal

tabe sugiru　食べ過ぎる
to eat too much

tabemono　食べ物
food

shokuyoku　食欲
appetite

tabenokoshi　食べ残し
leftovers

tadori

TRANSITIVE　　　*to pursue* (a course), *to follow* (a path), *to trace*

			AFFIRMATIVE	NEGATIVE
Indicative	**INFORMAL**		tadoru	tadoranai
	FORMAL		tadorimasu	tadorimasen
Imperative	**INFORMAL**	I	tadore	tadoru na
		II	tadorinasai	tadorinasaru na
		III	tadotte kudasai	tadoranai de kudasai
	FORMAL		otadori nasaimase	otadori nasaimasu na
Presumptive	**INFORMAL**	I	tadorō	tadorumai
		II	tadoru darō	tadoranai darō
	FORMAL	I	tadorimashō	tadorimasumai
		II	tadoru deshō	tadoranai deshō
Provisional	**INFORMAL**		tadoreba	tadoranakereba
	FORMAL		tadorimaseba	tadorimasen nara
			tadorimasureba	
Gerund	**INFORMAL**	I	tadotte	tadoranai de
		II		tadoranakute
	FORMAL		tadorimashite	tadorimasen de
Past Ind.	**INFORMAL**		tadotta	tadoranakatta
	FORMAL		tadorimashita	tadorimasen deshita
Past Presump.	**INFORMAL**		tadottarō	tadoranakattarō
			tadotta darō	tadoranakatta darō
	FORMAL		tadorimashitarō	tadorimasen deshitarō
			tadotta deshō	tadoranakatta deshō
Conditional	**INFORMAL**		tadottara	tadoranakattara
	FORMAL		tadorimashitara	tadorimasen deshitara
Alternative	**INFORMAL**		tadottari	tadoranakattari
	FORMAL		tadorimashitari	tadorimasen deshitari

		INFORMAL AFFIRMATIVE INDICATIVE
Passive		tadorareru
Potential		tadoreru
Causative		tadoraseru
Causative Pass.		tadoraserareru
Honorific	I	otadori ni naru
	II	otadori nasaru
Humble	I	otadori suru
	II	otadori itasu

-tagar.u　〜たがる　　　　　　　　　　　　　　　　　　　-tagari

to want to, to wish to, to be eager to (non-first person desiderative suffix*)

			AFFIRMATIVE	NEGATIVE
Indicative	**INFORMAL**		-tagaru	-tagaranai
	FORMAL		-tagarimasu	-tagarimasen
Imperative	**INFORMAL**	I	-tagare	-tagaru na
		II	-tagarinasai	-tagarinasaru na
		III	-tagatte kudasai	-tagaranai de kudasai
	FORMAL			
Presumptive	**INFORMAL**	I	-tagarō	-tagarumai
		II	-tagaru darō	-tagaranai darō
	FORMAL	I	-tagarimashō	-tagarimasumai
		II	-tagaru deshō	-tagaranai deshō
Provisional	**INFORMAL**		-tagareba	-tagaranakereba
	FORMAL		-tagarimaseba	-tagarimasen nara
			-tagarimasureba	
Gerund	**INFORMAL**	I	-tagatte	-tagaranai de
		II		-tagaranakute
	FORMAL		-tagarimashite	-tagarimasen de
Past Ind.	**INFORMAL**		-tagatta	-tagaranakatta
	FORMAL		-tagarimashita	-tagarimasen deshita
Past Presump.	**INFORMAL**		-tagattarō	-tagaranakattarō
			-tagatta darō	-tagaranakatta darō
	FORMAL		-tagarimashitarō	-tagarimasen deshitarō
			-tagatta deshō	-tagaranakatta deshō
Conditional	**INFORMAL**		-tagattara	-tagaranakattara
	FORMAL		-tagarimashitara	-tagarimasen deshitara
Alternative	**INFORMAL**		-tagattari	-tagaranakattari
	FORMAL		-tagarimashitari	-tagarimasen deshitari

		INFORMAL AFFIRMATIVE INDICATIVE
Passive		-tabetagarareru
Potential		-tabetagareru
Causative		-tagaraseru
Causative Pass.		-tagaraserareru
Honorific	I	
	II	
Humble	I	
	II	

*-*tagaru* is added to the infinitive of verbs, and like -*masu* does not have
any transitive/intransitive bias of its own.

takurami

TRANSITIVE   *to plot, to scheme, to conspire*

			AFFIRMATIVE	NEGATIVE
Indicative	**INFORMAL**		takuramu	takuramanai
	FORMAL		takuramimasu	takuramimasen
Imperative	**INFORMAL**	I	takurame	takuramu na
		II	takuraminasai	takuraminasaru na
		III	takurande kudasai	takuramanai de kudasai
	FORMAL		otakurami nasaimase	otakurami nasaimasu na
Presumptive	**INFORMAL**	I	takuramō	takuramumai
		II	takuramu darō	takuramanai darō
	FORMAL	I	takuramimashō	takuramimasumai
		II	takuramu deshō	takuramanai deshō
Provisional	**INFORMAL**		takurameba	takuramanakereba
	FORMAL		takuramimaseba	takuramimasen nara
			takuramimasureba	
Gerund	**INFORMAL**	I	takurande	takuramanai de
		II		takuramanakute
	FORMAL		takuramimashite	takuramimasen de
Past Ind.	**INFORMAL**		takuranda	takuramanakatta
	FORMAL		takuramimashita	takuramimasen deshita
Past Presump.	**INFORMAL**		takurandarō	takuramanakattarō
			takuranda darō	takuramanakatta darō
	FORMAL		takuramimashitarō	takuramimasen deshitarō
			takuranda deshō	takuramanakatta deshō
Conditional	**INFORMAL**		takurandara	takuramanakattara
	FORMAL		takuramimashitara	takuramimasen deshitara
Alternative	**INFORMAL**		takurandari	takuramanakattari
	FORMAL		takuramimashitari	takuramimasen deshitari

			INFORMAL AFFIRMATIVE INDICATIVE
Passive			takuramareru
Potential			takurameru
Causative			takuramaseru
Causative Pass.			takuramaserareru
Honorific		I	otakurami ni naru
		II	otakurami nasaru
Humble		I	
		II	

to save (money, etc.), *to store, to lay aside*　　　TRANSITIVE

			AFFIRMATIVE	NEGATIVE
Indicative	**INFORMAL**		takuwaeru	takuwaenai
	FORMAL		takuwaemasu	takuwaemasen
Imperative	**INFORMAL**	I	takuwaero	takuwaeru na
		II	takuwaenasai	takuwaenasaru na
		III	takuwaete kudasai	takuwaenai de kudasai
	FORMAL		otakuwae nasaimase	otakuwae nasaimasu na
Presumptive	**INFORMAL**	I	takuwaeyō	takuwaemai
		II	takuwaeru darō	takuwaenai darō
	FORMAL	I	takuwaemashō	takuwaemasumai
		II	takuwaeru deshō	takuwaenai deshō
Provisional	**INFORMAL**		takuwaereba	takuwaenakereba
	FORMAL		takuwaemaseba	takuwaemasen nara
			takuwaemasureba	
Gerund	**INFORMAL**	I	takuwaete	takuwaenai de
		II		takuwaenakute
	FORMAL		takuwaemashite	takuwaemasen de
Past Ind.	**INFORMAL**		takuwaeta	takuwaenakatta
	FORMAL		takuwaemashita	takuwaemasen deshita
Past Presump.	**INFORMAL**		takuwaetarō	takuwaenakattarō
			takuwaeta darō	takuwaenakatta darō
	FORMAL		takuwaemashitarō	takuwaemasen deshitarō
			takuwaeta deshō	takuwaenakatta deshō
Conditional	**INFORMAL**		takuwaetara	takuwaenakattara
	FORMAL		takuwaemashitara	takuwaemasen deshitara
Alternative	**INFORMAL**		takuwaetari	takuwaenakattari
	FORMAL		takuwaemashitari	takuwaemasen deshitari

			INFORMAL AFFIRMATIVE INDICATIVE
Passive			takuwaerareru
Potential			takuwaerareru
Causative			takuwaesaseru
Causative Pass.			takuwaesaserareru
Honorific		I	otakuwae ni naru
		II	otakuwae nasaru
Humble		I	otakuwae suru
		II	otakuwae itasu

tamari   たまる／貯まる／溜まる   tamar.u

to be saved, to be accumulated

			AFFIRMATIVE	NEGATIVE
Indicative	INFORMAL		tamaru	tamaranai
	FORMAL		tamarimasu	tamarimasen
Imperative	INFORMAL	I	tamare	tamaru na
		II		
		III	tamatte kudasai	tamaranai de kudasai
	FORMAL			
Presumptive	INFORMAL	I	tamarō	tamarumai
		II	tamaru darō	tamaranai darō
	FORMAL	I	tamarimashō	tamarimashumai
		II	tamaru deshō	tamaranai deshō
Provisional	INFORMAL		tamareba	tamaranakereba
	FORMAL		tamarimaseba	tamarimasen nara
			tamarimasureba	
Gerund	INFORMAL	I	tamatte	tamaranai de
		II		tamaranakute
	FORMAL		tamarimashite	tamarimasen de
Past Ind.	INFORMAL		tamatta	tamaranakatta
	FORMAL		tamarimashita	tamarimasen deshita
Past Presump.	INFORMAL		tamattarō	tamaranakattarō
			tamatta darō	tamaranakatta darō
	FORMAL		tamarimashitarō	tamarimasen deshitarō
			tamatta deshō	tamaranakatta deshō
Conditional	INFORMAL		tamattara	tamaranakattara
	FORMAL		tamarimashitara	tamarimasen deshitara
Alternative	INFORMAL		tamattari	tamaranakattari
	FORMAL		tamarimashitari	tamarimasen deshitari

		INFORMAL AFFIRMATIVE INDICATIVE
Passive		
Potential		tamareru
Causative		tamaraseru
Causative Pass.		tamaraserareru
Honorific	I	otamari ni naru
	II	otamari nasaru
Humble	I	
	II	

tamera.u　ためらう　　　　　　　　　　　　　　　　　　**tamerai**
to hesitate, to flinch, to waver　　　TRANSITIVE

			AFFIRMATIVE	NEGATIVE
Indicative	**INFORMAL**		tamerau	tamerawanai
	FORMAL		tameraimasu	tameraimasen
Imperative	**INFORMAL**	I	tamerae	tamerau na
		II	tamerainasai	tamerainasaru na
		III	tameratte kudasai	tamerawanai de kudasai
	FORMAL		otamerai nasaimase	otamerai nasaimasu na
Presumptive	**INFORMAL**	I	tameraō	tameraumai
		II	tamerau darō	tamerawanai darō
	FORMAL	I	tameraimashō	tameraimasumai
		II	tamerau deshō	tamerawanai deshō
Provisional	**INFORMAL**		tameraeba	tamerawanakereba
	FORMAL		tameraimaseba	tameraimasen nara
			tameraimasureba	
Gerund	**INFORMAL**	I	tameratte	tamerawanai de
		II		tamerawanakute
	FORMAL		tameraimashite	tameraimasen de
Past Ind.	**INFORMAL**		tameratta	tamerawanakatta
	FORMAL		tameraimashita	tameraimasen deshita
Past Presump.	**INFORMAL**		tamerattarō	tamerawanakattarō
			tameratta darō	tamerawanakatta darō
	FORMAL		tameraimashitarō	tameraimasen deshitarō
			tameratta deshō	tamerawanakatta deshō
Conditional	**INFORMAL**		tamerattara	tamerawanakattara
	FORMAL		tameraimashitara	tameraimasen deshitara
Alternative	**INFORMAL**		tamerattari	tamerawanakattari
	FORMAL		tameraimashitari	tameraimasen deshitari

			INFORMAL AFFIRMATIVE INDICATIVE
Passive			tamerawareru
Potential			tameraeru
Causative			tamerawaseru
Causative Pass.			tamerawaserareru
Honorific		I	otamerai ni naru
		II	otamerai nasaru
Humble		I	
		II	

			AFFIRMATIVE	NEGATIVE
Indicative	**INFORMAL**		tameru	tamenai
	FORMAL		tamemasu	tamemasen
Imperative	**INFORMAL**	I	tamero	tameru na
		II	tamenasai	tamenasaru na
		III	tamete kudasai	tamenai de kudasai
	FORMAL		otame nasaimase	otame nasaimasu na
Presumptive	**INFORMAL**	I	tameyō	tamerumai
		II	tameru darō	tamenai darō
	FORMAL	I	tamemashō	tamemasumai
		II	tameru deshō	tamenai deshō
Provisional	**INFORMAL**		tamereba	tamenakereba
	FORMAL		tamemaseba	tamemasen nara
			tamemasureba	
Gerund	**INFORMAL**	I	tamete	tamenai de
		II		tamenakute
	FORMAL		tamemashite	tamemasen de
Past Ind.	**INFORMAL**		tameta	tamenakatta
	FORMAL		tamemashita	tamemasen deshita
Past Presump.	**INFORMAL**		tametarō	tamenakattarō
			tameta darō	tamenakatta darō
	FORMAL		tamemashitarō	tamemasen deshitarō
			tameta deshō	tamenakatta deshō
Conditional	**INFORMAL**		tametara	tamenakattara
	FORMAL		tamemashitara	tamemasen deshitara
Alternative	**INFORMAL**		tametari	tamenakattari
	FORMAL		tamemashitari	tamemasen deshitari

		INFORMAL AFFIRMATIVE INDICATIVE
Passive		tamerareru
Potential		tamerareru
Causative		tamesaseru
Causative Pass.		tamesaserareru
Honorific	I	otame ni naru
	II	otame nasaru
Humble	I	otame suru
	II	otame itasu

T

tames.u　ためす／試す　　　　　　　　　　　　　　　　tameshi

to try, to test, to taste　　　TRANSITIVE

			AFFIRMATIVE	**NEGATIVE**
Indicative	**INFORMAL**		tamesu	tamesanai
	FORMAL		tameshimasu	tameshimasen
Imperative	**INFORMAL**	I	tamese	tamesu na
		II	tameshinasai	tameshinasaru na
		III	tameshite kudasai	tamesanai de kudasai
	FORMAL		otameshi nasaimase	otameshi nasaimasu na
Presumptive	**INFORMAL**	I	tamesō	tamesumai
		II	tamesu darō	tamesanai darō
	FORMAL	I	tameshimashō	tameshimasumai
		II	tamesu deshō	tamesanai deshō
Provisional	**INFORMAL**		tameseba	tamesanakereba
	FORMAL		tameshimaseba	tameshimasen nara
			tameshimasureba	
Gerund	**INFORMAL**	I	tameshite	tamesanai de
		II		tamesanakute
	FORMAL		tameshimashite	tameshimasen de
Past Ind.	**INFORMAL**		tameshita	tamesanakatta
	FORMAL		tameshimashita	tameshimasen deshita
Past Presump.	**INFORMAL**		tameshitarō	tamesanakattarō
			tameshita darō	tamesanakatta darō
	FORMAL		tameshimashitarō	tameshimasen deshitarō
			tameshita deshō	tamesanakatta deshō
Conditional	**INFORMAL**		tameshitara	tamesanakattara
	FORMAL		tameshimashitara	tameshimasen deshitara
Alternative	**INFORMAL**		tameshitari	tamesanakattari
	FORMAL		tameshimashitari	tameshimasen deshitari

			INFORMAL AFFIRMATIVE INDICATIVE
Passive			tamesareru
Potential			tameseru
Causative			tamesaseru
Causative Pass.			tamesaserareru
Honorific		I	otameshi ni naru
		II	otameshi nasaru
Humble		I	otameshi suru
		II	otameshi itasu

490

たのむ／頼む　**tanom.u**

TRANSITIVE　　*to ask* (a favor), *to request, to order*

			AFFIRMATIVE	NEGATIVE
Indicative	**INFORMAL**		tanomu	tanomanai
	FORMAL		tanomimasu	tanomimasen
Imperative	**INFORMAL**	I	tanome	tanomu na
		II	tanominasai	tanominasaru na
		III	tanonde kudasai	tanomanai de kudasai
	FORMAL		otanomi nasaimase	otanomi nasaimasu na
Presumptive	**INFORMAL**	I	tanomō	tanomumai
		II	tanomu darō	tanomanai darō
	FORMAL	I	tanomimashō	tanomimasumai
		II	tanomu deshō	tanomanai deshō
Provisional	**INFORMAL**		tanomeba	tanomanakereba
	FORMAL		tanomimaseba	tanomimasen nara
			tanomimasureba	
Gerund	**INFORMAL**	I	tanonde	tanomanai de
		II		tanomanakute
	FORMAL		tanomimashite	tanomimasen de
Past Ind.	**INFORMAL**		tanonda	tanomanakatta
	FORMAL		tanomimashita	tanomimasen deshita
Past Presump.	**INFORMAL**		tanondarō	tanomanakattarō
			tanonda darō	tanomanakatta darō
	FORMAL		tanomimashitarō	tanomimasen deshitarō
			tanonda deshō	tanomanakatta deshō
Conditional	**INFORMAL**		tanondara	tanomanakattara
	FORMAL		tanomimashitara	tanomimasen deshitara
Alternative	**INFORMAL**		tanondari	tanomanakattari
	FORMAL		tanomimashitari	tanomimasen deshitari

			INFORMAL AFFIRMATIVE INDICATIVE
Passive			tanomareru
Potential			tanomeru
Causative			tanomaseru
Causative Pass.			tanomaserareru
Honorific		I	otanomi ni naru
		II	otanomi nasaru
Humble		I	otanomi suru
		II	otanomi itasu

T

AN ESSENTIAL
55 VERB

Tanomu 頼む

to ask (a favor), to request, to order

Tanomu is a verb you need in common everyday situations to ask for things, order meals, ask favors, and much more. You can't get along without it!

Sentences Using *Tanomu*

Haha ni otsukai o suru yō ni tanomaremashita.
母にお遣いをするように頼まれました。
I was asked by mother to do errands.

Dezāto o tanomimashō ka.
デザートを頼みましょうか。
Shall we order dessert?

Tasuke o tanomu tsumori wa nai.
助けを頼むつもりはない。
I have no intention of asking for help.

Tomodachi ni kuruma o kashite kureru yō tanomimashita.
友達に車を貸してくれるよう頼みました。
I asked my friend to lend me her car.

Kanojo ni tanomeba nandemo shite kureru.
彼女に頼めば何でもしてくれる。
If you ask her, she will do anything for you.

Words and Expressions Related to This Verb

irai suru　依頼する
to ask, to request, to rely on

yōsei suru　要請する
to ask, to request

onegai suru　お願いする
to have a favor to ask

tanomi no tsuna　頼みの綱
one's mainstay

Proverb

Kurushii toki no kami danomi.
苦しい時の神頼み。
Once on shore, we pray no more.
(Ask the gods for help only when you're having a difficult time.)

たのしむ／楽しむ　tanoshim.u

TRANSITIVE　*to enjoy, to have fun, to have a good time*

			AFFIRMATIVE	NEGATIVE
Indicative	**INFORMAL**		tanoshimu	tanoshimanai
	FORMAL		tanoshimimasu	tanoshimimasen
Imperative	**INFORMAL**	I	tanoshime	tanoshimu na
		II	tanoshiminasai	tanoshiminasaru na
		III	tanoshinde kudasai	tanoshimanai de kudasai
	FORMAL		otanoshimi nasaimase	otanoshimi nasaimasu na
Presumptive	**INFORMAL**	I	tanoshimō	tanoshimumai
		II	tanoshimu darō	tanoshimanai darō
	FORMAL	I	tanoshimimashō	tanoshimimasumai
		II	tanoshimu deshō	tanoshimanai deshō
Provisional	**INFORMAL**		tanoshimeba	tanoshimanakereba
	FORMAL		tanoshimimaseba	tanoshimimasen nara
			tanoshimimasureba	
Gerund	**INFORMAL**	I	tanoshinde	tanoshimanai de
		II		tanoshimanakute
	FORMAL		tanoshimimashite	tanoshimimasen de
Past Ind.	**INFORMAL**		tanoshinda	tanoshimanakatta
	FORMAL		tanoshimimashita	tanoshimimasen deshita
Past Presump.	**INFORMAL**		tanoshindarō	tanoshimanakattarō
			tanoshinda darō	tanoshimanakatta darō
	FORMAL		tanoshimimashitarō	tanoshimimasen deshitarō
			tanoshinda deshō	tanoshimanakatta deshō
Conditional	**INFORMAL**		tanoshindara	tanoshimanakattara
	FORMAL		tanoshimimashitara	tanoshimimasen deshitara
Alternative	**INFORMAL**		tanoshindari	tanoshimanakattari
	FORMAL		tanoshimimashitari	tanoshimimasen deshitari

		INFORMAL AFFIRMATIVE INDICATIVE
Passive		tanoshimareru
Potential		tanoshimeru
Causative		tanoshimaseru
Causative Pass.		tanoshimaserareru
Honorific	I	otanoshimi ni naru
	II	otanoshimi nasaru
Humble	I	
	II	

AN ESSENTIAL 55 VERB

AN ESSENTIAL 55 VERB

Tanoshimu 楽しむ

to enjoy, to have fun, to have a good time

Tanoshimu is a verb you need every day for enjoying yourself, having fun, having a good time. You'll do all of that in Japan!

Sentences Using *Tanoshimu*

Nihon de tanoshinde imasu ka.
日本で楽しんでいますか。
Are you having a good time in Japan?

Kyonen Amerika ryokō o tanoshinda.
去年アメリカ旅行を楽しんだ。
I enjoyed my trip to the United States last year.

Musume mo musuko mo, natsu wa sāfin, fuyu wa sunōbōdo o tanoshimimasu.
娘も息子も、夏はサーフィン、冬はスノーボードを楽しみます。
Both my son and daughter enjoy surfing in summer, snowboarding in winter.

Kaigan ni itta keredo, samusugite tanoshimu koto ga dekinakatta.
海岸に行ったけど、寒すぎて楽しむことが出来なかった。
We went to the beach but couldn't have any fun because it was too cold.

Chichi wa shūmatsu ni hirune o tanoshimō to omotte iru.
父は週末に昼寝を楽しもうと思っている。
My father is planning to enjoy a nap during the weekend.

Words and Expressions Related to This Verb

raku suru 楽する
to live comfortably, to have an easy life

tanoshimu 楽しみ
enjoyment, fun, pleasure, joy

goraku 娯楽
entertainment, recreation, a pastime

rakuraku 楽々
easily, effortlessly

Proverb

Raku areba ku ari ku areba raku ari.
楽あれば苦あり苦あれば楽あり。
There is no pleasure without pain.

to fall over (from a standing position), *to collapse, to fall down*

			AFFIRMATIVE	**NEGATIVE**
Indicative	**INFORMAL**		taoreru	taorenai
	FORMAL		taoremasu	taoremasen
Imperative	**INFORMAL**	I	taorero	taoreru na
		II	taorenasai	taorenasaru na
		III	taorete kudasai	taorenai de kudasai
	FORMAL		otaore nasaimase	otaore nasaimasu na
Presumptive	**INFORMAL**	I	taoreyō	taoremai
		II	taoreru darō	taorenai darō
	FORMAL	I	taoremashō	taoremasumai
		II	taoreru deshō	taorenai deshō
Provisional	**INFORMAL**		taorereba	taorenakereba
	FORMAL		taoremaseba	taoremasen nara
			taoremasureba	
Gerund	**INFORMAL**	I	taorete	taorenai de
		II		taorenakute
	FORMAL		taoremashite	taoremasen de
Past Ind.	**INFORMAL**		taoreta	taorenakatta
	FORMAL		taoremashita	taoremasen deshita
Past Presump.	**INFORMAL**		taoretarō	taorenakattarō
			taoreta darō	taorenakatta darō
	FORMAL		taoremashitarō	taoremasen deshitarō
			taoreta deshō	taorenakatta deshō
Conditional	**INFORMAL**		taoretara	taorenakattara
	FORMAL		taoremashitara	taoremasen deshitara
Alternative	**INFORMAL**		taoretari	taorenakattari
	FORMAL		taoremashitari	taoremasen deshitari

		INFORMAL AFFIRMATIVE INDICATIVE
Passive		taorerareru
Potential		taorerareru
Causative		taoresaseru
Causative Pass.		taoresaserareru
Honorific	I	otaore ni naru
	II	otaore nasaru
Humble	I	
	II	

T

495

taos.u　たおす／倒す

to overthrow, to knock down, to throw down　TRANSITIVE

taoshi

			AFFIRMATIVE	NEGATIVE
Indicative	**INFORMAL**		taosu	taosanai
	FORMAL		taoshimasu	taoshimasen
Imperative	**INFORMAL**	I	taose	taosu na
		II	taoshinasai	taoshinasaru na
		III	taoshite kudasai	taosanai de kudasai
	FORMAL		otaoshi nasaimase	otaoshi nasaimasu na
Presumptive	**INFORMAL**	I	taosō	taosumai
		II	taosu darō	taosanai darō
	FORMAL	I	taoshimashō	taoshimasumai
		II	taosu deshō	taosanai deshō
Provisional	**INFORMAL**		taoseba	taosanakereba
	FORMAL		taoshimaseba	taoshimasen nara
			taoshimasureba	
Gerund	**INFORMAL**	I	taoshite	taosanai de
		II		taosanakute
	FORMAL		taoshimashite	taoshimasen de
Past Ind.	**INFORMAL**		taoshita	taosanakatta
	FORMAL		taoshimashita	taoshimasen deshita
Past Presump.	**INFORMAL**		taoshitarō	taosanakattarō
			taoshita darō	taosanakatta darō
	FORMAL		taoshimashitarō	taoshimasen deshitarō
			taoshita deshō	taosanakatta deshō
Conditional	**INFORMAL**		taoshitara	taosanakattara
	FORMAL		taoshimashitara	taoshimasen deshitara
Alternative	**INFORMAL**		taoshitari	taosanakattari
	FORMAL		taoshimashitari	taoshimasen deshitari

		INFORMAL AFFIRMATIVE INDICATIVE
Passive		taosareru
Potential		taoseru
Causative		taosaseru
Causative Pass.		taosaserareru
Honorific	I	otaoshi ni naru
	II	otaoshi nasaru
Humble	I	otaoshi suru
	II	otaoshi itasu

			AFFIRMATIVE	NEGATIVE
Indicative	**INFORMAL**		tariru	tarinai
	FORMAL		tarimasu	tarimasen
Imperative	**INFORMAL**	**I**		
		II		
		III		
	FORMAL			
Presumptive	**INFORMAL**	**I**	tariyō	tarimai
		II	tariru darō	tarinai darō
	FORMAL	**I**	tarimashō	tarimasumai
		II	tariru deshō	tarinai deshō
Provisional	**INFORMAL**		tarireba	tarinakereba
	FORMAL		tarimaseba	tarimasen nara
			tarimasureba	
Gerund	**INFORMAL**	**I**	tarite	tarinai de
		II		tarinakute
	FORMAL		tarimashite	tarimasen de
Past Ind.	**INFORMAL**		tarita	tarinakatta
	FORMAL		tarimashita	tarimasen deshita
Past Presump.	**INFORMAL**		taritarō	tarinakattarō
			tarita darō	tarinakatta darō
	FORMAL		tarimashitarō	tarimasen deshitarō
			tarita deshō	tarinakatta deshō
Conditional	**INFORMAL**		taritara	tarinakattara
	FORMAL		tarimashitara	tarimasen deshitara
Alternative	**INFORMAL**		taritari	tarinakattari
	FORMAL		tarimashitari	tarimasen deshitari

	INFORMAL AFFIRMATIVE INDICATIVE
Passive	
Potential	
Causative	
Causative Pass.	
Honorific **I**	
II	
Humble **I**	
II	

T

tashikame.ru　たしかめる／確かめる　tashikame

to make sure, to check　TRANSITIVE

			AFFIRMATIVE	**NEGATIVE**
Indicative	**INFORMAL**		tashikameru	tashikamenai
	FORMAL		tashikamemasu	tashikamemasen
Imperative	**INFORMAL**	**I**	tashikamero	tashikameru na
		II	tashikamenasai	tashikamenasaru na
		III	tashikamete kudasai	tashikamenai de kudasai
	FORMAL		otashikame nasaimase	otashikame nasaimasu na
Presumptive	**INFORMAL**	**I**	tashikameyō	tashikamemai
		II	tashikameru darō	tashikamenai darō
	FORMAL	**I**	tashikamemashō	tashikamemasumai
		II	tashikameru deshō	tashikamenai deshō
Provisional	**INFORMAL**		tashikamereba	tashikamenakereba
	FORMAL		tashikamemaseba	tashikamemasen nara
			tashikamemasureba	
Gerund	**INFORMAL**	**I**	tashikamete	tashikamenai de
		II		tashikamenakute
	FORMAL		tashikamemashite	tashikamemasen de
Past Ind.	**INFORMAL**		tashikameta	tashikamenakatta
	FORMAL		tashikamemashita	tashikamemasen deshita
Past Presump.	**INFORMAL**		tashikametarō	tashikamenakattarō
			tashikameta darō	tashikamenakatta darō
	FORMAL		tashikamemashitarō	tashikamemasen deshitarō
			tashikameta deshō	tashikamenakatta deshō
Conditional	**INFORMAL**		tashikametara	tashikamenakattara
	FORMAL		tashikamemashitara	tashikamemasen deshitara
Alternative	**INFORMAL**		tashikametari	tashikamenakattari
	FORMAL		tashikamemashitari	tashikamemasen deshitari

		INFORMAL AFFIRMATIVE INDICATIVE
Passive		tashikamerareru
Potential		tashikamerareru
Causative		tashikamesaseru
Causative Pass.		tashikamesaserareru
Honorific	**I**	otashikame ni naru
	II	otashikame nasaru
Humble	**I**	otashikame suru
	II	otashikame itasu

たすける／助ける　**tasuke.ru**

TRANSITIVE　*to help, to assist, to rescue, to save*

			AFFIRMATIVE	NEGATIVE
Indicative	**INFORMAL**		tasukeru	tasukenai
	FORMAL		tasukemasu	tasukemasen
Imperative	**INFORMAL**	I	tasukero	tasukeru na
		II	tasukenasai	tasukenasaru na
		III	tasukete kudasai	tasukenai de kudasai
	FORMAL		otasuke nasaimase	otasuke nasaimasu na
Presumptive	**INFORMAL**	I	tasukeyō	tasukemai
		II	tasukeru darō	tasukenai darō
	FORMAL	I	tasukemashō	tasukemasumai
		II	tasukeru deshō	tasukenai deshō
Provisional	**INFORMAL**		tasukereba	tasukenakereba
	FORMAL		tasukemaseba	tasukemasen nara
			tasukemasureba	
Gerund	**INFORMAL**	I	tasukete	tasukenai de
		II		tasukenakute
	FORMAL		tasukemashite	tasukemasen de
Past Ind.	**INFORMAL**		tasuketa	tasukenakatta
	FORMAL		tasukemashita	tasukemasen deshita
Past Presump.	**INFORMAL**		tasuketarō	tasukenakattarō
			tasuketa darō	tasukenakatta darō
	FORMAL		tasukemashitarō	tasukemasen deshitarō
			tasuketa deshō	tasukenakatta deshō
Conditional	**INFORMAL**		tasuketara	tasukenakattara
	FORMAL		tasukemashitara	tasukemasen deshitara
Alternative	**INFORMAL**		tasuketari	tasukenakattari
	FORMAL		tasukemashitari	tasukemasen deshitari

			INFORMAL AFFIRMATIVE INDICATIVE
Passive			tasukerareru
Potential			tasukerareru
Causative			tasukesaseru
Causative Pass.			tasukesaserareru
Honorific		I	otasuke ni naru
		II	otasuke nasaru
Humble		I	otasuke suru
		II	otasuke itasu

AN ESSENTIAL 55 VERB

Tasukeru 助ける

to help, to assist, to rescue, to save

Tasukeru is an essential verb because you often need help, you want to help others, and people need your help, too. This verb will help you to do many things.

Sentences Using *Tasukeru*

Onegai desu, tasukete kudasai.
お願いです、助けて下さい。
Please help me.

Nanika otetsudai dekimasu ka.
何かお手伝いできますか。
May I help you?

Koshō shita kuruma o osu no o tasukete ageta.
故障した車を押すのを助けてあげた。
I helped push a disabled car.

Ko inu ga kasai genba kara tasukerareta.
子犬が火災現場から助けられた。
A puppy was rescued from the fire.

Kare wa tomodachi no senkyo undō o tasukete imasu.
彼は友達の選挙運動を助けています。
He is assisting with his friend's election campaign.

Words and Expressions Related to This Verb

joryoku suru　助力する
to help, to aid

enjo suru　援助する
to help, to aid

tetsudau　手伝う
to help, to assist

jogen　助言
advice

joshu　助手
assistant

Proverb

Ten wa mizu kara tasukuru mono o tasuku.
天は自ら助くるものを助く。
Heaven helps those who help themselves.

たたかう／戦う／闘う　**tataka.u**

to fight against, to wage war on, to struggle against

			AFFIRMATIVE	NEGATIVE
Indicative	**INFORMAL**		tatakau	tatakawanai
	FORMAL		tatakaimasu	tatakaimasen
Imperative	**INFORMAL**	I	tatakae	tatakau na
		II	tatakainasai	tatakainasaru na
		III	tatakatte kudasai	tatakawanai de kudasai
	FORMAL		otatakai nasaimase	otatakai nasaimasu na
Presumptive	**INFORMAL**	I	tatakaō	tatakaumai
		II	tatakau darō	tatakawanai darō
	FORMAL	I	tatakaimashō	tatakaimasumai
		II	tatakau deshō	tatakawanai deshō
Provisional	**INFORMAL**		tatakaeba	tatakawanakereba
	FORMAL		tatakaimaseba	tatakaimasen nara
			tatakaimasureba	
Gerund	**INFORMAL**	I	tatakatte	tatakawanai de
		II		tatakawanakute
	FORMAL		tatakaimashite	tatakaimasen de
Past Ind.	**INFORMAL**		tatakatta	tatakawanakatta
	FORMAL		tatakaimashita	tatakaimasen deshita
Past Presump.	**INFORMAL**		tatakattarō	tatakawanakattarō
			tatakatta darō	tatakawanakatta darō
	FORMAL		tatakaimashitarō	tatakaimasen deshitarō
			tatakatta deshō	tatakawanakatta deshō
Conditional	**INFORMAL**		tatakattara	tatakawanakattara
	FORMAL		tatakaimashitara	tatakaimasen deshitara
Alternative	**INFORMAL**		tatakattari	tatakawanakattari
	FORMAL		tatakaimashitari	tatakaimasen deshitari

		INFORMAL AFFIRMATIVE INDICATIVE
Passive		tatakawareru
Potential		tatakaeru
Causative		tatakawaseru
Causative Pass.		tatakawaserareru
Honorific	I	otatakai ni naru
	II	otatakai nasaru
Humble	I	otatakai suru
	II	otatakai itasu

tatak.u たたく／叩く   tataki
to hit, to slap, to beat, to criticize   TRANSITIVE

			AFFIRMATIVE	NEGATIVE
Indicative	**INFORMAL**		tataku	tatakanai
	FORMAL		tatakimasu	tatakimasen
Imperative	**INFORMAL**	I	tatake	tataku na
		II	tatakinasai	tatakinasaru na
		III	tataite kudasai	tatakanai de kudasai
	FORMAL		otataki nasaimase	otataki nasaimasu na
Presumptive	**INFORMAL**	I	tatakō	tatakumai
		II	tataku darō	tatakanai darō
	FORMAL	I	tatakimashō	tatakimasumai
		II	tataku deshō	tatakanai deshō
Provisional	**INFORMAL**		tatakeba	tatakanakereba
	FORMAL		tatakimaseba	tatakimasen nara
			tatakimasureba	
Gerund	**INFORMAL**	I	tataite	tatakanai de
		II		tatakanakute
	FORMAL		tatakimashite	tatakimasen de
Past Ind.	**INFORMAL**		tataita	tatakanakatta
	FORMAL		tatakimashita	tatakimasen deshita
Past Presump.	**INFORMAL**		tataitarō	tatakanakattarō
			tataita darō	tatakanakatta darō
	FORMAL		tatakimashitarō	tatakimasen deshitarō
			tataita deshō	tatakanakatta deshō
Conditional	**INFORMAL**		tataitara	tatakanakattara
	FORMAL		tatakimashitara	tatakimasen deshitara
Alternative	**INFORMAL**		tataitari	tatakanakattari
	FORMAL		tatakimashitari	tatakimasen deshitari

		INFORMAL AFFIRMATIVE INDICATIVE
Passive		tatakareru
Potential		tatakeru
Causative		tatakaseru
Causative Pass.		tatakaserareru
Honorific	I	otataki ni naru
	II	otataki nasaru
Humble	I	otataki suru
	II	otataki itasu

たたむ／畳む　**tatam.u**

TRANSITIVE　*to fold, to close up* (one's shop)

			AFFIRMATIVE	NEGATIVE
Indicative	**INFORMAL**		tatamu	tatamanai
	FORMAL		tatamimasu	tatamimasen
Imperative	**INFORMAL**	I	tatame	tatamu na
		II	tataminasai	tataminasaru na
		III	tatande kudasai	tatamanai de kudasai
	FORMAL		otatami nasaimase	otatami nasaimasu na
Presumptive	**INFORMAL**	I	tatamō	tatamumai
		II	tatamu darō	tatamanai darō
	FORMAL	I	tatamimashō	tatamimasumai
		II	tatamu deshō	tatamanai deshō
Provisional	**INFORMAL**		tatameba	tatamanakereba
	FORMAL		tatamimaseba	tatamimasen nara
			tatamimasureba	
Gerund	**INFORMAL**	I	tatande	tatamanai de
		II		tatamanakute
	FORMAL		tatamimashite	tatamimasen de
Past Ind.	**INFORMAL**		tatanda	tatamanakatta
	FORMAL		tatamimashita	tatamimasen deshita
Past Presump.	**INFORMAL**		tatandarō	tatamanakattarō
			tatanda darō	tatamanakatta darō
	FORMAL		tatamimashitarō	tatamimasen deshitarō
			tatanda deshō	tatamanakatta deshō
Conditional	**INFORMAL**		tatandara	tatamanakattara
	FORMAL		tatamimashitara	tatamimasen deshitara
Alternative	**INFORMAL**		tatandari	tatamanakattari
	FORMAL		tatamimashitari	tatamimasen deshitari

			INFORMAL AFFIRMATIVE INDICATIVE
Passive			tatamareru
Potential			tatameru
Causative			tatamaseru
Causative Pass.			tatamaserareru
Honorific		I	otatami ni naru
		II	otatami nasaru
Humble		I	otatami suru
		II	otatami itasu

to erect, to build   TRANSITIVE

			AFFIRMATIVE	**NEGATIVE**
Indicative	**INFORMAL**		tateru	tatenai
	FORMAL		tatemasu	tatemasen
Imperative	**INFORMAL**	I	tatero	tateru na
		II	tatenasai	tatenasaru na
		III	tatete kudasai	tatenai de kudasai
	FORMAL		otate nasaimase	otate nasaimasu na
Presumptive	**INFORMAL**	I	tateyō	tatemai
		II	tateru darō	tatenai darō
	FORMAL	I	tatemashō	tatemasumai
		II	tateru deshō	tatenai deshō
Provisional	**INFORMAL**		tatereba	tatenakereba
	FORMAL		tatemaseba	tatemasen nara
			tatemasureba	
Gerund	**INFORMAL**	I	tatete	tatenai de
		II		tatenakute
	FORMAL		tatemashite	tatemasen de
Past Ind.	**INFORMAL**		tateta	tatenakatta
	FORMAL		tatemashita	tatemasen deshita
Past Presump.	**INFORMAL**		tatetarō	tatenakattarō
			tateta darō	tatenakatta darō
	FORMAL		tatemashitarō	tatemasen deshitarō
			tateta deshō	tatenakatta deshō
Conditional	**INFORMAL**		tatetara	tatenakattara
	FORMAL		tatemashitara	tatemasen deshitara
Alternative	**INFORMAL**		tatetari	tatenakattari
	FORMAL		tatemashitari	tatemasen deshitari

		INFORMAL AFFIRMATIVE INDICATIVE
Passive		taterareru
Potential		taterareru
Causative		tatesaseru
Causative Pass.		tatesaserareru
Honorific	I	otate ni naru
	II	otate nasaru
Humble	I	otate suru
	II	otate itasu

to stand, to be built

			AFFIRMATIVE	**NEGATIVE**
Indicative	**INFORMAL**		tatsu	tatanai
	FORMAL		tachimasu	tachimasen
Imperative	**INFORMAL**	I	tate	tatsu na
		II	tachinasai	tachinasaru na
		III	tatte kudasai	tatanai de kudasai
	FORMAL		otachi nasaimase	otachi nasaimasu na
Presumptive	**INFORMAL**	I	tatō	tatsumai
		II	tatsu darō	tatanai darō
	FORMAL	I	tachimashō	tachimasumai
		II	tatsu deshō	tatanai deshō
Provisional	**INFORMAL**		tateba	tatanakereba
	FORMAL		tachimaseba	tachimasen nara
			tachimasureba	
Gerund	**INFORMAL**	I	tatte	tatanai de
		II		tatanakute
	FORMAL		tachimashite	tachimasen de
Past Ind.	**INFORMAL**		tatta	tatanakatta
	FORMAL		tachimashita	tachimasen deshita
Past Presump.	**INFORMAL**		tattarō	tatanakattarō
			tatta darō	tatanakatta darō
	FORMAL		tachimashitarō	tachimasen deshitarō
			tatta deshō	tatanakatta deshō
Conditional	**INFORMAL**		tattara	tatanakattara
	FORMAL		tachimashitara	tachimasen deshitara
Alternative	**INFORMAL**		tattari	tatanakattari
	FORMAL		tachimashitari	tachimasen deshitari

		INFORMAL AFFIRMATIVE INDICATIVE
Passive		tatareru
Potential		tateru
Causative		tataseru
Causative Pass.		tataserareru
Honorific	I	otachi ni naru
	II	otachi nasaru
Humble	I	otachi suru
	II	otachi itasu

AN ESSENTIAL 55 VERB

Tatsu 立つ

to stand, to be built

Sentences Using *Tatsu*

Onaji basho ni ichi jikan tatte ita node tsukareta.
同じ場所に一時間立っていたので疲れた。
I got tired because I was standing in the same spot for one hour.

Fujisan no chōjō ni tatte mitai desu.
富士山の頂上に立ってみたいです。
I'd like to stand at the top of Mt. Fuji.

Densha wa suite ita node tatanai de sumimashita.
電車は空いていたので立たないですみました。
I didn't need to stand on the train because it wasn't crowded.

Kare wa tattari suwattari, itsumo ochitsukimasen.
彼は立ったり座ったり、いつも落ち着きません。
He doesn't stay calm, always standing up and sitting down.

Chichi wa koronde, shibaraku tatenakatta.
父は転んで、しばらく立てなかった。
My father fell and couldn't stand up for a while.

Tatsu is a verb you need often in everyday conversation. You may want to describe your commute, for example, or how it feels to stand after a long meal sitting on the tatami floor!

Words and Expressions Related to This Verb

tachiagaru　立ち上がる
to stand up

tachiyoru　立ち寄る
to drop by

tachidomaru　立ち止まる
to stop, to halt

tachiba　立場
a standpoint, a position

itemo tattemo irarenai
いても立ってもいられない
to be too nervous to be still

506

たよる／頼る **tayor.u**

to rely on, to depend on

			AFFIRMATIVE	NEGATIVE
Indicative	**INFORMAL**		tayoru	tayoranai
	FORMAL		tayorimasu	tayorimasen
Imperative	**INFORMAL**	I	tayore	tayoru na
		II	tayorinasai	tayorinasaru na
		III	tayotte kudasai	tayoranai de kudasai
	FORMAL		otayori nasaimase	otayori nasaimasu na
Presumptive	**INFORMAL**	I	tayorō	tayorumai
		II	tayoru darō	tayoranai darō
	FORMAL	I	tayorimashō	tayorimasumai
		II	tayoru deshō	tayoranaideshō
Provisional	**INFORMAL**		tayoreba	tayoranakereba
	FORMAL		tayorimaseba	tayorimasen nara
			tayorimasureba	
Gerund	**INFORMAL**	I	tayotte	tayoranai de
		II		tayoranakute
	FORMAL		tayorimashite	tayorimasen de
Past Ind.	**INFORMAL**		tayotta	tayoranakatta
	FORMAL		tayorimashita	tayorimasen deshita
Past Presump.	**INFORMAL**		tayottarō	tayoranakattarō
			tayotta darō	tayoranakatta darō
	FORMAL		tayorimashitarō	tayorimasen deshitarō
			tayotta deshō	tayoranakatta deshō
Conditional	**INFORMAL**		tayottara	tayoranakattara
	FORMAL		tayorimashitara	tayorimasen deshitara
Alternative	**INFORMAL**		tayottari	tayoranakattari
	FORMAL		tayorimashitari	tayorimasen deshitari

			INFORMAL AFFIRMATIVE INDICATIVE
Passive			tayorareru
Potential			tayoreru
Causative			tayoraseru
Causative Pass.			tayoraserareru
Honorific		I	otayori ni naru
		II	otayori nasaru
Humble		I	otayori suru
		II	otayori itasu

to ask (a question), *to look for, to visit*   TRANSITIVE

			AFFIRMATIVE	**NEGATIVE**
Indicative	**INFORMAL**		tazuneru	tazunenai
	FORMAL		tazunemasu	tazunemasen
Imperative	**INFORMAL**	I	tazunero	tazuneru na
		II	tazunenasai	lazunenasaru na
		III	tazunete kudasai	lazunenai de kudasai
	FORMAL		otazune nasaimase	otazune nasaimasu na
Presumptive	**INFORMAL**	I	tazuneyō	tazunemai
		II	tazuneru darō	tazunenai darō
	FORMAL	I	tazunemashō	tazunemasumai
		II	tazuneru deshō	tazunenai deshō
Provisional	**INFORMAL**		tazunereba	tazunenakereba
	FORMAL		tazunemaseba	tazunemasen nara
			tazunemasureba	
Gerund	**INFORMAL**	I	tazunete	tazunenai de
		II		tazunenakute
	FORMAL		tazunemashite	tazunemasen de
Past Ind.	**INFORMAL**		tazuneta	tazunenakatta
	FORMAL		tazunemashita	tazunemasen deshita
Past Presump.	**INFORMAL**		tazunetarō	tazunenakattarō
			tazuneta darō	tazunenakatta darō
	FORMAL		tazunemashitarō	tazunemasen deshitarō
			tazuneta deshō	tazunenakatta deshō
Conditional	**INFORMAL**		tazunetara	tazunenakattara
	FORMAL		tazunemashitara	tazunemasen deshitara
Alternative	**INFORMAL**		tazunetari	tazunenakattari
	FORMAL		tazunemashitari	tazunemasen deshitari

		INFORMAL AFFIRMATIVE INDICATIVE
Passive		tazunerareru
Potential		tazunerareru
Causative		tazunesaseru
Causative Pass.		tazunesaserareru
Honorific	I	otazune ni naru
	II	otazune nasaru
Humble	I	otazune suru
	II	otazune itasu

			AFFIRMATIVE	NEGATIVE
Indicative	INFORMAL		tetsudau	tetsudawanai
	FORMAL		tetsudaimasu	tetsudaimasen
Imperative	INFORMAL	I	tetsudae	tetsudau na
		II	tetsudainasai	tetsudainasaru na
		III	tetsudatte kudasai	tetsudawanai de kudasai
	FORMAL		otetsudai nasaimase	otetsudai nasaimasu na
Presumptive	INFORMAL	I	tetsudaō	tetsudaumai
		II	tetsudau darō	tetsudawanai darō
	FORMAL	I	tetsudaimashō	tetsudaimasumai
		II	tetsudau deshō	tetsudawanai deshō
Provisional	INFORMAL		tetsudaeba	tetsudawanakereba
	FORMAL		tetsudaimaseba	tetsudaimasen nara
			tetsudaimasureba	
Gerund	INFORMAL	I	tetsudatte	tetsudawanai de
		II		tetsudawanakute
	FORMAL		tetsudaimashite	tetsudaimasen de
Past Ind.	INFORMAL		tetsudatta	tetsudawanakatta
	FORMAL		tetsudaimashita	tetsudaimasen deshita
Past Presump.	INFORMAL		tetsudattarō	tetsudawanakattarō
			tetsudatta darō	tetsudawanakatta darō
	FORMAL		tetsudaimashitarō	tetsudaimasen deshitarō
			tetsudatta deshō	tetsudawanakatta deshō
Conditional	INFORMAL		tetsudattara	tetsudawanakattara
	FORMAL		tetsudaimashitara	tetsudaimasen deshitara
Alternative	INFORMAL		tetsudattari	tetsudawanakattari
	FORMAL		tetsudaimashitari	tetsudaimasen deshitari

		INFORMAL AFFIRMATIVE INDICATIVE
Passive		tetsudawareru
Potential		tetsudaeru
Causative		tetsudawaseru
Causative Pass.		tetsudawaserareru
Honorific	I	otetsudai ni naru
	II	otetsudai nasaru
Humble	I	otetsudai suru
	II	otetsudai itasu

509

tob.u とぶ／飛ぶ／跳ぶ   tobi
to fly, to jump

			AFFIRMATIVE	NEGATIVE
Indicative	INFORMAL		tobu	tobanai
	FORMAL		tobimasu	tobimasen
Imperative	INFORMAL	I	tobe	tobu na
		II	tobinasai	tobinasaru na
		III	tonde kudasai	tobanai de kudasai
	FORMAL		otobi nasaimase	otobi nasaimasu na
Presumptive	INFORMAL	I	tobō	tobumai
		II	tobu darō	tobanai darō
	FORMAL	I	tobimashō	tobimasumai
		II	tobu deshō	tobanai deshō
Provisional	INFORMAL		tobeba	tobanakereba
	FORMAL		tobimaseba	tobimasen nara
			tobimasureba	
Gerund	INFORMAL	I	tonde	tobanai de
		II		tobanakute
	FORMAL		tobimashite	tobimasen de
Past Ind.	INFORMAL		tonda	tobanakatta
	FORMAL		tobimashita	tobimasen deshita
Past Presump.	INFORMAL		tondarō	tobanakattarō
			tonda darō	tobanakatta darō
	FORMAL		tobimashitarō	tobimasen deshitarō
			tonda deshō	tobanakatta deshō
Conditional	INFORMAL		tondara	tobanakattara
	FORMAL		tobimashitara	tobimasen deshitara
Alternative	INFORMAL		tondari	tobanakattari
	FORMAL		tobimashitari	tobimasen deshitari

		INFORMAL AFFIRMATIVE INDICATIVE
Passive		tobareru
Potential		toberu
Causative		tobaseru
Causative Pass.		tobaserareru
Honorific	I	otobi ni naru
	II	otobi nasaru
Humble	I	otobi suru
	II	otobi itasu

510

とどける／届ける **todoke .ru**

TRANSITIVE *to deliver, to report*

			AFFIRMATIVE	NEGATIVE
Indicative	**INFORMAL**		todokeru	todokenai
	FORMAL		todokemasu	todokemasen
Imperative	**INFORMAL**	I	todokero	todokeru na
		II	todokenasai	todokenasaru na
		III	todokete kudasai	todokenai de kudasai
	FORMAL		otodoke nasaimase	otodoke nasaimasu na
Presumptive	**INFORMAL**	I	todokeyō	todokemai
		II	todokeru darō	todokenai darō
	FORMAL	I	todokemashō	todokemasumai
		II	todokeru deshō	todokenai deshō
Provisional	**INFORMAL**		todokereba	todokenakereba
	FORMAL		todokemaseba	todokemasen nara
			todokemasureba	
Gerund	**INFORMAL**	I	todokete	todokenai de
		II		todokenakute
	FORMAL		todokemashite	todokemasen de
Past Ind.	**INFORMAL**		todoketa	todokenakatta
	FORMAL		todokemashita	todokemasen deshita
Past Presump.	**INFORMAL**		todoketarō	todokenakattarō
			todoketa darō	todokenakatta darō
	FORMAL		todokemashitarō	todokemasen deshitarō
			todoketa deshō	todokenakatta deshō
Conditional	**INFORMAL**		todoketara	todokenakattara
	FORMAL		todokemashitara	todokemasen deshitara
Alternative	**INFORMAL**		todoketari	todokenakattari
	FORMAL		todokemashitari	todokemasen deshitari

			INFORMAL AFFIRMATIVE INDICATIVE
Passive			todokerareru
Potential			todokerareru
Causative			todokesaseru
Causative Pass.			todokesaserareru
Honorific		I	otodoke ni naru
		II	otodoke nasaru
Humble		I	otodoke suru
		II	otodoke itasu

todok.u　とどく／届く

to reach, to arrive

todoki

			AFFIRMATIVE	NEGATIVE
Indicative	**INFORMAL**		todoku	todokanai
	FORMAL		todokimasu	todokimasen
Imperative	**INFORMAL**	I	todoke	todoku na
		II		
		III	todoite kudasai	todokanai de kudasai
	FORMAL			
Presumptive	**INFORMAL**	I	todokō	todokumai
		II	todoku darō	todokanai darō
	FORMAL	I	todokimashō	todokimasumai
		II	todoku deshō	todokanai deshō
Provisional	**INFORMAL**		todokeba	todokanakereba
	FORMAL		todokimaseba	todokimasen nara
			todokimasureba	
Gerund	**INFORMAL**	I	todoite	todokanai de
		II		todokanakute
	FORMAL		todokimashite	todokimasen de
Past Ind.	**INFORMAL**		todoita	todokanakatta
	FORMAL		todokimashita	todokimasen deshita
Past Presump.	**INFORMAL**		todoitarō	todokanakattarō
			todoita darō	todokanakatta darō
	FORMAL		todokimashitarō	todokimasen deshitarō
			todoita deshō	todokanakatta deshō
Conditional	**INFORMAL**		todoitara	todokanakattara
	FORMAL		todokimashitara	todokimasen deshitara
Alternative	**INFORMAL**		todoitari	todokanakattari
	FORMAL		todokimashitari	todokimasen deshitari

		INFORMAL AFFIRMATIVE INDICATIVE
Passive		
Potential		todokeru
Causative		todokaseru
Causative Pass.		todokaserareru
Honorific	I	
	II	
Humble	I	
	II	

512

とける／溶ける／解ける　**toke .ru**

to melt, to dissolve, to get loose, to come untied

			AFFIRMATIVE	NEGATIVE
Indicative	**INFORMAL**		tokeru	tokenai
	FORMAL		tokemasu	tokemasen
Imperative	**INFORMAL**	I	tokero	tokeru na
		II		
		III	tokete kudasai	tokenai de kudasai
	FORMAL			
Presumptive	**INFORMAL**	I	tokeyō	tokemai
		II	tokeru darō	tokenai darō
	FORMAL	I	tokemashō	tokemasumai
		II	tokeru deshō	tokenai deshō
Provisional	**INFORMAL**		tokereba	tokenakereba
	FORMAL		tokemaseba	tokemasen nara
			tokemasureba	
Gerund	**INFORMAL**	I	tokete	tokenai de
		II		tokenakute
	FORMAL		tokemashite	tokemasen de
Past Ind.	**INFORMAL**		toketa	tokenakatta
	FORMAL		tokemashita	tokemasen deshita
Past Presump.	**INFORMAL**		toketarō	tokenakattarō
			toketa darō	tokenakatta darō
	FORMAL		tokemashitarō	tokemasen deshitarō
			toketa deshō	tokenakatta deshō
Conditional	**INFORMAL**		toketara	tokenakattara
	FORMAL		tokemashitara	tokemasen deshitara
Alternative	**INFORMAL**		toketari	tokenakattari
	FORMAL		tokemashitari	tokemasen deshitari

		INFORMAL AFFIRMATIVE INDICATIVE
Passive		
Potential		
Causative		tokesaseru
Causative Pass.		tokesaserareru
Honorific	I	otoke ni naru
	II	otoke nasaru
Humble	I	
	II	

T

tok.u　とく／解く

to solve, to untie, to dispel　　TRANSITIVE

toki

			AFFIRMATIVE	NEGATIVE
Indicative	**INFORMAL**		toku	tokanai
	FORMAL		tokimasu	tokimasen
Imperative	**INFORMAL**	I	toke	toku na
		II	tokinasai	tokinasaru na
		III	toite kudasai	tokanai de kudasai
	FORMAL		otoki nasaimase	otoki nasaimasu na
Presumptive	**INFORMAL**	I	tokō	tokumai
		II	toku darō	tokanai darō
	FORMAL	I	tokimashō	tokimasumai
		II	toku deshō	tokanai deshō
Provisional	**INFORMAL**		tokeba	tokanakereba
	FORMAL		tokimaseba	tokimasen nara
			tokimasureba	
Gerund	**INFORMAL**	I	toite	tokanai de
		II		tokanakute
	FORMAL		tokimashite	tokimasen de
Past Ind.	**INFORMAL**		toita	tokanakatta
	FORMAL		tokimashita	tokimasen deshita
Past Presump.	**INFORMAL**		toitarō	tokanakattarō
			toita darō	tokanakatta darō
	FORMAL		tokimashitarō	tokimasen deshitarō
			toita deshō	tokanakatta deshō
Conditional	**INFORMAL**		toitara	tokanakattara
	FORMAL		tokimashitara	tokimasen deshitara
Alternative	**INFORMAL**		toitari	tokanakattari
	FORMAL		tokimashitari	tokimasen deshitari

			INFORMAL AFFIRMATIVE INDICATIVE
Passive			tokareru
Potential			tokeru
Causative			tokaseru
Causative Pass.			tokaserareru
Honorific		I	otoki ni naru
		II	otoki nasaru
Humble		I	otoki suru
		II	otoki itasu

とまる／止まる／泊まる　**tomar.u**

to stop, to stay overnight

			AFFIRMATIVE	NEGATIVE
Indicative	INFORMAL		tomaru	tomaranai
	FORMAL		tomarimasu	tomarimasen
Imperative	INFORMAL	I	tomare	tomaru na
		II	tomarinasai	tomarinasaru na
		III	tomatte kudasai	tomaranai de kudasai
	FORMAL		otomari nasaimase	otomari nasaimasu na
Presumptive	INFORMAL	I	tomarō	tomarumai
		II	tomaru darō	tomaranai darō
	FORMAL	I	tomarimashō	tomarimasumai
		II	tomaru deshō	tomaranai deshō
Provisional	INFORMAL		tomareba	tomaranakereba
	FORMAL		tomarimaseba	tomarimasen nara
			tomarimasureba	
Gerund	INFORMAL	I	tomatte	tomaranai de
		II		tomaranakute
	FORMAL		tomarimashite	tomarimasen de
Past Ind.	INFORMAL		tomatta	tomaranakatta
	FORMAL		tomarimashita	tomarimasen deshita
Past Presump.	INFORMAL		tomattarō	tomaranakattarō
			tomatta darō	tomaranakatta darō
	FORMAL		tomarimashitarō	tomarimasen deshitarō
			tomatta deshō	tomaranakatta deshō
Conditional	INFORMAL		tomattara	tomaranakattara
	FORMAL		tomarimashitara	tomarimasen deshitara
Alternative	INFORMAL		tomattari	tomaranakattari
	FORMAL		tomarimashitari	tomarimasen deshitari

		INFORMAL AFFIRMATIVE INDICATIVE
Passive		tomarareru
Potential		tomareru
Causative		tomaraseru
Causative Pass.		tomaraserareru
Honorific	I	otomari ni naru
	II	otomari nasaru
Humble	I	otomari suru
	II	otomari itasu

515

to stop, to put up, to fasten　　　TRANSITIVE

			AFFIRMATIVE	NEGATIVE
Indicative	**INFORMAL**		tomeru	tomenai
	FORMAL		tomemasu	tomemasen
Imperative	**INFORMAL**	I	tomero	tomeru na
		II	tomenasai	tomenasaru na
		III	tomete kudasai	tomenai de kudasai
	FORMAL		otome nasaimase	otome nasaimasu na
Presumptive	**INFORMAL**	I	tomeyō	tomemai
		II	tomeru darō	tomenai darō
	FORMAL	I	tomemashō	tomemasumai
		II	tomeru deshō	tomenai deshō
Provisional	**INFORMAL**		tomereba	tomenakereba
	FORMAL		tomemaseba	tomemasen nara
			tomemasureba	
Gerund	**INFORMAL**	I	tomete	tomenai de
		II		tomenakute
	FORMAL		tomemashite	tomemasen de
Past Ind.	**INFORMAL**		tometa	tomenakatta
	FORMAL		tomemashita	tomemasen deshita
Past Presump.	**INFORMAL**		tometarō	tomenakattarō
			tometa darō	tomenakatta darō
	FORMAL		tomemashitarō	tomemasen deshitarō
			tometa deshō	tomenakatta deshō
Conditional	**INFORMAL**		tometara	tomenakattara
	FORMAL		tomemashitara	tomemasen deshitara
Alternative	**INFORMAL**		tometari	tomenakattari
	FORMAL		tomemashitari	tomemasen deshitari

		INFORMAL AFFIRMATIVE INDICATIVE
Passive		tomerareru
Potential		tomerareru
Causative		tomesaseru
Causative Pass.		tomesaserareru
Honorific	I	otome ni naru
	II	otome nasaru
Humble	I	otome suru
	II	otome itasu

TRANSITIVE　　*to take, to get, to hold, to pick up, to have*

			AFFIRMATIVE	NEGATIVE
Indicative	**INFORMAL**		toru	toranai
	FORMAL		torimasu	torimasen
Imperative	**INFORMAL**	I	tore	toru na
		II	torinasai	torinasaru na
		III	totte kudasai	toranai de kudasai
	FORMAL		otori nasaimase	otori nasaimasu na
Presumptive	**INFORMAL**	I	torō	torumai
		II	toru darō	toranai darō
	FORMAL	I	torimashō	torimasumai
		II	toru deshō	toranai deshō
Provisional	**INFORMAL**		toreba	toranakereba
	FORMAL		torimaseba	torimasen nara
			torimasureba	
Gerund	**INFORMAL**	I	totte	toranai de
		II		toranakute
	FORMAL		torimashite	torimasen de
Past Ind.	**INFORMAL**		totta	toranakatta
	FORMAL		torimashita	torimasen deshita
Past Presump.	**INFORMAL**		tottarō	toranakattarō
			totta darō	toranakatta darō
	FORMAL		torimashitarō	torimasen deshitarō
			totta deshō	toranakatta deshō
Conditional	**INFORMAL**		tottara	toranakattara
	FORMAL		torimashitara	torimasen deshitara
Alternative	**INFORMAL**		tottari	toranakattari
	FORMAL		torimashitari	torimasen deshitari

			INFORMAL AFFIRMATIVE INDICATIVE
Passive			torareru
Potential			toreru
Causative			toraseru
Causative Pass.			toraserareru
Honorific		I	otori ni naru
		II	otori nasaru
Humble		I	otori suru
		II	otori itasu

**AN ESSENTIAL
55 VERB**

AN ESSENTIAL 55 VERB

Toru 取る

to take, to get, to hold, to pick up, to have

Toru is an essential verb, just like its English counterpart. With its wide range of meanings and applicable situations, it's used all the time. Take your time and learn it well.

Sentences Using *Toru*

Rai gakki kara nihongo no kurasu o torimasu.
来学期から日本語のクラスを取ります。
Starting next semester, I'll take a Japanese language class.

Kurīningu ya kara doresu o totte kite kudasai.
クリーニング屋からドレスを取ってきてください。
Can you pick up my dress from the dry cleaner's?

Mijikai kankō ryokō nanode, biza wa toramakute ii desu.
短い観光旅行なので、ビザは取らなくていいです。
Since it's a brief sightseeing trip, you don't need to get a visa.

Unten menkyo shō o toreba, tsūkin ga raku ni naru.
運転免許証を取れば通勤が楽になる。
If I get a driver's license, my commute will become easier.

Sushi no demae o torimashō ka.
鮨の出前を取りましょうか。
Shall we get a sushi delivery?

Words and Expressions Related to This Verb

torikaeru
取り替える
to exchange

toru ni tarinai
取るに足らない
insignificant, trifling

toru mono mo toriaezu
取る物も取り敢えず
in a hurry

Proverb

toranu tanuki no kawa zanyō
捕らぬ（取らぬ）狸の皮算用
Don't count your chickens before they are hatched. (counting raccoon dogs' pelts before catching them)

518

tōri

とおる／通る　**tōr.u**

TRANSITIVE　　*to pass by, to go through, to pass*

			AFFIRMATIVE	NEGATIVE
Indicative	**INFORMAL**		tōru	tōranai
	FORMAL		tōrimasu	tōrimasen
Imperative	**INFORMAL**	**I**	tōre	tōru na
		II	tōrinasai	tōrinasaru na
		III	tōtte kudasai	tōranai de kudasai
	FORMAL		otōri nasaimase	otōri nasaimasu na
Presumptive	**INFORMAL**	**I**	tōrō	tōrumai
		II	tōru darō	tōranai darō
	FORMAL	**I**	tōrimashō	tōrimasumai
		II	tōru deshō	tōranai deshō
Provisional	**INFORMAL**		tōreba	tōranakereba
	FORMAL		tōrimaseba	tōrimasen nara
			tōrimasureba	
Gerund	**INFORMAL**	**I**	tōtte	tōranai de
		II		tōranakute
	FORMAL		tōrimashite	tōrimasen de
Past Ind.	**INFORMAL**		tōtta	tōranakatta
	FORMAL		tōrimashita	tōrimasen deshita
Past Presump.	**INFORMAL**		tōttarō	tōranakattarō
			tōtta darō	tōranakatta darō
	FORMAL		tōrimashitarō	tōrimasen deshitarō
			tōtta deshō	tōranakatta deshō
Conditional	**INFORMAL**		tōttara	tōranakattara
	FORMAL		tōrimashitara	tōrimasen deshitara
Alternative	**INFORMAL**		tōttari	tōranakattari
	FORMAL		tōrimashitari	tōrimasen deshitari

		INFORMAL AFFIRMATIVE INDICATIVE
Passive		tōrareru
Potential		tōreru
Causative		tōraseru
Causative Pass.		tōraserareru
Honorific	**I**	otōri ni naru
	II	otōri nasaru
Humble	**I**	
	II	

totonoe.ru ととのえる／整える totonoe

to prepare, to arrange, to adjust   TRANSITIVE

			AFFIRMATIVE	NEGATIVE
Indicative	**INFORMAL**		totonoeru	totonoenai
	FORMAL		totonoemasu	totonoemasen
Imperative	**INFORMAL**	I	totonoero	totonoeru na
		II	totonoenasai	totonoenasaru na
		III	totonoete kudasai	totonoenai de kudasai
	FORMAL		ototonoe nasaimase	ototonoe nasaimasu na
Presumptive	**INFORMAL**	I	totonoeyō	totonoemai
		II	totonoeru darō	totonoenai darō
	FORMAL	I	totonoemashō	totonoemasumai
		II	totonoeru deshō	totonoenai deshō
Provisional	**INFORMAL**		totonoereba	totonoenakereba
	FORMAL		totonoemaseba	totonoemasen nara
			totonoemasureba	
Gerund	**INFORMAL**	I	totonoete	totonoenai de
		II		totonoenakute
	FORMAL		totonoemashite	totonoemasen de
Past Ind.	**INFORMAL**		totonoeta	totonoenakatta
	FORMAL		totonoemashita	totonoemasen deshita
Past Presump.	**INFORMAL**		totonoetarō	totonoenakattarō
			totonoeta darō	totonoenakatta darō
	FORMAL		totonoemashitarō	totonoemasen deshitarō
			totonoeta deshō	totonoenakatta deshō
Conditional	**INFORMAL**		totonoetara	totonoenakattara
	FORMAL		totonoemashitara	totonoemasen deshitara
Alternative	**INFORMAL**		totonoetari	totonoenakattari
	FORMAL		totonoemashitari	totonoemasen deshitari

		INFORMAL AFFIRMATIVE INDICATIVE
Passive		totonoerareru
Potential		totonoerareru
Causative		totonoesaseru
Causative Pass.		totonoesaserareru
Honorific	I	ototonoe ni naru
	II	ototonoe nasaru
Humble	I	ototonoe suru
	II	ototonoe itasu

to make oneself understood, to transmit, to lead to, to be well informed

			AFFIRMATIVE	**NEGATIVE**
Indicative	**INFORMAL**		tsūjiru	tsūjinai
	FORMAL		tsūjimasu	tsūjimasen
Imperative	**INFORMAL**	I	tsūjiro	tsūjiru na
		II	tsūjinasai	tsūjinasaru na
		III	tsūjite kudasai	tsūjinai de kudasai
	FORMAL		otsūji nasaimase	otsūji nasaimasu na
Presumptive	**INFORMAL**	I	tsūjiyō	tsūjimai
		II	tsūjiru darō	tsūjinai darō
	FORMAL	I	tsūjimashō	tsūjimasumai
		II	tsūjiru deshō	tsūjinai deshō
Provisional	**INFORMAL**		tsūjireba	tsūjinakereba
	FORMAL		tsūjimaseba	tsūjimasen nara
			tsūjimasureba	
Gerund	**INFORMAL**	I	tsūjite	tsūjinai de
		II		tsūjinakute
	FORMAL		tsūjimashite	tsūjimasen de
Past Ind.	**INFORMAL**		tsūjita	tsūjinakatta
	FORMAL		tsūjimashita	tsūjimasen deshita
Past Presump.	**INFORMAL**		tsūjitarō	tsūjinakattarō
			tsūjita darō	tsūjinakatta darō
	FORMAL		tsūjimashitarō	tsūjimasen deshitarō
			tsūjita deshō	tsūjinakatta deshō
Conditional	**INFORMAL**		tsūjitara	tsūjinakattara
	FORMAL		tsūjimashitara	tsūjimasen deshitara
Alternative	**INFORMAL**		tsūjitari	tsūjinakattari
	FORMAL		tsūjimashitari	tsūjimasen deshitari

		INFORMAL AFFIRMATIVE INDICATIVE
Passive		tsūjirareru
Potential		tsūjirareru
Causative		tsūjisaseru
Causative Pass.		tsūjisaserareru
Honorific	I	otsūji ni naru
	II	otsūji nasaru
Humble	I	
	II	

T

tsukam.u　つかむ／掴む　　　　　　　　　　　　　　**tsukami**
to grasp, to catch, to grab　　　TRANSITIVE

			AFFIRMATIVE	**NEGATIVE**
Indicative	**INFORMAL**		tsukamu	tsukamanai
	FORMAL		tsukamimasu	tsukamimasen
Imperative	**INFORMAL**	I	tsukame	tsukamu na
		II	tsukaminasai	tsukaminasaru na
		III	tsukande kudasai	tsukamanai de kudasai
	FORMAL		otsukami nasaimase	otsukami nasaimasu na
Presumptive	**INFORMAL**	I	tsukamō	tsukaumai
		II	tsukamu darō	tsukamanai darō
	FORMAL	I	tsukamimashō	tsukamimasumai
		II	tsukamu deshō	tsukamanai deshō
Provisional	**INFORMAL**		tsukameba	tsukamanakereba
	FORMAL		tsukamimaseba	tsukamimasen nara
			tsukamimasureba	
Gerund	**INFORMAL**	I	tsukande	tsukamanai de
		II		tsukamanakute
	FORMAL		tsukamimashite	tsukamimasen de
Past Ind.	**INFORMAL**		tsukanda	tsukamanakatta
	FORMAL		tsukamimashita	tsukamimasen deshita
Past Presump.	**INFORMAL**		tsukandarō	tsukamanakattarō
			tsukanda darō	tsukamanakatta darō
	FORMAL		tsukamimashitarō	tsukamimasen deshitarō
			tsukanda deshō	tsukamanakatta deshō
Conditional	**INFORMAL**		tsukandara	tsukamanakattara
	FORMAL		tsukamimashitara	tsukamimasen deshitara
Alternative	**INFORMAL**		tsukandari	tsukamanakattari
	FORMAL		tsukamimashitari	tsukamimasen deshitari

		INFORMAL AFFIRMATIVE INDICATIVE
Passive		tsukamareru
Potential		tsukamarareru
Causative		tsukamaseru
Causative Pass.		tsukamaserareru
Honorific	I	otsukami ni naru
	II	otsukami nasaru
Humble	I	otsukami suru
	II	otsukami itasu

522

つかれる／疲れる　**tsukare.ru**

to be tired, to get weary

			AFFIRMATIVE	NEGATIVE
Indicative	**INFORMAL**		tsukareru	tsukarenai
	FORMAL		tsukaremasu	tsukaremasen
Imperative	**INFORMAL**	I	tsukarero	tsukareru na
		II	tsukarenasai	tsukarenasaru na
		III	tsukarete kudasai	tsukarenai de kudasai
	FORMAL		otsukare nasaimase	otsukare nasaimasu na
Presumptive	**INFORMAL**	I	tsukareyō	tsukaremai
		II	tsukareru darō	tsukarenai darō
	FORMAL	I	tsukaremashō	tsukaremasumai
		II	tsukareru deshō	tsukarenai deshō
Provisional	**INFORMAL**		tsukarereba	tsukarenakereba
	FORMAL		tsukaremaseba	tsukaremasen nara
			tsukaremasureba	
Gerund	**INFORMAL**	I	tsukarete	tsukarenai de
		II		tsukarenakute
	FORMAL		tsukaremashite	tsukaremasen de
Past Ind.	**INFORMAL**		tsukareta	tsukarenakatta
	FORMAL		tsukaremashita	tsukaremasen deshita
Past Presump.	**INFORMAL**		tsukaretarō	tsukarenakattarō
			tsukareta darō	tsukarenakatta darō
	FORMAL		tsukaremashitarō	tsukaremasen deshitarō
			tsukareta deshō	tsukarenakatta deshō
Conditional	**INFORMAL**		tsukaretara	tsukarenakattara
	FORMAL		tsukaremashitara	tsukaremasen deshitara
Alternative	**INFORMAL**		tsukaretari	tsukarenakattari
	FORMAL		tsukaremashitari	tsukaremasen deshitari

		INFORMAL AFFIRMATIVE INDICATIVE
Passive		
Potential		
Causative		tsukaresaseru
Causative Pass.		tsukaresaserareru
Honorific	I	otsukare ni naru
	II	otsukare nasaru
Humble	I	
	II	

523

tsuka.u　つかう／使う　　　　　　　　　　　　　　　tsukai

to use, to operate, to employ　　　　TRANSITIVE

			AFFIRMATIVE	**NEGATIVE**
Indicative	**INFORMAL**		tsukau	tsukawanai
	FORMAL		tsukaimasu	tsukaimasen
Imperative	**INFORMAL**	I	tsukae	tsukau na
		II	tsukainasai	tsukainasaru na
		III	tsukatte kudasai	tsukawanai de kudasai
	FORMAL		otsukai nasaimase	otsukai nasaimasu na
Presumptive	**INFORMAL**	I	tsukaō	tsukaumai
		II	tsukau darō	tsukawanai darō
	FORMAL	I	tsukaimashō	tsukaimasumai
		II	tsukau deshō	tsukawanai deshō
Provisional	**INFORMAL**		tsukaeba	tsukawanakereba
	FORMAL		tsukaimaseba	tsukaimasen nara
			tsukaimasureba	
Gerund	**INFORMAL**	I	tsukatte	tsukawanai de
		II		tsukawanakute
	FORMAL		tsukaimashite	tsukaimasen de
Past Ind.	**INFORMAL**		tsukatta	tsukawanakatta
	FORMAL		tsukaimashita	tsukaimasen deshita
Past Presump.	**INFORMAL**		tsukattarō	tsukawanakattarō
			tsukatta darō	tsukawanakatta darō
	FORMAL		tsukaimashitarō	tsukaimasen deshitarō
			tsukatta deshō	tsukawanakatta deshō
Conditional	**INFORMAL**		tsukattara	tsukawanakattara
	FORMAL		tsukaimashitara	tsukaimasen deshitara
Alternative	**INFORMAL**		tsukattari	tsukawanakattari
	FORMAL		tsukaimashitari	tsukaimasen deshitari

		INFORMAL AFFIRMATIVE INDICATIVE
Passive		tsukawareru
Potential		tsukaeru
Causative		tsukawaseru
Causative Pass.		tsukawaserareru
Honorific	I	otsukai ni naru
	II	otsukai nasaru
Humble	I	otsukai suru
	II	otsukai itasu

AN ESSENTIAL
55 VERB

Tsukau 使う

Sentences Using *Tsukau*

Kono dejikame wa tsukawanai kara,
hoshikereba agemashō.
このデジカメは使わないから、欲しけ
ればあげましょう。
*I don't use this digital camera, so if
you want it, I'll give it to you.*

Kanojo no mise dewa ten-in o jū nin
tsukatte imasu.
彼女の店では店員を十人使っていま
す。
*She's employing ten sales clerks at her
shop.*

Kono dōgu wa tsukaikata ga
wakarimasen.
この道具は使い方が分かりません。
I don't know how to operate this tool.

Sono denwa o tsukattemo ii desu ka.
その電話を使ってもいいですか。
Is it okay if I use the phone?

Kanji wa tsukawanai to wasureru.
漢字は使わないと忘れる。
*If you don't use kanji, you forget
them.*

to use, to operate, to employ

Tsukau is a verb you'll use in daily
conversation, just as you do its English
equivalent. You use computers and
phones, operate machinery, employ
people, and much more.

Words and Expressions Related to This Verb

mochiiru　用いる
to use, to employ

shiyō suru　使用する
to use, to employ

tsukaimono ni naranai
使い物にならない
useless

shiyō chū　使用中
occupied

to attach, to apply, to put on, to turn on　　TRANSITIVE

			AFFIRMATIVE	**NEGATIVE**
Indicative	**INFORMAL**		tsukeru	tsukenai
	FORMAL		tsukemasu	tsukemasen
Imperative	**INFORMAL**	I	tsukero	tsukeru na
		II	tsukenasai	tsukenasaru na
		III	tsukete kudasai	tsukenai de kudasai
	FORMAL		otsuke nasaimase	otsuke nasaimasu na
Presumptive	**INFORMAL**	I	tsukeyō	tsukemai
		II	tsukeru darō	tsukenai darō
	FORMAL	I	tsukemashō	tsukemasumai
		II	tsukeru deshō	tsukenai deshō
Provisional	**INFORMAL**		tsukereba	tsukenakereba
	FORMAL		tsukemaseba	tsukemasen nara
			tsukemasureba	
Gerund	**INFORMAL**	I	tsukete	tsukenai de
		II		tsukenakute
	FORMAL		tsukemashite	tsukemasen de
Past Ind.	**INFORMAL**		tsuketa	tsukenakatta
	FORMAL		tsukemashita	tsukemasen deshita
Past Presump.	**INFORMAL**		tsuketarō	tsukenakattarō
			tsuketa darō	tsukenakatta darō
	FORMAL		tsukemashitarō	tsukemasen deshitarō
			tsuketa deshō	tsukenakatta deshō
Conditional	**INFORMAL**		tsuketara	tsukenakattara
	FORMAL		tsukemashitara	tsukemasen deshitara
Alternative	**INFORMAL**		tsuketari	tsukenakattari
	FORMAL		tsukemashitari	tsukemasen deshitari

			INFORMAL AFFIRMATIVE INDICATIVE
Passive			tsukerareru
Potential			tsukerareru
Causative			tsukesaseru
Causative Pass.			tsukesaserareru
Honorific		I	otsuke ni naru
		II	otsuke nasaru
Humble		I	otsuke suru
		II	otsuke itasu

526

つきあう／付き合う　**tsukia.u**

to associate with, to be friendly with

			AFFIRMATIVE	NEGATIVE
Indicative	**INFORMAL**		tsukiau	tsukiawanai
	FORMAL		tsukiaimasu	tsukiaimasen
Imperative	**INFORMAL**	I	tsukiae	tsukiau na
		II	tsukiainasai	tsukiainasaru na
		III	tsukiatte kudasai	tsukiawanai de kudasai
	FORMAL		otsukiai nasaimase	otsukiai nasaimasu na
Presumptive	**INFORMAL**	I	tsukiaō	tsukiaumai
		II	tsukiau darō	tsukiawanai darō
	FORMAL	I	tsukiaimashō	tsukiaimasumai
		II	tsukiau deshō	tsukiawanai deshō
Provisional	**INFORMAL**		tsukiaeba	tsukiawanakereba
	FORMAL		tsukiaimaseba	tsukiaimasen nara
			tsukiaimasureba	
Gerund	**INFORMAL**	I	tsukiatte	tsukiawanai de
		II		tsukiawanakute
	FORMAL		tsukiaimashite	tsukiaimasen de
Past Ind.	**INFORMAL**		tsukiatta	tsukiawanakatta
	FORMAL		tsukiaimashita	tsukiaimasen deshita
Past Presump.	**INFORMAL**		tsukiattarō	tsukiawanakattarō
			tsukiatta darō	tsukiawanakatta darō
	FORMAL		tsukiaimashitarō	tsukiaimasen deshitarō
			tsukiatta deshō	tsukiawanakatta deshō
Conditional	**INFORMAL**		tsukiattara	tsukiawanakattara
	FORMAL		tsukiaimashitara	tsukiaimasen deshitara
Alternative	**INFORMAL**		tsukiattari	tsukiawanakattari
	FORMAL		tsukiaimashitari	tsukiaimasen deshitari

		INFORMAL AFFIRMATIVE INDICATIVE
Passive		
Potential		tsukiaeru
Causative		tsukiawaseru
Causative Pass.		tsukiawaserareru
Honorific	I	otsukiai ni naru
	II	otsukiai nasaru
Humble	I	otsukiai suru
	II	otsukiai itasu

			AFFIRMATIVE	NEGATIVE
Indicative	**INFORMAL**		tsuku	tsukanai
	FORMAL		tsukimasu	tsukimasen
Imperative	**INFORMAL**	I	tsuke	tsuku na
		II		
		III	tsuite kudasai	tsukanai de kudasai
	FORMAL			
Presumptive	**INFORMAL**	I	tsukō	tsukumai
		II	tsuku darō	tsukanai darō
	FORMAL	I	tsukimashō	tsukimasumai
		II	tsuku deshō	tsukanai deshō
Provisional	**INFORMAL**		tsukeba	tsukanakereba
	FORMAL		tsukimaseba	tsukimasen nara
			tsukimasureba	
Gerund	**INFORMAL**	I	tsuite	tsukanai de
		II		tsukanakute
	FORMAL		tsukimashite	tsukimasen de
Past Ind.	**INFORMAL**		tsuita	tsukanakatta
	FORMAL		tsukimashita	tsukimasen deshita
Past Presump.	**INFORMAL**		tsuitarō	tsukanakattarō
			tsuita darō	tsukanakatta darō
	FORMAL		tsukimashitarō	tsukimasen deshitarō
			tsuita deshō	tsukanakatta deshō
Conditional	**INFORMAL**		tsuitara	tsukanakattara
	FORMAL		tsukimashitara	tsukimasen deshitara
Alternative	**INFORMAL**		tsuitari	tsukanakattari
	FORMAL		tsukimashitari	tsukimasen deshitari

		INFORMAL AFFIRMATIVE INDICATIVE
Passive		tsukareru
Potential		tsukeru
Causative		tsukaseru
Causative Pass.		tsukaserareru
Honorific	I	otsuki ni naru
	II	otsuki nasaru
Humble	I	
	II	

AN ESSENTIAL 55 VERB

Tsuku 着く

Sentences Using *Tsuku*

Hikōki wa yotei yori juppun hayaku tsukimashita.
飛行機は予定より十分早く着きました。
The plane arrived 10 minutes earlier than scheduled.

Kono kisha wa Nagoya ni nan ji ni tsukimasu ka.
この汽車は名古屋に何時に着きますか。
What time does this train arrive at Nagoya?

Tegami ga asatte made ni tsukanakattara, shirasete kudasai.
手紙が明後日までに着かなかったら知らせてください。
Let me know it if the letter doesn't reach you by the day after tomorrow.

Nihon ni tsuitara sugu ni sushi o tabeni ikimasu.
日本に着いたら直ぐに鮨を食べにいきます。
When we arrive in Japan, we'll immediately go to eat sushi.

Gakkō ni ku ji ni tsuku yō, ie o shichi ji han ni deru.
学校に9時に着くよう、家を7時半に出る。
I leave home at 7:30 in order to arrive at my school at 9.

to arrive, to get to, to reach

Tsuku is a verb you'll use often in everyday conversation. Just remember that in Japan it's better to arrive for appointments on time or early, never late! The Japanese value punctuality. So allow for heavy traffic and rush hour delays as you try to reach your destination at the appointed time.

T

Words and Expressions Related to This Verb

tōchaku suru   到着する
to arrive, to reach

chakuriku suru   着陸する
to land, to touch down

chakuseki suru   着席する
to sit down, to take one's seat

shinchaku no   新着の
new, latest

to make, to cook, to create, to build　　　TRANSITIVE

			AFFIRMATIVE	NEGATIVE
Indicative	**INFORMAL**		tsukuru	tsukuranai
	FORMAL		tsukurimasu	tsukurimasen
Imperative	**INFORMAL**	I	tsukure	tsukuru na
		II	tsukurinasai	tsukurinasaru na
		III	tsukutte kudasai	tsukuranai de kudasai
	FORMAL		otsukuri nasaimase	otsukuri nasaimasu na
Presumptive	**INFORMAL**	I	tsukurō	tsukurumai
		II	tsukuru darō	tsukuranai darō
	FORMAL	I	tsukurimashō	tsukurimasumai
		II	tsukuru deshō	tsukuranai deshō
Provisional	**INFORMAL**		tsukureba	tsukuranakereba
	FORMAL		tsukurimaseba	tsukurimasen nara
			tsukurimasureba	
Gerund	**INFORMAL**	I	tsukutte	tsukuranai de
		II		tsukuranakute
	FORMAL		tsukurimashite	tsukurimasen de
Past Ind.	**INFORMAL**		tsukutta	tsukuranakatta
	FORMAL		tsukurimashita	tsukurimasen deshita
Past Presump.	**INFORMAL**		tsukuttarō	tsukuranakattarō
			tsukutta darō	tsukuranakatta darō
	FORMAL		tsukurimashitarō	tsukurimasen deshitarō
			tsukutta deshō	tsukuranakatta deshō
Conditional	**INFORMAL**		tsukuttara	tsukuranakattara
	FORMAL		tsukurimashitara	tsukurimasen deshitara
Alternative	**INFORMAL**		tsukuttari	tsukuranakattari
	FORMAL		tsukurimashitari	tsukurimasen deshitari

		INFORMAL AFFIRMATIVE INDICATIVE
Passive		tsukurareru
Potential		tsukureru
Causative		tsukuraseru
Causative Pass.		tsukuraserareru
Honorific	I	otsukuri ni naru
	II	otsukuri nasaru
Humble	I	otsukuri suru
	II	otsukuri itasu

AN ESSENTIAL 55 VERB

Tsukuru 作る

to make, to cook, to create, to build

Tsukuru is a verb you can hardly do without in your daily life. You'll use it many times in everyday conversation as you refer to making all sorts of things, and, of course, to cooking delicious food.

Sentences Using *Tsukuru*

Ani wa daiku shigoto ga suki de nandemo tsukuremasu.
兄は大工仕事が好きで何でも作れます。
My older brother likes carpentry, and he can make anything.

Konban wa watakushi ga ban gohan o tsukurimasu.
今晩は私が晩ご飯を作ります。
I'll cook dinner.

Kare ga tsukuru tōki wa subarashii.
彼が作る陶器は素晴らしい。
The pottery he makes is wonderful.

Kono kōjō dewa nani o tsukutte imasu ka.
この工場では何を作っていますか？
What are they making at this factory?

Kono tēburu wa watakushi ga tsukurimashita.
このテーブルは私が作りました。
I made this table.

Words and Expressions Related to This Verb

koshiraeru　こしらえる
to make

sakusei suru　作成する
to make

seisaku suru　製作する
to make, to manufacture, to produce

sakubun　作文
a composition, an essay

sakumotsu　作物
produce, farm products

T

tsukus.u つくす／尽くす   tsukushi

to use up, to exhaust, to do one's best   TRANSITIVE

			AFFIRMATIVE	NEGATIVE
Indicative	**INFORMAL**		tsukusu	tsukusanai
	FORMAL		tsukushimasu	tsukushimasen
Imperative	**INFORMAL**	I	tsukuse	tsukusu na
		II	tsukushinasai	tsukushinasaru na
		III	tsukushite kudasai	tsukusanai de kudasai
	FORMAL		otsukushi nasaimase	otsukushi nasaimasu na
Presumptive	**INFORMAL**	I	tsukusō	tsukusumai
		II	tsukusu darō	tsukusanai darō
	FORMAL	I	tsukushimashō	tsukushimasumai
		II	tsukusu deshō	tsukusanai deshō
Provisional	**INFORMAL**		tsukuseba	tsukusanakereba
	FORMAL		tsukushimaseba	tsukushimasen nara
			tsukushimasureba	
Gerund	**INFORMAL**	I	tsukushite	tsukusanai de
		II		tsukusanakute
	FORMAL		tsukushimashite	tsukushimasen de
Past Ind.	**INFORMAL**		tsukushita	tsukusanakatta
	FORMAL		tsukushimashita	tsukushimasen deshita
Past Presump.	**INFORMAL**		tsukushitarō	tsukusanakattarō
			tsukushita darō	tsukusanakatta darō
	FORMAL		tsukushimashitarō	tsukushimasen deshitarō
			tsukushita deshō	tsukusanakatta deshō
Conditional	**INFORMAL**		tsukushitara	tsukasanakattara
	FORMAL		tsukushimashitara	tsukushimasen deshitara
Alternative	**INFORMAL**		tsukushitari	tsukusanakattari
	FORMAL		tsukushimashitari	tsukushimasen deshitari

		INFORMAL AFFIRMATIVE INDICATIVE
Passive		tsukusareru
Potential		tsukuseru
Causative		tsukusaseru
Causative Pass.		tsukusaserareru
Honorific	I	otsukushi ni naru
	II	otsukushi nasaru
Humble	I	otsukushi suru
	II	otsukushi itasu

つもる／積もる　**tsumor.u**

to pile up, to accumulate

			AFFIRMATIVE	NEGATIVE
Indicative	**INFORMAL**		tsumoru	tsumoranai
	FORMAL		tsumorimasu	tsumorimasen
Imperative	**INFORMAL**	I	tsumore	tsumoru na
		II		
		III	tsumotte kudasai	tsumoranai de kudasai
	FORMAL			
Presumptive	**INFORMAL**	I	tsumorō	tsumorumai
		II	tsumoru darō	tsumoranai darō
	FORMAL	I	tsumorimashō	tsumorimasumai
		II	tsumoru deshō	tsumoranai deshō
Provisional	**INFORMAL**		tsumoreba	tsumoranakereba
	FORMAL		tsumorimaseba	tsumorimasen nara
			tsumorimasureba	
Gerund	**INFORMAL**	I	tsumotte	tsumoranai de
		II		tsumoranakute
	FORMAL		tsumorimashite	tsumorimasen de
Past Ind.	**INFORMAL**		tsumotta	tsumoranakatta
	FORMAL		tsumorimashita	tsumorimasen deshita
Past Presump.	**INFORMAL**		tsumottarō	tsumoranakattarō
			tsumotta darō	tsumoranakatta darō
	FORMAL		tsumorimashitarō	tsumorimasen deshitarō
			tsumotta deshō	tsumoranakatta deshō
Conditional	**INFORMAL**		tsumottara	tsumoranakattara
	FORMAL		tsumorimashitara	tsumorimasen deshitara
Alternative	**INFORMAL**		tsumottari	tsumoranakattari
	FORMAL		tsumorimashitari	tsumorimasen deshitari

INFORMAL AFFIRMATIVE INDICATIVE

Passive		
Potential		
Causative		
Causative Pass.		
Honorific	I	
	II	
Humble	I	
	II	

T

tsunag.u つなぐ／繋ぐ

to connect, to fasten, to join   TRANSITIVE

			AFFIRMATIVE	NEGATIVE
Indicative	**INFORMAL**		tsunagu	tsunaganai
	FORMAL		tsunagimasu	tsunagimasen
Imperative	**INFORMAL**	I	tsunage	tsunagu na
		II	tsunaginasai	tsunaginasaru na
		III	tsunaide kudasai	tsunaganai de kudasai
	FORMAL		otsunagi nasaimase	otsunagi nasaimasu na
Presumptive	**INFORMAL**	I	tsunagō	tsunagumai
		II	tsunagu darō	tsunaganai darō
	FORMAL	I	tsunagimashō	tsunagimasumai
		II	tsunagu deshō	tsunaganai deshō
Provisional	**INFORMAL**		tsunageba	tsunaganakereba
	FORMAL		tsunagimaseba	tsunagimasen nara
			tsunagimasureba	
Gerund	**INFORMAL**	I	tsunaide	tsunaganai de
		II		tsunaganakute
	FORMAL		tsunagimashite	tsunagimasen de
Past Ind.	**INFORMAL**		tsunaida	tsunaganakatta
	FORMAL		tsunagimashita	tsunagimasen deshita
Past Presump.	**INFORMAL**		tsunaidarō	tsunaganakattarō
			tsunaida darō	tsunaganakatta darō
	FORMAL		tsunagimashitarō	tsunagimasen deshitarō
			tsunaida deshō	tsunaganakatta deshō
Conditional	**INFORMAL**		tsunaidara	tsunaganakattara
	FORMAL		tsunagimashitara	tsunagimasen deshitara
Alternative	**INFORMAL**		tsunaidari	tsunaganakattari
	FORMAL		tsunagimashitari	tsunagimasen deshitari

			INFORMAL AFFIRMATIVE INDICATIVE
Passive			tsunagareru
Potential			tsunageru
Causative			tsunagaseru
Causative Pass.			tsunagaserareru
Honorific		I	otsunagi ni naru
		II	otsunagi nasaru
Humble		I	otsunagi suru
		II	otsunagi itasu

つたえる／伝える **tsutae.ru**

TRANSITIVE   *to tell, to convey, to report, to transmit*

			AFFIRMATIVE	**NEGATIVE**
Indicative	**INFORMAL**		tsutaeru	tsutaenai
	FORMAL		tsutaemasu	tsutaemasen
Imperative	**INFORMAL**	**I**	tsutaero	tsutaeru na
		II	tsutaenasai	tsutaenasaru na
		III	tsutaete kudasai	tsutaenai de kudasai
	FORMAL		otsutae nasaimase	otsutae nasaimasu na
Presumptive	**INFORMAL**	**I**	tsutaeyō	tsutaemai
		II	tsutaeru darō	tsutaenai darō
	FORMAL	**I**	tsutaemashō	tsutaemasumai
		II	tsutaeru deshō	tsutaenai deshō
Provisional	**INFORMAL**		tsutaereba	tsutaenakereba
	FORMAL		tsutaemaseba	tsutaemasen nara
			tsutaemasureba	
Gerund	**INFORMAL**	**I**	tsutaete	tsutaenai de
		II		tsutaenakute
	FORMAL		tsutaemashite	tsutaemasen de
Past Ind.	**INFORMAL**		tsutaeta	tsutaenakatta
	FORMAL		tsutaemashita	tsutaemasen deshita
Past Presump.	**INFORMAL**		tsutaetarō	tsutaenakattarō
			tsutaeta darō	tsutaenakatta darō
	FORMAL		tsutaemashitarō	tsutaemasen deshitarō
			tsutaeta deshō	tsutaenakatta deshō
Conditional	**INFORMAL**		tsutaetara	tsutaenakattara
	FORMAL		tsutaemashitara	tsutaemasen deshitara
Alternative	**INFORMAL**		tsutaetari	tsutaenakattari
	FORMAL		tsutaemashitari	tsutaemasen deshitari

T

		INFORMAL AFFIRMATIVE INDICATIVE
Passive		tsutaerareru
Potential		tsutaerareru
Causative		tsutaesaseru
Causative Pass.		tsutaesaserareru
Honorific	**I**	otsutae ni naru
	II	otsutae nasaru
Humble	**I**	otsutae suru
	II	otsutae itasu

to work for, to be employed

			AFFIRMATIVE	NEGATIVE
Indicative	**INFORMAL**		tsutomeru	tsutomenai
	FORMAL		tsutomemasu	tsutomemasen
Imperative	**INFORMAL**	I	tsutomero	tsutomeru na
		II	tsutomenasai	tsutomenasaru na
		III	tsutomete kudasai	tsutomenai de kudasai
	FORMAL		otsutome nasaimase	otsutome nasaimasu na
Presumptive	**INFORMAL**	I	tsutomeyō	tsutomemai
		II	tsutomeru darō	tsutomenai darō
	FORMAL	I	tsutomemashō	tsutomemasumai
		II	tsutomeru deshō	tsutomenai deshō
Provisional	**INFORMAL**		tsutomereba	tsutomenakereba
	FORMAL		tsutomemaseba	tsutomemasen nara
			tsutomemasureba	
Gerund	**INFORMAL**	I	tsutomete	tsutomenai de
		II		tsutomenakute
	FORMAL		tsutomemashite	tsutomemasen de
Past Ind.	**INFORMAL**		tsutometa	tsutomenakatta
	FORMAL		tsutomemashita	tsutomemasen deshita
Past Presump.	**INFORMAL**		tsutometarō	tsutomenakattarō
			tsutometa darō	tsutomenakatta darō
	FORMAL		tsutomemashitarō	tsutomemasen deshitarō
			tsutometa deshō	tsutomenakatta deshō
Conditional	**INFORMAL**		tsutometara	tsutomenakattara
	FORMAL		tsutomemashitara	tsutomemasen deshitara
Alternative	**INFORMAL**		tsutometari	tsutomenakattari
	FORMAL		tsutomemashitari	tsutomemasen deshitari

		INFORMAL AFFIRMATIVE INDICATIVE
Passive		tsutomerareru
Potential		tsutomerareru
Causative		tsutomesaseru
Causative Pass.		tsutomesaserareru
Honorific	I	otsutome ni naru
	II	otsutome nasaru
Humble	I	otsutome suru
	II	otsutome itasu

AN ESSENTIAL 55 VERB

Tsutomeru 勤める

Sentences Using *Tsutomeru*

Tsuma wa ginkō ni tsutomete imasu.
妻は銀行に勤めています。
My wife is working at a bank.

Chichi wa san jū go nen seifu ni
tsutomemashita.
父は３５年政府に勤めました。
*My father worked for the government
for 35 years.*

Kare wa bōeki gaisha ni tsutomeyō to
omotte imasu.
彼は貿易会社に勤めようと思っていま
す。
*He's thinking about working for a
trading company.*

Dai kigyō niwa tsutometakunai.
大企業には勤めたくない。
I don't work for a large corporation.

Kanojo wa sono mise ni mikka
tsutometa dake de yamete shimatta.
彼女はその店に三日勤めただけで辞め
てしまった。
*She quit after working at that store for
only three days.*

to work for, to be employed

Tsutomeru is an essential verb because
everyone talks about work, at least some
of the time. Where one works and how to
prepare for it is a big part of life in Japan.

Words and Expressions Related to This Verb

kinmu suru　勤務する
to work

tsūkin suru　　通勤する
to commute

tsutome/otsutome　　勤め／お勤め
work

tsutome saki　　勤め先
one's office, one's place of work

kinben na　　勤勉な
hard-working, diligent

Proverb

Kinben wa seikō no haha.
勤勉は成功の母。
Diligence is the mother of success.

tsutsum.u つつむ／包む   tsutsumi

to wrap   TRANSITIVE

			AFFIRMATIVE	NEGATIVE
Indicative	**INFORMAL**		tsutsumu	tsutsumanai
	FORMAL		tsutsumimasu	tsutsumimasen
Imperative	**INFORMAL**	I	tsutsume	tsutsumu na
		II	tsutsuminasai	tsutsuminasaru na
		III	tsutsunde kudasai	tsutsumanai de kudasai
	FORMAL		otsutsumi nasaimase	otsutsumi nasaimasu na
Presumptive	**INFORMAL**	I	tsutsumō	tsutsumumai
		II	tsutsumu darō	tsutsumanai darō
	FORMAL	I	tsutsumimashō	tsutsumimasumai
		II	tsutsumu deshō	tsutsumanai deshō
Provisional	**INFORMAL**		tsutsumeba	tsutsumanakereba
	FORMAL		tsutsumimaseba	tsutsumimasen nara
			tsutsumimasureba	
Gerund	**INFORMAL**	I	tsutsunde	tsutsumanai de
		II		tsutsumanakute
	FORMAL		tsutsumimashite	tsutsumimasen de
Past Ind.	**INFORMAL**		tsutsunda	tsutsumanakatta
	FORMAL		tsutsumimashita	tsutsumimasen deshita
Past Presump.	**INFORMAL**		tsutsundarō	tsutsumanakattarō
			tsutsunda darō	tsutsumanakatta darō
	FORMAL		tsutsumimashitarō	tsutsumimasen deshitarō
			tsutsunda deshō	tsutsumanakatta deshō
Conditional	**INFORMAL**		tsutsundara	tsutsumanakattara
	FORMAL		tsutsumimashitara	tsutsumimasen deshitara
Alternative	**INFORMAL**		tsutsundari	tsutsumanakattari
	FORMAL		tsutsumimashitari	tsutsumimasen deshitari

		INFORMAL AFFIRMATIVE INDICATIVE
Passive		tsutsumareru
Potential		tsutsumeru
Causative		tsutsumaseru
Causative Pass.		tsutsumaserareru
Honorific	I	otsutsumi ni naru
	II	otsutsumi nasaru
Humble	I	otsutsumi suru
	II	otsutsumi itasu

つづける／続ける　**tsuzuke.ru**

TRANSITIVE　　*to continue, to proceed*

			AFFIRMATIVE	NEGATIVE
Indicative	**INFORMAL**		tsuzukeru	tsuzukenai
	FORMAL		tsuzukemasu	tsuzukemasen
Imperative	**INFORMAL**	I	tsuzukero	tsuzukeru na
		II	tsuzukenai	tsuzukenasaru na
		III	tsuzukete kudasai	tsuzukenai de kudasai
	FORMAL		otsuzuke nasaimase	otsuzuke nasaimasu na
Presumptive	**INFORMAL**	I	tsuzukeyō	tsuzukemai
		II	tsuzukeru darō	tsuzukenai darō
	FORMAL	I	tsuzukemashō	tsuzukemasumai
		II	tsuzukeru deshō	tsuzukenai deshō
Provisional	**INFORMAL**		tsuzukereba	tsuzukenakereba
	FORMAL		tsuzukemaseba	tsuzukemasen nara
			tsuzukemasureba	
Gerund	**INFORMAL**	I	tsuzukete	tsuzukenai de
		II		tsuzukenakute
	FORMAL		tsuzukemashite	tsuzukemasen de
Past Ind.	**INFORMAL**		tsuzuketa	tsuzukenakatta
	FORMAL		tsuzukemashita	tsuzukemasen deshita
Past Presump.	**INFORMAL**		tsuzuketarō	tsuzukenakattarō
			tsuzuketa darō	tsuzukenakatta darō
	FORMAL		tsuzukemashitarō	tsuzukemasen deshitarō
			tsuzuketa deshō	tsuzukenakatta deshō
Conditional	**INFORMAL**		tsuzuketara	tsuzukenakattara
	FORMAL		tsuzukemashitara	tsuzukemasen deshitara
Alternative	**INFORMAL**		tsuzuketari	tsuzukenakattari
	FORMAL		tsuzukemashitari	tsuzukemasen deshitari

			INFORMAL AFFIRMATIVE INDICATIVE
Passive			tsuzukerareru
Potential			tsuzukerareru
Causative			tsuzukesaseru
Causative Pass.			tsuzukesaserareru
Honorific		I	otsuzuke ni naru
		II	otsuzuke nasaru
Humble		I	otsuzuke suru
		II	otsuzuke itaru

T

to continue, to follow, to lead to

			AFFIRMATIVE	NEGATIVE
Indicative	**INFORMAL**		tsuzuku	tsuzukanai
	FORMAL		tsuzukimasu	tsuzukimasen
Imperative	**INFORMAL**	I	tsuzuke	tsuzuku na
		II	tsuzukinasai	tsuzukinasaru na
		III	tsuzuite kudasai	tsuzukanai de kudasi
	FORMAL		otsuzuki nasaimase	otsuzuki nasaimasu na
Presumptive	**INFORMAL**	I	tsuzukō	tsuzukumai
		II	tsuzuku darō	tsuzukanai darō
	FORMAL	I	tsuzukimashō	tsuzukimasumai
		II	tsuzuku deshō	tsuzukanai deshō
Provisional	**INFORMAL**		tsuzukeba	tsuzukanakereba
	FORMAL		tsuzukimaseba	tsuzukimasen nara
			tsuzukimasureba	
Gerund	**INFORMAL**	I	tsuzuite	tsuzukanai de
		II		tsuzukanakute
	FORMAL		tsuzukimashite	tsuzukimasen de
Past Ind.	**INFORMAL**		tsuzuita	tsuzukanakatta
	FORMAL		tsuzukimashita	tsuzukimasen deshita
Past Presump.	**INFORMAL**		tsuzuitarō	tsuzukanakattarō
			tsuzuita darō	tsuzukanakatta darō
	FORMAL		tsuzukimashitarō	tsuzukimsen deshitarō
			tsuzuita deshō	tsuzukanakatta deshō
Conditional	**INFORMAL**		tsuzuitara	tsuzukanakattara
	FORMAL		tsuzukimashitara	tsuzukimasen deshitara
Alternative	**INFORMAL**		tsuzuitari	tsuzukanakattari
	FORMAL		tsuzukimashitari	tsuzukimasen deshitari

		INFORMAL AFFIRMATIVE INDICATIVE
Passive		
Potential		
Causative		tsuzukaseru
Causative Pass.		tsuzukaserareru
Honorific	I	otsuzuki ni naru
	II	otsuzuki nasaru
Humble	I	otsuzuki suru
	II	otsuzuki itasu

うえる／植える **ue.ru**

TRANSITIVE　　*to plant*

			AFFIRMATIVE	NEGATIVE
Indicative	**INFORMAL**		ueru	uenai
	FORMAL		uemasu	uemasen
Imperative	**INFORMAL**	I	uero	ueru na
		II	uenasai	uenasaru na
		III	uete kudasai	uenai de kudasai
	FORMAL		oue nasaimase	oue nasaimasu na
Presumptive	**INFORMAL**	I	ueyō	uemai
		II	ueru darō	uenai darō
	FORMAL	I	uemashō	uemasumai
		II	ueru deshō	uenai deshō
Provisional	**INFORMAL**		uereba	uenakereba
	FORMAL		uemaseba	uemasen nara
			uemasureba	
Gerund	**INFORMAL**	I	uete	uenai de
		II		uenakute
	FORMAL		uemashite	uemasen de
Past Ind.	**INFORMAL**		ueta	uenakatta
	FORMAL		uemashita	uemasen deshita
Past Presump.	**INFORMAL**		uetarō	uenakattarō
			ueta darō	uenakatta darō
	FORMAL		uemashitarō	uemasen deshitarō
			ueta deshō	uenakatta deshō
Conditional	**INFORMAL**		uetara	uenakattara
	FORMAL		uemashitara	uemasen deshitara
Alternative	**INFORMAL**		uetari	uenakattari
	FORMAL		uemashitari	uemasen deshitari

		INFORMAL AFFIRMATIVE INDICATIVE
Passive		uerareru
Potential		uerareru
Causative		uesaseru
Causative Pass.		uesaserareru
Honorific	I	oue ni naru
	II	oue nasaru
Humble	I	oue suru
	II	oue itasu

U

ugokas.u うごかす／動かす　　　　　　　　ugokashi
to move, to operate　　TRANSITIVE

			AFFIRMATIVE	NEGATIVE
Indicative	**INFORMAL**		ugokasu	ugokasanai
	FORMAL		ugokashimasu	ugokashimasen
Imperative	**INFORMAL**	I	ugokase	ugokasu na
		II	ugokashinasai	ugokashinasaru na
		III	ugokashite kudasai	ugokasanai de kudasai
	FORMAL		ougokashi nasaimase	ougokashi nasaimasu na
Presumptive	**INFORMAL**	I	ugokasō	ugokasumai
		II	ugokasu darō	ugokasanai darō
	FORMAL	I	ugokashimashō	ugokashimasumai
		II	ugokasu deshō	ugokasanai deshō
Provisional	**INFORMAL**		ugokaseba	ugokasanakereba
	FORMAL		ugokashimaseba	ugokashimasen nara
			ugokashimasureba	
Gerund	**INFORMAL**	I	ugokashite	ugokasanai de
		II		ugokasanakute
	FORMAL		ugokashimashite	ugokashimasen de
Past Ind.	**INFORMAL**		ugokashita	ugokasanakatta
	FORMAL		ugokashimashita	ugokashimasen deshita
Past Presump.	**INFORMAL**		ugokashitarō	ugokasanakattarō
			ugokashita darō	ugokasanakatta darō
	FORMAL		ugokashimashitarō	ugokashimasen deshitarō
			ugokashita deshō	ugokasanakatta deshō
Conditional	**INFORMAL**		ugokashitara	ugokasanakattara
	FORMAL		ugokashimashitara	ugokashimasen deshitara
Alternative	**INFORMAL**		ugokashitari	ugokasanakattari
	FORMAL		ugokashimashitari	ugokashimasen deshitari

		INFORMAL AFFIRMATIVE INDICATIVE
Passive		ugokasareru
Potential		ugokaseru
Causative		ugokasaseru
Causative Pass.		ugokasaserareru
Honorific	I	ougokashi ni naru
	II	ougokashi nasaru
Humble	I	ougokashi suru
	II	ougokashi itasu

うごく／動く **ugok.u**
to move (to make a motion)

			AFFIRMATIVE	NEGATIVE
Indicative	**INFORMAL**		ugoku	ugokanai
	FORMAL		ugokimasu	ugokimasen
Imperative	**INFORMAL**	I	ugoke	ugoku na
		II	ugokinasai	ugokinasaru na
		III	ugoite kudasai	ugokanai de kudasai
	FORMAL		ougoki nasaimase	ougoki nasaimasu na
Presumptive	**INFORMAL**	I	ugokō	ugokumai
		II	ugoku darō	ugokanai darō
	FORMAL	I	ugokimashō	ugokimasumai
		II	ugoku deshō	ugokanai deshō
Provisional	**INFORMAL**		ugokeba	ugokanakereba
	FORMAL		ugokimaseba	ugokimasen nara
			ugokimasureba	
Gerund	**INFORMAL**	I	ugoite	ugokanai de
		II		ugokanakute
	FORMAL		ugokimashite	ugokimasen de
Past Ind.	**INFORMAL**		ugoita	ugokanakatta
	FORMAL		ugokimashita	ugokimasen deshita
Past Presump.	**INFORMAL**		ugoitarō	ugokanakattarō
			ugoita darō	ugokanakatta darō
	FORMAL		ugokimashitarō	ugokimasen deshitarō
			ugoita deshō	ugokanakatta deshō
Conditional	**INFORMAL**		ugoitara	ugokanakattara
	FORMAL		ugokimashitara	ugokimasen deshitara
Alternative	**INFORMAL**		ugoitari	ugokanakattari
	FORMAL		ugokimashitari	ugokimasen deshitari

		INFORMAL AFFIRMATIVE INDICATIVE
Passive		ugokareru
Potential		ugokeru
Causative		ugokaseru
Causative Pass.		ugokaserareru
Honorific	I	ougoki ni naru
	II	ougoki nasaru
Humble	I	
	II	

U

to float, to show, to express　　　TRANSITIVE

			AFFIRMATIVE	NEGATIVE
Indicative	**INFORMAL**		ukaberu	ukabenai
	FORMAL		ukabemasu	ukabemasen
Imperative	**INFORMAL**	I	ukabero	ukaberu na
		II	ukabenasai	ukabenasaru na
		III	ukabete kudasai	ukabenai de kudasai
	FORMAL		oukabe nasaimase	oukabe nasaimasu na
Presumptive	**INFORMAL**	I	ukabeyō	ukaberumai
		II	ukaberu darō	ukabenai darō
	FORMAL	I	ukabemashō	ukabemasumai
		II	ukaberu deshō	ukabenai deshō
Provisional	**INFORMAL**		ukabereba	ukabenakereba
	FORMAL		ukabemsaseba	ukabemasen nara
			ukabemasureba	
Gerund	**INFORMAL**	I	ukabete	ukabenai de
		II		ukabenakute
	FORMAL		ukabemashite	ukabemasen de
Past Ind.	**INFORMAL**		ukabeta	ukabenakatta
	FORMAL		ukabemashita	ukabemasen deshita
Past Presump.	**INFORMAL**		ukabetarō	ukabenakattarō
			ukabeta darō	ukabenakatta darō
	FORMAL		ukabemashitarō	ukabemasen deshitarō
			ukabeta deshō	ukabenakatta deshō
Conditional	**INFORMAL**		ukabetara	ukabenakattara
	FORMAL		ukabemashitara	ukabemasen deshitara
Alternative	**INFORMAL**		ukabetari	ukabenakattari
	FORMAL		ukabemashitari	ukabemasen deshitari

		INFORMAL AFFIRMATIVE INDICATIVE
Passive		ukaberareru
Potential		ukaberareru
Causative		ukabesaseru
Causative Pass.		ukabesaserareru
Honorific	I	oukabe ni naru
	II	oukabe nasaru
Humble	I	oukabe suru
	II	oukabe itasu

うかぶ／浮かぶ **ukab.u**
to float, to come to the surface, to come to mind

			AFFIRMATIVE	NEGATIVE
Indicative	**INFORMAL**		ukabu	ukabanai
	FORMAL		ukabimasu	ukabimasen
Imperative	**INFORMAL**	I	ukabe	ukabu na
		II	ukabinasai	ukabinasaru na
		III	ukande kudasai	ukabanai de kudasai
	FORMAL		oukabi nasaimase	oukabi nasaimasu na
Presumptive	**INFORMAL**	I	ukabō	ukabumai
		II	ukabu darō	ukabanai darō
	FORMAL	I	ukabimashō	ukabimasumai
		II	ukabu deshō	ukabanai deshō
Provisional	**INFORMAL**		ukabeba	ukabanakereba
	FORMAL		ukabimaseba	ukabimasen nara
			ukabimasureba	
Gerund	**INFORMAL**	I	ukande	ukabanai de
		II		ukabanakute
	FORMAL		ukabimashite	ukabimasen de
Past Ind.	**INFORMAL**		ukanda	ukabanakatta
	FORMAL		ukabimashita	ukabimasen deshita
Past Presump.	**INFORMAL**		ukandarō	ukabanakattarō
			ukanda darō	ukabanakatta darō
	FORMAL		ukabimashitarō	ukabimasen deshitarō
			ukanda deshō	ukabanakatta deshō
Conditional	**INFORMAL**		ukandara	ukabanakattara
	FORMAL		ukabimashitara	ukabimasen deshitara
Alternative	**INFORMAL**		ukandari	ukabanakattari
	FORMAL		ukabimashitari	ukabimasen deshitari

		INFORMAL AFFIRMATIVE INDICATIVE
Passive		ukabareru
Potential		ukaberu
Causative		ukabaseru
Causative Pass.		ukabaserareru
Honorific	I	oukabi ni naru
	II	oukabi nasaru
Humble	I	
	II	

U

ukaga.u　うかがう／伺う　　　　　　　　　　　　　　ukagai

to visit, to ask, to hear (news, etc.)　　　TRANSITIVE

			AFFIRMATIVE	NEGATIVE
Indicative	**INFORMAL**		ukagau	ukagawanai
	FORMAL		ukagaimasu	ukagaimasen
Imperative	**INFORMAL**	I	ukagae	ukagau na
		II	ukagainasai	ukagainasaru na
		III	ukagatte kudasai	ukagawanai de kudasai
	FORMAL		oukagai nasaimase	oukagai nasaimasu na
Presumptive	**INFORMAL**	I	ukagaō	ukagaumai
		II	ukagau darō	ukagawanai darō
	FORMAL	I	ukagaimashō	ukagaimasumai
		II	ukagau deshō	ukagawanai deshō
Provisional	**INFORMAL**		ukagaeba	ukagawanakereba
	FORMAL		ukagaimaseba	ukagaimasen nara
			ukagaimasureba	
Gerund	**INFORMAL**	I	ukagatte	ukagawanai de
		II		ukagawanakute
	FORMAL		ukagaimashite	ukagaimasen de
Past Ind.	**INFORMAL**		ukagatta	ukagawanakatta
	FORMAL		ukagaimashita	ukagaimasen deshita
Past Presump.	**INFORMAL**		ukagattarō	ukagawanakattarō
			ukagatta darō	ukagawanakatta darō
	FORMAL		ukagaimashitarō	ukagaimasen deshitarō
			ukagatta deshō	ukagawanakatta deshō
Conditional	**INFORMAL**		ukagattara	ukagawanakattara
	FORMAL		ukagaimashitara	ukagaimasen deshitara
Alternative	**INFORMAL**		ukagattari	ukagawanakattari
	FORMAL		ukagaimashitari	ukagaimasen deshitari

		INFORMAL AFFIRMATIVE INDICATIVE
Passive		
Potential		ukagaeru
Causative		ukagawaseru
Causative Pass.		ukagawaserareru
Honorific	I	oukagai ni naru
	II	oukagai nasaru
Humble	I	oukagai suru
	II	oukagai itasu

TRANSITIVE　　*to get, to receive, to accept, to understand*

			AFFIRMATIVE	**NEGATIVE**
Indicative	**INFORMAL**		uketoru	uketoranai
	FORMAL		uketorimasu	uketorimasen
Imperative	**INFORMAL**	I	uketore	uketoru na
		II	uketorinasai	uketorinasaru na
		III	uketotte kudasai	uketoranai de kudasai
	FORMAL		ouketori nasaimase	ouketori nasaimasu na
Presumptive	**INFORMAL**	I	uketorō	uketorumai
		II	uketoru darō	uketoranai darō
	FORMAL	I	uketorimashō	uketorimasumai
		II	uketoru deshō	uketoranai deshō
Provisional	**INFORMAL**		uketoreba	uketoranakereba
	FORMAL		uketorimaseba	uketorimasen nara
			uketorimasureba	
Gerund	**INFORMAL**	I	uketotte	uketoranai de
		II		uketoranakute
	FORMAL		uketorimashite	uketorimasen de
Past Ind.	**INFORMAL**		uketotta	uketoranakatta
	FORMAL		uketorimashita	uketorimasen deshita
Past Presump.	**INFORMAL**		uketottarō	uketoranakattarō
			uketotta darō	uketoranakatta darō
	FORMAL		uketorimashitarō	uketorimasen deshitarō
			uketotta deshō	uketoranakatta deshō
Conditional	**INFORMAL**		uketottara	uketoranakattara
	FORMAL		uketorimashitara	uketorimasen deshitara
Alternative	**INFORMAL**		uketottari	uketoranakattari
	FORMAL		uketorimashitari	uketorimasen deshitari

		INFORMAL AFFIRMATIVE INDICATIVE
Passive		uketorareru
Potential		uketoreru
Causative		uketoraseru
Causative Pass.		uketoraserareru
Honorific	I	ouketori ni naru
	II	ouketori nasaru
Humble	I	ouketori suru
	II	ouketori itasu

U

umare.ru* うまれる／生まれる umare

to be born

			AFFIRMATIVE	NEGATIVE
Indicative	INFORMAL		umareru	umarenai
	FORMAL		umaremasu	umaremasen
Imperative	INFORMAL	I	umarero	umareru na
		II	umarenasai	umarenasaru na
		III	umarete kudasai	umarenai de kudasai
	FORMAL		oumare nasaimase	oumare nasaimasu na
Presumptive	INFORMAL	I	umareyō	umaremai
		II	umareru darō	umarenai darō
	FORMAL	I	umaremashō	umaremasumai
		II	umareru deshō	umarenai deshō
Provisional	INFORMAL		umarereba	umarenakereba
	FORMAL		umaremaseba	umaremasen nara
			umaremasureba	
Gerund	INFORMAL	I	umarete	umarenai de
		II		umarenakute
	FORMAL		umaremashite	umaremasen de
Past Ind.	INFORMAL		umareta	umarenakatta
	FORMAL		umaremashita	umaremasen deshita
Past Presump.	INFORMAL		umaretarō	umarenakattarō
			umareta darō	umarenakatta darō
	FORMAL		umaremashitarō	umaremasen deshitarō
			umareta deshō	umarenakatta deshō
Conditional	INFORMAL		umaretara	umarenakattara
	FORMAL		umaremashitara	umaremasen deshitara
Alternative	INFORMAL		umaretari	umarenakattari
	FORMAL		umaremashitari	umaremasen deshitari

		INFORMAL AFFIRMATIVE INDICATIVE
Passive		
Potential		
Causative		umaresaseru
Causative Pass.		umaresaserareru
Honorific	I	oumare ni naru
	II	oumare nasaru
Humble	I	
	II	

*This corresponds to the passive derived form of *um.u* "to give birth."

うむ／産む／生む　um.u

TRANSITIVE　*to produce, to give birth, to lay eggs*

			AFFIRMATIVE	NEGATIVE
Indicative	INFORMAL		umu	umanai
	FORMAL		umimasu	umimasen
Imperative	INFORMAL	I	ume	umuna
		II	uminasai	uminasaru na
		III	unde kudasai	umanai de kudasai
	FORMAL		oumi nasaimase	oumi nasaimasu na
Presumptive	INFORMAL	I	umō	umumai
		II	umu darō	umanai darō
	FORMAL	I	umimashō	umimasumai
		II	umu deshō	umanai deshō
Provisional	INFORMAL		umeba	umanakereba
	FORMAL		umimaseba	umimasen nara
			umimasureba	
Gerund	INFORMAL	I	unde	umanai de
		II		umanakute
	FORMAL		umimashite	umimasen de
Past Ind.	INFORMAL		unda	umanakatta
	FORMAL		umimashita	umimasen deshita
Past Presump.	INFORMAL		undarō	umanakattarō
			unda darō	umanakatta darō
	FORMAL		imimashitarō	umimasen deshitarō
			unda deshō	umanakatta deshō
Conditional	INFORMAL		undara	umanakattara
	FORMAL		umimashitara	umimasen deshitara
Alternative	INFORMAL		undari	umanakattari
	FORMAL		umimashitari	umimasen deshitari

			INFORMAL AFFIRMATIVE INDICATIVE
Passive			umareru
Potential			umeru
Causative			umaseru
Causative Pass.			umaserareru
Honorific		I	oumi ni naru
		II	oumi nasaru
Humble		I	oumi suru
		II	oumi itasu

U

uram.u うらむ／恨む   urami

to bear a grudge   TRANSITIVE

			AFFIRMATIVE	NEGATIVE
Indicative	**INFORMAL**		uramu	uramanai
	FORMAL		uramimasu	uramimasen
Imperative	**INFORMAL**	I	urame	uramu na
		II	uraminasai	uraminasaru na
		III	urande kudasai	uramanai de kudasai
	FORMAL		ourami nasaimase	ourami nasaimasu na
Presumptive	**INFORMAL**	I	uramō	uramumai
		II	uramu darō	uramanai darō
	FORMAL	I	uramimashō	uramimasumai
		II	uramu deshō	uramanai deshō
Provisional	**INFORMAL**		urameba	uramanakereba
	FORMAL		uramimaseba	uramimasen nara
			uramimasureba	
Gerund	**INFORMAL**	I	urande	uramanai de
		II		uramanakute
	FORMAL		uramimashite	uramimasen de
Past Ind.	**INFORMAL**		uranda	uramanakatta
	FORMAL		uramimashita	uramimasen deshita
Past Presump.	**INFORMAL**		urandarō	uramanakattarō
			uranda darō	uramanakatta darō
	FORMAL		uramimashitarō	uramimasen deshitarō
			uranda deshō	uramanakatta deshō
Conditional	**INFORMAL**		urandara	uramanakattara
	FORMAL		uramimashitara	uramimasen deshitara
Alternative	**INFORMAL**		urandari	uramanakattari
	FORMAL		uramimashitari	uramimasen deshitari

			INFORMAL AFFIRMATIVE INDICATIVE
Passive			uramareru
Potential			urameru
Causative			uramaseru
Causative Pass.			uramaserareru
Honorific		I	ourami ni naru
		II	ourami nasaru
Humble		I	ourami suru
		II	ourami itasu

550

uri

			AFFIRMATIVE	NEGATIVE
Indicative	**INFORMAL**		uru	uranai
	FORMAL		urimasu	urimasen
Imperative	**INFORMAL**	I	ure	uru na
		II	urinasai	urinasaru na
		III	utte kudasai	uranai de kudasai
	FORMAL		ouri nasaimase	ouri nasaimasu na
Presumptive	**INFORMAL**	I	urō	urumai
		II	uru darō	uranai darō
	FORMAL	I	urimashō	urimasumai
		II	uru deshō	uranai deshō
Provisional	**INFORMAL**		ureba	uranakereba
	FORMAL		urimaseba	urimasen nara
			urimasureba	
Gerund	**INFORMAL**	I	utte	uranai de
		II		uranakute
	FORMAL		urimashite	urimasen de
Past Ind.	**INFORMAL**		utta	uranakatta
	FORMAL		urimashita	urimasen deshita
Past Presump.	**INFORMAL**		uttarō	uranakattarō
			utta darō	uranakatta darō
	FORMAL		urimashitarō	urimasen deshitarō
			utta deshō	uranakatta deshō
Conditional	**INFORMAL**		uttara	uranakattara
	FORMAL		urimashitara	urimasen deshitara
Alternative	**INFORMAL**		uttari	uranakattari
	FORMAL		urimashitari	urimasen deshitari

		INFORMAL AFFIRMATIVE INDICATIVE
Passive		urareru
Potential		ureru
Causative		uraseru
Causative Pass.		uraserareru
Honorific	I	ouri ni naru
	II	ouri nasaru
Humble	I	ouri suru
	II	ouri itasu

AN ESSENTIAL 55 VERB

Uru 売る

to sell

Sentences Using *Uru*

Ima no kuruma o utte atarashii no o kaitai desu.
今の車を売って新しいのを買いたいです。
I want to buy a new car after selling the one I have now.

Anata no kamera o uru nara, watakushi ni utte kudasai.
貴方のカメラを売るなら私に売ってください。
If you're going to sell your camera, please sell it to me.

Ano mise dewa, takai hōseki shika uranai.
あの店では高い宝石しか売らない。
They sell only expensive jewelry at that shop.

Mingei hin wa doko de utte imasu ka.
民芸品はどこで売っていますか。
Where do you sell folk craft products?

Ano kaisha wa shin seihin ga urenakute komatte imasu.
あの会社は新製品が売れなくて困っています。
That company is in trouble because their new products are not selling.

Uru is an essential verb for everyday use because the acts of buying and selling are so common. And you must know how to ask where something you need is sold!

Words and Expressions Related to This Verb

hanbai suru　販売する
to sell

ō uridashi　大売り出し
a great bargain sale

tokubai　特売
a special bargain sale

urikire　売り切れ
sold out

Proverb

uri kotoba ni kaikotoba
売り言葉に買い言葉
One ill word asks another. (selling words and buying words)

552

うたがう／疑う **utaga.u**

TRANSITIVE   *to doubt, to suspect, to distrust*

			AFFIRMATIVE	**NEGATIVE**
Indicative	**INFORMAL**		utagau	utagawanai
	FORMAL		utagaimasu	utagaimasen
Imperative	**INFORMAL**	I	utagae	utagau na
		II	utagainasai	utagainasaru na
		III	utagatte kudasai	utagawanai de kudasai
	FORMAL		outagai nasaimase	outagai nasaimasu na
Presumptive	**INFORMAL**	I	utagaō	utagaumai
		II	utagau darō	utagawanai darō
	FORMAL	I	utagaimashō	utagaimasumai
		II	utagau deshō	utagawanai deshō
Provisional	**INFORMAL**		utagaeba	utagawanakereba
	FORMAL		utagaimaseba	utagaimasen nara
			utagaimasureba	
Gerund	**INFORMAL**	I	utagatte	utagawanai de
		II		utagawanakute
	FORMAL		utagaimashite	utagaimasen de
Past Ind.	**INFORMAL**		utagatta	utagawanakatta
	FORMAL		utagaimashita	utagaimasen deshita
Past Presump.	**INFORMAL**		utagattarō	utagawanakattarō
			utagatta darō	utagawanakatta darō
	FORMAL		utagaimashitarō	utagaimasen deshitarō
			utagatta deshō	utagawanakatta deshō
Conditional	**INFORMAL**		utagattara	utagawanakattara
	FORMAL		utagaimashitara	utagaimasen deshitara
Alternative	**INFORMAL**		utagattari	utagawanakattari
	FORMAL		utagaimashitari	utagaimasen deshitari

			INFORMAL AFFIRMATIVE INDICATIVE
Passive			utagawareru
Potential			utagaeru
Causative			utagawasaseru
Causative Pass.			utagawaserareru
Honorific		I	outagai ni naru
		II	outagai nasaru
Humble		I	outagai suru
		II	outagai itasu

U

uta.u　うたう／歌う／謳う　　　　　　　　　　　　　　**utai**

to sing, to express one's opinion　　　TRANSITIVE

			AFFIRMATIVE	**NEGATIVE**
Indicative	**INFORMAL**		utau	utawanai
	FORMAL		utaimasu	utaimasen
Imperative	**INFORMAL**	I	utae	utau na
		II	utainasai	utainasaru na
		III	utatte kudasai	utawanai de kudasai
	FORMAL		outai nasaimase	outai nasaimasu na
Presumptive	**INFORMAL**	I	utaō	utaumai
		II	utau darō	utawanai darō
	FORMAL	I	utaimashō	utaimasumai
		II	utau deshō	utawanai deshō
Provisional	**INFORMAL**		utaeba	utawanakereba
	FORMAL		utaimaseba	utaimasen nara
			utaimasureba	
Gerund	**INFORMAL**	I	utatte	utawanai de
		II		utawanakute
	FORMAL		utaimashite	utaimasen de
Past Ind.	**INFORMAL**		utatta	utawanakatta
	FORMAL		utaimashita	utaimasen deshita
Past Presump.	**INFORMAL**		utattarō	utawanakattarō
			utatta darō	utawanakatta darō
	FORMAL		utaimashitarō	utaimasen deshitarō
			utatta deshō	utawanakatta deshō
Conditional	**INFORMAL**		utattara	utawanakattara
	FORMAL		utaimashitara	utaimasen deshitara
Alternative	**INFORMAL**		utattari	utawanakattari
	FORMAL		utaimashitari	utaimasen deshitari

		INFORMAL AFFIRMATIVE INDICATIVE
Passive		utawareru
Potential		utaeru
Causative		utawaseru
Causative Pass.		utawaserareru
Honorific	I	outai ni naru
	II	outai nasaru
Humble	I	outai suru
	II	outai itasu

TRANSITIVE   *to hit, to strike, to shoot*

			AFFIRMATIVE	**NEGATIVE**
Indicative	**INFORMAL**		utsu	utanai
	FORMAL		uchimasu	uchimasen
Imperative	**INFORMAL**	I	ute	utsu na
		II	uchinasai	uchinasaru na
		III	utte kudasai	utanai de kudasai
	FORMAL		ouchi nasaimase	ouchi nasaimasu na
Presumptive	**INFORMAL**	I	utō	utsumai
		II	utsu darō	utanai darō
	FORMAL	I	uchimashō	uchimasumai
		II	utsu deshō	utanai deshō
Provisional	**INFORMAL**		uteba	utanakereba
	FORMAL		uchimaseba	uchimasen nara
			uchimasureba	
Gerund	**INFORMAL**	I	utte	utanai de
		II		utanakute
	FORMAL		uchimashite	uchimasen de
Past Ind.	**INFORMAL**		utta	utanakatta
	FORMAL		uchimashita	uchimasen deshita
Past Presump.	**INFORMAL**		uttarō	utanakattarō
			utta darō	utanakatta darō
	FORMAL		uchimashitarō	uchimasen deshitarō
			utta deshō	utanakatta deshō
Conditional	**INFORMAL**		uttara	utanakattara
	FORMAL		uchimashitara	uchimasen deshitara
Alternative	**INFORMAL**		uttari	utanakattari
	FORMAL		uchimashitari	uchimasen deshitari

			INFORMAL AFFIRMATIVE INDICATIVE
Passive			utareru
Potential			uteru
Causative			utaseru
Causative Pass.			utaserareru
Honorific		I	ouchi ni naru
		II	ouchi nasaru
Humble		I	ouchi suru
		II	ouchi itasu

U

うつす／写す／移す／映す   **utsushi**
to copy, to photograph, to move to, to infect, to reflect   TRANSITIVE

			AFFIRMATIVE	NEGATIVE
Indicative	**INFORMAL**		utsusu	utsusanai
	FORMAL		utsushimasu	utsushimasen
Imperative	**INFORMAL**	I	utsuse	utsusu na
		II	utsushinasai	utsushinasaru na
		III	utsushite kudasai	utsusanai de kudasai
	FORMAL		outsushi nasaimase	outsushi nasaimasu na
Presumptive	**INFORMAL**	I	utsusō	utsusumai
		II	utsusu darō	utsusanai darō
	FORMAL	I	utsushimashō	utsushimasumai
		II	utsusu deshō	utsusanai deshō
Provisional	**INFORMAL**		utsuseba	utsusanakereba
	FORMAL		utsushimaseba	utsushimasen nara
			utsushimasureba	
Gerund	**INFORMAL**	I	utsushite	utsusanai de
		II		utsusanakute
	FORMAL		utsushimashite	utsushimasen de
Past Ind.	**INFORMAL**		utsushita	utsusanakatta
	FORMAL		utsushimashita	utsushimasen deshita
Past Presump.	**INFORMAL**		utsushitarō	utsusanakattarō
			utsushita darō	utsusanakatta darō
	FORMAL		utsushimashitarō	utsushimasen deshitarō
			utsushita deshō	utsusanakatta deshō
Conditional	**INFORMAL**		utsushitara	utsusanakattara
	FORMAL		utsushimashitara	utsushimasen deshitara
Alternative	**INFORMAL**		utsushitari	utsusanakattari
	FORMAL		utsushimashitari	utsushimasen deshitari

			INFORMAL AFFIRMATIVE INDICATIVE
Passive			utsusareru
Potential			utsuseru
Causative			utsusaseru
Causative Pass.			utsusaserareru
Honorific		I	outsushi ni naru
		II	outsushi nasaru
Humble		I	outsushi suru
		II	outsushi itasu

uwamawari

うわまわる／上回る **uwamawar.u**

to top, to exceed, to surpass

			AFFIRMATIVE	NEGATIVE
Indicative	**INFORMAL**		uwamawaru	uwamawaranai
	FORMAL		uwamawarimasu	uwamawarimasen
Imperative	**INFORMAL**	I	uwamaware	uwamawaru na
		II	uwamawarinasai	uwamawarinasaru na
		III	uwamawatte kudasai	uwamawaranai de kudasai
	FORMAL		ouwamawari nasaimase	ouwamawari nasaimasu na
Presumptive	**INFORMAL**	I	uwamawarō	uwamawarumai
		II	uwamawaru darō	uwamawaranai darō
	FORMAL	I	uwamawarimashō	uwamawarimasumai
		II	uwamawaru deshō	uwamawaranai deshō
Provisional	**INFORMAL**		uwamawareba	uwamawaranakereba
	FORMAL		uwamawarimaseba	uwamawarimasen nara
			uwamawarimasureba	uwamawarimasen nara
Gerund	**INFORMAL**	I	uwamawatte	uwamaranai de
		II		uwamawaranakute
	FORMAL		uwamawarimashite	uwamawarimasen de
Past Ind.	**INFORMAL**		uwamawatta	uwamawaranakatta
	FORMAL		uwamawarimashita	uwamawarimasen deshita
Past Presump.	**INFORMAL**		uwamawattarō	uwamaranakattarō
			uwamawatta darō	uwamawaranakatta darō
	FORMAL		uwamawarimashitarō	uwamawarimasen deshitarō
			uwamawatta deshō	uwamawaranakatta deshō
Conditional	**INFORMAL**		uwamawattara	uwamawaranakattara
	FORMAL		uwamawarimashitara	uwamawarimasen deshitara
Alternative	**INFORMAL**		uwamawattari	uwamawaranakattari
	FORMAL		uwamawarimashitari	uwamawarimasen deshitari

		INFORMAL AFFIRMATIVE INDICATIVE
Passive		uwamawarareru
Potential		uwamawareru
Causative		uwamawaraseru
Causative Pass.		uwamawaraserareru
Honorific	I	ouwamawari ni naru
	II	ouwamawari nasaru
Humble	I	
	II	

wakare.ru わかれる／別れる／分かれる   wakare

to part, to separate from, to be divorced, to be divided

			AFFIRMATIVE	NEGATIVE
Indicative	INFORMAL		wakareru	wakarenai
	FORMAL		wakaremasu	wakaremasen
Imperative	INFORMAL	I	wakarero	wakareru na
		II	wakarenasai	wakarenasaru na
		III	wakarete kudasai	wakarenai de kudasai
	FORMAL		owakare nasaimase	owakare nasaimasu na
Presumptive	INFORMAL	I	wakareyō	wakaremai
		II	wakareru darō	wakarenai darō
	FORMAL	I	wakaremashō	wakaremasumai
		II	wakareru deshō	wakarenai deshō
Provisional	INFORMAL		wakarereba	wakarenakereba
	FORMAL		wakaremaseba	wakaremasen nara
			wakaremasureba	
Gerund	INFORMAL	I	wakarete	wakarenai de
		II		wakarenakute
	FORMAL		wakaremashite	wakaremasen de
Past Ind.	INFORMAL		wakareta	wakarenakatta
	FORMAL		wakaremashita	wakaremasen deshita
Past Presump.	INFORMAL		wakaretarō	wakarenakattarō
			wakareta darō	wakarenakatta darō
	FORMAL		wakaremashitarō	wakaremasen deshitarō
			wakareta deshō	wakarenakatta deshō
Conditional	INFORMAL		wakaretara	wakarenakattara
	FORMAL		wakaremashitara	wakaremasen deshitara
Alternative	INFORMAL		wakaretari	wakarenakattari
	FORMAL		wakaremashitari	wakaremasen deshitari

		INFORMAL AFFIRMATIVE INDICATIVE
Passive		wakarerareru
Potential		wakarerareru
Causative		wakaresaseru
Causative Pass.		wakaresaserareru
Honorific	I	owakare ni naru
	II	owakare nasaru
Humble	I	owakare suru
	II	owakare itasu

558

わかる／分かる／解る **wakar.u**

to understand, to know

			AFFIRMATIVE	NEGATIVE
Indicative	**INFORMAL**		wakaru	wakaranai
	FORMAL		wakarimasu	wakarimasen
Imperative	**INFORMAL**	I	wakare	
		II		
		III	wakatte kudasai	
	FORMAL			
Presumptive	**INFORMAL**	I	wakarō	wakarumai
		II	wakaru darō	wakaranai darō
	FORMAL	I	wakarimashō	wakarimasumai
		II	wakaru deshō	wakaranai deshō
Provisional	**INFORMAL**		wakareba	wakaranakereba
	FORMAL		wakarimaseba	wakarimasen nara
			wakarimasureba	
Gerund	**INFORMAL**	I	wakatte	wakaranai de
		II		wakaranakute
	FORMAL		wakarimashite	wakarimasen de
Past Ind.	**INFORMAL**		wakatta	wakaranakatta
	FORMAL		wakarimashita	wakarimasen deshita
Past Presump.	**INFORMAL**		wakattarō	wakaranakattarō
			wakatta darō	wakaranakatta darō
	FORMAL		wakarimashitarō	wakarimasen deshitarō
			wakatta deshō	wakaranakatta deshō
Conditional	**INFORMAL**		wakattara	wakaranakattara
	FORMAL		wakarimashitara	wakarimasen deshitara
Alternative	**INFORMAL**		wakattari	wakaranakattari
	FORMAL		wakarimashitari	wakarimasen deshitari

		INFORMAL AFFIRMATIVE INDICATIVE
Passive		
Potential		
Causative		wakaraseru
Causative Pass.		wakaraserareru
Honorific	I	owakari ni naru
	II	owakari nasaru
Humble	I	
	II	

W

AN ESSENTIAL
55 VERB

Wakaru 分かる

to understand, to know

Wakaru is an essential verb for so many everyday situations. What could be more basic than understanding? It's hard to imagine getting by without this verb.

Sentences Using *Wakaru*

Nihongo ga wakarimasu ka.
日本語が分かりますか。
Do you understand Japanese?

Kare wa yatto kanojo no kutsū ga wakatta.
彼はやっと彼女の苦痛が分かった。
He finally understood her pain.

Wakaranakereba setsumei shite agemashō.
分からなければ説明してあげましょう。
If you don't understand it, I'll explain it to you.

Kono machi no michi wa fukuzatsu de wakarinikui.
この町の道は複雑で分かりにくい。
The streets in this town are difficult to grasp because they're so complex.

Kekka ga wakattara shirasete kudasai.
結果が分かったら知らせてください。
When you get the results, please tell me.

Words and Expressions Related to This Verb

rikai suru　理解する
to understand, to grasp

wakariyasui　分かり易い
easy to understand

wakarinikui　分かりにくい
difficult to understand

wakarikitta　分かり切った
obvious, evident

monowakari ga ii　物分かりがいい
understanding, sensible

wakarazu ya　分からず屋
an obstinate person

560

わける／分ける／別ける　**wake.ru**

TRANSITIVE　*to divide, to separate, to distribute*

			AFFIRMATIVE	**NEGATIVE**
Indicative	**INFORMAL**		wakeru	wakenai
	FORMAL		wakemasu	wakemasen
Imperative	**INFORMAL**	**I**	wakero	wakeru na
		II	wakenasai	wakenasaru na
		III	wakete kudasai	wakenai de kudasai
	FORMAL		owake nasaimase	owake nasaimasu na
Presumptive	**INFORMAL**	**I**	wakeyō	wakemai
		II	wakeru darō	wakenai darō
	FORMAL	**I**	wakemashō	wakemasumai
		II	wakeru deshō	wakenai deshō
Provisional	**INFORMAL**		wakereba	wakenakereba
	FORMAL		wakemaseba	wakemasen nara
			wakemasureba	
Gerund	**INFORMAL**	**I**	wakete	wakenai de
		II		wakenakute
	FORMAL		wakemashite	wakemasen de
Past Ind.	**INFORMAL**		waketa	wakenakatta
	FORMAL		wakemashita	wakemasen deshita
Past Presump.	**INFORMAL**		waketarō	wakenakattarō
			waketa darō	wakenakatta darō
	FORMAL		wakemashitarō	wakemasen deshitarō
			waketa deshō	wakenakatta deshō
Conditional	**INFORMAL**		waketara	wakenakattara
	FORMAL		wakemashitara	wakemasen deshitara
Alternative	**INFORMAL**		waketari	wakenakattari
	FORMAL		wakemashitari	wakemasen deshitari

			INFORMAL AFFIRMATIVE INDICATIVE
Passive			wakerareru
Potential			wakerareru
Causative			wakesaseru
Causative Pass.			wakesaserareru
Honorific		**I**	owake ni naru
		II	owake nasaru
Humble		**I**	owake suru
		II	owake itasu

W

561

wara.u わらう／笑う — warai

to laugh, to smile, to grin

			AFFIRMATIVE	NEGATIVE
Indicative	INFORMAL		warau	warawanai
	FORMAL		waraimasu	waraimasen
Imperative	INFORMAL	I	warae	warau na
		II	warainasai	warainasaru na
		III	waratte kudasai	warawanai de kudasai
	FORMAL		owarai nasaimase	owarai nasaimasu na
Presumptive	INFORMAL	I	waraō	waraumai
		II	warau darō	warawanai darō
	FORMAL	I	waraimashō	waraimasumai
		II	warau deshō	warawanai deshō
Provisional	INFORMAL		waraeba	warawanakereba
	FORMAL		waraimaseba	waraimasen nara
			waraimasureba	
Gerund	INFORMAL	I	waratte	warawanai de
		II		warawanakute
	FORMAL		waraimashite	waraimasen de
Past Ind.	INFORMAL		waratta	warawanakatta
	FORMAL		waraimashita	waraimasen deshita
Past Presump.	INFORMAL		warattarō	warawanakattarō
			waratta darō	warawanakatta darō
	FORMAL		waraimashitarō	waraimasen deshitarō
			waratta deshō	warawanakatta deshō
Conditional	INFORMAL		warattara	warawanakattara
	FORMAL		waraimashitara	waraimasen deshitara
Alternative	INFORMAL		warattari	warawanakattari
	FORMAL		waraimashitari	waraimasen deshitari

		INFORMAL AFFIRMATIVE INDICATIVE
Passive		warawareru
Potential		waraeru
Causative		warawaseru
Causative Pass.		warawaserareru
Honorific	I	owarai ni naru
	II	owarai nasaru
Humble	I	
	II	

わる／割る **war.u**

TRANSITIVE   *to divide, to break*

			AFFIRMATIVE	NEGATIVE
Indicative	**INFORMAL**		waru	waranai
	FORMAL		warimasu	warimasen
Imperative	**INFORMAL**	I	ware	waru na
		II	warinasai	warinasaru na
		III	watte kudasai	waranai de kudasai
	FORMAL		owari nasaimase	owari nasaimasu na
Presumptive	**INFORMAL**	I	warō	warumai
		II	waru darō	waranai darō
	FORMAL	I	warimashō	warimasumai
		II	waru deshō	waranai deshō
Provisional	**INFORMAL**		wareba	waranakereba
	FORMAL		warimaseba	warimasen nara
			warimasureba	
Gerund	**INFORMAL**	I	watte	waranai de
		II		waranakute
	FORMAL		warimashite	warimasen de
Past Ind.	**INFORMAL**		watta	waranakatta
	FORMAL		warimashita	warimasen deshita
Past Presump.	**INFORMAL**		wattarō	waranakattarō
			watta darō	waranakatta darō
	FORMAL		warimashitarō	warimasen deshitarō
			watta deshō	waranakatta deshō
Conditional	**INFORMAL**		wattara	waranakattara
	FORMAL		warimashitara	warimasen deshitara
Alternative	**INFORMAL**		wattari	waranakattari
	FORMAL		warimashitari	warimasen deshitari

			INFORMAL AFFIRMATIVE INDICATIVE
Passive			warareru
Potential			wareru
Causative			waraseru
Causative Pass.			waraserareru
Honorific		I	owari ni naru
		II	owari nasaru
Humble		I	owari suru
		II	owari itasu

W

wasure.ru わすれる／忘れる

to forget   TRANSITIVE

			AFFIRMATIVE	NEGATIVE
Indicative	**INFORMAL**		wasureru	wasurenai
	FORMAL		wasuremasu	wasuremasen
Imperative	**INFORMAL**	I	wasurero	wasureru na
		II	wasurenasai	wasurenasaru na
		III	wasurete kudasai	wasurenai de kudasai
	FORMAL		owasure nasaimase	owasure nasaimasu na
Presumptive	**INFORMAL**	I	wasureyō	wasuremai
		II	wasureru darō	wasurenai darō
	FORMAL	I	wasuremashō	wasuremasumai
		II	wasureru deshō	wasurenai deshō
Provisional	**INFORMAL**		wasurereba	wasurenakereba
	FORMAL		wasuremaseba	wasuremasen nara
			wasuremasureba	
Gerund	**INFORMAL**	I	wasurete	wasurenai de
		II		wasurenakute
	FORMAL		wasuremashite	wasuremasen de
Past Ind.	**INFORMAL**		wasureta	wasurenakatta
	FORMAL		wasuremashita	wasuremasen deshita
Past Presump.	**INFORMAL**		wasuretarō	wasurenakattarō
			wasureta darō	wasurenakatta darō
	FORMAL		wasuremashitarō	wasuremasen deshitarō
			wasureta deshō	wasurenakatta deshō
Conditional	**INFORMAL**		wasuretara	wasurenakattara
	FORMAL		wasuremashitara	wasuremasen deshitara
Alternative	**INFORMAL**		wasuretari	wasurenakattari
	FORMAL		wasuremashitari	wasuremasen deshitari

		INFORMAL AFFIRMATIVE INDICATIVE
Passive		wasurerareru
Potential		wasurerareru
Causative		wasuresaseru
Causative Pass.		wasuresaserareru
Honorific	I	owasure ni naru
	II	owasure nasaru
Humble	I	owasure suru
	II	owasure itasu

わたる／渡る **watar.u**

to cross, to go across

			AFFIRMATIVE	NEGATIVE
Indicative	**INFORMAL**		wataru	wataranai
	FORMAL		watarimasu	watarimasen
Imperative	**INFORMAL**	I	watare	wataru na
		II	watarinasai	watarinasaru na
		III	watatte kudasai	wataranai de kudasai
	FORMAL		owatari nasaimase	owatari nasaimasu na
Presumptive	**INFORMAL**	I	watarō	watarumai
		II	wataru darō	wataranai darō
	FORMAL	I	watarimashō	watarimasumai
		II	wataru deshō	wataranai deshō
Provisional	**INFORMAL**		watareba	wataranakereba
	FORMAL		watarimaseba	watarimasen nara
			watarimasureba	
Gerund	**INFORMAL**	I	watatte	wataranai de
		II		wataranakute
	FORMAL		watarimashite	watarimasen de
Past Ind.	**INFORMAL**		watatta	wataranakatta
	FORMAL		watarimashita	watarimasen deshita
Past Presump.	**INFORMAL**		watattarō	wataranakattarō
			watatta darō	wataranakatta darō
	FORMAL		watarimashitarō	watarimasen deshitarō
			watatta deshō	wataranakatta deshō
Conditional	**INFORMAL**		watattara	wataranakattara
	FORMAL		watarimashitara	watarimasen deshitara
Alternative	**INFORMAL**		watattari	wataranakattari
	FORMAL		watarimashitari	watarimasen deshitari

		INFORMAL AFFIRMATIVE INDICATIVE
Passive		watarareru
Potential		watareru
Causative		wataraseru
Causative Pass.		wataraserarera
Honorific	I	owatari ni naru
	II	owatari nasaru
Humble	I	
	II	

W

to hand over, to carry across　　　TRANSITIVE

			AFFIRMATIVE	**NEGATIVE**
Indicative	**INFORMAL**		watasu	watasanai
	FORMAL		watashimasu	watashimasen
Imperative	**INFORMAL**	**I**	watase	watasu na
		II	watashinasai	watashinasaru na
		III	watashite kudasai	watasanai de kudasai
	FORMAL		owatashi nasaimase	owatashi nasaimasu na
Presumptive	**INFORMAL**	**I**	watasō	watasumai
		II	watasu darō	watasanai darō
	FORMAL	**I**	watashimashō	watashimasumai
		II	watasu deshō	watasanai deshō
Provisional	**INFORMAL**		wataseba	watasanakereba
	FORMAL		watashimaseba	watashimasen nara
			watashimasureba	
Gerund	**INFORMAL**	**I**	watashite	watasanai de
		II		watasanakute
	FORMAL		watashimashite	watashimasen de
Past Ind.	**INFORMAL**		watashita	watasanakatta
	FORMAL		watashimashita	watashimasen deshita
Past Presump.	**INFORMAL**		watashitarō	watasanakattarō
			watashita darō	watasanakatta darō
	FORMAL		watashimashitarō	watashimasen deshitarō
			watashita deshō	watasanakatta deshō
Conditional	**INFORMAL**		watashitara	watasanakattara
	FORMAL		watashimashitara	watashimasen deshitara
Alternative	**INFORMAL**		watashitari	watasanakattari
	FORMAL		watashimashitari	watashimasen deshitari

		INFORMAL AFFIRMATIVE INDICATIVE
Passive		watasareru
Potential		wataseru
Causative		watasaseru
Causative Pass.		watasarerareru
Honorific	**I**	owatashi ni naru
	II	owatashi nasaru
Humble	**I**	owatashi suru
	II	owatashi itasu

やぶれる／破れる／敗れる　yabure.ru
to tear, to rip, to break, to lose, to be beaten

			AFFIRMATIVE	NEGATIVE
Indicative	**INFORMAL**		yabureru	yaburenai
	FORMAL		yaburemasu	yaburemasen
Imperative	**INFORMAL**	I	yaburero	yabureru na
		II	yaburenasai	yaburenasaru na
		III	yaburete kudasai	yaburenai de kudasai
	FORMAL		oyabure nasaimase	oyabure nasaimasu na
Presumptive	**INFORMAL**	I	yabureyō	yaburemai
		II	yabureru darō	yaburenai darō
	FORMAL	I	yaburemashō	yaburemasumai
		II	yabureru deshō	yaburenai deshō
Provisional	**INFORMAL**		yaburereba	yaburenakereba
	FORMAL		yaburemaseba	yaburemasen nara
			yaburemasureba	
Gerund	**INFORMAL**	I	yaburete	yaburenai de
		II		yaburenakute
	FORMAL		yaburemashite	yaburemasen de
Past Ind.	**INFORMAL**		yabureta	yaburenakatta
	FORMAL		yaburemashita	yaburemasen deshita
Past Presump.	**INFORMAL**		yaburetarō	yaburenakattarō
			yabureta darō	yaburenakatta darō
	FORMAL		yaburemashitarō	taburemasen deshitarō
			yabureta deshō	yaburenakatta deshō
Conditional	**INFORMAL**		yaburetara	yaburenakattara
	FORMAL		yaburemashitara	yaburemasen deshitara
Alternative	**INFORMAL**		yaburetari	yaburenakattari
	FORMAL		yaburemashitari	yaburemasen deshitari

			INFORMAL AFFIRMATIVE INDICATIVE
Passive			
Potential			
Causative			yaburesaseru
Causative Pass.			yaburesaserareru
Honorific		I	oyabure ni naru
		II	oyabure nasaru
Humble		I	oyabure suru
		II	oyabure itasu

Y

to tear, to break, to beat, to defeat   TRANSITIVE

			AFFIRMATIVE	NEGATIVE
Indicative	**INFORMAL**		yaburu	yaburanai
	FORMAL		yaburimasu	yaburimasen
Imperative	**INFORMAL**	I	yabure	yaburu na
		II	yaburinasai	yaburinasaru na
		III	yabutte kudasai	yaburanai de kudasai
	FORMAL		oyaburi nasaimase	oyaburi nasaimasu na
Presumptive	**INFORMAL**	I	yaburō	yaburumai
		II	yaburu darō	yaburanai darō
	FORMAL	I	yaburimashō	yaburimasumai
		II	yaburu deshō	yaburanai deshō
Provisional	**INFORMAL**		tabureba	yaburanakereba
	FORMAL		yaburimaseba	yaburimasen nara
			yaburimasureba	
Gerund	**INFORMAL**	I	yabutte	yaburanai de
		II		yaburanakute
	FORMAL		yaburimashite	yaburimasen de
Past Ind.	**INFORMAL**		yabutta	yaburanakatta
	FORMAL		yaburimashita	yaburimasen deshita
Past Presump.	**INFORMAL**		yabuttarō	yaburanakattarō
			yabutta darō	yaburanakatta darō
	FORMAL		yaburimashitarō	yaburimasen deshitarō
			yabutta deshō	yaburanakatta deshō
Conditional	**INFORMAL**		yabuttara	yaburanakattara
	FORMAL		yaburimashitara	yaburimasen deshitara
Alternative	**INFORMAL**		yabuttari	yaburanakattari
	FORMAL		yaburimashitari	yaburimasen deshitari

			INFORMAL AFFIRMATIVE INDICATIVE
Passive			yaburareru
Potential			yabureru
Causative			yaburaseru
Causative Pass.			yaburaserareru
Honorific		I	oyaburi ni naru
		II	oyaburi nasaru
Humble		I	oyaburi suru
		II	oyaburi itasu

やける／焼ける　**yake.ru**

to burn, to be grilled, to be broiled, to be baked, to be toasted

			AFFIRMATIVE	NEGATIVE
Indicative	**INFORMAL**		yakeru	yakenai
	FORMAL		yakemasu	yakemasen
Imperative	**INFORMAL**	I	yakero	yakeru na
		II		
		III	yakete kudasai	yakenai de kudasai
	FORMAL			
Presumptive	**INFORMAL**	I	yakeyō	yakerumai
		II	yakeru darō	yakenai darō
	FORMAL	I	yakemashō	yakemasumai
		II	yakeru deshō	yakenai deshō
Provisional	**INFORMAL**		yakereba	takenakereba
	FORMAL		yakemaseba	yakemasen nara
			yakemasureba	
Gerund	**INFORMAL**	I	yakete	yakenai de
		II		yakenakute
	FORMAL		yakemashite	yakemasen de
Past Ind.	**INFORMAL**		yaketa	yakenakatta
	FORMAL		yakemashita	yakemasen deshita
Past Presump.	**INFORMAL**		yaketarō	yakenakattarō
			yaketa darō	yakenakatta darō
	FORMAL		yakemashitarō	yakemasen deshitarō
			yaketa deshō	yakenakatta deshō
Conditional	**INFORMAL**		yaketara	yakenakattara
	FORMAL		yakemashitara	yakemasen deshitara
Alternative	**INFORMAL**		yaketari	yakenakattari
	FORMAL		yakemashitari	yakemasen deshitari

		INFORMAL AFFIRMATIVE INDICATIVE
Passive		
Potential		
Causative		yakesaseru
Causative Pass.		yakesaserareru
Honorific	I	oyake ni naru
	II	oyake nasaru
Humble	I	
	II	

to burn, to set fire, to envy　　　TRANSITIVE

			AFFIRMATIVE	NEGATIVE
Indicative	**INFORMAL**		yaku	yakanai
	FORMAL		yakimasu	yakimasen
Imperative	**INFORMAL**	I	yake	yaku na
		II	yakinasai	yakinasaru na
		III	yaite kudasai	yakanai de kudasai
	FORMAL		oyaki nasaimase	oyaki nasaimasu na
Presumptive	**INFORMAL**	I	yakō	yakumai
		II	yaku darō	yakanai darō
	FORMAL	I	yakimashō	yakimasumai
		II	yaku deshō	yakanai deshō
Provisional	**INFORMAL**		yakeba	yakanakereba
	FORMAL		yakimaseba	yakimasen nara
			yakimasureba	
Gerund	**INFORMAL**	I	yaite	yakanai de
		II		yakanakute
	FORMAL		yakimashite	yakimasen de
Past Ind.	**INFORMAL**		yaita	yakanakatta
	FORMAL		yakimashita	yakimasen deshita
Past Presump.	**INFORMAL**		yaitarō	yakanakattarō
			yaita darō	yakanakatta darō
	FORMAL		yakimashitarō	yakimasen deshitarō
			yaita deshō	yakanakatta deshō
Conditional	**INFORMAL**		yaitara	yakanakattara
	FORMAL		yakimashitara	yakimasen deshitara
Alternative	**INFORMAL**		yaitari	yakanakattari
	FORMAL		yakimashitari	yakimasen deshitari

			INFORMAL AFFIRMATIVE INDICATIVE
Passive			yakareru
Potential			yakeru
Causative			yakaseru
Causative Pass.			yakaserareru
Honorific		I	oyaki ni naru
		II	oyaki nasaru
Humble		I	oyaki suru
		II	oyaki itasu

やめる／止める／辞める **yame.ru**

TRANSITIVE *to stop, to give up, to quit, to resign*

			AFFIRMATIVE	**NEGATIVE**
Indicative	**INFORMAL**		yameru	yamenai
	FORMAL		yamemasu	yamemasen
Imperative	**INFORMAL**	**I**	yamero	yameru na
		II	yamenasai	yamenasaru na
		III	yamete kudasai	yamenai de kudasai
	FORMAL		oyame nasaimase	oyame nasaimasu na
Presumptive	**INFORMAL**	**I**	yameyō	yamemai
		II	yameru darō	yamenai darō
	FORMAL	**I**	yamemashō	yamemasumai
		II	yameru deshō	yamenai deshō
Provisional	**INFORMAL**		yamereba	yamenakereba
	FORMAL		yamemaseba	yamemasen nara
			yamemasureba	
Gerund	**INFORMAL**	**I**	yamete	yamenai de
		II		yamenakute
	FORMAL		yamemashite	yamemasen de
Past Ind.	**INFORMAL**		yameta	yamenakatta
	FORMAL		yamemashita	yamemasen deshita
Past Presump.	**INFORMAL**		yametarō	yamenakattarō
			yameta darō	yamenakatta darō
	FORMAL		yamemashitarō	yamemasen deshitarō
			yameta deshō	yamenakatta deshō
Conditional	**INFORMAL**		yametara	yamenakattara
	FORMAL		yamemashitara	yamemasen deshitara
Alternative	**INFORMAL**		yametari	yamenakattari
	FORMAL		yamemashitari	yamemasen deshitari

		INFORMAL AFFIRMATIVE INDICATIVE
Passive		yamerareru
Potential		yamerareru
Causative		yamesaseru
Causative Pass.		yamesaserareru
Honorific	**I**	oyame ni naru
	II	oyame nasaru
Humble	**I**	oyame suru
	II	oyame itasu

Y

to do, to give   TRANSITIVE

			AFFIRMATIVE	NEGATIVE
Indicative	**INFORMAL**		yaru	yaranai
	FORMAL		yarimasu	yarimasen
Imperative	**INFORMAL**	I	yare	yaru na
		II	yarinasai	yarinasaru na
		III	yatte kudasai	yaranai de kudasai
	FORMAL		oyari nasaimase	oyari nasaimasu na
Presumptive	**INFORMAL**	I	yarō	yarumai
		II	yaru darō	yaranai darō
	FORMAL	I	yarimashō	yarimasumai
		II	yaru deshō	yaranai deshō
Provisional	**INFORMAL**		yareba	yaranakereba
	FORMAL		yarimaseba	yarimasen nara
			yarimasureba	
Gerund	**INFORMAL**	I	yatte	yaranai de
		II		yaranakute
	FORMAL		yarimashite	yarimasen de
Past Ind.	**INFORMAL**		yatta	yaranakatta
	FORMAL		yarimashita	yarimasen deshita
Past Presump.	**INFORMAL**		yattarō	yaranakattarō
			yatta darō	yaranakatta darō
	FORMAL		yarimashitarō	yarimasen deshitarō
			yatta deshō	yaranakatta deshō
Conditional	**INFORMAL**		yattara	yaranakattara
	FORMAL		yarimashitara	yarimasen deshitara
Alternative	**INFORMAL**		yattari	yaranakattari
	FORMAL		yarimashitari	yarimasen deshitari

		INFORMAL AFFIRMATIVE INDICATIVE
Passive		yarareru
Potential		yareru
Causative		yaraseru
Causative Pass.		yaraserareru
Honorific	I	oyari ni naru
	II	oyari nasaru
Humble	I	
	II	

やせる／痩せる　**yase.ru**
to lose weight, to get thin

			AFFIRMATIVE	NEGATIVE
Indicative	**INFORMAL**		yaseru	yasenai
	FORMAL		yasemasu	yasemasen
Imperative	**INFORMAL**	I	yasero	yaseru na
		II	yasenasai	yasenasaru na
		III	yasete kudasai	yasenai de kudasai
	FORMAL		oyase nasaimase	oyase nasaimasu na
Presumptive	**INFORMAL**	I	yaseyō	yasemai
		II	yaseru darō	yasenai darō
	FORMAL	I	yasemashō	yasemasumai
		II	yaseru deshō	yasenai deshō
Provisional	**INFORMAL**		yasereba	yasenakereba
	FORMAL		yasemaseba	yasemasen nara
			yasemasureba	
Gerund	**INFORMAL**	I	yasete	yasenai de
		II		yasenakute
	FORMAL		yasemashite	yasemasen de
Past Ind.	**INFORMAL**		yaseta	yasenakatta
	FORMAL		yasemashita	yasemasen deshita
Past Presump.	**INFORMAL**		yasetarō	yasenakattarō
			yaseta darō	yasenakatta darō
	FORMAL		yasemashitarō	yasemasen deshitarō
			yaseta deshō	yasenakatta deshō
Conditional	**INFORMAL**		yasetara	yasenakattara
	FORMAL		yasemashitara	yasemasen deshitara
Alternative	**INFORMAL**		yasetari	yasenakattari
	FORMAL		yasemashitari	yasemasen deshitari

			INFORMAL AFFIRMATIVE INDICATIVE
Passive			yaserareru
Potential			yaserareru
Causative			yasesaseru
Causative Pass.			yasesaserareru
Honorific		I	oyase ni naru
		II	oyase nasaru
Humble		I	
		II	

yasum.u やすむ／休む
to rest, to sleep, to be absent

			AFFIRMATIVE	NEGATIVE
Indicative	INFORMAL		yasumu	yasumanai
	FORMAL		yasumimasu	yasumimasen
Imperative	INFORMAL	I	yasume	yasumu na
		II	yasuminasai	yasuminasaru na
		III	yasunde kudasai	yasumanai de kudasai
	FORMAL		oyasumi nasaimase	oyasumi nasaimasu na
Presumptive	INFORMAL	I	yasumō	yasumumai
		II	yasumu darō	yasumanai darō
	FORMAL	I	yasumimashō	yasumimasumai
		II	yasumu deshō	yasumanai deshō
Provisional	INFORMAL		yasumeba	yasumanakereba
	FORMAL		yasumimaseba	yasumimasen nara
			yasumimasureba	
Gerund	INFORMAL	I	yasunde	yasumanai de
		II		yasumanakute
	FORMAL		yasumimashite	yasumimasen de
Past Ind.	INFORMAL		yasunda	yasumanakatta
	FORMAL		yasumimashita	yasumimasen deshita
Past Presump.	INFORMAL		yasundarō	yasumanakattarō
			yasunda darō	yasumanakatta darō
	FORMAL		yasumimashitarō	yasumimasen deshitarō
			yasunda deshō	yasumanakatta deshō
Conditional	INFORMAL		yasundara	yasumanakattara
	FORMAL		yasumimashitara	yasumimasen deshitara
Alternative	INFORMAL		yasundari	yasumanakattari
	FORMAL		yasumimashitari	yasumimasen deshitari

		INFORMAL AFFIRMATIVE INDICATIVE
Passive		yasumareru
Potential		yasumeru
Causative		yasumaseru
Causative Pass.		yasumaserareru
Honorific	I	oyasumi ni naru
	II	oyasumi nasaru
Humble	I	
	II	

			AFFIRMATIVE	NEGATIVE
Indicative	**INFORMAL**		yatou	yatowanai
	FORMAL		yatoimasu	yatoimasen
Imperative	**INFORMAL**	I	yatoe	yatou na
		II	yatoinasai	yatoinasaru na
		III	yatotte kudasai	yatowanai de kudasai
	FORMAL		oyatoi nasaimase	oyatoi nasaimasu na
Presumptive	**INFORMAL**	I	yatoō	yatoumai
		II	yatou darō	yatowanai darō
	FORMAL	I	yatoimashō	yatoimasumai
		II	yatou deshō	yatowanai deshō
Provisional	**INFORMAL**		yatoeba	yatowanakereba
	FORMAL		yatoimaseba	yatoimasen nara
			yatoimasureba	
Gerund	**INFORMAL**	I	yatotte	yatowanai de
		II		yatowanakute
	FORMAL		yatoimashite	yatoimasen de
Past Ind.	**INFORMAL**		yatotta	yatowanakatta
	FORMAL		yatomashita	yatoimasen deshita
Past Presump.	**INFORMAL**		yatottarō	yatowanakattarō
			yatotta darō	yatowanakatta darō
	FORMAL		yatoimashitarō	yatoimasen deshitarō
			yatotta deshō	yatowanakatta deshō
Conditional	**INFORMAL**		yatottara	yatowanakattara
	FORMAL		yatoimashitara	yatoimasen deshitara
Alternative	**INFORMAL**		yatottari	yatowanakattari
	FORMAL		yatoimashitari	yatoimasen deshitari

		INFORMAL AFFIRMATIVE INDICATIVE
Passive		yatowareru
Potential		yatoeru
Causative		yatowaseru
Causative Pass.		yatowaserareru
Honorific	I	oyatoi ni naru
	II	oyatoi nasaru
Humble	I	oyatoi suru
	II	oyatoi itasu

Y

to call, to invite, to cause　　　TRANSITIVE

			AFFIRMATIVE	**NEGATIVE**
Indicative	**INFORMAL**		yobu	yobanai
	FORMAL		yobimasu	yobimasen
Imperative	**INFORMAL**	I	yobe	yobu na
		II	yobinasai	yobinasaru na
		III	yonde kudasai	yobanai de kudasai
	FORMAL		oyobi nasaimase	oyobi nasaimasu na
Presumptive	**INFORMAL**	I	yobō	yobumai
		II	yobu darō	yobanai darō
	FORMAL	I	yobimashō	yobimasumai
		II	yobu deshō	yobanai deshō
Provisional	**INFORMAL**		yobeba	yobanakereba
	FORMAL		yobimaseba	yobimasen nara
			yobimasureba	
Gerund	**INFORMAL**	I	yonde	yobanai de
		II		yobanakute
	FORMAL		yobimashite	yobimasen de
Past Ind.	**INFORMAL**		yonda	yobanakatta
	FORMAL		yobimashita	yobimasen deshita
Past Presump.	**INFORMAL**		yondarō	yobanakattarō
			yonda darō	yobanakatta darō
	FORMAL		yobimashitarō	yobimasen deshitarō
			yonda deshō	yobanakatta deshō
Conditional	**INFORMAL**		yondara	yobanakattara
	FORMAL		yobimashitara	yobimasen deshitara
Alternative	**INFORMAL**		yondari	yobanakattari
	FORMAL		yobimashitari	yobimasen deshitari

			INFORMAL AFFIRMATIVE INDICATIVE
Passive			yobareru
Potential			yoberu
Causative			yobaseru
Causative Pass.			yobaserareru
Honorific		I	oyobi ni naru
		II	oyobi nasaru
Humble		I	oyobi suru
		II	oyobi itasu

よむ／読む **yom.u**
TRANSITIVE   *to read*

			AFFIRMATIVE	**NEGATIVE**
Indicative	**INFORMAL**		yomu	yomanai
	FORMAL		yomimasu	yomimasen
Imperative	**INFORMAL**	I	yome	yomu na
		II	yominasai	yominasaru na
		III	yonde kudasai	yomanai de kudasai
	FORMAL		oyomi nasaimase	oyomi nasaimasu na
Presumptive	**INFORMAL**	I	yomō	yomumai
		II	yomu darō	yomanai darō
	FORMAL	I	yomimashō	yomimasumai
		II	yomu deshō	yomanai deshō
Provisional	**INFORMAL**		yomeba	yomanakereba
	FORMAL		yomimaseba	yomimasen nara
			yomimasureba	
Gerund	**INFORMAL**	I	yonde	yomanai de
		II		yomanakute
	FORMAL		yomimashite	yomimasen de
Past Ind.	**INFORMAL**		yonda	yomanakatta
	FORMAL		yomimashita	yomimasen deshita
Past Presump.	**INFORMAL**		yondarō	yomanakattarō
			yonda darō	yomanakatta darō
	FORMAL		yomimashitarō	yomimasen deshitarō
			yonda deshō	yomanakatta deshō
Conditional	**INFORMAL**		yondara	yomanakattara
	FORMAL		yomimashitara	yomimasen deshitara
Alternative	**INFORMAL**		yondari	yomanakattari
	FORMAL		yomimashitari	yomimasen deshitari

		INFORMAL AFFIRMATIVE INDICATIVE
Passive		yomareru
Potential		yomeru
Causative		yomaseru
Causative Pass.		yomaserareru
Honorific	I	oyomi ni naru
	II	oyomi nasaru
Humble	I	oyomi suru
	II	oyomi itasu

AN ESSENTIAL
55 VERB

AN ESSENTIAL 55 VERB

Yomu 読む

to read

Sentences Using *Yomu*

Nihongo ga yomeru shi kakemasu.
日本語が読めるし書けます。
I can write and read Japanese.

Natsu yasumi niwa shōsetsu o go
satsu yomitai desu.
夏休みには小説を五冊読みたいです。
I'd like to read five novels during the
summer vacation.

Kyō wa shorui o takusan
yomanakereba narimasen.
今日は書類をたくさん読まなければな
りません。
I have to read a lot of papers today.

Kesa no shinbun o yomimashita ka.
今朝の新聞を読みましたか。
Did you read this morning's paper?

Manyuaru o yonde purintā no koshō
o naoshimashita.
マニュアルを読んでプリンターの故障
を直しました。
I fixed the printer's malfunction by
reading the manual.

Yomu is an essential verb because
reading is such an important part of life.
And if you're learning to read Japanese,
this verb is more meaningful than ever!

Words and Expressions Related to This Verb

ondoku suru　音読する
to read aloud

mokudoku suru　黙読する
to read silently

dokusho　読書
reading

dokusha　読者
reader

Proverb

seikō udoku　晴耕雨読
living a simple and carefree life
(tilling fields on sunny days and
reading books on rainy days)

			AFFIRMATIVE	NEGATIVE
Indicative	INFORMAL		yorokobu	yorokobanai
	FORMAL		yorokobimasu	yorokobimasen
Imperative	INFORMAL	I	yorokobe	yorokobu na
		II	yorokobinasai	yorokobinasaru na
		III	yorokonde kudasai	yorokobanai de kudasai
	FORMAL		oyorokobi nasaimase	oyorokobi nasaimasu na
Presumptive	INFORMAL	I	yorokobō	yorokobumai
		II	yorokobu darō	yorokobanai darō
	FORMAL	I	yorokobimashō	yorokobimasumai
		II	yorokobu deshō	yorokobanai deshō
Provisional	INFORMAL		yorokobeba	yorokobanakereba
	FORMAL		yorokobimaseba	yorokobimasen nara
			yorokobimasureba	
Gerund	INFORMAL	I	yorokonde	yorokobanai de
		II		yorokobanakute
	FORMAL		yorokobimashite	yorokobimasen de
Past Ind.	INFORMAL		yorokonda	yorokobanakatta
	FORMAL		yorokobimashita	yorokobimasen deshita
Past Presump.	INFORMAL		yorokondarō	yorokobanakattarō
			yorokonda darō	yorokobanakatta darō
	FORMAL		yorokobimashitarō	yorokobimasen deshitarō
			yorokonda deshō	yorokobanakatta deshō
Conditional	INFORMAL		yorokondara	yorokobanakattara
	FORMAL		yorokobimashitara	yorokobimasen deshitara
Alternative	INFORMAL		yorokondari	yorokobanakattari
	FORMAL		yorokobimashitari	yorokobimasen deshitari

		INFORMAL AFFIRMATIVE INDICATIVE
Passive		yorokobareru
Potential		yorokoberu
Causative		yorokobaseru
Causative Pass.		yorokobaserareru
Honorific	I	oyorokobi ni naru
	II	oyorokobi nasaru
Humble	I	oyorokobi suru
	II	oyorokobi itasu

yor.u　よる／因る／寄る　　　　　　　　　　　yori
to depend on, to be based on, to drop in

			AFFIRMATIVE	NEGATIVE
Indicative	INFORMAL		yoru	yoranai
	FORMAL		yorimasu	yorimasen
Imperative	INFORMAL	I	yore	yoru na
		II	yorinasai	yorinasaru na
		III	yotte kudasai	yoranai de kudasai
	FORMAL		oyori nasaimase	oyori nasaimasu na
Presumptive	INFORMAL	I	yorō	yorumai
		II	yoru darō	yoranai darō
	FORMAL	I	yorimashō	yorimasumai
		II	yoru deshō	yoranai deshō
Provisional	INFORMAL		yoreba	yoranakereba
	FORMAL		yorimaseba	yorimasen nara
			yorimasureba	
Gerund	INFORMAL	I	yotte	yoranai de
		II		yoranakute
	FORMAL		yorimashita	yorimasen de
Past Ind.	INFORMAL		yotta	yoranakatta
	FORMAL		yorimashita	yorimasen deshita
Past Presump.	INFORMAL		yottarō	yoranakattarō
			yotta darō	yoranakatta darō
	FORMAL		yorimashitarō	yorimasen deshitarō
			yotta deshō	yoranakatta deshō
Conditional	INFORMAL		yottara	yoranakattara
	FORMAL		yorimashitara	yorimasen deshitara
Alternative	INFORMAL		yottari	yoranakattari
	FORMAL		yorimashitari	yorimasen deshitari

		INFORMAL AFFIRMATIVE INDICATIVE
Passive		yorareru
Potential		yoreru
Causative		yoraseru
Causative Pass.		yoraserareru
Honorific	I	oyori ni naru
	II	oyori nasaru
Humble	I	oyori suru
	II	oyori itasu

580

よう／酔う **yo.u**

to get drunk, to get seasick, motion sickness

			AFFIRMATIVE	NEGATIVE
Indicative	**INFORMAL**		you	yowanai
	FORMAL		yoimasu	yoimasen
Imperative	**INFORMAL**	I	yoe	you na
		II	yoinasai	yoinasaru na
		III	yotte kudasai	yowanai de kudasai
	FORMAL		oyoi nasaimase	oyoi nasaimasu na
Presumptive	**INFORMAL**	I	yoō	youmai
		II	you darō	yowanai darō
	FORMAL	I	yoimashō	yoimasumai
		II	you deshō	yowanai deshō
Provisional	**INFORMAL**		yoeba	yowanakereba
	FORMAL		yoimaseba	yoimasen nara
			yoimasureba	
Gerund	**INFORMAL**	I	yotte	yowanai de
		II		yowanakute
	FORMAL		yoimashite	yoimasen de
Past Ind.	**INFORMAL**		yotta	yowanakautta
	FORMAL		yoimashita	yoimasen deshita
Past Presump.	**INFORMAL**		yottarō	yowanakattarō
			yotta darō	yowanakatta darō
	FORMAL		yoimashitarō	yoimasen deshitarō
			yotta deshō	yowanakatta deshō
Conditional	**INFORMAL**		yottara	yowanakattara
	FORMAL		yoimashitara	yoimasen deshitara
Alternative	**INFORMAL**		yottari	yowanakattari
	FORMAL		yoimashitari	yoimasen deshitari

		INFORMAL AFFIRMATIVE INDICATIVE
Passive		yowareru
Potential		yoeru
Causative		yowaseru
Causative Pass.		yowaserareru
Honorific	I	oyoi ni naru
	II	oyoi nasaru
Humble	I	
	II	

Y

to forgive, to permit, to allow, to approve   TRANSITIVE

			AFFIRMATIVE	**NEGATIVE**
Indicative	**INFORMAL**		yurusu	yurusanai
	FORMAL		yurushimasu	yurushimasen
Imperative	**INFORMAL**	I	yuruse	yurusu na
		II	yurushinasai	yurushinasaru na
		III	yurushite kudasai	yurusanai de kudasai
	FORMAL		oyurushi nasaimase	oyurushi nasaimasu na
Presumptive	**INFORMAL**	I	yurusō	yurusumai
		II	yurusu darō	yurusanai darō
	FORMAL	I	yurushimashō	yurushimasumai
		II	yurusu deshō	yurusanai deshō
Provisional	**INFORMAL**		yuruseba	yurusanakereba
	FORMAL		yurushimaseba	yurushimasen nara
			yurushimasureba	
Gerund	**INFORMAL**	I	yurushite	yurusanai de
		II		yurusanakute
	FORMAL		yurushimashite	yurushimasen de
Past Ind.	**INFORMAL**		yurushita	yurusanakatta
	FORMAL		yurushimashita	yurushimasen deshita
Past Presump.	**INFORMAL**		yurushitarō	yurusanakattarō
			yurushita darō	yurusanakatta darō
	FORMAL		yurushimashitarō	yurushimasen deshitarō
			yurushita deshō	yurusanakatta deshō
Conditional	**INFORMAL**		yurushitara	yurusanakattara
	FORMAL		yurushimashitara	yurushimasen deshitara
Alternative	**INFORMAL**		yurushitari	yurusanakattari
	FORMAL		yurushimashitari	yurushimasen deshitari

			INFORMAL AFFIRMATIVE INDICATIVE
Passive			yurusareru
Potential			yuruseru
Causative			yurusaseru
Causative Pass.			yurusaserareru
Honorific		I	oyurushi ni naru
		II	oyurushi nasaru
Humble		I	oyurushi suru
		II	oyurushi itasu

Appendixes

Verbs of Giving and Receiving

In Japanese many verbs of giving and receiving have an intrinsic "directionality" which helps to identify the person performing the act of giving. This is a big help to English-speaking students, because Japanese often omits explicit reference to the subject of a sentence.

The four verbs for giving which occur most often in spoken Japanese are *ageru, yaru, kudasaru*, and *kureru*.

Ageru means "I (you, he, she, or they) give TO SOMEONE OTHER THAN THE SPEAKER." Thus *Okane o agemashita.* could mean "I gave you money," "You gave him money," or "She gave them money," but it could not mean "You (he, she, or they) gave me money." *Ageru* also has an intrinsic element of politeness to the receiver of the gift, so it is used to describe giving to equals or superiors, or to anyone to whom the speaker wishes to express politeness or respect.

Examples:
Sensei ni agete mo ii desu.
"You may give it to the teacher."

Mō sukoshi agemashō ka.
"Shall I give you a little more?"

Okāsan ni agete kudasai.
"Please give it to your mother."

Yaru too means "give TO SOMEONE OTHER THAN THE SPEAKER," but it differs greatly in that it lacks the politeness of *ageru.* Thus it is used to describe giving to someone of equal or lower status when speaking very plainly and informally, but since such judgments are extremely difficult for students, and since using *yaru* at the wrong time could offend the person one is speaking to or about, you should to use *yaru* only when talking about giving things to plants and animals. This is a safe usage, and one which is common in Japan.

Examples:
Imōto ni okashi o takusan yarimashita.
"I gave a lot of candy to my little sister."

Sanji ni inu ni esa o yatta.
"She fed the dog at three o'clock."

Tarō wa mada hana ni mizu o yarimasen.
"Taro has not watered the flowers yet."

Kudasaru means "giving BY SOMEONE OTHER THAN THE SPEAKER," and is usually used to describe giving to the speaker or to a member of the speaker's in-group such as a family member. *Kudasaru* forms a pair with *ageru,* but while *ageru* shows politeness to the recipient of the gift, *kudasaru* shows politeness to the giver. It implies that the giver's position is superior to that of the speaker, or that the speaker is showing respect to the giver in order to be polite, as would commonly be done when the giver is present.

Examples:

Akai no o kudasai.
"Please give me the red one."

Sensei ga kudasatta hon desu.
"It's the book the teacher gave me."

Hiroko ni mo kudasatta no?
"You mean you gave some to (my child) Hiroko too?"

Kureru also means "giving BY SOMEONE OTHER THAN THE SPEAKER" but it implies that the status of the giver is equal to or lower than the receiver's, so it is not used when one wants to show politeness or respect to the giver. It is often used when the giver is an institution rather than a person. It is also often used when describing a gift to the speaker by a person of roughly equivalent status who is not present. Though it is sometimes used to mean "someone (other than the speaker) gives to you," this usage is best avoided by students because it could give offense if used with the wrong person.

Examples:

Tomodachi ga kudamono o kuremashita.
"My friend gave me some fruit."

Untenshu wa otsuri mo kurenai de itte shimatta.
"The driver went off without giving me my change."

Kodomotachi ga hankachi o kureta.
"The kids gave me some handkerchiefs."

The two common verbs for receiving are ***itadaku*** and ***morau***.

Itadaku means "something is received by me or by a member of my in-group such as a close relative." It is a humble verb which shows deference to the giver by placing the receiver in a lower position. Therefore, it would not be used for "you receive" unless the receiver is a lesser member of the speaker's in-group. A mother might say to her small child *Mā sensei ni itadaita no?* "Oh! Did you receive it from your teacher?" in order to show respect to the teacher.

Examples:

Okusan ni kippu o itadaita no de, shibai o mite kimashita.
"We received tickets from your wife, so we went to the play."

Tomita sensei kara itadaita shashin wa doko desu ka.
"Where is the photo you received from Professor Tomita?"

Ohenji o itadaite anshin itashimashita.
"I was relieved to receive your reply."

Morau lacks the directionality of the verbs discussed above. It can mean "I, you, he, she, or they receive." Since it has the standard honorific forms of *omorai ni naru* and *omorai nasaru,* it can be used to express deference or politeness to the receiver. Its humble form is *itadaku.*

Examples:
Tomodachi kara iroiro na mono o moraimashita.
"I (you, he, she, they) received all sorts of things from friends."

Zuibun ii tokei o omorai ni narimashita nē.
"My, you certainly got a nice watch."

Tanaka san ni moratta no wa dore deshō ka.
"Which is the one that we got from Mr. Tanaka?"

Mada moraimasen ka.
"Haven't you received it yet?"

Minna nani ka ii mono o morau deshō.
"Probably everyone will get something good."

A thorough grasp of these verbs is needed because, in addition to describing the giving and receiving of objects, they are also widely used in describing actions done for another person's benefit. In this construction the informal gerund of the verb which describes the action is used immediately before the appropriate form of the verb of giving or receiving. We have already encountered this construction in the imperative III in which the gerund is used before the informal imperative form of *kudasaru* to make a polite request. The same directionality applies as in the giving and receiving of objects. Therefore, just as *Ringo o ageta.* means "Someone gave an apple to someone other than the speaker," *Ringo o katte ageta.* means "Someone brought an apple for someone other than the speaker." and so on.

Examples:
Kodomotachi ni kurisumasu tsurī o katte yatta.
"We bought a Christmas tree for the children."

Kanai ga itsumo boku no suki na mono o tsukutte kureru.
"My wife always cooks things that I like for me."

Mō sukoshi matte kudasaimasen ka.
"Would you please wait a bit longer for me."

Okāsama ni oishii okashi o motte kite itadakimashita.
"Your mother brought some delicious cake for us." (Literally "We received the bringing of some delicious cake by your mother.")

Dare mo oshiete kuremasen deshita.
"Nobody told me."

Sono hana wa dare ni okutte moraimashita ka.
"Who sent you the flowers?" (Literally "As for those flowers, by whom did you receive the sending?")

Misete agemashō ka. *
"Shall 1 show it to you." *

Sensei ga nankai mo setsumei shite kudasaimashita.
"The teacher explained it to me many times."

A gerund plus *morau* or *itadaku* is also used when one person has another do something for him or her.

Examples:
Otetsudai san ni sentakumono o tatande moraimashita.
"She had the housekeeper fold the laundry."

Nikuya san ni tori no ii tokoro o totte oite moratta.
"I had the butcher save the good part of the chicken for me."

Sensei ni setsumei shite itadakimashita.
"I had the teacher explain it for me."

Bīru o todokete moraeru deshō.
"You can probably have the beer delivered."

You should also know that a gerund plus *moraitai* or *itadakitai* constitutes an indirect request meaning "I want to have something done by someone." With *itadakitai* it usually means "I want to have something done by you."

Examples:
Dare ka ni tana o tsukutte moraitai desu.
"I would like to have someone build me a shelf."

Isha ni mite moraitai.
"I want to have the doctor take a look at it."

Sanji ni irashite itadakitai desu.
"I want to have you come at three o'clock."

Ōkiku shite moraitai no desu ga.
"I want to have them enlarge it."

*Since this use of *ageru* implies the doing of a favor, it would not be used to a superior or to someone to whom special politeness or deference was intended. Instead, one would use the humble form of the verb describing the action. Thus, a clerk in a department store would not use this *ageru* construction when addressing a customer, but would say *Omise shimashō ka.* or *Omise itashimashō ka.* for "Shall I show it to you?"

Verb Exercises

Following is a series of drills and quizzes to let you practice using Japanese verb forms. All verb forms used in these drills and quizzes are found in the main body of the text.

Tips: To find the correct verb form consider such factors as transitive or intransitive, time words such as tomorrow and last month, which help to establish whether an action has been completed, and terms such as teacher and little brother, which provide clues regarding formality and deference levels.

Answers and explanations for all drills and quizzes are given beginning on page 599.

Verb Exercise 1 (Drill)

SENTENCE CONVERSION

Directions: The following is a series of simple sentences ending in a verb in formal style. Convert the same information into a sentence modifier and a new sentence ending in a noun plus the appropriate form of the copula. (Sentence modifiers were introduced on page 12 in connection with discussing the informal indicative form of the verb. There, examples were given of the sentence *mado o aketa* modifying a number of nouns.) Here, as in other sentence modifiers, *no* is often used as a general substitute for a specific noun.

Examples:
Mado o aketa no wa dare deshita ka.   *Who opened the window?*
Mado o aketa no wa itsu deshita ka.   *When did they open the window?*

In this exercise the noun that will stand before the copula at the end of the sentence is given as a prompt. In some cases more than one new sentence can be made from the original one. This is indicated by multiple prompts for the new sentences.

Example: Tomodachi ga Furansugo no jisho o kaimashita.
(My friend bought a French dictionary.)

—tomodachi—

Becomes: Furansugo no jisho o katta no wa tomodachi desu.
(The one who bought a French dictionary is my friend.)

1. Tanaka san ga ōkii tsukue o kaimashita.
   —Tanaka san—
   —ōkii tsukue—

2. Nobori wa sanji han ni tsukimasu.
   —nobori—
   —sanji han—

3. Imōto wa to o akete soto e demashita.
   —imōto—

4. Yūbe Shinjuku de omoshiroi hito ni aimashita.
   —yūbe—
   —omoshiroi hito—
   —Shinjuku—

5. Kinō gaikoku no eiga o mimashita.
   —gaikoku no eiga—
   —kinō—

6. Tarō wa Tōkyō no byōin ni tsutomete imasu.
   —Tarō—
   —Tōkyō no byōin—

7. Eki no mae de takushī o machimashita.
   —eki no mae—
   —takushī—

8. Tonari no otoko no ko wa Doitsu de umaremashita.
   —tonari no otoko no ko—
   —Doitsu—

9. Tomodachi ga watashi ni oishii kēki o katte kuremashita.
   —tomodachi—
   —oishii kēki—

10. Kusuri o nonde kara genki ni narimashita.
   —kusuri o nonde kara—

Verb Exercise 2 (Drill)

SENTENCE COMBINATION

> **Directions:** In this drill you will be given two short Japanese sentences that describe events or actions that occur in chronological order. Combine them into a single sentence that gives the same information.
>
> **Example:**   Asa gohan o tabemashita.
> Sore kara uchi o demashita.
>
> Becomes: Asa gohan o tabete uchi o demashita.

1. Tomodachi ni denwa o kakemashita.
   Nagaku hanashimashita.

2. Kaisha kara kaerimashita.
   Ofuro ni hairimashita.

3. Denwachō o hirakimashita.
   Bangō o sagashimashita.

4. Eki made aruku tsumori desu.
   Soko kara densha ni notte iku tsumori desu.

5. Sensei ni chūi saremashita.
   Hazukashiku narimashita.

6. Daigaku o sotsugyō shimashita.
   Ōkii kaisha ni hairimashita.

7. Nankai mo yatte mimashita.
   Tōtō seikō shimashita.

8. Kirei na hana o katte kimashō.
   Tokonoma ni kazarimashō.

9. Neko ga heya no naka ni haitte kimashita.
   Mizu o nomimashita.

10. Muzukashii hon o yomimashita.
    Zenzen wakarimasen deshita.

Verb Exercise 3 (Quiz)

VERBS OF GIVING AND RECEIVING

Directions: This quiz will test your understanding of verbs of giving or receiving. Each of the following sentences has an empty space to be filled by one of the verbs listed after the sentence. Write the letter of the correct verb in the empty space to complete the sentence. It may help to first review the section on verbs of giving and receiving on pages 585–588.

1. Sensei wa itsumo seito ni shinsetsu ni setsumei shite _____.

   Ⓐ agemasu   Ⓑ moraimasu   Ⓒ kudasaimasu

2. Otanjōbi ni otōto ga chichi ni hen na nekutai o _____.

   Ⓐ agemashita   Ⓑ kudasaimashita   Ⓒ yarimashita

3. Ima kaimono ni iku kara, tsuide ni nani ka katte kite _____.

   Ⓐ kuremashō ka   Ⓑ itadakimashō ka   Ⓒ agemashō ka

4. Boku wa dekinai kara, dare ka ni naoshite _____ tsumori desu.

   Ⓐ ageru   Ⓑ kureru   Ⓒ yaru   Ⓓ morau

5. Akachan no shashin ga dekitara obāsan ni misete _____ kudasai.

    Ⓐ kurete   Ⓑ agete   © itadaite   Ⓓ kudasatte

6. Atsui kara inu ni mizu o yobun ni _____ hō ga ii deshō.

    Ⓐ yaru   Ⓑ morau   © kudasaru   Ⓓ itadaku

7. Kōban de michi o oshiete _____ .

    Ⓐ moraimashita.   Ⓑ kudasaimashita   © agemashita   Ⓓ kuremashita

8. Otōto ga hitori de dekiru made, boku wa setsumei shite _____ .

    Ⓐ kudasaimashita   Ⓑ agemashita   © itadakimashita

9. Senjitsu goryōshin ni _____ okashi wa totemo oishikatta desu yo.

    Ⓐ yatta   Ⓑ kudasatta   © kureta   Ⓓ itadaita

10. Ane ga tokidoki watakushi no shukudai o tetsudatte _____ koto ga arimasu.

    Ⓐ morau   Ⓑ kureru   © ageru   Ⓓ yaru

Verb Exercise 4 (Quiz)

SENTENCE JOINING

Directions: The following quiz will test your understanding of the environments in which particular forms of verbs can occur in sentences. Ten sentences have been separated at the juncture between a verb and the item that follows it. The sentence-beginnings are numbered 1 through 10. The sentence-endings are designated by letters A through J. Check each beginning carefully and write the letter of an appropriate ending in the space at the end. You may find two items that can complete a particular sentence.

1. Hachiji han no densha ni notte_____   A. mo henji wa onaji deshita.

2. Sachiko wa isha ni me o mite_____   B. no wa donna eiga deshita ka.

3. Okane ga nakatta_____   C. aida rajio o kikimasu.

4. Yūhan o sumasete   D morau deshō.

5. Obāsan ga nete iru_____   E. Nihonjin ga takusan iru deshō.

6. Kagi ga kakatte_____   F. kara nani mo kaemasen deshita.

7. Eibun no shinbun o mainichi yomu_____   G. Nikkō ni ikimashita.

8. Kodomotachi ga senshū mita_____   H. kara shizuka ni shite kudasai.

9. Sara o aratte iru_____   I. iru kara to wa akeraremasen.

10. Dare ni kiite_____   J. kara sugu nemashita.

TRANSITIVE/INTRANSITIVE EXERCISE

Directions: A verb has been omitted from each of the following sentences. Choose the appropriate verb from the list given below the sentence, and write the letter in the blank space to complete the sentence. Pay special attention to any clues in the sentence that indicate whether the missing verb is transitive or intransitive.

1. Kuraku natta kara, denki o _____ kudasai.
   Ⓐ tsuite   Ⓑ tsukete   Ⓒ keshite   Ⓓ kiete

2. Kore o ichiban takai tana no ue ni _____ kudasai.
   Ⓐ nosete   Ⓑ dashite   Ⓒ notte   Ⓓ oroshite

3. Kono ji wa akiraka ni _____ imasu.
   Ⓐ mitsukete   Ⓑ machigaete   Ⓒ mitsukatte   Ⓓ machigatte

4. Denki ga _____ no de heya wa kuraku narimashita.
   Ⓐ tsuketa   Ⓑ keshita   Ⓒ kieta   Ⓓ tsuita

5. Tsugi no eki de _____ deshō.
   Ⓐ oriru   Ⓑ ochiru   Ⓒ otosu   Ⓓ noseru

6. Denwa bangō o _____ kara tsūjimasen deshita.
   Ⓐ mitsuketa   Ⓑ machigatta   Ⓒ machigaeta   Ⓓ mitsukatta

7. Mō osoi kara ginkō wa _____ iru deshō.
   Ⓐ shimatte   Ⓑ akete   Ⓒ shimete   Ⓓ aite

8. Chotto takai kara mō sukoshi yasuku _____ kuremasen ka.
   Ⓐ natte   Ⓑ oroshite   Ⓒ orite   Ⓓ shite

9. Genkan no to o _____ naka e hairimashita.
   Ⓐ shimete   Ⓑ aite   Ⓒ akete   Ⓓ shimatte

10. Neru mae ni kagi o _____ kudasai.
    Ⓐ kakete   Ⓑ kakatte   Ⓒ shimatte   Ⓓ aite

EXPRESSING SIMULTANEOUS ACTION WITH -*NAGARA*

Directions: Each of the following sentences has two blank spaces to be filled by verbs. The sentences are followed by a list of verbs in two separate columns. Insert the proper form of a verb from column A in the space before -nagara, and the proper form of a verb from column B in the space at the end of the sentence. Some verbs may fit in more than one space.

1. Michi o _____ nagara tomodachi to _____.

2. Shinbun o _____ nagara gohan o _____.

3. Kao o _____ nagara rajio o _____.

4. Dame da to _____ nagara _____ shimaimashita.

5. Terebi o _____ nagara shukudai o _____.

6. Kuruma o unten _____ nagara ongaku o _____.

7. Takushī o _____ nagara denwa o _____.

8. Kōhī o _____ nagara tegami o _____.

9. Chizu o _____ nagara tomodachi no uchi o _____.

10. Kare no hanashi o _____ nagara kowaku _____.

A		B	
yomu	taberu	suu	sagasu
aruku	matsu	taberu	suru
kiku	omou	hanasu	yomu
miru	suru	kiku	kakeru
nomu	arau	naru	yaru

SENTENCE JOINING

> **Directions:** As in exercise 4, correctly join the two parts of sentences that have been divided at the end of a verb form.

1. Kono mado wa aite iru _____
2. Ano ko wa nando shikatte _____
3. Yoku renshū shinakereba _____
4. Kinō okutta _____
5. Tsumaranai terebi o miru _____
6. Kono mittsu o kuraberu _____
7. Ōsaka ni yoku ikimasu _____
8. Nichiyōbi ni kodomotachi o tsurete _____
9. Kesa no shinbun ni yoru _____
10. Ano hito nara dekiru to omotta _____

a) tegami wa itsu tsuku deshō.
b) to dore ga ichiban ii desu ka.
c) to kyō wa mata ame da sō desu.
d) mo onaji itazura o shimasu.
e) ga Kyōto e itta koto wa arimasen.
f) keredomo mukō no wa shimatte imasu.
g) Ueno kōen ni iku tsumori desu.
h) no ni zenzen dame deshita.
i) Jōzu ni naru hazu ga arimasen.
j) yori hon o yonda hō ga ii desu.

Verb Exercise 8 (Drill)

VERB JUNCTURE

> **Directions:** Each of the following verbs is followed by five items, each of which can follow the verb in a sentence. Insert in each blank space the proper form of the verb to occur before that item.

1. **kaku**   _____ nagara   _____ kudasai   _____ hito
    _____ tai   _____ naosu

2. **yomu**   _____ toki   _____ hajimeru   _____ morau
    _____ kudasai   _____ hazu

3. **akeru**   _____ ageru   _____ hō   _____ aru
    _____ sugiru   _____ mado

4. **kuru**   _____ nai   _____ tsumori   _____ iru
    _____ deshō   _____ tai

5. **suru**   _____ koto   _____ masu   _____ nagara

                     _____ imasu   _____ moraimashita

6. **warau**   _____ toki   _____ no de   _____ taku nai

                     _____ nakatta   _____ imasu

7. **dasu**   _____ kureta   _____ tokoro   _____ tai

                     _____ nai   _____ okane

8. **isogu**   _____ kaerimashita   _____ nagara   _____ yomu

                     _____ hazu   _____ riyū

9. **miru**   _____ me   _____ toki   _____ sokonau

                     _____ imasu   _____ nagara

10. **ossharu**   _____ nai   _____ mashita   _____ kata

                     _____ itadakitai   _____ deshō

Verb Exercise 9 (Drill)

PASSIVE DRILL

Directions: Below are ten sentences using verbs in active forms. Convert them into sentences using passive forms that convey similar information. For some sentences two passive versions are possible, one version being the adversative passive in which the passive is used to show an unpleasant result.

     Example: Dorobō ga sono okane o nusumimashita.

                   Becomes: Sono okane wa dorobō ni nusumaremashita.

1. Inu ga neko o kamimashita.

2. Neko ga sakana o tabemashita.

3. Tarō ga boku no tegami o yomimashita.

4. Ani wa mainichi watashi o matasemasu.

5. Ojiisan ga Tarō o shikarimashita.

6. Ano hito ga boku no okane o zenbu tsukatte shimaimashita.

7. Tomodachi wa kare o waraimashita.

8. Sensei wa imōto o homemashita.

9. Keikan ga kuruma o tomemashita.

10. Sensei ga boku ni shitsumon shimashita.

Verb Exercise 10 (Drill)

SENTENCE CONVERSION

Directions: Below are ten pairs of short sentences ending in nonpast formal verb forms. Convert each pair into a single sentence as follows:

"If so and so, probably so and so."

Example:

Ji o ōkiku kakimasu. *Write the characters large.*
Ojiisan ga yoku yomemasu. *Grandfather can read it well.*

Becomes:

Ji o ōkiku kakeba, Ojiisan ga yoku yomeru deshō.
If you write the characters large, Grandfather can probably read it well.

1. Teinei ni tanomimasu.
   Oniisan ga kashite kuremasu.

2. Ji o chiisaku kakimasu.
   Obāsan wa hakkiri miemasen.

3. Yukkuri yasumimasu.
   Kitto genki ni narimasu.

4. Issho ni asonde yarimasu.
   Kodomotachi ga yorokobimasu.

5. Hima ga arimasu.
   Sanpo ni ikemasu.

6. Kippu o katte okimasu.
   Itsu demo ikemasu.

7. Tanaka san no tomodachi ni sōdan shimasu.
   Nani ka ii shigoto no kuchi ga arimasu.

8. Isshō kenmei ni doryoku shimasu.
   Kitto shusse shimasu.

9. Yasashii shigoto sae dekimasen.
   Muzukashii shigoto wa mochiron dekimasen.

10. Kōhī o takusan nomimasu.
    Sono yoru yoku neraremasen.

Exercise 11 (Quiz)

SENTENCE JOINING

Directions: Below are ten divided sentences. Select which parts go together, and write the letter of the second part in the space at the end of the first part. Note that the second parts all begin with either -no ni, which indicates a conrast between the parts, or -no de, which indicates a causal relationship. Make sure that the completed sentences reflect the appropriate relationship.

1. Asa kara ban made hataraita _____

2. Bukka wa dondon agaru _____

3. Kono seito wa yoku benkyō suru _____

4. Jibun ga yoku dekiru to itta _____

5. Harada san wa byōki ni natta _____

6. Minasan ga matte iru _____

7. Sanji goro chūmon shite oita _____

8. Kare wa utaenai to kiite ita _____

9. Ano seito wa benkyō shinai _____

10. Nimotsu ga ōsugiru _____

a) no ni jitsu wa jōzu deshita.

b) no ni kare wa isoide kuremasen deshita.

c) no de sukoshi herashitai desu.

d) no de totemo tsukaremashita.

e) no ni gekkyū wa zenzen agarimasen.

f) no ni nakanaka jōzu ni narimasen.

g) no de sensei ni shikararemashita.

h) no ni hontō wa dekimasen deshita.

i) no de rokuji made ni tsuku deshō.

j) no de kaisha o yasumimashita.

Exercise 1 Conversion Drill

The original sentences and their conversions are as follows:

1. Tanaka san ga ōkii tsukue o kaimashita.
   Mr. Tanaka bought a large desk.

   > Ōkii tsukue o katta no wa Tanaka san desu.
   > Tanaka san ga katta no wa ōkii tsukue desu.

2. Nobori wa sanji han ni tsukimasu.
   The inbound train arrives at 3:30.

   > Sanji han ni tsuku no wa nobori desu.
   > Nobori ga tsuku no wa saji han desu.

3. Imōto wa to o akete soto e demashita.
   My little sister opened the door and went outside.

   > To o akete soto e deta no wa imōto deshita.

4. Yūbe Shinjuku de omoshiroi hito ni aimashita.
   Last night I met someone interesting in Shinjuku.

   > Shinjuku de omoshiroi hito ni atta no wa yūbe deshita.
   > Yūbe Shinjuku de atta no wa omoshiroi hito deshita.
   > Yūbe omoshiroi hito ni atta no wa Shinjuku deshita.

5. Kinō gaikoku no eiga o mimashita.
   I saw a foreign movie yesterday.

   > Kinō mita no wa gaikoku no eiga deshita.
   > Gaikoku no eiga o mita no wa kinō deshita.

6. Tarō wa Tōkyō no byōin ni tsutomete imasu.
   Taro works at a Tokyo hospital.

   > Tōkyō no byōin ni tsutomete iru no wa Tarō desu.
   > Tarō ga tsutomete iru no wa Tōkyō no byōin desu.

7. Eki no mae de takushī o machimashita.
   I waited for a taxi in front of the station.

   > Takushī o matta no wa eki no mae deshita.
   > Eki no mae de matta no wa takushī deshita.

8. Tonari no otoko no ko wa Doitsu de umaremashita.
   The boy next door was born in Germany.

   Doitsu de umareta no wa tonari no otoko no ko desu.
   Tonari no otoko no ko ga umareta no wa Doitsu desu.

9. Tomodachi ga watashi ni oishii kēki o katte kuremashita.
   A friend bought me some delicious cake.

   Oishii kēki o katte kureta no wa tomodachi deshita.
   Tomodachi ga katte kureta no wa oishii kēki deshita.

10. Kusuri o nonde kara genki ni narimashita.
    I got better after taking the medicine.

    Genki ni natta no wa kusuri o nonde kara deshita.

Exercise 2   Sentence Combination Drill

The combined sentences and their English translations are as follows:

1. Tomodachi ni denwa o kakete, nagaku hanashimashita.
   I phoned my friend and talked a long time.

2. Kaisha kara kaette, ofuro ni hairimashita.
   I returned from the office and got into the tub.

3. Denwachō o hiraite, bangō o sagashimashita.
   I opened the phone book and looked up the number.

4. Eki made aruite, soko kara densha ni notte iku tsumori desu.
   I intend to walk as far as the station and take a train from there.

5. Sensei ni chūi sarete, hazukashiku narimashita.
   I was scolded by the teacher and became embarrassed.

6. Daigaku o sotsugyō shite ōkii kaisha ni hairimashita.
   I graduated from college and joined a large firm.

7. Nankai mo yatte mite tōtō seikō shimashita.
   I tried any number of times and finally succeeded.

8. Kirei na hana o katte kite tokonoma ni kazarimashō.
   Let's go buy some pretty flowers and display them in the tokonoma.

9. Neko ga heya no naka ni haitte kite mizu o nomimashita.
   The cat came into the room and drank some water.

10. Muzukashii hon o yonde, zenzen wakarimasen deshita.
    I read a difficult book and could not understand it at all.

Exercise 3 Quiz on Verbs of Giving and Receiving

The correct responses and their English translations are as follows:

1. Sensei wa itsumo seito ni shinsetsu ni setsumei shite kudasaimasu. Ⓒ
   The teacher always explains to the pupils in a kind manner.

2. Otanjōbi ni otōto ga chichi ni hen na nekutai o agemashita. Ⓐ
   My kid brother gave my dad a funny necktie on his birthday.

3. Ima kaimono ni iku kara tsuide ni nani ka katte kite agemashō ka Ⓒ
   I'm going shopping now, so shall I get something for you at the same time?

4. Boku wa dekinai kara dare ka ni naoshite morau Ⓓ tsumori desu.
   I can't do it, so I plan to have someone do it for me.

5. Akachan no shashin ga dekitara obāsan ni misete agete Ⓑ kudasai.
   Please show the baby's photos to Grandma when they are ready.

6. Atsui kara inu ni mizu o yobun ni yaru Ⓐ hō ga ii deshō.
   It's hot, so you'd better give the dog extra water.

7. Kōban de michi o oshiete moraimashita. Ⓐ
   I got the directions at a police booth.

8. Otōto ga hitori de dekiru made, boku wa setsumei shite agemashita. Ⓑ
   I explained it until my little brother could do it by himself.

9. Senjitsu goryōshin ni itadaita Ⓓ okashi wa totemo oishikatta desu yo.
   The candy we received from your parents the other day was delicious.

10. Ane ga tokidoki watakushi no shukudai o tetsudatte kureru Ⓑ koto ga arimasu.
    Sometimes my older sister helps with my homework.

Verb Exercise 4 Sentence Joining

The correct responses and their English translations are as follows:

1. Hachiji han no densha ni notte Nikkō ni ikimashita. (g)
   I boarded the 8:30 train and went to Nikko.

2. Sachiko wa isha ni me o mite morau deshō. (d)
   Sachiko will probably have a doctor check her eyes.

3. Okane ga nakatta kara nani mo kaemasen deshita. (f)
   I had no money so I couldn't buy anything.

4. Yūhan o sumasete kara sugu nemashita. (j)
   I went to bed soon after finishing dinner.

5. Obāsan ga nete iru kara shizuka ni shite kudasai. (h)
   Grandma is sleeping so please don't make any noise.

6. Kagi ga kakatte iru kara to wa akeraremasen. (i)
   It's locked, so I can't open the door.

7. Eibun no shinbun o mainichi yomu Nihonjin ga takusan iru deshō. (e)
   There are probably many Japanese who read English language newspapers every day.

8. Kodomotachi ga senshū mita no wa donna eiga deshita ka. (b)
   What kind of movie did the children see last week?

9. Sara o aratte iru aida rajio o kikumasu. (c)
   I listen to the radio while I wash the dishes.

10. Dare ni kiite mo henji wa onaji deshita. (a)
    No matter whom I asked, the answer was the same.

Exercise 5   Transitive/Intransitive Quiz

The correct answers are given below with their English translations. The choice of the proper verb involves two considerations. The first is deciding whether a transitive or intransitive verb is needed. Here, the presence of the particle *o* or a request pattern, or both, indicate a transitive verb. The second consideration is what kind of action fits the meaning of the sentence.

For example:

1. Kuraku natta kara, denki o tsukete Ⓑ kudasai.
   It has gotten dark, so please turn on the light.

Here:
Ⓐ tsuite will not do because the o————kudasai pattern demands a transitive verb
Ⓒ keshite (tr.) and Ⓓ kiete will not do because their meanings of "turn out" and "go out" do not fit the meaning of the rest of the sentence.

2. Kore o ichiban takai tana no ue ni nosete Ⓐ kudasai.
   Please put this on the highest shelf.

3. Kono ji wa akiraka ni machigatte imasu. Ⓓ
   This character is clearly wrong.

4. Denki ga kieta no de heya wa kuraku narimashita. Ⓒ
   The light went out so the room became dark.

5. Tsugi no eki de oriru deshō. Ⓐ
   He will probably get off at the next station.

6. Denwa bangō o machigaeta kara tsūjimasen deshita. Ⓒ
   I dialed the wrong number, so I didn't reach them.

7. Mō osoi kara ginkō wa shimatte iru deshō. Ⓐ
   It's already late, so the bank is probably closed.

8. Chotto takai kara mō sukoshi yasuku shite kuremasen ka. Ⓓ
   It's a bit expensive, so could you make it a little cheaper?

9. Genkan no to o akete naka e hairimashita. Ⓒ
   I opened the entrance door and stepped inside.

10. Neru mae ni kagi o kakete kudasai. Ⓐ
    Please lock up before you go to bed.

Exercise 6   Expressing Simultaneous Action with -nagara

The correct answers and their English translations are given below:

NOTE: The formal past indicative has been used for the final verb in all the sentences. The sentences would be equally correct if the informal past indicative had been used, and the translation would be the same. The formal or informal nonpast indicative could also be used for the final verb, in which case it would refer to a future or habitsual action rather than a completed action. Examples of all four types are given for the first sentence only, after which only the formal past indicative is given.

1. Michi o arukinagara tomodachi to hanashimashita.
   Or: Michi o arukinagara tomodachi to hanashita.
   I walked along the street while talking to my friends.

   Or: Michi o arukinagara tomodachi to hanashimasu.
   Or: Michi o arukinagara tomodachi to hanasu.
   I walk along the street while talking to my friends.

2. Shinbun o yominagara gohan o tabemashita.
   I ate while reading a newspaper.

3. Kao o arainagara rajio o kikimashita.
   I listened to the radio while washing my face.

4. Dame da to omoinagara yatte shimaimashita.
   I tried anyway although I thought it wouldn't work.

5. Terebi o minagara shukudai o shimashita.
   I did my homework while watching television.

6. Kuruma o unten shinagara ongaku o kikimashita.
   I listened to music while driving the car.

7. Takushī o machinagara denwa o kakemashita.
   I made a phone call while waiting for the taxi.

8. Kōhī o nominagara tegami o yomimashita.
   I read the letter while drinking coffee.

9. Chizu o minagara tomodachi no uchi o sagashimashita.
   I searched for my friend's house while looking at a map.

10. Kare no hanashi o kikinagara kowaku narimashita.
    I became frightened while listening to his story.

Exercise 7   Sentence Joining Quiz

The completed sentences and their English translations are as follows:

1. Kono mado wa aite iru keredomo mukō no wa shimatte imasu. (f)
   This window is open, but the one over there is closed.

2. Ano ko wa nando shikattemo onaji itazura o shimasu. (d)
   That child gets into the same mischief no matter how many times you scold him.

3. Yoku renshū shinakereba jōzu ni naru hazu ga arimasen. (i)
   You will never get good if you don't practice a lot.

4. Kinō okutta tegami wa itsu tsuku deshō. (a)
   When do you suppose the letter we sent yesterday will arrive?

5. Tsumaranai terebi o miru yori hon o yonda hō ga ii desu. (j)
   Reading a book is better than watching boring television.

6. Kono mittsu o kuraberu to dore ga ichiban ii desu ka. (b)
   When you compare these three, which is the best?

7. Ōsaka ni yoku ikimasu ga Kyōto e wa itta koto ga arimasen. (e)
   I often go to Osaka, but I have never been to Kyoto.

8. Nichiyōbi ni kodomotachi o tsurete Ueno kōen ni iku tsumori desu. (g)
   I intend to take the children to Ueno Park on Sunday.

9. Kesa no shinbun ni yoru to kyō wa mata ame da sō desu. (c)
   According to this morning's paper, it is going to rain again today.

10. Ano hito nara dekiru to omotta no ni zenzen dame deshita. (h)
    I was sure he could do it, but he couldn't do it at all.

Exercise 8   Verb Juncture Drill

The correct verb forms are given below. The basic principle is that the informal indicative occurs before the nouns, the gerund occurs before the verbs, and the infinitive occurs in compound words.

1. kakinagara   kaite kudasai   kaku hito (here and below, the past
        kakitai   kakinaosu   indicative would also be
                                                              acceptable)

2. yomu toki   yomihajimeru   yonde morau
        yonde kudasai   yomu hazu

3. akete ageru   akeru hō   akete aru
        akesugiru   akeru mado

4. konai   kuru tsumori   kite iru
        kuru deshō   kitai

5. suru koto   shimasu   shinagara
        shite imasu   shite moraimashita

6. warau toki   warau no de   waraitaku nai
        warawanakatta   waratte imasu

7. dashite kureta   dasu tokoro   dashitai
        dasanai   dasu okane

8. isoide kaerimashita   isoginagara   isoide yomu
        isogu hazu   isogu riyū

9. miru me   miru toki   misokonau
     mite imasu   minagara

10. ossharanai   osshaimashita   ossharu kata
     osshatte itadakitai   ossharu deshō

Exercise 9   Passive Drill

The passive sentences and their English translations, some literal, not colloquial, are as follows:

1. Neko wa inu ni kamaremashita.
   The cat was bitten by a dog.

2. Sakana wa neko ni taberaremashita.
   The fish was eaten by a cat.

3. Boku no tegami wa Tarō ni yomaremashita.
   My letter was read by Taro.

   Boku wa Tarō ni tegami o yomaremashita.
   I suffered having Taro read my letter.

4. Watashi wa mainichi ani ni mataseraremasu.
   I am made to wait by my elder brother every day.

5. Tarō wa ojiisan ni shikararemashita.
   Taro was scolded by Grandfather.

6. Boku no okane wa ano hito ni zenbu tsukawarete shimaimashita.
   My money was all spent by that person.

   Boku wa ano hito ni okane o zenbu tsukawarete shimaimashita.
   I suffered having that person spend all my money.

7. Kare wa tomodachi ni warawaremashita.
   He was laughed at by his friends.

8. Imōto wa sensei ni homeraremashita.
   My younger sister was praised by her teacher.

9. Kuruma wa keikan ni tomeraremashita.
   The car was stopped by a policeman.

   Boku wa keikan ni kuruma o tomeraremashita.
   I suffered having my car stopped by a policeman.

10. Boku wa sensei ni shitsumon saremashita.
    I was asked a question by the teacher.

Exercise 10   Sentence Conversion Drill

The converted sentences and their English translations are as follows:

1. Teinei ni tanomeba oniisan ga kashite kureru deshō.
   If you ask politely, big brother will probably lend it to you.

2. Ji o chiisaku kakeba obāsan wa hakkiri mienai deshō.
   If you write small, Grandmother probably won't be able to see it clearly.

3. Yukkuri yasumeba kitto genki ni naru deshō.
   If you get a good rest, you'll surely get better.

4. Issho ni asonde yareba kodomotachi ga yorokobu deshō.
   The children will probably enjoy it if you play with them.

5. Hima ga areba sanpo ni ikeru deshō.
   If I have free time, I will probably be able to go for a walk.

6. Kippu o katte okeba itsu demo ikeru deshō.
   If we buy tickets in advance, we probably can go anytime.

7. Tanaka san no tomodachi ni sōdan sureba nani ka ii shigoto no kuchi ga aru deshō.
   If you ask Mr. Tanaka's friend, he will probably have a lead on some good job.

8. Isshō kenmei ni doryoku sureba kitto shusse suru deshō.
   If you give it your best, you will surely get ahead in life.

9. Yasashii shigoto sae dekinakereba muzukashii shigoto wa mochiron dekinai deshō.
   If he can't even do easy work, of course he won't be able to do hard work.

10. Kōhī o takusan nomeba sono yoru yoku nerarenai deshō.
    If you drink a lot of coffee, you won't be able to sleep well that night.

Exercise 11   Sentence Joining Quiz

The correct answers and their English translations are as follows:

1. Asa kara ban made hataraita no de totemo tsukaremashita. (d)
   I worked from morning till night, so I got very tired.

2. Bukka wa dondon agaru no ni gekkyū wa zenzen agarimasen. (e)
   Although prices are going up steadily, salaries are not going up at all.

3. Kono seito wa yoku benkyō suru no ni nakanaka jōzu ni narimasen. (f)
   Although this student studies hard, he doesn't improve.

4. Jibun ga yoku dekiru to itta no ni hontō wa dekimasen deshita. (h)
   Despite his saying he was good at it, in fact he couldn't do it.

5. Harada san wa byōki ni natta no de kaisha o yasumimashita. (j)
   Mr. Harada got sick, so he took off from work.

6. Minasan ga matte iru no ni kare wa isoide kuremasen deshita. (b)
   In spite of everyone waiting, he did not hurry because of them.

7. Sanji goro chūmon shite oita no de rokuji made ni tsuku deshō. (i)
   I ordered it at about 3:00, so it will probably get here by 6:00.

8. Kare wa utaenai to kiite ita no ni jitsu wa jyōzu deshita. (a)
   Despite our hearing that he couldn't sing, actually his singing was very good.

9. Ano seito wa benkyō shinai no de sensei ni shikararemashita. (g)
   That student doesn't study, so he was scolded by the teacher.

10. Nimotsu ga ōsugiru no de sukoshi herashitai desu. (c)
    I have too much to carry, so I want to lighten it a bit.

Examples of Verbs Used in Sentences

This section includes many verbs from the 501 tables and others as well. Most sentences here end in informal forms, which is typical of casual speech and also of the impersonal style used in newspapers and other written material.

AFURERU あふれる／溢れる　well up, overflow
> Kare wa jishin ni afurete iru. *He's overflowing with confidence.*
> Ganjitsu no jinja wa hito de afureteita. *The shrine was overflowing with people on New Year's Day.*

AGARU あがる／上がる　rise, go up, improve, visit
> Seiseki ga agatta. *My grades improved.*
> Jūtaku rōn no rishi ga agarisō da. *The interest rates on housing loans seem to be going up.*

AGERU あげる／上げる　give (to second or third person), raise
> Haha ni agetai. *I want to give it to my mother.*
> Nikuya ga nedan o ageta. *The butcher raised his prices.*

AKERU あける／開ける　open, empty out, leave vacant
> Sono mado o akenai de kudasai. *Please don't open that window.*
> Yokusō o akete sōji shita. *I emptied out the bathtub and scrubbed it.*

AKIRAMERU あきらめる／諦める　abandon (an idea), resign oneself (to)
> Akirameru na. *Don't give up.*
> Shūmatsu no ryokō wa isogashikute akirameta. *I gave up the weekend trip because I was too busy.*

AKIRERU あきれる／呆れる　be disgusted, be shocked
> Kare no okonai niwa akireta. *I'm disgusted with his behavior.*
> Kanojo no rōhi niwa akireta. *We're shocked at her wasting money.*

AKIRU あきる／飽きる　get tired of, have enough of, lose interest in
> Akiru made pachinko o shita. *I played pachinko till I got tired of it.*
> Sushi wa nando tabetemo akinai. *No matter how many times I eat it, I never get tired of sushi.*

AKU あく／開く／空く　open, become empty, have time to spare
> Hon-ya wa jū ji made akimasen. *The bookstore won't open till ten o'clock.*
> Sono seki wa aite imasu ka. *Is that seat free?*
> Jikan ga aku to, hon o yomu. *If I have spare time, I read books.*

ANNAI SURU あんないする／案内する　guide, show around
> Tōkyō dewa tomodachi ga anata o annai shite kuremasu. *My friend will show you around Tokyo.*
> Soko made annai shite agemashō. *I'll guide you there.*

ANSHIN SURU　あんしんする／安心する　feel relieved, feel at ease
Otegami o itadaite anshin shimashita. *I was relieved to receive your letter.*
Ano byōin nara anshin dekiru. *With that hospital, you can rest assured.*

ARASOU　あらそう／争う　argue, fight, dispute
Arasowazu ni, mondai o kaiketsu shita. *We settled the issue without arguing.*
Mittsu no chīmu ga yūshō o arasotte iru. *The three teams are competing for the championship.*

ARATAMARU　あらたまる／改まる　be changed, become serious, become formal
Aratamatta fukusō wa hitsuyō dewa arimasen. *You don't need formal clothing.*
Kanojo wa aratamatta kuchō de hanashita. *She spoke in a serious tone of voice.*

ARATAMERU　あらためる／改める　change, renew, revise, adjust
Taido o aratamenasai. *Change your attitude!*
Sono hōshin o sugu ni aratameru darō. *They'll revise the policy soon.*

ARAWARERU　あらわれる／現れる　appear, show up
Fui ni tomodachi ga arawareta. *Some friends showed up unexpectedly.*
Kare wa mō sorosoro arawareru hazu desu. *He should be appearing sometime soon.*

ARAWASU　あらわす／現わす／表わす　display, reveal, express, show up
Kare wa idai na sainō o arawashi hajimeta. *He has begun to display great talent.*
Kanojo wa kangeki o egao de arawashita. *She expressed her enthusiasm with her smile.*

ARUKU　あるく／歩く　walk, pace
Aruku no ga suki da. *I like to walk.*
Ichinichi jū aruite ita node tsukareta. *I got tired because I was walking all day long.*

ARU　ある／有る／在る　be (inanimate), exist, have, be possible
Mada pan ga aru ka to omottara, nakatta. *Although I thought there would be some bread left, there wasn't any.*
Donna dezāto ga arimasu ka. *What kind of dessert do you have?*

ASOBU　あそぶ／遊ぶ　amuse oneself, play, be idle
Shūmatsu wa asonde bakari ita. *I just played around all weekend.*
Kodomo ga asobitagatta. *My children wanted to play with me.*

ATAERU　あたえる／与える　give, provide, bestow, grant
Kodomo no oyatsu ni ringo o ataeta. *I gave my children apples for their snack.*
Kega nin ni ōkyū sochi o ataeta. *They provided emergency aid to the injured.*

ATARU　あたる／当たる　strike, correspond, succeed, undertake
Kan ga atatta. *My hunch turned out to be correct.*
Ima, kono uta ga atatte iru. *Now this song is very popular.*

ATATAMARU　あたたまる／暖まる／温まる　get warm, be warmed
Ofuro ni haitte atatamarinasai. *Take a bath and get warm!*
Danbō ga nakute, nakanaka atatamarenakatta. *I couldn't get warm because there was no heat.*

ATATAMERU　あたためる／暖める／温める　heat, warm something
Sūpu o atatameta. *I warmed up some soup.*
Kono ie wa atatame nikui. *This house is difficult to heat.*

ATERU　あてる／当てる　hit the mark, put, assign to, guess correctly
Kare wa kyō no otenki o ateta. *He guessed today's weather correctly.*
Kanojo wa kodomo no hitai nite no hira o ateta. *She put her palm on her child's forehead.*

ATSUMARU　あつまる／集まる　gather together, assemble, center on
Eki mae ni gunshū ga atsumatta. *The crowd gathered in front of the station.*
Kokumin no chūmoku ga jishin no nyūsu ni atsumatte iru. *People's attention is focusing on the news of the earthquake.*

ATSUMERU　あつめる／集める　collect, put together, raise (funds)
Gakkō wa kifukin o atsumete iru. *The school is raising donations.*
Kanojo wa kaigara o atsumeru no ga shumi da. *Her hobby is collecting seashells.*

AU　あう／会う／逢う／合う　see, meet, encounter, fit
Kono kutsu wa saizu ga awanai. *These shoes don't fit.*
Ano hito niwa atta koto ga aru. *I've met him before.*
Mata oai shimashō. *Let's meet again.*

AWASERU　あわせる／合わせる　join together, combine, fit one thing to another
Kare wa kanojo no iken ni awaseta. *He adjusted his opinion to fit hers.*
Chikara o awasete mondai o kaiketsu shita. *We joined together and solved the problem.*

AWATERU　あわてる／慌てる　panic, lose one's composure, be flustered
Kare wa awatete ie o tobidashita. *He rushed home in a panic.*
Awateru na. *Don't panic.*

AYAMARU　あやまる／誤る　make a mistake
Seiken wa gaikō seisaku o ayamatta. *The administration made mistakes in foreign policy.*
Jikan o ayamatte, menkai ni okurete shimatta. *Mistaking the time, I was late for the appointment.*

AZUKARU あずかる／預かる   be entrusted with something, be in charge
   Tomodachi no inu o azukatte iru. *I'm keeping her dog for her.*
   Kodomo o haha ni azukatte moratta. *I got my mother to look after my children.*

AZUKERU あずける／預ける   entrust something to someone, deposit
   Kichō hin o hoteru no furonto ni azuketa. *We checked our valuables at the hotel reception desk.*
   Jon wa bōnasu o ginkō ni azukeru mae ni, zenbu tsukatte shimatta. *Before depositing his bonus, John spent it all.*

BENKYŌ SURU 勉強する   study, reduce (shop price)
   Hanako wa maiban go jikan benkyō shite iru. *Hanako studies five hours every night.*
   Kudamonoya wa itsumo benkyō shite kureru. *The fruit shop owner always reduces the prices for me.*

CHIGAU ちがう／違う   be different, differ, be incorrect
   Futari no iken wa mattaku chigatte iru. *The opinion of those two are completely different.*
   Sono setsumei wa chigau. *That explanation is not correct.*

CHIJIMU ちぢむ／縮む   shrink, contract
   Kono kiji wa chijimanai koto ga hoshō sarete iru. *The fabric is guaranteed not to shrink.*
   Kono sētā wa hidoku chijinde shimatte kirarenai. *This sweater shrank so much that I can't put it on.*

CHIKAU ちかう／誓う   promise, pledge, swear
   Kanojo wa nido to inshu unten o shinai koto o chikatta. *She swore she'd never drink and drive again.*
   Himitsu o mamoru koto o chikau. *I promise I'll keep it secret.*

CHIKAZUKU ちかづく／近づく   approach, get acquainted with
   Gakusei wa haru yasumi ga chikazuite ureshigatte iru. *My students are glad spring break is coming soon.*
   Dona to chikazuki ni naritai. *I'd like to get acquainted with Donna.*

CHŪMON SURU ちゅうもんする／注文する   place an order, make a request
   Sushi no demae o chūmon shiyō. *Let's order a sushi delivery.*
   Karera wa intānetto de irui o takusan chūmon suru. *They order a lot of clothing online.*

DAMARU だまる／黙る   become silent, stop talking
   Damatte irarenai. *I just can't be silent.*
   Kaigi chū kanojo wa zutto damatte ita. *She kept silent throughout the meeting.*

DAMASU だます／騙す　deceive, cheat, betray
Kare no seijitsu sō na yōsu ni damasareta. *I was fooled by his sincere manner.*
Kanojo ni damasareta hito ga ōzei iru. *There are many people who have been cheated by her.*

DASU だす／出す　take out, put out, expose, publish, embark, serve
Kono resutoran wa shinsen na sakana o dasu node yūmei desu. *This restaurant is famous for serving fresh fish.*
Kanojo wa tōtō hon-ne o dashita. *He finally revealed his true colors.*

DEKIRU できる／出来る　be finished, be formed, be able to do, be good at, be ready
Itsu dekimasu ka. *When will it be ready?*
Mada dekimasen. *I'm not finished yet.*

DERU でる／出る　come out, appear, attend a meeting, be revealed
Sono pātī niwa detakunai. *I don't want to attend that party.*
Chikatetsu o deru to, yuki ga futte ita. *When we came out of the subway, it was snowing.*

ENRYO SURU えんりょする／遠慮する　stand on ceremony, be reserved, defer to others
Otabako wa goenryo kudasai. *Please refrain from smoking.*
Dōzo goenryo nasaranai de kudasai. *We want you to feel at home.*

ERABU えらぶ／選ぶ　select, choose, elect
Umi no chikaku no hoteru o eranda. *We chose a hotel near the sea.*
Kaitai mono ga takusan atte, erabu no ni komatta. *Since there were so many things I wanted to buy, I had a hard time choosing.*

ERU える／得る　get, obtain, be able to, secure
Shushō wa kokumin no shinyō o eta. *The prime minister got the confidence of the people.*
Karera kara yakudatsu jōhō wa erarenakatta. *We couldn't get any useful information.*

FUERU ふえる／増える　increase, proliferate, multiply
Saikin hanzai ga fuete iru no niwa taerarenai. *The recent increase in crime is intolerable.*
Kare wa taijū ga fuete imasu ka. *Is he gaining weight?*

FUKU ふく／吹く　blow, exhale, talk big
Tsuyoi kita kaze ga fuite iru. *A strong north wind is blowing.*
Junko wa bāsudēkēki no rōsoku o fuki keshita. *Junko blew out the candles on her birthday cake.*

FUKUMU ふくむ／含む　contain, include, hold in one's mouth, imply
Kono kanjō wa sābisu ryō o fukunde iru. *The check includes a service charge.*
Sanka sha wa watakushi o fukumete zenbu de go nin da. *The participants are five people altogether, including me.*

FURERU　ふれる／触れる　touch, mention, infringe
Koko de no kitsuen wa hōritsu ni fureru. *Smoking here is against the law.*
Sono supīchi wa bimyō na mondai ni fureta. *The speech touched on a delicate subject.*

FURIKAERU　ふりかえる／振り返る　look back, look upon the past
Kyūyū to tomo ni kako o furikaeru no wa tanoshii. *It's fun to look back at the past with old friends.*
Kare wa ichi do mo furikaerazu ni tachisatta. *He left without looking back even once.*

FURU　ふる／振る　wave, shake, swing, nod
Mishiranu hito ni te o furanai yō ni. *Please don't wave at strangers.*
Fan wa kokki o futte Nihon chīmu o miokutta. *Fans sent the Japanese team off waving national flags.*

FURU　ふる／降る　fall from the sky, rain
Ame ga futtemo ii yō ni kasa o motte ikinasai. *Please take an umbrella in case it rains.*
Ame ga futtemo yuki ga futtemo gēmu wa tsuzuku. *The game will go on even if it rains or snows.*

FURUERU　ふるえる／震える　tremble, shake, shiver, vibrate
Pūru kara deru jikan da. Kodomo tachi ga furuete iru. *Time to get out of the pool; the kids are shivering.*
Satō san wa ikari de koe ga furueta. *Mr. Sato's voice shook with anger.*

FURUU　ふるう／振るう　flourish, exercise, be in high spirits
Kare wa kokusai kyōgi dewa furuwanakatta. *He didn't do well in the international competition.*
Kono kaisha de kenryoku o furutte iru no wa shachō no musuko da. *In this company, the one who wields the power is not the president, but his son.*

FUSEGU　ふせぐ／防ぐ　prevent, defend against, protect from
Undō sureba byōki ga fusegeru. *Exercise can protect you from some diseases.*
Tadashii yarikata de ha o migakeba mushiba ga fusegeru. *Proper brushing can prevent tooth decay.*

FUTORU　ふとる／太る　become heavy, put on weight
Futotte shimatte, karada ni au kimono ga nai. *I've put on weight and nothing fits right.*
Kare wa futoranai yō ni undō shita. *He exercised to keep from gaining weight.*

GAMAN SURU　がまんする／我慢する　endure, restrain oneself, tolerate
Gaman suru nimo gendo ga aru. *There's a limit to tolerance.*
Kanojo wa gaman dekizu ni nakidashita. *She couldn't control herself and started to cry.*

GANBARU がんばる／頑張る　persist, stand firm, insist on, exert oneself
Ganbare. *Keep going. Hang in there. Keep it up.*
Karera wa totemo isogashii no ni yoku ganbatte iru. *They're exerting themselves hard when they're extremely busy.*

GOMAKASU ごまかす／誤摩化す　cheat, embezzle, evade, impose upon
Kanojo niwa gomakasarenai. *I won't be cheated by her.*
Kare wa kaisha no okane o gomakashite tsukamatta. *He embezzled company money and was arrested.*

HAERU はえる／生える　grow, sprout
Utsukushii no no hana ga ichimen ni haeteita. *Beautiful wildflowers were growing everywhere.*
Akachan no ha ga haehajimeta. *The baby started teething.*

HAGEMASU はげます／励ます　encourage, urge on, cheer up
Byōki no tomodachi o hagemashita. *We cheered up our sick friend.*
Otagai o hagemashiatte yama o nobori tsuzuketa. *We urged each other on and kept climbing the mountain.*

HAGEMU はげむ／励む　strive for, devote oneself to a task
Benkyō ni hagende ii seiseki o totta. *I studied hard and got good grades.*
Kanojo wa piano no okeiko ni hagende iru. *She's devoting herself to practicing piano.*

HAIRU はいる／入る　enter, join, contain, hold
Kono hako niwa chokorēto ga haitte iru. *This box contains chocolate.*
Eiga kan wa kondeite hairenakatta. *The movie theater was crowded, and we couldn't get in.*

HAJIMARU はじまる／始まる　begin, be opened, originate
Kotoshi wa tsuyu ga hajimaru no ga osoi. *This year, the start of the rainy season is late.*
Senkyo undō ga hajimatta. *The election campaign has begun.*

HAJIMERU はじめる／始める　begin something, start
Ima sugu ni hajimereba ma ni au darō. *If you start right now, you'll make it.*
Sā, hajimeyō. *Let's begin.*

HAKARU はかる／計る／測る／量る　measure, calculate, estimate
Watakushi no kutsu no saizu o hakatte kudasai. *Please measure my shoe size.*
Kanojo no ito o hakaru koto ga dekinakatta. *I couldn't figure out her intentions.*

HAKOBU はこぶ／運ぶ　carry, go well, transport
Takushī no untenshu ga sūtsukēsu o hakonde kureta. *The cab driver carried the suitcase for me.*
Keikaku wa umaku hakobanakatta. *The plan didn't go well.*

HAKU はく／履く put on one's feet or legs
Haihīru o hakanakutemo ii. *It's okay if you don't wear high heels.*
Atsui node shōtsu o haita. *It was hot, so I put some shorts on.*

HANASU はなす／話す speak, talk, tell, state
Mō ichi do hanashite kudasai. *Repeat it please.*
Yukkuri hanashite kudasai. *Please speak slowly.*

HANTAI SURU はんたいする／反対する oppose, object to, stand against
Anata no iken ni hantai suru tsumori wa nai. *I have no intention of opposing your opinion.*
Kazoku wa watakushi no kekkon ni hantai shita. *My family objected to my marriage.*

HARAU はらう／払う pay
Kanjō wa genkin de haratta. *I paid the bill with cash.*
Kurejittokādo de haraemasu ka. *Can I pay with a credit card?*

HARERU はれる／晴れる clear up, disperse, be dispelled
Ashita wa hareru darō. *It'll clear up tomorrow.*
Kanojo e no utagai ga harenai. *My suspicions about her haven't cleared up.*

HARU はる／張る stretch, spread, pitch
Kawa no soba ni tento o hatta. *We pitched a tent near the river.*
Keikan wa jiko genba ni rōpu o hatta. *The police officers put ropes up at the accident site.*

HARU はる／貼る paste on, put up, stick on
Oshirase o iriguchi ni hatte kudasai. *Please put the announcement up at the entrance.*
Shashin o arubamu ni hatta. *I put some pictures in the photo album.*

HASHIRU はしる／走る run, rush, be carried away
Kono basu wa Tōkyō eki made hashitte iru. *This bus runs to Tokyo Station.*
Kare wa kakegoto ni hashitta. *He got carried away with gambling.*

HATARAKU はたらく／働く work, serve, function
Chichi wa seifu de hataraite iru. *My father works for the government.*
Ikura hataraitemo okane ga tamaranai. *No matter how much I work, I can't save any money.*

HAYARU はやる／流行る be in fashion, be popular, flourish, prosper, prevail
Kono uta wa hayaru darō. *This song will become popular.*
Ima ryūkan ga hayatte iru. *The flu is going around now.*

HERASU　へらす／減らす　decrease, reduce, cut down, curtail
Amai mono wa taberu no o herasshita hō ga ii. *You'd better cut down on sweets.*
Dō shitara shuppi o herasemasu ka. *How can we reduce our expenses?*

HERU　へる／減る　decrease, diminish, run low
Chosuichi no mizu ga hette iru. *The reservoir is running low.*
Tomu no shisan ga saikin herihajimeta. *Tom's assets began to decrease recently.*

HIKAKU SURU　ひかくする／比較する　compare, contrast
Kabushiki shijō wa, kyonen ni hikaku shite kōchō da. *Compared to last year, the market is doing well.*
Sakkā to futtobōru wa hikaku dekinai. *You can't compare soccer and football.*

HIKIUKERU　ひきうける／引き受ける　guarantee, undertake, take charge of, take on a job
Hideo wa muzukashii shigoto o hikiuketa. *Hideo undertook a difficult job.*
Tanaka san wa musuko no shakkin no hensai o hikiuketa. *Mr. Tanaka guaranteed he'd repay his son's debt.*

HIKU　ひく／引く／惹く　pull, drag, attract, subtract, draw, look up a word
Shūmatsu wa niwa no zassō o hikinuku. *I'll do some weeding this weekend.*
Sakanaya ga nedan o hiite kureta. *They gave me a discount at the fishmarket.*

HIRAKERU　ひらける／開ける　develop, become civilized, be opened to traffic
Toshiko wa kokoro ga hirakete iru. *Toshiko is open-minded.*
Doryoku sureba michi ga hirakeru. *If you try hard, anything is possible.*

HIRAKU　ひらく／開く　open, lift, uncover, start up, develop
Kinjo ni atarashiku subarashii resutoran ga hiraita. *A great new restaurant opened in our neighborhood.*
Sakura no hana ga hirakisō da. *The cherry blossoms are about to open.*

HIROGARU　ひろがる／広がる　spread out, extend, reach
Intānetto de uwasa ga kyūsoku ni hirogaru koto ga kanō da. *Rumors can spread quickly on the Internet.*
Kono resutoran no hyōban ga zenkoku ni hirogatte iru. *The reputation of this restaurant is spreading nationwide.*

HIROGERU　ひろげる／広げる　spread something out, widen, unfold
Eriko wa sunahama ni taoru o hirogeta. *Eriko spread a towel on the sand.*
Kanojo wa sensu o hirogeta. *She opened her fan.*

HIYASU　ひやす／冷やす　cool, chill, keep on ice
Suika o kawa de hiyashita. *We chilled a watermelon in the stream.*
Sūzan wa nenza shita ashikubi o hyōnō de hiyashita. *Susan put an ice pack on her sprained ankle.*

HOMERU ほめる／誉める praise, compliment, speak highly of
Kanojo wa anata o homete imasu. *She speaks highly of you.*
Dono hyōron ka mo kono eiga o homete iru. *All the critics are praising this movie.*

HORU ほる／掘る dig, burrow, excavate
Karera wa kyōryū no kaseki o hotte iru. *They're excavating dinosaur fossils.*
Inu ga niwa ni ana o hotta. *The dog dug a hole in my garden.*

HOSU ほす／干す dry up, drain off, empty, air
Futon o hosetara ii'n da kedo. *I wish we could air out the futon.*
Shimizu san no okusan wa sentakumono o soto de hosu. *Mrs. Shimizu dries her laundry outside.*

IJIMERU いじめる bully, tease, annoy, pick on, be mean to, mistreat
Kesshite dōbutsu o ijimenai yō ni. *Never mistreat an animal.*
Musuko wa gakkō de ijimerarete iru kamo shirenai. *Maybe my son is being bullied at school.*

IKIRU いきる／生きる live, be alive, revive
Ikite iru ebi wa dame desu. *No live shrimp, thank you.*
Hiiki no senshu ga tōnamento no jun kesshō made ikinokotta. *My favorite player survived and reached the semifinals of the tournament.*

IKU/YUKU いく／ゆく／行く
Ima sugu ikō. *Let's leave right now.*
Raishū kazoku ni ai ni ikitai. *I want to visit my family next week.*

IRASSHARU いらっしゃる come, go, be
Tanaka san wa irasshaimasu ka. *Is Mr. Tanaka there, please?*
Irasshai. Dōzo ohairi kudasai. *Welcome. Please come in.*

IRERU いれる／入れる insert, put in, add to, accommodate, admit
Kuruma ni go sen en bun no gasorin o ireta. *I put in five thousand yen worth of gas.*
Haha e no purezento o hako ni ireta. *We put the gift for mother in a box.*

IRU いる／居る be, live, remain, exist
Jirō wa ima imasen. *Jiro isn't here now.*
Minna ōrusutā gēmu o mite iru. *Everyone is watching the all-star game.*

IRU いる／要る need, require, want
Henji wa iranai. *You don't need to reply.*
Iru mono wa zenbu aru. *I have everything I need.*

ISOGU いそぐ／急ぐ   hurry, hasten
Isogō. *Let's get going.*
Jikan o kakete, isogazu ni. *Take your time. No hurry.*

ITADAKU いただく／頂く   I (or a person in my group) receive, accept, eat, drink
Jūbun itadakimashita. *I have had enough, thanks.*
Mizu o itadakemasu ka. *May I have some water, please?*

ITAMU いたむ／痛む／傷む   be sore, be damaged, feel pain, be soiled
Jishin de michi ga itande ita. *The road was damaged by the earthquake.*
Furu kizu ga ima demo tokidoki itamu. *Even now, my old wound hurts sometimes.*

ITARU いたる／至る   go, reach, arrive at, lead to, get to
Kare wa mokuteki o tassuru ni itaranakatta. *He didn't get to achieve his goal.*
Gēmu wa saigo no dankai ni itatte omoshiroku natta. *Toward the end, the game became interesting.*

IU いう／言う   say, speak, talk, state, tell, be called
Nani ga okotta no ka itte moraitai. *Tell me what happened.*
Sore wa Nihongo de nan to iimasu ka. *How do you say that in Japanese?*

KAERU かえる／変える／替える／換える／代える   change, exchange, replace, substitute
Kono purezento o ōkii saizu ni kaeraremasu ka. *May I exchange this gift for a larger size?*
Koko de doru o en ni kaete moraemasu ka. *Can you change dollars for yen here?*

KAERU かえる／帰る   return home, return
Okaerinasai. *Welcome home!*
Mō kaerō. *Let's go home.*

KAESU かえす／返す   give back, repay, return, send back
Ichigatsu ni shakkin o kaesanakereba naranai. *We have to repay the loan in January.*
Junko wa toshokan ni hon o kaesu no o wasureta. *Junko forgot to return the books to the library.*

KAGIRU かぎる／限る   limit, restrict
Koko no menyū wa totemo kagirarete iru. *The menu is quite limited.*
Kono eiga wa seijin ni kagirareteiru. *This film is restricted to adults only.*

KAKAERU かかえる／抱える   keep, hold in one's arm
Jeremī wa mondai o takusan kakaete iru. *Jeremy has a lot of problems.*
Kare wa kakaekirenai hodo no shakkin ga aru. *He's up to his ears in debt.*

KAKARU かかる／掛かる   be hanging, begin, require, depend on
Ii haiburiddokā o kau no ni dono kurai kakarimasu ka. *How much does it cost to buy a good hybrid car?*
Subete ga Satō san no ude ni kakatte iru. *Everything is depending on Mr. Sato's ability.*

KAKARU かかる／罹る   be taken ill, catch a disease
Kyonen no fuyu, watakushi tachi wa futari tomo ryūkan ni kakatte shimatta. *We both got the flu last winter.*
Sachiko wa byōki ni kakatta koto ga nai. *Sachiko has never become ill.*

KAKERU かける／掛ける   hang something, spend, sit down, place on top of
Dōzo okake kudasai. *Please have a seat.*
Karera wa Karibukai no kurūzu ni sugoku okane o kaketa. *They spent a lot on their Caribbean cruise.*

KAKERU かける／賭ける   risk, bet, wager
Keiba ni kakeru no ga suki desu ka. *Do you like to bet on horse races?*
Inochi o kakete chikau. *I swear on my life!*

KAKU かく／書く   write, draw up, compose
Karera wa wareware ni dasu teiansho o kaite iru. *They're writing a proposal to give us.*
Henji wa īmēru de kakimasu. *I'll compose an e-mail response.*

KAMAU かまう／構う   mind, care about, be concerned about, notice, care for, entertain
Kamaimasen. *I don't mind.*
Kare wa fukusō ni kamawanai. *He doesn't pay much attention to his clothes.*

KANGAERU かんがえる／考える   think, consider, believe, judge, suppose
Ima wa sono koto o kangaeru koto ga dekinai. *I can't think about that now.*
Tenshoku o kangaete mita koto ga arimasu ka. *Have you considered changing jobs?*

KANJIRU かんじる／感じる   feel, sense
Nanika ii koto ga okoru no o kanjiru. *I sense that something nice will happen.*
Kazuko wa koronda keredo itami o zenzen kanjinakatta. *Although Kazuko fell down, she didn't feel any pain at all.*

KARIRU かりる／借りる   borrow, lease, hire, lend
Ashita kuruma o karitemo ii desu ka. *May I borrow your car tomorrow?*
Kono natsu wa kaigan de ie o karite iru. *We're renting a house at the beach this summer.*

KASANARU　かさなる／重なる　overlap, be piled up
Kon shūmatsu wa kekkon shiki to sotsugyō shiki ga kasanatte iru. *I have a wedding and a graduation to attend this weekend.*
Tanaka san no desuku no ue niwa shorui ga tsumi kasanatte iru. *Files are piling up on Mr. Tanaka's desk.*

KASANERU　かさねる／重ねる　pile things up, repeat
Kasanete onegai itashimasu. *I'd like to ask you a favor again.*
Samui node tīshatsu ni sētā o kasanete kita. *Because it's cold, I put a sweater on over a tee shirt.*

KASU　かす／貸す　lend, rent, lease, help
Kodomo no inai fūfu ni ie o kashitai. *I want to rent my house to a couple with no children.*
Chotto pen o kashite moraemasu ka. *Could you let me use your pen for a moment?*

KATAMARU　かたまる／固まる　become hard, set, assemble, cake
Kare wa mada kangae ga katamatte inai. *His ideas haven't taken shape yet.*
Ikeda san wa tenshoku no ketsui ga katamatta. *Ms. Ikeda's decision to switch her job has become firm.*

KATAMERU　かためる／固める　strengthen, solidify
Kanojo wa seiji kiban o katameta. *She solidified her political base.*
Jakku wa rainen Nihon ni iku ketsui o katameta. *Jack decided to go to Japan next year.*

KATAZUKERU　かたづける／片付ける　put in order, tidy up, settle a problem
Heya o katazukenasai. *Tidy up your room.*
Sore wa ima kata o tsukeyō. *Let's settle this now.*

KATSU　かつ／勝つ　gain a victory, overcome, win, surpass, defeat
Marināzu ga Reddosokkusu ni katta. *The Mariners beat the Red Sox.*
Yamada san wa tōtō byōki ni katta. *Mr. Yamada finally got well.*

KAU　かう／買う　buy, provoke, have a high opinion of
Kare wa kanojo o takaku katte iru. *He has a high opinion of her.*
Kodomo ni poppukōn o katte ageyō. *Let's buy the kids some popcorn.*

KAWARU　かわる／変わる　change, be altered, turn into, be different
Kono kinjo ga donna ni kawatta ka shinjirarenai. *I can't believe how much this neighborhood has changed.*
Kare wa kekkon shite irai sukkari kawatta. *Since he got married, he's like a different person.*

KESU けす／消す　turn off, switch off, extinguish, erase
Yūbe wa denki o kesazu ni nemutte shimatta. *Last night I fell asleep without turning the light off.*
Kaji o kesu no ni ichi jikan kakatta. *It took one hour to extinguish the fire.*

KIERU きえる／消える　go out, die, melt away, vanish
Yama kaji ga nakanaka kienakatta. *The wildfire didn't die down easily.*
Haru ga kite yama no yuki ga kieta. *When spring arrived, the snow on the mountain melted away.*

KIKOERU きこえる／聞こえる　can hear, be audible
Yoku kikoeru yō ni boryūmu o agete kudasai. *Please turn up the volume so I can hear better.*
Kaminari ga kikoetara tatemono no naka ni haitta hō ga ii. *If you can hear the thunder, you'd better go inside.*

KIKU きく／聞く　ask, hear, listen
Watakushi no jogen o kikinasai. *Please take my advice.*
Ii nyūsu ga arunda kedo kikimashita ka. *Have you heard the good news?*

KIMERU きめる／決める　decide, settle, choose, make up one's mind
Sukejūru o kimeyō. *Let's decide on a schedule.*
Resutoran wa kimemashita ka. *Have you chosen a restaurant yet?*

KIRU きる／切る　cut, slice, turn off
Gekijō dewa keitai denwa o kitte kudasai. *Please turn off your cellphone in the theater.*
Raiu no aida wa konpyūta no suitchi o kitte kōdo o nuite oku. *I turn off and unplug the computer during a thunderstorm.*

KIRU きる／着る　wear (on the upper body), put on
Minna pātī niwa nani o kite ikundeshō. *What is everyone wearing to the party?*
Intabyū ni kite iku mono o kimeru no o tetsudatte kudasai. *Help me decide what to wear for the interview.*

KOMARU こまる／困る　be in trouble, have a hard time, be perplexed
Takushī ga mitsukaranai to komaru. *We'll be in trouble if we can't find a taxi.*
Sasaki san wa tomaru basho ga mitsukaranakute komatta. *Mr. Sasaki was in trouble because he couldn't find a place to stay.*

KOMU こむ／混む　be crowded, be congested
Kyūjitsu dakara mise ga komu darō. *The stores will be crowded because of the holiday.*
Konzatsu o sakete osome no dinā ni shimashō. *Let's have a late dinner and avoid the crowd.*

KOTOWARU ことわる／断る　refuse, reject, decline

Isogashii keredo shōtai o kotowarenakatta. *Although we were busy, we couldn't decline the invitation.*

Kare wa kanojo o dinā ni sasotta keredo, kotowararete shimatta. *He asked her to dinner but was refused.*

KUDASARU くださる／下さる　bestow upon, have the kindness to …, please

Wagaya no shinnen no pātī ni zehi irashite kudasai. *Please come to our New Year's party.*

Tetsudatte kudasai masen ka. *Could you please help us with this?*

KURABERU くらべる／比べる　compare, contrast

Betsumono dakara kuraberu beki dewa nai. *Don't compare apples and oranges.*

Kuraberu made mo naku akiraka da. *There's no comparison between the two.*

KURU くる／来る　come, reach, approach

Kayōbi no dinā ni kuru koto ga dekimasu ka. *Can you come to dinner on Tuesday?*

Kyonen wa taifū ga Nihon ni takusan kita. *Many typhoons came to Japan last year.*

MACHIGAU まちがう／間違う　be wrong, be mistaken, be incorrect

Sumimasen. Bangō o machigatte shimaimashita. *Sorry. I must have dialed the wrong number.*

Keisan ga machigatte imasu. *Your figures are incorrect.*

MAIRU まいる／参る　go, come, be defeated, be exhausted

Mieko wa isogashikute maitte shimatta. *Mieko was so busy that she became exhausted.*

Nan ji ni maireba yoroshii deshō ka. *What time may I come?*

MAKASERU まかせる／任せる　leave a matter to someone, leave a matter in someone's hands

Kodomo no kyōiku wa tsuma ni makaseru. *I leave our kids' education to my wife.*

Kanojo ni makasete okinasai. Chanto yatte kureru kara. *Leave it to her. She'll handle it.*

MAKERU まける／負ける　be defeated, lose a game, yield, cut the price

Kono shiai niwa makerarenai. *We can't lose this game!*

Nikuya wa itsumo makete kureru. *The butcher always gives me a discount.*

MAMORU まもる／護る／守る　protect, defend, guard, adhere to principles

Kare wa itta koto o kanarazu mamoru. *He always keeps his word.*

Chikagoro wa oya ga kodomo o mamoru no wa yōi dewa nai. *Protecting their children can be hard for parents these days.*

MATSU　まつ／待つ　wait
>Karera wa Nihon e no ryokō o machi ni matte iru. *They're eagerly awaiting their trip to Japan.*
>Machi kutabireta. *I'm tired of waiting.*

MAYOU　まよう／迷う　be at a loss, be bewildered, hesitate, get lost
>Tōkyō dewa michi ni mayoi yasui. *It's easy to get lost in Tokyo.*
>Mayowazu ni Nihon ni iku koto ni kimeta. *Without any hesitating, I decided to go to Japan.*

MEDATSU　めだつ／目立つ　be conspicuous, be prominent, attract attention
>Kare wa koe ga ōkii node medatsu. *He attracts attention because he's so loud.*
>Medatanai yō ni shiyō. *Let's try not to be conspicuous.*

MIKOMU　みこむ／見込む　expect, count on, have confidence in
>Ame o mikonde hayaku kaetta. *We went back home early because we expected rain.*
>Kaigi niwa san jū nin sanka o mikonde iru. *We're expecting 30 people to participate in the meeting.*

MINAOSU　みなおす／見直す　take another look at, reconsider, discover new merits
>Seifu wa gaikō seisaku o minaoshite iru. *The government is reviewing foreign policy.*
>Takusan no kaisha ga shūshin koyō seido o minaoshite iru. *Many companies are taking another look at life-long employment.*

MIRU　みる／見る　see, look at, read, observe
>Yūbe ōrusutā sen o mita. *We watched the all-star game last night.*
>Shinbun, zasshi de mita mono o subete shinjinai yō ni. *Don't believe everything you read in the press.*

MISERU　みせる／見せる　show, display, exhibit
>Katta mono o misete kudasai. *Please show me what you bought.*
>Kare wa shashin o ima Ginza no garō de misete iru. *He's exhibiting his photos at an art gallery in Ginza now.*

MITOMERU　みとめる／認める　recognize, acknowledge, admit, consider as
>Ano renchū wa jibun no hi o kesshite mitomenai. *Those folks never admit their mistakes.*
>Daremo ga kanojo no sainō o mitomete iru. *Everyone recognizes her talent.*

MITSUKARU　みつかる／見つかる　be found, be discovered, be detected
>Ikura sagashitemo mitsukaranakatta. *No matter how hard I looked, I couldn't find it.*
>Kare wa uso ga mitsukatte shimatta. *He was caught in a lie.*

MOERU もえる／燃える   burn, blaze
Furui otera ga moete shimatta. *Unfortunately the old temple burned down.*
Kono maki wa yoku moenai. *These logs don't burn well.*

MŌKARU もうかる／儲かる   gain, make a profit, be profitable
Ano mise wa totemo mōkatte iru. *That shop is quite profitable.*
Mōkaranai kabu o shobun shita. *I sold some unprofitable stocks.*

MORAU もらう／貰う   receive, get, be given, have someone do something
Sore o moraemasu ka. *May I have that?*
Ano sakka wa Nōberu bungaku shō o moratta. *That novelist received the Nobel prize for literature.*
Esu saizu no o moraimasu. *I'll take the one in size S.*

MOTOMERU もとめる／求める   call for, demand, ask for, look for
Mibun shōmei sho no teishutsu o motomerareta. *I was asked to submit an ID.*
Shain wa fuyu no bōnasu o motomete iru. *The company employees are demanding year-end bonuses.*
Ryōshin no iken o motometa. *I asked for my parents' advice.*

MOTSU もつ／持つ   have, take, hold, be durable, carry, bear expense
Chiisai osatsu o motte imasu ka. *Do you have any small bills with you?*
Kare wa kuruma o san dai motte iru. *He owns three cars.*

MUKAERU むかえる／迎える
Tomodachi ga kazoku zen-in de mukaete kureta. *My friend and his entire family welcomed us.*
Kare o mukae ni kūkō made itte moraemasu ka. *Will you go to the airport to meet him?*

MUKAU むかう／向かう   face, turn toward, head for
Taifū wa Kyūshū ni mukatte iru. *The typhoon is heading toward Kyushu.*
Sore wa yūbin kyoku ni mukatte hidari gawa ni arimasu *It's on the left as you face the post office.*

NAGARERU ながれる／流れる   flow, float, drift, be fortified
Nagarete shimawanai yō ni bōto o tsunage. *Secure the dinghy or it will drift away.*
Gēmu wa ame de nagareta. *The game was rained out.*

NAGERU なげる／投げる   throw, pitch, abandon, give up
Pitchā wa san kai tsuzukete sutoraiku o nageta. *The pitcher threw three consecutive strike balls.*
Kantan ni nageru na. *Don't give up so easily.*

NAGUSAMERU   なぐさめる／慰める   comfort, console, soothe
Karera wa kodomo o nagusameru koto ga dekinakatta. *They couldn't console the child.*
Kanojo o nagusamete mimasu. *I'll try to cheer her up.*

NAKU   なく／泣く   cry, weep, moan
Kono akachan wa hotondo naita koto ga nai. *This baby hardly ever cries.*
Karera wa sōshiki de naki ni naita. *They cried a lot at the funeral.*

NAKUNARU   なくなる／無くなる／亡くなる   be missing, disappear, run out of, pass away (polite for die)
Kanojo no nenpai no ojisan ga nakunatta. *Her elderly uncle passed away.*
Taisetsu na shorui ga nakunatta. *The important files are missing.*

NAORU   なおる／直る／治る   be mended, be repaired, get well, recover
Hason shita dōro o naoshite iru. *The damaged roads are being repaired.*
Mori san wa byōki ga naoru made ni shūkan nyūin shita. *Ms. Mori was hospitalized for two weeks before she got well.*

NAOSU   なおす／直す／治す   fix, mend, repair, revise, cure
Karera ga kanojo no byōki o naoseru to omoimasu ka. *Do you think they can cure her illness?*
Kutsu no kakato o naoshite moratta. *I got the heels of my shoes fixed.*

NARABU   ならぶ／並ぶ   line up, rank with, stand in a row
Yashi no ki ga narande iru no ga utsukushii. *The rows of palm trees are lovely.*
Fan wa ken o kau no ni gozen rei ji ni narabi hajimeta. *The fans started lining up for tickets at midnight.*

NARERU   なれる／慣れる   get used to, become tame, become familiar with
Kinjo no henka ni nareru koto ga dekinai. *I'm not used to the changes in the neighborhood.*
Edo wa yatto konpyūta ni nareta. *Ed finally got familiar with computers.*

NARU   なる   become, change into, get to be, turn out, result in
Kanojo wa tsui ni isha ni natta. *She finally became a doctor.*
Otenki ga yoku natta. *The weather turned out to be good.*

NEGAU   ねがう／願う   desire, hope, wish, request, pray for
Onegai shitai koto ga aru no desu ga. *May I ask you to do a favor for me?*
Okanjō o onegai shimasu. *Please bring the check.*

NERU   ねる／寝る   lie down, go to bed, go to sleep
Mērī wa ryūkan de nete imasu. *Mary is in bed with the flu.*
Kōhī o nomi sugiru to nerarenai. *Too much coffee keeps me awake.*

NIAU にあう／似合う suit, go with, befit, match well
Yakusoku no jikan ni okureru nante kare ni niawanai. *Being late for an appointment isn't like him.*
Sono fukusō ga Michiko ni totemo yoku niau. *Michiko looks really good in that outfit.*

NIRU にる／似る resemble, be similar
Kono kyōdai wa zenzen nite inai. *The two brothers are not at all alike.*
Karera no kuse wa nite iru. *Their habits are similar.*

NOBERU のべる／述べる express, tell, relate, state, mention
Goshinsetsu ni kansha no kimochi o nobesasete itadakimasu. *I'd like to express my gratitude for all your kindness.*
Nani ga osuki ka onobe kudasai. *Tell us what you'd like, please.*

NOBORU のぼる／登る／上る／昇る climb, ascend, go up, amount to
Fujisan ni nobotta koto ga arimasu ka. *Have you ever climbed Mt. Fuji?*
Kono kaidan wa kyū de otoshiyori ga noboru no wa muzukashii. *With these stairs so steep, it's difficult for the elderly to climb.*

NOKORU のこる／残る remain, stay behind, be left over
Sakura no hana ga mada sukoshi nokotte saite iru. *There are still a few cherry blossoms left.*
Ohiru gohan wa nokori mono de ii desu ka. *Do you mind having leftovers for lunch?*

NORU のる／乗る／載る ride on, board, be reported in the print media
Kuruma no nottori jiken ga shinbun ni notta. *The carjacking incident was reported in the paper.*
Jakku wa jitensha ni notte shokuryō hin no kaimono ni itta. *Jack went for grocery shopping on his bicycle.*

NOZOMU のぞむ／望む desire, wish, aspire to, hope for
Kanojo wa musuko ga bengoshi ni naru koto o nozonde imasu. *She wishes that her son would become a lawyer.*
Kare wa san nen inai ni kekkon shitai to nozonde imasu. *He hopes to get married within three years.*

OBOERU おぼえる／覚える remember, know, memorize, learn
Mainichi tango o ikuraka oboeru yō ni shinasai. *Try learning a few words each day.*
Oboete imasu ka. *Do you remember?*

OCHIRU おちる／落ちる fall, drop, come down, be omitted, fail, be inferior to
Kare wa nyūshi ni ochita. *He failed the school entrance exam.*
Maiku no namae ga risuto kara ochite ita. *Mike's name was inadvertently omitted from the list.*

ODOROKU おどろく／驚く　be surprised, be shocked, be frightened, be amazed
Kanojo no sainō niwa odoroku. *I'm amazed at her talent.*
Odorokanai de kudasai. *Please don't be shocked.*

OKIRU おきる／起きる　get up, wake up, happen, occur
Watakushi wa itsumo okiru no ga hayai desu. *I always wake up early.*
Kinō fushigi na koto ga okimashita. *A strange thing happened yesterday.*

OKORU おこる／怒る　get angry, lose one's temper
Kare wa okotte kao ga akaku natta. *He was so angry his face became red.*
Kanojo wa saikin okori yasui. *She loses her temper easily these days.*

OKORU おこる／起こる　happen, occur
Saikin wa jishin ga yoku okotte iru. *Earthquakes have been occuring often recently.*
Kesa kono kōsaten de ōkii kōtsū jiko ga okotta. *There was a serious traffic accident at this intersection this morning.*

OKU おく／置く　put, place, keep, leave
Soko ni oite kudasai. *Put it down there, please.*
Kanojo wa akachan o nekasete oita. *She let her baby sleep.*

OKURERU おくれる／遅れる　be late for, be delayed, be slow (a clock)
Hikōki no shuppatsu ga okurete iru. *My flight has been delayed.*
Jugyō ni okurenai yō ni. *Don't be late for class.*

OMOU おもう／思う　think, believe
Hitomebore to iu no wa arieru to omoimasu ka. *Do you believe in love at first sight?*
Kare ga daigaku no kyōju ni narō to wa omottemo inakatta. *We never thought he would become a college professor.*

OSHIERU おしえる／教える　teach, inform, show, point out, tell, explain
Yorokonde otetsudai shimasu. Nani o subeki ka oshiete kudasai. *I'll be glad to help. Just show me what to do.*
Tejun o oshiete moraemasu ka. *Can you explain the procedure to us, please?*

OWARU おわる／終わる　end, be over, close, be finished, be completed, result in
Shigoto ga owattara, mata aimashō. *Let's meet again when the job is finished.*
Kono hideri ga itsu owaru ka wakaranai. *We don't know when this drought will be over.*

RIKAI SURU りかいする／理解する　understand, comprehend, grasp, make out
Kanojo wa watakushi tachi no shinpai o rikai shite iru to omoimasu ka. *Do you think she understands our concerns?*
Anata no yōten ga rikai dekinai. *I don't quite get your point.*

SAGASU さがす／探す look for, hunt, seek, trace
Doko o sagashitemo sangurasu wa mitsukaranakatta. *I've looked everywhere, but I couldn't find my sunglasses.*
Kare wa yūnō na bengoshi o sagashite imasu. *He's looking for a good lawyer.*

SHABERU しゃべる／喋る talk, chatter, divulge
Kare wa shaberi sugiru. *He talks too much.*
Dare nimo shaberanai de kudasai. *Please keep this to yourself.*

SHIKARU しかる／叱る scold, chide, reprimand
Kare no okāsan wa kare ga ie mawari no shigoto o shinai node shikatta. *His mother scolded him for not doing his chores.*
Kanojo wa shigoto ni okurete, yoku shikararete iru. *She's often reprimanded for being late to work.*

SHIMARU しまる／閉まる shut, close, be shut, be fastened, be thrifty
Yūbin kyoku wa nan ji ni shimarimasu ka. *What time does the post office close?*
Ginkō wa kokumin no shukujitsu de shimatte iru. *Banks are closed for a national holiday.*

SHIMESU しめす／示す show, point out, tell
Ondo kei wa gaiki ga kashi kyūjū do o shimeshite iru. *The thermostat says it's 90 degrees Fahrenheit outside.*
Nenryō kei ga mantan o shimeshite iru. *The gas gauge shows we have a full tank.*

SHINJIRU しんじる／信じる believe, accept, believe in, trust
Watakushi wa ryōshin no handan o shinjiru. *I trust my parents' judgment.*
Kanojo wa kare ga iu koto o issai shinjinai. *She can't believe anything he says.*

SHINU しぬ／死ぬ die, pass away
Kare wa nagai byōki no ato shinda. *He passed away after a long illness.*
Jidōsha jiko de yonin ga shinda. *Four people died in the auto accident.*

SHIRABERU しらべる／調べる investigate, examine, inquire into, search, interrogate
Ima, keisatsu wa yogi sha o torishirabete iru. *The police are interrogating the suspects right now.*
Intānetto de shirabeta. *I did some research on the Internet.*

SHIRASERU しらせる／知らせる inform, notify, tell, report
Kensa no kekka wa itsu shirasete moraemasu ka. *When will you inform me of the test results?*
Kaigi no ato, kekka o shirasemasu. *I'll report back to you after the meeting.*

SHIRU しる／知る know, learn, find out, realize, become acquainted with
Ano hito wa shirimasen. *I don't know him.*
Dō yatte sono koto o shitta no desu ka. *How did you find out about that?*

SUGIRU すぎる／過ぎる   pass by, run past, exceed, go too far, expire
Bakansu, atto iu ma ni sugite shimatta ne. *Our vacation went by quickly, didn't it?*
Kore wa nanajussai sugi no hito no tame ni totte aru seki desu. *These seats are reserved for people over 70.*

SUGOSU すごす／過ごす   spend time, pass time, go too far
Tomu wa aite iru jikan wa zenbu bideo gēmu o shite sugosu. *Tom spends all his free time playing video games.*
Jon wa sen gakki Nihon no daigaku de sugoshita. *John spent the last semester at a university in Japan.*

SUMU すむ／住む   live, dwell, reside, inhabit
Karera wa kawa no soba no manshon ni sunde iru. *They live in a condo near the river.*
Kare wa Nihon de ni nen sumitai. *He wants to live in Japan for two years.*

SUMU すむ／済む   end, be settled, be over, be finished
Okurete sumimasen. *I'm sorry I'm late.* (lit. "endless apologies")
Sumimasen. *Thank you.* (lit. "endless indebtedness")

SURU する   do, try, make, be worth, play (a game)
Kore wa ikura shimasu ka. *How much does this cost?*
Doyōbi ni gorufu o shimashō. *Let's play golf Saturday.*

SUTERU すてる／捨てる   throw away, give up, abandon, desert, leave, forsake
Kare wa ano bakageta puran o zettai ni sutenai darō. *He'll never give up that stupid plan.*
Okane o suteru yō na koto o shite wa naranai. *Don't throw away your money.*

TABERU たべる／食べる   eat, feed on
Ban gohan wa nan ji ni tabetai desu ka. *What time would you like to eat dinner?*
Totemo oishikatta node tabe sugita. *It was so delicious that I ate too much.*

TANOMU たのむ／頼む   request, ask a favor, appeal to
Otanomi shitai koto ga arimasu. *I have a favor to ask of you.*
Miruku o katte kuru yō ni tanomareta. *I was asked to go buy some milk.*

TARIRU たりる／足りる   be enough, suffice, be worthy of
Hyaku doru de tarimasu ka. *Will a hundred dollars be enough?*
Kanojo wa shinyō suru ni tarinai. *She isn't worthy of our trust.*

TASHIKAMERU たしかめる／確かめる   ascertain, confirm, see if, verify
Yoyaku o tashikamete moraemasu ka. *Can you confirm the reservation?*
Karera wa Kawasaki san ga kaigi ni kuru no ka tashikametagatte imasu. *They'd like to know if Mr. Kawasaki is coming to the meeting.*

TASUKERU たすける／助ける   help, assist, aid, rescue, save, support, back up
Tasukete! Gōtō da! *Help! I've been robbed!*
Hitsuyō nara tasukete ageru. *We'll back you up if you need it.*

TATERU　たてる／立てる／建てる　stand, set up, erect, establish, create
Karera wa atarashii keikaku o tateta. *They made a new plan.*
Kono daigaku wa sen nana hyaku san jū go nen ni taterareta. *The university was founded in 1735.*

TATSU　たつ／立つ／建つ　stand up, rise, be built, be set up, be established, set out, start
Karera wa konda densha de zutto Shibuya made tatte ita. *They stood on the crowded train all the way to Shibuya.*
Sono jinja wa yama no teppen ni tatte ita. *The shrine was standing on the top of the mountain.*

TAZUNERU　たずねる／尋ねる　look for, seek, ask questions, inquire about something
Shitsumon ga aru nara, Jōnzu san ni tazunenasai. *If you have questions, ask Mrs. Jones.*
Michi jun ga iru nara, kōban de tazunemasu. *I'll inquire at the police booth if I need directions.*

TAZUNERU　たずねる／訪ねる　visit, call upon, pay a visit
Kare wa gakkō kara kaeru tochū, obāsan o tazuneta. *He visited his grandmother on the way home from school.*
Porutogaru ni iru oji to oba o tazunetai. *I want to visit my aunt and uncle in Portugal.*

TETSUDAU　てつだう／手伝う　help a person, assist, lend a hand
Tetsudatte moraemasu ka. *Can you lend me a hand?*
Tetsudaimashō ka. *Shall I lend you a hand?*

TOBU　とぶ／飛ぶ／跳ぶ　fly, jump, leap, hop, skip
Nyūyōku ni iku toki wa, tobu'n desu ka doraibu desu ka. *When you go to New York, will you fly or drive?*
Fuyu o kosu tame, tori ga minami ni mukatte tobi hajimete iru. *The birds are starting to fly south for winter.*

TODOKU　とどく／届く　reach, arrive at, get to, be received
Hashigo wa mado ni todoita. *The ladder reached the window.*
Tomodachi ni okutta tegami ga todokanakatta. *The letter I sent to my friend never reached her.*

TOMARU　とまる／止まる／停まる／泊まる　stop, halt, stand still, lodge, stay the night
Tokei ga tomatte shimatta. *My watch stopped.*
Tōkyō dewa doko ni tomarimasu ka. *Where are you staying in Tokyo?*

TŌRU　とおる／通る　pass by, pass through, be known as
Kono machi o tōri nuketara, shingō de hidari ni magarinasai. *After you drive through town, take a left at the traffic light.*
Kanojo wa unten menkyo no shiken ni tōtta. *She passed the test for her driver's license.*

TORU とる／取る take, hold, seize, get, obtain, receive, choose, remove, interpret
Kare wa atarashii pasupōto o toranakereba narimasen. *He has to get a new passport.*
Kaerigake ni kurīningu ya de sentaku mono o totte kimasu. *I'll pick up the dry cleaning on my way home.*

TSUKARERU つかれる／疲れる get tired of, grow weary, be worn out
Sugoku tsukarete ban gohan ga tsukurenakatta. *I was too tired to cook dinner.*
Hanku wa nan jikan konpyūta gēmu o shitemo tsukarenai. *No matter how many hours he plays, Hank doesn't get tired of computer games.*

TSUKAU つかう／使う use, make use of, employ, handle, operate, spend money
Arigatō. Yakudatete tsukaimasu. *Thanks. I'll make good use of it.*
Sono tsukai kata o oshiete kudasai. *Please teach me how to use it.*

TSUKU つく／着く arrive, reach
Karera wa ashita Narita ni tsukimasu. *They'll arrive at Narita tomorrow.*
Kanojo wa kaigi ni ichi jikan okurete tsuita. *She arrived at the conference one hour late.*

TSUKURU つくる／作る／創る／造る make, manufacture, create, build
Koko dewa utsukushii urushi nuri no seihin o tsukutte iru. *They make beautiful lacquer items here.*
Sushi o tsukuru no wa muzukashii desu ka. *Is it difficult to make sushi?*

TSUTAERU つたえる／伝える convey, report, tell, hand down
Yoroshiku tsutaete kudasai. *Please tell them I send my best regards.*
Shinbun wa akarui keizai tenbō o tsutaete iru. *The newspapers are reporting a good economic outlook.*

TSUTOMERU つとめる／勤める／努める／務める serve, be employed by, work for, exert oneself, perform
Kare ni reigi tadashiku suru yō ni isshōkenmei tsutometa. *I tried my best to be polite to him.*
Kare wa saisho kara saigo made soko de zutto tsutometa. *He worked there for his entire career.*

TSUZUKU つづく／続く continue, follow, succeed, last, lead to
Kono kokusho wa kore ijō tsuzukumai. *This heat wave can't go on much longer.*
Tochū no kyūkei jikan wa dono kurai tsuzukimasu ka. *How long does the intermission last?*

UMARERU うまれる／生まれる be born, come into existence, result from
Hachi gatsu ni Meiko ni akachan ga umareta. *Meiko had a baby in August.*
Kare wa kotoshi umarete hajimete gorufu o hajimeta. *He took up golf this year for the first time.*

USHINAU うしなう／失う　lose, miss, be deprived of
Kanojo wa wakai toki ni ryōshin o ushinatta. *She lost her parents at an early age.*
Kare wa daitōryō ni naru kikai o ushinatta. *He missed his opportunity to become president.*

UTAGAU うたがう／疑う　doubt, suspect, distrust, be skeptical of
Sono nyūsu no seikakusa o utagau. *I distrust the accuracy of the report.*
Ōzei no hito ga kanojo no dōki ni tsuite utagatte iru. *Many people are skeptical of her motivation.*

WAKARU わかる／分かる／解る　understand, see, learn, know, find out, come to light
Wakarimasu. *I understand.*
Sore ni tsuite wa zenzen wakarimasen. *We don't know anything about that.*

WASURERU わすれる／忘れる　forget, put out of one's mind, think no more of
Mazui koto ni, kare no namae o wasurete shimatta. *Unfortunately, I've forgotten his name.*
Yakusoku o wasurete wa naranai. *Don't forget your promise!*

YAMERU やめる／止める／辞める　stop doing, cease, discontinue, drop, end, resign, quit
Yamenasai. *Please stop that!*
Kare wa kaisha o yamete sekinin o totta. *He took responsibility by resigning from the company.*

YARU やる　give, send, do, try, take, hold, manage
Neko ni ichi nichi ni kai gohan o yaru. *I feed my cats twice a day.*
Nantoka yatte imasu. *Somehow we manage.*

YASUMU やすむ／休む　rest, have a day off, be absent (from school, etc.), go to bed
Sū jikan, yasumitai. *I could use a few hours' rest.*
Kinō wa, naze jugyō o yasunda o desu ka. *Why were you absent from class yesterday?*

YOMU よむ／読む　read
Kisha de yomu no ni ii hon ga aru. *I have a good book to read on the train.*
Kyō wa shinbun o yomu jikan ga nai. *We haven't had time to read the newspaper today.*

YORU よる／依る　depend on, lean on, by means of, be based on, be caused by, according to
Tenki ni yotte, doko ni iku ka kimeru. *Depending on the weather, we'll decide where to go.*
Tenki yohō ni yoru to, kono natsu wa totemo atsui sō da. *According to the weather forecast, this summer will be very hot.*

English-Japanese Verb Index

be broken   oreru   414
be built   tatsu   505
be burned   kogeru   262
be called off   nagareru   360
be changed   aratamaru   36
be charred   kogeru   262
be closed   fusagaru   97
be closed   shimaru   450
be conspicuous   medatsu   326
be cut off   kireru   251
be decided   kimaru   247
be defeated   makeru   316
be different   chigau   63
be different (from)   kotonaru   278
be divided   wakareru   558
be divorced   wakareru   558
be eager to   -tagaru   484
be effective   kiku   246
be employed   tsutomeru   536
be enough   tariru   497
be excellent   sugureru   467
be extinguished   kieru   241
be finished   owaru   429
be finished   sumu   473
be fixed   naoru   371
be formed   dekiru   78
be found   mitsukaru   340
be friendly with   tsukiau   527
be glad   yorokobu   T   579
be grilled   yakeru   569
be hanging (from)   kakaru   197
be hazy   kasumu   222
be in   hairu   108
be in a fix   komaru   265
be in awe of   osoreru   T   421
be in discord   kuichigau   286
be in disorder   chirakaru   68
be in trouble   komaru   265
be indebted   ou   T   428
be inferior to   otoru   425
be late   okureru   410
be lazy   namakeru   T   369
be left behind   nokoru   389
be left over   nokoru   389
be missing   nakunaru   367
be mistaken   machigau   308
be mixed   majiru   313

be necessary   iru   175
be out of order (a watch)   kuruu   300
be over   owaru   429
be over   sumaseru   T   470
be over   sumu   473
be piled up   kasanaru   218
be pleased   yorokobu   T   579
be popular   moteru   351
be possible   dekiru   78
be profitable   mōkaru   344
be puzzled   mayou   324
be raised   sodatsu   463
be ready   dekiru   78
be reluctant   oshimu   T   420
be renewed   aratamaru   36
be rowdy   sawagu   444
be sad   kanashimu   T   211
be saved   tamaru   487
be scattered about   chirakaru   68
be served   deru   80
be shut   shimaru   450
be similar to   niru   386
be startled   bikkuri suru   T   60
be sufficient   tariru   497
be superior   sugureru   467
be surprised   bikkuri suru   T   60
be surprised   odoroku   403
be suspicious of   ayashimu   T   54
be taken   fusagaru   97
be tired   tsukareru   523
be toasted   yakeru   569
be untidy   chirakaru   68
be visible   mieru   328
be well informed   tsūjiru   T   521
be worse than   otoru   425
be wrong   chigau   63
bear   ou   T   428
bear a grudge   uramu   T   550
bear fruit   minoru   334
beat   tataku   T   502
beat   yaburu   T   568
beckon to   maneku   T   319
become   naru   378
become acquainted with
   najimu   365
become blurred   kasumu   222
become crowded   komu   266

English-Japanese Verb Index

grieve kanashimu T 211
grin warau T 562
grow dark (at the end of the day)
  kureru 294
grow fertile (of land) koeru 260
grow tired of akiru 33
grow up sodatsu 463
guide oshieru T 418

H

hand over watasu T 566
hang kakeru T 199
hang sagaru 434
hang sageru T 436
harden katameru T 224
harm kizutsukeru T 257
hate iyagaru T 184
have aru 41
have iru 173
have kakaeru T 195
have motsu T 354
have toru T 517
have a good time tanoshimu T 493
have an insight into minuku T 335
have fun tanoshimu T 493
head toward mukau 357
hear kiku T 244
hear (news, etc.) ukagau T 546
help tasukeru T 499
help (to do work) tetsudau T 509
hesitate tamerau T 488
hide (oneself) kakureru 205
hide (something) kakusu T 206
hinder samatageru T 440
hint honomekasu T 149
hire yatou T 575
hit butsukaru 61
hit naguru T 363
hit tataku T 502
hit utsu T 555
hit against butsukeru T 62
hold motsu T 354
hold nigiru T 384
hold toru T 517
hold (a party, etc.) hiraku T 140
hold in one's arms kakaeru T 195
hold in trust azukaru T 56

hold up kakageru T 196
hurry isogu T 176
hurt itamu 178

I

imply fukumu 91
include fukumeru T 90
include fukumu T 91
include (in) kuwaeru T 303
increase fueru 85
increase (something) fuyasu T 103
incur maneku T 319
indicate shimesu T 453
infect utsusu T 556
inflict pain kurushimeru T 298
inform oshieru T 418
instruct oshieru T 418
intend kokorozasu T 264
investigate shiraberu T 456
invite maneku T 319
invite sasou T 442
invite yobu T 576

J

join hairu 108
join majiru 313
join tsunagu T 534
jump tobu 510

K

keep azukaru T 56
keep mamoru T 317
keep (an animal) kau T 231
keep a lookout miharu T 330
keep an eye on niramu T 385
kill korosu T 372
knock down taosu T 496
knot musubu T 358
know shiru T 457
know wakaru 559

L

lack kaku T 204
lag behind okureru 410
laugh warau T 562
lay shiku T 449
lay (something) face down
  fuseru T 100

English-Japanese Verb Index

N

need iru 175
neglect one's work namakeru T 369
nibble kajiru T 194
not speak damaru 72
notice kizuku 256

O

obey shitagau 459
obstruct samatageru T 440
omit nozoku T 396
open akeru T 31
open aku 34
open hiraku T 140
operate tsukau T 524
operate ugokasu T 542
order tanomu T 491
overflow koboreru 258
overlap kasanaru 218
overlook minogasu T 333
overthrow taosu T 496
own motsu T 354

P

pack away shimau T 451
paint nuru T 399
panic awateru 52
part wakareru 558
pass koeru T 261
pass kosu T 275
pass sugiru 465
pass tōru T 519
pass by tōru T 519
pass through heru T 133
pass time sugosu T 466
paste haru T 124
pay harau T 121
perish horobiru 151
permit yurusu T 582
persevere koraeru T 269
persuade kudoku T 285
photograph utsusu T 556
pick up toru T 517
pick up (from ground, etc.) hirou T 143
pile up kasaneru T 219
pile up tsumoru 533
pitch haru T 124

pitch nageru T 262
place oku T 409
plan hakaru T 114
plan kuwadateru T 302
plant ueru T 541
play asobu 45
play jokes on karakau T 215
pledge one's word chikau T 66
plot hakaru T 114
plot takuramu T 485
point out sasu T 443
point out shimesu T 453
polish migaku T 329
postpone nobasu T 387
pour nagasu T 361
praise homeru T 148
pray inoru T 170
prepare totonoeru T 520
press osu T 424
press down osaeru T 417
prevent fusegu T 99
proceed tsuzukeru T 539
produce umu T 549
profit mōkeru T 345
progress susumu 477
prohibit kinjiru T 250
promise chikau T 66
protect kabau T 186
protect mamoru T 317
pull hiku T 138
punch naguru T 363
pursue ou T 427
pursue (a course) tadoru T 483
push osu T 424
put oku T 409
put (on top of) noseru T 395
put away shimau T 451
put back modosu T 343
put in ireru T 172
put in someone's charge
    azukeru T 57
put on kaburu T 187
put on kiru T 253
put on nuru T 399
put on tsukeru T 526
put on airs ibaru T 156
put on airs kidoru 240

put on board   noseru   T   395

put on or wear on the feet or legs (shoes, socks, skirt, trousers)   haku   T   116

put out   dasu   T   74

put together   kumu   T   288

put up   sasu   T   443

put up   tomeru   T   516

Q

quit   yameru   T   571

R

raid   osou   T   422

raise (a flag)   kakageru   T   196

raise a child   sodateru   T   462

raise up   okosu   T   408

reach   oyobu   431

reach   todoku   512

reach   tsuku   528

read   miru   T   336

read   yomu   T   577

realize   kizuku   256

receive   itadaku   T   177

receive   morau   T   347

receive   uketoru   T   547

recline   neru   381

recognize   mitomeru   T   339

recommend   susumeru   T   476

reconsider   minaosu   T   331

recover from illness   naoru   371

reduce   chijimeru   T   64

reduce   herasu   T   132

reduce   heru   134

refer to   oyobu   431

reflect   utsusu   T   556

refrain from   hikaeru   T   135

refrigerate   hiyasu   T   145

refuse   kotowaru   T   279

regard   omou   T   412

regard as   minasu   T   332

regret   oshimu   T   420

release   hanasu   T   118

rely on   tayoru   507

remain   nokoru   389

remember   oboeru   T   401

remove   hazusu   T   131

remove   nakusu   T   368

remove   nozoku   T   396

remove (clothes, shoes, hats, etc.)   nugu   T   397

rent   kariru   T   217

rent (to)   kasu   T   221

repair   naosu   T   372

repeat   kasaneru   T   219

repeat   kurikaesu   T   295

rephrase   iinaosu   T   161

report   todokeru   T   511

report   tsutaeru   T   535

request   motomeru   T   352

request   tanomu   T   491

require (time, money, etc.)   kakaru   197

rescue   sukuu   T   469

rescue   tasukeru   T   499

resemble   niru   386

reside   sumu   471

resign   yameru   T   571

resign oneself (to)   akirameru   T   32

respond   kotaeru   276

rest   yasumu   574

restrain   osaeru   T   417

restrict   kagiru   T   193

retort   iikaesu   160

retrace one's steps   modoru   342

return   modoru   342

return   modosu   T   343

return (something to someone)   kaesu   T   191

return (to a place)   kaeru   189

reveal   akasu   T   30

revise   aratameru   T   37

ride   noru   393

rip   yabureru   567

ripen   jukusu   185

ripen   minoru   334

rise   agaru   27

risk   kakeru   T   200

ruin   horobosu   T   152

run   hashiru   126

run away   nigeru   383

run out   kireru   251

S

save   nokosu   T   390

save   sukuu   T   469

save   tameru   T   489

English-Japanese Verb Index

save   tasukeru   T   499
save (money, etc.)   takuwaeru   T   486
say   iu   T   181
say (honorific)   ossharu   T   423
scatter   chirakasu   T   69
scatter   chiru   70
scheme   kuwadateru   T   302
scheme   takuramu   T   485
scold   shikaru   T   448
search   shiraberu   T   456
search for   sagasu   T   435
see   au   51
see   miru   T   336
see off   okuru   T   411
see through   minuku   T   335
seek   motomeru   T   352
select   erabu   T   82
sell   uru   T   551
send   dasu   T   74
send (a package)   okuru   T   411
sense   kanjiru   T   214
sense   kizuku   256
separate   wakeru   T   561
separate from   hanareru   117
separate from   wakareru   558
set fire   yaku   T   570
set free   hanasu   T   118
settle (a dispute)   matomeru   T   320
shed   kobosu   T   259
shine   hikaru   136
shine   kagayaku   192
shoot   utsu   T   555
shorten   chijimeru   T   64
shout   sakebu   T   437
show   miseru   T   338
show   oshieru   T   418
show   shimesu   T   453
show   ukaberu   T   544
show up   arawasu   T   40
show up   kuru   T   296
shrink   chijimeru   T   64
shrink   chijimu   65
shut   shimeru   T   452
sing   utau   T   554
sink   shizumu   461
sip   suu   T   479
sit   kakeru   T   199

sit   suwaru   480
sit in   koshikakeru   273
slap   tataku   T   502
sleep   nemuru   380
sleep   neru   381
sleep   yasumu   574
slide   suberu   464
slip   suberu   464
smash   kowasu   T   282
smash   kudaku   T   283
smile   warau   562
smoke (a cigarette)   suu   T   479
snap   oreru   414
solve   toku   T   514
sparkle   kagayaku   192
speak   hanasu   T   119
spend time   sugosu   T   466
spill   koboreru   258
spill   kobosu   T   259
spread   hiromaru   141
spread   hiromeru   T   142
spread   nuru   T   399
spread (a story)   iifurasu   T   159
spread out flat (as a quilt)   shiku   T   449
stab   sasu   T   443
stand   tatsu   505
stand firm   ganbaru   104
stand guard   miharu   T   330
stand out   medatsu   326
stand prepared   kamaeru   T   207
start   hajimeru   T   111
start talking   iidasu   T   158
stay away from   sakeru   T   438
stay overnight   tomaru   515
steal   nusumu   T   400
step on   fumu   T   92
stick   haru   T   124
sting   sasu   T   443
stop   tomaru   515
stop   tomeru   T   516
stop   yameru   T   571
stop talking   damaru   72
store   takuwaeru   T   486
store   tameru   T   489
straighten up things
   katazukeru   T   226
strengthen   katameru   T   224

stretch   haru   T   124
strike   utsu   T   555
strike (against)   ataru   46
strive   hagemu   107
struggle against   tatakau   T   501
study   benkyō suru   T   58
study   manabu   T   318
submit   dasu   T   74
suffer   kurushimu   299
suggest   iidasu   T   158
suit   kanau   212
support   sasaeru   T   441
surpass   kosu   T   275
surpass   sugureru   467
surpass   uwamawaru   557
surround   kakomu   T   201
suspect   utagau   T   553
swallow   nomu   T   391
swear   chikau   T   66
swim   oyogu   432

T

take   toru   T   517
take a person under one's wing
   kabau   T   186
take a ride   noru   393
take a spill   korobu   271
take an oath   chikau   T   66
take charge of   hikiukeru   T   137
take food or drink
   (humble)   itadaku   T   177
take in   ireru   T   172
take off   nugu   T   397
take part in   kakawaru   198
take shape   katamaru   223
talk   hanasu   T   119
talk about   iu   T   181
talk back   iikaesu   160
taste   tamesu   T   490
teach   oshieru   T   418
team up   kumu   T   288
tear   yabureru   567
tear   yaburu   T   568
tease   hiyakasu   T   144
tease   karakau   T   215
telephone   kakeru   T   199
tell   hanasu   T   119

tell   iu   T   181
tell   tsutaeru   T   535
tell (a person to do
   something)   iitsukeru   T   162
tempt   sasou   T   442
test   kokoromiru   T   263
test   tamesu   T   490
think   omou   T   412
think about   kangaeru   T   213
think back   furikaeru   T   94
think of   kangaeru   T   213
throw   nageru   T   362
throw at   butsukeru   T   62
throw away   suteru   T   478
throw down   taosu   T   496
tie   musubu   T   358
tie up   shibaru   T   447
tilt   katamuku   225
top   uwamawaru   557
torment   ijimeru   T   163
torment   kurushimeru   T   298
torment   semeru   T   446
touch   fureru   93
touch   ijiru   T   164
touch or feel (with the hands)
   sawaru   445
trace   tadoru   T   483
train   sodateru   T   462
transmit   tsūjiru   521
transmit   tsutaeru   T   535
tremble   furueru   96
trick   damasu   T   73
trust   shinjiru   T   454
try   kokoromiru   T   263
try   tamesu   T   490
turn a corner   magaru   T   309
turn off   kesu   T   239
turn on   tsukeru   T   526
turn toward   mukau   357
twist   hineru   T   139
twist   mageru   T   310

U

understand   nigiru   T   384
understand   shiru   T   457
understand   uketoru   T   547
understand   wakaru   559

undertake hikiukeru T 137
unfasten hazusu T 131
unite kumu T 288
untie hodoku T 147
untie toku T 514
urge kudoku T 285
use tsukau T 524
use up tsukusu T 532

V

vanish kieru 241
vanish nakunaru 367
view nagameru T 359
visit tazuneru T 508
visit ukagau T 546
vomit modosu T 343

W

wage war on tatakau T 501
wager kakeru T 200
wait matsu T 321
wait for matsu T 321
wake up okiru 405
walk aruku 43
want hoshigaru T 154

want to -tagaru 484
warm atatameru T 48
warm oneself atatamaru 47
wash arau T 38
watch nagameru T 359
waver tamerau T 488
wear (on the body as with a coat, suit, or
　dress) kiru T 253
wear on one's head kaburu T 187
welcome mukaeru T 356
win katsu 227
wipe fuku T 89
wish for inoru T 170
wish to -tagaru 484
wither kareru 216
work hataraku 127
work kiku 246
work for tsutomeru 536
worry about kizukau T 255
worship matsuru T 323
wound kizutsukeru T 257
wrap tsutsumu T 538
write kaku T 202
write down hikaeru T 135

Index of Verbs by Gerund

A

agatte **agaru**
agete **ageru**
aite **aku**
akashite **akasu**
akete **akeru**
akiramete **akirameru**
akite **akiru**
arasotte **arasou**
aratamatte **aratamaru**
aratamete **aratameru**
aratte **arau**
arawarete **arawareru**
arawashite **arawasu**
aruite **aruku**
asonde **asobu**
atatamatte **atatamaru**
atatamete **atatameru**
atatte **ataru**
atsumatte **atsumaru**
atsumete **atsumeru**
atte **aru**
atte **au**
awatete **awateru**
ayamatte **ayamaru**
ayasinde **ayashimu**
ayatsutte **ayatsuru**
azukatte **azukaru**
azukete **azukeru**

B

benkyō shite **benkyō suru**
bikkuri shite **bikkuri suru**
butsukatte **butsukaru**
butsukete **butsukeru**

C

chigatte **chigau**
chijimete **chijimeru**
chijinde **chijimu**
chikatte **chikau**

chikazuite **chikazuku**
chirakashite **chirakasu**
chirakatte **chirakaru**
chitte **chiru**

D

daite **daku**
damashite **damasu**
damatte **damaru**
dashite **dasu**
deatte **deau**
dekakete **dekakeru**
dekite **dekiru**
dete **deru**

E

erande **erabu**
ete **eru**

F

fuete **fueru**
fuite **fuku**
fukamatte **fukamaru**
fukamete **fukameru**
fukumete **fukumeru**
fukunde **fukumu**
funde **fumu**
furete **fureru**
furikaette **furikaeru**
furuete **furueru**
fusagatte **fusagaru**
fusaide **fusagu**
fuseide **fusegu**
fusete **fuseru**
fusette **fuseru**
futotte **futoru**
futte **furu**
fuyashite **fuyasu**

G

ganbatte **ganbaru**

H

hagemashite **hagemasu**
hagende **hagemu**
haite **haku**
haitte **hairu**
hajimatte **hajimaru**
hajimete **hajimeru**
hakatte **hakaru**
hakonde **hakobu**
hanarete **hanareru**
hanashite **hanasu**
haratte **harau**
harete **hareru**
hasande **hasamu**
hashitte **hashiru**
hataraite **hataraku**
hatte **haru**
hayatte **hayaru**
hazurete **hazureru**
hazushite **hazusu**
herashite **herasu**
hete **heru**
hette **heru**
hiite **hiku**
hikaete **hikaeru**
hikatte **hikaru**
hikiukete **hikiukeru**
hinette **hineru**
hiraite **hiraku**
hiromatte **hiromaru**
hiromete **hiromeru**
hirotte **hirou**
hiyakashite **hiyakasu**
hiyashite **hiyasu**
hodoite **hodoku**
hodokete **hodokeru**
homete **homeru**
honomekashite **honomekasu**
horete **horeru**
horobite **horobiru**
horoboshite **horobosu**
hoshigatte **hoshigaru**
hoshite **hosu**
hotte **horu**

I

ibatte **ibaru**
iiarawashite **iiarawasu**

iidashite **iidasu**
iifurashite **iifurasu**
iikaeshite **iikaesu**
iinaoshite **iinaosu**
iitsukete **iitsukeru**
ijimete **ijimeru**
ijitte **ijiru**
ikite **ikiru**
imashimete **imashimeru**
inaotte **inaoru**
inotte **inoru**
irasshatte **irassharu**
irete **ireru**
isoide **isogu**
itadaite **itadaku**
itande **itamu**
itashite **itasu**
ite **iru**
itsuwatte **itsuwaru**
itte **iku**
itte **iru**
itte **iu**
iwatte **iwau**
iyagatte **iyagaru**

J

jukushite **jukusu**

K

kabatte **kabau**
kabutte **kaburu**
kaeshite **kaesu**
kaete **kaeru**
kaette **kaeru**
kagayaite **kagayaku**
kagitte **kagiru**
kaite **kaku**
kajitte **kajiru**
kakaete **kakaeru**
kakagete **kakageru**
kakatte **kakaru**
kakawatte **kakawaru**
kakete **kakeru**
kakonde **kakomu**
kakurete **kakureru**
kakushite **kakusu**
kamaete **kamaeru**
kamatte **kamau**

kanaete **kanaeru**
kanashinde **kanashimu**
kanatte **kanau**
kande **kamu**
kangaete **kangaeru**
kanjite **kanjiru**
karakatte **karakau**
karete **kareru**
karite **kariru**
kasanatte **kasanaru**
kasanete **kasaneru**
kaseide **kasegu**
kashite **kasu**
kasunde **kasumu**
katamatte **katamaru**
katamete **katameru**
katamuite **katamuku**
katazukete **katazukeru**
katsuide **katsugu**
katte **katsu**
katte **kau**
kawaigatte **kawaigaru**
kawaite **kawaku**
kawakashite **kawakasu**
kawatte **kawaru**
kayotte **kayou**
kazatte **kazaru**
kazoete **kazoeru**
keshite **kesu**
kidotte **kidoru**
kiete **kieru**
kiite **kiku**
kikaete **kikaeru**
kikoete **kikoeru**
kimatte **kimaru**
kimete **kimeru**
kinjite **kinjiru**
kite **kiru**
kite **kuru**
kitte **kiru**
kizuite **kizuku**
kizukatte **kizukau**
kizutsukete **kizutsukeru**
koborete **koboreru**
koboshite **kobosu**
koete **koeru**
kogete **kogeru**
kokoromite **kokoromiru**

kokorozashite **kokorozasu**
komatte **komaru**
konde **komu**
kononde **konomu**
koraete **koraeru**
korashite **korasu**
koronde **korobu**
koroshite **korosu**
koshikakete **koshikakeru**
koshiraete **koshiraeru**
koshite **kosu**
kotaete **kotaeru**
kotonatte **kotonaru**
kotowatte **kotowaru**
kōtte **kōru**
kowagatte **kowagaru**
kowarete **kowareru**
kowashite **kowasu**
kudaite **kudaku**
kudasatte **kudasaru**
kudoite **kudoku**
kuichigatte **kuichigau**
kumotte **kumoru**
kunde **kumu**
kurabete **kuraberu**
kurande **kuramu**
kurashite **kurasu**
kurete **kureru**
kurikaeshite **kurikaesu**
kurushimete **kurushimeru**
kurushinde **kurushimu**
kurutte **kuruu**
kusatte **kusaru**
kuwadatete **kuwadateru**
kuwaete **kuwaeru**
kuzurete **kuzureru**
kuzushite **kuzusu**

M

machigaete **machigaeru**
machigatte **machigau**
magatte **magaru**
magete **mageru**
magirashite **magirasu**
maitte **mairu**
majitte **majiru**
makasete **makaseru**
makashite **makasu**

makete **makeru**
mamotte **mamoru**
manande **manabu**
maneite **maneku**
matomete **matomeru**
matsutte **matsuru**
matte **matsu**
mayotte **mayou**
mazete **mazeru**
medatte **medatsu**
meshiagatte **meshiagaru**
miete **mieru**
migaite **migaku**
mihatte **miharu**
minaoshite **minaosu**
minashite **minasu**
minogashite **minogasu**
minotte **minoru**
minuite **minuku**
misete **miseru**
mite **miru**
mitomete **mitomeru**
mitsukatte **mitsukaru**
mitsukete **mitsukeru**
modoshite **modosu**
modotte **modoru**
mōkatte **mōkaru**
mōkete **mōkeru**
morashite **morasu**
moratte **morau**
morete **moreru**
motarashite **motarasu**
motete **moteru**
motomete **motomeru**
motozuite **motozuku**
motte **motsu**
mukaete **mukaeru**
mukatte **mukau**
musunde **musubu**

N

nagamete **nagameru**
nagarete **nagareru**
nagashite **nagasu**
nagete **nageru**
nagusamete **nagusameru**
nagutte **naguru**

naite **naku**
najinde **najimu**
nakunatte **nakunaru**
nakushite **nakusu**
namakete **namakeru**
namete **nameru**
naoshite **naosu**
naotte **naoru**
narabete **naraberu**
narande **narabu**
naratte **narau**
narete **nareru**
nasatte **nasaru**
natte **naru**
nemutte **nemuru**
nete **neru**
nigete **nigeru**
nigitte **nigiru**
nirande **niramu**
nite **niru**
nobashite **nobasu**
nobotte **noboru**
nokoshite **nokosu**
nonde **nomu**
nosete **noseru**
notte **noru**
nozoite **nozoku**
nuide **nugu**
nurete **nureru**
nusunde **nusumu**
nutte **nuru**

O

oboete **oboeru**
ochite **ochiru**
odoroite **odoroku**
odotte **odoru**
oite **oku**
okite **okiru**
okoshite **okosu**
okotte **okoru**
okurete **okureru**
okutte **okuru**
omotte **omou**
orete **oreru**
orite **oriru**
osaete **osaeru**

oshiete **oshieru**
oshinde **oshimu**
oshite **osu**
osorete **osoreru**
osotte **osou**
osshatte **ossharu**
otoshite **otosu**
ototte **otoru**
otte **ou**
owatte **owaru**
oyoide **oyogu**
oyonde **oyobu**

S

sadamete **sadameru**
sagashite **sagasu**
sagatte **sagaru**
sagete **sageru**
saite **saku**
sakende **sakebu**
sakete **sakeru**
samatagete **samatageru**
sasaete **sasaeru**
sashite **sasu**
sasotte **sasou**
sawaide **sawagu**
sawatte **sawaru**
semete **semeru**
shibatte **shibaru**
shiite **shiku**
shikatte **shikaru**
shimatte **shimaru**
shimatte **shimau**
shimeshite **shimesu**
shimete **shimeru**
shinde **shinu**
shinjite **shinjiru**
shirabete **shiraberu**
shitagatte **shitagau**
shitashinde **shitashimu**
shite **suru**
shitte **shiru**
shizunde **shizumu**
sodatete **sodateru**
sodatte **sodatsu**
subette **suberu**
sugite **sugiru**
sugoshite **sugosu**

sugurete **sugureru**
suite **suku**
sukutte **sukuu**
sumasete **sumaseru**
sunde **sumu**
susumete **susumeru**
susunde **susumu**
sutete **suteru**
sutte **suu**
suwatte **suwaru**

T

tabete **taberu**
tadotte **tadoru**
-tagatte **-tagaru**
takurande **takuramu**
takuwaete **takuwaeru**
tamatte **tamaru**
tameratte **tamerau**
tameshite **tamesu**
tamete **tameru**
tanonde **tanomu**
tanoshinde **tanoshimu**
taorete **taoreru**
taoshite **taosu**
tarite **tariru**
tashikamete **tashikameru**
tasukete **tasukeru**
tataite **tataku**
tatakatte **tatakau**
tatande **tatamu**
tatete **tateru**
tatte **tatsu**
tayotte **tayoru**
tazunete **tazuneru**
tetsudatte **tetsudau**
todoite **todoku**
todokete **todokeru**
toite **toku**
tokete **tokeru**
tomatte **tomaru**
tomete **tomeru**
tonde **tobu**
totonoete **totonoeru**
totte **toru**
tōtte **tōru**
tsuite **tsuku**

tsūjite **tsūjiru**
tsukande **tsukamu**
tsukarete **tsukareru**
tsukatte **tsukau**
tsukete **tsukeru**
tsukiatte **tsukiau**
tsukushite **tsukusu**
tsukutte **tsukuru**
tsumotte **tsumoru**
tsunaide **tsunagu**
tsutaete **tsutaeru**
tsutomete **tsutomeru**
tsutsunde **tsutsumu**
tsuzuite **tsuzuku**
tsuzukete **tsuzukeru**

U

uete **ueru**
ugoite **ugoku**
ugokashite **ugokasu**
ukabete **ukaberu**
ukagatte **ukagau**
ukande **ukabu**
uketotte **uketoru**
umarete **umareru**
unde **umu**
urande **uramu**
utagatte **utagau**
utatte **utau**
utsushite **utsusu**

utte **uru**
utte **utsu**
uwamawatte **uwamawaru**

W

wakarete **wakareru**
wakatte **wakaru**
wakete **wakeru**
waratte **warau**
wasurete **wasureru**
watashite **watasu**
watatte **wataru**
watte **waru**

Y

yaburete **yabureru**
yabutte **yaburu**
yaite **yaku**
yakete **yakeru**
yamete **yameru**
yasete **yaseru**
yasunde **yasumu**
yatotte **yatou**
yatte **yaru**
yonde **yobu**
yonde **yomu**
yorokonde **yorokobu**
yotte **yoru**
yotte **you**
yurushite **yurusu**